The Codewriting Workbook

The Codewriting Workbook

Creating Computational Architecture in AutoLISP

Robert J. Krawczyk

Foreword by William J. Mitchell

Princeton Architectural Press
New York

To my mother, Wladyslawa Krawczyk

Published by
Princeton Architectural Press
37 East Seventh Street
New York, New York 10003

For a free catalog of books, call 1.800.722.6657.
Visit our website at www.papress.com.

Printed and bound in China
11 10 09 08 4 3 2 1 First edition

Editor: Laurie Manfra
Designer: Arnoud Verhaeghe

Special thanks to: Nettie Aljian, Sara Bader, Dorothy Ball, Nicola Bednarek, Janet Behning, Becca Casbon, Carina Cha, Penny (Yuen Pik) Chu, Russell Fernandez, Pete Fitzpatrick, Wendy Fuller, Jan Haux, Clare Jacobson, Aileen Kwun, Nancy Eklund Later, Linda Lee, Aaron Lim, Katharine Myers, Lauren Nelson Packard, Jennifer Thompson, Paul Wagner, Joseph Weston, and Deb Wood of Princeton Architectural Press
—Kevin C. Lippert, publisher

Library of Congress Cataloging-in-Publication Data

Krawczyk, Robert J., 1949-
The codewriting workbook : creating computational architecture in AutoLISP / Robert J. Krawczyk ; foreword by William J. Mitchell.
p. cm.
Summary: "A primer on basic code-writing concepts for computer-aided design in the fields of architecture and engineering"--Provided by publisher.
ISBN 978-1-56898-792-7 (pbk. w/cd : alk. paper)
1. AutoLISP (Computer program language) 2. Computer-aided design. 3. Architectural design--Data processing. 4. Engineering design--Data processing. I. Title.
QA76.73.A89K73 2008
620'.00420285--dc22

2008032639

CONTENTS

FOREWORD

The creation of an artifact by moving a tool repeatedly across a surface or through a volume is one of the simplest and most fundamental human acts. It's how you make a drawing with pencil strokes, or shape a block of stone with a chisel. Today's computer graphics and digitally controlled fabrication techniques are highly evolved descendents of this act. The moving tool might leave a mark, as with a pencil, a pen, a paintbrush, or an electron-beam traversing a phosphor. It might remove material, as with a chisel, a plow, a saw, a lathe, or a drill. Or it might deposit material, as with a glue gun, a soldering iron, or a concrete hose. There are many variations and combinations, but these basic possibilities are all at the craftsperson's disposal.

You can hold the material being worked in a fixed position and move the tool relative to it; you can keep the tool fixed and move the material; or you can move both. You can use a single tool to work the material serially, or you can use multiple tools in parallel. You can switch among tools for different effects at different stages in the process. The basic motion of the tool may have one degree of spatial freedom, as with a drill moving up and down; two degrees of freedom, as with a pencil moving across paper; or three degrees of freedom, as with a chisel cutting through stone. The effect of the tool might be uniform, or it might vary with pressure, angle, and so on.

The tool's movements might be loosely controlled freehand actions; they might be tightly disciplined through training and practice; or they might be precisely constrained by guides or mechanisms, such as straightedges, compasses, and templates. In the last case, they are exactly repeatable. Or, to put it another way, all the repetitions can be regarded as mathematically equivalent. This element of repeatability served as the foundation for Euclid's geometric constructions. It eventually allowed for the description of lines, as figures swept-out by moving points in a Cartesian coordinate system; for surfaces, as figures swept out by moving lines; and for volumes, as figures swept-out by moving surfaces.

By the mid-twentieth century, the concept of a *toolpath*—the numerically specified route across a surface or through a material—had emerged. To meet the increasingly sophisticated demands of manufacturing, numerically controlled plotters, routers, lathes, and multi-axis milling machines were developed. Sequences of coordinates were put into them (usually punched on paper tape) and the corresponding machine-produced artifacts came out. This, however, posed a new problem: how to efficiently create the necessary sequences of coordinates. The emerging technology of digital computation soon provided a powerful answer. Operators could type in commands and coordinates for storage in computer memory and then use and reuse them, as necessary, in fabrication. Or, when they wanted to describe regular repeating forms, they could specify algorithms to generate the coordinates. These algorithms were, in effect, software tools that could be used in combination with numerically controlled devices to produce particular types of artifacts.

The first computer-aided design (CAD) systems, which emerged in the early 1960s, were modest collections of software tools. For the most part, they allowed for the efficient production of drawings composed of straight lines and circular arcs, through the use of numerically controlled pen plotters. These systems were also capable of quickly and accurately creating three-dimensional machine parts out of foam or metal. In the decades that followed, the broader potential of CAD and computer-aided manufacturing (CAM)—the combining of CAD with numerically controlled manufacturing—gradually became more apparent.

First, the new technology made artifacts composed of curved lines and surfaces much easier to design and produce. Building on a vast accumulation of knowledge of analysis and calculus, pioneering computer graphics researchers demonstrated that a great many curved lines and surfaces could be described by relatively simple formulas. They could also be varied by simply adjusting the parameters of these formulas; they could be expressed as sequences of coordinates, by running computer code that repeatedly evaluated the formulas; or they could be produced physically, by sending those sequences of coordinates to numerically controlled plotting, cutting, milling, and deposition devices.

More generally, any assemblage of points, lines, surfaces, or volumes could be described by a procedure for generating its coordinates. Such procedures could be "parameterized." That is, inputting different parameter values could yield many variants. The code within a given procedure could specify the essential properties of an artifact. In other words, the properties and parameters common to all instances established ways in which these instances might differ in size, position, or proportion. In fact, the possibilities were unlimited.

In the software of today's CAD systems, libraries of such procedures define the vocabularies of geometric, architectural, and other elements and put these systems at the disposal of users. A general purpose two-dimensional drafting system might, for example, provide straight lines, circular arcs, and spline curves. A three-dimensional modeling system might provide extrusions and solids of revolution. An architectural system might provide walls, doors, and windows. And a mechanical engineering system might provide a collection of standard mechanical parts. As a designer, you can simply accept the vocabulary elements of a CAD system, and create designs by selecting, transforming, and combining various instances of them. This is extremely efficient, since it takes advantage of previous efforts to think about and write the necessary code, which suffices for many practical purposes.

But you can also break away from such established structures and design conventions. You can define new vocabularies and ways of putting vocabulary elements together by writing your own procedures. You can do so by modifying existing procedures, by writing entirely new ones, or by recombining fragments of code. This is designing at a meta-level, by defining the underlying rules that structure your design explorations. It demands a capacity for abstraction and generalization, and the ability to express concepts in terms of the constructs provided by a given programming language. Often, it requires considerable effort and technical skill, but it is a powerful way to capture design knowledge for future reuse. It provides ways to explore variations on themes, adapt design elements to particular contexts and requirements, and innovate by setting up new domains of possibility. It can also fundamentally change the economics of design and construction. If you are clever, you can often write simple procedures to generate complex forms—ones that would be impossibly laborious to construct with manual drafting tools or in a command-by-command fashion with a CAD system. Then, today's increasingly versatile, efficient, and cost-effective numerically controlled fabrication devices could be used to materialize these forms at reasonable cost.

This book is for adventurers who want to embark on the exciting and rewarding path of meta-design. It introduces the basic principles of computer programming, relates these to the concerns of visual and spatial designers, and provides numerous examples as starting points for further development. It will challenge you to think critically about fundamental design ideas, question your assumptions, and liberate your imagination.

—William J. Mitchell

1.0

My God is machinery. The art of the future will be the expression of the individual artist through the thousand powers of the machine, doing all the things the individual worker cannot do, and the creative artist is the man who controls all this and understands it.

—Frank Lloyd Wright

1.0 INTRODUCTION

C. R. Ashbee, an English craftsman, visited Frank Lloyd Wright in Chicago in 1901. In his journal, he quoted Wright:

> My God is machinery. The art of the future will be the expression of the individual artist through the thousand powers of the machine, doing all the things the individual worker cannot do, and the creative artist is the man who controls all this and understands it.

At the turn of the last century, Wright and his contemporaries believed strongly in the power of mechanical technology—what it could do for architecture and for humankind. Today, the "thousand powers of the machine" refers to the potential for digital technology to improve the conceptual tools at the architect's disposal. We are no longer limited by the physical properties of the past, it is time that we break our reliance on what is available only as menu options.

Architectural design concepts can be approached in a number of different ways. One approach is to craft digitally based procedures through existing CAD-programming tools. The purpose of this workbook is to thoroughly introduce and deconstruct even the most basic CAD-programming concepts and to demonstrate how you can develop procedures for creating two-dimensional drawings and three-dimensional models using a variety of computational methods.

This workbook focuses as much on design development as it does on programming methodology. Each chapter begins with a simple design idea and develops that idea into a family of possible solutions. It teaches you how to specify and control design variations within a concept and how to develop your own personal approach to digital architectural design, through programming. The overall objective is to introduce the CAD-programming elements and concepts required for structuring procedures and to demonstrate how a variety of CAD entities can be used to express architectural design concepts in both two- and three-dimensions. As a thinking tool for developing design ideas, computers are much more powerful than when used simply for drawing or fabrication.

Consider each written procedure as a single sketch, one variation of many. Digital methods are excellent at computing singular results, but they are much more powerful at generating a range of possibilities. The question that will be raised over and over will be, "What if we tried this?"

All of the examples in this workbook utilize the most accessible CAD programming environment currently available: AutoLISP. The material is presented in a do-it-yourself, instruction-by-example, work-from-success fashion, with the intention of helping you acquire the skills necessary for expressing your own ideas while developing a better understanding of basic and complex architectural design concepts.

Why use a procedure to create a drawing or model?

- Procedures or functions are sequences of executed instructions. They can specify computations or create any entity supported within a given CAD environment.
- They codify design intent by explicitly specifying each required step and computation. If it is not in the procedure, it won't happen.
- They expose the parameters controlling a concept, making it easier for them to be evaluated, reviewed, and understood.
- Procedures are repeatable. Each time you run one, the same results are generated for the same conditions. The exception is, of course, if a procedure uses randomness to control certain parameters.
- Procedures encourage the development of alternatives. Since they are easily replicated, variations can be explored without the loss of previous work.

What are the limitations to using a procedure?

* Because procedures are computationally based, they are limited to what can be expressed numerically. They require some initial knowledge or intent to determine the best parameters for controlling a design.

* Another interesting but less obvious limitation is that variations can take you down a limitless path that may include generating and reviewing many alternatives. Procedures are relatively easy to refine when only a few evaluation rules are established, limiting the number of variations to the best possible alternatives.

What is the best way to approach the exercises in this workbook?

The exercises in this workbook are based on the premise that, when constructing a procedure, the first objective is to get an initial script running as soon as possible. The next step is to make subtle modifications, entering a small number of changes to the code to specify an alternative or refine an idea. After a number of changes and additions, the final architectural design will be complete; that is, until you think of another variation to consider. Consider each written procedure as a throwaway sketch. The goal being to better understand the design concept you started with, not simply to create a drawing or model.

Why use Autodesk's CAD programming environment?

Quite simply, almost every architect uses, or at least has, AutoCAD, which contains a simple but robust programming environment called AutoLISP. When developing procedures in AutoCAD, no other support software is needed. The purpose of this workbook, however, is not to instruct you on a specific programming language, but to demonstrate concepts for structuring procedures that can be applied to any CAD-programming language in any CAD environment. In other words, we are going to cover syntax, grammar, and art, but spend more time on creating art.

The advantages of working within a powerful CAD environment, such as AutoLISP in AutoCAD, are the greater number of types and varieties of graphic entities available for developing, representing, and communicating design concepts. The workbook begins with basic lines and geometric shapes, such as circles, and it progresses to more advanced representations, such as solids, meshes, regions, and polylines. Each exercise has a specific representational purpose: to create a plotted drawing, to develop a drawing for laser cutting, or to assemble a model that can be fabricated with subtractive or additive 3-D rapid-prototyping systems. All of these options will be demonstrated in a variety of ways, and these digital representations are as important as the algorithmic methods used to create them.

Who is this workbook written for?

The primary focus of this workbook is to introduce computational architecture, but any artist or sculptor who is interested in developing non-image-based digital methods will find much to discover here. Architecture students and practicing design professionals interested in exploring new digital design methods will also benefit from this workbook, which is meant to be a tool for demonstrating methods. With over 450 listed functions, these pages provide the roadmap for charting your own course, with each exercise providing an underlying design-and-programming concept to explore.

We start with the assumption that the reader has never written a program. All you need is a working knowledge of two- and three-dimensional AutoCAD. Any version will do, but this set of functions has been tested with AutoCAD 2008. On occasion, AutoCAD changes its commands, but such changes are included and explained in the text.

This workbook is intended to be executed, not read. As you work your way through the functions, try to consider all of the alternatives, even those that I have omitted. The most important aspect of this workbook is for you to develop the ability to implement your own ideas.

What does *The Codewriting Workbook* cover?

* Chapter 2: basic operations and expressions, the fundamental elements of AutoLISP, and how computations are developed

* Chapter 3: how to create a drawing using a function, how information within a drawing is communicated, and how to develop simple drawing elements

* Chapter 4: how decisions and repetition are specified and how language elements are used to create drawings and models

* Chapter 5: how to first create a simple lineal form, then a more complex one along a circular path, and how to explore a form starting with a simple representation and expanding it to include complex architectural concepts

* Chapter 6: methods for developing a variety of two- and three-dimensional constructions based on randomness; both vertical and horizontal forms are explored

* Chapter 7: techniques for generating forms based on external data, such as weather information or images

Sometimes, dealing with drawings and models requires a background in mathematics. When necessary, equations are included within the workbook. You will also find that certain examples are very similar to existing commands in AutoCAD, such as drawing an n-sided polygon.

It is always practical to understand how basic CAD operations are implemented. You may never need to use your own polygon function, but knowing how the vertices in a polygon are computed may be very important for other, more complex functions. Often times, a basic procedure provides the point of departure for developing the methods you specifically require.

Now, let's get started.

—Robert J. Krawczyk

2.0

AutoLISP's programming environment is based on the concept of evaluating a function. This chapter covers the most rudimentary functions consisting of basic operations and mathematical expressions. Associated with these operations are data types that can be processed, such as individual numbers, strings, and lists.

Operations and expressions are the basic methods used to relate numeric and character values. AutoLISP is based on the simple concept of evaluating a function. The function requires an operator and some values. This section covers data types that can be used as values, as well as basic, built-in operators.

Definitions

Real number: a set of digits containing a decimal point, it can be positive or negative

Integer: whole numbers, positive or negative (and without a decimal point)

String: any set of printable characters—such as numbers and spaces—enclosed between two sets of double quotes and including a single character

List: a collection of any number of data elements contained within parentheses; it may include real, integer, string values, other lists and symbols, or it can be empty

Constant: an actual numeric or string value

Variable: a symbol to represent a specific value for a real, integer, string, or list

Function: a list that can be evaluated, some functions have an assigned name; others have a symbol, such as the plus sign (+) for addition

Expression: a combination of functions, variables, and constants to be evaluated

Nil: a special value representing the absence of a value; it is different from a space and the value zero

Instructions

Simply type each function at the AutoCAD command line.

For example, type:

```
(+ 1 2)
```

Press the Enter key after closing the parentheses, and try to anticipate the answer. Once you get the answer, try to understand why it evaluated the way it did.

In this example, the plus sign is the function or operator, and the integers `1` and `2` are the arguments. The function + is applied to arguments `1` and `2`. The result of this evaluation will be an integer, `3`.

Exercises

This series of exercises includes a number of examples that demonstrate what to do and, more importantly, what not to do. Pay close attention. Later, when an error occurs in one of your functions, the explanation will most likely be found in this chapter. Not all conditions or potential variations are covered here. This is a good time to try a variation of a function, just to see what happens. It may not make sense at first, but try substituting a number for a string. You should know what happens if you do. Be sure to try many combinations. And finally, get your left and right parentheses to match.

* In the next set of exercises, notice the use of integers and real numbers, the way each function is structured, the function keyword or symbol, and the arguments that the function requires. Order and data type are critical.

* If you do not get the expected result, just type it again. To get out of an error condition, press the Escape key.

* In all of these examples, type the text following >> at the AutoCAD command line. To end the text, press the Enter key.

* Start a new drawing. Set the drawing units to architectural. Turn off all snaps, including object snap `(OSNAP)` and dynamic input `(DYN)`.

2.1 Addition

Add integers:

```
>> (+ 1 2)
3
```

Separate the function from the argument:

```
>> (+1 2)
; error: bad function: 1
```

```
>> (+1 2)
; error: bad function: 1
```

```
>>( + 1     2     )
3
```

Add an integer to a real number:

```
>> (+ 1 0.0)
1.0
```

```
>> (+ 1 2.0)
3.0
```

```
>> (+ 1 2.2)
3.2
```

Add real numbers:

```
>> (+ 1.7 2.2)
3.9
```

Add negative and positive numbers, integer or real:

```
>> (+ -5.0 2)
-3.0
```

```
>> (+ 5.0 -2)
3.0
```

```
>> (+ -5 -2)
-7
```

Add fractions less than 1.0:

```
>> (+ 1 .5)
; error: misplaced dot on input
```

```
>> (+ 1 0.5)
1.5
```

Add a series of numbers:

```
>> (+ 1 2 3 4 5)
15
```

```
>> (+ 1 2 3 4 5.0)
15.0
```

Some common typos:

```
>> (+ 1 2))
; error: extra right paren on input
```

Press the Escape key to return to the command line:

```
>> (+ 1 2(
((_>
```

```
>> (+ 1 2
((_>
```

```
>> (+- 1 2)
; error: no function definition: +-
```

```
>> (+ 1.. 2)
; error: bad argument type: numberp:
nil
```

```
>> (+ 1 2..)
; error: bad argument type: numberp:
nil

>> ( 1 + 2)
; error: bad function: 1

>> (+ 1-2)
; error: bad argument type: numberp:
nil

>> (+1-2)
; error: no function definition: +1-2
```

What if numbers include unit designations?

```
>> (+ 1 $2.00)
; error: bad argument type: numberp:
nil

>> (+ 1 12,000)
; error: bad argument type: numberp:
nil

>> (+ 1 1")
("_>
```

Press the Escape key to return to the command line.

2.2 Subtraction

Subtract integers:

```
>> (- 6 1)
5

>> (- 1 6)
-5

>> (- 6)
-6

>> (- 0 6)
-6
```

Subtract integers and real numbers:

```
>> (- 1 0.0)
1.0

>> (- 0.0 1)
-1.0

>> (- 1 6.6)
-5.6

>> (- -5.0 2)
-7.0

>> (- 5.0 -2)
7.0

>> (- 1 0.5)
0.5
```

Subtract real numbers:

```
>> (- 4.0 2.5)
1.5

>> (- 0.5 0.75)
-0.25

>> (- 1.0 -3.0)
4.0
```

Subtract a series of numbers:

```
>> (- 1 2 3 4 5)
-13

>> (- 1 2 3 4 5.0)
-13.0
```

2.3 Multiplication

Multiply integers:

```
>> (* 2 2)
4

>> (* 2 0)
0
```

Multiply integers and real numbers:

```
>> (* 2 2.0)
4.0

>> (* 2.0 2)
4.0

>> (* 2 2.5)
5.0

>> (* 2 -2.5)
-5.0

>> (* -2 -2.5)
5.0

>> (* 2 0.5)
1.0

>> (* 2 0.0)
0.0

>> (* 0.0 2)
0.0
```

Multiply real numbers:

```
>> (* 2.0 2.5)
5.0

>> (* 3.0 0.5)
1.5

>> (* 3.0 0.0000001)
3.0e-007
```

Multiply a series of numbers:

```
>> (* 1 2 3 4 5)
120

>> (* 1 2 3 4 5.0)
120.0
```

2.4 Division

Divide integers:

```
>> (/ 6 2)
3

>> (/ 6 4)
1

>> (/ 2 6)
0
```

Divide integers and real numbers:

```
>> (/ 6 4.0)
1.5

>> (/ 14 3)
4

>> (/ 14 3.0)
4.66667

>> (/ 4 6)
0

>> (/ 4 6.0)
0.666667

>> (/ 4.0 6)
0.666667
```

Divide real numbers:

```
>> (/ 4.0 0.5)
8.0

>> (/ 4.0 3.0)
1.33333

>> (/ 4.0 2.0)
2.0
```

Divide with zeros:

```
>> (/ 0 4)
0

>> (/ 0 4.0)
0.0
```

The division-by-zero error will terminate a function:

```
>> (/ 4 0)
; error: divide by zero

>> (/ 4.0 0)
; error: divide by zero
```

Divide a series of numbers:

```
>> (/ 1 2 3 4 5)
0

>> (/ 1.0 2.0 3.0 4.0 5.0)
0.00833333

>> (/ 1 2 3 4.0 5.0)
0.00833333

>> (/ 1.0 2 3 4.0 5.0)
0.00833333
```

2.5 Increment and Decrement

```
>> (1+ 6)
7

>> (1+ 6.5)
7.5

>> (1- 6)
5

>> (1- 6.5)
5.5

>> (2+ 3)
; error: no function definition: 2+
```

2.6 Assign a Variable a Value

Assign integers and real numbers:

```
>> (setq a 2.5)
2.5

>> (setq a 2)
2
```

Convert a number to a real:

```
>> (setq a (float 2))
2.0
```

Convert a number to an integer:

```
>> (setq a (fix 2.5))
2

>> (setq a (+ 3 2.5))
5.5
```

Convert an addition operation to an integer:

```
>> (setq a (fix (+ 3 2.5)))
5

>> (setq a (float (fix (+ 3 2.5))))
5.0
```

Convert a division operation to a real number:

```
>> (setq a (/ 1 6))
0

>> (setq a (float (/ 1 6)))
0.0

>> (setq a (/ (float 1) 6))
0.166667

>> (setq a (/ 1.0 6))
0.166667

>> (setq a (/ 1.0 6.0))
0.166667
```

Does case matter in variable names?

```
>> (setq a 2)
2

>> (setq A 4)
4

>> (setq b (+ a A))
8
```

Display the current value of a variable:

```
>> !a
4

>> !A
4
```

Set a variable to a negative value:

```
>> (setq b -a)
nil

>> (setq b (-a))
:error; no function: -A

>> (setq b (- a))
-4

>> (setq b (* a -1))
-4

>> (setq b (* a -1.0))
-4.0
```

Compute an expression with an undefined variable:

```
>> (setq b (+ a z))
; error: bad argument type: numberp:
nil

>> !z
nil
```

Variable names:

```
>> (setq b_1 (+ a 1))
5

>> (setq b 1 (+ a 1))
; error: syntax error

>> (setq 1b (+ a 1))
5

>> (setq 000b (+ a 1))
5

>> (setq b1 (+ a 1))
5

>> (setq b01 (+ a 1))
5
```

2.7 Division and the Remainder Function

```
>> (setq a 6.0)
6.0

>> (setq b 4.0)
4.0

>> (setq c (/ a b))
1.5

>> (setq c (/ (fix a) (fix b)))
1

>> (setq c (rem a b))
2.0

>> (setq c (rem 6 2))
0

>> (setq c (rem 7 2))
1

>> (setq c (rem 7 2.0))
1.0

>> (setq c (rem 7 2.5))
2.0
```

```
>> (setq c (rem 2 6))
2

>> (setq c (rem 2 0.5))
0.0

>> (setq c (rem 2.25 0.5))
0.25

>> (setq c (rem 2 5.0))
2.0

>> (setq c (rem 7 -2))
1

>> (setq c (rem 2 0))
; error: divide by zero
```

Use the remainder function to determine if a number is even or odd:

```
>> (setq c (rem 4 2))
0

>> (setq c (rem 5 2))
1
```

2.8 Absolute and Square Root Functions

Absolute values of integers and real numbers:

```
>> (setq a -6.0)
-6.0

>> (setq b 6)
6

>> (setq c (abs a))
6.0

>> (setq c (abs b))
6
```

Square roots of integers and real numbers:

```
>> (setq c sqrt b))
2.44949

>> (setq c (sqrt a))
; error: function undefined for
argument: -6.0

>> (setq c (sqrt (abs a)))
2.44949

>> (setq c (sqrt (/ b 10)))
0.0
```

2.9 Powers and Roots

Powers of integers and real numbers:

```
>> (setq c (expt 2 2))
4

>> (setq c (expt 2 2.0))
4.0

>> (setq c (expt 2 4))
16

>> (setq c (expt -2 4))
16

>> (setq c (expt 2 4.0))
16.0

>> (setq c (expt 2 -4))
0

>> (setq c (expt 2 1))
2

>> (setq c (expt 2 0))
1
```

Use a fraction to compute a root:

```
>> (setq c (expt 25 (/ 1.0 2.0)))
5.0

>> (setq c (expt 25 0.5))
5.0

>> (setq c (expt 25 -0.5))
0.2

>> (setq c (expt -25 0.5))
; error: x**y is undefined when x is
real >> 0, and y is not a whole number
```

Compare the computation of a cube and a cube root:

```
>> (setq c (expt 3 3))
27

>> (setq d (expt c 0.33333))
2.99997

>> (setq d (expt c (/ 1 3)))
1

>> (setq d (expt c (/ 1.0 3.0)))
3.0

>> (setq d (expt c (/ 1 3.0)))
3.0
```

2.10 Expressions

Initialize variables a and b:

```
>> (setq a 1)
1

>> (setq b 2)
2
```

Increase or decrease a variable by the value of 1. Note that the variable appears twice in the assignment:

```
>> (setq a (+ a 1))
2

>> (setq a (- a 1))
1
```

Accumulate values into a variable:

```
>> (setq a (+ a b))
3

>> (setq a (+ a b))
5
```

Reset the value of variables a and b:

```
>> (setq a 1)
1

>> (setq b 2)
2

>> !b
2
```

The innermost function is evaluated first:

```
>> (setq c (/ (+ a b) 2))
1

>> (setq c (/ 2 (+ a b)))
0

>> (setq c (/ 2.0 (+ a b)))
0.666667

>> (setq c (* 2 (+ a b)))
6

>> (setq c (* 2.0 (+ a b)))
6.0
```

```
>> (setq c (/ (+ a b) 2.0))
1.0

>> (setq c (+ (/ a 2) 2.0))
2.0

>> (setq c (/ (+ a b) 2))
1.5

>> (setq c (/ 1 2))
0

>> (setq c (/ 1 2.0))
0.5

>> (setq c (/ 1 a))
1

>> (setq c (/ 1 b))
0

>> (setq c (/ a b))
0

>> (setq a 1)
1

>> (setq b 2.0)
2.0

>> (setq c (/ a b))
0.5

>> (setq c (* a b))
2.0

>> (setq c (/ 1 (/ a 2)))
; error: divide by zero

>> (setq c (/ 1 (/ a 2.0)))
2.0

>> (setq c (/ 1 (/ 1 b)))
2.0
```

2.11 Translating Expressions

One of the common challenges when writing functions is translating equations from mathematical and engineering texts.

Here are some examples:

$$c = \frac{1}{3} + 2$$

```
>> (setq c (+ (/ 1 3) 2))
2
```

$$c = \frac{6}{3} + 2$$

```
>> (setq c (+ (/ 6 3) 2))
4
```

$$c = \frac{7}{3} + 2$$

```
>> (setq c (+ (/ 7 3) 2))
4
```

$$c = \frac{7}{3} + 2.0$$

```
>> (setq c (+ (/ 7 3) 2.0))
4.0
```

$$c = \frac{6+2}{3}$$

```
>> (setq c (/ (+ 6 2) 3))
2
```

$$c = \frac{6+2}{3.0}$$

```
>> (setq c (/ (+ 6 2) 3.0))
2.66667
```

$$c = \frac{10(6+2)}{3+2}$$

```
>> (setq c (/ (* 10 (+ 6 2)) (+ 3 2)))
16
```

$$c=\frac{6}{3}+\frac{2}{4}$$

```
>> (setq c (+ (/ 6 3) (/ 2 4)))
2
```

$$c=\frac{6}{3}+\frac{2}{4}+4.5$$

```
>> (setq c (+ (+ (/ 6 3) (/ 2 4)) 4.5))
6.5
```

$$c=\frac{\frac{6-9}{8+4}+5.5(6-3)}{3}$$

```
>> (setq c (/ (+ (/ (- 6 9) (+ 8 4)) (*
5.5 (- 6 3))) 3))
5.5
```

$$c=0.1+0.2+0.3+0.5+0.8+1.3+2.1+3.4$$

```
>> (setq c (+ 0.1 0.2 0.3 0.5 0.8 1.3 2.1
3.4))
8.7
```

What is the next term in the sequence?

```
5.5; the subsequent term is the
addition of the last two terms.
```

What is this sequence of numbers called?

```
Fibonacci; look up the Fibonacci number
on the web. Investigate other number
sequences.
```

Consider what these numbers might look like if they were plotted as the changing radius in a spiral.

2.12 Degrees, Radians, and Trigonometric Functions

All variables first have to be defined. Here is one that is predefined:

```
>> !pi
3.14159
```

```
>> (setq a pi)
3.14159
```

The trigonometric functions needed for programming use radian measure, so you need to know how to convert degrees to radians and radians to degrees.

Use the function `defun` to define other functions. Define two functions, one that converts degrees to radians and one that converts radians to degrees:

```
>> (defun dtr (ang) (* pi (/ ang 180.0)))
DTR
```

```
>> (defun rtd (rad) (/ (*rad 180.0) pi))
RTD
```

Try each one:

```
>> (setq b (dtr 45))
0.785398
```

```
>> (setq c (rtd b))
45.0
```

Compute the sine of 30 degrees:

```
>> (setq b (sin 30))
-0.988032
```

Now compute the sine of 30 degrees in radian measure:

```
>> (setq b (sin (dtr 30)))
0.5
```

Other built-in trigonometric functions include cosine and arctangent:

```
>> (setq b (cos (dtr 30)))
0.866025
```

```
>> (setq b (atan (dtr 30)))
0.482348
```

Compute the tangent of an angle in radians:

```
>> (defun tan (ang) (/ (sin ang) (cos
ang)))
TAN
```

```
>> (setq b (tan (dtr 45)))
1.0
```

```
>> (setq b (tan (dtr 0)))
0.0
```

```
>> (setq b (tan (dtr 90)))
1.63312e+016
```

Compute the cotangent of an angle in radians:

```
>> (defun cotan (ang) (if (= (sin ang)
0) 0 (/ (cos ang) (sin ang))))
COTAN
```

Compute the arc-cosine in radians:

```
>> (defun acos (num) (- (/ pi 2.0) (atan
(/ num (sqrt (- 1.0 (* num num)))))))
ACOS
```

Compute the arcsine in radians:

```
>> (defun asin (num) (atan (/ num (sqrt
(- 1.0 (* num num))))))
ASIN
```

```
>> (setq b (sin (dtr 30)))
0.5
```

```
>> (setq c (asin b))
0.523599
```

```
>> (setq c (rtd (asin b)))
30.0
```

2.13 String Functions

Assign a string to a variable:

```
>> (setq s "ABCDE")
"ABCDE"
```

For string length, upper case, and substring functions, note that the same variable is redefined in these examples:

```
>> (setq a (strlen s))
5
```

```
>> (setq s (strcase "abcde"))
"ABCDE"
```

```
>> (setq s (strcat s "FG"))
"ABCDEFG"
```

```
>> (setq s (substr s 1 5))
"ABCDE"
```

```
>> (setq s (substr s 3))
"CDE"
```

Spaces count as characters in a string:

```
>> (setq s "ABC D E ")
"ABC D E "
```

```
>> (setq a (strlen s))
8
```

2.14 List Functions

Assign a list to a variable. A list can consist of numeric values, strings, and other lists:

```
>> (setq s (list "A" "B" "C" "D"))
("A" "B" "C" "D")
```

Get the first member of a list using the `car` function:

```
>> (setq x (car s))
"A"
```

Get all the members of a list except the first, using the `cdr` function:

```
>> (setq x (cdr s))
("B" "C" "D")
```

Combine the `car` and `cdr` functions to get other members of the list:

```
>> (setq x (car (cdr s)))
"B"
```

```
>> (setq x (cdr (cdr s)))
("C" "D")
```

```
>> (setq x (car (cdr (cdr s))))
"C"
```

Get the last member of a list:

```
>> (setq x (last s))
"D"
```

Get any member of the list by its index:

```
>> (setq x (nth 0 s))
"A"
```

```
>> (setq x (nth 3 s))
"D"
```

Index is set beyond the list:

```
>> (setq x (nth 4 s))
nil
```

An index can be a constant, a variable, or an expression:

```
>> (setq n 2)
2
```

```
>> (setq x (nth n s))
"C"
```

Get the length of a list or number of members:

```
>> (setq x (length s))
4
```

Reverse the members of a list:

```
>> (setq x (reverse s))
("D" "C" "B" "A")
```

Substitute one member of the list for another:

```
>> (setq x (subst "E" "D" s))
("A" "B" "C" "E")
```

Add a member to the beginning of the same list:

```
>> (setq s (cons "A" s))
("A" "A" "B" "C" "D")
```

Create a special kind of list, the dotted pair:

```
>> (setq x (cons 0 "LINE"))
(0 . "LINE")
```

```
>> (setq x (cons 0 LINE))
(0)
```

```
>> (setq x (cons 0 (list LINE)))
(0 nil)
```

Append a list to another list:

```
>> (setq s (append s (list "D")))
("A" "A" "B" "C" "D" "D")

>> (setq s (append s "D"))
; error: bad argument type: listp "D"

>> (setq s (append s (list "D" "D")))
("A" "A" "B" "C" "D" "D" "D" "D")

>> (setq x (subst "E" "D" s))
("A" "A" "B" "C" "E" "E" "E" "E")

>> !s
("A" "A" "B" "C" "D" "D" "D" "D")

>> (setq t (list 1 2 3 4))
(1 2 3 4)

>> (setq s (append s t))
("A" "A" "B" "C" "D" "D" "D" 1 2 3 4)

>> (setq s (append s (list t)))
("A" "A" "B" "C" "D" "D" "D" 1 2 3 4 (1
2 3 4))
```

Try some operations on individual members of a list:

```
>> (setq s (list "A" "B" "C" "D"))
("A" "B" "C" "D")

>> (setq x (+ (nth 0 s) (nth 3)))
; error: too few arguments

>> (setq x (+ (nth 0 s) (nth 3 s)))
; error: bad argument type: numberp:
"A"

>> (setq x (strcat (nth 0 s) (nth 3 s)))
"AD"

>> (setq x (list (nth 0 s) (nth 3 s)))
("A" "D")

>> (setq s (list 1 2 3 4))
(1 2 3 4)

>> (setq x (+ (nth 0 s) (nth 3 s)))
5

>> (setq x (list (nth 0 s) (nth 3 s)))
(1 4)

>> (setq x (list (nth 0 s) (nth 4 s)))
(1 nil)

>> (setq x (list (nth 0 s) (nth 3 r)))
; error: bad argument type: consp nil

>> !r
nil
```

Create a list of lists:

```
>> (setq s (list (list 1 10) (list 4 40)
(list 2 20)))
((1 10) (4 40) (2 20))
```

Use the first member of each sublist as an index. Then get individual members of that sublist:

```
>> (setq x (assoc 4 s))
(4 40)

>> (setq x (cdr (assoc 4 s)))
(40)

>> (setq x (car (cdr (assoc 4 s))))
40

>> (setq x (assoc 6 s))
nil

>> (setq s (list (list 1 10 "a") (list 4
40 "d") (list 2 20 "b")))
((1 10 "a") (4 40 "d") (2 20 "b"))

>> (setq x (assoc 4 s))
(4 40 "d")

>> (setq x (cdr (assoc 4 s)))
(40 "d")
```

```
>> (setq x (car (cdr (assoc 4 s))))
40

>> (setq x (cdr (cdr (assoc 4 s))))
("d")

>> (setq x (car (cdr (cdr (assoc 4 s)))))
"d"

>> (setq x (nth 0 (assoc 4 s)))
4

>> (setq x (nth 1 (assoc 4 s)))
40

>> (setq x (nth 2 (assoc 4 s)))
"d"

>> (setq x (nth 3 (assoc 4 s)))
nil

>> (setq x (nth 3 (assoc 4 r)))
; error: bad argument type: consp nil

>> !r
nil
```

2.15 Coordinate Lists, and Polar, Distance, and Angle Functions

Coordinates form the basis of all entity definitions in AutoCAD: a line is specified between two points, a circle has a centerpoint, and a rectangle is defined by two corner points. A point consists of three values. These points are defined as computationally absolute. That is, they represent actual x, y, and z values. Points are defined as relative when the value of the x, y, or z is offset from a current point or polar, which requires an angle showing a direction and a distance from a current point. An absolute point needs no computation. A relative point simply adds an offset distance to each coordinate. A polar point requires a bit more explanation.

The computation of polar coordinates requires a stationary point, a compass direction, and a distance. The standard compass is shown in the AutoCAD coordinate system. North is along the positive y-axis at 90 degrees. East is along the positive x-axis at 0 degrees. Note that compass angles increase counterclockwise. The origin for the coordinate system is (0.0, 0.0, 0.0). Each axis is labeled.

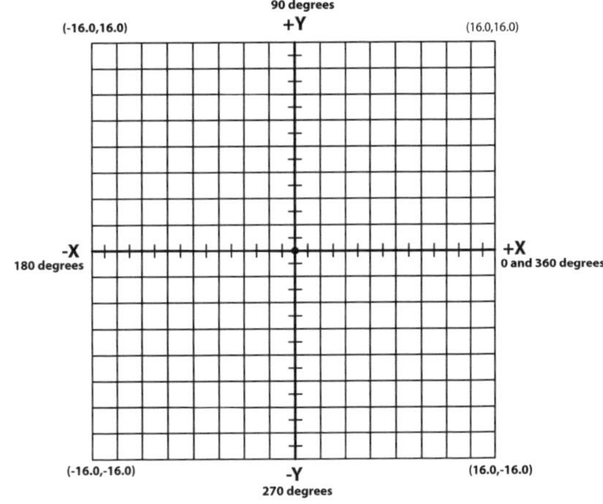

AutoCAD coordinate system

To be able to work with points, you must first create a list of three real numbers. This list represents the x, y, and z coordinates of a point.

First create the origin point using constants:

```
>> (setq pt0 (list 0.0 0.0 0.0))
(0.0 0.0 0.0)
```

Define the functions for degree and radian conversions:

```
>> (defun dtr (ang) (* pi (/ ang 180.0)))
DTR

>> (defun rtd (rad) (/ (* rad 180.0) pi))
RTD
```

Create a series of points with differing angles at a distance of ten architectural units. Is the distance value feet or inches? Locate these on the grid before computing them. All are located relative to the origin point.

```
>> (setq pt1 (polar pt0 (dtr 0) 10.0))
(10.0 0.0 0.0)
```

Compute a point at 90 degrees. Notice how close the x-coordinate is to zero:

```
>> (setq pt1 (polar pt0 (dtr 90) 10.0))
(6.12323e-016 10.0 0.0)
```

Enter the angle as degrees, not radians:

```
>> (setq pt1 (polar pt0 90 10.0))
(-4.48074 8.93997 0.0)
```

Try to enter the distance as feet:

```
>> (setq pt1 (polar pt0 (dtr 90) 10.0'))
; error: extra right paren on input
```

Compute points at 180 degrees and 270 degrees:

```
>> (setq pt1 (polar pt0 (dtr 180) 10.0))
(-10.0 1.22465e-015 0.0)

>> (setq pt1 (polar pt0 (dtr 270) 10.0))
(-1.83697e-015 -10.0 0.0)
```

Are the results for an angle of 0 degrees the same as for 360 degrees?

```
>> (setq pt1 (polar pt0 (dtr 360) 10.0))
(10.0 -2.44929e-015 0.0)
```

Is a negative compass setting different from a positive one?

```
>> (setq pt1 (polar pt0 (dtr -180) 10.0))
(-10.0 -1.22465e-015 0.0)
```

Is a negative distance the same as a positive distance?

```
>> (setq pt1 (polar pt0 (dtr 180) -10.0))
(10.0 -1.22465e-015 0.0)

>> (setq pt1 (polar pr0 ) dtr 45) 10.0))
(7.07107 7.07107 0.0)
```

What if the stationary point was not at a z-coordinate of 0.0?

```
>> (setq pt0 (list 0.0 0.0 10.0))
(0.0 0.0 10.0)

>> (setq pt1 (polar pt0 (dtr 45) 10.0))
(7.07107 7.07107 10.0)
```

Once you have a point, use the `car` and `cdr` functions to extract the x, y, and z coordinates:

```
>> (setq xpt1 (car pt1))
7.07107

>> (setq zpt1 (cdr pt1))
(7.07107 10.0)

>> (setq ypt1 (car (cdr pt1)))
7.07107

>> (setq ypt1 (cadr pt1))
7.07107

>> (setq zpt1 (cdr (cdr pt1)))
(10.0)

>> (setq zpt1 (car (cdr (cdr pt1))))
10.0

>> (setq zpt1 (car (cddr pt1)))
10.0
```

An easier method is to use the `nth` function:

```
>> (setq xpt1 (nth 0 pt1))
7.07107

>> (setq ypt1 (nth 1 pt1))
7.07107

>> (setq zpt1 (nth 2 pt1))
10.0

>> (setq npt1 (nth 3 pt1))
nil
```

Find the distance between two points:

```
>> !pt0
(0.0 0.0 10.0)

>> !pt1
(7.07107 7.07107 10.0)

>> (setq d (distance pt0 pt1))
10.0

>> (setq d (distance pt1 pt0))
10.0
```

Find the angle, in radians or degrees, between two points:

```
>> (setq a (angle pt0 pt1))
0.785398

>> (setq a (rtd (angle pt0 pt1)))
45.0

>> (setq a (angle pt1 pt0))
3.92699

>> (setq a (rtd (angle pt1 pt0)))
225.0
```

Create two new points and find the included angle between them:

```
>> (setq pt1 (polar pt0 (dtr 45) 10.0))
(7.07107 7.07107 10.0)

>> (setq pt2 (polar pt0 (dtr 0) 10.0))
(10.0 0.0 10.0)

>> (setq ang1 (angle pt0 pt1))
0.785398

>> (setq ang1 (rtd (angle pt0 pt1)))
45.0

>> (setq ang2 (rtd (angle pt0 pt2)))
0.0

>> (setq inc (- ang2 ang1))
-45.0
```

Create another point from coordinates previously extracted as variables:

```
>> (setq pt3 (list xpt1 ypt1 zpt1))
(7.07107 7.07107 10.0)
```

Create a point with offsets in the x and y directions:

```
>> (setq pt4 (list (+ xpt1 4.0) (+ ypt1
4.0) zpt1))
(11.0711 11.0711 10.0)
```

Create a point with an offset in the z direction:

```
>> (setq pt5 (list xpt1 ypt1 (- zpt1
5.0)))
(7.07107 7.07107 5.0)
```

Create a point using the `nth` function and an offset in the z-direction:

```
>> (setq pt6 (list (nth 0 pt3) (nth 1
pt3) (+ (nth 2 pt3) 5.0)))
(7.07107 7.07107 15.0)
2-23 2-24
```

The z-coordinates in the previously shown distance and angle functions had the same value, but what if they did not?

```
>> (setq pt0 (list 0.0 0.0 0.0))
(0.0 0.0 0.0)

>> !pt1
(7.07107 7.07107 10.0)

>> (setq d (distance pt0 pt1))
14.1421

>> (setq a (angle pt0 pt1))
0.785398
```

Notice that the angle computation remains in the xy-plane:

```
>> (setq a (rtd (angle pt0 pt1)))
45.0
```

3.0

Functions that define architectural design concepts must be capable of handling a variety of situations, and they must be able to ask for the data needed for computation. AutoLISP has a variety of functions for obtaining these values, and a number of data types for computing points: real, integer, string, distance, angle, and points picked directly from the drawing. We will first start with points picked from the screen.

For these examples, start a new drawing and set the drawing units to architectural. Turn off all snaps, including object snap (OSNAP) and dynamic input (DYN), if available.

3.1 Getting Points and Drawing Lines

To pick a point from the screen, enter the getpoint function at the command line. Then pick a point with the left click of the mouse button:

```
>>(getpoint)    [pick point]
```

Assign the point to a variable:

```
>>(setq pnt1 (getpoint))   [pick point]
```

Check the coordinates of the point:

```
!pnt1
```

Relative to architectural units, do the selected coordinates represent feet, feet and inches, or inches?

Inches.

Notice that for this version of the getpoint function, a prompt or message is not displayed on the command line. This let's you know that the function is waiting for you to pick a point.

Get two points to draw a line, with an added prompt:

```
>>(setq pnt1 (getpoint "From point:"))
[pick point]
```

```
>>!pnt1
```

```
>>(setq pnt2 (getpoint "To point:"))
[pick point]
```

```
>>!pnt2
```

Draw a line between the picked points:

```
>>(command ".LINE" pnt1 pnt2 "")
```

The command function accepts any AutoCAD command that can be executed at the command line. The first argument is the command keyword preceded by a period. The period tells AutoCAD to use the native meaning of the keyword, not an alias. Next, you must input the arguments for that command. Order and data type are critical. To determine the arguments, execute the command keyword at the command line and record how it is answered. Take careful note of the order and type of entries, such as numbers, options, points, and selections. Double quotation marks represent the Enter key.

Some AutoCAD commands display a dialog box. To suppress the dialog box and see the required entries, enter a dash as a prefix before the command keyword. For example, the ARRAY command would be entered:

```
>>-array
```

What happens when a point is not picked? In the following examples, press the Escape and Enter keys, as shown.

```
>>(setq pnt3 (getpoint "To point:"))
[ESC]
```

```
>>!pnt3
```

```
>>(setq pnt3 (getpoint "To point:"))
[Enter]
```

```
>>!pnt3
```

Try a few more entries. Enter points as coordinates; absolute, relative, or polar numbers; and real numbers, integers, and distances.

Always check the command line to see what coordinate values are returned.

An alternate method would be to get a point with a longer prompt and a function to display its value:

```
>>(prompt "First point:")
```

```
>>(setq pnt3 (getpoint)) [pick point]
```

```
>>(prompt pnt3)
```

```
>>(princ pnt3)
```

Draw a line using the start point as a reference for the endpoint. Notice that a rubberband line is displayed when it asks for the endpoint:

```
>>(setq pnt1 (getpoint "Start point:"))
[pick point]
```

```
>>(setq pnt2 (getpoint pnt1
"Endpoint:")) [pick point]
```

```
>>(command ".LINE" pnt1 pnt2 "")
```

Draw a line using start and corner points. Notice that a rubberband rectangle is displayed when it asks for the endpoint:

```
>>(setq pnt1 (getpoint "From point:"))
[pick point]
```

```
>>(setq pnt2 (getcorner pnt1 "To
point:")) [pick point]
```

```
>>(command ".LINE" pnt1 pnt2 "")
```

Draw a polyline, a single object composed of one or more connected line segments or circular arcs treated as a single object, from three points:

```
>>(setq pnt1 (getpoint "First point:"))
[pick point]
```

```
>>(setq pnt2 (getpoint "Second point:"))
[pick point]
```

```
>>(setq pnt3 (getpoint "Third point:"))
[pick point]
```

```
>>(command ".PLINE" pnt1 pnt2 pnt3 pnt1
"")
```

Why use a `PLINE` instead of three line-commands?

`Because a polyline is one graphic entity. Three lines would be three entities. A polyline is defined as any continuous series of lines or arcs.`

Is there another `PLINE` sequence you could use to create the closed triangle?

Erase the current polyline and enter:

```
>>(command ".PLINE" pnt1 pnt2 pnt3 "c")
```

The `c-option` closes the polyline. Execute the `PLINE` command, and see what other options are available:

```
>> pline
```

```
Specify start point:
```

```
Specify next point or [Arc/Halfwidth/
Length/Undo/Width]:
```

```
Specify next point or [Arc/Close/
Halfwidth/Length/Undo/Width]:
```

What are the PLINE's current properties, including layer, color, and line type? Later, we will discuss how to assign properties when creating a graphic entity.

To prepare for the next section, try entering functions that display text on the screen:

```
>>(textscr)

>>(princ "TEXT")

>>(princ "\nTEXT again")

>>(princ "\n\nTEXT still again")

>>(princ)

>>(graphscr)
```

The textscr and graphscr functions turn the text window on and off. Notice that the princ function, by itself, returns nothing.

What is the purpose of \n?

It adds a new line character.

3.2 Defining a Function

To draw a line, it took a number of commands to get the points and create the line. What we want to do next is place these instructions in a file and define our own function for executing them. This way, we won't have to retype the function at the command line. For this, we will use AutoCAD's Text Editor.

To execute the AutoLISP Editor, select the Tools drop-down menu from the AutoCAD toolbar, then click AutoLISP and Visual LISP Editor. In the Editor Toolbar, select File and then New File.

A new window will open in Text Editor. This window contains a set of AutoLISP functions. First, add the rtd and dtr functions by typing the following:

```
;----------------------------------
(defun dtr (a) (* pi (/ a 180.0)))
(defun rtd (a) (/ (* a 180.0) pi))
;----------------------------------
```

Enter the following function:

```
;----------------------------------
(defun prog01 ()
 (graphscr)
 ; get line points
 (prompt "\nLine")
 (setq pnt1
   (getpoint "\nFrom point:"))
 (setq pnt2
   (getpoint pnt1 "\nTo point:"))
 ; draw line
 (command ".LINE" pnt1 pnt2 "")
 ; display coordinates
 (textscr)
 (princ "\nStart/endpoints: ")
 (princ pnt1) (princ "-")
 (princ pnt2)
 (princ)
)
;----------------------------------
```

As you type, notice the color coding. Every time you type an open parenthesis mark, the program automatically prompts the corresponding close parenthesis mark. Type all of the instructions in lowercase, except for lines that begin with a semicolon, which are comments. Any text that appears inside of double quotation marks will not be processed by AutoLISP. Indenting is optional.

* Save the file as CH03.LSP.

* From the Editor Toolbar, select File and Save As.

* Return to AutoCAD.

* From the Main Toolbar, select Tools, AutoLISP, and Load Application.

* Select the file you just saved.

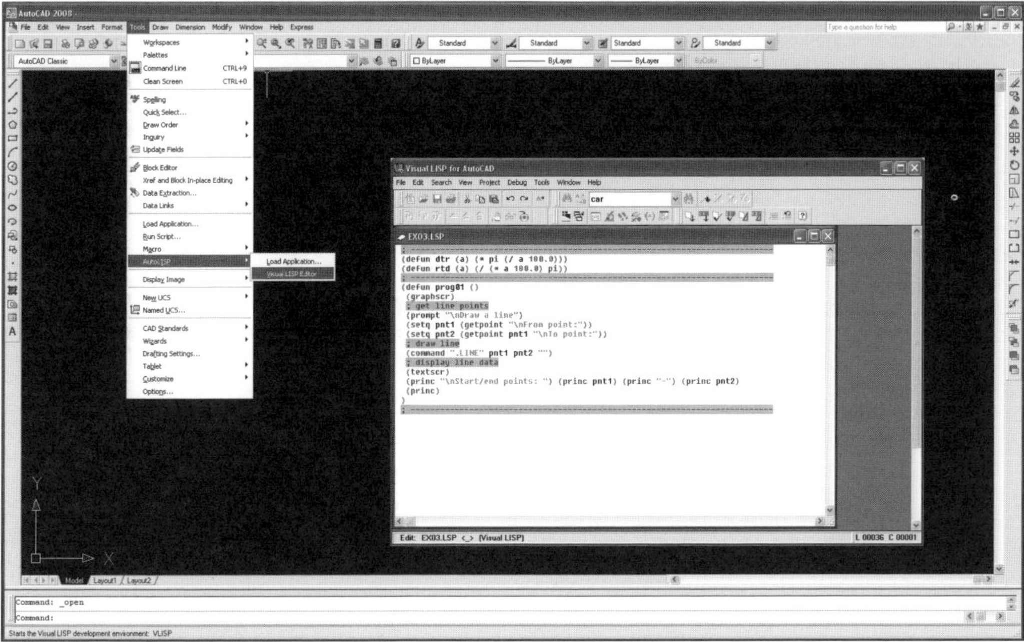

How to execute the AutoLISP editor

* Close the Load Application dialog box and press function-key F2 to see if the LSP file has loaded without errors. If errors are listed, go back to Text Editor and make the changes.

* At the AutoCAD command line, execute the function by entering it and pressing the Enter key:

```
>>(prog01)
```

* Answer the prompts as the function executes.

* Use function-key F2 to close the text window.

* Test the function.

* If changes are needed, return to Text Editor, save it again, load it again, and execute it until it is correct.

Review the structure of function `PROG01`.

In `PROG01`, the function executes `graphscr` to set the current window to graphics. Next, use the `getpoint` function to pick two points, then execute the AutoCAD `LINE` command to draw a line between these points. Finally, the text screen opens, and the coordinates for the two points are displayed.

In file `CH03.LSP`, copy function `PROG01` and rename it `PROG02`. Modify the function so that the text screen displays the drawn line coordinates, x and y offsets, length, and angle in degrees. For example:

```
Start/endpoints: (0.00 0.00 0.00)-(0.00
0.00 0.00)
X offset:  0.00  Y offset:  0.00
Length: 0.00  Angle: 0.00
```

After the line is drawn, compute and display the coordinate data for the line.

The final function will be:

```
;----------------------------------
(defun prog02 ()
 (graphscr)
 ; get line points
 (prompt "\nLine")
 (setq pnt1
   (getpoint "\nFrom point:"))
 (setq pnt2
   (getpoint pnt1 "\nTo point:"))
 ; draw line
 (command ".LINE" pnt1 pnt2 "")
 ; compute offsets
 (setq xoff (- (nth 0 pnt2)
   (nth 0 pnt1)))
 (setq yoff (- (nth 1 pnt2)
   (nth 1 pnt1)))
 ; display coordinates
 (textscr)
 (princ "\nStart/endpoints: ")
 (princ pnt1) (princ "-")
 (princ pnt2)
 (princ "\nX offset: ") (princ xoff)
 (princ "  Y offset: ") (princ yoff)
 (princ "\nLength: ")
 (princ (distance pnt1 pnt2))
 (princ "  ") (princ "Angle: ")
 (princ (rtd (angle pnt1 pnt2)))
 (princ)
)
;----------------------------------
```

Use AutoCAD's `LIST` or `PROPERTIES` command to verify your results.

3.3 Drawing a Triangle

Using the concepts in `PROG02`, add function `PROG03` to draw a right triangle. Use the lower-left and upper-right corner points to compute the lower-right corner.

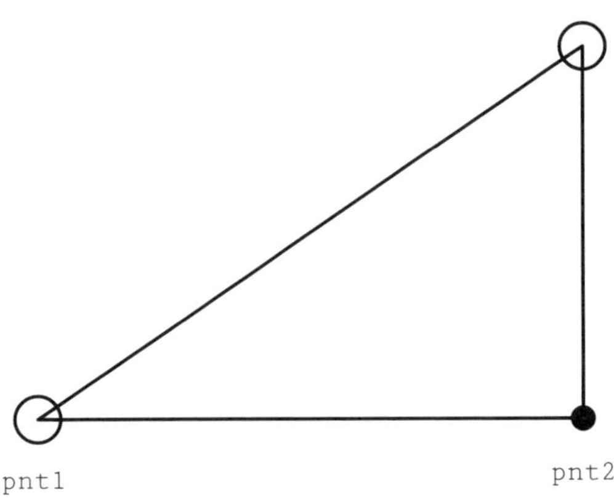

`PROG03`: drawing a triangle

Construct the right triangle as a polyline and display the following on the text screen:

```
Base:  0.00  Height:  0.00  Area:  0.00
Perimeter:  0.00
```

The corner point is computed based on the locations of the other two points:

```
X of pnt2 = X of pnt3
Y of pnt2 = Y of pnt1
Z of pnt2 = Z of pnt1
```

Note that when computing the second point, you are using the first point's z-coordinate value. This takes into account the previous elevation setting or a three-dimensional point that has been entered.

Completed function `PROG03`:

```
;----------------------------------
(defun prog03 ()
 (graphscr)
 ; get corner and top points
 (prompt "\nRight triangle")
 (setq pnt1
```

```
    (getpoint "\nCorner of base:"))
  (setq pnt3
    (getcorner pnt1 "\nTop corner:"))
  ; compute second point
  (setq pnt2 (list (nth 0 pnt3)
    (nth 1 pnt1) (nth 2 pnt1)))
  ; draw triangle
  (command ".PLINE" pnt1 pnt2 pnt3
    pnt1 "")
  ; display triangle data
  (textscr)
  ; base and height
  (setq xside (abs (- (nth 0 pnt2)
    (nth 0 pnt1))))
  (setq yside (abs (- (nth 1 pnt3)
    (nth 1 pnt2))))
  (princ "\nBase: ") (princ xside)
  (princ "  ")
  (princ "Height: ") (princ yside)
  ; area and perimeter
  (setq tarea (/ (* xside yside) 2))
  (setq tperm (+ (distance pnt1 pnt2)
    (distance pnt2 pnt3)
    (distance pnt3 pnt1)))
  (princ "\nArea: ") (princ tarea)
  (princ "  ")
  (princ "Perimeter: ") (princ tperm)
  (princ)
)
;---------------------------------
```

Execute PROG03 for a number of different points. Use AutoCAD's LIST or PROPERTIES command to verify your results.

Additional exercises:

* Does PROG03 work if the right base and upper-left corners are picked?

* Always test each function for alternative ways to answer each prompt.

* Review the computation of the base, height, area, and perimeter of PROG03.

* Consider how you could draw other types of triangles.

* How else could you specify the dimensions of a triangle?

* How much of a graphic shape can be defined visually by picked points?

* When are actual dimensions required or preferred?

* Consider what kinds of information AutoCAD asks for when specifying lines, rectangles, polylines, polygons, circles, and arcs.

3.4 Drawing a Rectangle

Using the concepts in PROG03, add function PROG04 to draw a rectangle. Use the lower-left and upper-right corner points to compute the two remaining corners.

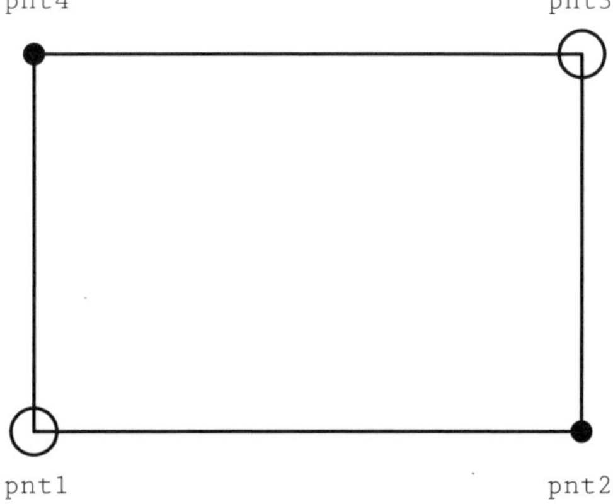

PROG04: draw a rectangle by computing two corners points

Create the rectangle by asking for the opposite corners. Construct it as a polyline and display the following on the text screen:

```
Length:  0.00  Width:  0.00  Area:  0.00
Perimeter:  0.00
```

The corner points are computed based on the two given points:

```
X of pnt2 = X of pnt3
Y of pnt2 = Y of pnt1
Z of pnt2 = Z of pnt1
```

Write PROG04 using this outline:

```
; ----------------------------
; PROG04 - draw a rectangle,
; by corners
(defun prog04 ()
(graphscr)
(prompt
  "\nDraw a rectangle, by corners")
; get bottom-left corner
  .
; get top-right corner
  .
; compute the two remaining points
  .
; draw rectangle
  .
; display rectangle data
  .
(princ)
)
; ----------------------------
```

Execute PROG04 for a number of different points. Use AutoCAD's LIST or PROPERTIES command to verify your results.

Additional exercises:

* Does the first point have to be the bottom-left corner?

* What are some other choices?

* Consider how you would draw the rectangle using its dimensions.

* What happens when points other than the lower-left and upper-right corners are selected?

* Test a number of different ways of executing your function.

Completed function PROG04:

```
;----------------------------------
(defun prog04 ()
 (graphscr)
 ; get corner points
 (prompt
   "\nRectangle, corners")
 (setq pnt1
   (getpoint "\nFirst corner:"))
 (setq pnt3
   (getcorner pnt1
   "\nSecond corner:"))
 ; compute other two points
 (setq pnt2 (list (nth 0 pnt3)
   (nth 1 pnt1) (nth 2 pnt1)))
 (setq pnt4 (list (nth 0 pnt1)
   (nth 1 pnt3) (nth 2 pnt1)))
 ; draw rectangle
 (command ".PLINE" pnt1 pnt2 pnt3
   pnt4 pnt1 "")
 ; display rectangle data
 (textscr)
 ; length and width
 (setq xside (abs (- (nth 0 pnt2)
   (nth 0 pnt1))))
 (setq yside (abs (- (nth 1 pnt3)
   (nth 1 pnt2))))
 (princ "\nLength: ") (princ xside)
 (princ "  ")
 (princ "Width: ") (princ yside)
 ; area and perimeter
 (setq tarea (* xside yside))
 (setq tperm (+ (* xside 2)
   (* yside 2)))
 (princ "\nArea: ") (princ tarea)
 (princ "  ")
 (princ "Perimeter: ") (princ tperm)
 (princ)
)
;----------------------------------
```

3.5 Getting Numeric Values

In addition to getting points from the screen, numeric values are sometimes needed.

If it's not already loaded, load `CH03.LSP` so that the functions `rtd` and `dtr` are defined. To get real and integer values use the `getreal` and `getint` functions. Execute each of these several times from the AutoCAD command line. Enter an integer, a real, a string, a dimension, and take note of the results. Also enter a few typos and watch for error messages.

For example:

```
>>(setq xside (getreal "Enter a
number:"))

>>(setq xside (getint "Enter a
number:"))
```

To get an angle, use the `getorient` function and enter the angle in degrees or by specifying two points:

```
>>(setq ang (getorient "Enter angle:"))

>>!ang
```

Is `ang` in degrees or radians? Try entering:

```
>>!(rtd ang)
```

To get a distance, use the `getdist` function. Execute it a number of times using an integer, a real, a string, and a dimension, as well as a few mistyped entries. Take note of the results and watch for error messages.

For example:

```
>>(setq xside (getdist "Enter a
number:"))
```

Consider when you would use each of these `get` functions, such as for length, number of sides in a polygon, or weight.

3.6 Displaying Numeric Values

The `rtos` real-to-string function can convert a numeric value to a variety of units.

Note how units and precision are specified:

```
>>(setq xside 15.5)
15.5

>>(rtos xside 1)
"1.5500E+01"

>>(rtos xside 2)
"15.5000"

>>(rtos xside 3)
"1'-3.5000\""

>>(rtos xside 4)
"1'-3 1/2\""

>>(rtos xside)
"15.5000"

>>(setq xside 15.25)
15.25

>>(rtos xside 2 2)
"15.25"

>>(rtos xside 2 1)
"15.3"

>>(rtos xside 2 0)
"15"

>>(rtos xside 4 2)
"1'-3 1/4\""

>>(rtos xside 4 1)
"1'-3 1/2\""
```

```
>>(rtos xside 4 0)
"1'-3\""

>>(setq r (rtos xside 4 0))
"1'-3\""

>>!r
1'-3""
```

The `angtos` angle-to-string function can convert an angle to a variety of units:

```
>>(angtos 45)
"58"

>>(angtos (dtr 45))
"45"

>>(angtos pi)
"180"

>>(angtos pi 0 3)
"180.000"

>>(angtos pi 1 3)
"180d0'0\""

>>(angtos pi 2 3)
"200.000g"

>>(angtos pi 3 3)
"3.142r"

>>(angtos pi 4 3)
"W"
```

3.7 Drawing a Rectangle by Dimensions

Many shapes are based on known geometry and are defined by simple sets of dimensions. Creating these shapes by their dimensions is called parametric design or modeling. In other words, they are shapes and forms based on parameters. The rectangle is a simple example. It is defined by length and width. If you give a starting point and origin, all other points can be computed relative to the origin.

The origin can be set depending on the application. For example, rectangular box columns would be easier to place if their origin was in the center of the rectangle, not in the corner.

The other advantage to developing parametric models as functions is that shapes created by other methods, such as a `BLOCK`, can only be scaled. For example, the thickness of the flange-of-a-beam section would increase proportional to the depth of that section, which may not be the actual case. In parametric modeling, any dimension can be uniquely computed or specified.

Using `PROG04`, add function `PROG05` to draw a rectangle. Use a centerpoint, length, and width to compute the four corner points.

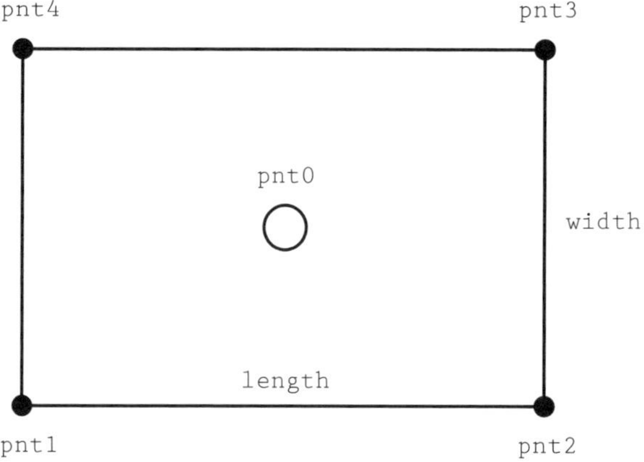

`PROG05`: draw a rectangle using a centerpoint

Write `PROG05` using this outline:

```
; ----------------------------
; PROG05 - draw a rectangle,
; by center and dimensions
(defun prog05 ()
(graphscr)
```

```
; get centerpoint
(prompt
  "\nDraw a rectangle, by center")
  .
; get length and width
  .
; compute corner points
  .
; draw rectangle
  .
; display rectangle data
  .
(princ)
)
; ---------------------------
```

Create the rectangle by asking for the centerpoint, length, and width. Then construct it as a polyline. Display the following on the text screen:

```
Length:  0'-0"  Width:  0'-0"  Area
sqft:  0.00  Perimeter:  0'-0"
```

The corner points are computed relative to the centerpoint, for example:

```
X of pnt2 = X of pnt0 + 1/2 of the
length
Y of pnt2 = Y of pnt0 - 1/2 of the
width
Z of pnt2 = Z of pnt0
```

Additional exercises:

* What `get` function will you use for the length and width values and why? Your options are `getint`, `getreal`, or `getdistance`.
* Note the data displayed on the text screen now includes units.
* Execute `PROG05` for a variety of rectangles. Check your dimensions, area, and perimeter using the `PROPERTIES` or `LIST` command.
* Are dimensions really needed for this type of rectangle?
* What can be input numerically?
* When is it better to input visually?

Completed function `PROG05`:

```
;-----------------------------------
(defun prog05 ()
 (graphscr)
 ; get centerpoint and dimensions
 (prompt
   "\nRectangle, centerpoint")
 (setq pnt0 (getpoint "\nCenter:"))
 (setq xside
   (getdist "\nEnter length:"))
 (setq yside
   (getdist "\nEnter width:"))
 ; compute corner points
 (setq pnt1 (list
   (- (nth 0 pnt0) (/ xside 2))
   (- (nth 1 pnt0) (/ yside 2))
   (nth 2 pnt0)))
 (setq pnt2 (list
   (+ (nth 0 pnt0) (/ xside 2))
   (- (nth 1 pnt0) (/ yside 2))
   (nth 2 pnt0)))
 (setq pnt3 (list
   (+ (nth 0 pnt0) (/ xside 2))
   (+ (nth 1 pnt0) (/ yside 2))
   (nth 2 pnt0)))
 (setq pnt4 (list
   (- (nth 0 pnt0) (/ xside 2))
   (+ (nth 1 pnt0) (/ yside 2))
   (nth 2 pnt0)))
 ; draw rectangle
 (command ".PLINE" pnt1 pnt2 pnt3
   nt4 pnt1 "")
 ; display rectangle data
 (textscr)
 (princ "\nLength: ")
 (princ (rtos xside)) (princ "  ")
 (princ "Width: ")
 (princ (rtos yside))
 (setq tarea
```

```
    (/ (* xside yside) 144))
  (setq tperm
    (+ (* xside 2) (* yside 2)))
  (princ "\nArea: ") (princ tarea)
  (princ "  ") (princ "Perimeter: ")
  (princ (rtos tperm))
  (princ)
)
;---------------------------------
```

Setting the origin to the lower-left corner is the same as using AutoCAD's RECTANGLE command, and it is easily duplicated. Another possible location would be the midpoint of the bottom edge.

Using PROG05, add function PROG05a.

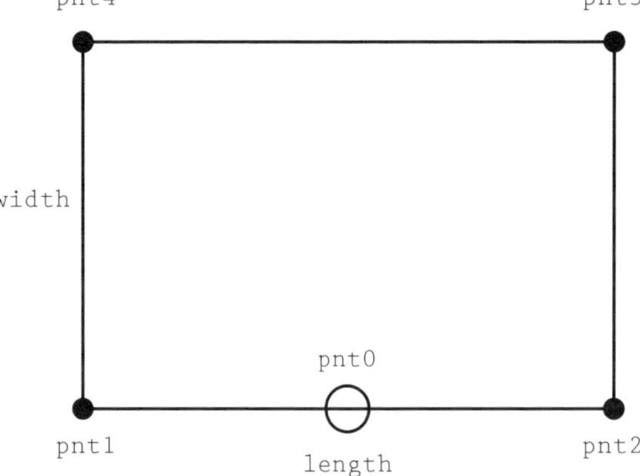

PROG05a: draw a rectangle using the midpoint of the bottom edge.
Structural sections

Completed function PROG05a:

```
;---------------------------------
(defun prog05a ()
 (graphscr)
 ; get centerpoint and dimensions
 (prompt
   "\nRectangle, bottom midpoint")
 (setq pnt0 (getpoint "\nCenter:"))
 (setq xside
   (getdist "\nEnter length:"))
 (setq yside
   (getdist "\nEnter width:"))
 ; compute corner points
 (setq pnt1 (list
   (- (nth 0 pnt0) (/ xside 2))
   (nth 1 pnt0) (nth 2 pnt0)))
 (setq pnt2 (list
   (+ (nth 0 pnt0) (/ xside 2))
   (nth 1 pnt0) (nth 2 pnt0)))
 (setq pnt3 (list
   (+ (nth 0 pnt0) (/ xside 2))
   (+ (nth 1 pnt0) yside)
   (nth 2 pnt0)))
 (setq pnt4 (list
   (- (nth 0 pnt0) (/ xside 2))
   (+ (nth 1 pnt0) yside)
   (nth 2 pnt0)))
 ; draw rectangle
 (command ".PLINE" pnt1 pnt2 pnt3
   pnt4 pnt1 "")
 ; display rectangle data
 (textscr)
 (princ "\nLength: ")
 (princ (rtos xside)) (princ "  ")
 (princ "Width: ")
 (princ (rtos yside))
 (setq tarea
   (/ (* xside yside) 144))
 (setq tperm
   (+ (* xside 2) (* yside 2)))
 (princ "\nArea: ") (princ tarea)
 (princ "  ")
 (princ "Perimeter: ")
 (princ (rtos tperm))
 (princ)
)
;---------------------------------
```

Consider the variety of triangles, rectangles, diamonds, trapezoids, parallelograms, and other basic shapes that could be created in a similar fashion. All you need to do is determine the minimum number of dimensions and the origin that best serves the application.

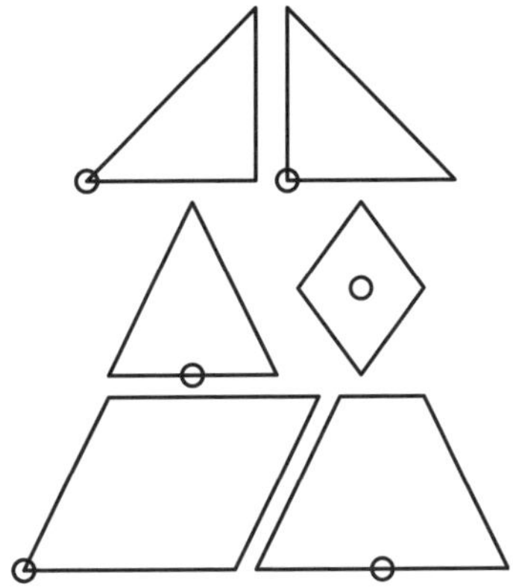

Other basic shapes

3.8 Drawing Structural Sections

Another common shape consisting only of straight line segments that can be created as a simple polyline is a structural section. For each type of section, the depth, width, flange thickness, and web thicknesses are specified. For rolled sections that include the taper and the root and toe radii, the polyline must include arcs. The use of arcs will be demonstrated in detail in section 3.12.

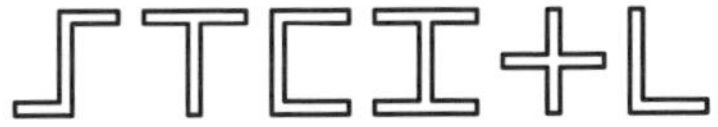

I-beam sections

Add PROG06 to draw an I-Beam section using the beam depth, width, thickness of the flange, and web. Set the origin at the center.

Completed function PROG06:

```
;---------------------------------
(defun prog06 ()
 (graphscr)
 ; get centerpoint and dimensions
 (prompt "\n3D I-beam, by center")
 (setq pnt0 (getpoint "\nCenter:"))
 (setq dbeam
   (getdist "\nEnter depth:"))
 (setq wbeam
   (getdist "\nEnter width:"))
 (setq wthk
   (getdist
   "\nEnter web thickness:"))
 (setq fthk
   (getdist
   "\nEnter flange thickness:"))
 ; compute corner points
 ; starting lower left corner
 (setq pnt1  (list
   (- (nth 0 pnt0) (/ wbeam 2))
   (- (nth 1 pnt0) (/ dbeam 2))
   (nth 2 pnt0)))
 (setq pnt2  (list
   (+ (nth 0 pnt0) (/ wbeam 2))
   (- (nth 1 pnt0) (/ dbeam 2))
   (nth 2 pnt0)))
 (setq pnt3  (list
   (+ (nth 0 pnt0) (/ wbeam 2))
   (+ (- (nth 1 pnt0)
     (/ dbeam 2)) fthk)
   (nth 2 pnt0)))
 (setq pnt4  (list
   (+ (nth 0 pnt0) (/ wthk 2))
   (+ (- (nth 1 pnt0)
     (/ dbeam 2)) fthk)
   (nth 2 pnt0)))
 (setq pnt5  (list
   (+ (nth 0 pnt0) (/ wthk 2))
   (- (+ (nth 1 pnt0)
     (/ dbeam 2)) fthk)
   (nth 2 pnt0)))
 (setq pnt6  (list
```

```
    (+ (nth 0 pnt0) (/ wbeam 2))
    (- (+ (nth 1 pnt0)
      (/ dbeam 2)) fthk)
    (nth 2 pnt0)))
  (setq pnt7  (list
    (+ (nth 0 pnt0) (/ wbeam 2))
    (+ (nth 1 pnt0) (/ dbeam 2))
    (nth 2 pnt0)))
  (setq pnt8  (list
    (- (nth 0 pnt0) (/ wbeam 2))
    (+ (nth 1 pnt0) (/ dbeam 2))
    (nth 2 pnt0)))
  (setq pnt9  (list
    (- (nth 0 pnt0) (/ wbeam 2))
    (- (+ (nth 1 pnt0)
      (/ dbeam 2)) fthk)
    (nth 2 pnt0)))
  (setq pnt10 (list
    (- (nth 0 pnt0) (/ wthk 2))
    (- (+ (nth 1 pnt0)
      (/ dbeam 2)) fthk)
    (nth 2 pnt0)))
  (setq pnt11 (list
    (- (nth 0 pnt0) (/ wthk 2))
    (+ (- (nth 1 pnt0)
      (/ dbeam 2)) fthk)
    (nth 2 pnt0)))
  (setq pnt12 (list
    (- (nth 0 pnt0) (/ wbeam 2))
    (+ (- (nth 1 pnt0)
      (/ dbeam 2)) fthk)
    (nth 2 pnt0)))
  ; draw I-Beam
  (command ".PLINE" pnt1 pnt2 pnt3
    pnt4 pnt5 pnt6 pnt7 pnt8 pnt9
    pnt10 pnt11 pnt12 pnt1 "")
  (princ)
)
;--------------------------------
```

Add PROG06a using a copy of PROG06. Enter a section height and extrude it to that height.

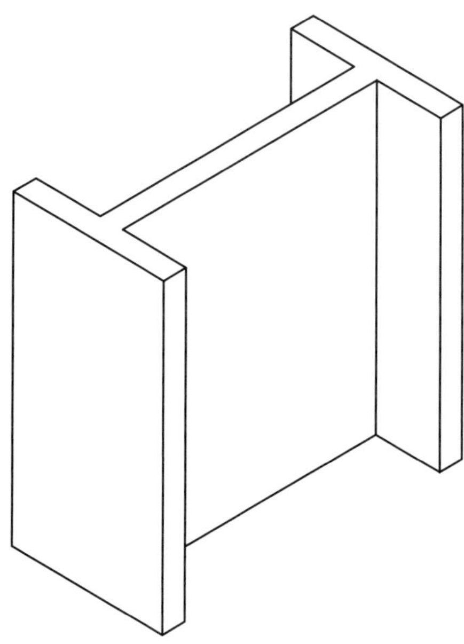

PROG06a: extrude a section to a height

To include the section height, add to the existing series of entered values:

```
(setq bhgt
  (getdist "\nEnter beam height:"))
```

After the PLINE command, add the EXTRUDE command:

```
; extrude section
(command ".EXTRUDE" "last" "" bhgt)
```

For AutoCAD versions released prior to 2007, the EXTRUDE command requires a taper angle. In this example, it can be set to zero, if needed.

```
;(command ".EXTRUDE" "last" "" bhgt "0")
```

The EXTRUDE command converts the PLINE to a three-dimensional solid. It requires a selection list and height. In this case, use the last selection-list option to get the last entity created. Double-quotation marks indicate the end of the selection list.

Completed function PROG06a:

```
 ;----------------------------------
(defun prog06a ()
 (graphscr)
 ; get centerpoint and dimensions
 (prompt "\n3D I-beam, by center")
 (setq pnt0 (getpoint "\nCenter:"))
 (setq dbeam
   (getdist "\nEnter depth:"))
 (setq wbeam
   (getdist "\nEnter width:"))
 (setq wthk
   (getdist
     "\nEnter web thickness:"))
 (setq fthk
   (getdist
     "\nEnter flange thickness:"))
 (setq bhgt
   (getdist "\nEnter beam height:"))
 ; compute corner points
 ; starting lower left corner
 (setq pnt1  (list
   (- (nth 0 pnt0) (/ wbeam 2))
   (- (nth 1 pnt0) (/ dbeam 2))
   (nth 2 pnt0)))
 (setq pnt2  (list
   (+ (nth 0 pnt0) (/ wbeam 2))
   (- (nth 1 pnt0) (/ dbeam 2))
   (nth 2 pnt0)))
 (setq pnt3  (list
   (+ (nth 0 pnt0) (/ wbeam 2))
   (+ (- (nth 1 pnt0)
     (/ dbeam 2)) fthk)
   (nth 2 pnt0)))
 (setq pnt4  (list
   (+ (nth 0 pnt0) (/ wthk 2))
   (+ (- (nth 1 pnt0)
     (/ dbeam 2)) fthk)
   (nth 2 pnt0)))
 (setq pnt5  (list
   (+ (nth 0 pnt0) (/ wthk 2))
   (- (+ (nth 1 pnt0)
     (/ dbeam 2)) fthk)
   (nth 2 pnt0)))
 (setq pnt6  (list
   (+ (nth 0 pnt0) (/ wbeam 2))
   (- (+ (nth 1 pnt0)
     (/ dbeam 2)) fthk)
   (nth 2 pnt0)))
 (setq pnt7  (list
   (+ (nth 0 pnt0) (/ wbeam 2))
   (+ (nth 1 pnt0) (/ dbeam 2))
   (nth 2 pnt0)))
 (setq pnt8  (list
   (- (nth 0 pnt0) (/ wbeam 2))
   (+ (nth 1 pnt0) (/ dbeam 2))
   (nth 2 pnt0)))
 (setq pnt9  (list
   (- (nth 0 pnt0) (/ wbeam 2))
   (  (+ (nth 1 pnt0)
     (/ dbeam 2)) fthk)
   (nth 2 pnt0)))
 (setq pnt10 (list
   (- (nth 0 pnt0) (/ wthk 2))
   (- (+ (nth 1 pnt0)
     (/ dbeam 2)) fthk)
   (nth 2 pnt0)))
 (setq pnt11 (list
   (- (nth 0 pnt0) (/ wthk 2))
   (+ (- (nth 1 pnt0)
     (/ dbeam 2)) fthk)
   (nth 2 pnt0)))
 (setq pnt12 (list
   (- (nth 0 pnt0) (/ wbeam 2))
   (+ (- (nth 1 pnt0)
     (/ dbeam 2)) fthk)
   (nth 2 pnt0)))
 ; draw I-Beam
 (command ".PLINE" pnt1 pnt2 pnt3
   pnt4 pnt5 pnt6 pnt7 pnt8 pnt9
   pnt10 pnt11 pnt12 pnt1 "")
```

```
  ; extrude section
  (command ".EXTRUDE" "last" "" bhgt)
  ; for versions prior to 2007 add a
  ; taper parameter
  ;(command ".EXTRUDE" "last" ""
     bhght "0")
  (princ)
)
;---------------------------------
```

3.9 Draw a Nested Triangle

Some shapes require additional computations of points.

Add PROG07 to draw a nested triangle. Create a triangle with another triangle inside of it based on connecting the midpoints of the sides. Ask for three points to define the outside triangle. Construct the two triangles as polylines.

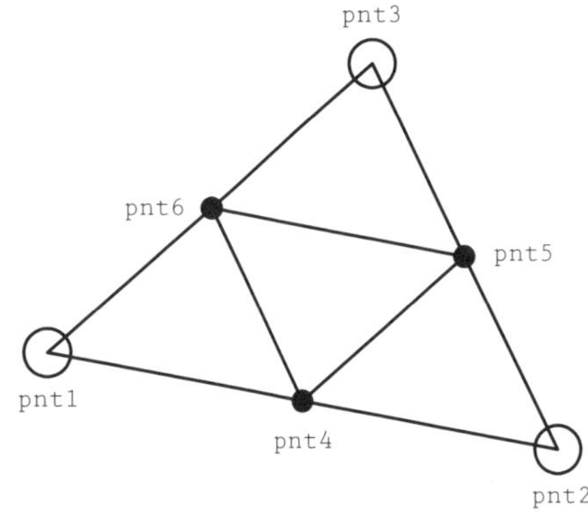

PROG07: a nested triangle

Write PROG07 using this outline:

```
;---------------------------------
; PROG07 - draw a set of nested
triangle
(defun prog07 ()
  (graphscr)
  ; get 3 points for triangle
  (prompt "\nDraw a nested triangle")
     .
  ; draw outside triangle
     .
  ; compute midpoints
     .
  ; draw inside triangle
     .
  (princ)
)
;---------------------------------
```

To compute the midpoints, one possible method is to add one-half of the x and y offsets, from the start and endpoints of one edge to the start of another edge.

For example:

```
X of pnt4 = (X of pnt2 - X of pnt1) / 2
+ X of pnt1
Y of pnt4 = (Y of pnt2 - Y of pnt1) / 2
+ Y of pnt1
Z of pnt4 = Z of pnt1
```

Another method is to compute the length and angle of an edge, and then use the polar function to compute the midpoint.

For example:

```
ang = angle of the edge pnt1 and pnt2
dist = distance between pnt1 and pnt2
pnt4 = polar from pnt1, direction at
ang radians, distance at dist/2
```

Completed function PROG07 using the polar midpoint computations:

```
;----------------------------------
(defun prog07 ()
 (graphscr)
 ; get corner points
 (prompt "\nNested triangle")
 (setq pnt1
   (getpoint "\nFirst point:"))
 (setq pnt2
   (getpoint "\nSecond point:"))
 (setq pnt3
   (getpoint "\nThird point:"))
 ; draw outside triangle
 (command ".PLINE" pnt1 pnt2 pnt3
   pnt1 "")
 ; compute midpoints
 (setq ang (angle pnt1 pnt2))
 (setq dist (distance pnt1 pnt2))
 (setq pnt4
   (polar pnt1 ang (/ dist 2)))
 (setq ang (angle pnt2 pnt3))
 (setq dist (distance pnt2 pnt3))
 (setq pnt5
   (polar pnt2 ang (/ dist 2)))
 (setq ang (angle pnt3 pnt1))
 (setq dist (distance pnt3 pnt1))
 (setq pnt6
   (polar pnt3 ang (/ dist 2)))
 ; draw inside triangle
 (command ".PLINE" pnt4 pnt5 pnt6
   pnt4 "")
 (princ)
)
;----------------------------------
```

Consider how to modify this function to create a three-dimensional model of these triangles, where the inside triangle is thicker or thinner than the outside triangle.

Add PROG07a and consider a nested four-sided polygon. The outside rectangle is given by four points.

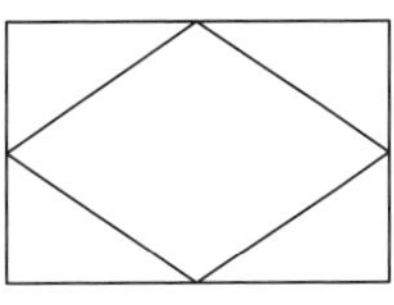

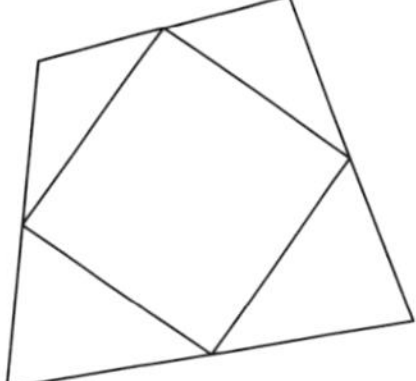

PROG07a: a nested four-sided polygon

Completed function PROG07a:

```
;----------------------------------
(defun prog07a ()
 (graphscr)
 ; get corner points
 (prompt "\nNested 3D rectangle")
 (setq pnt1
   (getpoint "\nFirst point:"))
 (setq pnt2
   (getpoint "\nSecond point:"))
 (setq pnt3
   (getpoint "\nThird point:"))
 (setq pnt4
   (getpoint "\nFourth point:"))
 ; draw outside rectangle
 (command ".PLINE" pnt1 pnt2 pnt3
   pnt4 pnt1 "")
 ; compute midpoints
 (setq ang (angle pnt1 pnt2))
 (setq dist (distance pnt1 pnt2))
 (setq pnt5
   (polar pnt1 ang (/ dist 2)))
 (setq ang (angle pnt2 pnt3))
 (setq dist (distance pnt2 pnt3))
 (setq pnt6
   (polar pnt2 ang (/ dist 2)))
 (setq ang (angle pnt3 pnt4))
 (setq dist (distance pnt3 pnt4))
 (setq pnt7
```

```
    (polar pnt3 ang (/ dist 2)))
  (setq ang (angle pnt4 pnt1))
  (setq dist (distance pnt4 pnt1))
  (setq pnt8
    (polar pnt4 ang (/ dist 2)))
  ; draw inside rectangle
  (command ".PLINE" pnt5 pnt6 pnt7
    pnt8 pnt5 "")
  (princ)
)
;---------------------------------
```

Later, we will revisit this example and modify it to become any number of nested rectangles or triangles.

3.10 Draw a Circle Based on Area

Some shapes are based on a geometric property.

Add PROG08 to draw a circle based on area.

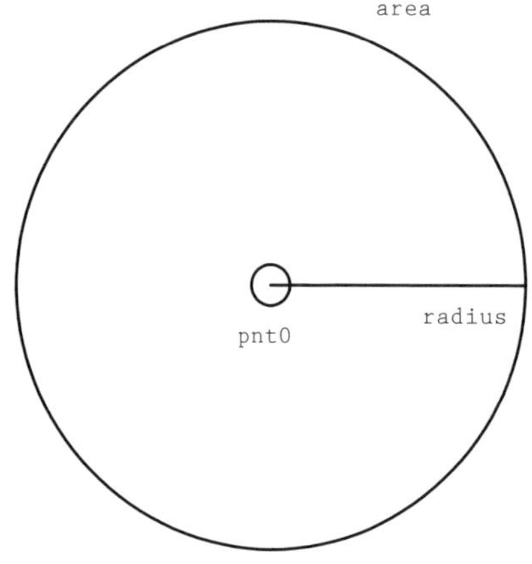

PROG08: draw a circle based on area

One application for this function is to create bubble diagrams with circles based on the area of each space.

Create a circle based on a given area in square feet and a centerpoint. The radius can be computed based on the area of the circle.

```
area = pi * radius2

radius = sqrt(area / pi)
```

Note that the area will be in square feet, but the CIRCLE command expects the radius to be in inches. Convert square feet to square inches.

Write PROG08 using this outline:

```
;---------------------------------
; PROG08 - draw circle based on area
(defun prog08 ()
 (graphscr)
 ; get circle area
 (prompt "\nDraw circle based on area")
 ; get circle area
    .
 ; get circle centerpoint
    .
 ; compute circle radius
    .
 ; draw circle
    .
 (princ)
)
;---------------------------------
```

Use the LIST or PROPERTIES command to check the radius and area of the drawn circle.

Completed function PROG08:

```
;---------------------------------
(defun prog08 ()
 (graphscr)
 ; get corner points
 (prompt "\nCircle based on area")
 (setq carea (getreal "\nArea:"))
 (setq pnt0 (getpoint "\nCenter:"))
 ; compute radius
 (setq crad
   (sqrt (/ (* carea 144) pi)))
 ; draw circle
 (command ".CIRCLE" pnt0 crad)
 (princ)
)
;---------------------------------
```

3.11 Draw a Pentagon

Some shapes have complex relationships between sides.

Add PROG09a to draw a pentagon. Consider options for its origin and what will determine its size, radius, or length of side.

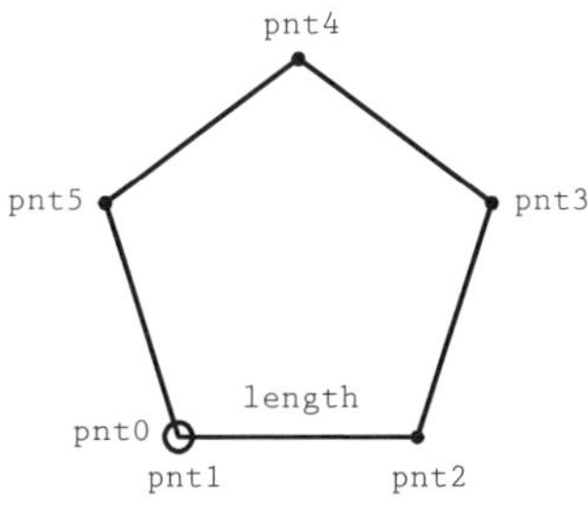

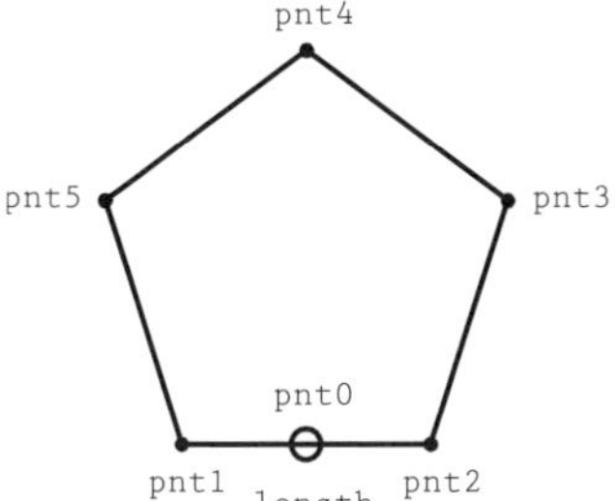

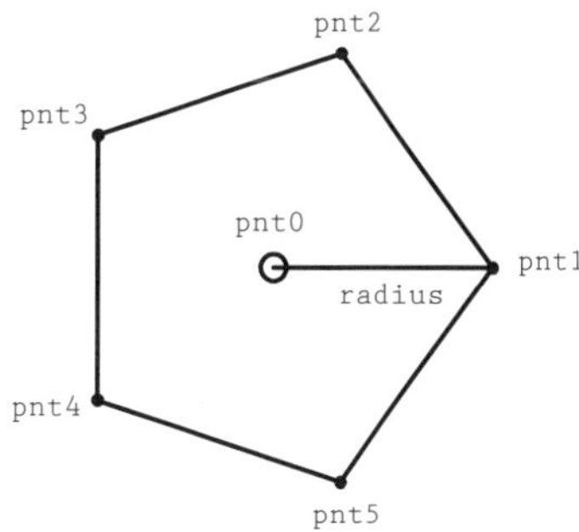

PROG09a, b, c: drawing pentagons

For PROG09a, consider the origin to be the start of an edge. The size of the circle will be determined by the length of an edge.

The five-sided inscribed polygon can be drawn according to its edge-length using the polar function to compute each edge-endpoint. The end of one edge becomes the start of the next edge. For a sixty-degree pentagon, increment the turning angle after each point computation by 360 over the number of sides.

For PROG09a, create a function for a pentagon by starting with:

```
;---------------------------------
 (defun prog09a ()
 (graphscr)
 ; get corner and edge length
 (prompt
  "\nPpentagon, corner and edge
length")
 (setq pnt0
   (getpoint "\nPick bottom-left
corner:"))
 (setq ledge
  (getdist "\nEnter edge length:"))
 ; compute turning angle
   .
 ; set starting angle and point
 (setq sang 0.0)
 (setq pnt1 pnt0)
```

```
 ; compute end of first edge
 (setq pnt2
  (polar pnt1 (dtr sang) ledge))
 ; inc turning angle
 (setq sang (+ sang tang))
 ; compute end of second edge
   .
 ; do the same for the third and
 ; fourth edge
   .
 ; draw polygon
 (command ".PLINE" pnt1 pnt2 pnt3
   pnt4 pnt5 "c")
 (princ)
)
```

Completed function PROG09a:

```
;-----------------------------------
(defun prog09a ()
 (graphscr)
 ; get corner and edge
 (prompt
   "\nPentagon, corner/edge length")
 (setq pnt0
   (getpoint
     "\nBottom-left corner:"))
 (setq ledge
   (getdist
     "\nEdge length:"))
 ; set turning angle
 (setq tang (/ 360.0 5))
 ; set starting angle and point
 (setq sang 0.0)
 (setq pnt1 pnt0)
 ; compute end of first edge
 (setq pnt2
   (polar pnt1 (dtr sang) ledge))
 ; inc turning angle
 (setq sang (+ sang tang))
 ; compute end of second edge
 (setq pnt3
   (polar pnt2 (dtr sang) ledge))
 ; inc turning angle
 (setq sang (+ sang tang))
 ; compute end of third edge
 (setq pnt4
   (polar pnt3 (dtr sang) ledge))
 ; inc turning angle
 (setq sang (+ sang tang))
 ; compute end of fourth edge
 (setq pnt5
   (polar pnt4 (dtr sang) ledge))
 ; draw polygon
 (command ".PLINE" pnt1 pnt2 pnt3
   pnt4 pnt5 "c")
 (princ)
)
;-----------------------------------
```

Add PROG09b. Draw the pentagon based on its bottom midpoint and edge-length. This version is almost exactly the same as PROG09a, except that the starting point (pnt1) is computed as one-half the edge-length from the origin (pnt0).

Completed function PROG09b:

```
;-----------------------------------
(defun prog09b ()
 (graphscr)
 ; get corner and edge
 (prompt
 "\nPentagon, midpoint/edge length")
 (setq pnt0
   (getpoint
     "\nBottom edge midpoint:"))
 (setq ledge
  (getdist "\nEdge length:"))
 ; set turning angle
 (setq tang (/ 360.0 5))
 ; set starting angle and point
 (setq sang 0.0)
 (setq pnt1 (list
   (- (nth 0 pnt0) (/ ledge 2))
   (nth 1 pnt0) (nth 2 pnt0)))
 ; compute end of first edge
 (setq pnt2
   (polar pnt1 (dtr sang) ledge))
 ; inc turning angle
 (setq sang (+ sang tang))
 ; compute end of second edge
 (setq pnt3
   (polar pnt2 (dtr sang) ledge))
```

```
 ; inc turning angle
 (setq sang (+ sang tang))
 ; compute end of third edge
 (setq pnt4
   (polar pnt3 (dtr sang) ledge))
 ; inc turning angle
 (setq sang (+ sang tang))
 ; compute end of fourth edge
 (setq pnt5
   (polar pnt4 (dtr sang) ledge))
 ; draw polygon
 (command ".PLINE" pnt1 pnt2 pnt3
   pnt4 pnt5 "c")
 (princ)
)
;---------------------------------
```

Add PROG09c. Draw the pentagon based on its centerpoint and radius.

For this version, the polar coordinate is always computed from the center, incrementing the angle, as before, for all five points.

Completed function PROG09c:

```
;---------------------------------
(defun prog09c ()
 (graphscr)
 ; get center and radius
 (prompt
   "\nPentagon, center and radius")
 (setq pnt0 (getpoint "\nCenter:"))
(setq radius (getdist "\nRadius:"))
 ; set turning angle
 (setq tang (/ 360.0 5))
 ; set starting angle
 (setq sang 0.0)
 ; compute first point
 (setq pnt1
   (polar pnt0 (dtr sang) radius))
 ; inc turning angle
 (setq sang (+ sang tang))
 ; compute second point
 (setq pnt2
   (polar pnt0 (dtr sang) radius))
 ; inc turning angle
 (setq sang (+ sang tang))
 ; compute third point
 (setq pnt3
   (polar pnt0 (dtr sang) radius))
 ; inc turning angle
 (setq sang (+ sang tang))
 ; compute fourth point
 (setq pnt4
   (polar pnt0 (dtr sang) radius))
 ; inc turning angle
 (setq sang (+ sang tang))
 ; compute fifth point
 (setq pnt5
   (polar pnt0 (dtr sang) radius))
 ; draw polygon
 (command ".PLINE" pnt1 pnt2 pnt3
   pnt4 pnt5 "c")
 (princ)
)
;---------------------------------
```

Additional exercises:

* How would you modify this version to have the same orientation as the previous ones?

```
The start angle (sang) would be changed
to (tang / 2).
```

* Consider what you need to draw any n-sided polygon.

* For reference, here are a few computations that relate the geometric properties of regular polygons:

Given the inscribed radius, number of sides, and centerpoint:

```
; compute chord length,
; circumscribed radius,
; bottom-left edge point and
; bottom-left edge midpoint
(setq chord (* 2.0 irad
   (sin (dtr (/ (/ 360.0 nsides)
     2.0)))))
 (setq crad (sqrt (- (expt irad 2)
```

```
    (expt (/ chord 2.0) 2))))
  (setq epnt (list
    (- (nth 0 cpnt) (/ chord 2.0))
    (- (nth 1 cpnt) crad)
    (nth 2 cpnt)))
  (setq mpnt (list (nth 0 cpnt)
    (- (nth 1 cpnt) crad)
    (nth 2 cpnt)))
```

Given the chord length, number of sides, and bottom-left edge-point:

```
; compute inscribed radius,
; circumscribed radius, and
; centerpoint and bottom-left
; edge midpoint
(setq irad (/ chord (* 2
  (sin (dtr (/ (/ 360.0 nsides)
    2.0))))))
(setq crad (sqrt (- (expt irad 2)
  (expt (/ chord 2.0) 2))))
(setq cpnt (list
  (+ (nth 0 epnt) (/ chord 2.0))
  (+ (nth 1 epnt) crad)
  (nth 2 epnt)))
 (setq mpnt (list
   (+ (nth 0 epnt) (/ chord 2.0))
   (nth 1 epnt) (nth 2 epnt)))
```

Given the chord length, number of sides, and bottom-left edge-midpoint:

```
; compute inscribed radius,
; circumscribed radius,
; centerpoint and bottom-left midpoint
(setq irad (/ chord (* 2
  (sin (dtr (/ (/ 360.0 nsides) 2.0))))))
(setq crad (sqrt (- (expt irad 2)
  (expt (/ chord 2.0) 2))))
(setq cpnt (list
  (nth 0 mpnt)
  (- (nth 1 mpnt) crad)
  (nth 2 mpnt)))
(setq epnt (list
  (- (nth 0 mpnt) (/ chord 2.0))
  (nth 1 mpnt) (nth 2 mpnt)))
```

Then:

```
; perimeter and area
(setq pperm (* chord nsides))
(setq parea (/ (* crad pperm) 2.0))
```

3.12 Draw a Rounded Rectangle

Some shapes consist of lines and arcs.

Add PROG10 to draw a rectangle with rounded ends using the centerpoint, total length, and width.

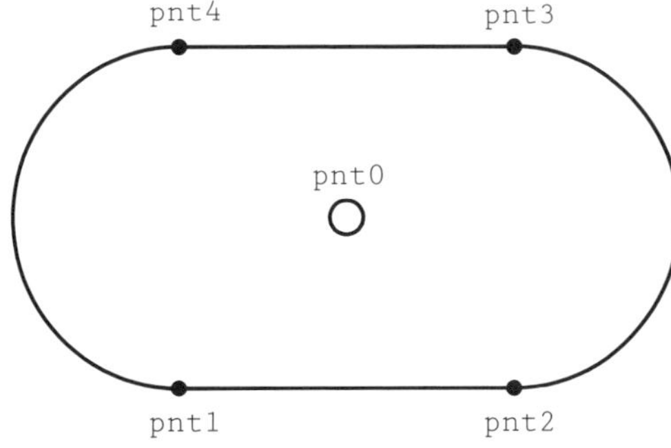

PROG10: a rounded rectangle

The critical points for this shape are the start and end points for each arc. Note the option sequence for the PLINE command. The four start and endpoints of the arcs are computed. The a option in the PLINE command draws an arc. The l option draws a line. The counterclockwise sequence starting at pnt1 is: line, arc, line, arc, close. It is best to test such sequences manually at the command line, before entering the command function.

Notice that because the last segment is an arc, the close option is cl.

Completed function PROG10:

```
;-----------------------------------
(defun prog10 ()
 (graphscr)
 ; get center and dimensions
 (prompt "\nRounded rectangle")
 (setq pnt0 (getpoint "\nCenter:"))
 (setq xdim (getdist "\nLength:"))
 (setq ydim (getdist "\nWidth:"))
 ; starting point for pline
 (setq pnt1 (list
   (- (nth 0 pnt0)
     (/ (- xdim ydim) 2))
   (- (nth 1 pnt0) (/ ydim 2))
   (nth 2 pnt0)))
 ; start of right curve
 (setq pnt2 (list
   (+ (nth 0 pnt0)
     (/ (- xdim ydim) 2))
   (- (nth 1 pnt0) (/ ydim 2))
   (nth 2 pnt0)))
 ; end of right curve
 (setq pnt3 (list
   (+ (nth 0 pnt0)
     (/ (- xdim ydim) 2))
   (+ (nth 1 pnt0) (/ ydim 2))
   (nth 2 pnt0)))
 ; start of left curve
 (setq pnt4 (list
   (- (nth 0 pnt0)
     (/ (- xdim ydim) 2))
   (+ (nth 1 pnt0) (/ ydim 2))
   (nth 2 pnt0)))
 ; draw PLINE
 (command ".PLINE" pnt1 pnt2 "a"
   pnt3 "l" pnt4 "a" "cl")
 (princ)
)
;-----------------------------------
```

3.13 Draw a Shape Using a Solid

Some shapes consist of multiple graphic entities, which are not connected to each other, such as a circular tube. A polyline cannot be used to define this shape as a single entity. In AutoCAD, either a REGION or a BLOCK can be used. You will first do an example using a REGION. A region is a two-dimensional solid that can accept Boolean operations of union and subtraction.

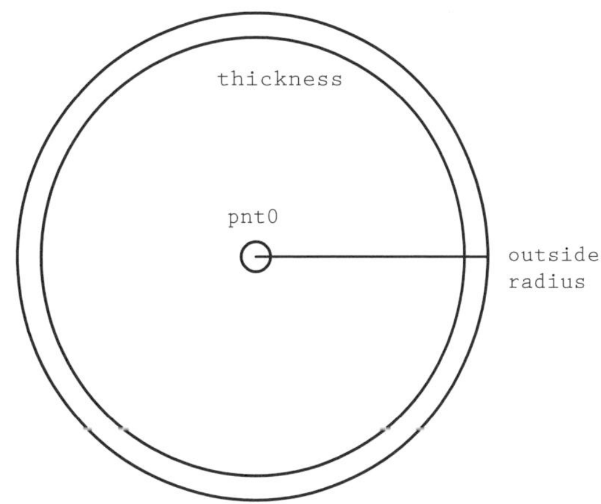

PROG11: a circular tube.

Add PROG11. Create a function for a circular tube given a center, outside radius, and thickness. The approach will be to draw the outside circle; make it into a region; place it into a selection list; draw the inside circle; make it into a region; place it into a selection list; and then subtract the inside region from the outside region, leaving the tube itself.

Completed PROG11:

```
;----------------------------------
(defun prog11 ()
 (graphscr)
 ; get center, outside radius, and
 ; thickness
 (prompt "\nDraw a circular tube")
 (setq pnt0 (getpoint "\nCenter:"))
 (setq crad
   (getdist "\nOutside radius:"))
 (setq cthk
   (getdist "\nThickness:"))
 ; outside circle
 (command ".CIRCLE" pnt0 crad)
 ; make region
 (command ".REGION" "last" "" )
 ; place into selection list
 (setq obj1 (ssadd (entlast)))
 ; inside circle
 (command
   ".CIRCLE" pnt0 (- crad cthk))
 ; make region
 (command ".REGION" "last" "" )
 ; place into a second selection
 ; list
 (setq obj2 (ssadd (entlast)))
 ; subtract inside from outside
 (command
   ".SUBTRACT" obj1 "" obj2 "")
 (princ)
)
;----------------------------------
```

Note the following sequence of commands:

```
; outside circle
(command ".CIRCLE" pnt0 crad)
; make region
(command ".REGION" "last" "" )
; place into selection list
(setq obj1 (ssadd (entlast)))
```

The REGION command requires a selection. To get the last entity drawn, use the last selection option. Then create a selection list using the ssadd function with the argument (entlast), the function that gets the name of the last entity created.

Once the two selection lists are created, the entities of one can be subtracted from the other. The SUBTRACT command requires two selections; in this case, each will be a list containing a single entity. By setting these types of entities as regions, we will later be able to create larger, more complex patterns by repeating and then uniting them into a single entity.

Add PROG11a. Create a function for drawing a circular plate with four intersecting openings, also known as a quatrefoil, using a centerpoint, outside radius, and thickness.

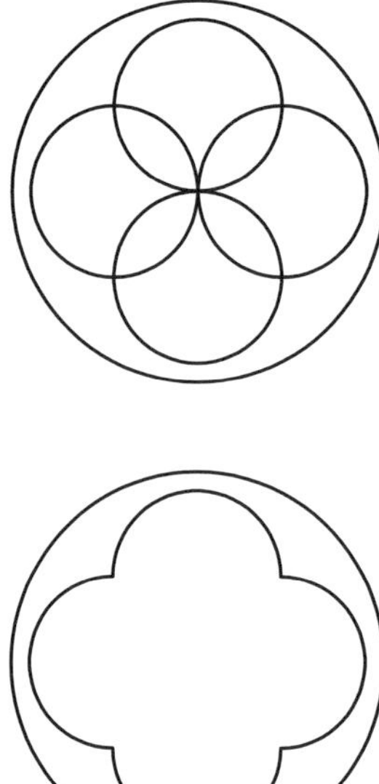

PROG11a: a quatrefoil, before and after subtraction

To create this pattern, draw the outside circle; make it into a region; place it in a selection list; and then draw the four inside circles, making each a region and placing all of them into another selection list. Then subtract the inside circles from the outside circle. The radius of the inside circle is computed based on the outside radius and thickness and distance from the outside circle-edge.

Completed PROG11a:

```
;---------------------------------
(defun prog11a ()
 (graphscr)
 ; get center, outside radius, and
 ; thickness
 (prompt
   "\nQuatrefoil opening in plate")
 (setq pnt0 (getpoint "\nCenter:"))
 (setq crad
   (getdist "\nOutside radius:"))
 (setq cthk
   (getdist "\nThickness:"))
 ; outside circle
 (command ".CIRCLE" pnt0 crad)
 ; make region
 (command ".REGION" "last" "" )
 ; place into selection list
 (setq obj1 (ssadd (entlast)))
 ; inside circle radius
 (setq inrad (/ (- crad cthk) 2.0))
 ; inside circle
 (setq cpt (list
   (- (nth 0 pnt0) inrad)
   (nth 1 pnt0) (nth 2 pnt0)))
 (command ".CIRCLE" cpt inrad)
 ; make region
 (command ".REGION" "last" "" )
 ; place into a second selection
 ; list
 (setq obj2 (ssadd (entlast)))
 ; inside circle
 (setq cpt (list
   (+ (nth 0 pnt0) inrad)
   (nth 1 pnt0) (nth 2 pnt0)))
 (command ".CIRCLE" cpt inrad)
 ; make region
 (command ".REGION" "last" "" )
 ; place into a second selection
 ; list
 (setq obj2 (ssadd (entlast) obj2))
 ; inside circle
 (setq cpt (list
  (nth 0 pnt0)
  (+ (nth 1 pnt0) inrad)
  (nth 2 pnt0)))
 (command ".CIRCLE" cpt inrad)
 ; make region
 (command ".REGION" "last" "" )
 ; place into a second selection
 ; list
 (setq obj2 (ssadd (entlast) obj2))
 ; inside circle
 (setq cpt (list
   (nth 0 pnt0)
   (- (nth 1 pnt0) inrad)
   (nth 2 pnt0)))
 (command ".CIRCLE" cpt inrad)
 ; make region
 (command ".REGION" "last" "" )
 ; place into a second selection
 ; list
 (setq obj2 (ssadd (entlast) obj2))
 ; subtract inside from outside
 (command
   ".SUBTRACT" obj1 "" obj2 "")
 (princ)
)
;---------------------------------
```

Note the difference when placing the first entity into the selection list:

```
; place into a second selection list
(setq obj2 (ssadd (entlast)))
```

Note the difference when placing additional entities into the same selection list:

```
; add into a second selection list
(setq obj2 (ssadd (entlast) obj2))
```

Add PROG11b. Create a function for a set of three intersecting circles, also known as a trefoil, using a centerpoint and a circle radius. Each of the circles is drawn 120 degrees apart, placed in a single selection list, and combined using the UNION command. The polar function is used to compute each circle center based on the distance of the circle radius. Then, a smaller circle is placed in the center with one-fourth the entered circle radius, which is subtracted from the UNION of the three drawn circles.

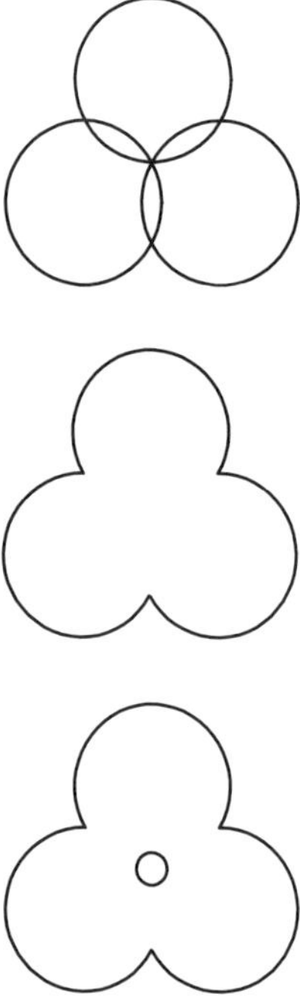

PROG11b: a trefoil before and after the union, and with centerhole added

Completed function PROG11b:

```
;---------------------------------
(defun prog11b ()
 (graphscr)
 ; get center, radius
 (prompt "\nTrefoil with hole")
 (setq pnt0 (getpoint "\nCenter:"))
 (setq crad (getdist "\nRadius:"))
 ; first circle
 (setq pnt1
   (polar pnt0 (dtr 90) crad))
 (command ".CIRCLE" pnt1 crad)
 ; make region
 (command ".REGION" "last" "" )
 ; place into selection list
 (setq objl (ssadd (entlast)))
 ; second circle
 (setq pnt2
   (polar pnt0 (dtr 210) crad))
 (command ".CIRCLE" pnt2 crad)
 ; make region
 (command ".REGION" "last" "" )
 ; place into selection list
 (setq objl (ssadd (entlast) objl))
 ; third circle
 (setq pnt3
   (polar pnt0 (dtr 330) crad))
 (command ".CIRCLE" pnt3 crad)
 ; make region
 (command ".REGION" "last" "" )
 ; place into selection list
 (setq objl (ssadd (entlast) objl))
 ; union are three
 (command ".UNION" objl "")
 ; place union into selection
 (setq objl (ssadd (entlast)))
 ; inside circular hole
 (command
   ".CIRCLE" pnt0 (* crad 0.25))
 ; make region
 (command ".REGION" "last" "" )
 ; place into selection list
 (setq obj2 (ssadd (entlast)))
 ; subtract
 (command
   ".SUBTRACT" objl "" obj2 "")
 (princ)
)
;---------------------------------
```

Note that when making the selection list for the combined circles, the same selection list name is used to combine them before the hole is subtracted.

Add PROG11c. Create a function for a cross-shaped opening in an elliptical plate using the center, cross length and width, thickness, and plate-edge distance.

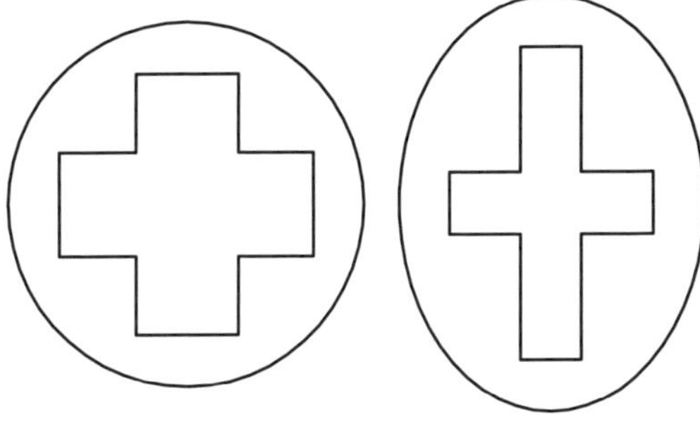

PROG11c: a cross-shaped opening in an elliptical plate

Completed function PROG11c:

```
;-----------------------------------
(defun prog11c ()
 (graphscr)
 ; get centerpoint and dimensions
 (prompt
  "\nOpening in elliptical plate")
 (setq pnt0 (getpoint "\nCenter:"))
 (setq xside
   (getdist "\nEnter length:"))
 (setq yside
   (getdist "\nEnter width:"))
 (setq cthk
   (getdist
     "\nEnter cross thickness:"))
 (setq pthk
   (getdist "\nEnter plate edge:"))
 ; compute corner points
 ; starting lower left corner
 (setq pnt1  (list
   (- (nth 0 pnt0) cthk)
   (- (nth 1 pnt0) (/ yside 2))
   (nth 2 pnt0)))
(setq pnt2  (list
   (+ (nth 0 pnt0) cthk)
   (- (nth 1 pnt0) (/ yside 2))
   (nth 2 pnt0)))
(setq pnt3  (list
   (+ (nth 0 pnt0) cthk)
   (- (nth 1 pnt0) cthk)
   (nth 2 pnt0)))
(setq pnt4  (list
   (+ (nth 0 pnt0) (/ xside 2))
   (- (nth 1 pnt0) cthk)
   (nth 2 pnt0)))
(setq pnt5  (list
   (+ (nth 0 pnt0) (/ xside 2))
   (+ (nth 1 pnt0) cthk)
   (nth 2 pnt0)))
(setq pnt6  (list
   (+ (nth 0 pnt0) cthk)
   (+ (nth 1 pnt0) cthk)
   (nth 2 pnt0)))
(setq pnt7  (list
   (+ (nth 0 pnt0) cthk)
   (+ (nth 1 pnt0) (/ yside 2))
   (nth 2 pnt0)))
(setq pnt8  (list
   (- (nth 0 pnt0) cthk)
   (+ (nth 1 pnt0) (/ yside 2))
   (nth 2 pnt0)))
(setq pnt9  (list
   (- (nth 0 pnt0) cthk)
   (+ (nth 1 pnt0) cthk)
   (nth 2 pnt0)))
(setq pnt10 (list
   (- (nth 0 pnt0) (/ xside 2))
   (+ (nth 1 pnt0) cthk)
   (nth 2 pnt0)))
(setq pnt11 (list
   (- (nth 0 pnt0) (/ xside 2))
   (- (nth 1 pnt0) cthk)
   (nth 2 pnt0)))
(setq pnt12 (list
   (- (nth 0 pnt0) cthk)
   (- (nth 1 pnt0) cthk)
   (nth 2 pnt0)))
; draw cross
(command ".PLINE" pnt1 pnt2 pnt3
  pnt4 pnt5 pnt6 pnt7 pnt8 pnt9
  pnt10 pnt11 pnt12 pnt1 "")
```

```
  ; make region
  (command ".REGION" "last" "" )
  ; place into selection list
  (setq obj2 (ssadd (entlast)))
  ; draw ellipse
  (setq xpt (list
    (+ (nth 0 pnt0)
      (+ (/ xside 2) pthk))
    (nth 1 pnt0) (nth 2 pnt0)))
  (setq ypt (list
    (nth 0 pnt0)
    (+ (nth 1 pnt0)
      (+ (/ yside 2) pthk))
    (nth 2 pnt0)))
  (command
    ".ELLIPSE" "c" pnt0 xpt ypt)
  ; make region
  (command ".REGION" "last" "" )
  ; place into selection list
  (setq obj1 (ssadd (entlast)))
  ; subtract
  (command
    ".SUBTRACT" obj1 "" obj2 "")
  (princ)
)
;---------------------------------
```

Note that a polyline and an ellipse can also be made into regions.

Add PROG11d. Create a function similar to PROG11c, except add a thickness so that the plate is three-dimensional.

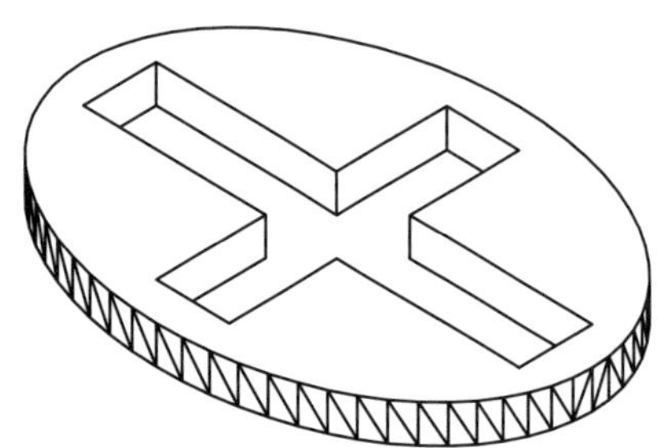

Subtract from a plate thickness

Add the value for the plate thickness:

```
(setq plthk  (getdist "\nEnter plate
thickness:"))
```

After the SUBTRACT command, EXTRUDE the plate:

```
; extrude plate
(command ".EXTRUDE" "last" "" plthk)
; for versions prior to 2007 add a
taper parameter
;(command ".EXTRUDE" "last" "" plthk
"0")
```

Add PROG11e. Use the same concept as in PROG11d. Set the cross-thickness to two times the plate thickness. Instead of subtracting one from the other, use the UNION command to combine them.

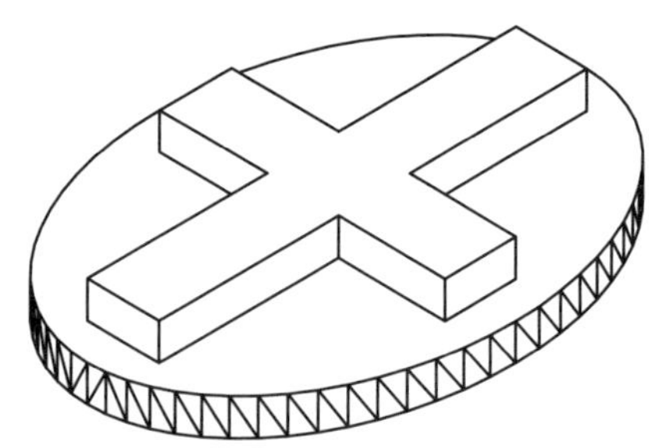

Add to the plate thickness

Completed function PROG11e:

```
;---------------------------------
(defun prog11e ()
 (graphscr)
 ; get centerpoint and dimensions
 (prompt
   "\n3D cross elliptical plate")
 (setq pnt0 (getpoint "\nCenter:"))
 (setq xside
   (getdist "\nEnter length:"))
```

```
(setq yside
  (getdist "\nEnter width:"))
(setq cthk
  (getdist
    "\nEnter cross thickness:"))
(setq pthk
  (getdist "\nEnter plate edge:"))
(setq plthk
 (getdist
   "\nEnter plate thickness:"))
; compute corner points
; starting lower left corner
(setq pnt1  (list
  (- (nth 0 pnt0) cthk)
  (- (nth 1 pnt0) (/ yside 2))
  (nth 2 pnt0)))
(setq pnt2  (list
  (+ (nth 0 pnt0) cthk)
  (- (nth 1 pnt0) (/ yside 2))
  (nth 2 pnt0)))
(setq pnt3  (list
  (+ (nth 0 pnt0) cthk)
  (- (nth 1 pnt0) cthk)
  (nth 2 pnt0)))
(setq pnt4  (list
  (+ (nth 0 pnt0) (/ xside 2))
  (- (nth 1 pnt0) cthk)
  (nth 2 pnt0)))
(setq pnt5  (list
  (+ (nth 0 pnt0) (/ xside 2))
  (+ (nth 1 pnt0) cthk)
  (nth 2 pnt0)))
(setq pnt6  (list
  (+ (nth 0 pnt0) cthk)
  (+ (nth 1 pnt0) cthk)
  (nth 2 pnt0)))
(setq pnt7  (list
  (+ (nth 0 pnt0) cthk)
  (+ (nth 1 pnt0) (/ yside 2))
  (nth 2 pnt0)))
(setq pnt8  (list
  (- (nth 0 pnt0) cthk)
  (+ (nth 1 pnt0) (/ yside 2))
  (nth 2 pnt0)))
(setq pnt9  (list
  (- (nth 0 pnt0) cthk)
  (+ (nth 1 pnt0) cthk)
  (nth 2 pnt0)))
(setq pnt10 (list
  (- (nth 0 pnt0) (/ xside 2))
  (+ (nth 1 pnt0) cthk)
  (nth 2 pnt0)))
(setq pnt11 (list
  (- (nth 0 pnt0) (/ xside 2))
  (- (nth 1 pnt0) cthk)
  (nth 2 pnt0)))
(setq pnt12 (list
  (- (nth 0 pnt0) cthk)
  (- (nth 1 pnt0) cthk)
  (nth 2 pnt0)))
; draw cross
(command ".PLINE" pnt1 pnt2 pnt3
  pnt4 pnt5 pnt6 pnt7 pnt8 pnt9
  pnt10 pnt11 pnt12 pnt1 "")
; extrude cross
(command
  ".EXTRUDE" "last" "" (* plthk 2))
; for versions prior to 2007 add a
; taper parameter
;(command
;   ".EXTRUDE" "last" "" plthk "0")
; place into selection list
(setq obj2 (ssadd (entlast)))
; draw ellipse
(setq xpt (list
 (+ (nth 0 pnt0)
   (+ (/ xside 2) pthk))
 (nth 1 pnt0) (nth 2 pnt0)))
(setq ypt (list
 (nth 0 pnt0)
 (+ (nth 1 pnt0)
   (+ (/ yside 2) pthk))
 (nth 2 pnt0)))
(command
  ".ELLIPSE" "c" pnt0 xpt ypt)
; extrude plate
(command
  ".EXTRUDE" "last" "" plthk)
; for versions prior to 2007 add a
; taper parameter
;(command
;   ".EXTRUDE" "last" "" plthk "0")
; place into selection list
(setq obj1 (ssadd (entlast)))
; union plate and cross
(command ".UNION" obj1 obj2 "")
(princ)
)
;---------------------------------
```

Note that REGION commands were replaced by using the EXTRUDE command. Because a polyline can be extruded, there is no need to convert it to a region first. Also, in this exercise, the SUBTRACT command was changed to the UNION command.

3.14 Draw a Shape Using Blocks

Another method for creating shapes composed of multiple graphic entities is to define them as a block.

Add PROG12. Create a function for a set of five circles. With this set, we will create a block. As before, a selection list is made and the BLOCK command is executed followed by the INSERT command to place the block into the drawing.

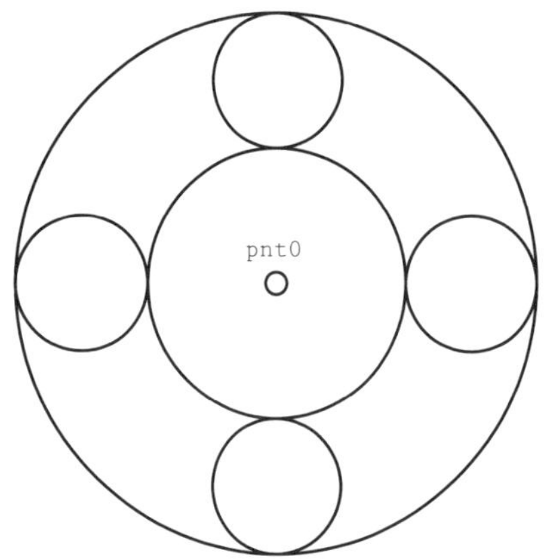

PROG12: combination of circles.

Completed function PROG12:

```
;-----------------------------------
(defun prog12 ()
 (graphscr)
 ; get center, radius
 (prompt "\nSet of five circles")
(setq pnt0 (getpoint "\nCenter:"))
(setq crad
  (getdist
    "\nCenter circle radius:"))
(setq erad
  (getdist "\nEdge circle radius:"))
(setq bname
  (getstring "\nBLOCK name:"))
; center circle
(command ".CIRCLE" pnt0 crad)
; place into selection list
(setq obj1 (ssadd (entlast)))
; first circle
(setq pnt1
  (polar pnt0 (dtr 0)
  (+ crad erad)))
(command ".CIRCLE" pnt1 erad)
; place into selection list
(setq obj1 (ssadd (entlast) obj1))
; second circle
(setq pnt2
  (polar pnt0 (dtr 90)
  (+ crad erad)))
(command ".CIRCLE" pnt2 erad)
; place into selection list
(setq obj1 (ssadd (entlast) obj1))
; third circle
(setq pnt3
 (polar pnt0 (dtr 180)
 (+ crad erad)))
(command ".CIRCLE" pnt3 erad)
; place into selection list
(setq obj1 (ssadd (entlast) obj1))
; fourth circle
(setq pnt4
  (polar pnt0 (dtr 270)
  (+ crad erad)))
(command ".CIRCLE" pnt4 erad)
; place into selection list
(setq obj1 (ssadd (entlast) obj1))
; outside circle
(command ".CIRCLE" pnt0
  (+ crad (* erad 2)))
; place into selection list
(setq obj1 (ssadd (entlast) obj1))
; make into a BLOCK
(command
  ".BLOCK" bname pnt0 obj1 "")
```

```
  ; INSERT back
  (command
    ".INSERT" bname pnt0 "1" "1" "0")
  (princ)
)
;---------------------------------
```

Setting the shapes into a block allows us to scale them nonproportionally. The `INSERT` command has a scale-x-and-y option. The scale option could also be used as dimensions, if the block was initially created as a single entity with a one-unit dimension.

This function assumes that the block name is unique and not already defined in the drawing. If it already exists, the `BLOCK` command requires you to answer a prompt to redefine the previous version, which this function is not set up to do.

One method is to give a `BLOCK` a unique internal name using the date-system variable:

```
(setq bname(rtos (getvar "date") 2 10))
"2454361.815545243"
```

And to make it more unique:

```
(setq bname (strcat "$" (rtos (getvar
"date") 2 10) "$"))
"$2454361.815545243$"
```

The date-system variable returns the Julian day, number, and decimal fraction of a day.

At the command line, check the values:

```
>>(rtos (getvar "date") 2 10)
```

The `getvar` function returns the value of system variables.

To see all of the system variables in AutoCAD, enter:

```
>>setvar
Enter variable name or [?]: ?
Enter variable(s) to list <*>: *
```

3.15 Functions as Shapes

All of these shape functions were written to be executed from the command line or assigned to a menu, and the parameters entered when requested. We can convert these so that they can be executed or called from other functions.

For example, the line drawing function as a stand-alone function was:

```
;---------------------------------
(defun prog01 ()
  (graphscr)
  ; get line points
  (prompt "\nLine")
  (setq pnt1
    (getpoint "\nFrom point:"))
  (setq pnt2
    (getpoint pnt1 "\nTo point:"))
  ; draw line
  (command ".LINE" pnt1 pnt2 "")
  ; display coordinates
  (textscr)
  (princ "\nStart/end points: ")
  (princ pnt1) (princ "-")
  (princ pnt2)
  (princ)
)
;---------------------------------
```

As a callable function, it would be:

```
;---------------------------------
; doline - draw a line
(defun doline (pnt1 pnt2 / )
  ; draw the line
  (command ".LINE" pnt1 pnt2 "")
  (princ)
)
;---------------------------------
```

At the command line, you would enter:

```
>>(doline (list 0.0 0.0 0.0) (list 10.0
10.0 0.0))
```

Or, within another function:

```
(setq p1 (list 0.0 0.0 0.0))
(setq p2 (list 10.0 10.0 0.0))
(doline p1 p2)
```

Or:

```
(doline (list 0.0 0.0 0.0) (list 10.0
10.0 0.0))
```

The function now includes an argument list of two points. One is the start and the other is the end of the line. In argument lists, order and data types are critical.

If you take PROG05a and create a rectangle using the bottom midpoint and convert it to a callable function, it would be:

```
;-----------------------------------
(defun dorectbtm (pnt0 xside yside
  / pnt1 pnt2 pnt3 pnt4)
 ; compute points
 (setq pnt1 (list
   (- (nth 0 pnt0) (/ xside 2))
   (nth 1 pnt0) (nth 2 pnt0)))
 (setq pnt2 (list
   (+ (nth 0 pnt0) (/ xside 2))
   (nth 1 pnt0) (nth 2 pnt0)))
 (setq pnt3 (list
   (+ (nth 0 pnt0) (/ xside 2))
   (+ (nth 1 pnt0) yside)
   (nth 2 pnt0)))
 (setq pnt4 (list
   (- (nth 0 pnt0) (/ xside 2))
   (+ (nth 1 pnt0) yside)
   (nth 2 pnt0)))
 ; draw rectangle
 (command ".PLINE" pnt1 pnt2 pnt3
   pnt4 pnt1 "")
 (princ)
)
;-----------------------------------
```

Note that all of the variables initialized in this function are called "local variables," and they are listed to the right of the function arguments following the right-slash symbol. All variables used in functions are assumed to be global, unless listed as local. Local variables do not exist once the function is complete, and they can be used by the `calling` function without being changed. The argument list requires a location point followed by the x and y dimensions. All three must be included, and they must appear in this order.

The function used at the command line would be:

```
>>(dorectbtm (list 0.0 0.0 0.0) 14.0 10.0)
```

In another function, it would be:

```
>>(setq p1 (list 0.0 0.0 0.0))
>>(setq xdim 14.0)
>>(setq ydim 10.0)
>>(dorectbtm p1 xdim ydim)
```

Or:

```
>>(dorectbtm (list 0.0 0.0 0.0) 14.0 10.0)
```

These basic shape-functions can be executed from the command line, from other functions, or from a menu.

Add PROG13. Using PROG11b, convert it to a three-dimensional ring trefoil.

PROG13: a three-dimensional ring trefoil

Copy PROG11 and convert it to a callable function called DOCRING:

```
;-----------------------------------
(defun docring (pnt0 crad cthk
  / obj1 obj2)
 ; requires center, outside radius,
 ; and thicknes
 ; outside circle
 (command ".CIRCLE" pnt0 crad)
 ; make region
 (command ".REGION" "last" "" )
 ; place into selection list
 (setq obj1 (ssadd (entlast)))
 ; inside circle
 (command
   ".CIRCLE" pnt0 (- crad cthk))
 ; make region
 (command ".REGION" "last" "" )
 ; place into second selection list
 (setq obj2 (ssadd (entlast)))
 ; subtract inside from outside
 (command
   ".SUBTRACT" obj1 "" obj2 "")
 (princ)
)
;-----------------------------------
```

Then copy function PROG11b and rename it PROG13. Modify the function to enter the ring radius and thickness. Change the CIRCLE commands to use the DOCRING function, and EXTRUDE the rings after they are combined using the UNION command.

Completed function PROG13:

```
;-----------------------------------
(defun prog13 ()
 (graphscr)
 ; get center, radius
 (prompt "\nDraw a 3D ring trefoil")
 (setq pnt0 (getpoint "\nCenter:"))
 (setq rrad
   (getdist "\nRing radius:"))
 (setq rthk
   (getdist "\nRing thickness:"))
 ; first ring
 (setq pnt1
   (polar pnt0 (dtr 90) rrad))
 (docring pnt1 rrad rthk)
 ; place into selection list
 (setq obj1 (ssadd (entlast)))
 ; second ring
 (setq pnt2
   (polar pnt0 (dtr 210) rrad))
 (docring pnt2 rrad rthk)
 ; place into selection list
 (setq obj1 (ssadd (entlast) obj1))
 ; third ring
 (setq pnt3
   (polar pnt0 (dtr 330) rrad))
 (docring pnt3 rrad rthk)
 ; place into selection list
 (setq obj1 (ssadd (entlast) obj1))
 ; union are three
 (command ".UNION" obj1 "")
 ; extrude rings
 (command ".EXTRUDE" "last" "" rthk)
 ; for versions prior to 2007 add a
 ; taper parameter
 ;(command
 ; ".EXTRUDE" "last" "" rthk "0")
 (princ)
)
;-----------------------------------
```

3.16 Converting Numeric and String Values

This section presents some miscellaneous functions for converting numeric values to character strings and vice versa.

Convert an integer to a string:

```
>>(itoa 1)
"1"

>>(itoa -1)
"-1"

>>(itoa 6.75)
; error: bad argument type: fixnump:
6.75
```

Convert an integer to a number with leading zeros, so it can be used when generating a file name:

```
>>(substr (itoa (+ 10000 25)) 2)
"0025"

>>(strcat "file" (substr (itoa (+ 10000
25)) 2) ".jpg")
"file0025.jpg"
```

Convert a string to a real number:

```
>>(atof "4.56")
4.56

>>(atof "4")
4.0

>>(atof "4'")
4.0

>>(atof "a1")
0.0
```

Convert a string to an integer:

```
>>(atoi "4.56")
4

>>(atoi "4")
4

>>(atoi "a1")
0
```

Every character is represented by an ASCII code ranging from zero to 255.

Get the ASCII code of a character.

```
>>(ascii " ")
32
```

In AutoLISP, the back slash is a special control-character. Since double quotation marks would not be valid, a back slash is used if the quote needs to be in a string:

```
>>(ascii "\"")
34

>>(chr 34)
"\""

>>(setq chara "A")
"A"

>>(strcat (chr 34) chara (chr 34))
"\"A\""

>>(strcat "\"" chara "\"")
"\"A\""
```

The back slash also needs to be used when a back slash is included in a string:

```
>>(strcat "\\" chara "\\")
"\\A\\"
```

For example, a full file name would be:

```
>>(setq fname "c:\\temp\\temp01.jpg")
"c:\\temp\\temp01.jpg"
```

In this case, the `t` would be processed and eliminated from the string if used in an AutoCAD command or AutoLISP function:

```
>>(setq fname "c:\temp\temp01.jpg")
"c:\temp\temp01.jpg"
```

Placing a comma into a string:

```
>>(setq a 10.0)
10.0

>>(setq b 5)
5

>>(strcat (rtos a 2 2) "," (rtos b 2 0))
"10.00,5"
```

The `read` function evaluates a string and returns the most logical conversion of the string's contents:

```
>>(read "4.56")
4.56

>>(read "4")
4

>>(read "ABC")
ABC

>>(setq indata "1 2 3 5.9 4")
"1 2 3 5.9 4"
```

Convert the string to a list:

```
>>(setq inlist (read (strcat "(" indata
")")))
(1 2 3 5.9 4)

>>(nth 3 inlist)
5.9
```

Rounding functions for integers and real numbers:

```
>>(defun roundi (rnum) (fix (+ rnum
0.5)))
ROUNDI

>>(roundi 4.50)
5

>>(roundi 4.4999)
4

>>(roundi 0.25)
0

>>(defun round (xnum ndec)  (atof (rtos
xnum 2 ndec)))
ROUND

>>(round 4.50 1)
4.5

>>(round 4.50 0)
5.0

>>(round 4.4999 2)
4.5

>>(round 0.25 1)
0.3

>>(round 0.25 0)
0.0
```

Rounding point coordinates:

```
>>(setq pt (list 10.567 12.5678 9.2345))
(10.567 12.5678 9.2345)

>>(setq pt (list
  (round (nth 0 pt) 2)
  (round (nth 1 pt) 2)
  (round (nth 2 pt) 1)))
(10.57 12.57 9.2)
```

4.0

All of the functions previously developed in Chapter 3.0 were based on sequences of computations and drawing operations. In many functions, you will need to decide which portion of the function to execute and repeat certain parts of the function. This chapter explains how decisions and repetition are developed.

Start a new drawing and set the units to architectural. Turn off all snaps and dynamic input.

Start a new AutoLISP file in the editor: `CH04.LSP`

4.1 Making Decisions

The `if` function can be used in a number of ways to make a decision and determine what should happen based on that decision.

Do a single statement if true:

```
(if (condition)
 (do this if true)
 (do this if false)
)
```

Do a single statement if true and false:

```
(if (condition)
  (progn
    do this if true
  )
)
```

Do multiple statements if true:

```
(if (condition)
      (progn
       do this if true
      )
    )
```

Do multiple statements if true and false:

```
(if (condition)
  (progn
    do this if true
  )
  (progn
    do this if false
  )
)
```

The `progn` function can include any number of AutoLISP statements.

The condition part of the `if` function can include one of the following functions:

```
= (equal to)
compares arguments for numerical
equality

/= (not equal to)
compares arguments for numerical
inequality

< (less than)
returns true if argument is numerically
less than the argument to its right

<= (less than or equal to)
returns true if argument is numerically
less than or equal to the argument to
its right

> (greater than)
returns true if argument is numerically
greater than the argument to its right

>= (greater than or equal to)
returns true if argument is numerically
greater than or equal to the argument
to its right
```

If a condition is true, `T` is returned; if false, `nil` is returned.

The conditions of the `if` function can be compounded by the `and` or `or` relationships:

```
(and (condition) (condition))

(or (condition) (condition))
```

Each condition must be complete. For and, both conditions have to be true for the compounded condition to be true; for or, only one condition must to be true for the compounded condition to be true.

Add function EX01:

```
;-----------------------------------
(defun ex01 ()
 (repeat 100000
  ; get number
  (setq num
    (getint
      "\nEnter a number from
      -10 to 10: "))
  ; check number
  (if (= num 0)
    (princ
      "\nNumber is equal to 0"))
  (if (> num 0)
    (princ
      "\nNumber is greater than 0"))
  (if (< num 0)
    (princ
      "\nNumber is less than 0"))
  (if (= (rem num 2) 0)
    (princ "\nNumber is even")
    (princ "\nNumber is odd") )
  (if (>= num 0)
    (princ "\nNumber is Positive")
    (princ "\nNumber is Negative"))
  (if (/= num 5)
    (princ
      "\nNumber is not equal to 5"))
  (if (or (= num 5) (= num 6))
    (princ
      "\nNumber is either 5 or 6"))
  (if (and (< num 5) (> num 0))
    (princ
      "\nNumber is in the range
     1 to 4"))
  (if (and (<= num 5) (>= num 0))
    (princ
      "\nNumber is in the range
      0 to 5"))
  (if (> num 6)
    (princ
      "\nNumber is greater than 6"))
   (if (= num 0) (exit))
 )
 (princ)
)
;-----------------------------------
```

Execute function EX01 for at least the following values:

5, 6, 4, 3, -4, -2, 10, 0

Take note of how each condition is specified and when each if statement is executed. Also note that each and and or relationship consists of complete individual conditions.

4.2 Repetition When the Number of Repeats Is Known

The repeat function is used when a section of a function repeats some number of times.

Add function EX02 and execute it:

```
;-----------------------------------
(defun ex02 ()
 (setq a 1)
 (setq n 10)
 (repeat n
  (princ a) (princ " ")
  (setq a (+ a 1))
 )
(princ)
)
;-----------------------------------
```

What are the values for variable a? Note that the variable a acts as a counter. Try setting the variable n to a real or negative number.

The general form of the `repeat` function is:

```
(repeat ntimes
  .
  do this
  .
)
```

Any number of instructions can exist within a repeat, including other repeats.

4.3 Repetition Based on the Evaluation of an Expression

The `while` function can be used even when you don't know how many times to repeat a set of operations, but a condition may arise that triggers the termination of the repetition.

Add function `EX03` and execute it:

```
;---------------------------------
(defun ex03 ()
 (setq a 1)
 (while (< a 10)
  (princ a) (princ " ")
  (setq a (+ a 1))
 )
 (princ)
)
;---------------------------------
```

What are the values for variable `a`?

Add function `EX04`:

```
;---------------------------------
(defun ex04 ()
 (setq a 10)
 (while (> a 1)
  (princ a) (princ " ")
  (setq a (- a 1))
 )
 (princ)
)
;---------------------------------
```

What are the values for variable `a`?

The general form of the `while` function is:

```
(while (expression is true)
  .
  do this
  .
)
```

The condition in the `while` expression is modified to a value that will terminate the repetition.

Add function `EX04a`:

```
;---------------------------------
(defun ex04a ()
 (setq a 10)
 (while (> a 1)
  (princ a) (princ " ")
  (setq b (- a 1))
 )
 (princ)
)
;---------------------------------
```

How many times does this function execute? Press the Escape key to terminate the function. Check the contents of the text screen for what has been displayed.

4.4 Repetition Determined Within the Body of a Loop by Value

If multiple conditions terminate a repetition, you can set up a flag for the `while` function to be lowered when the repetition is complete.

Add function `EX05` and execute it:

```
;-----------------------------------
(defun ex05 ()
 (setq doit 1)
 (setq a 0)
 (while (= doit 1)
  (princ a) (princ " ")
  (setq a (+ a 1))
  (if (> a 10) (setq doit 0))
 )
 (princ)
)
;-----------------------------------
```

The variable `doit` acts as a flag to signal termination.

4.5 Repetition Determined Within the Body of a Loop by Input

The flag value can also be controlled by input to signal the end of the repetition.

Add function `EX06` and execute it:

```
;-----------------------------------
(defun ex06 ()
 (setq doit 1)
 (setq a 1)
 (while (= doit 1)
  (princ "\n") (princ a)
  (setq a (+ a a))
  (setq ans (getstring "\nMore?"))
  (if (= (strcase ans) "NO")
    (setq doit 0))
 )
 (princ)
)
;-----------------------------------
```

Note that the input string becomes uppercase and the comparison determines a positive or negative response.

4.6 Nested Loops

Here is an example of two nested loops.

Add function `EX07` and execute it:

```
;-----------------------------------
(defun ex07 ()
 (setq xside 1)
 (while (< xside 10)
  (setq yside 1)
  (while (< yside 10)
   (princ "\n") (princ xside)
   (princ " x ") (princ yside)
   (setq yside (+ yside 1))
  )
  (setq xside (+ xside 1))
 )
 (princ)
)
;-----------------------------------
```

What are the values for the variables `xside` and `yside`? Note that the inside loop must complete before the outside loop continues. Also note how the initial values for variables `xside` and `yside` are set.

4.7 Draw a Set of Nested Rectangles

The sections that follow demonstrate a variety of repetitive operations and computations, including lines in a spiral path, simple linear paths, the modification of objects in repeating patterns, rectangular array repetition, and polar array repetition. Some of the exercises duplicate standard CAD operations and others extend their capabilities by allowing for modifications while a repetition is performed.

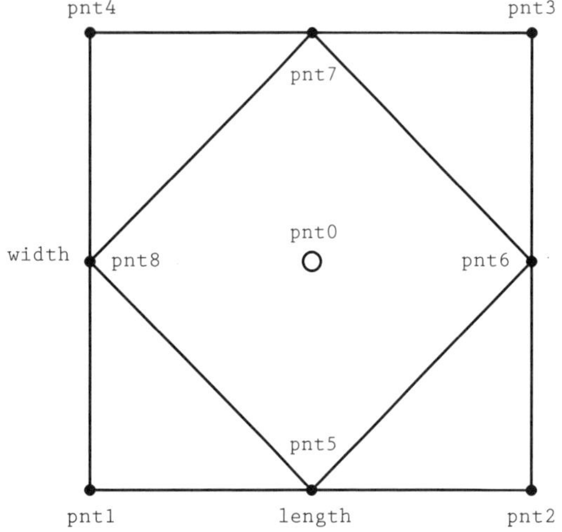

PROG01: nested rectangle parameters

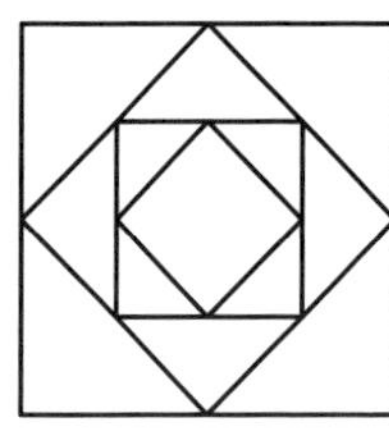

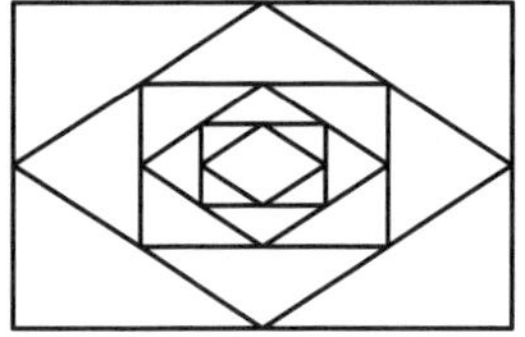

PROG01: nested rectangle variations

Add function PROG01 to CH04.LSP to draw a set of nested rectangles. Input includes the center, length, width, and number of rectangles.

The drawing of each rectangle is placed within the repeat loop using the polyline for points labeled 1 through 4. Prior to entering the repeat loop, the corners of the outside rectangle are computed as points 1 through 4. After the rectangle is drawn, the four midpoints are computed as points 5 through 8. Then points 1 through 4 are set to 5 through 8 and are ready to be drawn when the repeat loop continues.

Review function PROG07a in Chapter 3 (p. 46) on how to compute midpoints.

Add PROG01 using this outline:

```
;---------------------------------
(defun prog01 ()
 (graphscr)
 ; get centerpoint and dimensions
 (prompt
   "\nNested rectangles, by center")
 (setq pnt0
   (getpoint "\nPick center:"))
 (setq xside
   (getdist "\nEnter length:"))
 (setq yside
   (getdist "\nEnter width:"))
 (setq numrects
   (getint
   "\nEnter number of rectangles:"))
 ; compute outside rectangle corners
   .
(repeat numrects
  ; draw rectangle
   .
  ; compute midpoints
   .
  ; reset points
   .
)
 (princ)
)
;---------------------------------
```

Completed function PROG01:

```
;----------------------------------
(defun prog01 ()
 (graphscr)
 ; get centerpoint and dimensions
 (prompt
   "\nNested rectangles, by center")
 (setq pnt0
   (getpoint "\nPick center:"))
 (setq xside
   (getdist "\nEnter length:"))
 (setq yside
   (getdist "\nEnter width:"))
 (setq numrects
   (getint
   "\nEnter number of rectangles:"))
 ; compute outside rectangle corners
 (setq pnt1 (list
   (- (nth 0 pnt0) (/ xside 2))
   (- (nth 1 pnt0) (/ yside 2))
   (nth 2 pnt0)))
 (setq pnt2 (list
   (+ (nth 0 pnt0) (/ xside 2))
   (- (nth 1 pnt0) (/ yside 2))
   (nth 2 pnt0)))
 (setq pnt3 (list
   (+ (nth 0 pnt0) (/ xside 2))
   (+ (nth 1 pnt0) (/ yside 2))
   (nth 2 pnt0)))
 (setq pnt4 (list
   (- (nth 0 pnt0) (/ xside 2))
   (+ (nth 1 pnt0) (/ yside 2))
   (nth 2 pnt0)))
 (repeat numrects
  ; draw rectangle
  (command ".PLINE" pnt1 pnt2 pnt3
    pnt4 pnt1 "")
  ; compute midpoints
  (setq ang (angle pnt1 pnt2))
  (setq dist (distance pnt1 pnt2))
  (setq pnt5
    (polar pnt1 ang (/ dist 2)))
  (setq ang (angle pnt2 pnt3))
  (setq dist (distance pnt2 pnt3))
  (setq pnt6
    (polar pnt2 ang (/ dist 2)))
  (setq ang (angle pnt3 pnt4))
  (setq dist (distance pnt3 pnt4))
  (setq pnt7
    (polar pnt3 ang (/ dist 2)))
  (setq ang (angle pnt4 pnt1))
  (setq dist (distance pnt4 pnt1))
  (setq pnt8
    (polar pnt4 ang (/ dist 2)))
  ; reset points
  (setq pnt1 pnt5)
  (setq pnt2 pnt6)
  (setq pnt3 pnt7)
  (setq pnt4 pnt8)
 )
 (princ)
)
;----------------------------------
```

We used four temporary point variables since we couldn't do this:

```
pnt1 = midpoint pnt1 to pnt2
pnt2 = midpoint pnt2 to pnt3
pnt3 = midpoint pnt3 to pnt4
pnt4 = midpoint pnt4 to pnt1
```

Note that an unchanged pnt1 is needed for the new pnt4. This method could be modified by saving the values of pnt1 first:

```
savepnt1 = pnt1
pnt1 = midpoint pnt1 to pnt2
pnt2 = midpoint pnt2 to pnt3
pnt3 = midpoint pnt3 to pnt4
pnt4 = midpoint pnt4 to savepnt1
```

Add function PROG01a, a variation that accepts any four corner points and the number of nested rectangles.

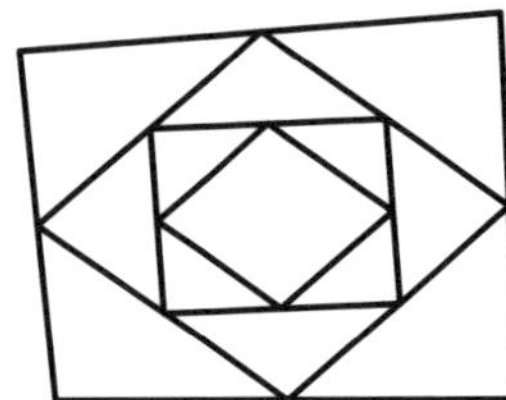

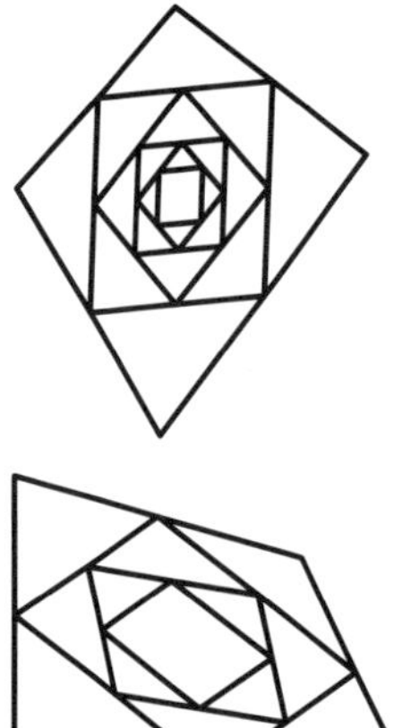

PROG01a: nested rectangles based on four points

Completed function PROG01a:

```
;-----------------------------------
(defun prog01a ()
 (graphscr)
 ; get four corner points
 (prompt
   "\nNested rectangles, by four
   points")
 (setq pnt1
   (getpoint "\nPick 1st corner:"))
 (setq pnt2
   (getpoint pnt1
   "\nPick 2nd corner:"))
 (setq pnt3
   (getpoint pnt2
   "\nPick 3rd corner:"))
 (setq pnt4
   (getpoint pnt3
   "\nPick 4th corner:"))
 (setq numrects
   (getint
   "\nEnter number of rectangles:"))
 (repeat numrects
  ; draw rectangle
  (command ".PLINE" pnt1 pnt2 pnt3
   pnt4 pnt1 "")
  ; save first point
  (setq savepnt1 pnt1)
  ; compute midpoints
  (setq ang (angle pnt1 pnt2))
  (setq dist (distance pnt1 pnt2))
  (setq pnt1
    (polar pnt1 ang (/ dist 2)))
  (setq ang (angle pnt2 pnt3))
  (setq dist (distance pnt2 pnt3))
  (setq pnt2
    (polar pnt2 ang (/ dist 2)))
  (setq ang (angle pnt3 pnt4))
  (setq dist (distance pnt3 pnt4))
  (setq pnt3
    (polar pnt3 ang (/ dist 2)))
  (setq ang (angle pnt4 savepnt1))
  (setq dist
    (distance pnt4 savepnt1))
  (setq pnt4
    (polar pnt4 ang (/ dist 2)))
 )
 (princ)
)
;-----------------------------------
```

4.8 Draw a Radial Spiral

Add function PROG02 to draw a set of radial spiral lines within a circle. Input consists of a center, radius, and number of lines. The approach is to draw a set number of lines, starting in the center of the circle. Each one increases in length and orientation, going through a 360-degree circle. The outside circle can be drawn before or after the repeat loop.

The value of the initial angle determines where the last line is drawn because 0 and 360 degrees are the same orientation. The starting angle can be

0 degrees or at one-increment degrees. Both the angle and line length require a starting value and a computed increment. The starting length of the line needs to be one increment, because a zero-length line cannot be drawn. Each is accumulated for the number of lines requested.

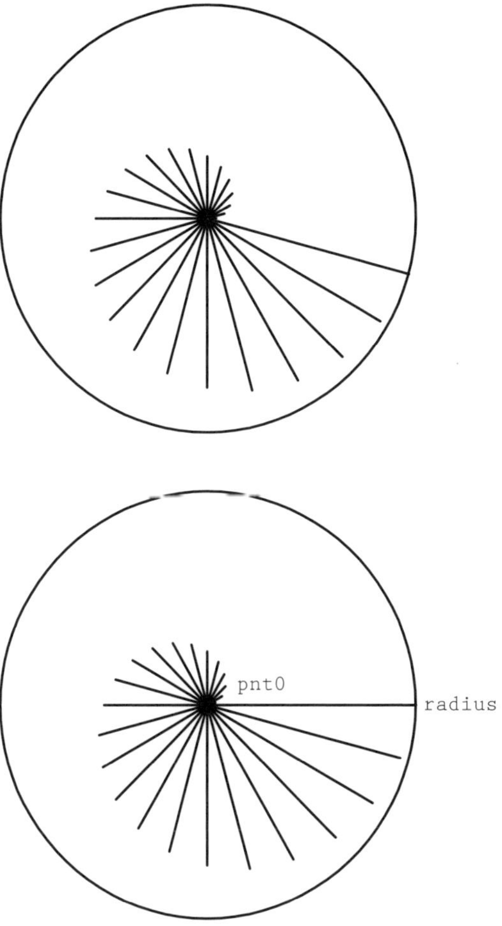

PROG02: radial lines starting at 0 degrees; PROG02a, starting at one-increment degrees

Completed function PROG02:

```
;----------------------------------
(defun prog02 ()
 (graphscr)
 ; get centerpoint and dimensions
 (prompt "\nDraw radial spiral")
 (setq pnt0
   (getpoint "\nPick center:"))
 (setq crad
   (getdist pnt0 "\nEnter radius:"))
 (setq numlines
  (getint
    "\nEnter number of lines:"))
 ; compute angle and line length
 ; increments
 (setq anginc (/ 360.0  numlines))
 (setq radinc (/ crad numlines))
 ; initial angle and line length
 (setq angline 0)
 (setq radline radinc)
 ; draw circle
 (command ".CIRCLE" pnt0 crad)
 (repeat numlines
  ; compute endpoint
  (setq pnt1 (polar
    pnt0 (dtr angline) radline))
  ; draw line
  (command ".LINE" pnt0 pnt1 "")
  ; inc ang and length
  (setq angline (+ angline anginc))
  (setq radline (+ radline radinc))
 )
 (princ)
)
;----------------------------------
```

Note that the computation of the variable anginc is based on real 360 degrees; otherwise an integer division would not always give the correct increment.

Also review how variables angline and radline are initialized and how increments are added to them as accumulations.

Execute PROG02 for a number of different parameters.

Add function PROG02a. It is identical to PROG02, except for the starting angle, which is set to:

```
(setq angline anginc)
```

Graphically, the second method provides a better solution, but both approaches are correct. Choose the approach based on the results you are looking to get.

The sequences that follow are simple variations of the radial spiral. This series of functions demonstrates how a simple starting concept can evolve into something much more complex. When reviewing these variations, consider the parameters or directions that were not selected.

Add function PROG02b to flip the length of the lines when half the number of lines is reached. One method is to start the radius increment as a positive number and set it to negative at the point when half the lines have been drawn.

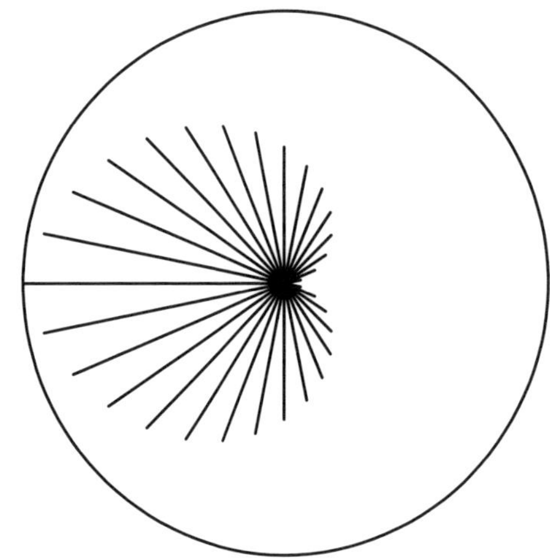

PROG02b: increasing and decreasing radial lines

Completed function PROG02b:

```
;----------------------------------
(defun prog02b ()
 (graphscr)
 ; get centerpoint and dimensions
 (prompt
   "\nDraw radial spiral, inc/dec")
 (setq pnt0
   (getpoint "\nPick center:"))
 (setq crad
   (getdist pnt0 "\nEnter radius:"))
 (setq numlines
   (getint
   "\nEnter number of lines:"))
 ; compute inc
 (setq anginc (/ 360.0  numlines))
 ; set the radius inc for half
 ; the lines
 (setq radinc (/ crad
   (/ numlines 2)))
 (setq angline anginc)
 (setq radline radinc)
 ; line counter
 (setq lsegs 0)
 ; draw circle
 (command ".CIRCLE" pnt0 crad)
 (repeat numlines
  ; compute endpoint
  (setq pnt1 (polar
    pnt0 (dtr angline) radline))
  ; draw line
  (command ".LINE" pnt0 pnt1 "")
  ; inc line count
  (setq lsegs (+ lsegs 1))
  ; decrease inc at half point
  (if (= lsegs (/ numlines 2))
    (setq radinc (* radinc -1.0)))
  ; inc ang and length
  (setq angline (+ angline anginc))
  (setq radline (+ radline radinc))
 )
 (princ)
)
;----------------------------------
```

Modify the radius-increment variable `radinc` to reach the circle edge at half of the number of lines. To determine when half the lines have been drawn, initialize a line-counter variable, `lsegs`, before the repeat loop and after each line is drawn, increment it by one. Then a simple check is made to see if half the lines have been drawn. The radius increment is multiplied by a negative one to flip it from positive to negative, changing it from increasing to decreasing. Note that the value of the variable `numlines` is entered as an integer and the division is by an integer so that an integer is compared to an integer. Otherwise, the `fix` function should be used to convert the computation to an integer:

```
; set the radius inc for half
; the lines
(setq radinc (/ crad
  (fix (/ numlines 2))))
```

And:

```
; decrease inc at half point
(if (= lsegs
  (fix (/ numlines 2)))
  (setq radinc (* radinc -1.0)))
```

Try PROG02b for an even and odd numbers of lines. Consider another approach if an odd number of lines is required.

Add function PROG02c, where the increase and decrease occurs at one-fourth the radial lines drawn.

Function PROG02c is the same as PROG02b, except for the computation of the radius increment and the check when the increment direction reverses, changing to:

```
; set the radius inc for 1/4 the lines
(setq radinc (/ crad (/ numlines 4)))
```

And:

```
; flip inc at 1/4 point
(if (= (rem lsegs (/ numlines 4)) 0)
  (setq radinc (* radinc -1.0)))
```

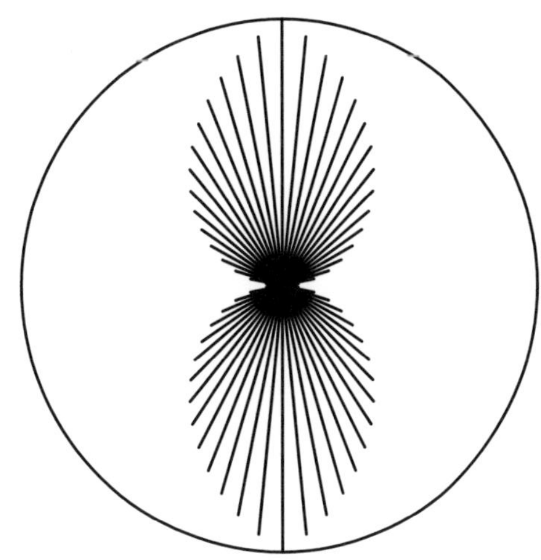

PROG02c: two sets of increasing and decreasing radial lines

Completed function PROG02c:

```
;-----------------------------------
(defun prog02c ()
 (graphscr)
 ; get centerpoint and dimensions
 (prompt
   "\nDraw radial spiral, inc/dec
   twice")
 (setq pnt0
   (getpoint "\nPick center:"))
 (setq crad
   (getdist pnt0 "\nEnter radius:"))
 (setq numlines
   (getint
   "\nEnter number of lines:"))
 ; compute inc
 (setq anginc (/ 360.0  numlines))
 ; set the radius inc for 1/4
 ; the lines
 (setq radinc
   (/ crad (fix (/ numlines 4))))
 (setq angline anginc)
 (setq radline radinc)
```

```
 ; line counter
 (setq lsegs 0)
 ; draw circle
 (command ".CIRCLE" pnt0 crad)
 (repeat numlines
  ; compute endpoint
  (setq pnt1 (polar
    pnt0 (dtr angline) radline))
  ; draw line
  (command ".LINE" pnt0 pnt1 "")
  ; inc line count
  (setq lsegs (+ lsegs 1))
  ; flip inc at 1/4 point
  (if (= (rem lsegs
     (fix (/ numlines 4))) 0)
     (setq radinc (* radinc -1.0)))
  ; inc ang and length
  (setq angline (+ angline anginc))
  (setq radline (+ radline radinc))
 )
 (princ)
)
;----------------------------------
```

Add function PROG02d. Starting with PROG02, instead of drawing radial lines from the center, connect each line-endpoint to form a spiral starting at the center. The number of lines and endpoints determines the smoothness of the spiral.

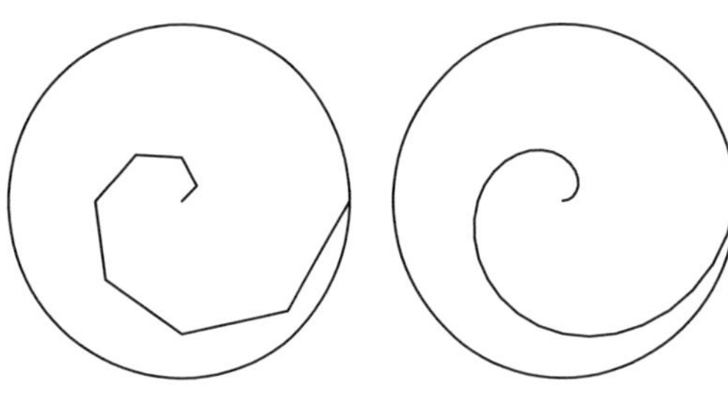

PROG02d: spiral connecting endpoints, 8 line segments and 32 line segments

Two points are needed to draw each line segment of the spiral. Before the repeat loop starts, set the variable pnt1 to pnt0, the center. Then compute the radial endpoint as pnt2 and draw a line between pnt1 and pnt2. After the angle and radius are incremented, pnt1 is set to pnt2. The endpoint of the current line becomes the start point of the next.

Completed function PROG02d:

```
;----------------------------------
(defun prog02d ()
 (graphscr)
 ; get centerpoint and dimensions
 (prompt "\nDraw radial spiral")
 (setq pnt0
   (getpoint "\nPick center:"))
 (setq crad
   (getdist pnt0
   "\nEnter radius:"))
 (setq numlines
   (getint
   "\nEnter number of lines:"))
 ; compute inc
 (setq anginc (/ 360.0 numlines))
 (setq radinc (/ crad numlines))
 (setq angline anginc)
 (setq radline radinc)
 ; draw circle
 (command ".CIRCLE" pnt0 crad)
 ; first point
 (setq pnt1 pnt0)
 (repeat numlines
  ; compute second point
  (setq pnt2 (polar
    pnt0 (dtr angline) radline))
  ; draw line
  (command ".LINE" pnt1 pnt2 "")
  ; inc ang and length
  (setq angline (+ angline anginc))
  (setq radline (+ radline radinc))
  ; make the last point first
  (setq pnt1 pnt2)
 )
 (princ)
)
;----------------------------------
```

In function PROG02d, the spiral has been drawn as a series of individual line segments. Using function PROG02d, add function PROG02e to draw the spiral as a single entity.

In previous exercises, the polylines included all points in one command. In the next example, the number of points is unknown. The implementation of AutoCAD commands within AutoLISP allows for this situation in a very interesting manner. The PLINE command can be executed and then points can be added to it until it is closed. The actual number of points does not need to be known.

Completed function PROG02e:

```
;-----------------------------------
(defun prog02e ()
 (graphscr)
 ; get centerpoint and dimensions
 (prompt "\nDraw radial spiral")
 (setq pnt0
   (getpoint "\nPick center:"))
 (setq crad
   (getdist pnt0 "\nEnter radius:"))
 (setq numlines
   (getint
   "\nEnter number of lines:"))
 ; compute inc
 (setq anginc (/ 360.0 numlines))
 (setq radinc (/ crad numlines))
 (setq angline anginc)
 (setq radline radinc)
 ; draw circle
 (command ".CIRCLE" pnt0 crad)
 ; start the polyline
 (command ".PLINE" pnt0)
 (repeat numlines
  ; compute second point
  (setq pnt2
    (polar pnt0 (dtr angline)
    radline))
  ; add point
  (command pnt2)
  ; inc ang and length
  (setq angline (+ angline anginc))
  (setq radline (+ radline radinc))
 )
 ; close polyline
 (command "")
 (princ)
)
;-----------------------------------
```

Review how the PLINE command is started with the first point, how the next point is added, and how it is ended. Note that the variable pnt1 is no longer required and that we closed the PLINE command but did not close the polyline itself. The only restriction to this method is that no other AutoCAD command can be executed until the current one is complete. This method can be used with any AutoCAD command requiring multiple arguments.

Add function PROG02f in the same way as PROG02, except with the start line at the end of the previous line. It is always drawn to the edge of the circle, the inverse of the PROG02 version.

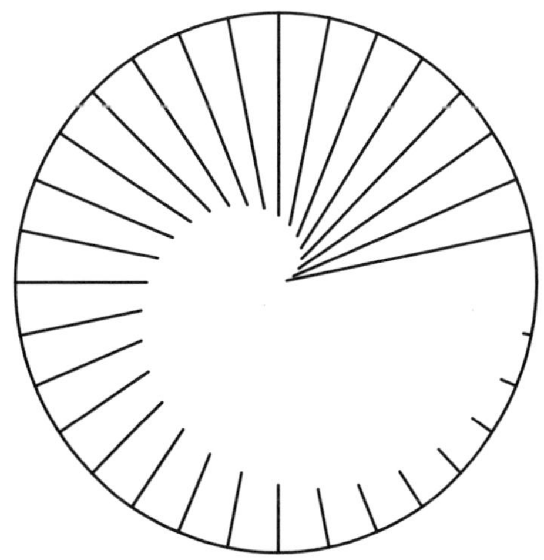

PROG02f: spiral, radial lines to edge

Review and compare the difference in function PROG02:

```
; compute endpoint
(setq pnt1
  (polar pnt0 (dtr angline)
  radline))
; draw line
(command ".LINE" pnt0 pnt1 "")
```

when it is replaced with:

```
; compute endpoint
(setq pnt1 (polar
  pnt0 (dtr angline) radline))
(setq pnt2 (polar
  pnt0 (dtr angline) crad))
; draw line
(command ".LINE" pnt1 pnt2 "")
```

Completed function PROG02f:

```
;----------------------------------
(defun prog02f ()
 (graphscr)
 ; get centerpoint and dimensions
 (prompt
   "\nDraw the inverse of the
   radial spiral")
 (setq pnt0
   (getpoint "\nPick center:"))
 (setq crad
   (getdist pnt0 "\nEnter radius:"))
 (setq numlines
   (getint
   "\nEnter number of lines:"))
 ; compute inc
 (setq anginc (/ 360.0  numlines))
 (setq radinc (/ crad numlines ))
 (setq angline anginc)
 (setq radline radinc)
 ; draw circle
 (command ".CIRCLE" pnt0 crad)
 (repeat numlines
  ; compute endpoint
  (setq pnt1 (polar
    pnt0 (dtr angline)  radline))
  (setq pnt2 (polar
   pnt0 (dtr angline) crad))
  ; draw line
  (command ".LINE" pnt1 pnt2 "")
  ; inc ang and length
  (setq angline (+ angline anginc))
  (setq radline (+ radline radinc))
 )
 (princ)
)
;----------------------------------
```

Add function PROG02g. Draw the radial line in the same way as PROG02f, except with each line length equal to the full radius.

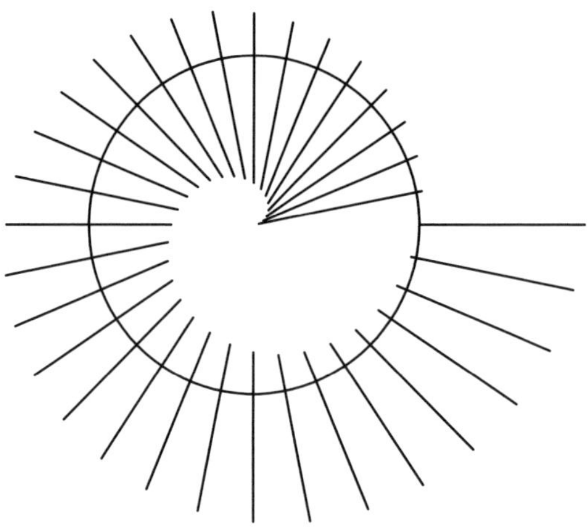

PROG02g: spiral radial lines at full radius length

Review and compare the difference in PROG02f:

```
; compute endpoint
(setq pnt1 (polar
  pnt0 (dtr angline) radline))
(setq pnt2 (polar
  pnt0 (dtr angline) crad))
; draw line
(command ".LINE" pnt1 pnt2 "")
```

when it is replaced with:

```
; compute endpoint
(setq pnt1 (polar
  pnt0 (dtr angline) radline))
(setq pnt2 (polar pnt0
  (dtr angline) (+ radline crad)))
; draw line
(command ".LINE" pnt1 pnt2 "")
```

Completed function PROG02g:

```
;----------------------------------
(defun prog02g ()
 (graphscr)
 ; get centerpoint and dimensions
 (prompt
   "\nDraw inverse radial spiral")
 (setq pnt0
   (getpoint "\nPick center:"))
 (setq crad
   (getdist pnt0 "\nEnter radius:"))
 (setq numlines
   (getint
   "\nEnter number of lines:"))
 ; compute inc
 (setq anginc (/ 360.0  numlines))
 (setq radinc (/ crad numlines ))
 (setq angline anginc)
 (setq radline radinc)
 ; draw circle
 (command ".CIRCLE" pnt0 crad)
 (repeat numlines
  ; compute endpoint
  (setq pnt1  (polar
   pnt0 (dtr angline) radline))
  (setq pnt2 (polar pnt0
    (dtr angline) (+ radline crad)))
  ; draw line
  (command ".LINE" pnt1 pnt2 "")
  ; inc ang and length
  (setq angline (+ angline anginc))
  (setq radline (+ radline radinc))
 )
 (princ)
)
;----------------------------------
```

Add function PROG02h by adding a third dimension to the spiral. PROG02h is the same as PROG02g, except we set the z-value of each line, the start and endpoints, to one-half the radial length, which is the distance from the center of the circle.

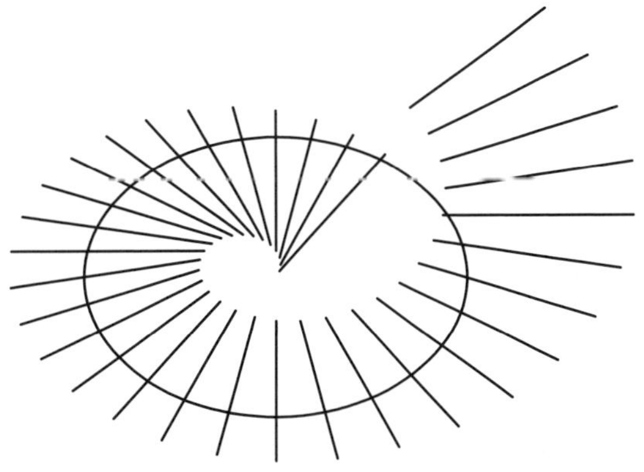

PROG02h: 3-D spiral of radial lines

The z-value is computed as:

```
; compute endpoint
(setq pnt1 (polar
  pnt0 (dtr angline) radline))
(setq pnt2 (polar pnt0
  (dtr angline) (+ radline crad)))
```

```
; set Z elev
(setq pnt1 (list
  (nth 0 pnt1) (nth 1 pnt1)
  (/ radline 2)))
(setq pnt2 (list
  (nth 0 pnt2) (nth 1 pnt2)
  (/ radline 2)))
; draw line
(command ".LINE" pnt1 pnt2 "")
```

An alternate method is to determine the z-height as a ratio to the radial line length and to use a separate parameter for the total height.

Completed function PROG02h:

```
;---------------------------------
(defun prog02h ()
 (graphscr)
 ; get centerpoint and dimensions
 (prompt
   "\nDraw inverse radial spiral,
   3D lines")
 (setq pnt0
   (getpoint "\nPick center:"))
 (setq crad
   (getdist pnt0 "\nEnter radius:"))
 (setq numlines
   (getint
   "\nEnter number of lines:"))
 ; compute inc
 (setq anginc (/ 360.0  numlines))
 (setq radinc (/ crad numlines ))
 (setq angline anginc)
 (setq radline radinc)
 ; draw circle
 (command ".CIRCLE" pnt0 crad)
 (repeat numlines
  ; compute endpoint
  (setq pnt1 (polar
    pnt0 (dtr angline) radline))
  (setq pnt2 (polar pnt0
    (dtr angline) (+ radline crad)))
  ; set Z elev
  (setq pnt1 (list
    (nth 0 pnt1) (nth 1 pnt1)
    (/ radline 2)))
  (setq pnt2 (list
    (nth 0 pnt2) (nth 1 pnt2)
    (/ radline 2)))
  ; draw line
  (command ".LINE" pnt1 pnt2 "")
  ; inc ang and length
  (setq angline (+ angline anginc))
  (setq radline (+ radline radinc))
 )
 (princ)
)
;---------------------------------
```

Add function PROG02i to create a spiral ramp. Function PROG02i is the same as PROG02h, except that the start and endpoints of the line are used as points in a mesh. The result will be a ramp, which is a continuous surface.

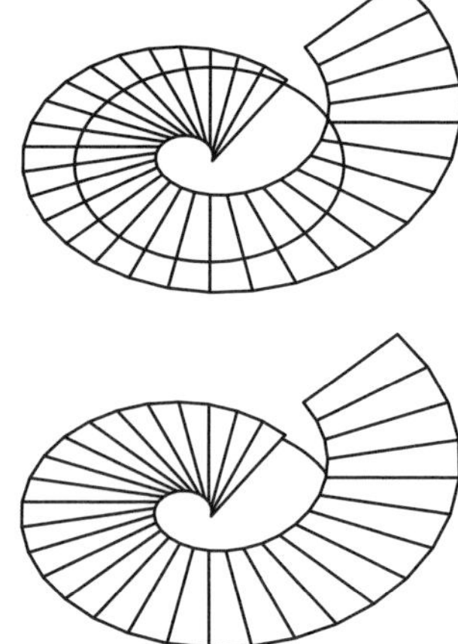

PROG02i: 3-D spiral ramp as a mesh, wireframe, and hidden line views

The three-dimensional mesh is created by specifying how many points in a grid need to be entered. For our spiral, the grid is made of two points for each segment and the number of lines is the number of segments. The `3DMESH` command is expecting the number of lines times two points.

Before the repeat loop begins, start the mesh with:

```
; start mesh
(command ".3DMESH" numlines "2")
```

Instead of drawing a line, the two computed points are given to the open mesh command:

```
; sendpoints to mesh
(command pnt1 pnt2)
```

The `3DMESH` command will terminate automatically when it receives all of the points it is expecting. Unlike the `PLINE` command, it does not have a close option.

Completed function `PROG02i`:

```
;-----------------------------------
(defun prog02i ()
 (graphscr)
 ; get centerpoint and dimensions
 (prompt
   "\nDraw inverse radial spiral,
   3D mesh ramp")
 (setq pnt0
   (getpoint "\nPick center:"))
 (setq crad
   (getdist pnt0 "\nEnter radius:"))
 (setq numlines
   (getint
   "\nEnter number of lines:"))
 ; compute inc
 (setq anginc (/ 360.0  numlines))
 (setq radinc (/ crad numlines ))
 (setq angline anginc)
 (setq radline radinc)
 ; draw circle
 (command ".CIRCLE" pnt0 crad)
 ; start mesh
 (command ".3DMESH" numlines "2")
 (repeat numlines
  ; compute endpoint
  (setq pnt1 (polar pnt0
    (dtr angline) radline))
  (setq pnt2 (polar pnt0
    (dtr angline) (+ radline crad)))
  ; set Z elev
  (setq pnt1 (list
    (nth 0 pnt1) (nth 1 pnt1)
    (/ radline 2)))
  (setq pnt2 (list
    (nth 0 pnt2) (nth 1 pnt2)
    (/ radline 2)))
  ; sendpoints to mesh
  (command pnt1 pnt2)
  ; inc ang and length
  (setq angline (+ angline anginc))
  (setq radline (+ radline radinc))
 )
 (princ)
)
;-----------------------------------
```

Add function `PROG02j` and modify the ramp to steps. Function `PROG02j` is the same as `PROG02i`, except that instead of two points per segment, four points are needed for the front and back edges of each step. The flat-ramping surface in `PROG02j` is bent at the back edge of each segment.

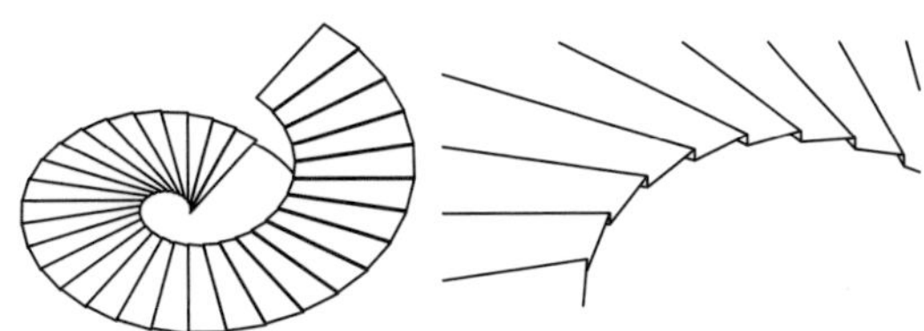

`PROG02j`: 3-D spiral ramp converted to steps

The two points currently being computed, `pnt1` and `pnt2`, represent the front edge of the step. Now compute the back edge of the step by computing the next endpoints at the same z-value. Next, angle and radial line length are used to determine `pnt3` and `pnt4`, as follows:

```
; compute next endpoint
(setq pnt3 (polar pnt0
  (dtr (+ angline anginc))
  (+ radline radinc)))
(setq pnt4 (polar pnt0
  (dtr (+ angline anginc))
  (+ (+ radline radinc) crad)))
; set Z elev
(setq pnt3 (list
  (nth 0 pnt3) (nth 1 pnt3)
  (/ radline 2)))
(setq pnt4 (list
  (nth 0 pnt4) (nth 1 pnt4)
  (/ radline 2)))
; sendpoints to mesh
(command pnt3 pnt4)
```

Compare this computation to the front edge.

Now that each segment has four points, change the `3DMESH` command to:

```
; start mesh
(command
  ".3DMESH" (* numlines 2) "2")
```

Completed function `PROG02j`:

```
;---------------------------------
(defun prog02j ()
 (graphscr)
 ; get centerpoint and dimensions
 (prompt
   "\nDraw inverse radial spiral,
   3D mesh steps")
 (setq pnt0
   (getpoint "\nPick center:"))
 (setq crad
   (getdist pnt0 "\nEnter radius:"))
 (setq numlines
   (getint
   "\nEnter number of lines:"))
 ; compute inc
 (setq anginc (/ 360.0  numlines))
 (setq radinc (/ crad numlines ))
 (setq angline anginc)
 (setq radline radinc)
 ; draw circle
 (command ".CIRCLE" pnt0 crad)
 ; start mesh
 (command
   ".3DMESH" (* numlines 2) "2")
 (repeat numlines
  ; compute endpoint
  (setq pnt1 (polar pnt0
    (dtr angline) radline))
  (setq pnt2 (polar pnt0
    (dtr angline) (+ radline crad)))
  ; set Z elev
  (setq pnt1 (list
    (nth 0 pnt1) (nth 1 pnt1)
    (/ radline 2)))
  (setq pnt2 (list
    (nth 0 pnt2) (nth 1 pnt2)
    (/ radline 2)))
  (command pnt1 pnt2)
  ; compute next endpoint
  (setq pnt3 (polar pnt0
    (dtr (+ angline anginc))
    (+ radline radinc)))
  (setq pnt4 (polar pnt0
    (dtr (+ angline anginc))
    (+ (+ radline radinc) crad)))
  ; set Z elev
  (setq pnt3 (list
    (nth 0 pnt3) (nth 1 pnt3)
    (/ radline 2)))
  (setq pnt4 (list
    (nth 0 pnt4) (nth 1 pnt4)
    (/ radline 2)))
  ; sendpoints to mesh
  (command pnt3 pnt4)
  ; inc ang and length
  (setq angline (+ angline anginc))
  (setq radline (+ radline radinc))
 )
 (princ)
)
;---------------------------------
```

Add function PROG02k. Modify the stepping mesh from a simple bent surface to a series of individual steps with a thickness.

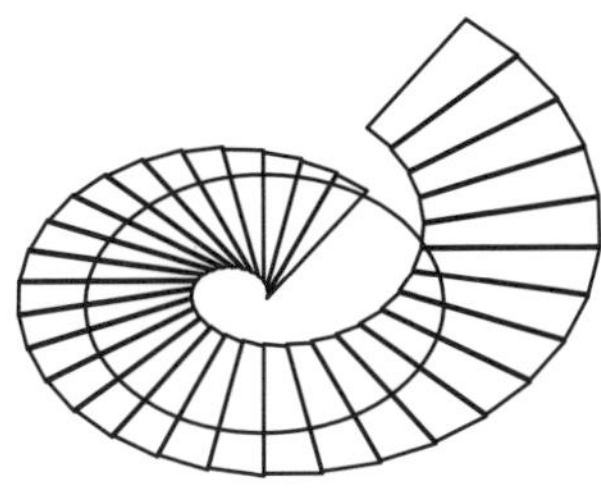

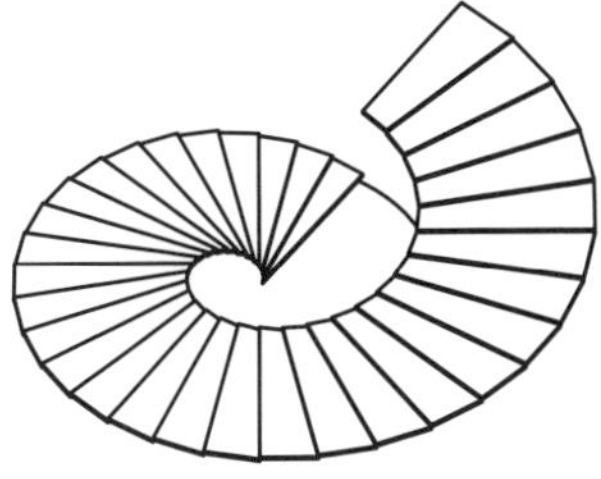

PROG02k: 3-D spiral steps as polylines and extruded polylines

Function PROG02j already computes four points for each segment. Instead of specifying them as a mesh, use the four points to create a polyline, which can be extruded for the thickness of each step.

The start and endpoints of the 3DMESH are removed. A polyline is created and extruded:

```
; make polyline
(command ".PLINE" pnt1 pnt2
  pnt4 pnt3 "c")
; extrude step
(command ".EXTRUDE"
  "last" "" (/ radinc 2))
; versions prior to 2007 use
;(command ".EXTRUDE"
; "last" "" (/ radinc 2) "0")
```

The EXTRUDE command converts the PLINE to a three-dimensional solid. It requires a selection list and a height. In this case, use the last selection list option to get the last entity created. Double quotation marks indicate the end of the selection list.

In AutoCAD versions released prior to 2007, the EXTRUDE command requires a taper angle. In this example, set it to zero:

```
; versions prior to 2007 use
(command ".EXTRUDE"
  "last" "" (/ radinc 2) "0")
```

Similar to the spiral height, this version could also include a step thickness as an alternate parameter. In this example, use a value related to the radius increment.

Completed function PROG02k:

```
;-----------------------------------
(defun prog02k ()
 (graphscr)
 ; get centerpoint and dimensions
 (prompt
   "\nDraw inverse radial spiral,
   3D steps")
 (setq pnt0
   (getpoint "\nPick center:"))
 (setq crad
   (getdist pnt0 "\nEnter radius:"))
 (setq numlines
   (getint
   "\nEnter number of lines:"))
 ; compute inc
 (setq anginc (/ 360.0  numlines))
 (setq radinc (/ crad numlines ))
 (setq angline anginc)
 (setq radline radinc)
 ; draw circle
 (command ".CIRCLE" pnt0 crad)
 (repeat numlines
  ; compute endpoint
  (setq pnt1 (polar pnt0
    (dtr angline) radline))
```

```
  (setq pnt2 (polar pnt0
    (dtr angline) (+ radline crad)))
  ; set Z elev
  (setq pnt1 (list
    (nth 0 pnt1) (nth 1 pnt1)
    (/ radline 2)))
  (setq pnt2 (list
    (nth 0 pnt2) (nth 1 pnt2)
    (/ radline 2)))
  ; compute next endpoint
  (setq pnt3 (polar pnt0
    (dtr (+ angline anginc))
    (+ radline radinc)))
  (setq pnt4 (polar pnt0
    (dtr (+ angline anginc))
    (+ (+ radline radinc) crad)))
  ; set Z elev
  (setq pnt3 (list
    (nth 0 pnt3) (nth 1 pnt3)
    (/ radline 2)))
  (setq pnt4 (list
    (nth 0 pnt4) (nth 1 pnt4)
    (/ radline 2)))
  ; make polyline
  (command ".PLINE" pnt1 pnt2
   pnt4 pnt3 "c")
  ; extrude step
  (command ".EXTRUDE"
   "last" "" (/ radinc 2))
  ; versions prior to 2007 use
  ;(command ".EXTRUDE"
  ;  "last" "" (/ radinc 2) "0")
  ; inc ang and length
  (setq angline (+ angline anginc))
  (setq radline (+ radline radinc))
 )
 (princ)
)
;---------------------------------
```

Add function PROG021. Extend the steps for another revolution. PROG021 is the same as PROG02k, except that the repeat loop is completed for twice the number of lines.

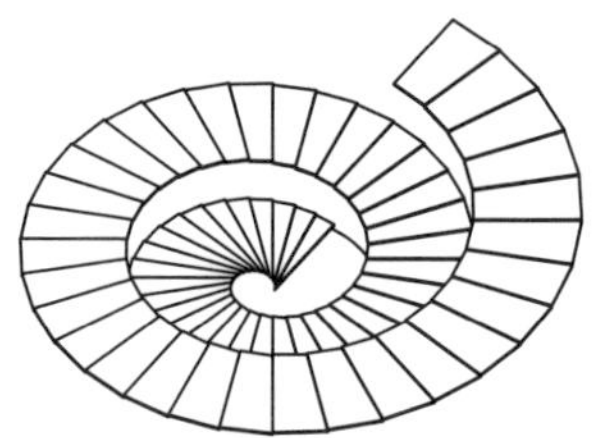

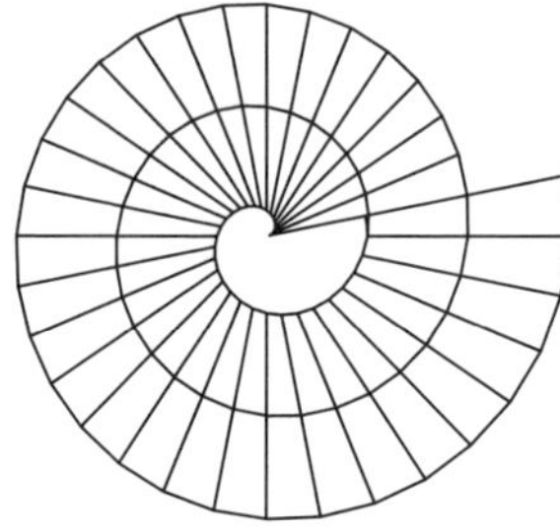

PROG021: 3-D spiral of two revolutions, isometric and plan views

The `repeat` function parameter changes to:

```
(repeat (* numlines 2)
```

An alternate method would be to use the number of revolutions as the input parameter. The `repeat` function only accepts an integer value. When using a fractional number, use the `fix` function to convert the computation to an integer value.

For example:

```
(repeat (fix (* numlines 2.5))
```

Or, if using a real variable:

```
(repeat (fix (* numlines nrevs))
```

Add function PROG02m. Change the spiral steps to a simple helix.

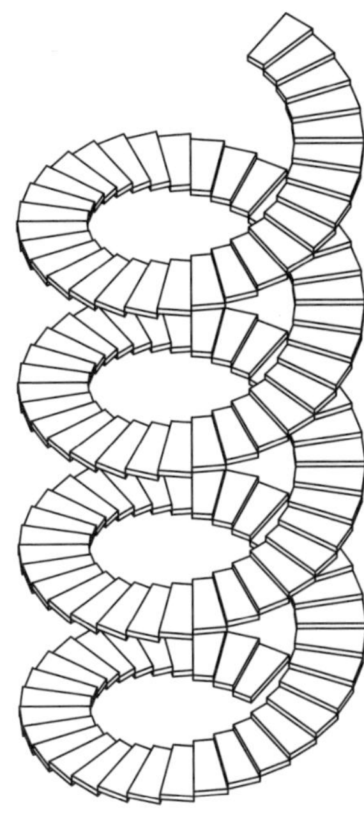

PROG02m: 3-D spiral steps with multiple revolutions

Use function PROG02l as a basis for PROG02m. The spiral is simplified by including parameters for inside and outside radii, number of segments per turn, number of turns, and step thickness.

Note how the number of turns determines the angle increment, the total number of steps and the starting value for the z-coordinate. Also note how it is incremented.

Compare the differences between functions PROG02l and PROG02m.

Completed function PROG02m:

```
;----------------------------------
(defun prog02m ()
 (graphscr)
 ; get centerpoint and dimensions
 (prompt
   "\nDraw a helix, 3D steps")
 (setq pnt0
   (getpoint "\nPick center:"))
 (setq icrad
   (getdist pnt0
   "\nEnter inside radius:"))
 (setq ocrad
   (getdist pnt0
   "\nEnter outside radius:"))
 (setq numsegs
   (getint
   "\nEnter number segments/turn:"))
 (setq numturns
   (getint
   "\nEnter number of turns:"))
 (setq zoff
   (getdist
   "\nEnter Z incremental height:"))
 ; compute inc
 (setq anginc (/ 360.0 numsegs))
 (setq angline anginc)
 ; start Z
 (setq zpt 0.0)
 (repeat (* numsegs numturns)
  ; compute endpoint
  (setq pnt1 (polar pnt0
    (dtr angline) icrad))
  (setq pnt2 (polar pnt0
    (dtr angline) ocrad))
  ; set Z elev
  (setq pnt1 (list
    (nth 0 pnt1) (nth 1 pnt1) zpt))
  (setq pnt2 (list
    (nth 0 pnt2) (nth 1 pnt2) zpt))
  ; compute next endpoint
  (setq pnt3 (polar pnt0
    (dtr (+ angline anginc)) icrad))
  (setq pnt4 (polar pnt0
    (dtr (+ angline anginc)) ocrad))
  ; set Z elev
  (setq pnt3 (list
    (nth 0 pnt3) (nth 1 pnt3) zpt))
```

```
    (setq pnt4 (list
      (nth 0 pnt4) (nth 1 pnt4) zpt))
    ; make polyline
    (command ".PLINE" pnt1 pnt2 pnt4
      pnt3 "c")
    ; extrude step
    (command ".EXTRUDE"
     "last" "" zoff)
    ; versions prior to 2007 use
    ;(command ".EXTRUDE"
    ;   "last" "" zoff "0")
    ; inc ang and Z point
    (setq angline (+ angline anginc))
    (setq zpt (+ zpt zoff))
  )
  (princ)
)
;----------------------------------
```

4.9 Draw a Linear Series of Objects

The previous examples consisted of repeating lines in a circular pattern. Now we demonstrate basic object repetition that is usually unavailable as a native CAD command.

Start with a simple repetition of a circle using start and endpoints. Add function PROG03. Input start and end centers, radius, and number of repeats. The repeats will be along the x-axis only. Draw a line showing the path for the repeats, from start to end centerpoints.

The first circle is drawn at the start center, and the last circle is drawn at the end center. Based on the distance between the start and end centerpoints, the remaining circles are drawn. The distance between each center is based on the x-distance divided by the number of repeats minus one. The x-coordinate of the center is incremented by this distance for each repeat, and a new centerpoint is computed.

This function is the same as the linear ARRAY command in AutoCAD, except that the y-coordinate is not being considered.

Completed function PROG03:

```
;----------------------------------
(defun prog03 ()
 (graphscr)
 ; get start and endpoint
 (prompt
   "\nDraw a linear series of
   circles")
 (setq pnt1
   (getpoint
   "\nPick start center:"))
 (setq pnt2
   (getpoint pnt1
   "\nPick end center:"))
 (setq crad
   (getdist pnt1
   "\nEnter circle radius:"))
 (setq numrepeat
   (getint
```

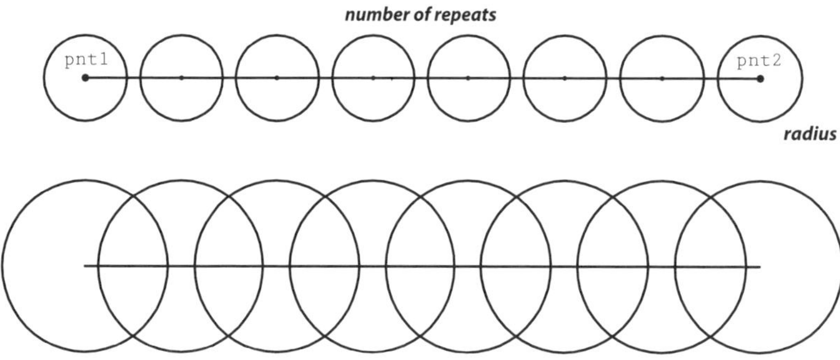

PROG03: simple repetition of a circle

```
    "\nEnter number of repeats:"))
  ; compute inc
  (setq xdist (- (nth 0 pnt2)
    (nth 0 pnt1)))
  (setq xinc
    (/ xdist (- numrepeat 1)))
  ; draw line between start/end
  (command ".LINE" pnt1 pnt2 "")
  ; start
  (setq pntc pnt1)
  (repeat numrepeat
   ; draw circle
   (command ".CIRCLE" pntc crad)
   ; inc X
   (setq pntc (list
     (+ (nth 0 pntc) xinc)
     (nth 1 pntc) (nth 2 pntc)))
  )
  (princ)
)
;---------------------------------
```

If the y-coordinate was considered, then a y-increment based on the y-offset distance would be computed and incremented for each repeat, just as the x-coordinate was.

Add function PROG03a. Using PROG03, modify the function to increase the radii of the circles as they are repeated.

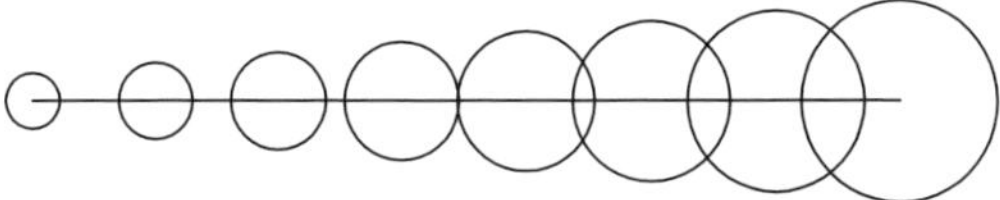

PROG03a: repetition with increasing circle radius

The single radius in PROG03 is replaced with a start and end radius. A radius increment is computed, a stating value for the radius is set, and the radius is incremented for each repeat.

Completed function PROG03a:

```
;---------------------------------
(defun prog03a ()
 (graphscr)
 ; get start and endpoint
 (prompt
   "\nDraw a linear series of
   increasing circles")
 (setq pnt1
   (getpoint
   "\nPick start center:"))
 (setq pnt2
   (getpoint pnt1
   "\nPick end center:"))
 (setq scrad
   (getdist pnt1
   "\nEnter start circle radius:"))
 (setq ecrad
   (getdist pnt1
   "\nEnter end circle radius:"))
 (setq numrepeat
   (getint
   "\nEnter number of repeats:"))
 ; compute inc
 (setq xdist (- (nth 0 pnt2)
   (nth 0 pnt1)))
 (setq xinc
   (/ xdist (- numrepeat 1)))
 (setq xrad (- ecrad scrad))
 (setq radinc
   (/ xrad (- numrepeat 1)))
 ; draw line between start/end
 (command ".LINE" pnt1 pnt2 "")
 ; start
 (setq pntc pnt1)
 (setq crad scrad)
 (repeat numrepeat
  ; draw circle
  (command ".CIRCLE" pntc crad)
  ; inc X
  (setq pntc (list
    (+ (nth 0 pntc) xinc)
    (nth 1 pntc) (nth 2 pntc)))
  ; inc radius
  (setq crad (+ crad radinc))
 )
 (princ)
)
;---------------------------------
```

Add function PROG03b. Increase the radius to one-half the number of repeats, then decrease the radius for the remaining repeats.

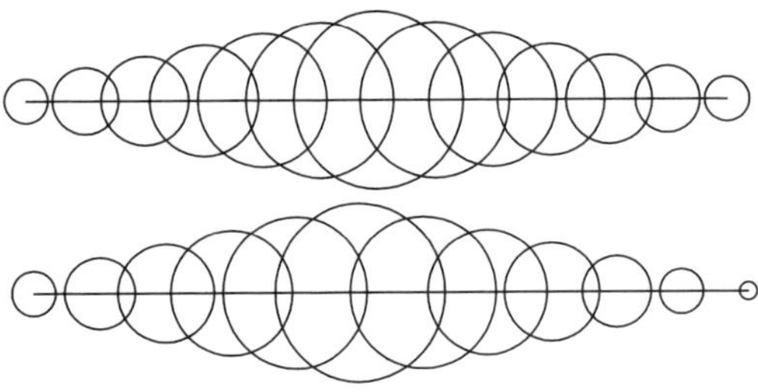

PROG03b: repetition with increasing and decreasing circle radius, 12 and 13 repeats

In a manner similar to function PROG02b, compute the midpoint repeat and the radius increment. To get the correct midpoint repeat value, the division is rounded to the next higher integer:

```
; compute mid number of repeats
 (setq midrepeat
   (fix (+ (/ numrepeat 2.0) 0.5)))
```

Try this function for an even and odd number of repeats. For an even number of repeats, the radius for the last circle could become negative, and the CIRCLE command would fail, terminating the function. Set the radius in the CIRCLE command to an absolute value so that a negative value does not terminate the function.

For example:

```
; draw circle
(command ".CIRCLE" pntc
  (abs crad))
```

A better solution is to have the function correctly draw an even and odd number of repeats.

Completed function PROG03b:

```
;----------------------------------
(defun prog03b ()
 (graphscr)
 ; get start and endpoint
 (prompt
   "\nDraw a linear series of
   increasing/decreasing circles")
 (setq pnt1
   (getpoint
   "\nPick start center:"))
 (setq pnt2
   (getpoint pnt1
   "\nPick end center:"))
 (setq scrad
   (getdist pnt1
   "\nEnter start circle radius:"))
 (setq ecrad
   (getdist pnt1
   "\nEnter end circle radius:"))
 (setq numrepeat
   (getint
   "\nEnter number of repeats:"))
 ; compute inc
 (setq xdist (- (nth 0 pnt2)
   (nth 0 pnt1)))
 (setq xinc (/ xdist
   (- numrepeat 1)))
 (setq xrad (- ecrad scrad))
 ; compute mid number of repeats
 (setq midrepeat
   (fix (+ (/ numrepeat 2.0) 0.5)))
 (setq radinc
   (/ xrad (- midrepeat 1)))
 ; draw line between start/end
 (command ".LINE" pnt1 pnt2 "")
 ; start
 (setq pntc pnt1)
 (setq crad scrad)
 ; object counter
 (setq ncnt 0)
 (repeat numrepeat
  ; draw circle
  (command ".CIRCLE" pntc crad)
  ; inc objs drawn
  (setq ncnt (+ ncnt 1))
  ; inc X
```

```
  (setq pntc (list
    (+ (nth 0 pntc) xinc)
    (nth 1 pntc) (nth 2 pntc)))
  ; check number of circles drawn
  (if (= ncnt midrepeat)
    (setq radinc (* radinc -1)))
  ; inc radius
  (setq crad (+ crad radinc))
 )
 (princ)
)
;---------------------------------
```

Add function PROG03c to correctly draw an even or odd number of circles.

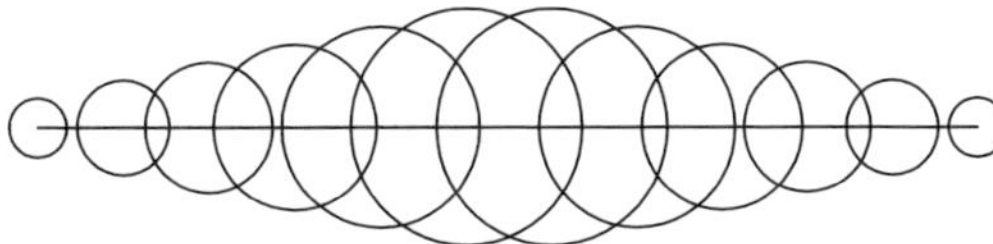

PROG03c: repetition with increasing and decreasing circle radius, 13 repeats revised

If the number of repeats is odd, nothing additional needs to be done. If the number of repeats is even, the repeat following the midpoint should have the same radius, or the radius should not be changed at the midpoint repeat.

This can be written as:

```
  ; check number of objs drawn
  (if (= ncnt midrepeat)
    (setq radinc (* radinc -1)))
  ; check for odd/even number
  ; of repeats
  ; inc radius
  (if (= (rem numrepeat 2) 1)
    (setq crad (+ crad radinc)))
  (if (and (= (rem numrepeat 2) 0)
    (/= ncnt midrepeat))
    (setq crad (+ crad radinc)))
```

The rem function is used to determine if the number of repeats is even or odd.

Completed function PROG03c:

```
;---------------------------------
(defun prog03c ()
 (graphscr)
 ; get start and endpoint
 (prompt
   "\nDraw a linear series of
   increasing/decreasing circles")
 (setq pnt1
   (getpoint
   "\nPick start center:"))
 (setq pnt2
   (getpoint pnt1
   "\nPick end center:"))
 (setq scrad
   (getdist pnt1
   "\nEnter start circle radius:"))
 (setq ecrad
   (getdist pnt1
   "\nEnter end circle radius:"))
 (setq numrepeat
   (getint
   "\nEnter number of repeats:"))
 ; compute inc
 (setq xdist (- (nth 0 pnt2)
   (nth 0 pnt1)))
 (setq xinc (/ xdist
   (- numrepeat 1)))
 (setq xrad (- ecrad scrad))
 ; compute mid number of repeats
 (setq midrepeat
   (fix (+ (/ numrepeat 2.0) 0.5)))
 (setq radinc
   (/ xrad (- midrepeat 1)))
 ; draw line between start/end
 (command ".LINE" pnt1 pnt2 "")
 ; start
 (setq pntc pnt1)
 (setq crad scrad)
 ; object counter
 (setq ncnt 0)
 (repeat numrepeat
  ; draw circle
  (command ".CIRCLE" pntc crad)
```

```
  ; inc objs drawn
  (setq ncnt (+ ncnt 1))
  ; inc X
  (setq pntc (list
    (+ (nth 0 pntc) xinc)
    (nth 1 pntc) (nth 2 pntc)))
  ; check number of objs drawn
  (if (= ncnt midrepeat)
    (setq radinc (* radinc -1)))
  ; check for odd/even number
  ; of repeats
  ; inc radius
  (if (= (rem numrepeat 2) 1)
    (setq crad (+ crad radinc)))
  (if (and (= (rem numrepeat 2) 0)
    (/= ncnt midrepeat))
    (setq crad (+ crad radinc)))
 )
 (princ)
)
;---------------------------------
```

Add function PROG03d. Using PROG03c, substitute a rectangle for the circle. Also replace the start and end radii with the start and end length and width.

The dimensions for this example are length from 6 to 2 and width from 8 to 2, with 9 repeats.

Copy the DORECTEN function from CH03.LSP into CH04.LSP.

```
;---------------------------------
(defun dorectcen (pnt0 xside yside
  / pnt1 pnt2 pnt3 pnt4)
 ; compute points
 (setq pnt1 (list
   (- (nth 0 pnt0) (/ xside 2))
   (- (nth 1 pnt0) (/ yside 2))
   (nth 2 pnt0)))
 (setq pnt2 (list
   (+ (nth 0 pnt0) (/ xside 2))
   (- (nth 1 pnt0) (/ yside 2))
   (nth 2 pnt0)))
 (setq pnt3 (list
   (+ (nth 0 pnt0) (/ xside 2))
   (+ (nth 1 pnt0) (/ yside 2))
   (nth 2 pnt0)))
 (setq pnt4 (list
   (- (nth 0 pnt0) (/ xside 2))
   (+ (nth 1 pnt0) (/ yside 2))
   (nth 2 pnt0)))
 ; draw rectangle
 (command ".PLINE" pnt1 pnt2 pnt3
   pnt4 pnt1 "")
 (princ)
)
;---------------------------------
```

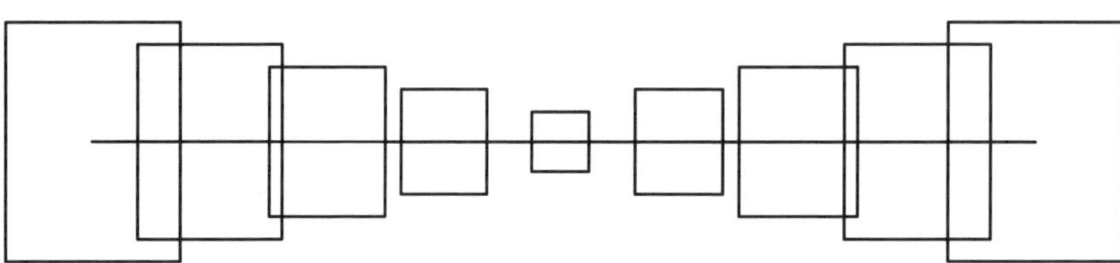

PROG03d: repetition with increasing and decreasing rectangle dimensions

Using function PROG03c, expand the incrementing of the radius to the incrementing of the length and width of the rectangle. The length and width will each need incrementing values.

Completed function PROG03d:

```
;-----------------------------------
(defun prog03d ()
 (graphscr)
 ; get start and endpoint
 (prompt
   "\nDraw a linear series of
   increasing/decreasing rectangles")
 (setq pnt1
   (getpoint
   "\nPick start center:"))
 (setq pnt2
   (getpoint pnt1
   "\nPick end center:"))
 (setq slen
   (getdist pnt1
   "\nEnter start rect length:"))
 (setq elen
   (getdist pnt1
   "\nEnter end rect length:"))
 (setq swid
   (getdist pnt1
   "\nEnter start rect width:"))
 (setq ewid
   (getdist pnt1
   "\nEnter end rect width:"))
 (setq numrepeat
   (getint
   "\nEnter number of repeats:"))
 ; compute inc
 (setq xdist
   (- (nth 0 pnt2) (nth 0 pnt1)))
 (setq xinc
   (/ xdist (- numrepeat 1)))
 ; compute mid number of repeats
 (setq midrepeat
   (fix (+ (/ numrepeat 2.0) 0.5)))
 ; compute length and width inc
 (setq linc
   (/ (- elen slen) (- midrepeat 1)))
 (setq winc
   (/ (- ewid swid) (- midrepeat 1)))
 ; draw line between start/end
 (command ".LINE" pnt1 pnt2 "")
 ; start
 (setq pntc pnt1)
 (setq rlen slen)
 (setq rwid swid)
 ; object counter
 (setq ncnt 0)
 (repeat numrepeat
  ; draw rectangle
  (dorectcen pntc rlen rwid)
  ; inc objs drawn
  (setq ncnt (+ ncnt 1))
  ; inc X
  (setq pntc (list
    (+ (nth 0 pntc) xinc)
    (nth 1 pntc) (nth 2 pntc)))
  ; check number of objs drawn
  (if (= ncnt midrepeat) (progn
    (setq linc (* linc -1))
    (setq winc (* winc -1))
  ))
  ; check for odd/even number
  ; of repeats
  ; inc dims
  (if (= (rem numrepeat 2) 1) (progn
    (setq rlen (+ rlen linc))
    (setq rwid (+ rwid winc))
  ))
  (if (and (= (rem numrepeat 2) 0)
    (/= ncnt midrepeat)) (progn
    (setq rlen (+ rlen linc))
    (setq rwid (+ rwid winc))
  ))
 )
 (princ)
)
;-----------------------------------
```

Add function PROG03e. Using PROG03d, include a z-start-and-end dimension and extrude each rectangle to the z-value. Collect all of the rectangles into a selection list. When completed, unite all the solid rectangles using the UNION command.

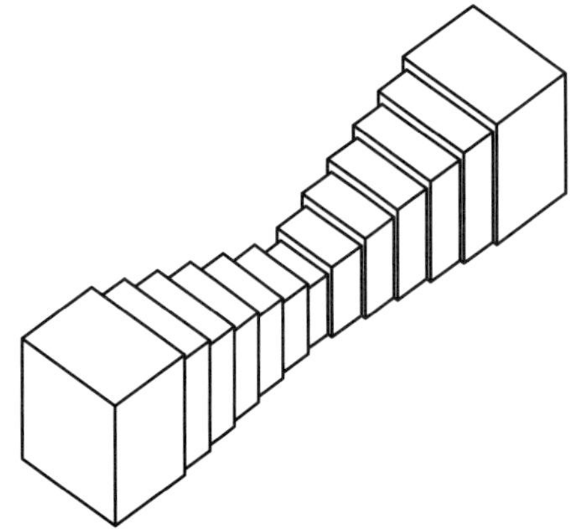

PROG03e: repetition with increasing and decreasing rectangle height

A height increment is computed and increased and decreased in the same manner as the length and width.

Completed function PROG03e:

```
;----------------------------------
(defun prog03e ()
 (graphscr)
 ; get start and endpoint
 (prompt
   "\nDraw a linear series of
   increasing/decreasing 3D
   rectangles")
 (setq pnt1
   (getpoint
   "\nPick start center:"))
 (setq pnt2
   (getpoint pnt1
   "\nPick end center:"))
 (setq slen
   (getdist pnt1
   "\nEnter start rect length:"))
 (setq elen
   (getdist pnt1
   "\nEnter end rect length:"))
 (setq swid
   (getdist pnt1
   "\nEnter start rect width:"))
 (setq ewid
   (getdist pnt1
   "\nEnter end rect width:"))
 (setq shgt
   (getdist pnt1
   "\nEnter start rect height:"))
 (setq ehgt
   (getdist pnt1
   "\nEnter end rect height:"))
 (setq numrepeat
   (getint
   "\nEnter number of repeats:"))
 ; compute inc
 (setq xdist
   (- (nth 0 pnt2) (nth 0 pnt1)))
 (setq xinc
   (/ xdist (- numrepeat 1)))
 ; compute mid number of repeats
 (setq midrepeat
   (fix (+ (/ numrepeat 2.0) 0.5)))
 ; compute length, width, height inc
 (setq linc
   (/ (- elen slen)
   (- midrepeat 1)))
 (setq winc
   (/ (- ewid swid)
   (- midrepeat 1)))
 (setq hinc
   (/ (- ehgt shgt)
   (- midrepeat 1)))
 ; draw line between start/end
 (command ".LINE" pnt1 pnt2 "")
 ; start
 (setq pntc pnt1)
 (setq rlen slen)
 (setq rwid swid)
 (setq rhgt shgt)
 ; object counter
 (setq ncnt 0)
 ; start an empty selection list
```

```
  (setq objs (ssadd))
  (repeat numrepeat
   ; draw rectangle
   (dorectcen pntc rlen rwid)
   ; extrude
   (command ".EXTRUDE"
     "last" "" rhgt)
   ; add to selection list
   (setq objs
     (ssadd (entlast) objs))
   ; inc objs drawn
   (setq ncnt (+ ncnt 1))
   ; inc X
   (setq pntc (list
     (+ (nth 0 pntc) xinc)
     (nth 1 pntc) (nth 2 pntc)))
   ; check number of objs drawn
   (if (= ncnt midrepeat)  (progn
     (setq linc (* linc -1))
     (setq winc (* winc -1))
     (setq hinc (* hinc -1))
   ))
   ; check for odd/even number of
   ; repeats
   ; inc dims
   (if (= (rem numrepeat 2) 1) (progn
     (setq rlen (+ rlen linc))
     (setq rwid (+ rwid winc))
     (setq rhgt (+ rhgt hinc))
   ))
   (if (and (= (rem numrepeat 2) 0)
     (/= ncnt midrepeat)) (progn
     (setq rlen (+ rlen linc))
     (setq rwid (+ rwid winc))
     (setq rhgt (+ rhgt hinc))
   ))
  )
  ; union objs
  (command ".UNION" objs "")
  (princ)
)
;---------------------------------
```

Add function PROG03f. Using PROG03e, add a start-and-end rotation angle.

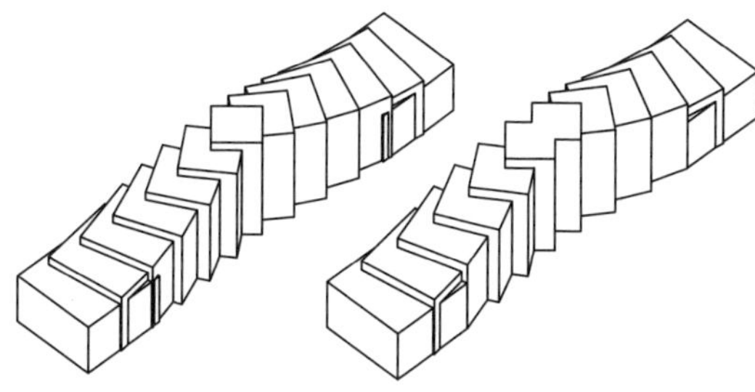

PROG03f: repetition with increasing and decreasing rectangle rotation, even and odd number of repeats

The rotation increment is computed and the rectangle is rotated before it is extruded. The rotation should increase and decrease in the same manner as the length and width dimensions.

For the rotation angle, set the current angle to a negative value, not the increment. We want the rotation to reverse itself. Just subtracting an increment will not work.

The reverse should be:

```
; check number of objs drawn
(if (= ncnt midrepeat)  (progn
  (setq linc (* linc -1))
  (setq winc (* winc -1))
  (setq hinc (* hinc -1))
  (setq rang (* rang -1))
))
```

If the variable rang is replaced with the variable ainc, the rotation will be mirrored, not symmetrical. Do the replacement and note the difference. Also note the conversion of the entered angles to degrees in the getorient function.

Completed function PROG03f:

```
;--------------------------------
(defun prog03f ()
 (graphscr)
 ; get start and endpoint
 (prompt
   "\nDraw a linear series of
   increasing/decreasing 3D
   rectangles")
 (setq pnt1
   (getpoint
   "\nPick start center:"))
 (setq pnt2
   (getpoint pnt1
   "\nPick end center:"))
 (setq slen
   (getdist pnt1
   "\nEnter start rect length:"))
 (setq elen
   (getdist pnt1
   "\nEnter end rect length:"))
 (setq swid
   (getdist pnt1
   "\nEnter start rect width:"))
 (setq ewid
   (getdist pnt1
   "\nEnter end rect width:"))
 (setq shgt
   (getdist pnt1
   "\nEnter start rect height:"))
 (setq ehgt
   (getdist pnt1
   "\nEnter end rect height:"))
 (setq sang
   (rtd (getorient
   "\nEnter start rot angle:")))
 (setq eang
   (rtd (getorient
   "\nEnter end rot angle:")))
 (setq numrepeat
   (getint
   "\nEnter number of repeats:"))
 ; compute inc
 (setq xdist
   (- (nth 0 pnt2) (nth 0 pnt1)))
 (setq xinc
   (/ xdist (- numrepeat 1)))
; compute mid number of repeats
(setq midrepeat
  (fix (+ (/ numrepeat 2.0) 0.5)))
; compute length, width, height,
; angle inc
(setq linc
  (/ (- elen slen) (- midrepeat 1)))
(setq winc
  (/ (- ewid swid) (- midrepeat 1)))
(setq hinc
  (/ (- ehgt shgt) (- midrepeat 1)))
(setq ainc
  (/ (- eang sang) (- midrepeat 1)))
; draw line between start/end
(command ".LINE" pnt1 pnt2 "")
; start
(setq pntc pnt1)
(setq rlen slen)
(setq rwid swid)
(setq rhgt shgt)
(setq rang sang)
; object counter
(setq ncnt 0)
; start an empty selection list
(setq objs (ssadd))
(repeat numrepeat
 ; draw rectangle
 (dorectcen pntc rlen rwid)
 ; rotate
 (command ".ROTATE"
   "last" "" pntc rang)
 ; extrude
 (command ".EXTRUDE"
   "last" "" rhgt)
 ; add to selection list
 (setq objs
   (ssadd (entlast) objs))
 ; inc objs drawn
 (setq ncnt (+ ncnt 1))
 ; inc X
 (setq pntc (list
   (+ (nth 0 pntc) xinc)
   (nth 1 pntc) (nth 2 pntc)))
 ; check number of objs drawn
 (if (= ncnt midrepeat) (progn
   (setq linc (* linc -1))
   (setq winc (* winc -1))
   (setq hinc (* hinc -1))
```

```
    (setq rang (* rang -1))
  ))
  ; check for odd/even number of
  ; repeats
  ; inc dims
  (if (= (rem numrepeat 2) 1) (progn
    (setq rlen (+ rlen linc))
    (setq rwid (+ rwid winc))
    (setq rhgt (+ rhgt hinc))
    (setq rang (+ rang ainc))
  ))
  (if (and (= (rem numrepeat 2) 0)
    (/= ncnt midrepeat)) (progn
    (setq rlen (+ rlen linc))
    (setq rwid (+ rwid winc))
    (setq rhgt (+ rhgt hinc))
    (setq rang (+ rang ainc))
  ))
 )
 ; union objs
 (command ".UNION" objs "")
 (princ)
)
;----------------------------------
```

The amount of input has increased so that for function PROG03f we are now entering eleven parameters. Answering all of these prompts over and over at the command line can be tedious. With that many parameters, it is also difficult to remember or document them for future review. Another method is to use the script file feature within AutoCAD. This consists of preparing a text file in Microsoft Notepad that contains the answers to the get functions. Order and data type are critical. Very simply, the entries in the script file are sent to the command line when requested.

Here is an example of a script file to execute function PROG03f. This script file was saved as: PROG03f_01.SCR:

```
;----------------------------------
; prog03f_01
(command ".ERASE" "all" "")
(prog03f)
;Pick start center:
0,0,0
;Pick end center:
@33,0,0
;Enter start rectangle length:
8
;Enter end rectangle length:
4
;Enter start rectangle width:
8
;Enter end rectangle width:
4
;Enter start rectangle height:
5
;Enter end rectangle height:
10
;Enter start rotation angle:
0
;Enter end rotation angle:
45
;Enter number of repeats:
13
(command ".VIEW" "swiso")
(command ".ZOOM" "e")
(command ".HIDE")
;----------------------------------
```

Start entering each line as shown here. The first line is the comment with dashes. Do not add any spaces at the end of the lines. A line should not have a space or several spaces. All lines starting with a semicolon are comments; they are ignored when the script file is read. The last line, the one after the last comment of dashes, is blank with no spaces. Hitting the space bar at AutoCAD's command line will execute the previous command entered. The same will happen from a script file.

Note that for function PROG03f the answers to the prompts follow the execution of the function, as in the line containing (prog03f).

Also note that the script file can include normal AutoLISP functions. This script file includes an ERASE command before PROG03f is executed, and a change to an isometric view, zoom, and HIDE command after the function executes.

Once the script file is edited and saved, select it from the Main Menu bar to run it:

```
Tools > Run > Script
```

Select the script file to run and select `Open`. The functions that are to be executed must already be loaded. If an error occurs, return to the script file, make changes, and run it again.

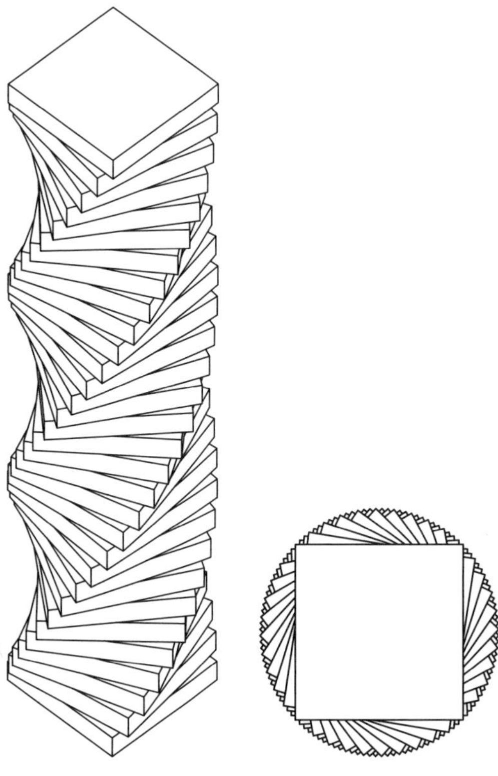

`PROG03g`: vertical repetition of a rotated rectangle, isometric and plan view

Add function `PROG03g` to draw a column of squares. Using `PROG03` and what was covered in `PROG03f`, replace the circle with the `DORECTEN` function. The input parameters consist of center location, height of column, number of squares, and total rotation angle.

This function differs in that repetition is along the z axis. Compute an increment for the height and rotation. The starting rotation is zero. A selection list is created to unite the squares. One major difference is the inclusion of the `ZOOM` command directly following the drawing of the square. Since we are using commands with the last option for selections, the entity selected must be visible in the current window. Inclusion of the `ZOOM` command ensures that this will occur.

Completed function `PROG03g`:

```
;----------------------------------
(defun prog03g ()
 (graphscr)
 ; get start and endpoint
 (prompt
   "\nDraw a column of rotated
   squares")
 (setq pnt1
   (getpoint
   "\nPick start center:"))
 (setq chgt
   (getdist pnt1
   "\nEnter column height:"))
 (setq sdim
   (getdist pnt1
   "\nEnter square size:"))
 (setq numrepeat
   (getint
   "\nEnter number of squares:"))
 (setq trot
   (rtd (getorient
   "\nEnter total rotation:")))
 ; compute inc
 (setq zinc
   (/ chgt (- numrepeat 1)))
 (setq ainc
   (/ trot (- numrepeat 1)))
 ; start
```

```
 (setq pntc pntl)
 (setq tang 0.0)
 ; start selection list
 (setq objs (ssadd))
 (repeat numrepeat
  ; draw rectangle
  (dorectcen pntc sdim sdim)
  (command ".ZOOM" "e")
  ; rotate
  (command ".ROTATE"
    "last" "" pntc tang)
  ; extrude
  (command ".EXTRUDE"
    "last" "" zinc)
  ; add to selection list
  (setq objs
    (ssadd (entlast) objs))
  ; inc Z
  (setq pntc (list
    (nth 0 pntc) (nth 1 pntc)
    (+ (nth 2 pntc) zinc)))
  ; inc angle
  (setq tang (+ tang ainc))
 )
 ; union column
 (command ".UNION" objs "")
 (princ)
)
;----------------------------------
```

Consider other sections that could be stacked in this manner: circular cylinder, elliptical cylinder, rectangles, n-sided polygons, or any shape defined by the methods in Chapter 3. Rotation is just one variable parameter. Size and thickness can also be considered.

Add function `PROG03h`. The square section changes to an ellipse. The appearance of the rotation is created by incremental changes in the x and y radii of the ellipse.

Review how the x and y radii are specified for the ellipse, and how the incremental values are computed.

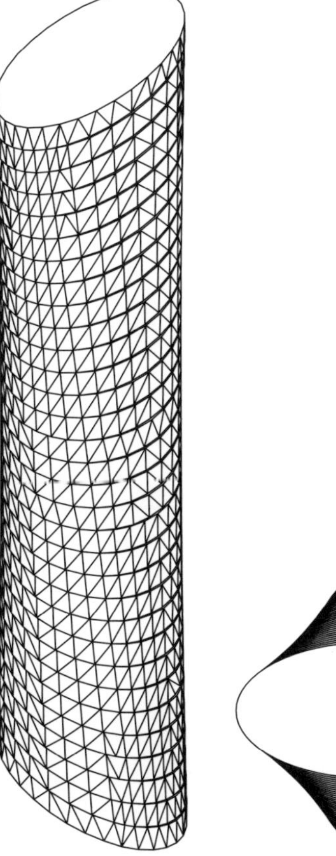

`PROG03h`: vertical repetition of a rotated ellipse, isometric and plan view

Completed function PROG03h:

```
;--------------------------------
(defun prog03h ()
 (graphscr)
 ; get start and endpoint
 (prompt
   "\nDraw a column of ellipses")
 (setq pnt1
   (getpoint
   "\nPick start center:"))
 (setq chgt
   (getdist pnt1
   "\nEnter column height:"))
 (setq sxrad
   (getdist pnt1
   "\nEnter start X radius:"))
 (setq exrad
   (getdist pnt1
   "\nEnter end X radius:"))
 (setq syrad
   (getdist pnt1
   "\nEnter start Y radius:"))
 (setq eyrad
   (getdist pnt1
   "\nEnter end Y radius:"))
 (setq numrepeat
   (getint
   "\nEnter number of ellipses:"))
 ; compute inc
 (setq zinc
   (/ chgt (- numrepeat 1)))
 (setq xinc
   (/ (- exrad sxrad)
   (- numrepeat 1)))
 (setq yinc
   (/ (- eyrad syrad)
   (- numrepeat 1)))
 ; start
 (setq pntc pnt1)
 (setq xrad sxrad)
 (setq yrad syrad)
 ; start selection list
 (setq objs (ssadd))
 (repeat numrepeat
  ; draw ellipse
  (setq xpt (list
    (+ (nth 0 pntc) xrad)
    (nth 1 pntc) (nth 2 pntc)))
  (setq ypt (list
   (nth 0 pntc)
   (+ (nth 1 pntc) yrad)
   (nth 2 pntc)))
  (command ".ELLIPSE"
    "c" pntc xpt ypt)
  (command ".ZOOM" "e")
  ; extrude
  (command ".EXTRUDE"
    "last" "" zinc)
  ; add to selection list
  (setq objs
    (ssadd (entlast) objs))
  ; inc Z
  (setq pntc (list
    (nth 0 pntc) (nth 1 pntc)
    (+ (nth 2 pntc) zinc)))
  ; inc dims
  (setq xrad (+ xrad xinc))
  (setq yrad (+ yrad yinc))
 )
 ; union column
 (command ".UNION" objs "")
 (princ)
)
;--------------------------------
```

4.10 Draw a Rectangular Array of Objects

Add function PROG04 to draw an array of cylinders. Vary the height of each row, x-direction, low to high in the y-direction. Input includes the number of x and y repeats, x and y offset distances, circle radius, and start and end heights. Once placed, UNION all of the cylinders.

PROG04: array of increasing height cylinders, to one edge

This function is an extension of the ones just completed. Instead of one repeat loop, two are required: one to compute the x-coordinate of the cylinder center and another to compute the y-coordinate. For every y-increment, all locations along the x-axis will compute in order. Note where the x, y, and z values start and where the increments occur.

Here is an outline for the nested loops in this function:

```
; start Z coordinate
  .
; start Y coordinate
  .
(repeat ytimes
  ; start X coordinate
    .
  (repeat xtimes
    ; draw cylinder
      .
    ; increment X coordinate
      .
  )
  ; increment Y coordinate
    .
  ; increment Z coordinate
    .
)
```

Completed function PROG04:

```
;----------------------------------
(defun prog04 ()
 (graphscr)
 ; get centerpoint and dimensions
 (prompt "\nDraw array of circles")
 (setq pnt0
   (getpoint
   "\nPick start center:"))
 (setq xtimes
   (getint
   "\nEnter repeat X times:"))
 (setq ytimes
   (getint
   "\nEnter repeat Y times:"))
 (setq xoff
   (getdist pnt0
   "\nEnter X offset:"))
 (setq yoff
   (getdist pnt0
   "\nEnter Y offset:"))
 (setq crad
   (getdist pnt0
   "\nEnter circle radius:"))
 (setq shgt
   (getdist pnt0
   "\nEnter start height:"))
 (setq ehgt
   (getdist pnt0
   "\nEnter end height:"))
 ; compute inc
 (setq zinc
   (/ (- ehgt shgt) (- ytimes 1)))
 ; start
 (setq ypt (nth 1 pnt0))
 (setq zhgt shgt)
 ; start selection list
 (setq objs (ssadd))
 (repeat ytimes
  (setq xpt (nth 0 pnt0))
  (repeat xtimes
   ; array location
   (setq pntc
     (list xpt ypt (nth 2 pnt0)))
   ; draw circle
   (command ".CIRCLE" pntc crad)
   (command ".ZOOM" "e")
```

```
    (command ".EXTRUDE"
      "last" "" zhgt)
    ; add to selection list
    (setq objs
      (ssadd (entlast) objs))
    ; inc X
    (setq xpt (+ xpt xoff))
   )
   ; inc Y
   (setq ypt (+ ypt yoff))
   ; inc height
   (setq zhgt (+ zhgt zinc))
  )
  ; union objs
  (command ".UNION" objs "")
  (princ)
)
;----------------------------------
```

Add function PROG04a to change the method of computing the height of each cylinder. The ones at the center are higher than the ones at the edges. All of the cylinders have the same radius.

PROG04a: array of increasing height cylinders, to center

Using a copy of PROG04, remove the z-increment and compute the height of each cylinder based on its distance to the center of the array. Compute the center of the array, and for each location determine the percent of that distance:

```
; distance to center
(setq cdist (distance pntc cpt))
; compute height
(setq zprct
  (- 1.0 (/ cdist
  (distance pnt0 cpt))))
(setq zhgt
  (+ shgt (* zprct
  (- ehgt shgt))))
; draw circle
(command ".CIRCLE" pntc crad)
```

To reverse this relationship from high-at-edges to low-at-center, use:

```
; compute height
(setq zprct
  (/ cdist
  (distance pnt0 cpt))))
(setq zhgt
  (+ shgt (* zprct
  (- ehgt shgt))))
```

What other relationship to edges or corners can be considered?

Completed function PROG04a:

```
;----------------------------------
(defun prog04a ()
 (graphscr)
 ; get centerpoint and dimensions
 (prompt
   "\nDraw array of circles, height
   to center")
 (setq pnt0
   (getpoint
   "\nPick start center:"))
 (setq xtimes
   (getint
   "\nEnter repeat X times:"))
 (setq ytimes
   (getint
   "\nEnter repeat Y times:"))
```

```
(setq xoff
  (getdist pnt0
  "\nEnter X offset:"))
(setq yoff
  (getdist pnt0
  "\nEnter Y offset:"))
(setq crad
  (getdist pnt0
  "\nEnter circle radius:"))
(setq shgt
  (getdist pnt0
  "\nEnter start height:"))
(setq ehgt
  (getdist pnt0
  "\nEnter end height:"))
; compute center
(setq cpt (list
  (+ (nth 0 pnt0) (/ (* xoff
  (- xtimes 1)) 2))
  (+ (nth 1 pnt0) (/ (* yoff
  (- ytimes 1)) 2))
  (nth 2 pnt0)))
; start
(setq ypt (nth 1 pnt0))
; start selection list
(setq objs (ssadd))
(repeat ytimes
 (setq xpt (nth 0 pnt0))
 (repeat xtimes
  ; array location
  (setq pntc
    (list xpt ypt (nth 2 pnt0)))
  ; distance to center
  (setq cdist (distance pntc cpt))
  ; compute height
  (setq zprct
    (- 1.0 (/ cdist
    (distance pnt0 cpt))))
  (setq zhgt
    (+ shgt (* zprct
    (- ehgt shgt))))
  ; draw circle
  (command ".CIRCLE" pntc crad)
  (command ".ZOOM" "e")
  (command ".EXTRUDE"
    "last" "" zhgt)
  ; add to selection list
  (setq objs
    (ssadd (entlast) objs))
  ; inc X
  (setq xpt (+ xpt xoff))
 )
 ; inc Y
 (setq ypt (+ ypt yoff))
)
; union objs
(command ".UNION" objs "")
(princ)
)
;-----------------------------------
```

Add function PROG04b to place circular rings at each location, and vary their radii according to the horizontal distance from the edge.

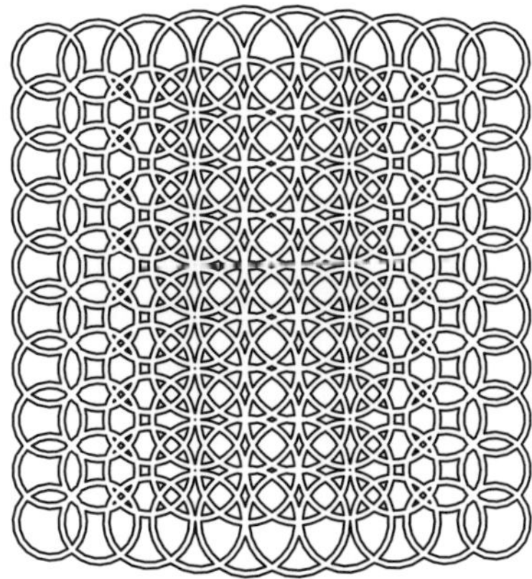

PROG04b: array of increasing radius circular rings

Copy function DOCRING, the circular ring from Chapter 3 in file CH03.LSP, into CH04.LSP.

Completed DOCRING function:

```
;---------------------------------
(defun docring (pnt0 crad cthk
  / obj1 obj2)
 ; requires center, outside radius,
 ; and thickness
 ; outside circle
 (command ".CIRCLE" pnt0 crad)
 ; make region
 (command ".REGION" "last" "" )
 ; place into selection list
 (setq obj1 (ssadd (entlast)))
 ; inside circle
 (command ".CIRCLE" pnt0
   (- crad cthk))
 ; make region
 (command ".REGION" "last" "" )
 ; place into a second selection
 ; list
 (setq obj2 (ssadd (entlast)))
 ; subtract inside from outside
 (command ".SUBTRACT"
   obj1 "" obj2 "")
 (princ)
)
;---------------------------------
```

Using a copy of PROG04a, replace the extruded circle with the circular ring, and change the radius to be determined by distances from the left and right edges.

The distance is computed as:

```
; X distance to center
(setq xdist
  (abs (- (nth 0 pntc)
  (nth 0 cpt))))
; compute height
(setq xprct
  (- 1.0 (/ xdist
  (abs (- (nth 0 pnt0)
  (nth 0 cpt))))))
(setq xrad
  (+ scrad (* xprct
  (- ecrad scrad))))
; draw ring
(docring pntc xrad rthk)
```

Completed function PROG04b:

```
;---------------------------------
(defun prog04b ()
 (graphscr)
 ; get centerpoint and dimensions
 (prompt
   "\nDraw array of rings, radius
   to vertical center")
 (setq pnt0
   (getpoint
   "\nPick start center:"))
 (setq xtimes
   (getint
   "\nEnter repeat X times:"))
 (setq ytimes
   (getint
   "\nEnter repeat Y times:"))
 (setq xoff
   (getdist pnt0
   "\nEnter X offset:"))
 (setq yoff
   (getdist pnt0
   "\nEnter Y offset:"))
 (setq scrad
   (getdist pnt0
   "\nEnter start ring radius:"))
 (setq ecrad
   (getdist pnt0
   "\nEnter end ring radius:"))
 (setq rthk
   (getdist pnt0
   "\nEnter ring thickness:"))
 ; compute center
 (setq cpt (list
   (+ (nth 0 pnt0) (/ (* xoff
   (- xtimes 1)) 2))
   (+ (nth 1 pnt0) (/ (* yoff
   (- ytimes 1)) 2))
   (nth 2 pnt0)))
 ; start
 (setq ypt (nth 1 pnt0))
 ; start selection list
 (setq objs (ssadd))
 (repeat ytimes
  (setq xpt (nth 0 pnt0))
  (repeat xtimes
   ; array location
```

```
    (setq pntc
      (list xpt ypt (nth 2 pnt0)))
    ; X distance to center
    (setq xdist
      (abs (- (nth 0 pntc)
      (nth 0 cpt))))
    ; compute height
    (setq xprct
      (- 1.0 (/ xdist
      (abs (- (nth 0 pnt0)
      (nth 0 cpt))))))
    (setq xrad
      (+ scrad (* xprct
      (- ecrad scrad))))
    ; draw ring
    (docring pntc xrad rthk)
    (command ".ZOOM" "e")
    ; add to selection list
    (setq objs
      (ssadd (entlast) objs))
    ; inc X
    (setq xpt (+ xpt xoff))
  )
  ; inc Y
  (setq ypt (+ ypt yoff))
 )
 ; union objs
 (command ".UNION" objs "")
 (princ)
)
;-----------------------------------
```

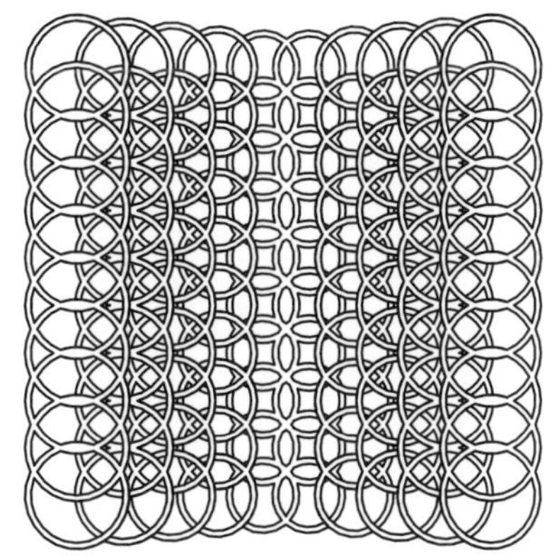

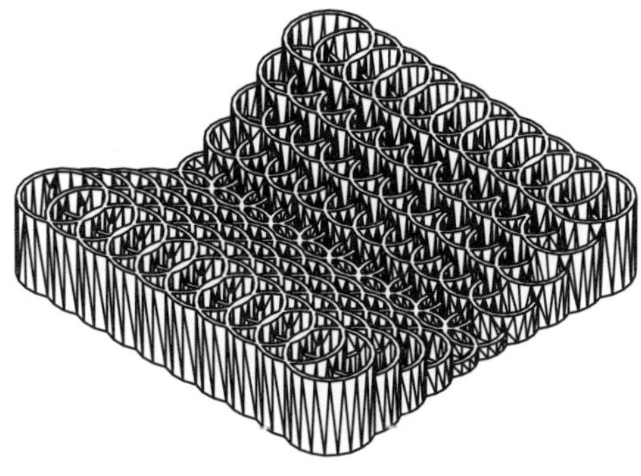

PROG04c: array of decreasing radius and height circular rings

Add function PROG04c. Using PROG04b, add a computation to vary the height in the same manner as the radii of the rings, except reverse the change from high-at-the-edges and low-at-the-center. Review PROG04a for the height computations.

Completed function PROG04c:

```
;-----------------------------------
(defun prog04c ()
 (graphscr)
 ; get centerpoint and dimensions
 (prompt
   "\nDraw array of rings, radius
   to vertical center")
 (setq pnt0
   (getpoint
   "\nPick start center:"))
 (setq xtimes
   (getint
   "\nEnter repeat X times:"))
 (setq ytimes
```

```
  (getint
   "\nEnter repeat Y times:"))
(setq xoff
  (getdist pnt0
  "\nEnter X offset:"))
(setq yoff
  (getdist pnt0
  "\nEnter Y offset:"))
(setq scrad
  (getdist pnt0
  "\nEnter start ring radius:"))
(setq ecrad
  (getdist pnt0
  "\nEnter end ring radius:"))
(setq rthk
  (getdist pnt0
  "\nEnter ring thickness:"))
(setq shgt
  (getdist pnt0
  "\nEnter start height:"))
(setq ehgt
  (getdist pnt0
  "\nEnter end height:"))
; compute center
(setq cpt (list
  (+ (nth 0 pnt0) (/ (* xoff
  (- xtimes 1)) 2))
  (+ (nth 1 pnt0) (/ (* yoff
  (- ytimes 1)) 2))
  (nth 2 pnt0)))
; start
(setq ypt (nth 1 pnt0))
; start selection list
(setq objs (ssadd))
(repeat ytimes
 (setq xpt (nth 0 pnt0))
 (repeat xtimes
  ; array location
  (setq pntc
    (list xpt ypt (nth 2 pnt0)))
  ; X distance to center
  (setq xdist
    (abs (- (nth 0 pntc)
    (nth 0 cpt))))
  ; compute height
  (setq xprct
    (/ xdist (abs (- (nth 0 pnt0)
    (nth 0 cpt)))))
  (setq xrad
    (+ scrad (* xprct
    (- ecrad scrad))))
  (setq zhgt
    (+ shgt (* xprct
    (- ehgt shgt))))
  ; draw ring
  (docring pntc xrad rthk)
  (command ".ZOOM" "e")
  (command ".EXTRUDE"
    "last" "" zhgt)
  ; add to selection list
  (setq objs
    (ssadd (entlast) objs))
  ; inc X
  (setq xpt (+ xpt xoff))
 )
 ; inc Y
 (setq ypt (+ ypt yoff))
)
; union objs
(command ".UNION" objs "")
(princ)
)
;----------------------------------
```

Add function PROG04d. Using PROG02a, create a mesh from the computed points previously used for the extruded circles.

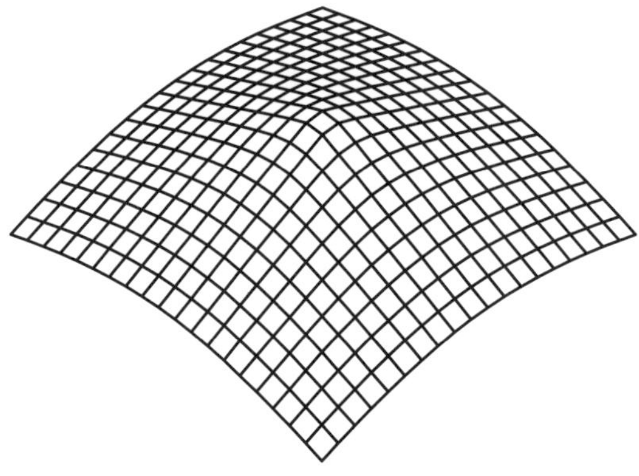

PROG04d: array of increasing heights as a mesh

The extruded circle commands are removed, and the location point with height as the z-coordinate becomes the mesh point. At the start of the 3DMESH command, specify the number of points along the x- and y-axis:

```
; start mesh
(command ".3DMESH" ytimes xtimes)
```

For each point computed, add it to the mesh using:

```
; add point to mesh
(command pntc)
```

All of the points along the x-axis are computed for each y-increment. The mesh command terminates when it receives all of the points it expects.

Completed function PROG04d:

```
;---------------------------------
(defun prog04d ()
 (graphscr)
 ; get centerpoint and dimensions
 (prompt
   "\nDraw mesh, height to center")
 (setq pnt0
   (getpoint
   "\nPick start center:"))
 (setq xtimes
   (getint
   "\nEnter repeat X times:"))
 (setq ytimes
   (getint
   "\nEnter repeat Y times:"))
 (setq xoff
   (getdist pnt0
   "\nEnter X offset:"))
 (setq yoff
   (getdist pnt0
   "\nEnter Y offset:"))
 (setq shgt
   (getdist pnt0
   "\nEnter start height:"))
 (setq ehgt
   (getdist pnt0
   "\nEnter end height:"))
 ; compute center
 (setq cpt (list
   (+ (nth 0 pnt0) (/ (* xoff
   (- xtimes 1)) 2))
   (+ (nth 1 pnt0) (/ (* yoff
   (- ytimes 1)) 2))
   (nth 2 pnt0)))
 ; start
 (setq ypt (nth 1 pnt0))
 ; start mesh
 (command ".3DMESH" ytimes xtimes)
 (repeat ytimes
  (setq xpt (nth 0 pnt0))
  (repeat xtimes
   ; array location
   (setq pntc
     (list xpt ypt (nth 2 pnt0)))
   ; distance to center
   (setq cdist (distance pntc cpt))
   ; compute height
   (setq zprct
     (- 1.0 (/ cdist
     (distance pnt0 cpt))))
   (setq zhgt
     (+ shgt (* zprct
     (- ehgt shgt))))
   ; add Z value
   (setq pntc (list
     (nth 0 pntc) (nth 1 pntc)
     zhgt))
   ; add point to mesh
   (command pntc)
   ; inc X
   (setq xpt (+ xpt xoff))
  )
  ; inc Y
  (setq ypt (+ ypt yoff))
 )
 (command ".ZOOM" "e")
 (princ)
)
;---------------------------------
```

Add function PROG04e. Using PROG04d, change the method of computing the height of mesh points from a simple distance relationship to a mathematical function. Replace the start and end heights with a single curve height.

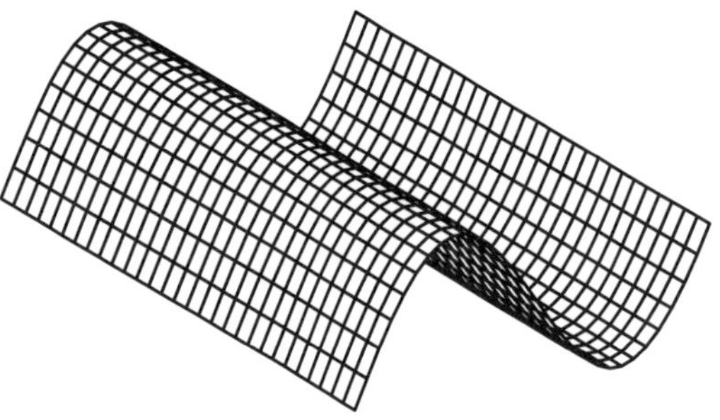

PROG04e: array of mathematically computed heights as a mesh

The height of the mesh is determined by a number of different mathematical functions. For this example, compute the height as a factor of the sine function along the x-direction of the mesh. The smoothness of the mesh depends on the number of points computed in each direction.

The sine of the angle is used as a factor for the height:

```
; curve value
(setq cval (sin (dtr xang)))
; compute height
(setq zpt (* cval chgt))
; add point to mesh
(setq pntc (list xpt ypt zpt))
(command pntc)
```

The angle for the sine function ranges from 0 to 360 degrees. The angle increment is computed based on the number of points in the x-direction:

```
; ang inc
(setq xanginc (/ 360.0 xtimes))
```

Note where the x, y, and angle values start, and where the increments occur. Here is an outline for the nested loops in this function:

```
; start Y coordinate
  .
(repeat ytimes
  ; start X coordinate
    .
  ; start X angle
    .
  (repeat xtimes
    ; compute point
      .
    ; increment X coordinate
      .
    ; increment X angle
      .
  )
  ;increment Y coordinate
   .
)
```

Completed function PROG04e:

```
;-----------------------------------
(defun prog04e ()
 (graphscr)
 ; get centerpoint and dimensions
 (prompt "\nDraw mesh, X function")
 (setq pnt0
   (getpoint
   "\nPick start center:"))
 (setq xtimes
   (getint
   "\nEnter repeat X times:"))
 (setq ytimes
   (getint
   "\nEnter repeat Y times:"))
 (setq xoff
   (getdist pnt0
   "\nEnter X offset:"))
 (setq yoff
   (getdist pnt0
   "\nEnter Y offset:"))
 (setq chgt
   (getdist pnt0
```

```
    "\nEnter curve height:"))
  ; ang inc
  (setq xanginc (/ 360.0 xtimes))
  ; start
  (setq ypt (nth 1 pnt0))
  ; start mesh
  (command ".3DMESH" ytimes xtimes)
  (repeat ytimes
   (setq xpt (nth 0 pnt0))
   (setq xang 0.0)
   (repeat xtimes
    ; curve value
    (setq cval (sin (dtr xang)))
    ; compute height
    (setq zpt (* cval chgt))
    ; add point to mesh
    (setq pntc (list xpt ypt zpt))
    (command pntc)
    ; inc X
    (setq xpt (+ xpt xoff))
    ; inc ang
    (setq xang (+ xang xanginc))
   )
   ; inc Y
   (setq ypt (+ ypt yoff))
  )
  (command ".ZOOM" "e")
  (princ)
)
;--------------------------------
```

Add function PROG04f to allow a curve function in both the x and y directions of the mesh.

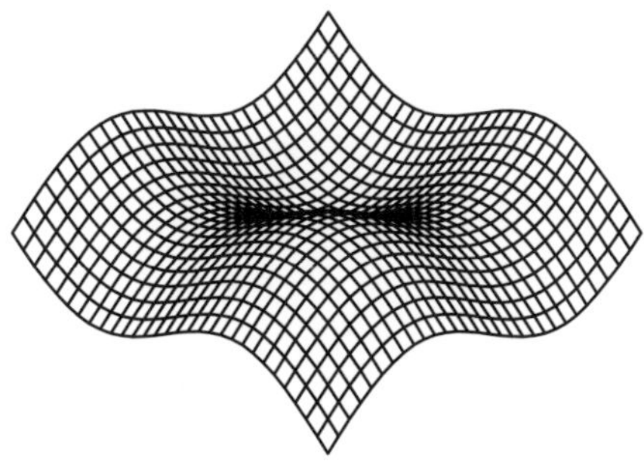

PROG04f: mesh heights based on sin(x)+sin(y)

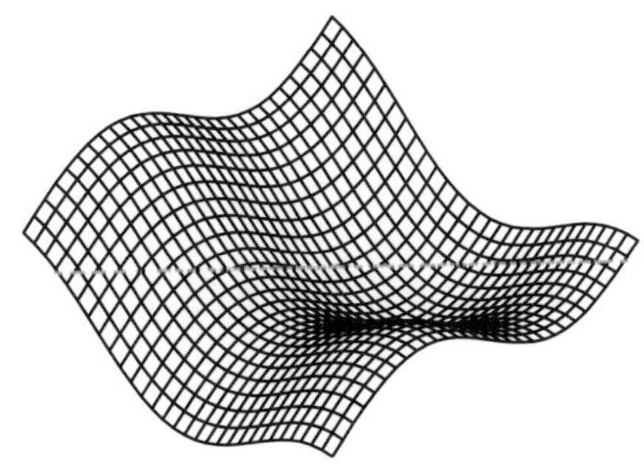

PROG04f: mesh heights based on sin(x)+cos(y)

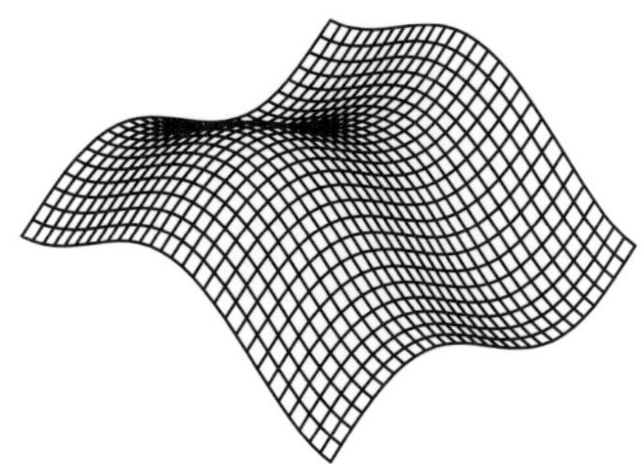

PROG04f: mesh heights based on sin(x)-cos(y)

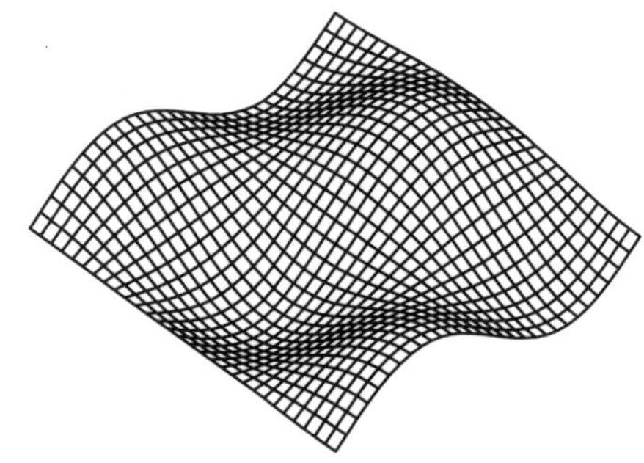

PROG04f: mesh heights based on sin(x)cos(y)

Modify PROG04e to compute an angle in the y-direction. The curve is computed using angles in both the x- and y-direction:

```
; curve value
(setq cval
  (+ (sin (dtr xang))
  (sin (dtr yang))))
```

Note where the x, y, and angle values start, and where the increments occur. Here is an outline for the nested loops in this function:

```
; start Y coordinate
  .
; start Y angle
  .
(repeat ytimes
  ; start X coordinate
    .
  ; start X angle
    .
  (repeat xtimes
    ; compute point
      .
    ; increment X coordinate
      .
    ; increment X angle
      .
  )
  ; increment Y coordinate
    .
  ; increment Y angle
    .
)
```

There are many curve functions worth investigating; here are a few simple ones to explore:

```
sin(x)+sin(y)
sin(x)+cos(y)
sin(x)-cos(y)
sin(x)*cos(y)
```

Completed function PROG04f:

```
;-----------------------------------
(defun prog04f ()
 (graphscr)
 ; get centerpoint and dimensions
 (prompt
   "\nDraw mesh, X and Y function")
 (setq pnt0
   (getpoint
   "\nPick start center:"))
 (setq xtimes
   (getint
   "\nEnter repeat X times:"))
 (setq ytimes
   (getint
   "\nEnter repeat Y times:"))
 (setq xoff
   (getdist pnt0
   "\nEnter X offset:"))
 (setq yoff
   (getdist pnt0
   "\nEnter Y offset:"))
 (setq chgt
   (getdist pnt0
   "\nEnter curve height:"))
 ; ang inc
 (setq xanginc (/ 360.0 xtimes))
 (setq yanginc (/ 360.0 ytimes))
 ; start
 (setq ypt (nth 1 pnt0))
 (setq yang 0.0)
```

```
 ; start mesh
 (command ".3DMESH" ytimes xtimes)
 (repeat ytimes
  (setq xpt (nth 0 pnt0))
  (setq xang 0.0)
  (repeat xtimes
   ; curve value
   (setq cval
     (* (sin (dtr xang))
     (cos (dtr yang))))
   ; compute height
   (setq zpt (* cval chgt))
   ; add point to mesh
   (setq pntc (list xpt ypt zpt))
   (command pntc)
   ; inc X
   (setq xpt (+ xpt xoff))
   ; inc ang
   (setq xang (+ xang xanginc))
  )
  ; inc Y
  (setq ypt (+ ypt yoff))
  ; inc ang
  (setq yang (+ yang yanginc))
 )
 (command ".ZOOM" "e")
 (princ)
)
;----------------------------------
```

Add function PROG04g to execute any mathematical expression as part of the input of the function.

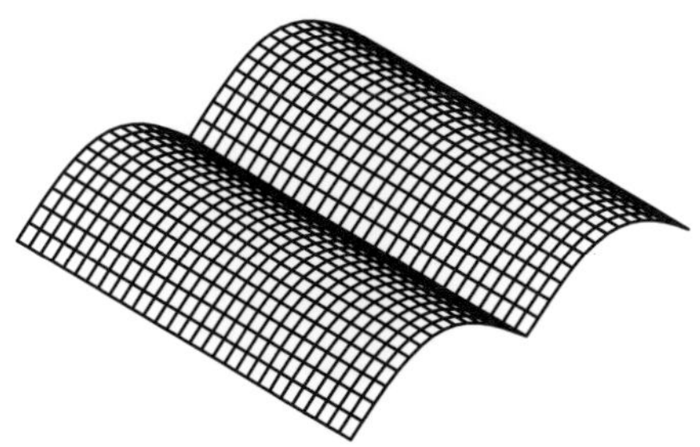

PROG04g: mesh heights based on (abs (sin (dtr xang)))

A script file example for PROG04g:

```
;----------------------------------
; prog04g_01
(command ".ERASE" "all" "")
(prog04g)
;Pick start center:
0,0,0
;Enter repeat X times:
30
;Enter repeat Y times:
30
;Enter X offset:
1
;Enter Y offset:
1
;Enter curve height:
4
;Enter curve expression:
(abs (sin (dtr xang)))
(command ".VIEW" "swiso")
(command ".ZOOM" "e")
(command ".HIDE")
;----------------------------------
```

Modify PROG04f to accept an expression based on variables in the function, input as:

```
(setq cexp
   (getstring
   "\nEnter curve expression:"))
```

The processing of the expression occurs at:

```
; curve value
(setq cval (eval (read cexp)))
```

The string variable cexp is first converted to a list by the read function and then evaluated by the eval function. This combination of functions allows you to insert AutoLISP code at the time of execution. The expression has to have a valid syntax and use variables and functions that are already available when PROG04g executes. These include functions dtr, sin, cos, and abs; mathematical operations of +, -, /, and *; variables xang and yang; and any valid numeric constant.

In the script file, the expression is entered on a single line. Here are a few expressions to try.

Examples of one-directional curves, with the sine function, absolute value, and negative absolute value:

```
(sin (* 1.00 (dtr xang)))
(abs (sin (* 1.00 (dtr xang))))
(* (abs (* 1.00 (sin (dtr xang)))) -1)

(* 1.00 (sin (dtr xang)))
(* 1.00 (abs (sin (dtr xang))))
(* 1.00 (* (abs (sin (dtr xang))) -1))
```

Now compute each of the above by replacing:

`sin` with `cos`
`xang` with `yang`
`1.0` with any other constant

```
(+ (sin (* 1.00 (dtr xang)))
```
For example: `(sin (* 2.00 (dtr xang))))`

```
(+ (* 1.00 (sin (dtr xang)))
```
For example: `(* 2.00 (sin (dtr xang))))`

Now replace:

`1.0` and `2.0` with other constants
`+` with `-` or `*`
the absolute value with the negative of the absolute value

For two-directional curves, replace any combination of one-directional functions (listed above).

For example:

```
(+ (sin (* 1.00 (dtr xang)))
     (sin (* 1.00 (dtr yang))))

(+ (sin (* 1.00 (dtr xang)))
     (cos (* 1.00 (dtr yang))))
```

Now replace:

`1.0` with any other constant
`+` with `-` or `*`
the absolute value with the negative of the absolute value

If division is used in any of the expressions, division by zero will terminate the function and display an error.

Completed function `PROG04g`:

```
;-----------------------------------
(defun prog04g ()
 (graphscr)
 ; get centerpoint and dimensions
 (prompt
   "\nDraw mesh, entered expression
   for height")
 (setq pnt0
   (getpoint
   "\nPick start center:"))
 (setq xtimes
   (getint
   "\nEnter repeat X times:"))
 (setq ytimes
   (getint
   "\nEnter repeat Y times:"))
 (setq xoff
   (getdist pnt0
   "\nEnter X offset:"))
 (setq yoff
   (getdist pnt0
   "\nEnter Y offset:"))
 (setq chgt
   (getdist pnt0
   "\nEnter curve height:"))
 (setq cexp
   (getstring
   "\nEnter curve expression:"))
 ; ang inc
 (setq xanginc (/ 360.0 xtimes))
 (setq yanginc (/ 360.0 ytimes))
 ; start
 (setq ypt (nth 1 pnt0))
 (setq yang 0.0)
```

```
; start mesh
(command ".3DMESH" ytimes xtimes)
(repeat ytimes
 (setq xpt (nth 0 pnt0))
 (setq xang 0.0)
 (repeat xtimes
  ; curve value
  (setq cval (eval (read cexp)))
  ; compute height
  (setq zpt (* cval chgt))
  ; add point to mesh
  (setq pntc (list xpt ypt zpt))
  (command pntc)
  ; inc X
  (setq xpt (+ xpt xoff))
  ; inc ang
  (setq xang (+ xang xanginc))
 )
 ; inc Y
 (setq ypt (+ ypt yoff))
 ; inc ang
 (setq yang (+ yang yanginc))
)
(command ".ZOOM" "e")
(princ)
)
;---------------------------------
```

Add PROG04h. Using the height for the mesh points computed in PROG04g, place a square at each location.

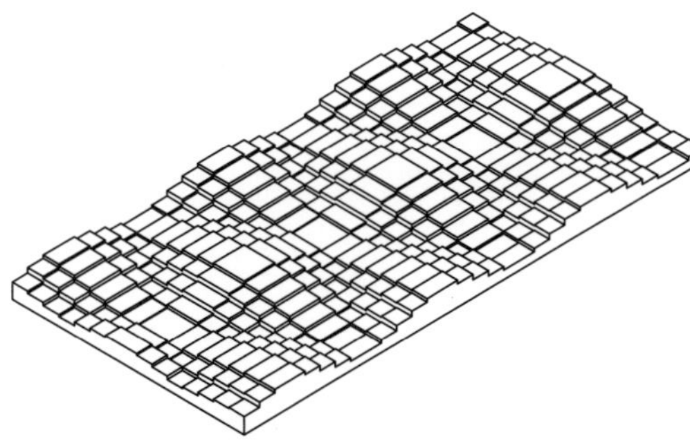

PROG04h: array of rectangles at heights based on a mathematical curve

This function is a combination of PROG04g and PROG04, but replaces the cylinder with a rectangular solid. Input includes: rectangle dimensions, x and y sides, and start and end heights.

The height is computed based on the entered expression:

```
; curve value
(setq cval (eval (read cexp)))
; compute height
(setq zhgt
  (+ shgt (* cval
  (- ehgt shgt))))
```

In this example, the expression is:

```
(abs (+ (sin (* 3.00 (dtr xang)))
  (cos (dtr yang))))
```

Example of a script file for PROG04h:

```
;---------------------------------
; prog04h_01
(command ".ERASE" "all" "")
(prog04h)
;Pick start center:
0,0,0
;Enter repeat X times:
30
;Enter repeat Y times:
15
;Enter X offset:
1.0
;Enter Y offset:
1.0
;Enter X rectangle side:
1.0
;Enter Y rectangle side:
1.0
;Enter start rectangle height:
0.5
;Enter end rectangle height:
1
```

```
;Enter curve expression:
(abs (+ (sin (* 3.00 (dtr xang)))
  (cos (dtr yang))))
(command ".VIEW" "swiso")
(command ".ZOOM" "e")
(command ".HIDE")
;---------------------------------
```

Completed function PROG04h:

```
;---------------------------------
(defun prog04h ()
 (graphscr)
 ; get centerpoint and dimensions
 (prompt
   "\nDraw rectangles, entered
   expression for height")
 (setq pnt0
   (getpoint
   "\nPick start center:"))
 (setq xtimes
   (getint
   "\nEnter repeat X times:"))
 (setq ytimes
   (getint
   "\nEnter repeat Y times:"))
 (setq xoff
   (getdist pnt0
   "\nEnter X offset:"))
 (setq yoff
   (getdist pnt0
   "\nEnter Y offset:"))
 (setq xdim
   (getdist pnt0
   "\nEnter X rect side:"))
 (setq ydim
   (getdist pnt0
   "\nEnter Y rect side:"))
 (setq shgt
   (getdist pnt0
   "\nEnter start rect height:"))
 (setq ehgt
   (getdist pnt0
   "\nEnter end rect height:"))
 (setq cexp
   (getstring
   "\nEnter curve expression:"))
 ; ang inc
 (setq xanginc (/ 360.0 xtimes))
 (setq yanginc (/ 360.0 ytimes))
 ; start
 (setq ypt (nth 1 pnt0))
 (setq yang 0.0)
 ; start selection list
 (setq objs (ssadd))
 (repeat ytimes
  (setq xpt (nth 0 pnt0))
  (setq xang 0.0)
  (repeat xtimes
   ; curve value
   (setq cval (eval (read cexp)))
   ; compute height
   (setq zhgt
     (+ shgt (* cval
     (- ehgt shgt))))
   ; location
   (setq pntc
     (list xpt ypt (nth 2 pnt0)))
   ; draw rectangle
   (dorectcen pntc xdim ydim)
   (command ".ZOOM" "e")
   ; extrude
   (command ".EXTRUDE"
     "last" "" zhgt)
   ; add to selection list
   (setq objs
     (ssadd (entlast) objs))
   ; inc X
   (setq xpt (+ xpt xoff))
   ; inc ang
   (setq xang (+ xang xanginc))
  )
  ; inc Y
  (setq ypt (+ ypt yoff))
  ; inc ang
  (setq yang (+ yang yanginc))
 )
 ; union objs
 (command ".UNION" objs "")
 (princ)
)
;---------------------------------
```

4.11 Draw a Circular Array of Objects

In the preceding exercises, repeating patterns were computed for a spiral, along a simple linear path and in a rectangular array. This section develops patterns along a circular path.

Add function PROG05 to draw a series of rotated rectangles.

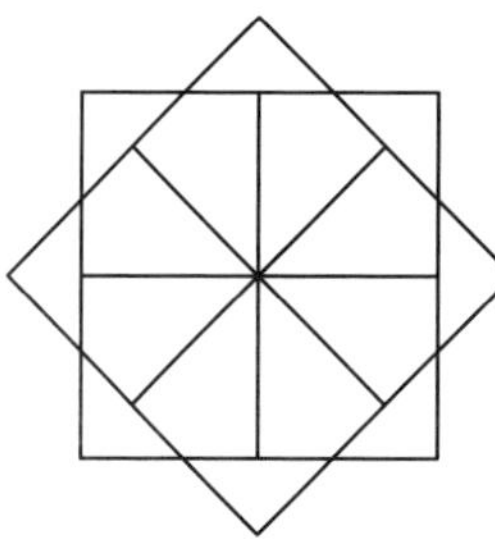

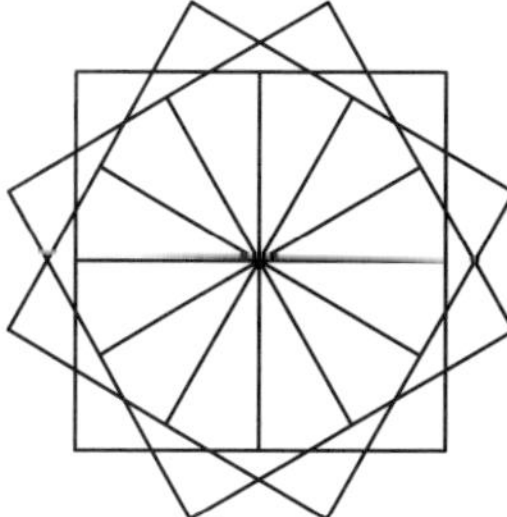

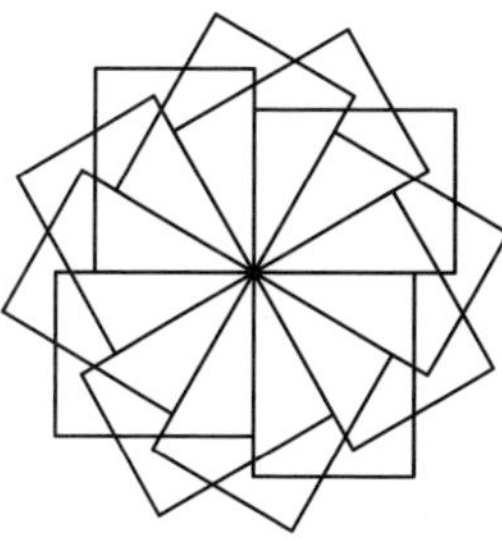

PROG05: repeated and rotated square 8 and 12 times, rectangle 12 times

The rectangle is drawn using AutoCAD's RECTANGLE command. The lower-left corner is located at the center of the rotation, and the upper-right corner is computed based on the x- and y-side dimensions. The rectangle is then rotated based on the number of repeats, passing through 360 degrees and starting at 0 degrees.

Completed function PROG05:

```
;-----------------------------------
(defun prog05 ()
 (graphscr)
 ; get centerpoint and dimensions
 (prompt
   “\nDraw rotated rectangles”)
 (setq pnt0
   (getpoint “\nPick center:”))
 (setq xside
   (getdist pnt0 “\nEnter X side:”))
 (setq yside
   (getdist pnt0 “\nEnter Y side:”))
 (setq ntimes
   (getint
   “\nEnter number repeats:”))
 ; compute inc
 (setq anginc (/ 360.0 ntimes))
 (setq ang 0)
 (repeat ntimes
  ; draw rectangle by corner points
  (setq pnt1 (list
    (+ (nth 0 pnt0) xside)
    (+ (nth 1 pnt0) yside)
    (nth 2 pnt0)))
  ; draw rectangle
  (command “.RECTANGLE” pnt0 pnt1)
  (command “.ZOOM” “e”)
  (command “.ROTATE”
    “last” “” pnt0 ang)
  ; inc ang
  (setq ang (+ ang anginc))
 )
 (princ)
)
;-----------------------------------
```

Execute function PROG05 a few times and explore some of the patterns formed by the rotation. Consider how the patterns would differ if the origin, the center of rotation, is at the center of the rectangle or the midpoint of the bottom edge. Also consider if the point of rotation is not the origin of the rectangle, but somewhere separate from the rectangle itself.

Add function PROG05a by converting PROG05 to a callable function:

```
;----------------------------------
(defun prog05a (pnt0 xside yside
  ntimes / anginc ang pnt1)
 ; draw rotated rectangles, origin
 ; at bottom-left corner
 ; center, X side, Y side,
 ; number of times
 ; compute inc
 (setq anginc (/ 360.0  ntimes))
 (setq ang 0)
 (repeat ntimes
  ; draw rectangle by corner points
  (setq pnt1 (list
    (+ (nth 0 pnt0) xside)
    (+ (nth 1 pnt0) yside)
    (nth 2 pnt0)))
  ; draw rectangle
  (command ".RECTANGLE" pnt0 pnt1)
  (command ".ZOOM" "e")
  (command ".ROTATE"
    "last" "" pnt0 ang)
  ; inc ang
  (setq ang (+ ang anginc))
 )
 (princ)
)
;----------------------------------
```

Previously we used script files to execute the functions. Another method is to create entire drawings as functions.

Create function DRWG05_01 using PROG05a to make a complete drawing by overlaying a set of rotated rectangles.

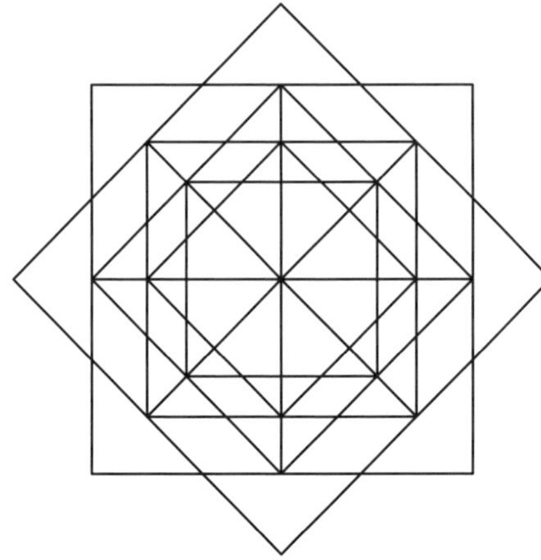

DRWG05_01: overlay three sets of rotated squares

Function DRWG05_01 overlays three sets of rotated squares of differing sizes. The sizes were selected so that they nest inside each other.

Try some of your own combinations.

Completed function DRWG05_01:

```
;----------------------------------
(defun drwg05_01 ()
 (command ".ERASE" "all" "")
 (setq pntc (list 0.0 0.0 0.0))
 (prog05a pntc 10.0 10.0 8)
 (prog05a pntc 7.07 7.07 8)
 (prog05a pntc 5.0 5.0 8)
 (command ".ZOOM" "e")
 (princ)
)
;----------------------------------
```

Add a callable function PROG05b to draw a series of rotated polygons.

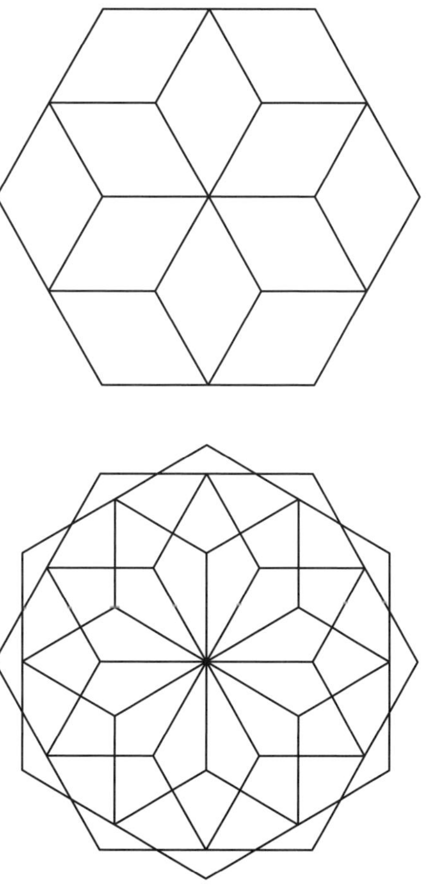

PROG05b: six-sided polygon, rotated 6 and 12 times

Using a copy of PROG05a, replace the RECTANGLE command with the POLYGON command. The polygon is specified by its lower-left corner and edge length. Instead of the upper-right corner being computed, the polygon requires the endpoint for the bottom edge.

Completed function PROG05b:

```
;-----------------------------------
(defun prog05b (pnt0 nsides xside
  ntimes / anginc ang pnt1)
 ; draw rotated polygons, origin at
 ; bottom-left edge
 ; compute inc
 (setq anginc (/ 360.0  ntimes))
 (setq ang 0)
 (repeat ntimes
  ; endpoint of edge
  (setq pnt1 (list
    (+ (nth 0 pnt0) xside)
    (nth 1 pnt0) (nth 2 pnt0)))
  ; draw polygon
  (command ".POLYGON"
    nsides "edge" pnt0 pnt1)
  (command ".ZOOM" "e")
  (command ".ROTATE"
    "last" "" pnt0 ang)
  ; inc ang
  (setq ang (+ ang anginc))
 )
 (princ)
)
;-----------------------------------
```

At the command line, execute function PROG05b:

```
(prog05b (list 0 0 0) 6 10 6)
```

Add a series of DRWG05 functions to draw a set of overlaid polygons.

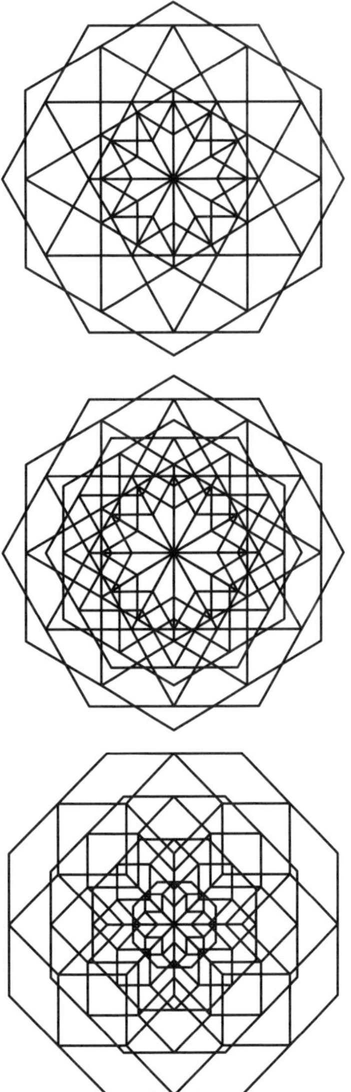

DRWG05_02, 03, and 04: examples of overlaid rotated polygons

Completed functions for DRWG05_02, 03, and 04 :

```
;-----------------------------------
(defun drwg05_02 ()
 (command ".ERASE" "all" "")
 (setq pntc (list 0.0 0.0 0.0))
 (prog05b pntc 6 10 12)
 (prog05b pntc 6 5 12)
 (command ".ZOOM" "e")
 (princ)
)
;-----------------------------------
(defun drwg05_03 ()
 (command ".ERASE" "all" "")
 (setq pntc (list 0.0 0.0 0.0))
 (prog05b pntc 6 10 12)
 (prog05b pntc 6 7.5 12)
 (prog05b pntc 6 5 12)
 (command ".ZOOM" "e")
 (princ)
)
;-----------------------------------
(defun drwg05_04 ()
 (command ".ERASE" "all" "")
 (setq pntc (list 0.0 0.0 0.0))
 (prog05b pntc 8 8 8)
 (prog05b pntc 8 6 8)
 (prog05b pntc 8 4 8)
 (prog05b pntc 8 2 8)
 (command ".ZOOM" "e")
 (princ)
)
;-----------------------------------
```

Additional exercises:

Explore the great variety of patterns that are possible by simply overlaying one or more polygons. Consider the dimensional relationship of one-half, one-fourth, or some other regular proportion of the radius of one polygon to another. Observe the relationship of the number of sides of each polygon within the repeating patterns of polygons. These are all developed by trial and error.

* Trying different variations or changing the parameters allows interesting patterns to emerge. Many of the results are unexpected.

* The patterns in the function PROG05 are single line drawings. Consider a version of function PROG05 where a rotated polygon is created from subtracted regions; when they are all placed, a simple union will create the double edges needed for laser cutting or extruding a three-dimensional object.

* The approach is to create a set of nested polygons using the OFFSET command, converting them to regions, and subtracting the inside polygon from the outside polygon. Since we are doing a simple rotation, the ARRAY polar command is used.

* Place each repetition on its own layer so that the OFFSET command selects the most current polygon ring. The OFFSET command requires an object to be selected by a point, not a selection list. Having each set of repetitions on a separate layer ensures that the correct polygon is always selected. The added parameter for this function is the thickness of the polygon ring.

* In the DRWG06 functions, we used a LAYER command to make sure the entire drawing was erased. Place each repetition on its own layer, and turn on all layers before executing the UNION command to create the required intersecting edges. When the final drawing is complete, scale the polygon pattern to the actual size for laser-cutting. Check the thickness of the individual members. If the members are too thin or too thick, modify the input thickness and regenerate the pattern.

Completed function PROG06a:

```
;----------------------------------
(defun prog06a (pnt0 psides pxside
   ptimes pthk player
   / pnt1 pnt2 pnt3)
 ; polygon start point of bottom
 ; edge
 ; set current layer
 (command ".LAYER" "MAKE" player "")
 ; endpoint of edge
 (setq pnt1 pnt0)
 (setq pnt2 (list
   (+ (nth 0 pnt1) pxside)
   (nth 1 pnt1) (nth 2 pnt1)))
 ; draw polygon
 (command ".POLYGON"
   psides "edge" pnt1 pnt2)
 (command ".ZOOM" "e")
 ; point inside polygon
 (setq pnt3 (polar
   pnt1 (dtr (/ 360.0 psides))
   (/ pxside 2.0)))
 ;offset thickness
 (command ".OFFSET"
   pthk pnt1 pnt3 "")
 ; convert to regions
 (command ".REGION" "all" "")
 ; subtract inside from outside
 (command ".SUBTRACT"
   "all" "r" "last" "" "last" "")
 ; rotate it
 (command ".ARRAY"
   "last" "" "P" pnt0 ptimes "360" "Y")
 ; hide layer
 (command ".LAYER" "SET" "0"
   "LOCK" player "FREEZE" player "")
 (princ)
)
;----------------------------------
```

Note the series of LAYER commands. The last LAYER command, which sets the current one to Layer 0, sets all of the layers (including the one just created) to locked and frozen.

For the offset, a point inside the polygon is required. Note how that point is computed.

In this example, the SUBTRACT command is executed without the use of selection lists, as shown previously. Review use of the last selection options.

The best method to understand or test new variations of AutoCAD commands and the options they include, as used in these functions, is to execute them on any polyline at the command line and to record the sequence of options needed for a particular operation.

To execute function PROG06a, add DRWG06_01. This drawing function unlocks, thaws, turns on all layers, and erases all objects from the drawing. A series of polygon repetitions are overlaid on separate layers; then the layers are released to union.

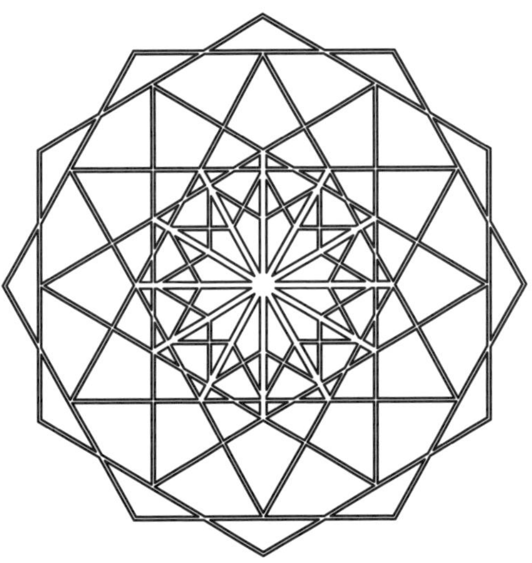

DRWG06_01: overlaid rotated polygons with edge thickness

Completed function DRWG06_01:

```
;-----------------------------------
(defun drwg06_01 ()
 (command ".LAYER" "UNLOCK" "*"
   "THAW" "*" "ON" "*" "")
 (command ".ERASE" "all" "")
 (setq pntc (list 0.0 0.0 0.0))
 (prog06a pntc 6 10 12 0.25
   "LAYER01")
 (prog06a pntc 6 5 12 0.25
   "LAYER02")
 (command ".LAYER" "UNLOCK" "*"
   "THAW" "*" "ON" "*" "")
 (command ".ZOOM" "e")
 (command ".UNION" "all" "")
 (princ)
)
;-----------------------------------
```

Here are three more examples: DRWG06_02, DRWG06_03, and DRWG06_04.

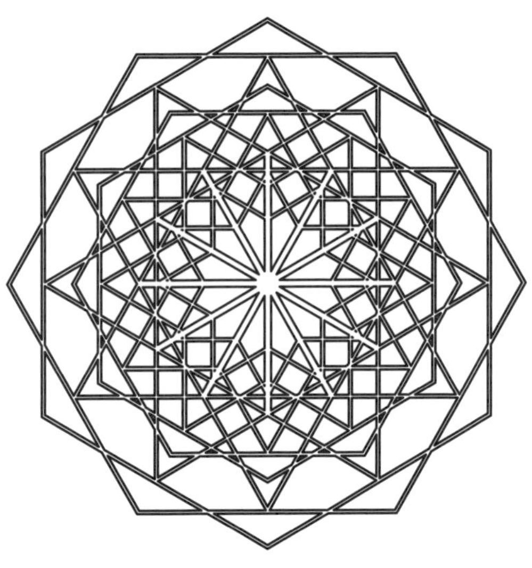

DRWG06_02: overlaid rotated polygons with edge thickness

Completed function DRWG06_02:

```
;-----------------------------------
(defun drwg06_02 ()
 (command ".LAYER" "UNLOCK" "*"
   "THAW" "*" "ON" "*" "")
 (command ".ERASE" "all" "")
 (setq pntc (list 0.0 0.0 0.0))
 (prog06a pntc 6 10 12 0.25
   "LAYER01")
 (prog06a pntc 6 7.5 12 0.25
   "LAYER02")
 (prog06a pntc 6 5 12 0.25
   "LAYER03")
 (command ".LAYER" "UNLOCK" "*"
   "THAW" "*" "ON" "*" "")
 (command ".ZOOM" "e")
 (command ".UNION" "all" "")
 (princ)
)
;-----------------------------------
```

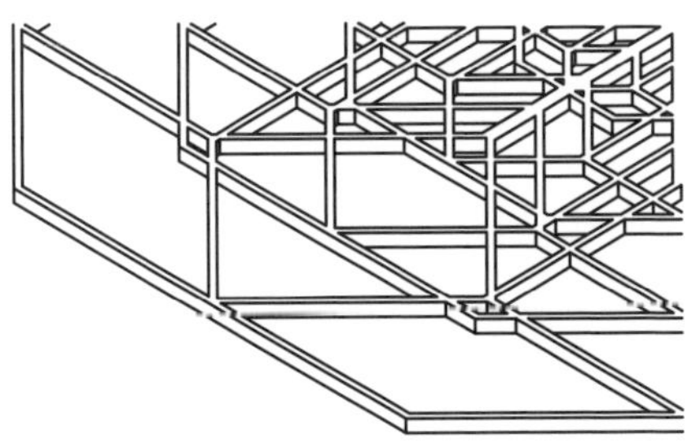

DRWG06_03 and 04: overlaid rotated polygons with edge thickness and extruded height

Completed function DRWG06_03:

```
;---------------------------------
(defun drwg06_03 ()
 (command “.LAYER” “UNLOCK” “*”
   “THAW” “*” “ON” “*” “”)
 (command “.ERASE” “all” “”)
 (setq pntc (list 0.0 0.0 0.0))
 (prog06a pntc 8 8 8 0.25 “LAYER01”)
 (prog06a pntc 8 6 8 0.25 “LAYER02”)
 (prog06a pntc 8 4 8 0.25 “LAYER03”)
 (prog06a pntc 8 2 8 0.25 “LAYER04”)
 (command “.LAYER” “UNLOCK” “*”
   “THAW” “*” “ON” “*” “”)
 (command “.ZOOM” “e”)
 (command “.UNION” “all” “”)
 (princ)
)
;---------------------------------
```

Function DRWG06_04 is a copy of DRWG06_03, with an added EXTRUDE command that creates a three-dimensional version of these patterns.

Completed function DRWG06_04:

```
;---------------------------------
(defun drwg06_04 ()
 (command “.LAYER” “UNLOCK” “*”
   “THAW” “*” “ON” “*” “”)
 (command “.ERASE” “all” “”)
 (setq pntc (list 0.0 0.0 0.0))
 (prog06a pntc 8 8 8 0.25 “LAYER01”)
 (prog06a pntc 8 6 8 0.25 “LAYER02”)
 (prog06a pntc 8 4 8 0.25 “LAYER03”)
 (prog06a pntc 8 2 8 0.25 “LAYER04”)
 (command “.LAYER” “UNLOCK” “*”
   “THAW” “*” “ON” “*” “”)
 (command “.ZOOM” “e”)
 (command “.UNION” “all” “”)
 (command “.EXTRUDE” “last” “” 0.5)
 ; include taper for versions prior
 ; to 2007
 ;(command “.EXTRUDE” “last” “” 0.25
 ;  “0”)
 (princ)
)
;---------------------------------
```

Consider other anchor points for the polygon, which can be rotated and repeated. A polygon can be created in a number of ways depending on what is known, the radius or the edge length. Three possible conditions are shown here.

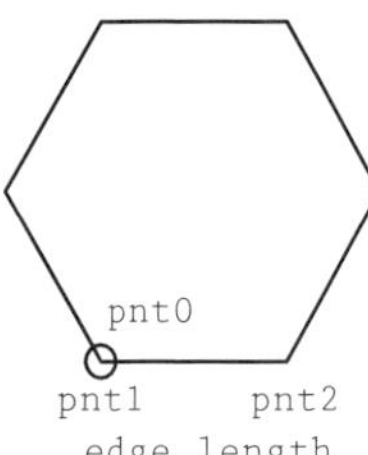

PROG06a: polygon with origin at start of bottom edge

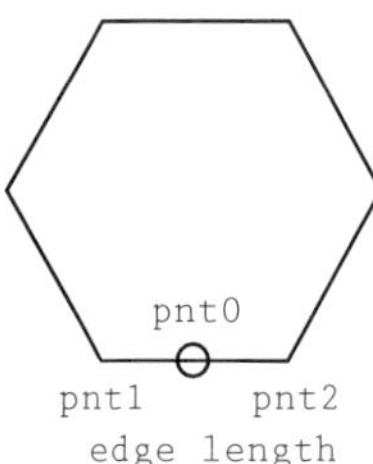

PROG06b: polygon with origin at midpoint of bottom edge

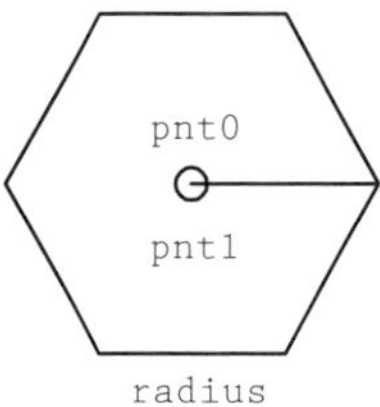

PROG06c: polygon with origin at center

Function PROG06a includes the start of the bottom edge and the edge length. Add function PROG06b using the midpoint of the bottom edge and the edge length. Add function PROG06c using the center and radius.

For function PROG06b, use PROG06a and change the following:

```
; endpoints of edge
 (setq pnt1 pnt0)
 (setq pnt2 (list
   (+ (nth 0 pnt1) pxside)
   (nth 1 pnt1) (nth 2 pnt1)))
```

To:

```
; endpoints of edge
 (setq pnt1 (list
   (- (nth 0 pnt0) (/ pxside 2.0))
   (nth 1 pnt0) (nth 2 pnt0)))
 (setq pnt2 (list
   (+ (nth 0 pnt0) (/ pxside 2.0))
   (nth 1 pnt0) (nth 2 pnt0)))
```

Completed function PROG06b:

```
;----------------------------------
(defun prog06b (pnt0 psides pxside
  ptimes pthk player
  / pnt1 pnt2 pnt3)
 ; polygon midpoint of bottom edge
 ; set current layer
 (command ".LAYER" "MAKE" player "")
 ; endpoints of edge
 (setq pnt1 (list
   (- (nth 0 pnt0) (/ pxside 2.0))
   (nth 1 pnt0) (nth 2 pnt0)))
 (setq pnt2 (list
   (+ (nth 0 pnt0) (/ pxside 2.0))
   (nth 1 pnt0) (nth 2 pnt0)))
 ; draw polygon
 (command ".POLYGON"
   psides "edge" pnt1 pnt2)
 (command ".ZOOM" "e")
 ; point inside polygon
 (setq pnt3 (polar pnt1
```

```
    (dtr (/ 360.0 psides))
    (/ pxside 2.0)))
 ;offset thickness
 (command ".OFFSET"
   pthk pnt1 pnt3 "")
 ; convert to regions
 (command ".REGION" "all" "")
 ; subtract inside from outside
 (command ".SUBTRACT"
   "all" "r" "last" "" "last" "")
 ; rotate it
 (command ".ARRAY"
   "last" "" "P" pnt0 ptimes "360" "Y")
 ; hide layer
 (command ".LAYER" "SET" "0"
   "LOCK" player "FREEZE" player "")
 (princ)
)
;----------------------------------
```

Add function PROG06c. This change-to-radius function does not require use of the OFFSET command.

Completed function PROG06c:

```
;----------------------------------
(defun prog06c (pnt0 psides prad
  ptimes pthk player / pnt1)
 ; polygon center
 ; set current layer
 (command ".LAYER" "MAKE" player "")
 ; center of polygon
 (setq pnt1 pnt0)
 ; draw polygon
 (command ".POLYGON"
   psides pnt1 "I" prad)
 (command ".ZOOM" "e")
 ;offset thickness
 (command ".POLYGON"
   psides pnt1 "I" (- prad pthk))
 ; convert to regions
 (command ".REGION" "all" "")
 ; subtract inside from outside
 (command ".SUBTRACT"
   "all" "r" "last" "" "last" "")
 ; rotate it
 (command ".ARRAY"
   "last" "" "P" pnt0 ptimes "360" "Y")
 ; hide layer
 (command ".LAYER" "SET" "0"
   "LOCK" player "FREEZE" player "")
 (princ)
)
;----------------------------------
```

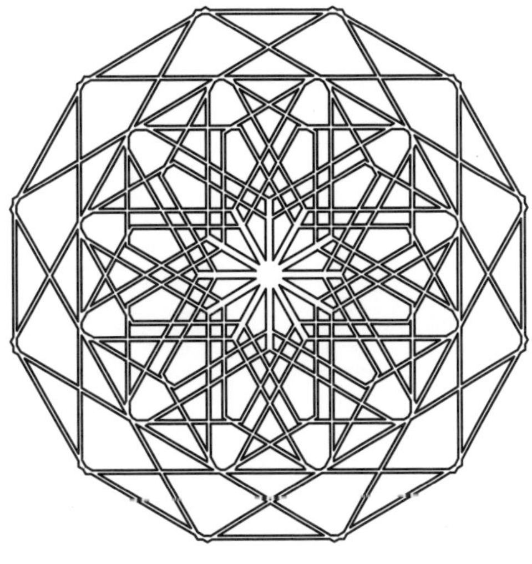

DRWG06_05: example of PROG06b, overlaid rotated polygons

Completed function DRWG06_05 using function PROG06b:

```
;----------------------------------
(defun drwg06_05 ()
 (command ".LAYER" "UNLOCK" "*"
   "THAW" "*" "ON" "*" "")
 (command ".ERASE" "all" "")
 (setq pntc (list 0.0 0.0 0.0))
 (prog06b pntc 6 10 12 0.25
   "LAYER01")
 (prog06b pntc 6 7.5 12 0.25
   "LAYER02")
 (command ".LAYER" "UNLOCK" "*"
```

```
    "THAW" "*" "ON" "*" "")
  (command ".ZOOM" "e")
  (command ".UNION" "all" "")
  (princ)
)
;-----------------------------------
```

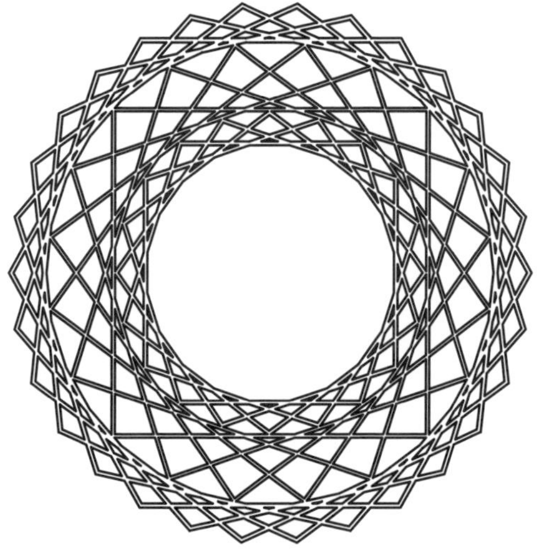

DRWG06_06: example of PROG06c, overlaid rotated polygons

Completed function DRWG06_06 using function PROG06c:

```
;-----------------------------------
(defun drwg06_06 ()
  (command ".LAYER" "UNLOCK" "*"
    "THAW" "*" "ON" "*" "")
  (command ".ERASE" "all" "")
  (setq pntc (list 0.0 0.0 0.0))
  (prog06c pntc 6 10 5 0.175
    "LAYER01")
  (prog06c pntc 4 8.6 5 0.175
    "LAYER02")
  (prog06c pntc 5 6.0 4 0.175
    "LAYER03")
  (command ".LAYER" "UNLOCK" "*"
```


```
    "THAW" "*" "ON" "*" "")
  (command ".ZOOM" "e")
  (command ".UNION" "all" "")
  (princ)
)
;-----------------------------------
```


Next create alternate versions of PROG06a, PROG06b, and PROG06c that include a y-axis offset for the start of the polygon. The rotation will still remain at pnt0.

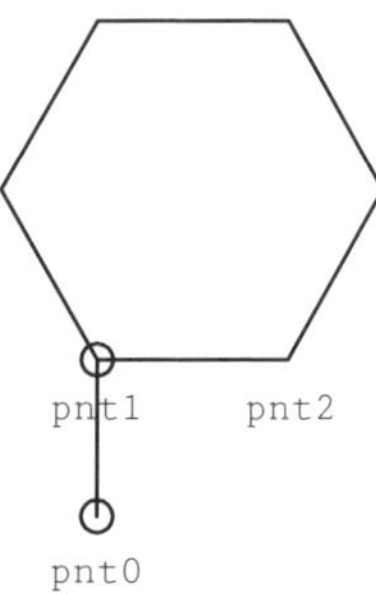

PROG06d: polygon with offset from start of bottom edge

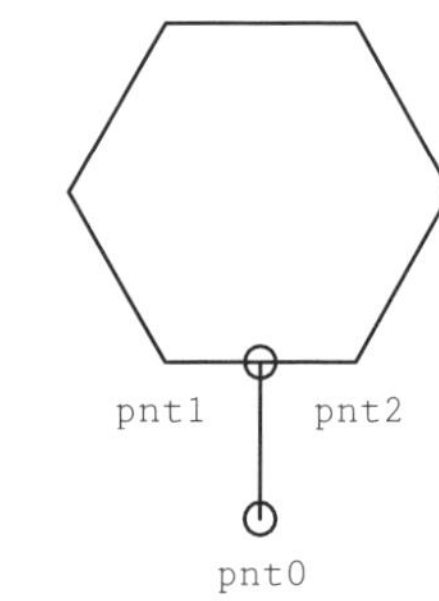

PROG06e: polygon with offset from midpoint of bottom edge

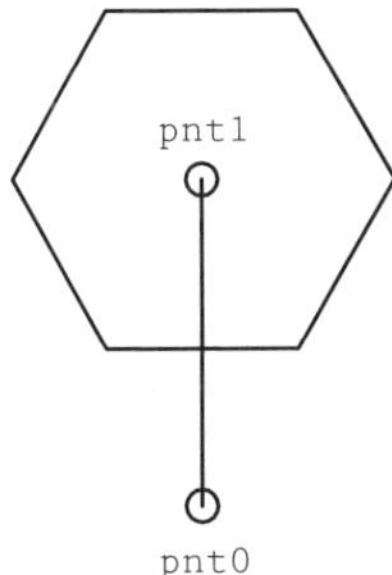

PROG06f: polygon with offset from center

Functions PROG06a, PROG06b, and PROG06c are modified for functions PROG06d, PROG06e, and PROG06f. For all of these, pnt1 is modified by adding the y-offset. The y-offset is also added to the argument list.

Completed function PROG06d:

```
;-----------------------------------
(defun prog06d (pnt0 psides pxside
  ptimes pthk pyoff player
  / pnt1 pnt2 pnt3)
 ; polygon start point of bottom
 ; edge w/Y offset
 ; set current layer
 (command “.LAYER” “MAKE” player “”)
 ; endpoint of edge
 (setq pnt1 (list
   (nth 0 pnt0)
   (+ (nth 1 pnt0) pyoff)
   (nth 2 pnt0)))
 (setq pnt2 (list
   (+ (nth 0 pnt1) pxside)
   (nth 1 pnt1) (nth 2 pnt1)))
 ; draw polygon
 (command “.POLYGON”
   psides “edge” pnt1 pnt2)
 (command “.ZOOM” “e”)
 ; point inside polygon
 (setq pnt3 (polar pnt1
   (dtr (/ 360.0 psides))
   (/ pxside 2.0)))
 ;offset thickness
 (command “.OFFSET”
   pthk pnt1 pnt3 “”)
 ; convert to regions
 (command “.REGION” “all” “”)
 ; subtract inside from outside
 (command “.SUBTRACT”
   “all” “r” “last” “” “last” “”)
 ; rotate it
 (command “.ARRAY”
   “last” “” “P” pnt0 ptimes “360” “Y”)
 ; hide layer
 (command “.LAYER” “SET” “0”
   “LOCK” player “FREEZE” player “”)
 (princ)
)
;-----------------------------------
```

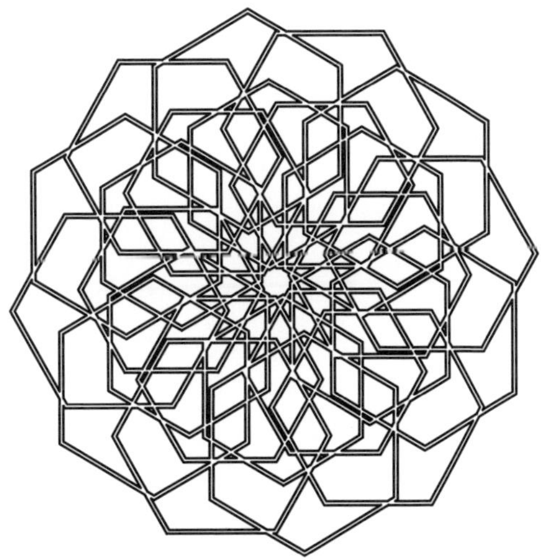

DRWG-06_07: example of PROG06d, overlaid rotated polygons

Completed function DRWG06_07 using function PROG06f:

```
;----------------------------------
(defun drwg06_07 ()
 (command ".LAYER" "UNLOCK" "*"
   "THAW" "*" "ON" "*" "")
 (command ".ERASE" "all" "")
 (setq pntc (list 0.0 0.0 0.0))
 (prog06d pntc 6 10 12 0.35 5.0
   "LAYER01")
 (prog06d pntc 6 8.5 12 0.35 1.25
   "LAYER02")
 (command ".LAYER" "UNLOCK" "*"
   "THAW" "*" "ON" "*" "")
 (command ".ZOOM" "e")
 (command ".UNION" "all" "")
 (princ)
)
;----------------------------------
```

Completed function PROG06e:

```
;----------------------------------
(defun prog06e (pnt0 psides pxside
  ptimes pthk pyoff player
  / pnt1 pnt2 pnt3)
 ; polygon midpoint of bottom edge
 ; w/Y offset
 ; set current layer
 (command ".LAYER" "MAKE" player "")
 ; endpoints of edge
 (setq pnt1 (list
   (- (nth 0 pnt0) (/ pxside 2.0))
   (+ (nth 1 pnt0) pyoff)
   (nth 2 pnt0)))
 (setq pnt2 (list
   (+ (nth 0 pnt0) (/ pxside 2.0))
   (+ (nth 1 pnt0) pyoff)
   (nth 2 pnt0)))
 ; draw polygon
 (command ".POLYGON"
   psides "edge" pnt1 pnt2)
 (command ".ZOOM" "e")
 ; point inside polygon
 (setq pnt3 (polar pnt1
   (dtr (/ 360.0 psides))
   (/ pxside 2.0)))
 ;offset thickness
 (command ".OFFSET"
   pthk pnt1 pnt3 "")
 ; convert to regions
 (command ".REGION" "all" "")
 ; subtract inside from outside
 (command ".SUBTRACT"
   "all" "r" "last" "" "last" "")
 ; rotate it
 (command ".ARRAY"
   "last" "" "P" pnt0 ptimes "360" "Y")
 ; hide layer
 (command ".LAYER" "SET" "0"
   "LOCK" player "FREEZE" player "")
 (princ)
)
;----------------------------------
```

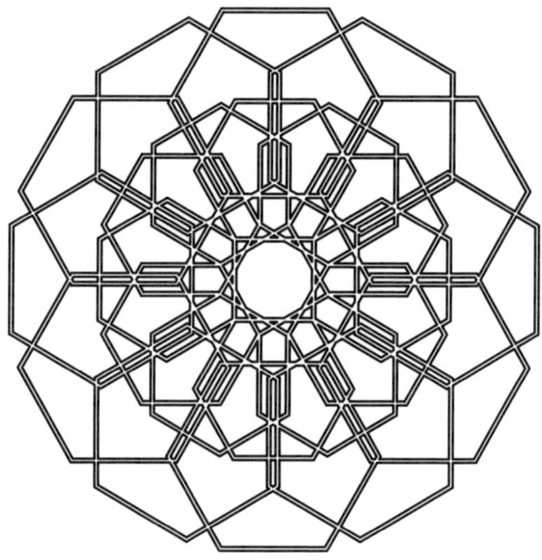

DRWG-06_08: example of PROG06e, overlaid rotated polygons

Completed function DRWG06_08 using function PROG06e:

```
;-----------------------------------
(defun drwg06_08 ()
 (command ".LAYER" "UNLOCK" "*"
   "THAW" "*" "ON" "*" "")
 (command ".ERASE" "all" "")
 (setq pntc (list 0.0 0.0 0.0))
 (prog06e pntc 6 10 12 0.35 7.5
   "LAYER01")
 (prog06e pntc 6 7.5 12 0.35 3.5
   "LAYER02")
 (command ".LAYER" "UNLOCK" "*"
   "THAW" "*" "ON" "*" "")
 (command ".ZOOM" "e")
 (command ".UNION" "all" "")
 (princ)
)
;-----------------------------------
```

Completed function PROG06f:

```
;-----------------------------------
(defun prog06f (pnt0 psides prad
  ptimes pthk pyoff player / pnt1)
 ; polygon center w/Y offset
 ; set current layer
 (command ".LAYER" "MAKE" player "")
 ; center of polygon
 (setq pnt1 (list
   (nth 0 pnt0)
   (+ (nth 1 pnt0) pyoff)
   (nth 2 pnt0)))
 ; draw polygon
 (command ".POLYGON"
   psides pnt1 "I" prad)
 (command ".ZOOM" "e")
 ;offset thickness
 (command ".POLYGON"
   psides pnt1 "I" (- prad pthk))
 ; convert to regions
 (command ".REGION" "all" "")
 ; subtract inside from outside
 (command ".SUBTRACT"
   "all" "r" "last" "" "last" "")
 ; rotate it
 (command ".ARRAY"
   "last" "" "P" pnt0 ptimes "360" "Y")
 ; hide layer
 (command ".LAYER" "SET" "0"
   "LOCK" player "FREEZE" player "")
 (princ)
)
;-----------------------------------
```

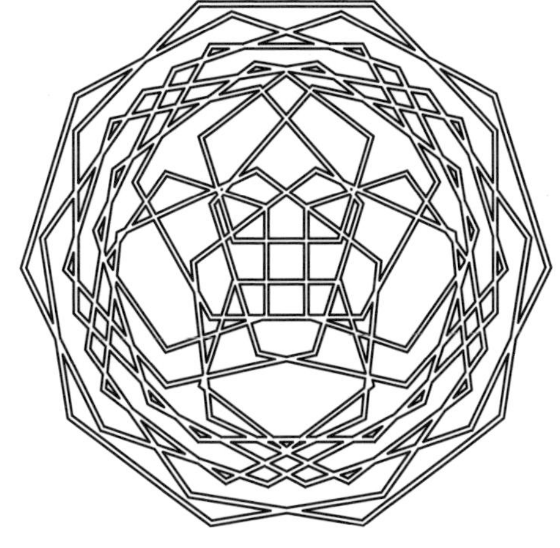

DRWG-06_09: example of PROG06f, overlaid rotated polygons

Completed function DRWG06_09 using function PROG06f:

```
;-----------------------------------
(defun drwg06_09 ()
 (command ".LAYER" "UNLOCK" "*"
   "THAW" "*" "ON" "*" "")
 (command ".ERASE" "all" "")
 (setq pntc (list 0.0 0.0 0.0))
 (prog06f pntc 6 10 5 0.35 5.0
   "LAYER01")
 (prog06f pntc 8 15 5 0.35 2.5
   "LAYER02")
 (prog06f pntc 5 6.0 4 0.35 6.0
   "LAYER03")
```

```
  (command ".LAYER" "UNLOCK" "*"
    "THAW" "*" "ON" "*" "")
  (command ".ZOOM" "e")
  (command ".UNION" "all" "")
  (princ)
)
;---------------------------------
```

Consider if the edges of the polygon are arcs, not simple lines. Since we cannot use AutoCAD's POLYGON command, we must develop our own polygon function: DOLPOLYGON. Using the approach in PROG09a (shown in Chapter 3), begin at the start point of the bottom edge and compute the endpoint based on the edge length. Then increment the turning angle and compute the next endpoint.

Completed function DOLPOLYGON:

```
;---------------------------------
(defun dolpolygon (pnts psides
  pxside / spnt npnt cang tang)
 ; line polygon start point bottom
 ; edge
 ; compute turning ang
 (setq cang (/ 360.0 psides))
 ; set initial ang
 (setq tang 0.0)
 ; start polyline
 (setq spnt pnts)
 ; draw polygon
 (command ".PLINE" spnt)
 (repeat psides
  ; compute next point
  (setq npnt
    (polar spnt (dtr tang) pxside))
  ; add point
  (command npnt)
  ; inc ang
  (setq tang (+ tang cang))
  ; set next start point
  (setq spnt npnt)
 )
 ; close PLINE
 (command "c")
 (princ)
)
;---------------------------------
```

Examples of DOLPOLYGON executed from the command line:

```
(dolpolygon (list 0 0 0) 4 3)
(dolpolygon (list 0 0 0) 5 3)
(dolpolygon (list 0 0 0) 6 3)
(doalolygon (list 0 0 0) 8 3)
```

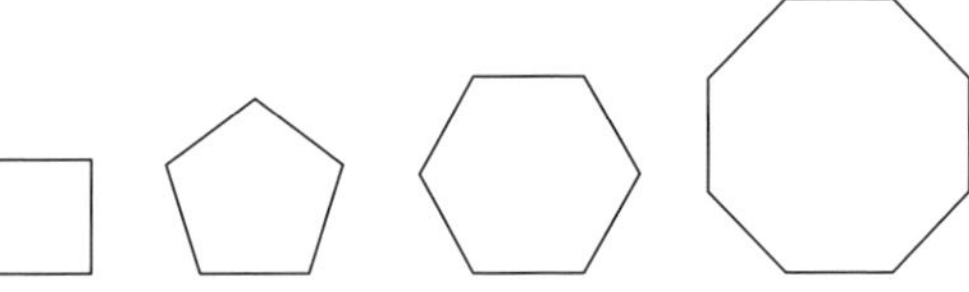

DOLPOLYGON: line polygon examples

We can now take PROG06a, copy it, and rename it PROG07a. Then replace AutoCAD's POLYGON command with our function. The other change is that variable pnt2 is no longer needed and can be removed.

Completed function PROG07a:

```
;---------------------------------
(defun prog07a (pnt0 psides pxside
  ptimes pthk player / pnt1 pnt3)
 ; polygon start point of bottom
 ; edge
 ; set current layer
 (command ".LAYER" "MAKE" player "")
 ; start point of edge
 (setq pnt1 pnt0)
 ; draw polygon
 (dolpolygon pnt0 psides pxside)
 (command ".ZOOM" "e")
 ; point inside polygon
 (setq pnt3 (polar pnt1
   (dtr (/ 360.0 psides))
   (/ pxside 2.0)))
 ;offset thickness
 (command ".OFFSET"
   pthk pnt1 pnt3 "")
 ; convert to regions
```

```
 (command ".REGION" "all" "")
 ; subtract inside from outside
 (command ".SUBTRACT"
    "all" "r" "last" "" "last" "")
 ; rotate it
 (command ".ARRAY"
   "last" "" "P" pnt0 ptimes "360" "Y")
 ; hide layer
 (command ".LAYER" "SET" "0"
   "LOCK" player "FREEZE" player "")
 (princ)
)
;---------------------------------
```

Verify PROG07a with function DRWG07_01.

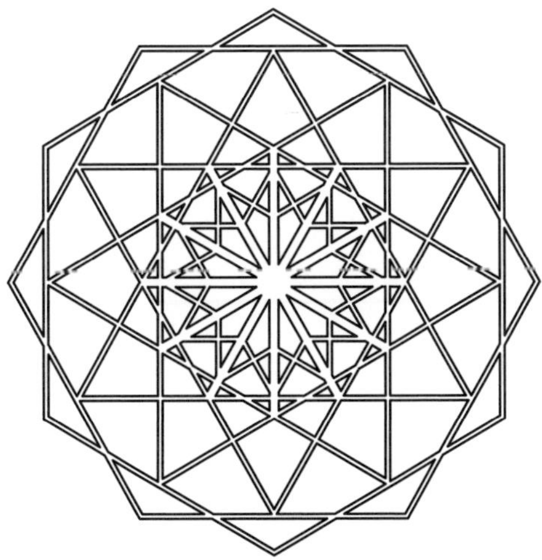

DRWG07_01: example of PROG07a with the line polygon

Completed function DRWG07_01 using function PROG07a:

```
;---------------------------------
(defun drwg07_01 ()
 (command ".LAYER" "UNLOCK" "*"
   "THAW" "*" "ON" "*" "")
 (command ".ERASE" "all" "")
 (setq pntc (list 0.0 0.0 0.0))
 (prog07a pntc 6 10 12 0.35
   "LAYER01")
 (prog07a pntc 6 5 12 0.35
   "LAYER02")
 (command ".LAYER" "UNLOCK" "*"
   "THAW" "*" "ON" "*" "")
 (command ".ZOOM" "e")
 (command ".UNION" "all" "")
 (princ)
)
;---------------------------------
```

Once the POLYGON command is replaced with the DOLPOLYGON function, change the lines in the polyline to arcs. In this version, the arcs will be concave and face toward the center.

Add function DOAIPOLYGON using DOLPOLYGON.

Completed function DOAIPOLYGON:

```
;---------------------------------
(defun doaipolygon (pnts psides
  pxside / spnt npnt cang tang)
 ; concave arc polygon start point
 ; of start point bottom edge
 ; compute turning ang
 (setq cang (/ 360.0 psides))
 ; set initial ang
 (setq tang (- 180.0 cang))
 ; start polyline
 (setq spnt pnts)
 ; draw polygon
 (command ".PLINE" spnt "a")
 (repeat psides
  ; compute next point
  (setq npnt
    (polar spnt (dtr tang) pxside))
  ; add point
```

```
    (command "r" (* pxside 1.0) npnt)
    ; inc ang
    (setq tang (- tang cang))
    ; set next start point
    (setq spnt npnt)
  )
  ; close PLINE
  (command "cl")
  (princ)
)
;----------------------------------
```

Examples of DOAIPOLYGON executed from the command line:

```
(doaipolygon (list 0 0 0) 4 3)
(doaipolygon (list 0 0 0) 5 3)
(doaipolygon (list 0 0 0) 6 3)
(doaipolygon (list 0 0 0) 8 3)
```

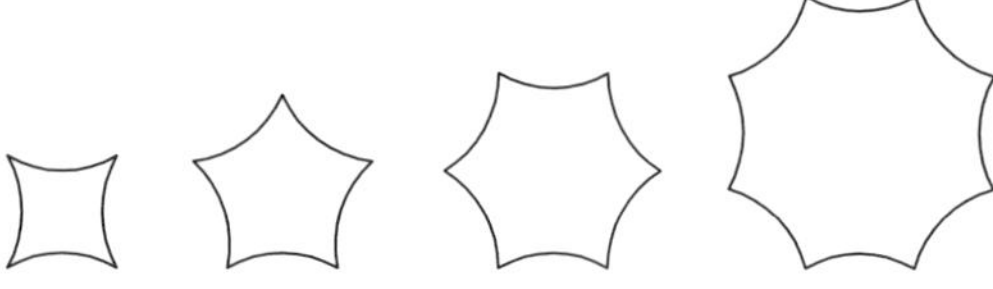

DOAIPOLYGON: concave arc polygon examples

Compare this version to DOLPOLYGON. Note the starting turning angle; the start of the polyline (including the arc option); how each arc endpoint is specified with a radius; and that the angle increment is decremented. The starting turning angle was modified due to the arcs being drawn clockwise; in the line-polygon version, the lines were drawn counterclockwise. The curvature radius is dependent on a factor of the edge length: `(* pxside 1.0)` (`1.0` in this example, try others). Also note that the polyline close is now `cl` not `c`. This is due to the use of the arc option. To better understand the sequence of options specified, execute the PLINE command from the command line and try drawing a similar arc polygon.

Add PROG08a using a copy of PROG07a and replace:

```
; draw polygon
(dolpolygon pnt0 psides pxside)
```

With:

```
; draw polygon
(doaipolygon pnt0 psides pxside)
```

Verify PROG08a with function DRWG08_01, a copy of DRWG07_01.

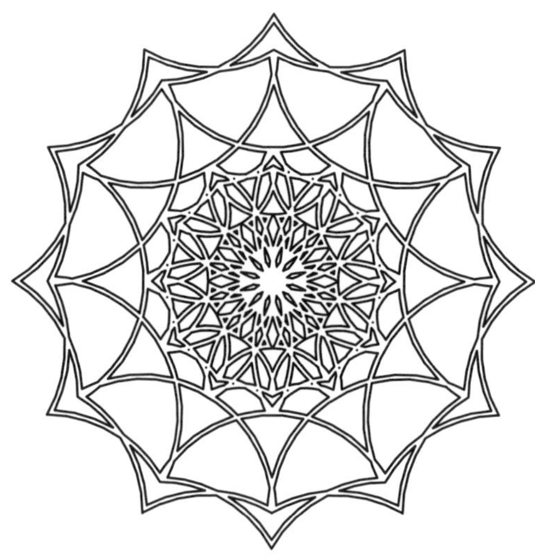

DRWG08_01: example of PROG08a with the concave arc polygon

Completed function DRWG08_01 using function PROG08a:

```
;----------------------------------
(defun drwg08_01 ()
 (command ".LAYER" "UNLOCK" "*"
   "THAW" "*" "ON" "*" "")
 (command ".ERASE" "all" "")
 (setq pntc (list 0.0 0.0 0.0))
 (prog08a pntc 6 10 12 0.35
```

```
    "LAYER01")
  (prog08a pntc 6 5 12 0.35
    "LAYER02")
  (command ".LAYER" "UNLOCK" "*"
    "THAW" "*" "ON" "*" "")
  (command ".ZOOM" "e")
  (command ".UNION" "all" "")
  (princ)
)
;---------------------------------
```

Once we have a concave arc polygon, add function DOAOPOLYGON to draw a convex arc polygon, with the arcs facing out from the center.

Add function DOAOPOLYGON using DOAIPOLYGON.

Completed function DOAOPOLYGON:

```
;---------------------------------
(defun doaopolygon (pnts psides
   pxside / spnt npnt cang tang)
  ; convex arc polygon start point
  ; of start point bottom edge
  ; compute turning ang
  (setq cang (/ 360.0 psides))
  ; set initial ang
  (setq tang 0.0)
  ; start polyline
  (setq spnt pnts)
  ; draw polygon
  (command ".PLINE" spnt "a")
  (repeat psides
   ; compute next point
   (setq npnt
     (polar spnt (dtr tang)
     pxside))
   ; add point
   (command "r" (* pxside 0.5) npnt)
   ; inc ang
   (setq tang (+ tang cang))
   ; set next start point
   (setq spnt npnt)
  )
  ; close PLINE
  (command "cl")
  (princ)
)
;---------------------------------
```

Examples of DOAOPOLYGON executed from the command line:

```
(doaopolygon (list 0 0 0) 4 3)
(doaopolygon (list 0 0 0) 5 3)
(doaopolygon (list 0 0 0) 6 3)
(doaopolygon (list 0 0 0) 8 3)
```

DOAOPOLYGON: convex arc polygon examples

Compare this version to DOAIPOLYGON. Note the starting turning angle; the start of the polyline (including the arc option); how each arc endpoint is specified with a radius; and the angle increment. The starting turning angle is set back to 0, and the arcs are drawn counterclockwise. The curvature radius is dependent on a factor of the edge length: (* pxside 0.5) (0.5 in this example, try others). To better understand the sequence of options, execute the PLINE command from the command line and try drawing a similar arc polygon.

Add PROG09a using a copy of PROG07a and replace:

```
; draw polygon
(dolpolygon pnt0 psides pxside)
```

With:

```
; draw polygon
(doaopolygon pnt0 psides pxside)
```

Verify PROG09a with function DRWG09_01, a copy of DRWG07_01.

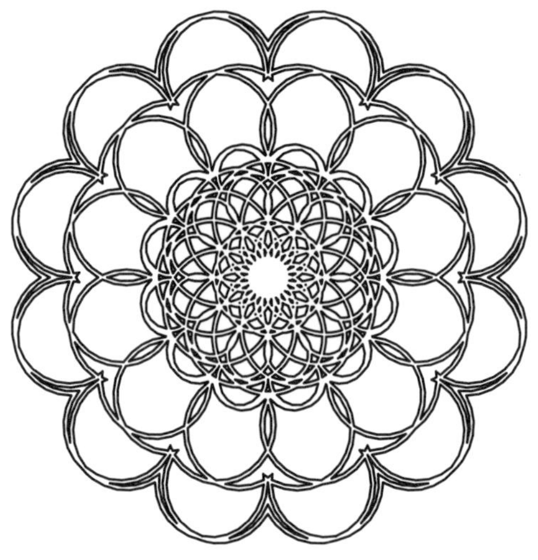

DRWG09_01: example of PROG09a with the convex arc polygon

Completed function DRWG09_01 using function PROG09a:

```
;-----------------------------------
(defun drwg09_01 ()
 (command ".LAYER" "UNLOCK" "*"
   "THAW" "*" "ON" "*" "")
 (command ".ERASE" "all" "")
 (setq pntc (list 0.0 0.0 0.0))
 (prog09a pntc 6 10 12 0.35
   "LAYER01")
 (prog09a pntc 6 5 12 0.35
   "LAYER02")
 (command ".LAYER" "UNLOCK" "*"
   "THAW" "*" "ON" "*" "")
 (command ".ZOOM" "e")
 (command ".UNION" "all" "")
 (princ)
)
;-----------------------------------
```

To complete all versions of the polygon arc, function PROG08a and PROG09a were arc polygons with origins based at the start of the bottom edge. A similar set of functions could be developed to account for the other two origins of a polygon; midpoint of the bottom edge and center; and by taking a y-offset into consideration.

Instead of a polygon for these designs, use a copy of PROG06f and add function PROG10f, replacing the polygon with a circle. Of course, function PROG06f could be used to draw a sixty-sided polygon, or greater for a circle pattern.

Completed function PROG10f:

```
;-----------------------------------
(defun prog10f (pnt0 prad ptimes
  pthk pyoff player / pnt1)
 ; circle center w/Y offset
 ; set current layer
 (command ".LAYER" "MAKE" player "")
 ; center of circle
 (setq pnt1 (list
   (nth 0 pnt0)
   (+ (nth 1 pnt0) pyoff)
   (nth 2 pnt0)))
 ; draw circle
 (command ".CIRCLE" pnt1 prad)
 (command ".ZOOM" "e")
 ; offset thickness
 (command ".CIRCLE"
   pnt1 (- prad pthk))
 ; convert to regions
 (command ".REGION" "all" "")
 ; subtract inside from outside
 (command ".SUBTRACT"
   "all" "r" "last" "" "last" "")
 ; rotate it
 (command ".ARRAY"
   "last" "" "P" pnt0 ptimes "360" "Y")
 ; hide layer
 (command ".LAYER" "SET" "0"
   "LOCK" player "FREEZE" player "")
 (princ)
)
;-----------------------------------
```

Execute PROG10f with an offset equal to the radius.

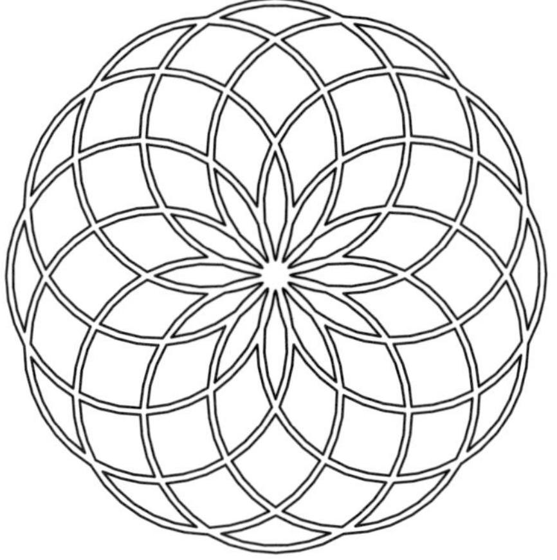

DRWG10_01: example of PROG10f, repeating rotated circles

Execute PROG10f with an offset greater than the radius.

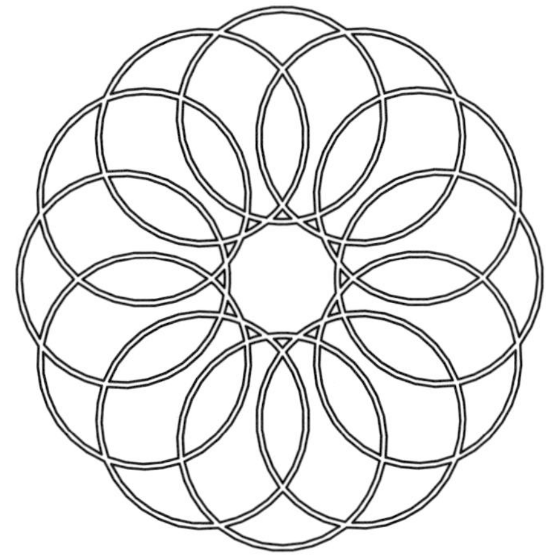

DRWG10_02: example of PROG10f, repeating rotated circles with center offset

Completed function DRWG10_01 using function PROG10f:

```
;-----------------------------------
(defun drwg10_01 ()
 (command ".LAYER" "UNLOCK" "*"
   "THAW" "*" "ON" "*" "")
 (command ".ERASE" "all" "")
 (setq pntc (list 0.0 0.0 0.0))
 (prog10f pntc 5 12 0.25 5.0
   "LAYER01")
 (command ".LAYER" "UNLOCK" "*"
   "THAW" "*" "ON" "*" "")
 (command ".ZOOM" "e")
 (command ".UNION" "all" "")
 (princ)
)
;-----------------------------------
```

Completed function DRWG10_02 using function PROG10f:

```
;-----------------------------------
(defun drwg10_02 ()
 (command ".LAYER" "UNLOCK" "*"
   "THAW" "*" "ON" "*" "")
 (command ".ERASE" "all" "")
 (setq pntc (list 0.0 0.0 0.0))
 (prog10f pntc 5 12 0.25 7.5
   "LAYER01")
 (command ".LAYER" "UNLOCK" "*"
   "THAW" "*" "ON" "*" "")
 (command ".ZOOM" "e")
 (command ".UNION" "all" "")
 (princ)
)
;-----------------------------------
```

Using PROG10f, add function PROG11f with the circle replaced by an ellipse. Replace the input of a single radius with a major and minor radius, and x- and y-axis distances. Review requirements for the ELLIPSE command (in this example, an ellipse with a center specified).

Completed function PROG11f:

```
;----------------------------------
(defun prog11f (pnt0 pxrad pyrad
  ptimes pthk pyoff player
  / pnt1 pnt2)
 ; ellipse center w/Y offset
 ; set current layer
 (command ".LAYER" "MAKE" player "")
 ; center of ellipse
 (setq pnt1 (list
   (nth 0 pnt0)
   (+ (nth 1 pnt0) pyoff)
   (nth 2 pnt0)))
 ; draw ellipses
 (setq pnt2 (list
   (- (nth 0 pnt1) pxrad)
   (nth 1 pnt1) (nth 2 pnt1)))
 (command ".ELLIPSE"
   "c" pnt1 pnt2 pyrad)
 (command ".ZOOM" "e")
 ; offset thickness
 (setq pnt2 (list
   (+ (- (nth 0 pnt1) pxrad) pthk)
   (nth 1 pnt1) (nth 2 pnt1)))
 (command ".ELLIPSE"
   "c" pnt1 pnt2 (- pyrad pthk))
 (command ".ZOOM" "e")
 ; convert to regions
 (command ".REGION" "all" "")
 ; subtract inside from outside
 (command ".SUBTRACT"
   "all" "r" "last" "" "last" "")
 ; rotate it
 (command ".ARRAY"
   "last" "" "P" pnt0 ptimes "360" "Y")
 ; hide layer
 (command ".LAYER" "SET" "0"
   "LOCK" player "FREEZE" player "")
 (princ)
)
;----------------------------------
```

Execute PROG11f with an offset greater than the radius.

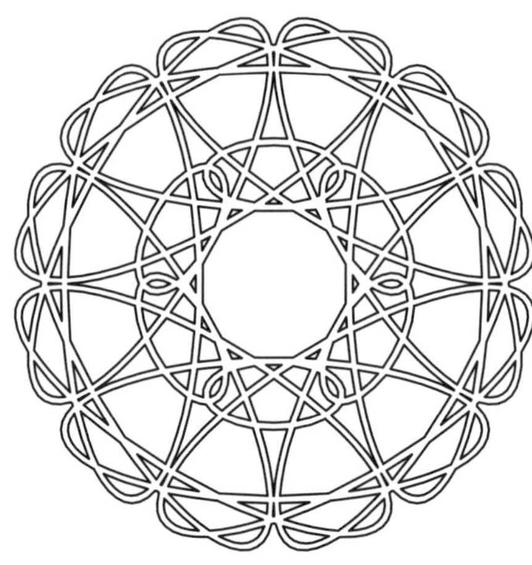

DRWG11_01: example of PROG11f, repeating rotated ellipses with center offset

Completed function DRWG11_01 using function PROG11f:

```
;----------------------------------
(defun drwg11_01 ()
 (command ".LAYER" "UNLOCK" "*"
   "THAW" "*" "ON" "*" "")
 (command ".ERASE" "all" "")
 (setq pntc (list 0.0 0.0 0.0))
 (prog11f pntc 7.5 2.5 12 0.25 5.0
   "LAYER01")
 (prog11f pntc 2.5 1.25 6 0.25 3.75
   "LAYER02")
 (command ".LAYER" "UNLOCK" "*"
   "THAW" "*" "ON" "*" "")
 (command ".ZOOM" "e")
 (command ".UNION" "all" "")
 (princ)
)
;----------------------------------
```

Execute PROG11f with a zero offset.

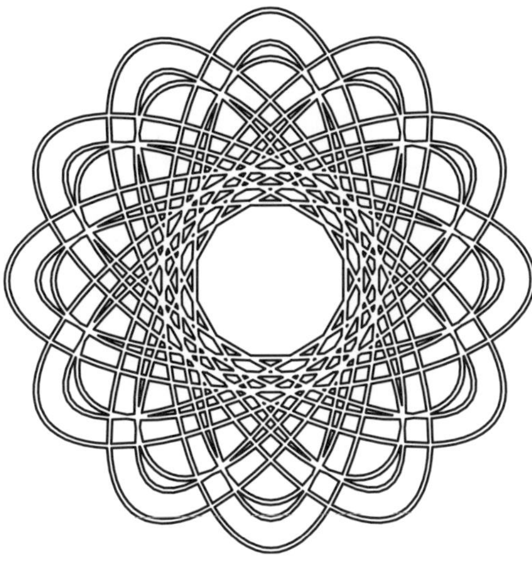

DRWG11_02: example of PROG11f, repeating rotated ellipses with no offset

Completed function DRWG11_02 using function PROG11f:

```
;-----------------------------------
(defun drwg11_02 ()
 (command ".LAYER" "UNLOCK" "*"
   "THAW" "*" "ON" "*" "")
 (command ".ERASE" "all" "")
 (setq pntc (list 0.0 0.0 0.0))
 (prog11f pntc 8.5 3.5 12 0.15 0
   "LAYER01")
 (prog11f pntc 7.0 3.0 12 0.15 0
   "LAYER02")
 (prog11f pntc 7.5 2.5 12 0.15 0
   "LAYER03")
 (command ".LAYER" "UNLOCK" "*"
   "THAW" "*" "ON" "*" "")
 (command ".ZOOM" "e")
 (command ".UNION" "all" "")
 (princ)
)
;-----------------------------------
```

Draw an elliptical polygon. The normal polygon is based on a circle. We can also develop a polygon based on an ellipse. In Chapter 3, we created our own polygons using the polar function to compute the corner points. For an elliptical polygon, we compute the equivalent of the polar function, but control both the x and y radii. The polar function-equivalent equations for a circle are:

```
xpt = X of the center +
    radius (sin angle)
ypt = Y of the center +
    radius (cos angle)
```

The polar function-equivalent equations for an ellipse are:

```
xpt = X of the center +
    X radius (sin angle)
ypt = Y of the center +
    Y radius (cos angle)
```

In both cases, a small change in the angle gives a circle or ellipse, and a large change gives a polygon.

Input now includes x and y radii and number of sides.

Completed function DOEPOLYGON:

```
;-----------------------------------
(defun doepolygon (pnt0 psides pxrad
  pyrad / npnt cang tang xpt ypt)
 ; elliptical polygon by center
 ; compute turning ang
 (setq cang (/ 360.0 psides))
 ; set initial ang
 (setq tang 0.0)
 ; draw polygon
 (command ".PLINE")
 (repeat psides
  ; compute next point
  (setq xpt
    (+ (nth 0 pnt0)
    (* pxrad (sin (dtr tang)))))
  (setq ypt
    (+ (nth 1 pnt0)
```

```
    (* pyrad (cos (dtr tang)))))
  (setq npnt
    (list xpt ypt (nth 2 pnt0)))
  ; add point
  (command npnt)
  ; inc ang
  (setq tang (+ tang cang))
 )
 ; close PLINE
 (command "c")
 (princ)
)
;---------------------------------
```

Examples of function DOEPOLYGON executed from the command line:

```
(doepolygon (list 0 0 0) 4 1 3)
(doepolygon (list 0 0 0) 5 2 3)
(doepolygon (list 0 0 0) 6 3 2.5)
(doepolygon (list 0 0 0) 8 2 3)
(doepolygon (list 0 0 0) 32 1 3)
```

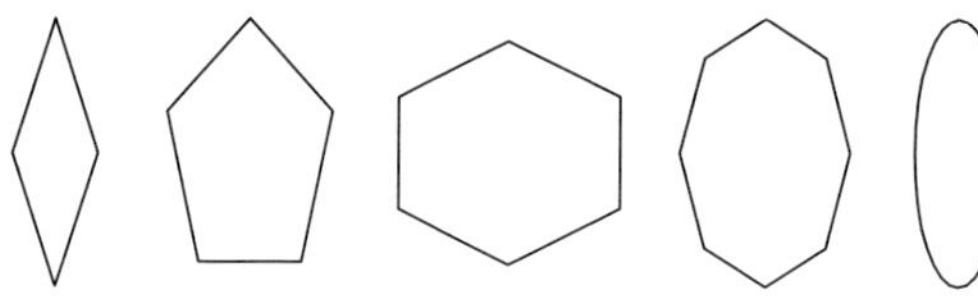

DOEPOLYGON examples

Using PROG11f, add function PROG12f using the ELLIPSE commands replaced with the function DOEPOLYGON, as follows:

```
; draw polygon
 (doepolygon pnt1 psides pxrad
   pyrad)
;offset thickness
 (doepolygon pnt1 psides
   (- pxrad pthk) (- pyrad pthk))
```

Completed function PROG12f:

```
;---------------------------------
(defun prog12f (pnt0 psides pxrad
  pyrad ptimes pthk pyoff player
  / pnt1 pnt2)
 ; ellipse polygon w/Y offset
 ; set current layer
 (command ".LAYER" "MAKE" player "")
 ; center of polygon
 (setq pnt1 (list
   (nth 0 pnt0)
   (+ (nth 1 pnt0) pyoff)
   (nth 2 pnt0)))
 ; draw polygon
 (doepolygon pnt1 psides pxrad
   pyrad)
 (command ".ZOOM" "e")
 ;offset thickness
 (doepolygon pnt1 psides
   (- pxrad pthk) (- pyrad pthk))
 (command ".ZOOM" "e")
 ; convert to regions
 (command ".REGION" "all" "")
 ; subtract inside from outside
 (command ".SUBTRACT"
   "all" "r" "last" "" "last" "")
 ; rotate it
 (command ".ARRAY"
   "last" "" "P" pnt0 ptimes "360" "Y")
 ; hide layer
 (command ".LAYER" "SET" "0"
   "LOCK" player "FREEZE" player "")
 (princ)
)
;---------------------------------
```

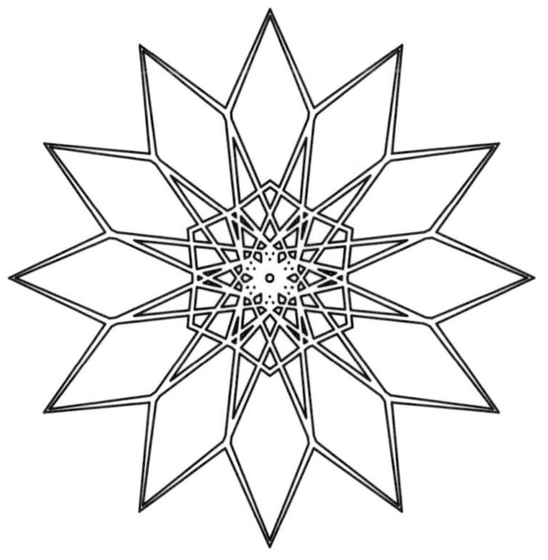

DRWG12_01: example of PROG12f, repeating rotated elliptical polygon

Completed function DRWG12_01 using function PROG12f:

```
;-----------------------------------
(defun drwg12_01 ()
 (command ".LAYER" "UNLOCK" "*"
   "THAW" "*" "ON" "*" "")
 (command ".ERASE" "all" "")
 (setq pntc (list 0.0 0.0 0.0))
 (prog12f pntc 5 2.5 7.5 12 0.35
   6.25 "LAYER01")
 (prog12f pntc 5 2.5 2.5 6 0.35
   2.5 "LAYER02")
 (command ".LAYER" "UNLOCK" "*"
   "THAW" "*" "ON" "*" "")
 (command ".ZOOM" "e")
 (command ".UNION" "all" "")
 (princ)
)
;-----------------------------------
```

Objects repeated in a polar array can be modified. For example, a circle repeated in a circular pattern can have a changing radius, from a start to end value. The ARRAY command does not give an opportunity to vary the dimensions of the repeating object. What is required is a function that duplicates the polar array command so that each location along the array is available. The object is modified before it is placed at that location.

In this case, compute the angle increment based on the number of repeats. For every repeat, rotate the object. That angle can be used to rotate the circle around pnt0, which includes a y-offset. Also included is a computed radius-increment based on the number of repeats, and the input start-and-end radius. A new radius is computed for the circle, for each rotation. If the y-offset is 0, the result is a series of concentric circles.

Add function PROG13f using a copy of PROG10f and drawing circles for the overall structure.

Completed function PROG13f:

```
;-----------------------------------
(defun prog13f (pnt0 prads prade
  ptimes pthk pyoff player
  / pnt1 ranginc rang pradinc prad
  obj1 obj2)
 ; circle by center, changing radius
 ; w/Y offset
 ; set current layer
 (command ".LAYER" "MAKE" player "")
 ; angs for repeat
 (setq ranginc (/ 360.0 ptimes))
 (setq rang 0.0)
 ; radius inc
 (setq pradinc
   (/ (- prade prads) ptimes))
 (setq prad prads)
 (repeat ptimes
  ; center of circle
  (setq pnt1 (list
    (nth 0 pnt0)
    (+ (nth 1 pnt0) pyoff)
    (nth 2 pnt0)))
  ; draw circles
  (command ".CIRCLE" pnt1 prad)
  (command ".ZOOM" "e")
  (command ".REGION" "last" "")
```

```
  (setq obj1 (ssadd (entlast)))
  ;offset thickness
  (command ".CIRCLE"
    pnt1 (- prad pthk))
  (command ".ZOOM" "e")
  (command ".REGION" "last" "")
  (setq obj2 (ssadd (entlast)))
  ; subtract inside from outside
  (command ".SUBTRACT"
    obj1 "" obj2 "")
  ; rotate
  (command ".ROTATE"
    "last" "" pnt0 rang)
  ; inc rotation
  (setq rang (+ rang ranginc))
  ; inc radius
  (setq prad (+ prad pradinc))
 )
 ; hide layer
 (command ".LAYER" "SET" "0"
   "LOCK" player "FREEZE" player "")
 (princ)
)
;----------------------------------
```

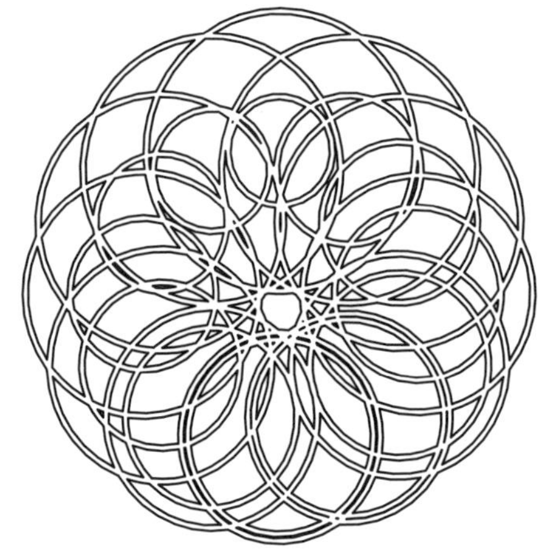

DRWG13_01: using PROG13f, repeating rotated circle with increasing radius

Completed function DRWG13_01 using function PROG13f:

```
;----------------------------------
(defun drwg13_01 ()
 (command ".LAYER" "UNLOCK" "*"
   "THAW" "*" "ON" "*" "")
 (command ".ERASE" "all" "")
 (setq pntc (list 0.0 0.0 0.0))
 (prog13f pntc 2.0 5.0 12 0.2 5.0
   "LAYER01")
 (prog13f pntc 5.0 2.5 12 0.2 5.0
   "LAYER02")
 (command ".LAYER" "UNLOCK" "*"
   "THAW" "*" "ON" "*" "")
 (command ".ZOOM" "e")
 (command ".UNION" "all" "")
 (princ)
)
;----------------------------------
```

In addition to changing the dimensions of an object while it is repeated, we may also want to change the y-offset.

Add function PROG14f using a copy of PROG13f and modify the radius for every repeat to a change in the y-offset distance. A start-and-end y-offset is input, from which a y-offset increment can be computed based on the number of repeats.

Completed function PROG14f:

```
;----------------------------------
(defun prog14f (pnt0 prad ptimes
  pthk pyoffs pyoffe player
  / pnt1 ranginc rang pyoffinc pyoff
  obj1 obj2)
 ; circle by center, changing Y
 ; offset
 ; set current layer
 (command ".LAYER" "MAKE" player "")
 ; angs for repeat
 (setq ranginc (/ 360.0 ptimes))
 (setq rang 0.0)
 ; offset inc
```

```
 (setq pyoffinc
   (/ (- pyoffe pyoffs) ptimes))
 (setq pyoff pyoffs)
 (repeat ptimes
  ; center of circle
  (setq pnt1 (list
    (nth 0 pnt0)
    (+ (nth 1 pnt0) pyoff)
    (nth 2 pnt0)))
  ; draw circles
  (command ".CIRCLE" pnt1 prad)
  (command ".REGION" "last" "")
  (setq obj1 (ssadd (entlast)))
  ;offset thickness
  (command ".CIRCLE"
    pnt1 (- prad pthk))
  (command ".REGION" "last" "")
  (setq obj2 (ssadd (entlast)))
  ; subtract inside from outside
  (command ".SUBTRACT"
    obj1 "" obj2 "")
  (command ".ZOOM" "e")
  ; rotate
  (command ".ROTATE"
    "last" "" pnt0 rang)
  ; inc rotation
  (setq rang (+ rang ranginc))
  ; inc offset
  (setq pyoff (+ pyoff pyoffinc))
 )
 ; hide layer
 (command ".LAYER" "SET" "0"
   "LOCK" player "FREEZE" player "")
 (princ)
)
;----------------------------------
```

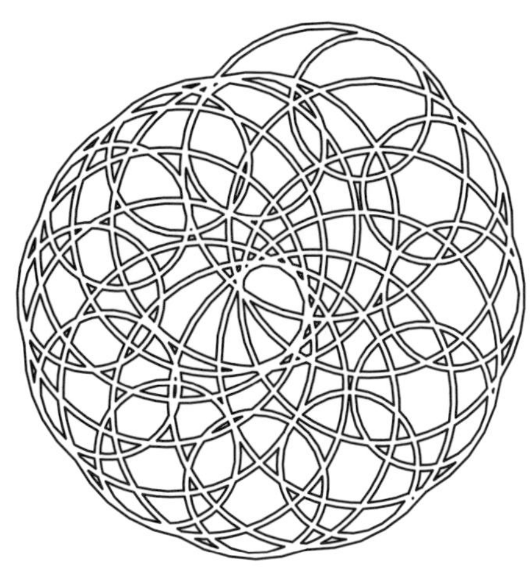

DRWG14_01: using PROG14f, repeating rotated circle with increasing offset

Completed function DRWG14_01 using function PROG14f:

```
;----------------------------------
(defun drwg14_01 ()
 (command ".LAYER" "UNLOCK" "*"
   "THAW" "*" "ON" "*" "")
 (command ".ERASE" "all" "")
 (setq pntc (list 0.0 0.0 0.0))
 (prog14f pntc 5.0 12 0.2 2.5 5.0
   "LAYER01")
 (prog14f pntc 2.5 12 0.2 5.0 7.5
   "LAYER02")
 (command ".LAYER" "UNLOCK" "*"
   "THAW" "*" "ON" "*" "")
 (command ".ZOOM" "e")
 (command ".UNION" "all" "")
 (princ)
)
;----------------------------------
```

Most of the examples shown for repetition have been basic AutoCAD shapes. We can also use one of the shapes created in Chapter 3.

Add function PROG15f using a copy of PROG10f and replacing the circle with the trefoil from Chapter 3. To create concentric trefoils, the computation of the radial distance for each puff is modified. The function includes the center of the trefoil, radius to the center of each puff, and the radius of each puff.

Review function DOTREFOIL and use it in PROG15f.

Complete function DOTREFOIL:

```
;----------------------------------
(defun dotrefoil (pnt0 lrad crad
  / pnt1 pnt2 pnt3 obj1)
 ; first circle
 (setq pnt1
   (polar pnt0 (dtr 90) lrad))
 (command ".CIRCLE" pnt1 crad)
 ; make region
 (command ".REGION" "last" "" )
 ; place into selection list
 (setq obj1 (ssadd (entlast)))
 ; second circle
 (setq pnt2
   (polar pnt0 (dtr 210) lrad))
 (command ".CIRCLE" pnt2 crad)
 ; make region
 (command ".REGION" "last" "" )
 ; place into selection list
 (setq obj1 (ssadd (entlast) obj1))
 ; third circle
 (setq pnt3 (polar
   pnt0 (dtr 330) lrad))
 (command ".CIRCLE" pnt3 crad)
 ; make region
 (command ".REGION" "last" "" )
 ; place into selection list
 (setq obj1 (ssadd (entlast) obj1))
 ; union are three
 (command ".UNION" obj1 "")
 (princ)
)
;----------------------------------
```

Completed function PROG15f:

```
;----------------------------------
(defun prog15f (pnt0 prad ptimes
  pthk pyoff player / pnt1)
 ; circle center w/Y offset
 ; set current layer
 (command ".LAYER" "MAKE" player "")
 ; center of circle
 (setq pnt1 (list
   (nth 0 pnt0)
   (+ (nth 1 pnt0) pyoff)
   (nth 2 pnt0)))
 ; draw circle
 (dotrefoil pnt1 prad prad)
 (command ".ZOOM" "e")
 ;offset thickness
 (dotrefoil pnt1 prad (- prad pthk))
 ; subtract inside from outside
 (command ".SUBTRACT"
   "all" "r" "last" "" "last" "")
 ; rotate it
 (command ".ARRAY"
   "last" "" "P" pnt0 ptimes "360" "Y")
 ; hide layer
 (command ".LAYER" "SET" "0"
   "LOCK" player "FREEZE" player "")
 (princ)
)
;----------------------------------
```

DRWG15_01: using PROG15f, repeating rotated trefoil

Completed function DRWG15_01 using function PROG15f:

```
;-----------------------------------
(defun drwg15_01 ()
 (command ".LAYER" "UNLOCK" "*"
   "THAW" "*" "ON" "*" "")
 (command ".ERASE" "all" "")
 (setq pntc (list 0.0 0.0 0.0))
 (prog15f pntc 5 6 0.35 2.5
   "LAYER01")
 (command ".LAYER" "UNLOCK" "*"
   "THAW" "*" "ON" "*" "")
 (command ".ZOOM" "e")
 (command ".UNION" "all" "")
 (princ)
)
;-----------------------------------
```

Varying repeated objects:

Now that we have a replacement for the ARRAY command, any parameter of any object can repeat. This can be a y-offset from the center of rotation, the radius of a circle or regular polygon, the x- and/or y-radius of an ellipse or elliptical polygon, or the x- and/or y-dimensions of a rectangle. These polar array patterns can be constructed as callable functions to be further repeated in a linear or rectangular array. Note that each DRWG function unioned all of the patterns into one. The single object can now be used in other operations, as well as repeated to form more complex patterns.

All of these patterns can be used for drawing, etched onto a surface such as glass, engraved with CNC-controlled routers, used for laser-cutting or by adding an extruded dimension, or used to create three-dimensional objects with a rapid-prototyping system or 3-D printer.

5.0

Simple patterns lead to simple forms; simple forms lead to complex constructions. In this chapter, we start with a simple horizontal-linear form. Its many representations will lead us to more complex vertical forms. This sequence also teaches you how to develop software using small steps and very few changes from one function to the next.

5.1 Generating a Simple Linear Form

Starting with a simple set of lines, we will progress to planes, frames, open surfaces, and finally a closed surface model. Each digital representation has some value for a particular phase of investigative design. Some are appropriate for drawing, others are for modeling, rendering, and fabrication.

This series of exercises demonstrates how a simple concept can be expanded one step at a time, to a more complex concept, as well as how to approach designs incrementally. At each step, consider a variation or parameter that was not included. These will be left out so that you can explore them on your own.

Start a new drawing and set the units to architectural. Set the grid to 1 foot, and turn off all snaps and dynamic input.

Start a new AutoLISP file in the editor: CH05A.LSP.

We will start with the simple task of drawing a series of lines within a specified boundary. In file CH05A.LSP, add the radians-to-degrees and degrees-to-radians functions, then add function PROG01.

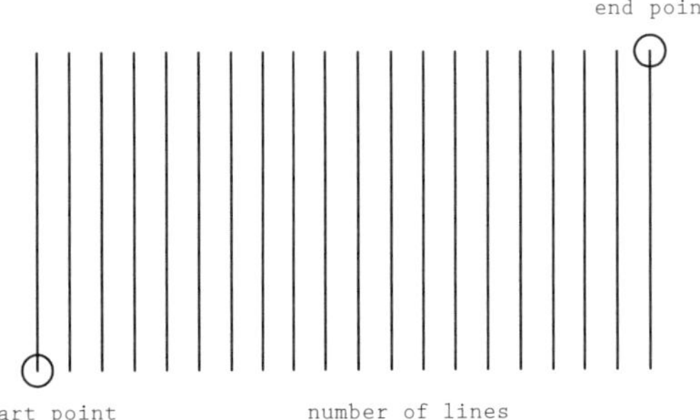

PROG01: draw a series of lines

Function PROG01 asks for a rectangular boundary and then fills it with lines in the y-direction and across the x-axis, similar to the rectangular ARRAY command with the number of lines requested placed equally across this boundary. First determine what we are given and what is needed to draw these lines. Input consists of the lower-left and upper-right corners of the boundary and the number of lines to draw.

To be able to draw these lines, compute the x-dimension that the lines will be repeated across, the distance between each line, and the length of each line. All of the lines will be drawn along the y-axis.

These are computed as:

```
line length =
  Y side of the boundary
X dimension =
  X side of the boundary
distance between lines =
  X dimension / (number of lines - 1)
```

The general outline for this function is:

```
(prog01 ()
 ; get input
 ; compute line length
 ; compute distance between lines
 ; set initial line start point and
 ;  X coordinate
 (repeat for number of lines
  ; compute endpoint for line
  ; draw line
  ; increment the X coordinate
 ; define next start point for line
 )
)
```

Completed functions dtr, rtd, and PROG01:

```
;--------------------------------
(defun dtr (a) (* pi (/ a 180.0)))
(defun rtd (a) (/ (* a 180.0) pi))
;--------------------------------
 (defun prog01 ()
 (graphscr)
 ; set extrude height
 (command ".ELEV" 0.0 0.0)
 ; get boundary points and
 ; parameters
 (prompt "\nPROG01:")
 (setq spnt
   (getpoint
    "\nPick start point:"))
 (setq cpnt
   (getcorner spnt
   "\nPick endpoint:"))
 (setq numtimes
   (getint
   "\nEnter number of lines:"))
 ; compute line length, width of
 ; boundary
 (setq linelen
   (- (nth 1 cpnt) (nth 1 spnt)))
 ; compute increment across boundary
 (setq xinc (/ (- (nth 0 cpnt)
   (nth 0 spnt)) (- numtimes 1)))
 ; set first point and first x coord
 (setq xpnt spnt)
 (setq xpt (nth 0 spnt))
 ; loop to repeat lines
 (repeat numtimes
  ; compute endpoint
  (setq epnt (polar
    xpnt (dtr 90) linelen))
  ; draw line
  (command ".LINE" xpnt epnt "")
  ; inc x coord
  (setq xpt (+ xpt xinc))
  (setq xpnt (list
    xpt (nth 1 xpnt) (nth 2 xpnt)))
 )
 (princ)
)
;--------------------------------
```

Save the file and execute PROG01 for a series of values. Review the structure of this function, including the way the x-coordinate is computed and modified in the loop. The ELEV command is executed to reset the current elevation and thickness.

Convert the lines into planes

Copy PROG01 to PROG02. Add a thickness to the lines to extrude them into three dimensions. AutoCAD has a simple feature for extruding objects when a thickness is specified.

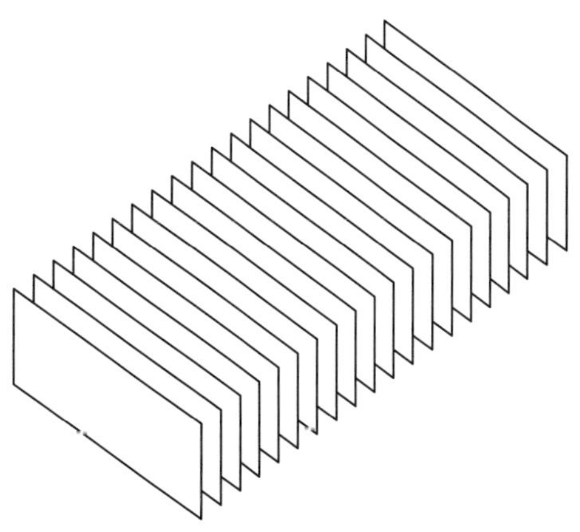

PROG02: convert lines to planes

Modify the input for PROG02 by adding a prompt to get the height of the line extrusion:

```
(setq zheight
  (getdist spnt
  "\nEnter height:"))
```

Set the height of each line by adding the following command prior to drawing the line:

```
(command ".ELEV"  0.0 zheight)
```

Both elevation and thickness are set with the ELEV command. Note that the line thickness is interpreted as height and that planes do not have a thickness or width dimension. Consider how they could be represented as solid planes with a width.

Completed function PROG02:

```
;----------------------------------
(defun prog02 ()
 (graphscr)
 ; set extrude height
 (command ".ELEV" 0.0 0.0)
 ; get boundary points and
 ; parameters
 (prompt "\nPROG02:")
 (setq spnt
   (getpoint
   "\nPick start point:"))
 (setq cpnt
   (getcorner spnt
   "\nPick endpoint:"))
 (setq zheight
   (getdist spnt
   "\nEnter Height:"))
 (setq numtimes (getint
   "\nEnter number of lines:"))
 ; compute line length, width of
 ; boundary
 (setq linelen
   (- (nth 1 cpnt) (nth 1 spnt)))
 ; compute increment across boundary
 (setq xinc (/ (- (nth 0 cpnt)
   (nth 0 spnt)) (- numtimes 1)))
 ; set first point and first x coord
 (setq xpnt spnt)
 (setq xpt (nth 0 spnt))
 ; loop to repeat lines
 (repeat numtimes
  ; compute endpoint
  (setq epnt (polar
    xpnt (dtr 90) linelen))
  ; set extrude height
  (command ".ELEV" 0.0 zheight)
  ; draw line
  (command ".LINE" xpnt epnt "")
  ; inc x coord
  (setq xpt (+ xpt xinc))
  (setq xpnt (list
    xpt (nth 1 xpnt) (nth 2 xpnt)))
 )
 ; set extrude height
 (command ".ELEV" 0.0 0.0)
 (princ)
)
;----------------------------------
```

Note that the thickness is reset to zero at the end of the function by the ELEV command.

Vary the length of the plane and articulate the far edges of these planes

A number of approaches could be taken to vary the length of each plane: a simple increase or decrease from start to end (or to the midpoint of the boundary); or a simple mathematical function to vary the length, in this case using the sine function.

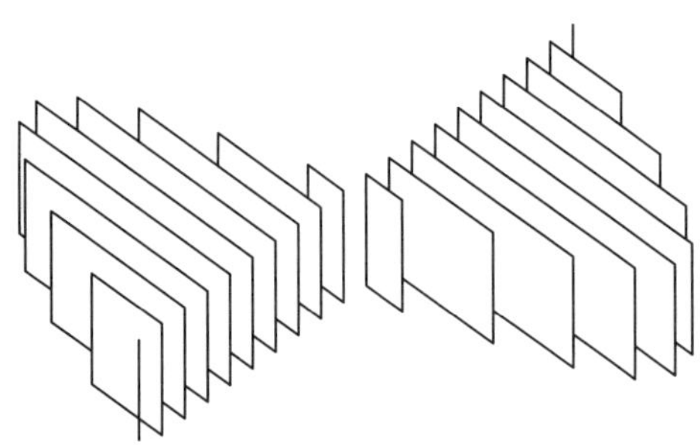

PROG03: vary length of each plane by the sine function

Copy PROG02 to PROG03. Vary the length of each line by multiplying the original line length by the sine of an angle. Assume that the angle covers 360 degrees over the repetition of lines.

Next:

* Create a variable that computes an angle-increment based on the number of lines specified.

* Create a variable to keep track of the current angle and initialize it to zero.

* Modify the line-length by the sine of the angle; the angle is in degrees.

* Increment the angle value after the line is drawn.

Determine which of the new variables should be integer or real, and if they are created or used before or within the loop. Notice that the total angle is set to 360.0, not 360, (a real number, not an integer). What happens when an integer is specified? Try it for an even and odd number of lines.

Completed function PROG03:

```
;----------------------------------
(defun prog03 ()
 (graphscr)
 ; set extrude height
 (command ".ELEV" 0.0 0.0)
 ; get boundary points and
 ; parameters
 (prompt "\nPROG03:")
 (setq spnt
   (getpoint "\nPick start point:"))
 (setq cpnt
   (getcorner spnt
   "\nPick endpoint:"))
 (setq zheight
   (getdist spnt "\nEnter Height:"))
 (setq numtimes
   (getint
   "\nEnter number of lines:"))
 ; compute line length, width of
 ; boundary
 (setq linelen
   (- (nth 1 cpnt) (nth 1 spnt)))
 ; compute increment across boundary
 (setq xinc (/ (- (nth 0 cpnt)
   (nth 0 spnt)) (- numtimes 1)))
 ; computer ang inc
 (setq anginc
   (/ 360.0 (- numtimes 1)))
 ; set first point and first x coord
 (setq xpnt spnt)
 (setq xpt (nth 0 spnt))
 ; start ang
 (setq ang 0)
 ; loop to repeat lines
 (repeat numtimes
  ; compute line length
  (setq newlinelen
    (* linelen (sin (dtr ang))))
  ; compute endpoint
  (setq epnt (polar
    xpnt (dtr 90) newlinelen))
  ; set extrude height
  (command ".ELEV" 0.0 zheight)
  ; draw line
  (command ".LINE" xpnt epnt "")
  ; inc x coord
  (setq xpt (+ xpt xinc))
  (setq xpnt (list
    xpt (nth 1 xpnt) (nth 2 xpnt)))
  ; inc ang
  (setq ang (+ ang anginc))
 )
 ; set extrude height
 (command ".ELEV" 0.0 0.0)
 (princ)
)
;----------------------------------
```

Notice that values of the sine function become zero, so that the plane-length is zero. Also note that this function generates negative values, forcing the plane to be outside of the original boundary selected.

Vary the length of the plane by the cosine function

Copy PROG03 to PROG04. Modify the line-length computation by changing the sine function to the cosine function.

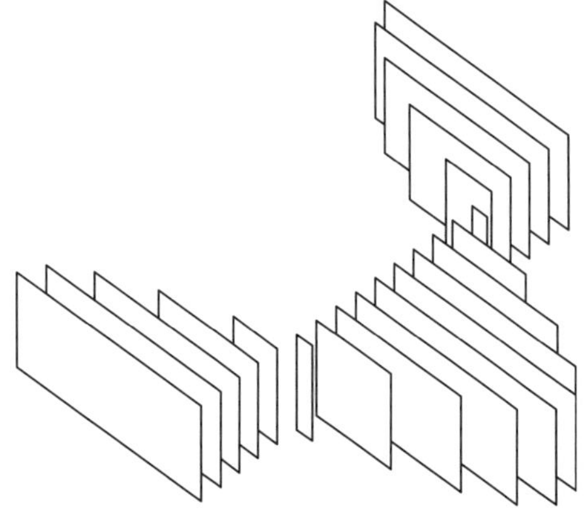

PROG04: vary length of each plane by the cosine function

Change the line-length computation from:

```
; compute line length
(setq newlinelen
  (* linelen (sin (dtr ang))))
```

To:

```
; compute line length
(setq newlinelen
  (* linelen (cos (dtr ang))))
```

Note that the lengths of the planes also go to zero and that they extend outside of the boundary, as they did previously. What other mathematical functions could be used? What if we used some of those mentioned in Chapter 4?

Modify the line-length computation so that it stays within the boundary

Copy PROG04 to PROG05. Modify the line-length computation using the absolute value of the cosine function.

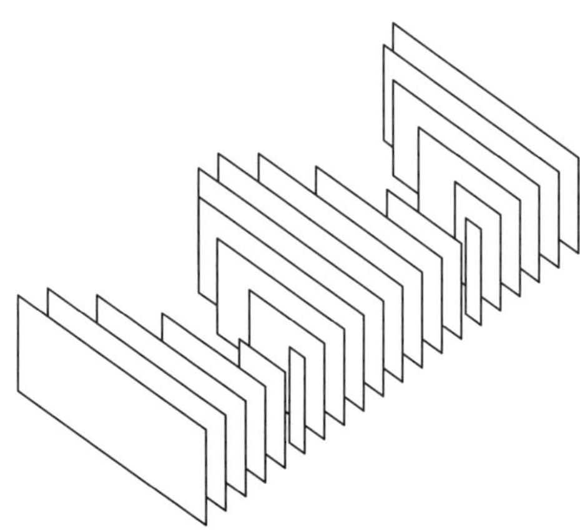

PROG05: vary length of each plane by the absolute value of the cosine function

Change the line-length computation from:

```
; compute line length
(setq newlinelen
  (* linelen (cos (dtr ang))))
```

To:

```
; compute line length
(setq newlinelen
  (* linelen (abs (cos (dtr ang)))))
```

This step considers the use of symmetry so that you only have to develop half of the form, where the bottom edge becomes the centerline. The issue of zero line-lengths remains. An alternative is to find a mathematical function that stays inside of the boundary, but it is possible to use an absolute value with any function.

Modify the line length so part of it always remains

Copy PROG05 to PROG06. Modify the line-length computation so that only one quarter of the length is determined by the cosine function and the remaining three quarters of the length is based on the original length specified.

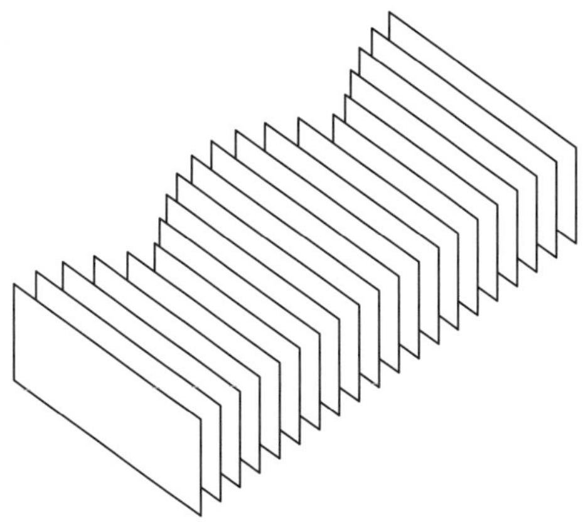

PROG06. keep a portion of the line length

Change the line-length computation from:

```
; compute line length
(setq newlinelen
  (* linelen (abs (cos (dtr ang)))))
```

To:

```
; compute line length
(setq linepart1
  (* linelen linefact))
(setq linepart2
  (* (* linelen (- 1.0 linefact))
  (abs (cos (dtr ang)))))
(setq newlinelen
  (+ linepart1 linepart2))
```

Once this modification is working, further modify the program by adding an input that determines what this ratio should be.

For example:

```
(setq linefact
  (getreal
  "\nEnter keep line factor:"))
```

Modify the line-length computation to use this entered value, not the constants already there. Since the planes tended to decrease to zero, a length-factor is added to control the minimum depth of the edges. Execute this function for a number of values.

Completed function PROG06:

```
;----------------------------------
(defun prog06 ()
 (graphscr)
 ; set extrude height
 (command ".ELEV" 0.0 0.0)
 ; get boundary points and
 ; parameters
 (prompt "\nPROG06:")
 (setq spnt
   (getpoint "\nPick start point:"))
 (setq cpnt
   (getcorner spnt
   "\nPick endpoint:"))
 (setq zheight
   (getdist spnt "\nEnter Height:"))
 (setq numtimes
   (getint
   "\nEnter number of lines:"))
 (setq linefact
   (getreal
   "\nEnter keep line factor:"))
 ; compute line length, width of
 ; boundary
 (setq linelen
   (- (nth 1 cpnt) (nth 1 spnt)))
 ; compute increment across boundary
 (setq xinc (/ (- (nth 0 cpnt)
   (nth 0 spnt)) (- numtimes 1)))
 ; computer ang inc
 (setq anginc
```

```
    (/ 360.0 (- numtimes 1)))
  ; set first point and first x coord
  (setq xpnt spnt)
  (setq xpt (nth 0 spnt))
  ; start ang
  (setq ang 0)
  ; loop to repeat lines
  (repeat numtimes
   ; compute line length
   (setq linepart1
     (* linelen linefact))
   (setq linepart2
     (* (* linelen (- 1.0 linefact))
     (abs (cos (dtr ang)))))
   (setq newlinelen
     (+ linepart1 linepart2))
   ; compute endpoint
   (setq epnt (polar
    xpnt (dtr 90) newlinelen))
   ; set extrude height
   (command ".ELEV" 0.0 zheight)
   ; draw line
   (command ".LINE" xpnt epnt "")
   ; inc x coord
   (setq xpt (+ xpt xinc))
   (setq xpnt (list
    xpt (nth 1 xpnt) (nth 2 xpnt)))
   ; inc ang
   (setq ang (+ ang anginc))
  )
  ; set extrude height
  (command ".ELEV" 0.0 0.0)
  (princ)
)
;----------------------------------
```

Modify the included angle for the curve

Copy PROG06 to PROG07. The current version is based on computing the cosine through 360 degrees. Modify PROG07 to consider any multiple of 360 degrees.

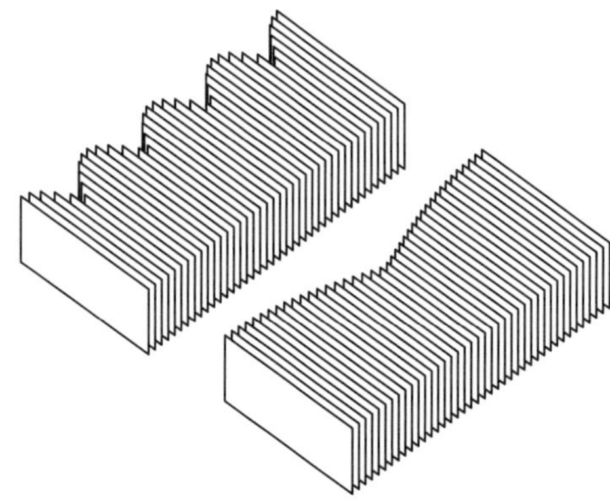

PROG07: for 2.0 and 0.5 curve cycles

Add input to get the number of cycles:

```
(setq numcycles
  (getreal
  "\nEnter number of curve cycles:"))
```

Compute the total angle by multiplying this factor by 360. Try values less than and greater than 1.0.

Change the angle increment from:

```
; computer ang inc
(setq anginc
  (/ 360.0 (- numtimes 1)))
```

To:

```
; computer ang inc
 (setq anginc (/ (* 360.0 numcycles)
   (- numtimes 1)))
```

This step adds more control over the edges of the planes. Note that the curve still starts at zero degrees. An alternate method is to input start and end angles for the curve.

Vary the height of the planes

Copy PROG07 to PROG08. Use the same type of computations used for line-length to modify the height of the line. The new height becomes the current ELEV command thickness-value.

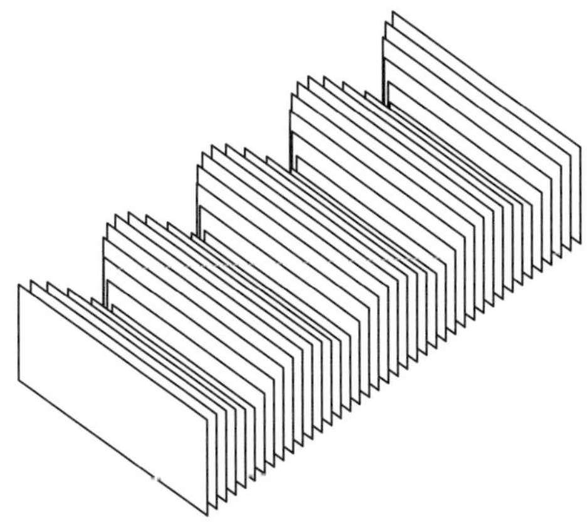

PROG08: vary the height of each plane

Change the setting of the plane height from:

```
; set extrude height
(command ".ELEV" 0.0 zheight)
```

To:

```
; compute height
(setq linepart1
  (* zheight linefact))
(setq linepart2
  (* (* zheight (- 1.0 linefact))
  (abs (cos (dtr ang)))))
(setq newzheight
  (+ linepart1 linepart2))
; set extrude height
(command ".ELEV" 0.0 newzheight)
```

Both length and height are still articulated by the cosine curve.

Mirror the planes

Copy PROG08 to PROG09. Modify the function to mirror all of the planes across the lower edge. Review the method used to draw the current line.

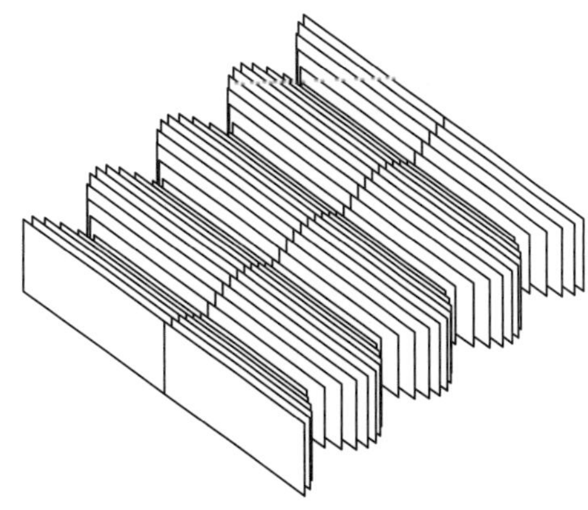

PROG09: mirror the planes

Change the computation of the line endpoint from:

```
; compute endpoint
(setq epnt (polar xpnt
  (dtr 90) newlinelen))
```

And the drawing of the line from:

```
; draw line
(command ".LINE" xpnt epnt "")
```

To:

```
; compute endpoint
(setq epnt1 (polar xpnt
  (dtr 90) newlinelen))
(setq epnt2 (polar xpnt
  (dtr 270) newlinelen))
```

And:

```
; draw line
(command ".LINE" xpnt epnt1 "")
(command ".LINE" xpnt epnt2 "")
```

This step adds symmetry to the form. The lower edge now becomes the centerline.

Vary the height differently than the edges

Copy PROG09 to PROG10. Modify the program by changing the cosine function in the computation of the height to the sine function. Leave the length computation using the cosine function.

Change the computation of the height from:

```
(setq linepart2
  (* (* zheight (- 1.0 linefact))
  (abs (cos (dtr ang)))))
```

To:

```
(setq linepart2
  (* (* zheight (- 1.0 linefact))
  (abs (sin (dtr ang))))
```

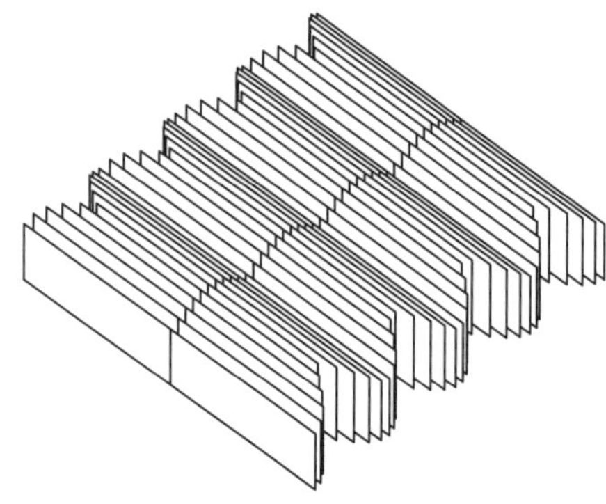

PROG10: vary height differently from edge

Switch the curve functions for the height and length

Copy PROG10 to PROG11. Modify the function by switching the cosine and sine functions in the computation of line-length and height.

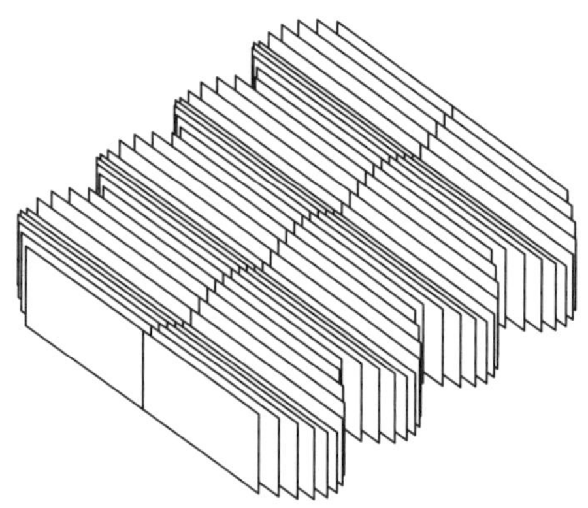

PROG11: switch functions on length and height

Convert planes to frames

Copy PROG11 to PROG12.

Instead of using thickness to extrude lines into planes, replace the planes with frames: two horizontal lines for the top members and two vertical lines at either side for the columns.

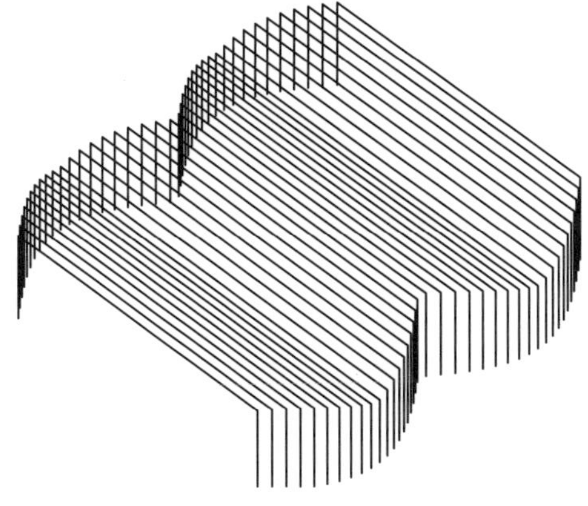

PROG12: convert planes to a frame

Compute all five points and use the 3DPOLY, PLINE, or LINE command to create the frame. PLINE only supports points in a single plane, and LINES are individual entities. 3DPOLY is the preferred method.

Remove the ELEV command from the body of the loop and replace the LINE command with the 3DPOLY command.

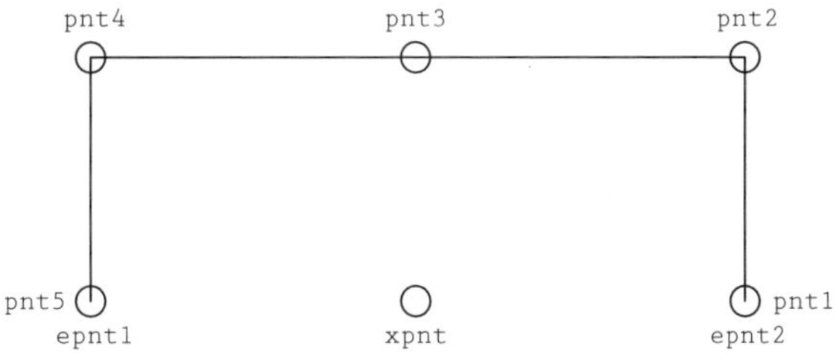

PROG11: relationship of plane points to frame points

Note how the frame points are computed based on the points defining each plane:

```
; compute frame points
(setq pnt1 epnt2)
(setq pnt2 (list
  (nth 0 epnt2) (nth 1 epnt2)
  (+ (nth 2 epnt2) newzheight)))
(setq pnt3 (list
  (nth 0 xpnt) (nth 1 xpnt)
  (+ (nth 2 xpnt) newzheight)))
(setq pnt4 (list
  (nth 0 epnt1) (nth 1 epnt1)
  (+ (nth 2 epnt1) newzheight)))
(setq pnt5 epnt1)
; draw 3DPOLY
(command ".3DPOLY" pnt1 pnt2 pnt3
  pnt4 pnt5 "")
```

Completed function PROG12:

```
;----------------------------------
(defun prog12 ()
 (graphscr)
 ; set extrude height
 (command ".ELEV" 0.0 0.0)
 ; get boundary points and
 ; parameters
 (prompt "\nPROG12:")
 (setq spnt
   (getpoint "\nPick start point:"))
 (setq cpnt
   (getcorner spnt
   "\nPick endpoint:"))
 (setq zheight
   (getdist spnt "\nEnter Height:"))
 (setq numtimes
   (getint
   "\nEnter number of lines:"))
 (setq linefact
   (getreal
   "\nEnter keep line factor:"))
 (setq numcycles
   (getreal
   "\nNumber of curve cycles:"))
 ; compute line length, width of
 ; boundary
 (setq linelen
```

```
  (- (nth 1 cpnt) (nth 1 spnt)))
; compute increment across boundary
(setq xinc (/ (- (nth 0 cpnt)
  (nth 0 spnt)) (- numtimes 1)))
; computer ang inc
(setq anginc (/ (* 360.0 numcycles)
  (- numtimes 1)))
; set first point and first x coord
(setq xpnt spnt)
(setq xpt (nth 0 spnt))
; start ang
(setq ang 0)
; loop to repeat lines
(repeat numtimes
 ; compute line length
 (setq linepart1
   (* linelen linefact))
 (setq linepart2
   (* (* linelen (- 1.0 linefact))
   (abs (sin (dtr ang)))))
 (setq newlinelen
   (+ linepart1 linepart2))
 ; compute endpoint
 (setq epnt1 (polar
   xpnt (dtr 90) newlinelen))
 (setq epnt2 (polar
   xpnt (dtr 270) newlinelen))
 ; compute height
 (setq linepart1
   (* zheight linefact))
 (setq linepart2
   (* (* zheight (- 1.0 linefact))
   (abs (cos (dtr ang)))))
 (setq newzheight
   (+ linepart1 linepart2))
 ; compute frame points
 (setq pnt1 epnt2)
 (setq pnt2 (list
   (nth 0 epnt2) (nth 1 epnt2)
   (+ (nth 2 epnt2) newzheight)))
 (setq pnt3 (list
   (nth 0 xpnt) (nth 1 xpnt)
   (+ (nth 2 xpnt) newzheight)))
 (setq pnt4 (list
   (nth 0 epnt1) (nth 1 epnt1)
   (+ (nth 2 epnt1) newzheight)))
 (setq pnt5 epnt1)
 ; draw 3DPOLY
 (command ".3DPOLY" pnt1 pnt2 pnt3
   pnt4 pnt5 "")
 ; inc x coord
 (setq xpt (+ xpt xinc))
 (setq xpnt (list
   xpt (nth 1 xpnt) (nth 2 xpnt)))
 ; inc ang
 (setq ang (+ ang anginc))
)
; set extrude height
(command ".ELEV" 0.0 0.0)
(princ)
)
;---------------------------------
```

Articulate the center-top point of the frame

Copy PROG12 to PROG13. The top member-height is computed by the cosine function. The height is the same value for the edge of the structure as it is for the midpoint. Modify this function to compute a new height for the midpoint based on the sine function, using the same computations as the others.

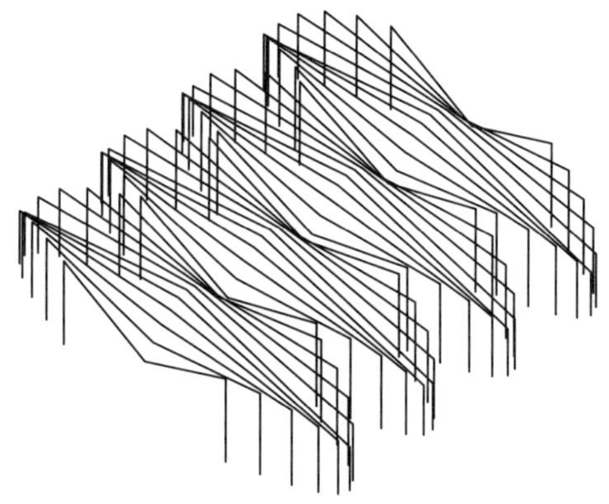

PROG13: add centerpoint to top of frame

After the edge height is computed, add:

```
; compute midpoint height
(setq linepart1
  (* zheight linefact))
(setq linepart2
  (* (* zheight (- 1.0 linefact))
  (abs (sin (dtr ang)))))
(setq newmidzheight
  (+ linepart1 linepart2))
```

Change the setting of the midpoint from:

```
(setq pnt3 (list
  (nth 0 xpnt) (nth 1 xpnt)
  (+ (nth 2 xpnt) newzheight)))
```

To:

```
(setq pnt3 (list
  (nth 0 xpnt) (nth 1 xpnt)
  (+ (nth 2 xpnt) newmidzheight)))
```

At this point, the lengths of the top members are computed by the sine function; the edge height by cosine; and the midpoint height by sine. Another variation is to try cosine, sine, and cosine, respectively. The midpoint height of the frame is independently computed from the edge points.

Add an independent midpoint height

Copy PROG13 to PROG14. The height of the edge and the midpoint are both computed from one entered height. Modify this function to accept two different heights: one for the edge and one for the midpoint. Replace the variable `zheight` with `zedge` and `zmid`, throughout.

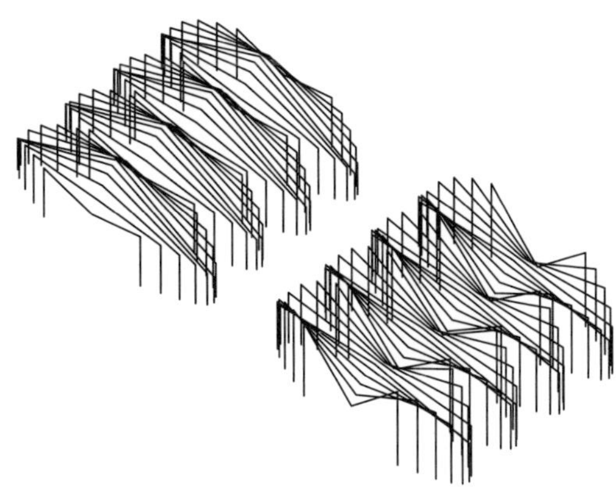

PROG14: separate midpoint frame height

Completed function PROG14:

```
;---------------------------------
(defun prog14 ()
 w(graphscr)
 ; set extrude height
 (command ".ELEV" 0.0 0.0)
 ; get boundary points and
 ; parameters
 (prompt "\nPROG14:")
 (setq spnt
   (getpoint "\nPick start point:"))
 (setq cpnt
   (getcorner spnt
   "\nPick endpoint:"))
 (setq zedge
   (getdist spnt
   "\nEnter edge height:"))
 (setq zmid
   (getdist spnt
   "\nEnter midpoint height:"))
 (setq numtimes
   (getint
   "\nEnter number of lines:"))
 (setq linefact
   (getreal
   "\nEnter keep line factor:"))
 (setq numcycles
```

```
  (getreal
  "\nNumber of curve cycles:"))
; compute line length, width of
; boundary
(setq linelen
  (- (nth 1 cpnt) (nth 1 spnt)))
; compute increment across boundary
(setq xinc (/ (- (nth 0 cpnt)
  (nth 0 spnt)) (- numtimes 1)))
; computer ang inc
(setq anginc (/ (* 360.0 numcycles)
  (- numtimes 1)))
; set first point and first x coord
(setq xpnt spnt)
(setq xpt (nth 0 spnt))
; start ang
(setq ang 0)
; loop to repeat lines
(repeat numtimes
 ; compute line length
 (setq linepart1
   (* linelen linefact))
 (setq linepart2
   (* (* linelen (- 1.0 linefact))
   (abs (sin (dtr ang)))))
 (setq newlinelen
   (+ linepart1 linepart2))
 ; compute endpoint
 (setq epnt1 (polar
   xpnt (dtr 90) newlinelen))
 (setq epnt2 (polar
   xpnt (dtr 270) newlinelen))
 ; compute edge height
 (setq linepart1
   (* zedge linefact))
 (setq linepart2
   (* (* zedge (- 1.0 linefact))
   (abs (cos (dtr ang)))))
 (setq newzedge
   (+ linepart1 linepart2))
 ; compute midpoint height
 (setq linepart1
   (* zmid linefact))
 (setq linepart2
   (* (* zmid (- 1.0 linefact))
   (abs (sin (dtr ang)))))
 (setq newzmid
   (+ linepart1 linepart2))
 ; compute frame points
 (setq pnt1 epnt2)
 (setq pnt2 (list
   (nth 0 epnt2) (nth 1 epnt2)
   (+ (nth 2 epnt2) newzedge)))
 (setq pnt3 (list
   (nth 0 xpnt) (nth 1 xpnt)
   (+ (nth 2 xpnt) newzmid)))
 (setq pnt4 (list
   (nth 0 epnt1) (nth 1 epnt1)
   (+ (nth 2 epnt1) newzedge)))
 (setq pnt5 epnt1)
 ; draw 3DPOLY
 (command ".3DPOLY" pnt1 pnt2 pnt3
   pnt4 pnt5 "")
 ; inc x coord
 (setq xpt (+ xpt xinc))
 (setq xpnt (list
   xpt (nth 1 xpnt) (nth 2 xpnt)))
 ; inc ang
 (setq ang (+ ang anginc))
)
; set extrude height
(command ".ELEV" 0.0 0.0)
(princ)
)
;---------------------------------
```

Set bottom of columns to boundary edge

Copy PROG14 to PROG15. The columns currently start at the edge of the top members and go straight down to the same x and y locations. Modify the base point of the columns, so that it is located along the edge of the boundary first specified. This requires modifying the y-coordinate for both bottom column locations.

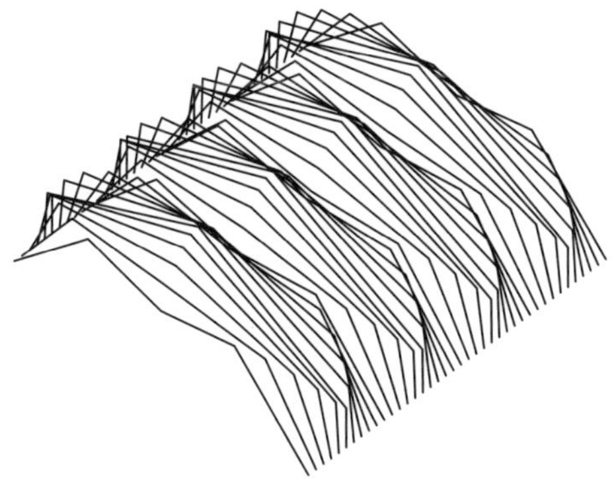

PROG15: modify column-base location to edge

Change the base location of the column from:

```
(setq pnt1 epnt2)
(setq pnt5 epnt1)
```

To:

```
(setq pnt1 (list
  (nth 0 xpnt)
  (- (nth 1 xpnt) linelen)
  (nth 2 xpnt)))
(setq pnt5 (list
  (nth 0 xpnt)
  (+ (nth 1 xpnt) linelen)
  (nth 2 xpnt)))
```

An alternate variation is to set the top of the columns to the edge of the boundary, instead of the bottom of the columns.

PROG15a: modify column-top location to edge

Copy PROG14 to PROG15a. Modify the top point of the columns, so that it is located along the edge of the boundary first specified. This requires modiyfing the y-coordinate for both top-column locations.

Change the top location of the column from:

```
(setq pnt2 (list
  (nth 0 epnt2) (nth 1 epnt2)
  (+ (nth 2 epnt2) newzedge)))
(setq pnt4 (list
  (nth 0 epnt1) (nth 1 epnt1)
  (+ (nth 2 epnt1) newzedge)))
```

To:

```
(setq pnt2 (list
  (nth 0 xpnt)
  (- (nth 1 xpnt) linelen)
  (+ (nth 2 xpnt) newzedge)))
(setq pnt4 (list
  (nth 0 xpnt)
  (+ (nth 1 xpnt) linelen)
  (+ (nth 2 xpnt) newzedge)))
```

Two variations for using the boundary to define the frame.

Convert the frames to a surface

Copy either PROG14, PROG15, or PROG15a to PROG16. These earlier exercises started with lines and then developed into vertical planes and frames. Now, based on the same computed points, replace the frames with a surface. We will use the 3DMESH command to create a single surface from these points.

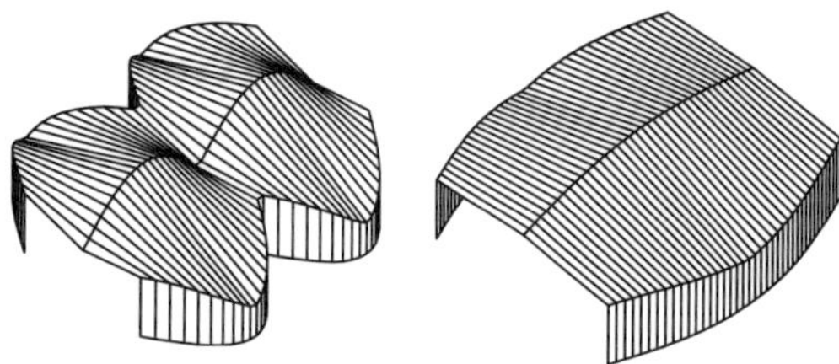

PROG16: convert frame to a surface

Start the 3DMESH command. Just prior to the start of the loop, add:

```
(command ".3DMESH"
  numtimes "5")
```

Remove the 3DPOLY command and replace it with:

```
(command pnt1 pnt2 pnt3 pnt4 pnt5)
```

The five points computed for each frame generated become the section points for the definition of the mesh.

Develop a series of forms by varying the length factor, number of cycles, and angle computation.

Length	Edge	Midpoint
SIN	COS	SIN
COS	SIN	COS
SIN	SIN	SIN
COS	COS	COS
SIN	SIN	COS
COS	COS	SIN
SIN	COS	COS
COS	SIN	SIN

Since the mesh is a single surface, the model will be displayed smooth if rendered.

Convert to a closed surface model. Copy PROG16 to PROG17. Modify the 3DMESH to create surfaces at the bottom and at both ends.

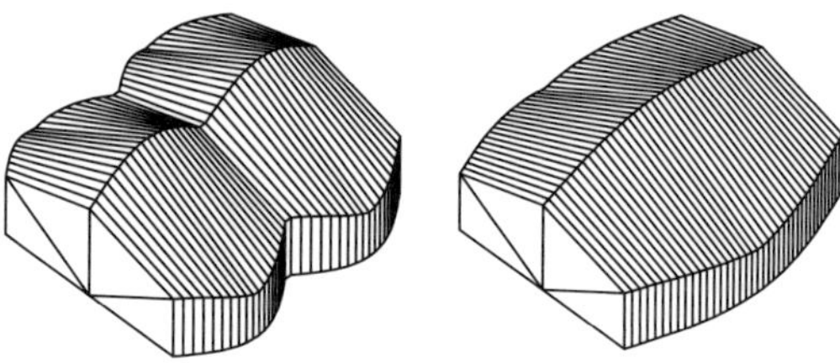

PROG17: close the bottom and ends of the mesh

For the bottom, modify the 3DMESH to 6 points, not 5; the sixth point is the same as the first:

```
(command pnt1 pnt2 pnt3 pnt4
  pnt5 pnt1)
```

This closes the mesh in the y-direction by including a bottom surface. For the ends, use the xpnt immediately before the first frame and directly after the last. Place a counter within the loop. When the counter is at 1, send 3DMESH the following:

```
(command xpnt xpnt xpnt xpnt
   xpnt xpnt)
```

Do the same after the frame points are sent, if the counter is equal to the number of lines.

With the addition of these two sets of six points, the start of the 3DMESH command must also be modified to:

```
(command ".3DMESH"
  (+ numtimes 2) "6")
```

These examples of PROG17 use the dimensions 40 feet x 20 feet; and heights ranging from 10 to 20 feet, and 40 lines.

The closed-surface model, being watertight, can be used in many rapid-prototyping systems.

Completed function PROG17:

```
;-----------------------------------
(defun prog17 ()
 (graphscr)
 ; set extrude height
 (command ".ELEV" 0.0 0.0)
 ; get boundary points and
 ; parameters
 (prompt "\nPROG17:")
 (setq spnt
   (getpoint "\nPick start point:"))
 (setq cpnt
   (getcorner spnt
   "\nPick endpoint:"))
 (setq zedge
   (getdist spnt
   "\nEnter edge height:"))
 (setq zmid
   (getdist spnt
   "\nEnter midpoint height:"))
 (setq numtimes
   (getint
   "\nEnter number of lines:"))
 (setq linefact
   (getreal
   "\nEnter keep line factor:"))
 (setq numcycles
   (getreal
   "\nNumber of curve cycles:"))
 ; compute line length, width of
 ; boundary
 (setq linelen
   (- (nth 1 cpnt) (nth 1 spnt)))
 ; compute increment across boundary
 (setq xinc (/ (- (nth 0 cpnt)
   (nth 0 spnt)) (- numtimes 1)))
 ; computer ang inc
 (setq anginc (/ (* 360.0 numcycles)
   (- numtimes 1)))
 ; set first point and first x coord
 (setq xpnt spnt)
 (setq xpt (nth 0 spnt))
 ; start ang
 (setq ang 0)
 ; start 3DMESH
 (command ".3DMESH"
   (+ numtimes 2) "6")
 ; frame counter
 (setq cnt 0)
 ; loop to repeat lines
 (repeat numtimes
  ; compute line length
  (setq linepart1
    (* linelen linefact))
  (setq linepart2
    (* (* linelen (- 1.0 linefact))
    (abs (sin (dtr ang)))))
  (setq newlinelen
    (+ linepart1 linepart2))
  ; compute endpoint
  (setq epnt1 (polar
   xpnt (dtr 90) newlinelen))
  (setq epnt2 (polar
   xpnt (dtr 270) newlinelen))
  ; compute edge height
  (setq linepart1
    (* zedge linefact))
  (setq linepart2
    (* (* zedge (- 1.0 linefact))
    (abs (cos (dtr ang)))))
  (setq newzedge
    (+ linepart1 linepart2))
  ; compute midpoint height
  (setq linepart1
    (* zmid linefact))
  (setq linepart2
    (* (* zmid (- 1.0 linefact))
    (abs (sin (dtr ang)))))
  (setq newzmid
```

```
    (+ linepart1 linepart2))
  ; compute frame points
  (setq pnt1 epnt2)
  (setq pnt2 (list
    (nth 0 epnt2)
    (nth 1 epnt2)
    (+ (nth 2 epnt2) newzedge)))
  (setq pnt3 (list
    (nth 0 xpnt)
    (nth 1 xpnt)
    (+ (nth 2 xpnt) newzmid)))
  (setq pnt4 (list
    (nth 0 epnt1)
    (nth 1 epnt1)
    (+ (nth 2 epnt1) newzedge)))
  (setq pnt5 epnt1)
  ; inc frames
  (setq cnt (+ cnt 1))
  ; check if before first frame
  (if (= cnt 1) (progn
   ; add front face to mesh
   (command xpnt xpnt xpnt xpnt xpnt
     xpnt xpnt)
  ))
  ; add points to 3DMESH
  (command pnt1 pnt2 pnt3 pnt4
    pnt5 pnt1)
  ; check if before first frame
  (if (= cnt numtimes) (progn
   ; add front face to mesh
   (command xpnt xpnt xpnt xpnt xpnt
     xpnt xpnt)
  ))
  ; inc x coord
  (setq xpt (+ xpt xinc))
  (setq xpnt (list
    xpt (nth 1 xpnt) (nth 2 xpnt)))
  ; inc ang
  (setq ang (+ ang anginc))
 )
 ; set extrude height
 (command ".ELEV" 0.0 0.0)
 (princ)
)
;----------------------------------
```

Add a horizontal offset to the midpoint height

Copy either PROG16 or PROG17 to PROG18. Modify the midpoint to accept a y-offset controlled by a curve.

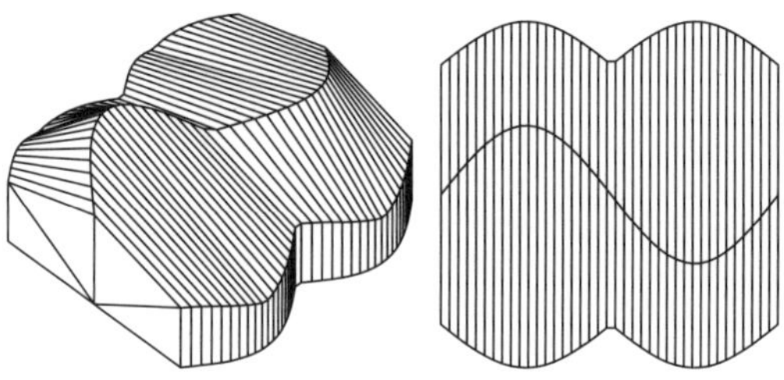

PROG18: horizontal offset to the midpoint height

Add input for an offset:

```
(setq yoff
  (getdist spnt
  "\nEnter midpoint offset:"))
```

Modify the y-coordinate of the midpoint by adding:

```
; compute midpoint offset
(setq newyoff
  (* yoff (sin (dtr ang))))
```

Change the setting of the midpoint from:

```
(setq pnt3 (list
  (nth 0 xpnt) (nth 1 xpnt)
  (+ (nth 2 xpnt) newzmid)))
```

To:

```
(setq pnt3 (list
  (nth 0 xpnt)
  (+ (nth 1 xpnt) newyoff)
  (+ (nth 2 xpnt) newzmid)))
```

The absolute value of the function is not used in the offset computation because it should be able to be positive or negative, right or left of the midpoint.

Completed function PROG18:

```
;----------------------------------
(defun prog18 ()
 (graphscr)
 ; set extrude height
 (command ".ELEV" 0.0 0.0)
 ; get boundary points and
 ; parameters
 (prompt "\nPROG18:")
 (setq spnt
   (getpoint "\nPick start point:"))
 (setq cpnt
   (getcorner spnt
   "\nPick endpoint:"))
 (setq zedge
   (getdist spnt
   "\nEnter edge height:"))
 (setq zmid
   (getdist spnt
   "\nEnter midpoint height:"))
 (setq yoff
   (getdist spnt
   "\nEnter midpoint offset:"))
 (setq numtimes
   (getint
   "\nEnter number of lines:"))
 (setq linefact
   (getreal
   "\nEnter keep line factor:"))
 (setq numcycles
   (getreal
   "\nNumber of curve cycles:"))
 ; compute line length, width of
 ; boundary
 (setq linelen
   (- (nth 1 cpnt) (nth 1 spnt)))
 ; compute increment across boundary
 (setq xinc (/ (- (nth 0 cpnt)
   (nth 0 spnt)) (- numtimes 1)))
 ; computer ang inc
 (setq anginc (/ (* 360.0 numcycles)
   (- numtimes 1)))
 ; set first point and first x coord
 (setq xpnt spnt)
(setq xpt (nth 0 spnt))
; start ang
(setq ang 0)
; start 3DMESH
(command ".3DMESH"
  (+ numtimes 2) "6")
; frame counter
(setq cnt 0)
; loop to repeat lines
(repeat numtimes
 ; compute line length
 (setq linepart1
   (* linelen linefact))
 (setq linepart2
   (* (* linelen (- 1.0 linefact))
   (abs (sin (dtr ang)))))
 (setq newlinelen
   (+ linepart1 linepart2))
 ; compute endpoint
 (setq epnt1 (polar
  xpnt (dtr 90) newlinelen))
 (setq epnt2 (polar
  xpnt (dtr 270) newlinelen))
 ; compute edge height
 (setq linepart1
   (* zedge linefact))
 (setq linepart2
   (* (* zedge (- 1.0 linefact))
   (abs (cos (dtr ang)))))
 (setq newzedge
   (+ linepart1 linepart2))
 ; compute midpoint height
 (setq linepart1
   (* zmid linefact))
 (setq linepart2
   (* (* zmid (- 1.0 linefact))
   (abs (sin (dtr ang)))))
 (setq newzmid
   (+ linepart1 linepart2))
 ; compute midpoint offset
 (setq newyoff
   (* yoff (sin (dtr ang))))
 ; compute frame points
 (setq pnt1 epnt2)
 (setq pnt2 (list
   (nth 0 epnt2)
   (nth 1 epnt2)
   (+ (nth 2 epnt2) newzedge)))
 (setq pnt3 (list
```

```
    (nth 0 xpnt)
    (+ (nth 1 xpnt) newyoff)
    (+ (nth 2 xpnt) newzmid)))
  (setq pnt4 (list
    (nth 0 epnt1)
    (nth 1 epnt1)
    (+ (nth 2 epnt1) newzedge)))
  (setq pnt5 epnt1)
  ; inc frames
  (setq cnt (+ cnt 1))
  ; check if before first frame
  (if (= cnt 1) (progn
   ; add front face to mesh
   (command xpnt xpnt xpnt xpnt
     xpnt xpnt xpnt)
  ))
  ; add points to 3DMESH
  (command pnt1 pnt2 pnt3 pnt4
    pnt5 pnt1)
  ; check if before first frame
  (if (= cnt numtimes) (progn
   ; add front face to mesh
   (command xpnt xpnt xpnt xpnt
     xpnt xpnt xpnt)
  ))
  ; inc x coord
  (setq xpt (+ xpt xinc))
  (setq xpnt (list
    xpt (nth 1 xpnt) (nth 2 xpnt)))
  ; inc ang
  (setq ang (+ ang anginc))
 )
 ; set extrude height
 (command ".ELEV" 0.0 0.0)
 (princ)
)
;--------------------------------
```

Other curve functions

A number of different curve variations could be explored beyond the basic sine and cosine functions. Here are a few to start with.

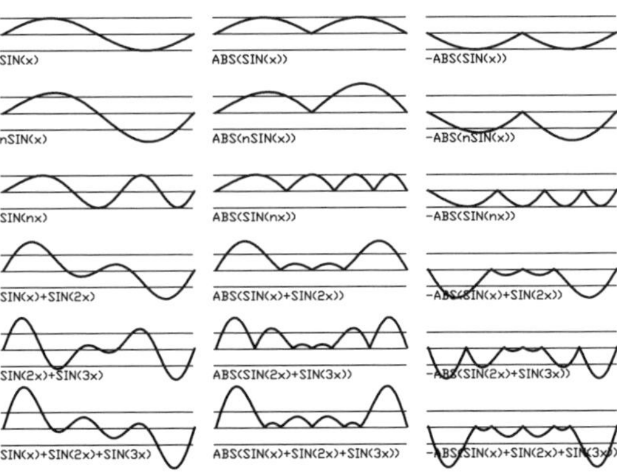

Variations of the sine function

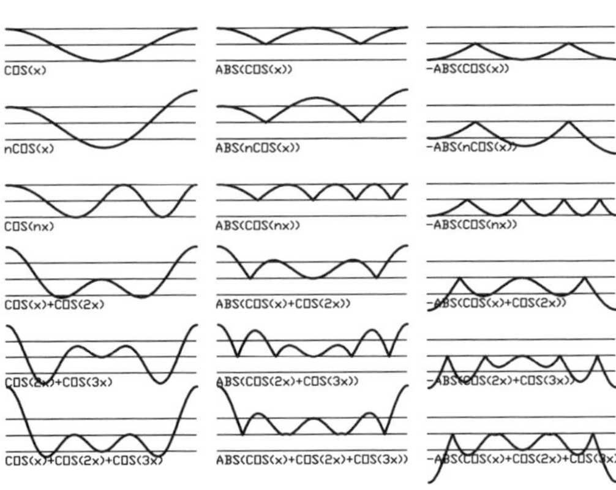

Variations of the cosine function

To be able to explore some mathematical functions of your own, add the DOCURVE function.

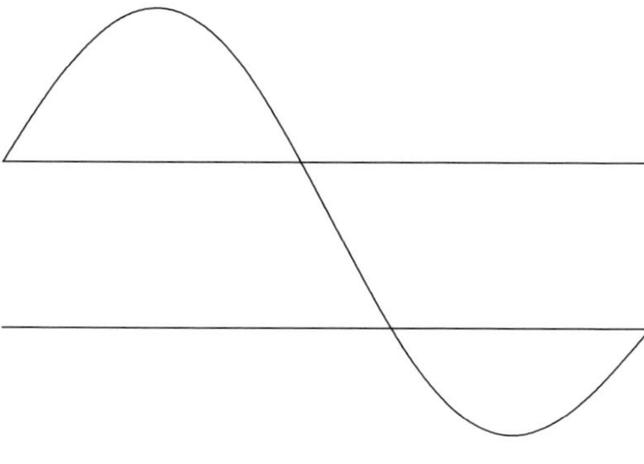

(+ (sin (dtr ang)) (cos (dtr (* 0.25 ang)))) from: 0 to: 360

DOCURVE example

Completed function DOCURVE:

```
;-----------------------------
(defun docurve ()
 ; get centerpoint and dimensions
 (prompt "\nDraw curve by entered
   expression")
 (setq pt0
   (getpoint "\nPick start:"))
 (setq cexp
   (getstring
   "\nEnter curve expression:"))
 (setq sang
   (getint
   "\nEnter start angle:"))
 (setq eang
   (getint "\nEnter end angle:"))
 ; set Y and X dims
 (setq ymax 50.0)
 (setq xmax 200.0)
 ; draw axis lines
 (setq pt1 (list
   (+ (nth 0 pt0) xmax)
   (nth 1 pt0) 0))
 (command ".LINE" pt0 pt1 "")
 (setq pt1 (list
   (nth 0 pt0)
   (+ (nth 1 pt0) ymax) 0))
 (setq pt2 (list
   (+ (nth 0 pt0) xmax)
   (+ (nth 1 pt0) ymax) 0))
 (command ".LINE" pt1 pt2 "")
 (setq pt1 (list
   (nth 0 pt0)
   (- (nth 1 pt0) ymax) 0))
 (setq pt2 (list
   (+ (nth 0 pt0) xmax)
   (- (nth 1 pt0) ymax) 0))
 (command ".LINE" pt1 pt2 "")
 (setq ytext
   (* (/ ymax 10.0) 0.8))
 (setq pt1 (list
   (nth 0 pt0)
   (- (- (nth 1 pt0) ymax) ytext)
   0))
 (setq ytext
   (* (/ ymax 10.0) 0.5))
 (setq stext
   (strcat cexp " from: "
   (itoa sang) " to: " (itoa eang)))
 (command ".TEXT" pt1 ytext "0.0"
    stext)
 (command ".ZOOM" "e")
 ; ang inc
 (setq anginc 1.0)
 (setq ang sang)
 ; start and X
 (setq xinc (/ xmax (- eang sang)))
 (setq xpt 0.0)
 ; start
 (command ".PLINE")
 (while (<= ang eang)
  ; compute height
  (setq ypt
    (* ymax (eval (read cexp))))
  ; add point
  (command (list
    (+ (nth 0 pt0) xpt)
    (+ (nth 1 pt0) ypt) 0))
  ; inc ang and x coord
  (setq ang (+ ang anginc))
```

```
    (setq xpt (+ xpt xinc))
  )
  ; close
  (command "")
  (command ".ZOOM" "e"
    ".ZOOM" "0.9x")
  (princ)
)
;-----------------------------------
```

The DOCURVE function is based on PROG04g (in Chapter 4), the function for generating a mesh based on an entered function. It draws any entered expression using a start-and-end angle in degrees. The expression has to use valid AutoLISP syntax and variables and functions that are already available when DOCURVE executes. These include:

* Functions: dtr, sin, cos, and abs
* Operations: +, -, / and *
* Variables: ang
* Constants: any valid numeric constant

Some examples of possible expressions include:

```
(sin (* 1.00 (dtr ang)))
(abs (sin (* 1.00 (dtr ang))))
(* (abs (* 1.00
  (sin (dtr ang)))) -1)
```

Or:

```
(+ (sin (* 1.00 (dtr ang)))
  (cos (* 2.00 (dtr ang))))
(+ (* 1.00 (sin (dtr ang)))
   (* 2.00 (cos (dtr ang))))
```

Within the DOCURVE function, note the use of the TEXT command to document the parameters executed. These are included at the bottom of the curve drawing.

Documenting multiple sets of parameters

Another issue to consider is how to organize a set of trials for a particular series of forms. One way is to execute functions through script files. A script file contains the keyboard entries for a series of steps. These steps can include AutoCAD commands, AutoLISP commands, or input values asked for by an AutoLISP function.

For example, the following script file was created using Microsoft Notepad and saved as DOCURVE01.SCR:

```
;-----------------------------------
; docurve01
(command ".ERASE" "all" "")
(docurve)
;Pick start:
0,0,0
;Curve expression
(sin (* 1.00 (dtr ang)))
;Start angle:
0
;End angle:
360
;-----------------------------------
```

The AutoCAD RUN SCRIPT command is used to start a script file. It is found under the Tools, and Run menu options.

This script executes PROG18 for two different forms:

```
;-----------------------------------
;Script for PROG18
(command "erase" "all" "")
(prog18)
;lower-left
0',0'
;upper-right
@40',20'
;edge height
10'
;center height
20'
;mid offset
```

```
0'
;lines
40
;keep line factor
0.75
;cycles
1.0
(prog18)
;lower-left
0',50'
;upper-right
@40',20'
;edge height
10'
;center height
20'
;mid offset
4'
;lines
40
;keep line factor
0.75
;cycles
0.5
view
swiso
zoom
e
hide
;---------------------------------
```

All the lines starting with " ; " are comments. Blank lines are treated as the Enter key. All text lines are typed starting in column one, without spaces at the end of any line. The last line is empty, with no spaces. Note that this script file executes function PROG18 twice, and viewing commands are included at the end.

CH05A.LSP must be loaded before these scripts are executed.

Documenting the parameters embedded in the drawing

For PROG18a, add the TEXT command to PROG18 to document the parameters used.

After the loop at the end of the function, insert the following:

```
; design parameters
 (setq xdim
   (- (nth 0 cpnt) (nth 0 spnt)))
 (setq ydim
   (- (nth 1 cpnt) (nth 1 spnt)))
 (setq textpt (list
   (- (nth 0 spnt) 18)
   (+ (nth 1 spnt) ydim) 0.0))
 (command ".TEXT" textpt 12 270
   (strcat "PROG18a"
   "/" (rtos xdim 4 2) " X "
   (rtos ydim 4 2)
   "/Edge Hght=" (rtos zedge 4 2)
   "/Mid Hght=" (rtos zmid 4 2)
 ))
 (setq textpt (list
   (- (nth 0 textpt) 18)
   (nth 1 textpt) 0.0))
 (command ".TEXT" textpt 12 270
   (strcat "/Lines="
   (rtos numtimes 2 0)
   "/Line Factor=" (rtos linefact 2 2)
   "/Cycles=" (rtos numcycles 2 2)
))
```

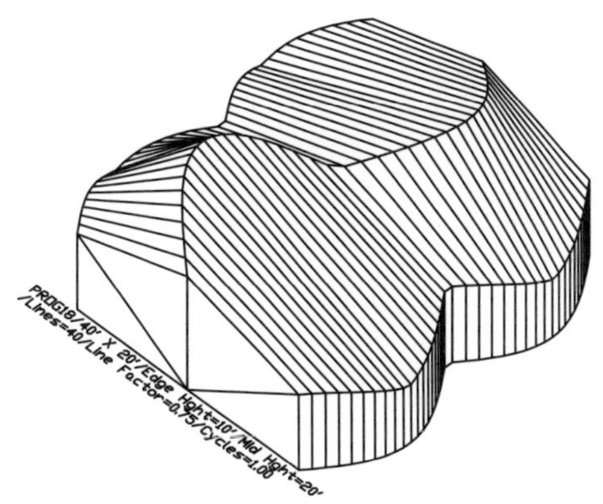

PROG18a: parameter description included as text

Note how the text-location points are computed, how the text is constructed using the `rtos` function, and how it is made into a single string using the `strcat` function. Also review the `TEXT` command parameters: how the text size of 12 inches and orientation of 270 degrees are specified. The function can fully identify all parameters, or it can simply identify the name of the function or some other variation by only showing the values.

For example:

```
PROG18a/40' x 20'/10'/20'/40/0.75/1.00
```

Convert a horizontal form to a vertical form

Another way to view this linear form is to consider it vertical. This can be done by rotating the entire form into a vertical position.

Copy `PROG17` or `PROG18` to `PROG19`, and add the following after the loop completes:

```
(command ".ZOOM" "e")
(command ".ROTATE3D"
  "all" "" "Y" "" "-90")
(command ".ZOOM" "e")
```

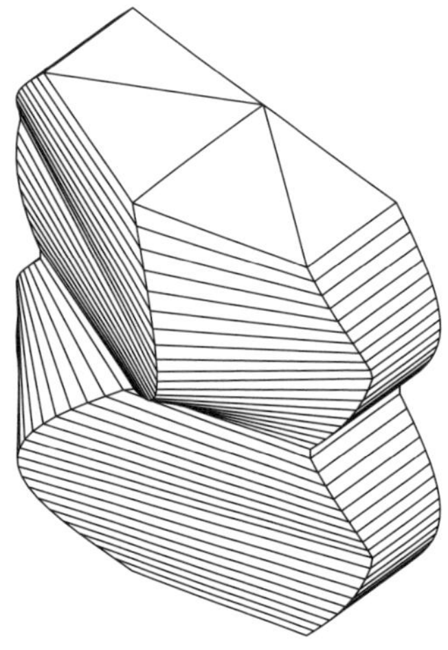

`PROG19`: converting to a vertical linear form

Vertical variation with symmetry

Another vertical variation is to mirror the entire form below the xy-plane and then rotate it vertically.

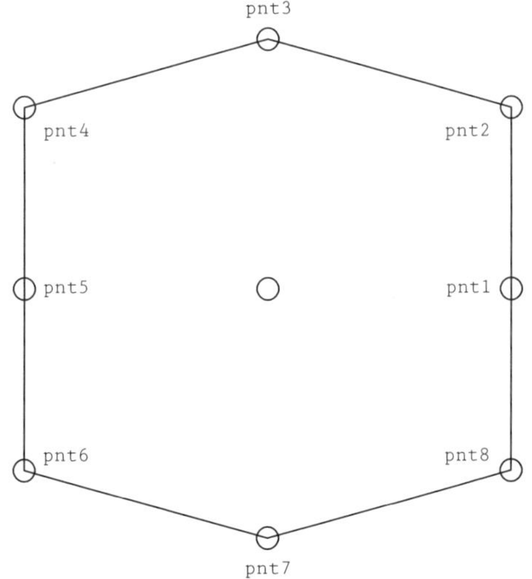

`PROG20`: additional points for symmetry

Additional points 6, 7, and 8 are computed. The `3DMESH` command parameters are changed to include three more points for every section.

Modify the start of the `3DMESH` command to:

```
; start 3DMESH
(command ".3DMESH"
   (+ numtimes 2) "9")
```

Add these three points:

```
(setq pnt6 (list
   (nth 0 pnt5) (nth 1 pnt5)
   (- newzedge)))
(setq pnt7 (list
  (nth 0 pnt3) (nth 1 pnt3)
  (- newzmid)))
(setq pnt8 (list
  (nth 0 pnt1) (nth 1 pnt1)
  (- newzedge)))
```

Modify the number of points for the front and back faces:

```
(command xpnt xpnt xpnt xpnt
   xpnt xpnt xpnt xpnt xpnt)
```

And modify the mesh points to:

```
  ; add points to 3DMESH
  (command pnt1 pnt2 pnt3 pnt4 pnt5
    pnt6 pnt7 pnt8 pnt1)
```

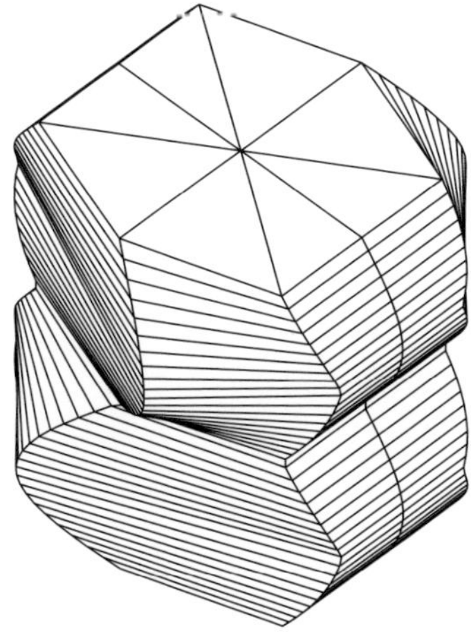

PROG20: converting to a vertical symmetrical linear form

Completed function PROG20:

```
;----------------------------------
(defun prog20 ()
 (graphscr)
 ; set extrude height
 (command ".ELEV" 0.0 0.0)
 ; get boundary points and
 ; parameters
 (prompt "\nPROG20:")
 (setq spnt
   (getpoint "\nPick start point:"))
 (setq cpnt
   (getcorner spnt
   "\nPick endpoint:"))
 (setq zedge
   (getdist spnt
   "\nEnter edge height:"))
 (setq zmid
   (getdist spnt
   "\nEnter midpoint height:"))
 (setq yoff
    getdist spnt
    "\nEnter midpoint offset:"))
 (setq numtimes
   (getint
   "\nEnter number of lines:"))
 (setq linefact
   (getreal
   "\nEnter keep line factor:"))
 (setq numcycles
   (getreal
   "\nNumber of curve cycles:"))
 ; compute line length, width of
 ; boundary
 (setq linelen
   (- (nth 1 cpnt) (nth 1 spnt)))
 ; compute increment across boundary
 (setq xinc (/ (- (nth 0 cpnt)
   (nth 0 spnt)) (- numtimes 1)))
 ; computer ang inc
 (setq anginc (/ (* 360.0 numcycles)
   (- numtimes 1)))
 ; set first point and first x coord
 (setq xpnt spnt)
 (setq xpt (nth 0 spnt))
 ; start ang
 (setq ang 0)
```

```
; start 3DMESH
(command ".3DMESH"
  (+ numtimes 2) "9")
; frame counter
(setq cnt 0)
; loop to repeat lines
(repeat numtimes
 ; compute line length
 (setq linepart1
   (* linelen linefact))
 (setq linepart2
   (* (* linelen (- 1.0 linefact))
   (abs (sin (dtr ang)))))
 (setq newlinelen
   (+ linepart1 linepart2))
 ; compute endpoint
 (setq epnt1 (polar
   xpnt (dtr 90) newlinelen))
 (setq epnt2 (polar
   xpnt (dtr 270) newlinelen))
 ; compute edge height
 (setq linepart1
   (* zedge linefact))
 (setq linepart2
   (* (* zedge (- 1.0 linefact))
   (abs (cos (dtr ang)))))
 (setq newzedge
   (+ linepart1 linepart2))
 ; compute midpoint height
 (setq linepart1
   (* zmid linefact))
 (setq linepart2
   (* (* zmid (- 1.0 linefact))
   (abs (sin (dtr ang)))))
 (setq newzmid
   (+ linepart1 linepart2))
 ; compute midpoint offset
 (setq newyoff
   (* yoff (sin (dtr ang))))
 ; compute frame points
 (setq pnt1 epnt2)
 (setq pnt2 (list
   (nth 0 epnt2)
   (nth 1 epnt2)
   (+ (nth 2 epnt2) newzedge)))
 (setq pnt3 (list
   (nth 0 xpnt)
   (+ (nth 1 xpnt) newyoff)
   (+ (nth 2 xpnt) newzmid)))
 (setq pnt4 (list
   (nth 0 epnt1)
   (nth 1 epnt1)
   (+ (nth 2 epnt1) newzedge)))
 (setq pnt5 epnt1)
 (setq pnt6 (list
   (nth 0 pnt5)
   (nth 1 pnt5) (- newzedge)))
 (setq pnt7 (list
   (nth 0 pnt3)
   (nth 1 pnt3) (- newzmid)))
 (setq pnt8 (list
   (nth 0 pnt1)
   (nth 1 pnt1) (- newzedge)))
 ; inc frames
 (setq cnt (+ cnt 1))
 ; check if before first frame
 (if (= cnt 1) (progn
  ; add front face to mesh
  (command xpnt xpnt xpnt xpnt xpnt
    xpnt xpnt xpnt xpnt)
 ))
 ; add points to 3DMESH
 (command pnt1 pnt2 pnt3 pnt4 pnt5
   pnt6 pnt7 pnt8 pnt1)
 ; check if before first frame
 (if (= cnt numtimes) (progn
  ; add front face to mesh
  (command xpnt xpnt xpnt xpnt xpnt
    xpnt xpnt xpnt xpnt)
 ))
 ; inc x coord
 (setq xpt (+ xpt xinc))
 (setq xpnt (list
   xpt (nth 1 xpnt) (nth 2 xpnt)))
 ; inc ang
 (setq ang (+ ang anginc))
)
; set extrude height
(command ".ELEV" 0.0 0.0)
; rotate vertical
(command ".ZOOM" "e")
(command ".ROTATE3D"
  "all" "" "Y" "" "-90")
(command ".ZOOM" "e")
(princ)
)
;---------------------------------
```

With either function PROG18 or PROG20, generate your own series of forms. Using a set of control points that can be varied is one possible method of creating forms. Can you begin to define other methods?

5.2 Generating a Form on a Circular Path

The linear path that we previously explored is an open path that closes at each end. Another common form is a path that closes on itself. A family of circular forms can be used to explore a variety of architectural concepts; consider them as base forms for further development. The first is a simple circle.

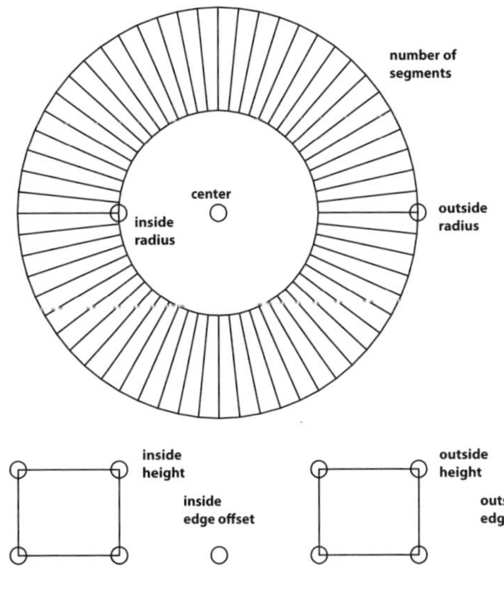

PROG01: circle parameters

The basic parameters consist of the centerpoint, outside radius, top height, and number of segments.

Start a new drawing and set the units to architectural. Set the grid to 1 foot, and turn off all snaps and dynamic input. Start a new AutoLISP file in the editor: CH05B.LSP.

We will start with a simple model of a circular-disc shape by computing the center and outside offsets and bottom- and top-height elevations. Those four points will be repeated for the number of segments in a 3DMESH. The points we need to compute were covered in Chapter 4 using the DOLPOLYGON function, where the polar function was used to compute points along the edge of a polygon.

The general outline for PROG01 is:

```
defun prog01 ()
 ; set center
 ; get input
 ; make and erase current layer
 ; compute angle increment
 ; set start angle
 ; set ground elevation
 ; start 3DMESH
 (repeat for number of segments
  ; compute outside top and
  ;  bottom points
  ; compute inside top and
  ;  bottom points
  ; add points to 3DMESH
  ; increment angle
 )
)
```

Completed function PROG01:

```
;----------------------------------
(defun dtr (a) (* pi (/ a 180.0)))
(defun rtd (a) (/ (* a 180.0) pi))
;----------------------------------
(defun prog01 ()
 (graphscr)
 ; circular curve
 (setvar "CMDECHO" 0)
 ; centerpoint
 (setq cpnt (list 0.0 0.0 0.0))
 ; get curve parameters
 (princ "\nProg01 - Circle")
 (setq CurveLayer
   (getstring
   "\nEnter layer name: "))
 (setq oRad
   (getdist cpnt
```

```
  "\nEnter outside radius: "))
(setq oHeight
  (getdist cpnt
  "\nEnter outside height: "))
(setq NumSegs
  (getint
  "\nEnter number of segments: "))
; clear layer
(command ".LAYER" "THAW" "*"
  "ON" "*" "")
(command ".LAYER"
  "MAKE" CurveLayer "")
(command ".LAYER" "SET" 0 "")
(command ".LAYER" "OFF" "@*"
  "FREEZE" "@*" "")
(command ".LAYER" "THAW" CurveLayer
  "ON" CurveLayer
  "SET" CurveLayer "")
(command ".ERASE" "ALL" "")
; calculate curve variables
(setq SweepAngle 360.0)
(setq anginc
  (/ SweepAngle NumSegs))
; start angle
(setq ang 0.0)
; set ground elev
(setq grdelev 0.0)
; start mesh
(command ".3DMESH"
  (+ NumSegs 1) "5")
(repeat (+ NumSegs 1)
 ; compute top
 (setq top oHeight)
 ; compute outside edge
 (setq oradpt (polar cpnt
   (dtr ang) oRad))
 (setq xoff (nth 0 oradpt))
 (setq yoff (nth 1 oradpt))
 ; outside edge
 (setq pnt1 (list
   (+ (nth 0 cpnt) xoff)
   (+ (nth 1 cpnt) yoff) grdelev))
 (setq pnt2 (list
   (+ (nth 0 cpnt) xoff)
   (+ (nth 1 cpnt) yoff) top))
 ; compute inside edge
 (setq iradpt cpnt)
 (setq xoff (nth 0 iradpt))
 (setq yoff (nth 1 iradpt))
 (setq pnt3 (list
   (+ (nth 0 cpnt) xoff)
   (+ (nth 1 cpnt) yoff) top))
 (setq pnt4 (list
   (+ (nth 0 cpnt) xoff)
   (+ (nth 1 cpnt) yoff) grdelev))
 ; add to mesh
 (command pnt1 pnt2 pnt3
   pnt4 pnt1)
 ; inc ang
 (setq ang (+ ang anginc))
)
(command ".ZOOM" "e")
(setvar "CMDECHO" 1)
(princ)
)
;----------------------------------
```

Review PROG01. As part of the input, we have added a layer name, so that multiple models can be saved in the same drawing file, on different layers.

To make and erase the current layer, the following series of layer commands are included:

```
; clear layer
 (command ".LAYER" "THAW" "*"
   "ON" "*" "")
 (command ".LAYER"
   "MAKE" CurveLayer "")
 (command ".LAYER" "SET" 0 "")
 (command ".LAYER" "OFF" "@*"
   "FREEZE" "@*" "")
 (command ".LAYER" "THAW" CurveLayer
   "ON" CurveLayer
   "SET" CurveLayer "")
 (command ".ERASE" "ALL" "")
```

The only requirement is for the layer's name to start with a letter, so that layer 0 can be set before all other layers are turned off. Start the mesh by specifying the number of segments plus one and a set of five points.

The plus one is needed to close the mesh on itself:

```
; start mesh
(command ".3DMESH"
  (+ NumSegs 1) "5")
```

For each set of points, use:

```
; add to mesh
(command pnt1 pnt2 pnt3
  pnt4 pnt1)
```

The four points that define the section of the disc are computed based on offsets from the center of the disc. The first point is repeated so that the disc has a bottom surface.

For the outside edge, use:

```
; compute outside edge
(setq oradpt (polar cpnt
  (dtr ang) oRad))
(setq xoff (nth 0 oradpt))
(setq yoff (nth 1 oradpt))
; outside edge
(setq pnt1 (list
  (+ (nth 0 cpnt) xoff)
  (+ (nth 1 cpnt) yoff)
  grdelev))
(setq pnt2 (list
  (+ (nth 0 cpnt) xoff)
  (+ (nth 1 cpnt) yoff)
  top))
```

The remaining coordinate to be entered represents the heights. The inner two points are computed in the same manner, except in this case the inside point is the center. There is no offset. Another method to control the AutoCAD environment is to set system variables.

System variable `CMDECHO` is set to disable and enable the echo display of commands to the text screen.

For this example, the input is:

```
layer c01a, radius 10 feet, height 5
feet, and segments 64.
```

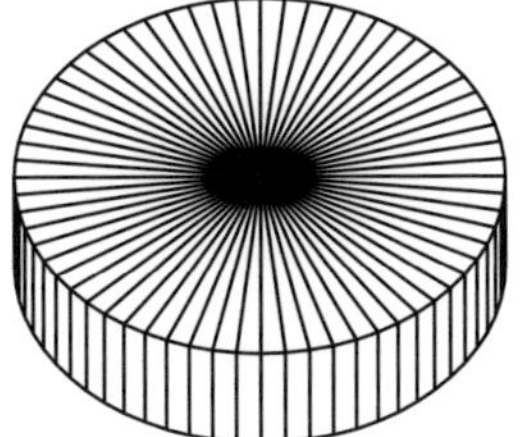
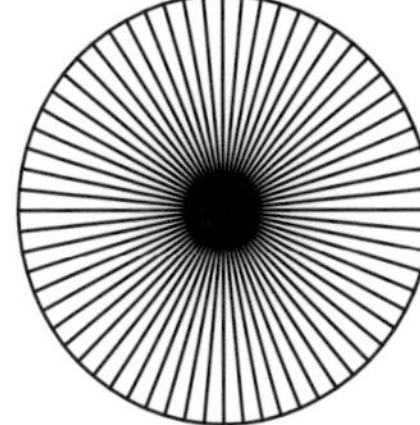

PROG01: example of simple circular disc

Note that one of the input parameters is the number of segments. That parameter can turn a circular form into a polygonal form.

For this example, the input is:

```
layer c01b, radius 10 feet, height 5
feet, and segments 12
```

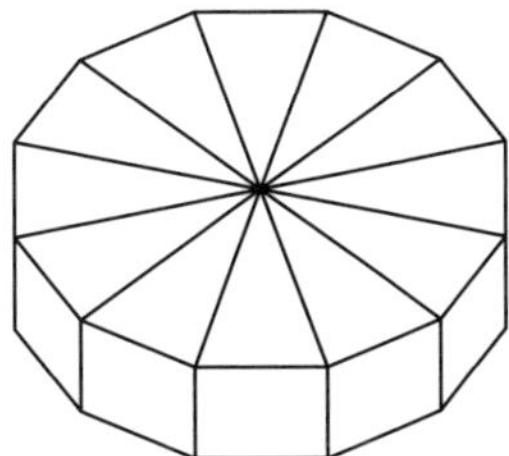
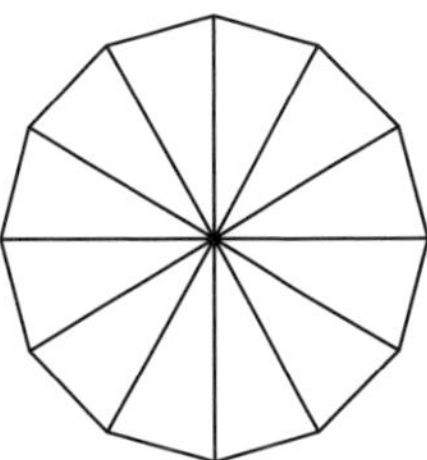

PROG01: example of a simple polygonal disc

Add an inside radius

To convert the circular disc to a donut or ring shape, add an inside radius and compute the offsets. Add PROG02, and using a copy of PROG01 make the following changes.

Add input for the inside radius:

```
(setq iRad
  (getdist cpnt
  "\nEnter inside radius: "))
```

The computation for the inside offset is modified to:

```
(setq iradpt (polar cpnt
  (dtr ang) iRad))
```

For this example, the input is:

```
layer c02a, outside radius 10 feet,
inside radius 5 feet, height 5 feet,
and segments 64.
```

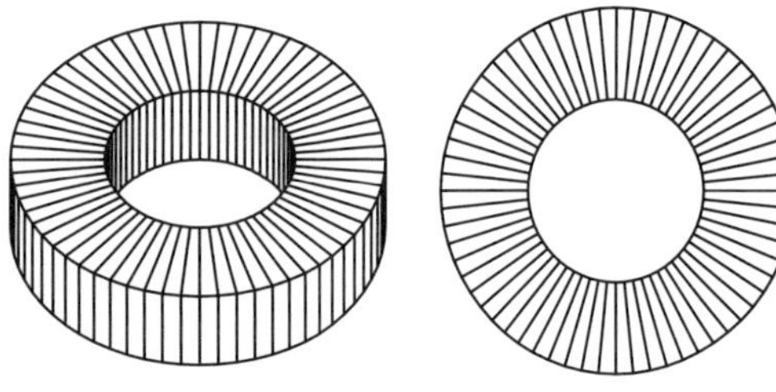

PROG02: convert circular disc to a ring

Convert the circular form to elliptical

The computations for this segmented circular form enables us to model circles and n-sided polygons. Using the same type of computations, we can extend this form to elliptical. The polar function was adequate for the circular-offset computation, but we now need access to both the x and y radii. Review the DOEPOLYGON function in Chapter 4 for computations of elliptical polygons.

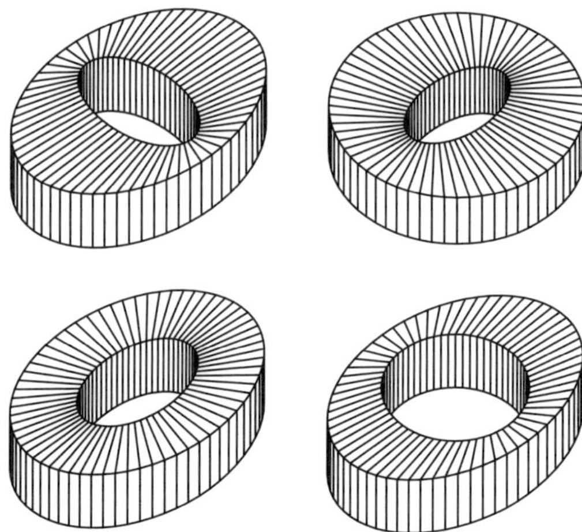

PROG03: convert circular form to elliptical

Add function PROG03 using a copy of PROG2. The polar function is replaced with the equivalent computation but allowing us to access both the x and y radii.

Offsets are computed as:

```
; compute outside edge
(setq xoff
  (* oXRad (cos (dtr ang))))
(setq yoff
  (* oYRad (sin (dtr ang))))
```

To fully control the inside and outside radii, each has an x- and y-component. The number of segments determines if it forms an ellipse or an elliptical polygon.

Completed function PROG03:

```
;----------------------------------
(defun prog03 ()
 (graphscr)
 ; circular curve
 (setvar "CMDECHO" 0)
 ; centerpoint
 (setq cpnt (list 0.0 0.0 0.0))
 ; get curve parameters
 (princ "\nProg03 - Circle")
 (setq CurveLayer
   (getstring
   "\nEnter layer name: "))
 (setq oXRad
   (getdist cpnt
   "\nEnter outside X radius: "))
 (setq oYRad
   (getdist cpnt
   "\nEnter outside Y radius: "))
 (setq iXRad
   (getdist cpnt
   "\nEnter inside X radius: "))
 (setq iYRad
   (getdist cpnt
   "\nEnter inside Y radius: "))
 (setq oHeight
   (getdist cpnt
   "\nEnter outside height: "))
 (setq NumSegs
   (getint
   "\nEnter number of segments: "))
 ; clear layer
 (command ".LAYER" "THAW" "*"
   "ON" "*" "")
 (command ".LAYER"
   "MAKE" CurveLayer "")
 (command ".LAYER" "SET" 0 "")
 (command ".LAYER" "OFF" "@*"
   "FREEZE" "@*" "")
 (command ".LAYER" "THAW" CurveLayer
   "ON" CurveLayer
   "SET" CurveLayer "")
 (command ".ERASE" "ALL" "")
 ; calculate curve variables
 (setq SweepAngle 360.0)
 (setq anginc
   (/ SweepAngle NumSegs))
 ; start angle
 (setq ang 0.0)
 ; set ground elev
 (setq grdelev 0.0)
 ; start mesh
 (command ".3DMESH"
   (+ NumSegs 1) "5")
 (repeat (+ NumSegs 1)
  ; compute top
  (setq top oHeight)
  ; compute outside edge
  (setq xoff
    (* oXRad (cos (dtr ang))))
  (setq yoff
    (* oYRad (sin (dtr ang))))
  ; outside edge
  (setq pnt1 (list
    (+ (nth 0 cpnt) xoff)
    (+ (nth 1 cpnt) yoff) grdelev))
  (setq pnt2 (list
    (+ (nth 0 cpnt) xoff)
    (+ (nth 1 cpnt) yoff) top))
  ; compute inside edge
  (setq xoff
    (* iXRad (cos (dtr ang))))
  (setq yoff
    (* iYRad (sin (dtr ang))))
  (setq pnt3 (list
    (+ (nth 0 cpnt) xoff)
    (+ (nth 1 cpnt) yoff) top))
  (setq pnt4 (list
    (+ (nth 0 cpnt) xoff)
    (+ (nth 1 cpnt) yoff) grdelev))
  ; add to mesh
  (command pnt1 pnt2 pnt3
    pnt4 pnt1)
  ; inc ang
  (setq ang (+ ang anginc))
 )
 (command ".ZOOM" "e")
 (setvar "CMDECHO" 1)
 (princ)
)
;----------------------------------
```

Define outside and inside heights

The current form uses a single value to define the height of the top surface. The outside height is used for both the outside and inside edges.

Add PROG04 using a copy of PROG03. Add input for an inside height to the current outside height. Prior to the computation of the inside points, change the top elevation to the inside height.

For the inside height, add:

```
(setq iHeight
  (getdist cpnt
  "\nEnter inside height: "))
```

And set the points by:

```
; compute top
(setq top iHeight)
; compute inside edge
(setq xoff
  (* iXRad (cos (dtr ang))))
(setq yoff
  (* iYRad (sin (dtr ang))))
(setq pnt3 (list
  (+ (nth 0 cpnt) xoff)
  (+ (nth 1 cpnt) yoff)
  top))
(setq pnt4 (list
  (+ (nth 0 cpnt) xoff)
  (+ (nth 1 cpnt) yoff)
  grdelev))
```

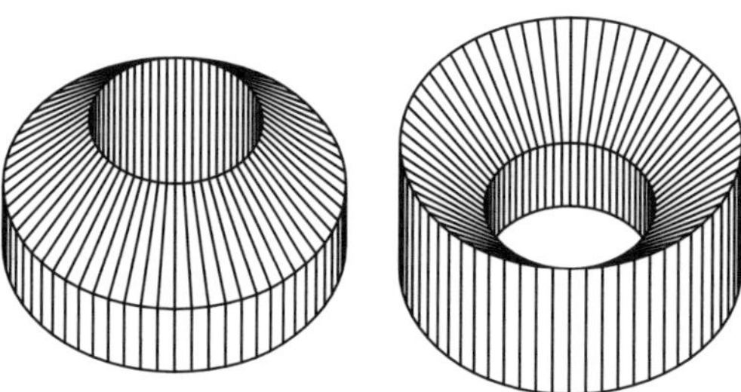

PROG04: variations of inside and outside heights

The inside radius, the inside height, or the outside height can be zero.

Less than a full circle

Each of these circular forms has been closed and swept a full 360 degrees. To sweep through less than 360 degrees, the open ends have to close, as they were previously in the linear form. Since the circular section does not have a centerline point, the midpoint of the bottom edge can be used to define the end surfaces.

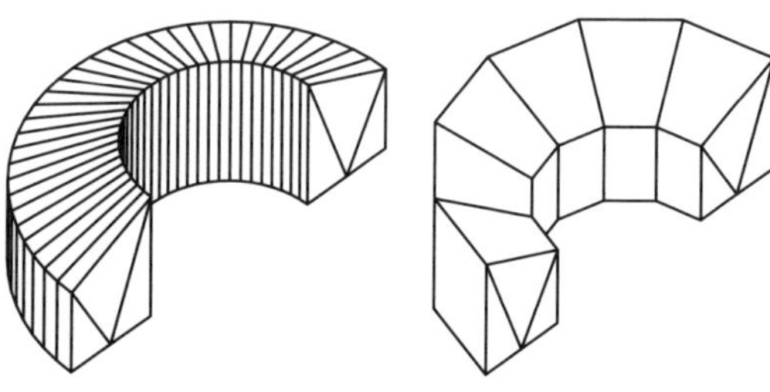

PROG05: circular form swept less than 360 degrees

Add PROG05 using a copy of PROG04. Add input for the sweep angle, and remove its current setting of 360 degrees. Add a counter for the segments, so we can determine when the sweep reaches the first and last segments. Also note that the 3DMESH start has to be set, depending on whether the ends need to be added.

The start of the 3DMESH changes to:

```
; start mesh, check sweep angle
 (if (= SweepAngle 360)
  (command ".3DMESH"
    (+ NumSegs 1) "5")
  (command ".3DMESH"
   (+ NumSegs 3) "5")
 )
```

The starting face of the mesh is included by:

```
; inc segment
(setq nseg (+ nseg 1))
; compute midpoint of bottom
(setq mpnt (polar pnt4
  (angle pnt4 pnt1)
  (/ (distance pnt4 pnt1) 2)))
; check if to close at start
(if (and (/= SweepAngle 360)
  (= nseg 1))
 (command mpnt mpnt mpnt mpnt
   mpnt)
)
```

Also review how the ending face is added to the mesh.

Completed function PROG05:

```
;----------------------------------
(defun prog05 ()
 (graphscr)
 ; circular curve
 (setvar "CMDECHO" 0)
 ; centerpoint
 (setq cpnt (list 0.0 0.0 0.0))
 ; get curve parameters
 (princ "\nProg05 - Circle")
 (setq CurveLayer
   (getstring
   "\nEnter layer name: "))
 (setq oXRad
   (getdist cpnt
   "\nEnter outside X radius: "))
 (setq oYRad
   (getdist cpnt
   "\nEnter outside Y radius: "))
 (setq iXRad
   (getdist cpnt
   "\nEnter inside X radius: "))
 (setq iYRad
   (getdist cpnt
   "\nEnter inside Y radius: "))
 (setq oHeight
   (getdist cpnt
   "\nEnter outside height: "))
 (setq iHeight
   (getdist cpnt
   "\nEnter inside height: "))
(setq NumSegs
   (getint
   "\nEnter number of segments: "))
(setq SweepAngle
   (getreal
   "\nEnter total sweep angle:"))
; clear layer
(command ".LAYER" "THAW" "*"
   "ON" "*" "")
(command ".LAYER"
   "MAKE" CurveLayer "")
(command ".LAYER" "SET" 0 "")
(command ".LAYER" "OFF" "@*"
   "FREEZE" "@*" "")
(command ".LAYER" "THAW" CurveLayer
   "ON" CurveLayer
   "SET" CurveLayer "")
(command ".ERASE" "ALL" "")
; calculate curve variables
(setq anginc
   (/ SweepAngle NumSegs))
; start angle
(setq ang 0.0)
; set ground elev
(setq grdelev 0.0)
; segment count
(setq nseg 0)
; start mesh, check sweep angle
(if (= SweepAngle 360)
 (command ".3DMESH"
    (+ NumSegs 1) "5")
 (command ".3DMESH"
   (+ NumSegs 3) "5")
)
(repeat (+ NumSegs 1)
 ; compute top
 (setq top oHeight)
 ; compute outside edge
 (setq xoff
    (* oXRad (cos (dtr ang))))
 (setq yoff
    (* oYRad (sin (dtr ang))))
 ; outside edge
 (setq pnt1 (list
    (+ (nth 0 cpnt) xoff)
    (+ (nth 1 cpnt) yoff) grdelev))
```

```
    (setq pnt2 (list
      (+ (nth 0 cpnt) xoff)
      (+ (nth 1 cpnt) yoff) top))
    ; compute top
    (setq top iHeight)
    ; compute inside edge
    (setq xoff
      (* iXRad (cos (dtr ang))))
    (setq yoff
      (* iYRad (sin (dtr ang))))
    (setq pnt3 (list
      (+ (nth 0 cpnt) xoff)
      (+ (nth 1 cpnt) yoff) top))
    (setq pnt4 (list
      (+ (nth 0 cpnt) xoff)
      (+ (nth 1 cpnt) yoff) grdelev))
    ; inc segment
    (setq nseg (+ nseg 1))
    ; compute midpoint of bottom
    (setq mpnt (polar pnt4
      (angle pnt4 pnt1)
      (/ (distance pnt4 pnt1) 2)))
    ; check if to close at start
    (if (and (/= SweepAngle 360)
      (= nseg 1))
     (command mpnt mpnt mpnt mpnt
       mpnt)
    )
    ; add to mesh
    (command pnt1 pnt2 pnt3
      pnt4 pnt1)
    ; check if to close at end
    (if (and (/= SweepAngle 360)
      (= nseg (+ NumSegs 1)))
     (command mpnt mpnt mpnt mpnt
       mpnt)
    )
    ; inc ang
    (setq ang (+ ang anginc))
  )
  (command ".ZOOM" "e")
  (setvar "CMDECHO" 1)
  (princ)
)
;----------------------------------
```

Control the height offsets

All major dimensional components of the text have been addressed. Similar to the linear path example, each edge and height can include a mathematical function to compute an offset. For example, the inside and outside heights can be controlled by sine and cosine functions.

Add PROG06 using a copy of PROG05. Add input for inside and outside height offsets. In the computation of the height, add the offset using a mathematical function.

For example, the outside-height offset could be varied by:

```
; compute top
(setq top (+ oHeight
  (* (sin (dtr (* ang 2)))
  oHeightOff)))
```

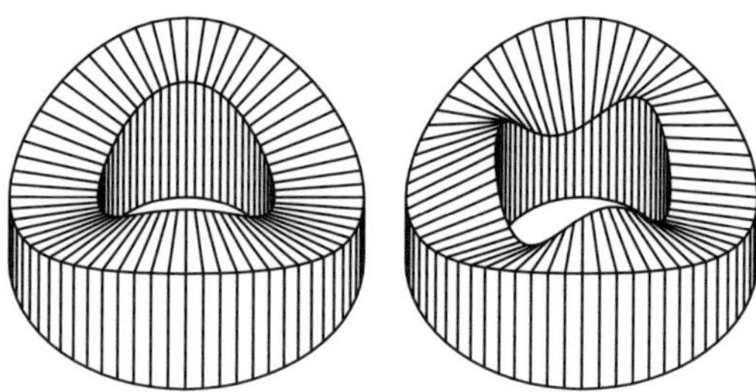

PROG06: variations of height using a mathematical function

For these examples, first the outside and inside height offsets vary by the sine of two times the angle; in the second, the inside varies by the cosine of three times the angle.

Completed function PROG06:

```
;---------------------------------
(defun prog06 ()
 (graphscr)
 ; circular curve
 (setvar "CMDECHO" 0)
 ; centerpoint
 (setq cpnt (list 0.0 0.0 0.0))
 ; get curve parameters
 (princ "\nProg06 - Circle")
 (setq CurveLayer
   (getstring
   "\nEnter layer name: "))
 (setq oXRad
   (getdist cpnt
   "\nEnter outside X radius: "))
 (setq oYRad
   (getdist cpnt
   "\nEnter outside Y radius: "))
 (setq iXRad
   (getdist cpnt
   "\nEnter inside X radius: "))
 (setq iYRad
   (getdist cpnt
   "\nEnter inside Y radius: "))
 (setq oHeight
   (getdist cpnt
   "\nEnter outside height: "))
 (setq oHeightOff
   (getdist cpnt
   "\nEnter outside height
   offset: "))
 (setq iHeight
   (getdist cpnt
   "\nEnter inside height: "))
 (setq iHeightOff
   (getdist cpnt
   "\nEnter inside height
   offset: "))
 (setq NumSegs
   (getint
   "\nEnter number of segments: "))
 (setq SweepAngle
   (getreal
   "\nEnter total sweep angle:"))
 ; clear layer
 (command ".LAYER" "THAW" "*"
   "ON" "*" "")
 (command ".LAYER"
   "MAKE" CurveLayer "")
 (command ".LAYER" "SET" 0 "")
 (command ".LAYER" "OFF" "@*"
   "FREEZE" "@*" "")
 (command ".LAYER" "THAW" CurveLayer
   "ON" CurveLayer
   "SET" CurveLayer "")
 (command ".ERASE" "ALL" "")
 ; calculate curve variables
 (setq anginc
   (/ SweepAngle NumSegs))
 ; start angle
 (setq ang 0.0)
 ; set ground elev
 (setq grdelev 0.0)
 ; segment count
 (setq nseg 0)
 ; start mesh, check sweep angle
 (if (= SweepAngle 360)
  (command ".3DMESH"
    (+ NumSegs 1) "5")
  (command ".3DMESH"
    (+ NumSegs 3) "5")
 )
 (repeat (+ NumSegs 1)
  ; compute top
  (setq top (+ oHeight
    (* (sin (dtr (* ang 2)))
    oHeightOff)))
  ; compute outside edge
  (setq xoff
    (* oXRad (cos (dtr ang))))
  (setq yoff
    (* oYRad (sin (dtr ang))))
  ; outside edge
  (setq pnt1 (list
    (+ (nth 0 cpnt) xoff)
    (+ (nth 1 cpnt) yoff) grdelev))
  (setq pnt2 (list
    (+ (nth 0 cpnt) xoff)
    (+ (nth 1 cpnt) yoff) top))
  ; compute top
  (setq top (+ iHeight
    (* (cos (dtr (* ang 3)))
    iHeightOff)))
  ; compute inside edge
```

```
  (setq xoff
    (* iXRad (cos (dtr ang))))
  (setq yoff
    (* iYRad (sin (dtr ang))))
  (setq pnt3 (list
    (+ (nth 0 cpnt) xoff)
    (+ (nth 1 cpnt) yoff) top))
  (setq pnt4 (list
    (+ (nth 0 cpnt) xoff)
    (+ (nth 1 cpnt) yoff) grdelev))
  ; inc segment
  (setq nseg (+ nseg 1))
  ; compute midpoint of bottom
  (setq mpnt (polar pnt4
    (angle pnt4 pnt1)
    (/ (distance pnt4 pnt1) 2)))
  ; check if to close at start
  (if (and (/= SweepAngle 360)
    (= nseg 1))
   (command mpnt mpnt mpnt mpnt
     mpnt)
  )
  ; add to mesh
  (command pnt1 pnt2 pnt3
    pnt4 pnt1)
  ; check if to close at end
  (if (and (/= SweepAngle 360)
    (= nseg (+ NumSegs 1)))
   (command mpnt mpnt mpnt mpnt
     mpnt)
  )
  ; inc ang
  (setq ang (+ ang anginc))
 )
 (command ".ZOOM" "e")
 (setvar "CMDECHO" 1)
 (princ)
)
;---------------------------------
```

Additional offsets and parameters

Considering the concepts covered in the final set of exercises, we can expand the list of parameters to include every point in the section, with independent articulations in the horizontal and vertical directions.

The following input can be considered:

* Layer name

* Centerpoint or set to 0,0,0

* Start angle (0 to 360)

* End angle (greater than start angle to 360) or set to 0–360 or 270–540 for selected curves

* Number of segments

* Radius
  - outside upper x-radius
  - outside upper y-radius
  - outside lower x-radius
  - outside lower y-radius
  - inside upper x-radius
  - inside upper y-radius
  - inside lower x-radius
  - inside lower y-radius

* Height, assume base is at z=0
  - outside z-height
  - inside z-height

* Curve specifications
  - outside z-height curve type
  - outside z-height offset
  - outside z-height start angle
  - outside z-height end angle
  - inside z-height curve type
  - inside z-height offset
  - inside z-height start angle
  - inside z-height end angle
  - outside-edge curve type
  - outside-edge x-offset
  - outside-edge y-offset
  - outside-edge start angle

- outside-edge end angle
- have a separate set for upper and lower edges
- inside-edge curve type
- inside-edge x-offset
- inside-edge y-offset
- inside-edge start angle
- inside-edge end angle

* Center offset
  - outside upper x-offset
  - outside upper y-offset
  - outside lower x-offset
  - outside lower y-offset
  - inside upper x-offset
  - inside upper y-offset
  - inside lower x-offset
  - inside lower y-offset

5.3 Other Curves to Explore

Other curves to explore

Mathematically defined curves have a long history. For example, the Hippopede Curve is attributed to Proclus in 75 BCE. Many others were developed in the seventeenth and nineteenth centuries. These curves are an excellent starting point for developing families of new forms. They can be used horizontally or vertically as closed figures and as portions for defining surfaces and forms. Additional background information for each of these forms can be found in *A Catalog of Special Plane Curves* by J. Dennis Lawrence (Dover Publications, 1972) or *Handbook and Atlas of Curves* by Eugene V. Shikin (CRC Press, 1995). Another excellent source is the website http://mathworld.wolfram.com, the contents of which were developed by Eric W. Weisstein. All of the equations in the following section are based on an underlying circular curve. These curves can also be defined as elliptical, by replacing the single radius for the x and y offsets with an x- and y-radius. The following series of curves include enough segments to read as smooth outlines. By lowering the number of segments, any regular polygon can be generated, including elliptical polygons.

Some of these curves have constants for controlling their shapes. Suggested values for these constants are included, but many variations exist when constants are misapplied. Many equations depend on simple operations, such as addition or subtraction, for their unique shapes. Feel free to replace addition with subtraction or any other operation. This is also true when adding multipliers—found in the previously discussed section on curves—to any of these equations.

Depending on the parameters specified, some of the curves transform from one shape to another. For example, the superellipse can be circular or square with rounded corners, depending on the value of one of its parameters. Explore this aspect of curves, for generating shapes that change with distance. Also, some of these curves have a puff or a pedal parameter. Most are demonstrated with four or fewer puffs or pedals, but try increasing those values also. Being surprised with the resultant shape and discovering new shapes are the major benefits of developing functions to express architectural design concepts.

Circular Curve

0 to 360 degrees:

```
xoff = (radius * COS(angle))
yoff = (radius * SIN(angle))
```

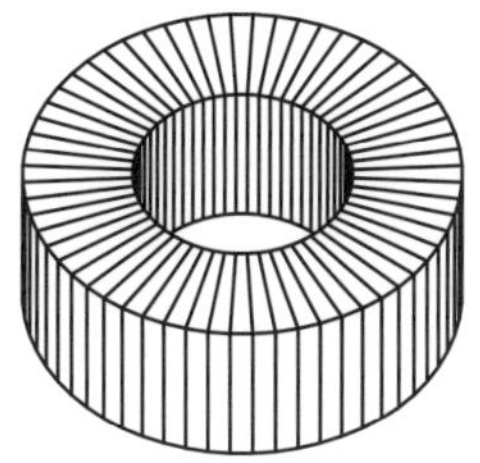
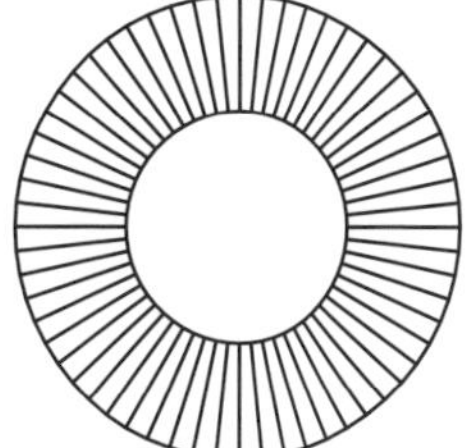

Circular Curve

Lame Curve

0 to 360 degrees:

```
xoff = (radius * ABS(COS(angle))^(2.0/n))
  * SIGN(COS(angle))
yoff = (radius * ABS(SIN(angle))^(2.0/n))
  * SIGN(SIN(angle))
```

Try different values of `n`: greater than, less than, and equal to 1.0.

For an ellipse, the x and y radii are different. In this example `n=4`, try `n=2/3` for an asteroid; `n=3` for a Witch of Agnesi, and `n=5/2` for a superellipse.

Add the `sign` function:

```
(defun sign (a) (if (< a 0.0)
  (- 0 1.0) (+ 0 1.0)))
```

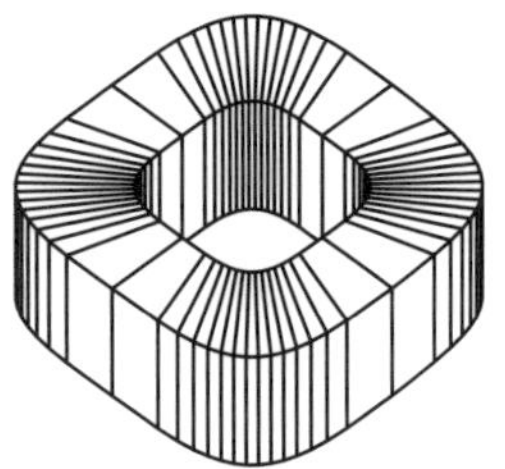

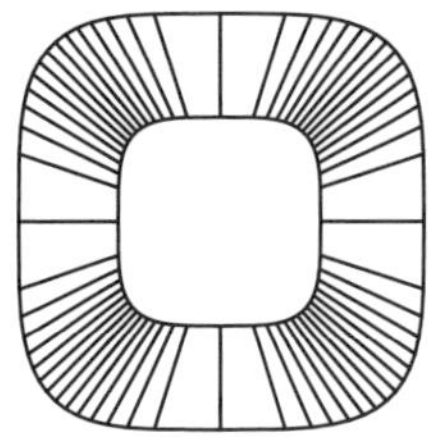

Lame Curve as a Superellipse

Curve of Watt

0 to 360 degrees:

```
r = SQRT(b^2 - (a * SIN(angle) -
  SQRT(c^2 - a^2 *
  COS(angle)^2))^2)
xoff = (r * radius) * COS(angle))
yoff = (r * radius) * SIN(angle))
```

Suggested values:

```
c = 1.25
b = 3.0
a = 1.0
```

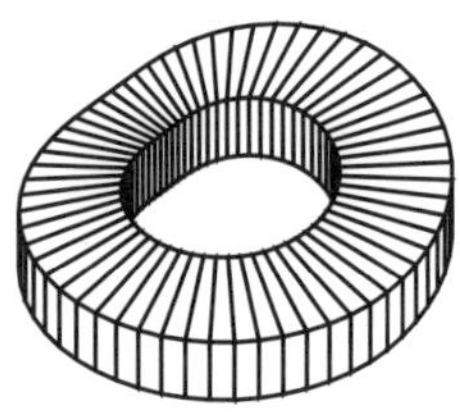

Curve of Watt

Epicycloid Curve or Puff

Related curves: Cardioid (1 cusp) and Nephroid (2 cusps)

0 to 360 degrees:

```
xoff = ((length of side * COS(angle)) -
  (radius * COS((length of side /
  radius) * angle)) )
yoff = ((length of side * SIN(angle)) -
  (radius * SIN((length of side /
  radius) * angle)) )

Where length of side =
  radius * (number of cusps + 1)
```

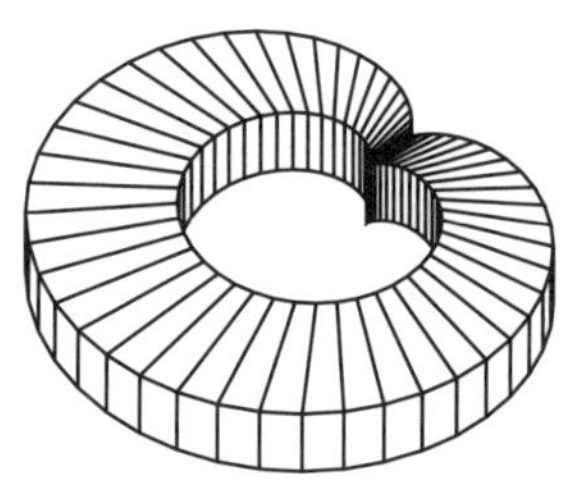

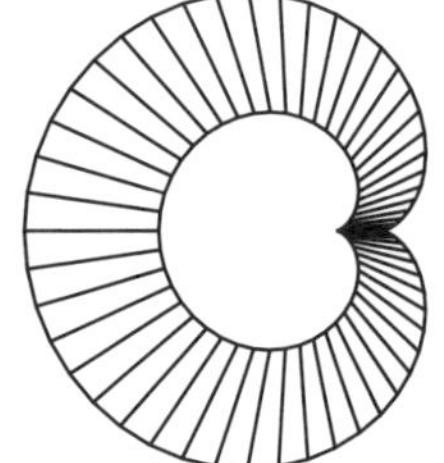

Epicycloid Curve, 1 cusp, a Cardoid

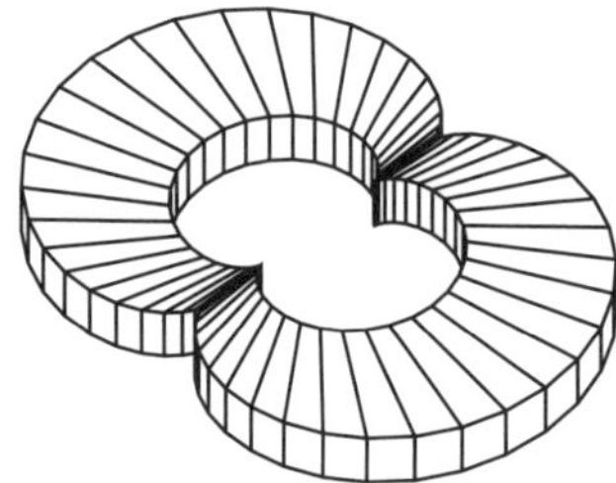

Epicycloid Curve, 2 cusps, a Nephroid

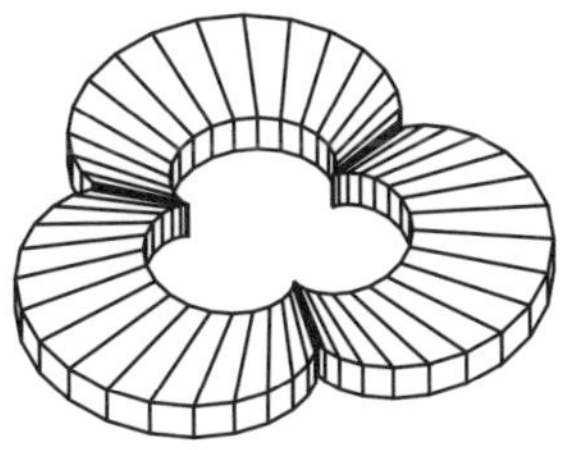

Epicycloid Curve, 3 cusps

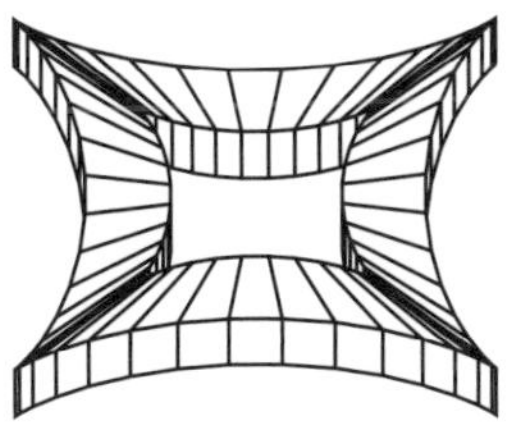

Hypocycloid Curve, 4 cusps

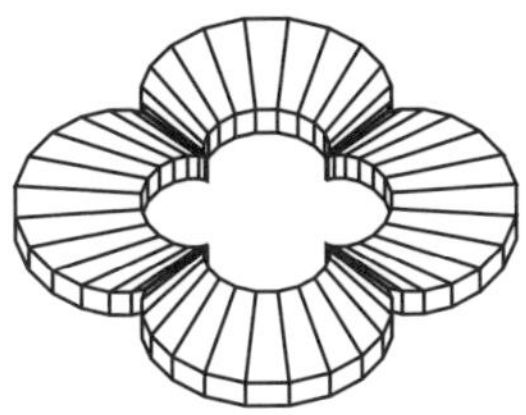

Epicycloid Curve, 4 cusps

Hypocycloid Curve or Roulette

0 to 360 degrees:

```
xoff = (radius * (((number of cusps - 1)
  * COS(angle)) +
  COS((number of cusps - 1) * angle))
yoff = (radius * (((number of cusps - 1)
  * SIN(angle)) -
  SIN((number of cusps - 1) * angle))
```

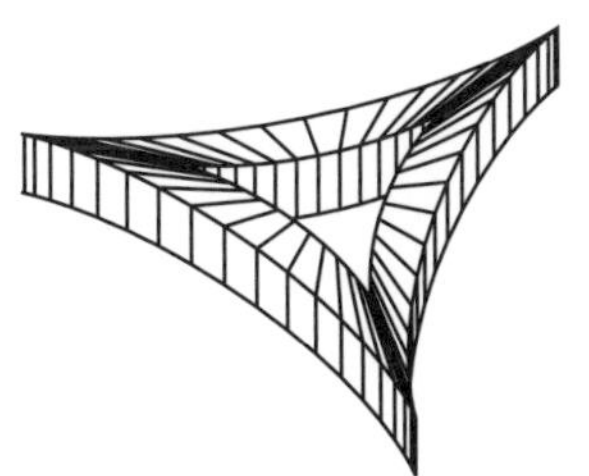

Hypocycloid Curve, 3 cusps

Lips Curve

0 to 360 degrees:

```
xoff = radius * COS(angle)
yoff = radius * SIN(angle)^5
```

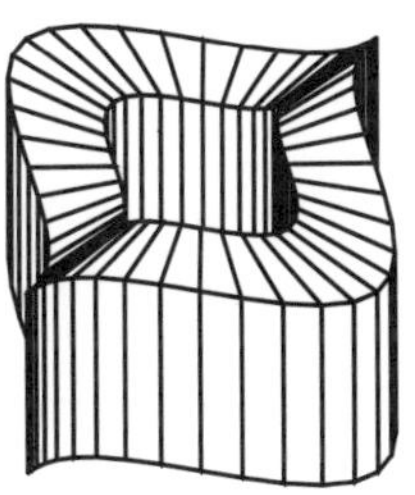
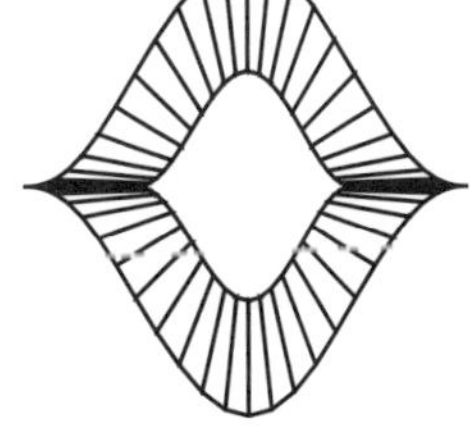

Lips Curve

Bicorn Curve

0 to 360 degrees:

```
xoff = (radius * SIN(angle))
yoff = ((radius * COS(angle)^2) *
  (2 + COS(angle))) / (3 + SIN(angle)^2)
```

Bicorn Curve

Piriform Curve

0 to 360 degrees:

```
xoff = (major radius *
  (1 + SIN(angle)))
yoff = ((minor radius *
  COS(angle)) * (1 + SIN(angle)))
```

For an inside curve, add to the x-coordinate:

```
(outside radius - inside radius)
```

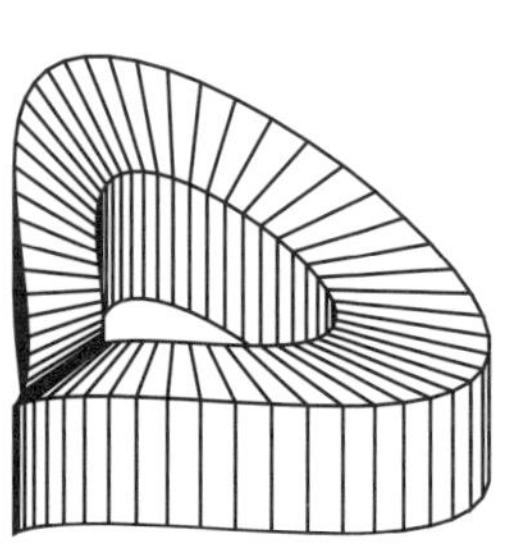

Piriform Curve

Eight Curve

Due to the crossover in the center, only half of the eight curve is considered.

270 to 540 degrees:

```
xoff = (radius * COS(angle))
yoff = ((radius * SIN(angle)) *
  COS(angle))
```

For an inside curve, add to the x-coordinate the value:

```
(outside radius - inside radius) / 2
```

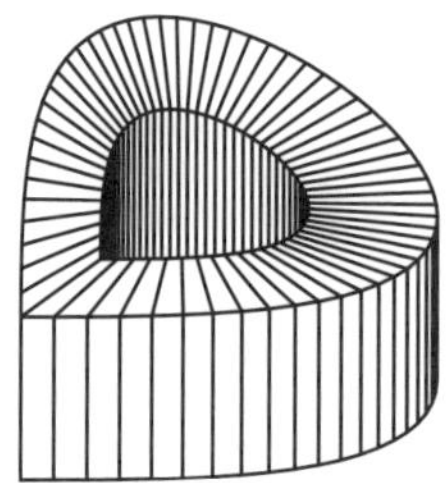

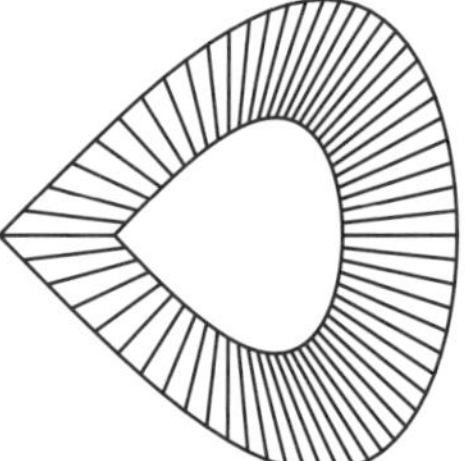

Eight Curve

Lemniscate of Bernoulli Curve

Due to the crossover in the center, only of half this Lemniscate is considered.

270 to 540 degrees:

```
xoff = ((radius * COS(angle)) /
  (1 + SIN(angle)^2))
yoff = ((radius * SIN(angle) *
  COS(angle)) / (1 + SIN(angle)^2))
```

For an inside curve, add to the x-coordinate:

```
(outside radius - inside radius) / 2
```

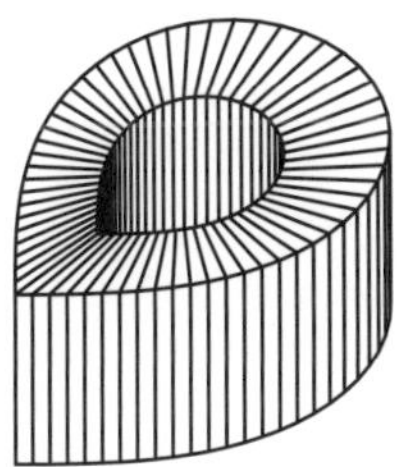

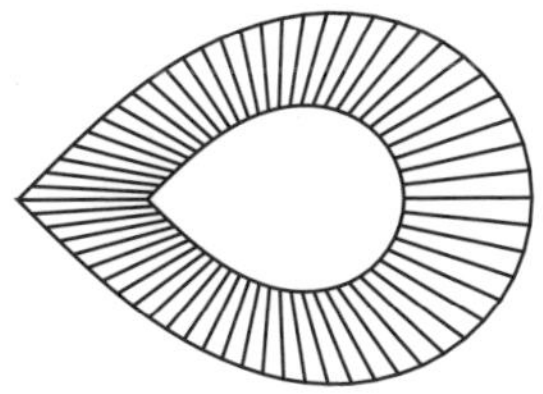

Leminiscate of Bernoulli Curve

Cranioid Curve

0 to 360 degrees:

```
r = a * COS(angle) + b *
  SQRT(1.0 - (m * SIN(angle)^2)) +
  SQRT(1.0 - (k * SIN(angle)^2))
xoff = (r * radius) * COS(angle)
yoff = (r * radius) * SIN(angle)
```

Suggested values:

```
a = 1.0
b = 2.0
k = 0.95^2
m = 0.90^2
```

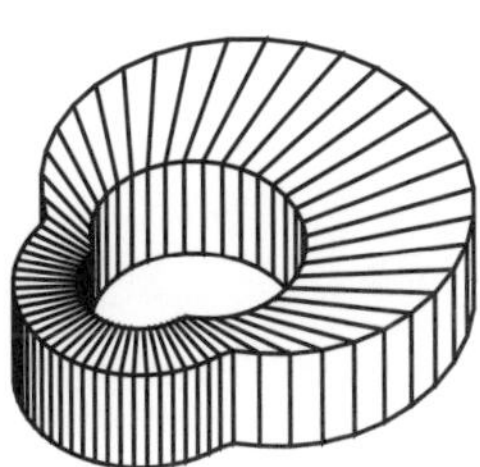

Cranioid Curve

Curve of Convexities

0 to 360 degrees:

```
r = (1.0 + (e * COS(angle * pedals))) / p
xoff = (r * radius) * COS(angle)
yoff = (r * radius) * SIN(angle)
```

Suggested values:

```
p = 1.0
pedals = 3 or 4
e = 0.3
```

Increase the value of `e` to expand the side curves.

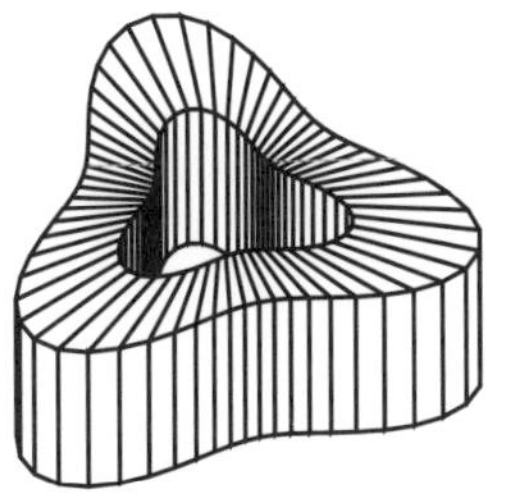

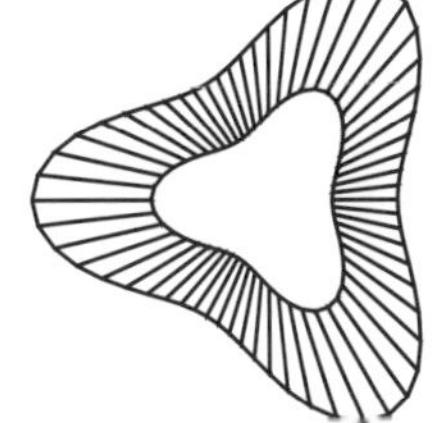

Curve of Convexities, 3 pedals

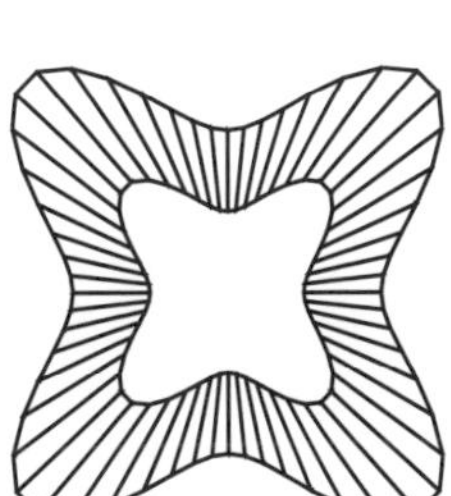

Curve of Convexities, 4 pedals

Hippopede Curve

0 to 360 degrees:

```
xoff = (2 * COS(angle)) *
  SQRT((major radius * minor radius) -
  (minor radius^2 * SIN(angle)^2))
yoff = (2 * SIN(angle)) *
  SQRT((major radius * minor radius) -
  (minor radius^2 * SIN(angle)^2))
```

The major radius is less than the minor radius. In this example, the minor radius is $\frac{9}{10}$ of the major radius. Try values for the minor radius. The indentation appears between the extremes of an oval and two circles.

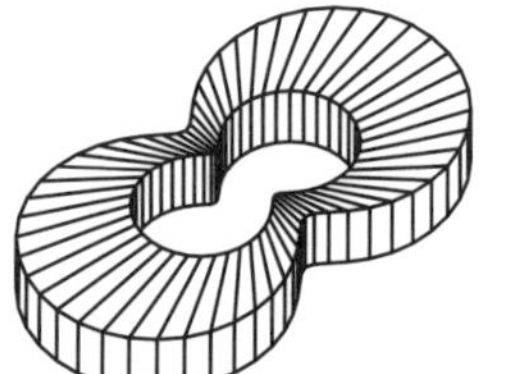

Hippopede Curve

Geometric Pedal B

0 to 360 degrees:

```
r = a + (b * COS(angle)^2n)
xoff = (r * radius) * COS(angle)
yoff = (r * radius) * SIN(angle)
```

Suggested values:

```
a = 2.0
b = 1.0
n = 8.0
```

Values of `n` are typically 1 to 8.

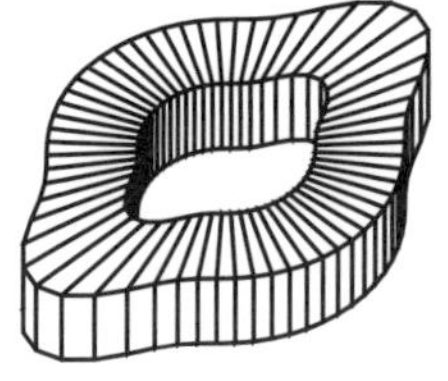
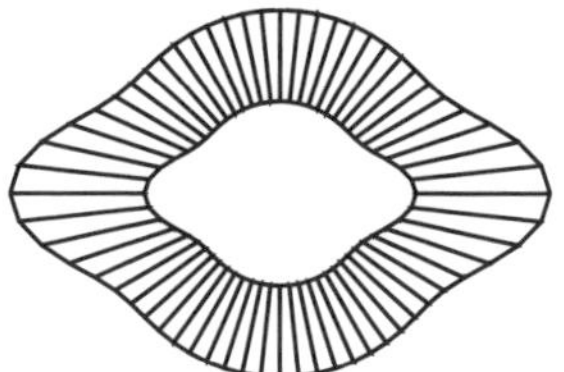

Geometric Pedal B

Geometric Pedal C

0 to 360 degrees:

```
r = a * (1.0 + COS(angle)^2n+1)
xoff = (r * radius) * COS(angle)
yoff = (r * radius) * SIN(angle)
```

For an inside curve, add to the x-coordinate:

```
(outside radius - inside radius)
```

Suggested values:

```
a = 1.0
n = 8.0
```

Values of `n` are typically 1 to 8.

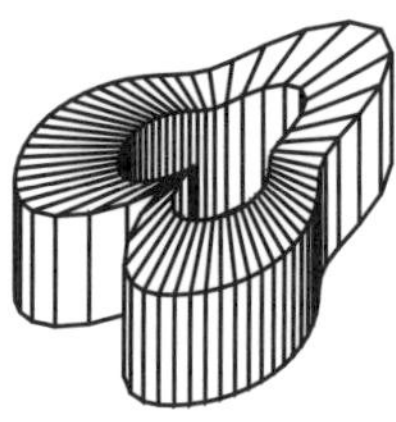
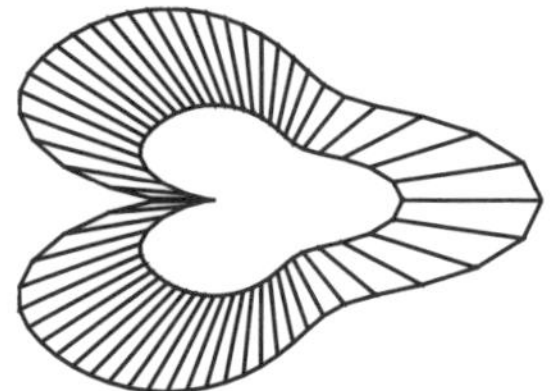

Geometric Pedal C

Functions to explore these curves

To test any of these curves, such as the Lips Curve, copy PROG01 to PROG08.

The Lips Curve offsets are computed as:

```
xoff = radius * COS(angle)
yoff = radius * SIN(angle)^5
```

Replace the computation of the points on a circle from:

```
(setq oradpt (polar cpnt
  (dtr ang) oRad))
(setq xoff (nth 0 oradpt))
(setq yoff (nth 1 oradpt))
```

To the Lips Curve offsets:

```
(setq xoff
  (* oRad (cos (dtr ang))))
(setq yoff
  (* oRad (expt (sin
  (dtr ang)) 5.0)))
```

Execute function PROG08 for different segment values.

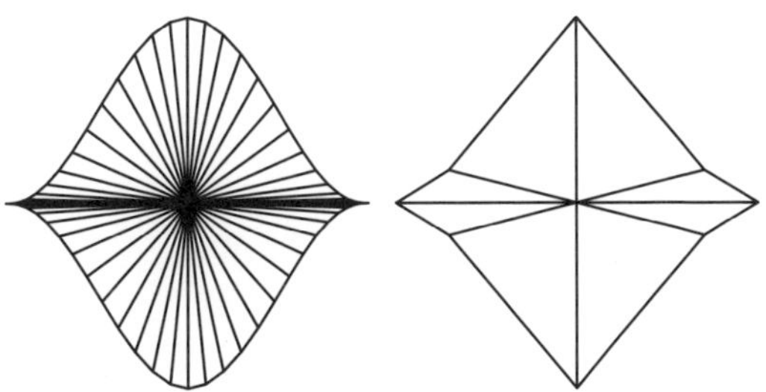

PROG08: Lips Curve with 64 and 8 segments

Note that the Lips Curve uses the sine function to the 5th power. What aspect of the curve does that control? Change it to another value and rerun function PROG08. I will leave it up to you to discover what happens if the power is an even number.

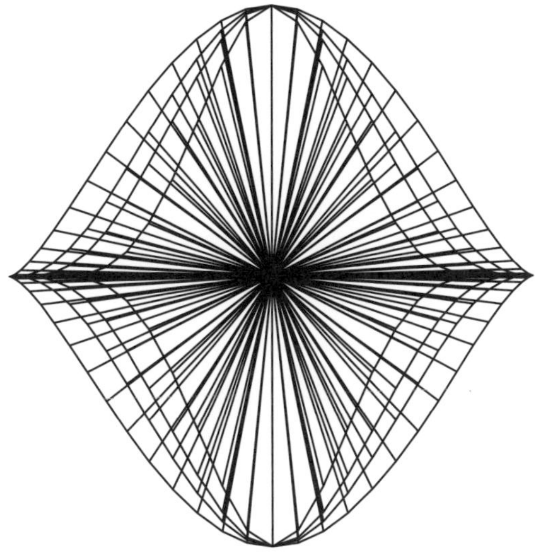

PROG08: Lips Curve, from the outside, 3rd, 5th, 7th, and 13th powers

5.4 Generating a Form Along a Vertical Path

A mass model for the exploration of tall building forms can be constructed from a series of stacked sections. Each section has a shape and a size, and it is repeated some number of times at some interval. Basic parameters include: section shape, dimension of section, number of floors, and floor-to-floor height. The section shape can be a simple polygon; circular or elliptical; curve equations that generate a closed boundary; or any set of points that form a closed boundary. As the section is repeated it can be transformed by size, radius, or dimensions. It can include angle of a polygon; rotation, or an offset in plan, along the x and y axes; or morphed from one section to another, such as an ellipse to a circle. All of these transformations can be varied linearly or using a curve function.

These models have a number of digital representations that serve different functions:

* All edges as `LINEs`, for structural analysis

* All sections as a `3DMESH`, for rendering and rapid prototyping, with a closed top and bottom

* Each floorplate as a `POLYLINE`, for computation of gross floor area

* Each floorplate as a `POLYLINE` converted to a `REGION`, to model floorplates only

All of the examples included here are demonstrated as standalone functions. If each were to be converted to a callable function and a starting elevation and centerpoint added, they could be used as a kit-of-parts to assemble a complete multiuse tall building having different shaped floorplates as well as, floor-to-floor heights appropriate for each use.

Tower with a simple polygon section

For the first version, use a simple polygon section for the floorplan. The parameters include number of floors, floor-to-floor height, and number of sides for the polygon section.

Start a new drawing and set the units to architectural. Set the grid to 1 foot, and turn off all snaps and dynamic input. Start a new AutoLISP file in the editor: `CH05C.LSP`.

The tower will be represented as a single `3DMESH`. The mesh will consist of `(NumLevels + 1)` by `(NumSides + 1)` points: one closed set of points for every floor and the roof. Since we have to generate each point for the section, each individual point of the polygon will have to be computed.

The general outline for `PROG01` is:

```
(defun prog01 ()
 ; set center
 ; get input
 ; make and erase current layer
 ; set floor elevation
 ; start 3DMESH
 (repeat for number of floors
  ; compute angle increment
  ; set start angle
  (repeat for number of polygon sides
   ; compute point
   ; add points to the 3DMESH
   ;increment polygon angle
  )
 ; increment floor elevation
 )
)
```

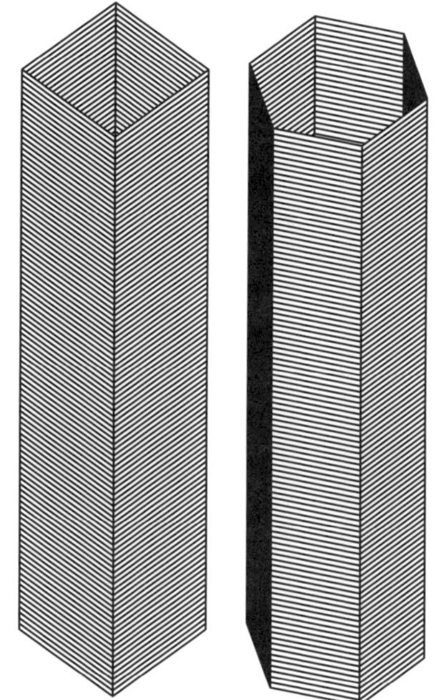

`PROG01`: polygon section of 4 and 5 sides

Sample script file for PROG01:

```
;----------------------------------
(prog01)
; Layer name:
LAYER01a
; number of floors
100
; floor height
10'
; number polygon sides
4
; radius
120'
;----------------------------------
```

Completed function PROG01, add to CH04C.LSP:

```
;----------------------------------
(defun dtr (a) (* pi (/ a 180.0)))
(defun rtd (a) (/ (* a 180.0) pi))
;----------------------------------
(defun prog01 ()
 (graphscr)
 ; tower polygon section
 (setvar “CMDECHO” 0)
 ; centerpoint
 (setq cpnt (list 0.0 0.0 0.0))
 ; get tower parameters
 (princ “\nProg01 - Tower”)
 (setq TowerLayer
   (getstring
   “\nEnter layer name: “))
 (setq NumLevels
   (getint
   “\nEnter number of levels: “))
 (setq LevelHeight
   (getdist
   “\nEnter level height: “))
 (setq NumSides
   (getint
   “\nEnter number of polygon
   sides: “))
 (setq Rad
   (getdist “\nEnter radius: “))
 ; clear layer
 (command “.LAYER” “THAW” “*”
   “ON” “*” “”)
 (command “.LAYER”
   “MAKE” TowerLayer “”)
 (command “.LAYER” “SET” 0 “”)
 (command “.LAYER” “OFF” “@*”
   “FREEZE” “@*” “”)
 (command “.LAYER” “THAW” TowerLayer
   “ON” TowerLayer
   “SET” TowerLayer “”)
 (command “.ERASE” “ALL” “”)
 ; set elev
 (setq LevelElev 0.0)
 ; start mesh
 (command “.3DMESH”
   (+ NumLevels 1) (+ NumSides 1))
 ; create each level
 (repeat (+ NumLevels 1)
  ; draw polygon
  (setq panginc
    (/ 360.0 NumSides))
  (setq pang (/ panginc 2.0))
  (repeat (+ NumSides 1)
   ; compute point
   (setq xpt (+ (nth 0 cpnt)
     (* Rad (sin (dtr pang)))))
   (setq ypt (+ (nth 1 cpnt)
     (* Rad (cos (dtr pang)))))
   (setq npnt
     (list xpt ypt LevelElev))
   ; add to mesh
   (command npnt)
   ; inc ang
   (setq pang (+ pang panginc))
  )
 ; inc elev
 (setq LevelElev
   (+ LevelElev LevelHeight))
 )
 (setvar “CMDECHO” 1)
 (command “.VIEW” “swiso”)
 (command “.ZOOM” “e”)
 (command “.HIDE”)
 (princ)
)
;----------------------------------
```

Review PROG01. The nested loops for the floors and polygon section, the generation of the polygon section, and the incrementing of the floor elevation.

Add top and bottom surfaces to the tower

Add surfaces to close the `3DMESH` at both ends. Add function `PROG02`. Using a copy of `PROG01`, add bottom and top surfaces to the tower.

Modify the `3DMESH` command for two additional sets of points:

```
; start mesh
(command ".3DMESH"
  (+ (+ NumLevels 1) 2)
  (+ NumSides 1))
```

Based on the number of sides, add those points. For example, for the bottom before the first section is computed:

```
; add bottom
(setq npnt cpnt)
(repeat (+ NumSides 1)
 (command npnt)
)
```

Do the same for the top of the tower, after all levels are specified.

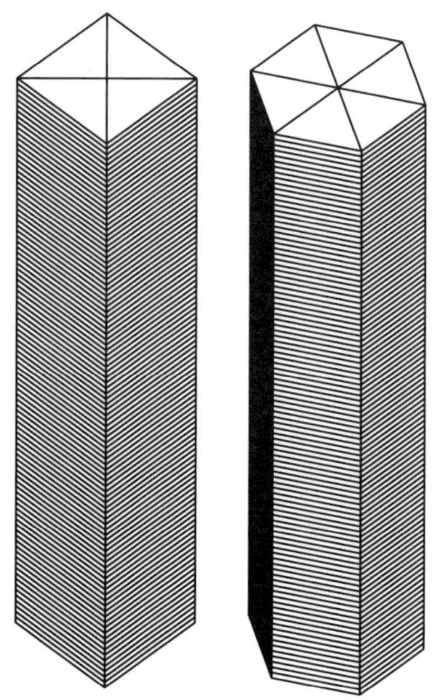

`PROG02`: top and bottom surfaces added

Completed function `PROG02`:

```
;-----------------------------------
(defun prog02 ()
 (graphscr)
 ; tower polygon section
 ; add bottom and top
 (setvar "CMDECHO" 0)
 ; centerpoint
 (setq cpnt (list 0.0 0.0 0.0))
 ; get tower parameters
 (princ "\nProg02 - Tower")
 (setq TowerLayer
   (getstring
   "\nEnter layer name: "))
```

```
(setq NumLevels
  (getint
  "\nEnter number of levels: "))
(setq LevelHeight
  (getdist
  "\nEnter level height: "))
(setq NumSides
  (getint "\nEnter number of polygon
  sides: "))
(setq Rad
  (getdist "\nEnter radius: "))
; clear layer
(command ".LAYER" "THAW" "*"
  "ON" "*" "")
(command ".LAYER"
  "MAKE" TowerLayer "")
(command ".LAYER" "SET" 0 "")
(command ".LAYER" "OFF" "@*"
  "FREEZE" "@*" "")
(command ".LAYER" "THAW" TowerLayer
  "ON" TowerLayer
  "SET" TowerLayer "")
(command ".ERASE" "ALL" "")
; set elev
(setq LevelElev 0.0)
; start mesh
(command ".3DMESH"
  (+ (+ NumLevels 1) 2)
  (+ NumSides 1))
; add bottom
(setq npnt cpnt)
(repeat (+ NumSides 1)
 (command npnt)
)
; create each level
(repeat (+ NumLevels 1)
 ; draw polygon
 (setq panginc (/ 360.0 NumSides))
 (setq pang (/ panginc 2.0))
 (repeat (+ NumSides 1)
  ; compute point
  (setq xpt (+ (nth 0 cpnt)
   (* Rad (sin (dtr pang)))))
  (setq ypt (+ (nth 1 cpnt)
   (* Rad (cos (dtr pang)))))
  (setq npnt
    (list xpt ypt LevelElev))
  ; add to mesh
  (command npnt)
  ; inc ang
  (setq pang (+ pang panginc))
 )
 ; inc elev
 (setq LevelElev
   (+ LevelElev LevelHeight))
)
; add top
(setq npnt (list
  (nth 0 cpnt) (nth 1 cpnt)
  (- LevelElev LevelHeight)))
(repeat (+ NumSides 1)
 (command npnt)
)
(setvar "CMDECHO" 1)
(command ".VIEW" "swiso")
(command ".ZOOM" "e")
(command ".HIDE")
(princ)
)
;----------------------------------
```

Taper the tower section

Add function PROG03. Using a copy of PROG02, taper the tower by changing the radius of the polygon section at each floor.

Replace the input for a single radius with:

```
(setq RadStart
  (getdist
  "\nEnter start radius: "))
(setq RadEnd
  (getdist
  "\nEnter end radius: "))
```

Compute a radius increment based on the number of floors; set the radius starting value; and increment the radius at each level.

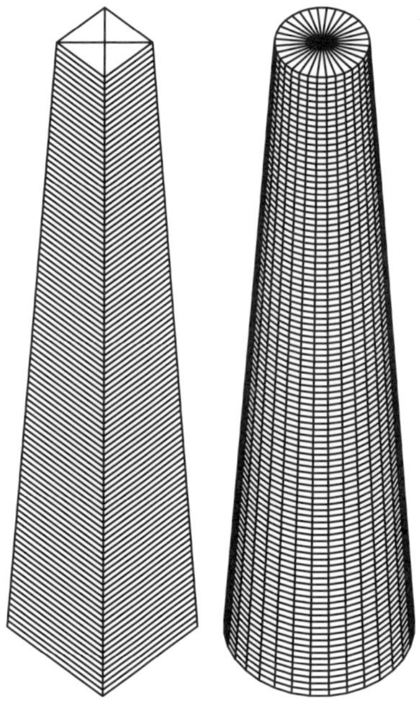

PROG03: tapered polygon shaped floors, 4 and 32 sides

Sample script file for PROG03:

```
;----------------------------------
(prog03)
; Layer name:
LAYER03b
; number of levels
100
; level height
10'
; number polygon sides
32
; radius start
120'
; radius end
60'
;----------------------------------
```

Completed function PROG03:

```
;----------------------------------
(defun prog03 ()
 (graphscr)
 ; tower by polygon repeats
 ; taper
 (setvar "CMDECHO" 0)
 ; centerpoint
 (setq cpnt (list 0.0 0.0 0.0))
 ; get curve parameters
 (princ "\nProg03 - Tower")
 (setq TowerLayer
   (getstring
   "\nEnter layer name: "))
 (setq NumLevels
   (getint
   "\nEnter number of levels: "))
 (setq LevelHeight
   (getdist
   "\nEnter level height: "))
 (setq NumSides
   (getint
   "\nEnter number of polygon
   sides: "))
 (setq RadStart
   (getdist
   "\nEnter start radius: "))
 (setq RadEnd
   (getdist
   "\nEnter end radius: "))
 ; clear layer
 (command ".LAYER" "THAW" "*"
   "ON" "*" "")
 (command ".LAYER"
   "MAKE" TowerLayer "")
 (command ".LAYER" "SET" 0 "")
 (command ".LAYER" "OFF" "@*"
   "FREEZE" "@*" "")
 (command ".LAYER" "THAW" TowerLayer
   "ON" TowerLayer
   "SET" TowerLayer "")
 (command ".ERASE" "ALL" "")
 ; set elev
 (setq LevelElev 0.0)
 ; start mesh
 (command ".3DMESH"
   (+ (+ NumLevels 1) 2)
   (+ NumSides 1))
 ; add bottom
```

```
  (setq npnt cpnt)
  (repeat (+ NumSides 1)
   (command npnt)
  )
  ; radius inc
  (setq RadInc
    (/ (- RadEnd RadStart)
    NumLevels))
  (setq Rad RadStart)
  ; create each level
  (repeat (+ NumLevels 1)
   ; draw polygon
   (setq panginc (/ 360.0 NumSides))
   (setq pang (/ panginc 2.0))
   (repeat (+ NumSides 1)
    ; compute point
    (setq xpt (+ (nth 0 cpnt)
      (* Rad (sin (dtr pang)))))
    (setq ypt (+ (nth 1 cpnt)
      (* Rad (cos (dtr pang)))))
    (setq npnt
      (list xpt ypt LevelElev))
    ; add to mesh
    (command npnt)
    ; inc ang
    (setq pang (+ pang panginc))
   )
   ; inc radius
   (setq Rad (+ Rad RadInc))
   ; inc elev
   (setq LevelElev
     (+ LevelElev LevelHeight))
  )
  ; add top
  (setq npnt (list
    (nth 0 cpnt) (nth 1 cpnt)
    (- LevelElev LevelHeight)))
  (repeat (+ NumSides 1)
   (command npnt)
  )
  (setvar "CMDECHO" 1)
  (command ".VIEW" "swiso")
  (command ".ZOOM" "e")
  (command ".HIDE")
  (princ)
)
;---------------------------------
```

Twist the tower section

Add function PROG04. Using a copy of PROG03, twist the tower by rotating each floor.

Then add:

```
(setq RotTotal
  (getreal
  "\nEnter total rotation angle: "))
```

To twist each floor, each point of the polygon section must be rotated by the current twist angle:

```
; compute point
(setq xpt (+ (nth 0 cpnt)
  (* Rad (sin (dtr pang)))))
(setq ypt (+ (nth 1 cpnt)
  (* Rad (cos (dtr pang)))))
; rotate point
(setq rxpt
  (- (* xpt (cos (dtr Rotang)))
   (* ypt (sin (dtr Rotang)))))
(setq rypt
  (+ (* xpt (sin (dtr Rotang)))
   (* ypt (cos (dtr Rotang)))))
(setq npnt
  (list rxpt rypt LevelElev))
```

Add a rotation-angle increment based on the number of floors; set the angle starting value to zero; and increment the angle at each floor.

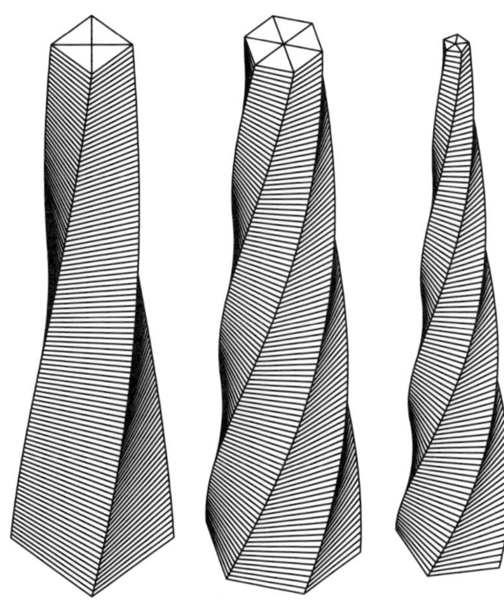

PROG04: tapered polygon sections with four, five, and six sides, and rotated 90, 180, and 270 degrees.

Sample script file for PROG04:

```
;-----------------------------------
(prog04)
; Layer name:
LAYER04c
; number of levels
100
; level height
10'
; number polygon sides
5
; radius start
90'
; radius end
20'
; rotation
270
;-----------------------------------
```

Completed function PROG04:

```
;-----------------------------------
(defun prog04 ()
 (graphscr)
 ; tower by polygon repeats
 ; twist
 (setvar "CMDECHO" 0)
 ; centerpoint
 (setq cpnt (list 0.0 0.0 0.0))
 ; get curve parameters
 (princ "\nProg04 - Tower")
 (setq TowerLayer
   (getstring
   "\nEnter layer name: "))
 (setq NumLevels
   (getint
   "\nEnter number of levels: "))
 (setq LevelHeight
   (getdist
   "\nEnter level height: "))
 (setq NumSides
   (getint
   "\nEnter number of polygon
   sides: "))
 (setq RadStart
   (getdist
   "\nEnter start radius: "))
 (setq RadEnd
   (getdist
   "\nEnter end radius: "))
 (setq RotTotal
   (getreal
   "\nEnter total rotation
   angle: "))
 ; clear layer
 (command ".LAYER" "THAW" "*"
   "ON" "*" "")
 (command ".LAYER"
   "MAKE" TowerLayer "")
 (command ".LAYER" "SET" 0 "")
 (command ".LAYER" "OFF" "@*"
   "FREEZE" "@*" "")
 (command ".LAYER" "THAW" TowerLayer
   "ON" TowerLayer
   "SET" TowerLayer "")
 (command ".ERASE" "ALL" "")
 ; set elev
```

```
(setq LevelElev 0.0)
; start mesh
(command ".3DMESH"
  (+ (+ NumLevels 1) 2)
  (+ NumSides 1))
; add bottom
(setq npnt cpnt)
(repeat (+ NumSides 1)
 (command npnt)
)
; radius inc
(setq RadInc
  (/ (- RadEnd RadStart)
  NumLevels))
(setq Rad RadStart)
; rotation inc
(setq RotInc
  (/ RotTotal NumLevels))
(setq Rotang 0.0)
; create each level
(repeat (+ NumLevels 1)
 ; draw polygon
 (setq panginc (/ 360.0 NumSides))
 (setq pang (/ panginc 2.0))
 (repeat (+ NumSides 1)
  ; compute point
  (setq xpt (+ (nth 0 cpnt)
    (* Rad (sin (dtr pang)))))
  (setq ypt (+ (nth 1 cpnt)
    (* Rad (cos (dtr pang)))))
  ; rotate point
  (setq rxpt
    (- (* xpt (cos (dtr Rotang)))
    (* ypt (sin (dtr Rotang)))))
  (setq rypt
    (+ (* xpt (sin (dtr Rotang)))
    (* ypt (cos (dtr Rotang)))))
  (setq npnt
    (list rxpt rypt LevelElev))
  ; add to mesh
  (command npnt)
  ; inc ang
  (setq pang (+ pang panginc))
 )
 ; inc radius
 (setq Rad (+ Rad RadInc))
 ; inc elev
 (setq LevelElev
    (+ LevelElev LevelHeight))
  ; inc rotation
  (setq Rotang (+ Rotang Rotinc))
 )
 ; add top
 (setq npnt (list
   (nth 0 cpnt) (nth 1 cpnt)
   (- LevelElev LevelHeight)))
 (repeat (+ NumSides 1)
  (command npnt)
 )
 (setvar "CMDECHO" 1)
 (command ".VIEW" "swiso")
 (command ".ZOOM" "e")
 (command ".HIDE")
 (princ)
)
;---------------------------------
```

Offset top section of the tower

Add function PROG05. Using a copy of PROG03, offset the top by adding an x- and y-offset at each level, starting from the bottom.

Add input for the offsets:

```
(setq Xoffset
  (getdist
  "\nEnter top X offset: "))
(setq Yoffset
  (getdist
  "\nEnter top Y offset: "))
```

Compute an x- and y-offset increment based on the number of floors, set each offset starting value to 0.0; add the offset increment to the polygon center; and increment the offsets at each floor.

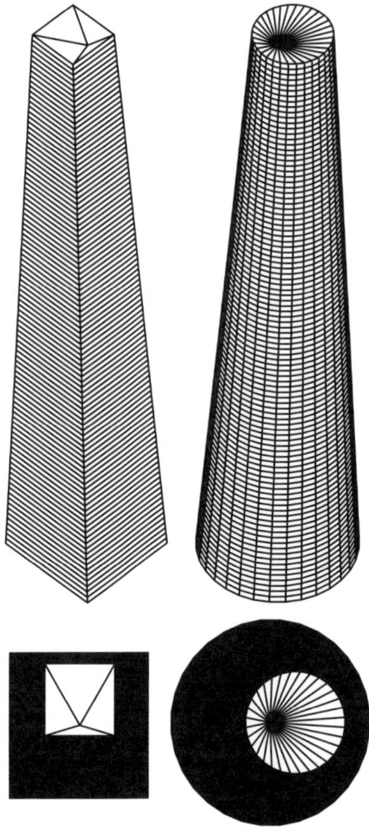

PROG05: tapered polygon sections with four and thirty-two sides, and with an x- and y-offset

Sample script file for PROG05:

```
;----------------------------------
(prog05)
; Layer name:
LAYER05b
; number of levels
100
; level height
10'
; number polygon sides
32
; radius start
120'
; radius end
60'
; X Y offset
30'
;----------------------------------
```

Completed function PROG05:

```
;----------------------------------
(defun prog05 ()
 (graphscr)
 ; tower by polygon repeats
 ; offsets
 (setvar "CMDECHO" 0)
 ; centerpoint
 (setq cpnt (list 0.0 0.0 0.0))
 ; get tower parameters
 (princ "\nProg05 - Tower")
 (setq TowerLayer
   (getstring
   "\nEnter layer name: "))
 (setq NumLevels
   (getint
   "\nEnter number of levels: "))
 (setq LevelHeight
   (getdist
   "\nEnter level height: "))
 (setq NumSides
   (getint
   "\nEnter number of polygon
   sides: "))
 (setq RadStart
   (getdist
```

```
  "\nEnter start radius: "))
(setq RadEnd
  (getdist
  "\nEnter end radius: "))
(setq Xoffset
  (getdist
  "\nEnter top X offset: "))
(setq Yoffset
  (getdist
  "\nEnter top Y offset: "))
; clear layer
(command ".LAYER" "THAW" "*"
  "ON" "*" "")
(command ".LAYER"
  "MAKE" TowerLayer "")
(command ".LAYER" "SET" 0 "")
(command ".LAYER" "OFF" "@*"
  "FREEZE" "@*" "")
(command ".LAYER" "THAW" TowerLayer
  "ON" TowerLayer
  "SET" TowerLayer "")
(command ".ERASE" "ALL" "")
; set elev
(setq LevelElev 0.0)
; start mesh
(command ".3DMESH"
  (+ (+ NumLevels 1) 2)
  (+ NumSides 1))
; add bottom
(setq npnt cpnt)
(repeat (+ NumSides 1)
 (command npnt)
)
; radius inc
(setq RadInc
  (/ (- RadEnd RadStart)
  NumLevels))
(setq Rad RadStart)
; offset inc
(setq XoffInc
  (/ Xoffset NumLevels))
(setq Xoff 0.0)
(setq YoffInc
  (/ Yoffset NumLevels))
(setq Yoff 0.0)
; create each level
(repeat (+ NumLevels 1)
 ; draw polygon
  (setq panginc (/ 360.0 NumSides))
  (setq pang (/ panginc 2.0))
  (repeat (+ NumSides 1)
   ; compute point
   (setq xpt (+ (+ (nth 0 cpnt)
     (* Rad (sin (dtr pang))))
     Xoff))
   (setq ypt (+ (+ (nth 1 cpnt)
     (* Rad (cos (dtr pang))))
     Yoff))
   (setq npnt
     (list xpt ypt LevelElev))
   ; add to mesh
   (command npnt)
   ; inc ang
   (setq pang (+ pang panginc))
  )
  ; inc radius
  (setq Rad (+ Rad RadInc))
  ; inc elev
  (setq LevelElev
    (+ LevelElev LevelHeight))
  ; inc offset
  (setq Xoff (+ Xoff XoffInc))
  (setq Yoff (+ Yoff YoffInc))
 )
 ; add top
 (setq npnt (list
   (nth 0 cpnt) (nth 1 cpnt)
   (- LevelElev LevelHeight)))
 (repeat (+ NumSides 1)
  (command npnt)
 )
 (setvar "CMDECHO" 1)
 (command ".VIEW" "swiso")
 (command ".ZOOM" "e")
 (command ".HIDE")
 (princ)
)
;---------------------------------
```

Elliptical tower section

Add function PROG06. Using a copy of PROG02, modify the polygon-point computation to model an elliptical section by using an x and y-radius.

Replace the single radius input with:

```
(setq XRad
  (getdist "\nEnter X radius: "))
(setq YRad
  (getdist "\nEnter Y radius: "))
```

Modify the polygon-point computation to both an x- and y-radius:

```
; compute point
(setq xpt
  (+ (nth 0 cpnt)
  (* XRad (sin (dtr pang)))))
(setq ypt
  (+ (nth 1 cpnt)
  (* YRad (cos (dtr pang)))))
(setq npnt
  (list xpt ypt LevelElev))
```

The number of sides for the polygon will determine if you model a smooth ellipse or an elliptical polygon.

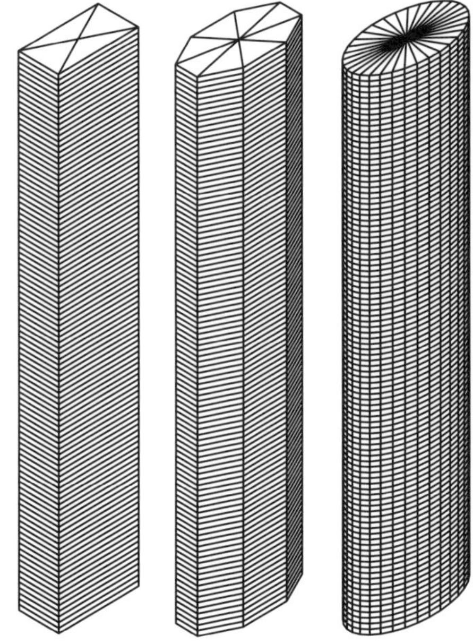

PROG06: elliptical floors, 4, 8, and 32 sides

Sample script file for PROG06:

```
;---------------------------------
(prog06)
; Layer name:
LAYER06b
; number of levels
100
; level height
10'
; number polygon sides
8
; X radius
120'
; Y radius
60'
;---------------------------------
```

Completed function PROG06:

```
;----------------------------------
(defun prog06 ()
 (graphscr)
 ; tower by polygon repeats
 ; elliptical form
 (setvar "CMDECHO" 0)
 ; centerpoint
 (setq cpnt (list 0.0 0.0 0.0))
 ; get tower parameters
 (princ "\nProg06 - Tower")
 (setq TowerLayer
   (getstring
   "\nEnter layer name: "))
 (setq NumLevels
   (getint
   "\nEnter number of levels: "))
 (setq LevelHeight
   (getdist
   "\nEnter level height: "))
 (setq NumSides
   (getint
   "\nEnter number of polygon
   sides: "))
 (setq XRad
   (getdist "\nEnter X radius: "))
 (setq YRad
   (getdist "\nEnter Y radius: "))
 ; clear layer
 (command ".LAYER" "THAW" "*"
   "ON" "*" "")
 (command ".LAYER"
   "MAKE" TowerLayer "")
 (command ".LAYER" "SET" 0 "")
 (command ".LAYER" "OFF" "@*"
   "FREEZE" "@*" "")
 (command ".LAYER" "THAW" TowerLayer
   "ON" TowerLayer
   "SET" TowerLayer "")
 (command ".ERASE" "ALL" "")
 ; set elev
 (setq LevelElev 0.0)
 ; start mesh
 (command ".3DMESH"
   (+ (+ NumLevels 1) 2)
   (+ NumSides 1))
 ; add bottom
 (setq npnt cpnt)
 (repeat (+ NumSides 1)
  (command npnt)
 )
 ; create each level
 (repeat (+ NumLevels 1)
  ; draw polygon
  (setq panginc (/ 360.0 NumSides))
  (setq pang (/ panginc 2.0))
  (repeat (+ NumSides 1)
   ; compute point
   (setq xpt (+ (nth 0 cpnt)
     (* XRad (sin (dtr pang)))))
   (setq ypt (+ (nth 1 cpnt)
     (* YRad (cos (dtr pang)))))
   (setq npnt
     (list xpt ypt LevelElev))
   ; add to mesh
   (command npnt)
   ; inc ang
   (setq pang (+ pang panginc))
  )
  ; inc elev
  (setq LevelElev
    (+ LevelElev LevelHeight))
 )
 ; add top
 (setq npnt (list
   (nth 0 cpnt) (nth 1 cpnt)
   (- LevelElev LevelHeight)))
 (repeat (+ NumSides 1)
  (command npnt)
 )
 (setvar "CMDECHO" 1)
 (command ".VIEW" "swiso")
 (command ".ZOOM" "e")
 (command ".HIDE")
 (princ)
)
;----------------------------------
```

Taper the elliptical section of the tower

Add function PROG07. Using a copy of PROG06, add a start and end x- and y-radius for the elliptical section. Compute an x- and y-radius increment based on the number of floors, set the x- and y-radius starting value, and increment the x- and y-radius for each level.

Replace the single x- and y-radius input with:

```
(setq XRadStart
  (getdist
  "\nEnter start X radius: "))
(setq XRadEnd
  (getdist
  "\nEnter end X radius: "))
(setq YRadStart
  (getdist
  "\nEnter start Y radius: "))
(setq YRadEnd
  (getdist
  "\nEnter end Y radius: "))
```

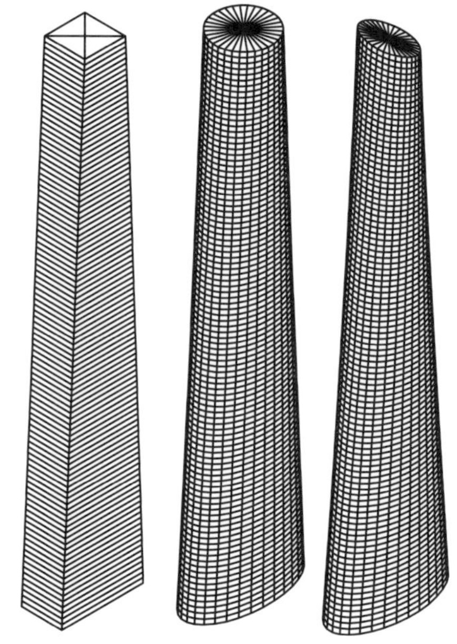

PROG07: elliptical section transformations

PROG07 examples include a transformation of a rectangle to a square, an ellipse to a circle, and an ellipse to another ellipse rotated 90 degrees.

Sample script file for PROG07:

```
;---------------------------------
(prog07)
; Layer name:
LAYER07c
; number of levels
100
; level height
10'
; number polygon sides
32
; X radius start
120'
; X radius end
30'
; Y radius start
60'
; Y radius end
60'
;---------------------------------
```

Completed function PROG07:

```
;----------------------------------
(defun prog07 ()
 (graphscr)
 ; tower by polygon repeats
 ; elliptical form
 (setvar "CMDECHO" 0)
 ; centerpoint
 (setq cpnt (list 0.0 0.0 0.0))
 ; get tower parameters
 (princ "\nProg07 - Tower")
 (setq TowerLayer
   (getstring
   "\nEnter layer name: "))
 (setq NumLevels
   (getint
   "\nEnter number of levels: "))
 (setq LevelHeight
   (getdist
   "\nEnter level height: "))
 (setq NumSides
   (getint
   "\nEnter number of polygon
   sides: "))
 (setq XRadStart
   (getdist
   "\nEnter start X radius: "))
 (setq XRadEnd
   (getdist
   "\nEnter end X radius: "))
 (setq YRadStart
   (getdist
   "\nEnter start Y radius: "))
 (setq YRadEnd
   (getdist
   "\nEnter end Y radius: "))
 ; clear layer
 (command ".LAYER" "THAW" "*"
   "ON" "*" "")
 (command ".LAYER"
   "MAKE" TowerLayer "")
 (command ".LAYER" "SET" 0 "")
 (command ".LAYER" "OFF" "@*"
   "FREEZE" "@*" "")
 (command ".LAYER" "THAW" TowerLayer
   "ON" TowerLayer
   "SET" TowerLayer "")
 (command ".ERASE" "ALL" "")
 ; set elev
 (setq LevelElev 0.0)
 ; start mesh
 (command ".3DMESH"
   (+ (+ NumLevels 1) 2)
   (+ NumSides 1))
 ; add bottom
 (setq npnt cpnt)
 (repeat (+ NumSides 1)
  (command npnt)
 )
 ; radius inc
 (setq XRadInc
   (/ (- XRadEnd XRadStart)
   NumLevels))
 (setq XRad XRadStart)
 ; radius inc
 (setq YRadInc
   (/ (- YRadEnd YRadStart)
   NumLevels))
 (setq YRad YRadStart)
 ; create each level
 (repeat (+ NumLevels 1)
  ; draw polygon
  (setq panginc (/ 360.0 NumSides))
  (setq pang (/ panginc 2.0))
  (repeat (+ NumSides 1)
   ; compute point
   (setq xpt (+ (nth 0 cpnt)
     (* XRad (sin (dtr pang)))))
   (setq ypt (+ (nth 1 cpnt)
     (* YRad (cos (dtr pang)))))
   (setq npnt
     (list xpt ypt LevelElev))
   ; add to mesh
   (command npnt)
   ; inc ang
   (setq pang (+ pang panginc))
  )
  ; inc radius
  (setq XRad (+ XRad XRadInc))
  (setq YRad (+ YRad YRadInc))
  ; inc elev
  (setq LevelElev
    (+ LevelElev LevelHeight))
 )
 ; add top
 (setq npnt (list
   (nth 0 cpnt) (nth 1 cpnt)
```

```
    (- LevelElev LevelHeight)))
  (repeat (+ NumSides 1)
   (command npnt)
  )
  (setvar "CMDECHO" 1)
  (command ".VIEW" "swiso")
  (command ".ZOOM" "e")
  (command ".HIDE")
  (princ)
)
;----------------------------------
```

Vary the dimensions of the section in the tower

Add function PROG08. Using a copy of PROG02, modify the single radius to include a radius-offset distance and an angle for controlling the amount of the offset used at each floor, in this case by the sine function.

Add input for the radius offset and angle as:

```
(setq RadOff
  (getdist
  "\nEnter radius offset: "))
(setq RadOffAng
  (getreal
  "\nEnter radius offset angle: "))
```

The modified radius is computed as:

```
(setq NewRad
  (+ Rad (* (sin (dtr rang))
  RadOff)))
```

Compute a radius-offset angle increment based on the number of floors, set it to a starting value of 0.0, and increment it for each floor.

A further modification would be to use the cosine function or any other mathematical curve function. Place the same controls on the elliptical version. You could also include a start and end angle, assuming it does not have 0 degrees as the start.

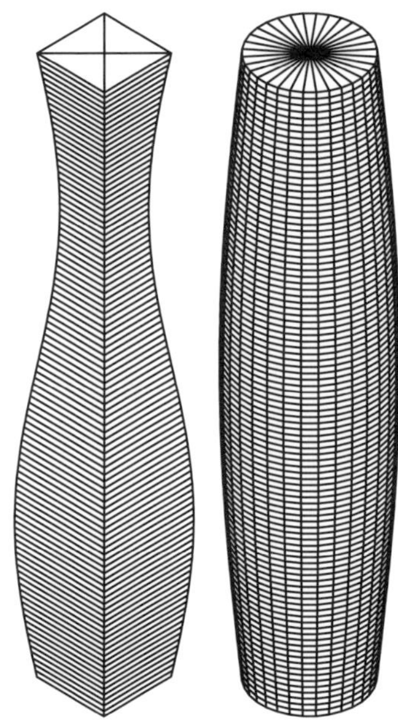

PROG08: polygon sections with four and thirty-two sides, varied by a sine curve

Sample script file for PROG08:

```
;----------------------------------
(prog08)
; Layer name:
LAYER08b
; number of levels
100
; level height
10'
; number polygon sides
32
; radius
90'
; radius offset
30'
; radius offset angle
180
;----------------------------------
```

Completed function PROG08:

```
;--------------------------------
(defun prog08 ()
 (graphscr)
 ; tower by polygon repeats
 ; curve applied to offset
 (setvar "CMDECHO" 0)
 ; centerpoint
 (setq cpnt (list 0.0 0.0 0.0))
 ; get tower parameters
 (princ "\nProg08 - Tower")
 (setq TowerLayer
   (getstring
   "\nEnter layer name: "))
 (setq NumLevels
   (getint
   "\nEnter number of levels: "))
 (setq LevelHeight
   (getdist
   "\nEnter level height: "))
 (setq NumSides
   (getint
   "\nEnter number of polygon
   sides: "))
 (setq Rad
   (getdist "\nEnter radius: "))
 (setq RadOff
   (getdist
   "\nEnter radius offset: "))
 (setq RadOffAng
   (getreal
   "\nEnter radius offset
   angle: "))
 ; clear layer
 (command ".LAYER" "THAW" "*"
   "ON" "*" "")
 (command ".LAYER"
   "MAKE" TowerLayer "")
 (command ".LAYER" "SET" 0 "")
 (command ".LAYER" "OFF" "@*"
   "FREEZE" "@*" "")
 (command ".LAYER" "THAW" TowerLayer
   "ON" TowerLayer
   "SET" TowerLayer "")
 (command ".ERASE" "ALL" "")
 ; set elev
 (setq LevelElev 0.0)
 ; start mesh
 (command ".3DMESH"
   (+ (+ NumLevels 1) 2)
   (+ NumSides 1))
 ; add bottom
 (setq npnt cpnt)
 (repeat (+ NumSides 1)
  (command npnt)
 )
 ; offset ang
 (setq ranginc
   (/ RadOffAng Numlevels))
 (setq rang 0.0)
 ; create each level
 (repeat (+ NumLevels 1)
  ; draw polygon
  (setq panginc (/ 360.0 NumSides))
  (setq pang (/ panginc 2.0))
  (repeat (+ NumSides 1)
   ; compute point
   (setq NewRad
     (+ Rad (* (sin (dtr rang))
     RadOff)))
   (setq xpt (+ (nth 0 cpnt)
     (* NewRad (sin (dtr pang)))))
   (setq ypt (+ (nth 1 cpnt)
     (* NewRad (cos (dtr pang)))))
   (setq npnt
     (list xpt ypt LevelElev))
   ; add to mesh
   (command npnt)
   ; inc ang
   (setq pang (+ pang panginc))
  )
  ; inc offset angle
  (setq rang (+ rang ranginc))
  ; inc elev
  (setq LevelElev
    (+ LevelElev LevelHeight))
 )
 ; add top
 (setq npnt (list
   (nth 0 cpnt) (nth 1 cpnt)
   (- LevelElev LevelHeight)))
 (repeat (+ NumSides 1)
  (command npnt)
 )
 (setvar "CMDECHO" 1)
```

```
  (command ".VIEW" "swiso")
  (command ".ZOOM" "e")
  (command ".HIDE")
  (princ)
)
;---------------------------------
```

Vary selective edges of a section of the tower

Add function PROG09. Using a copy of PROG08, instead of varying the radius by an offset on all points in the polygon, only vary a selective list of points. This is the same as PROG08, except that if the computed point number is in the list, use a modified radius value.

First add the list of points to be modified:

```
(setq ModPts
  (read (getstring
  "\nEnter list of points to modify:
")))
```

The read function will convert the string to a list. For example, if point 2 was to be modified, the input would be the string (2).

In the computation of polygon points, a test is added to check if the point is in the entered list:

```
; compute point
(setq NewRad Rad)
; check to modify point
(if (> (length
  (member pcnt ModPts)) 0)
(setq NewRad
  (+ Rad (* (sin (dtr rang))
  RadOff)))
)
(setq xpt (+ (nth 0 cpnt)
  (* NewRad (sin (dtr pang)))))
(setq ypt (+ (nth 1 cpnt)
  (* NewRad (cos (dtr pang)))))
(setq npnt
  (list xpt ypt LevelElev))
```

The new radius is set to the entered value, and then a point counter is checked against the list of points to be modified. If the member function finds it, it will return a list; otherwise nil will be returned or the empty list. If the returned list's length is greater than zero, the point is in the list and the radius is recomputed.

At the command line, review the member and length functions for lists:

```
>> (member 5 (list 1 4 5))
(5)
>> (member 1 (list 1 4 5))
(1 4 5)
>> (member 6 (list 1 4 5))
nil
>> (length (member 4 (list 1 4 5)))
2
>> (length (member 8 (list 1 4 5)))
0
```

PROG09 examples include a three-sided section with one point modified and a four-sided section with opposite points modified.

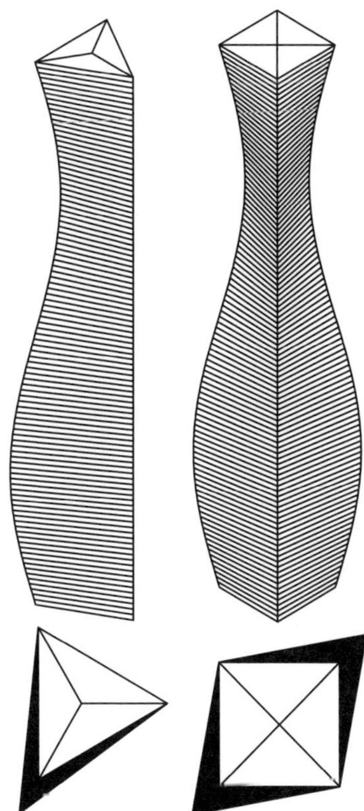

PROG09: vary the section radius of selected points

Sample script files for PROG09:

```
;----------------------------------
(prog09)
; Layer name:
LAYER09a
; number of levels
100
; level height
10'
; number of sides
3
; radius start
90'
; radius offset
40'
; radius angle
360
; points to modify
( 3 )
;----------------------------------
```

And:

```
;----------------------------------
(prog09)
; Layer name:
LAYER09b
; number of levels
100
; level height
10'
; number of sides
4
; radius start
90'
; radius offset
40'
; radius angle
360
; points to modify
( 2  4 )
;----------------------------------
```

Completed function PROG09:

```
;----------------------------------
(defun prog09 ()
 (graphscr)
 ; tower repeats
 ; curve on selective edges
 (setvar "CMDECHO" 0)
 ; centerpoint
 (setq cpnt (list 0.0 0.0 0.0))
 ; get curve parameters
 (princ "\nProg09 - Tower")
 (setq TowerLayer
   (getstring
   "\nEnter layer name: "))
 (setq NumLevels
   (getint
```

```
    "\nEnter number of levels: "))
  (setq LevelHeight
    (getdist
    "\nEnter level height: "))
  (setq NumSides
    (getint
    "\nEnter number of polygon
    sides: "))
  (setq Rad
    (getdist "\nEnter radius: "))
  (setq RadOff
    (getdist
    "\nEnter radius offset: "))
  (setq RadOffAng
    (getreal
    "\nEnter radius offset
    angle: "))
  (setq ModPts
    (read (getstring
    "\nEnter list of points to
    modify: ")))
  ; clear layer
  (command ".LAYER" "THAW" "*"
    "ON" "*" "")
  (command ".LAYER"
    "MAKE" TowerLayer "")
  (command ".LAYER" "SET" 0 "")
  (command ".LAYER" "OFF" "@*"
     "FREEZE" "@*" "")
  (command ".LAYER" "THAW" TowerLayer
    "ON" TowerLayer
    "SET" TowerLayer "")
  (command ".ERASE" "ALL" "")
  ; set elev
  (setq LevelElev 0.0)
  ; start mesh
  (command ".3DMESH"
    (+ (+ NumLevels 1) 2)
    (+ NumSides 1))
  ; add bottom
  (setq npnt cpnt)
  (repeat (+ NumSides 1)
   (command npnt)
  )
  ; offset ang
  (setq ranginc
    (/ RadOffAng Numlevels))
  (setq rang 0.0)
  ; create each level
  (repeat (+ NumLevels 1)
   ; draw polygon
   (setq panginc (/ 360.0 NumSides))
   (setq pang (/ panginc 2.0))
   ; point counter
   (setq pcnt 1)
   (repeat (+ NumSides 1)
    ; compute point
    (setq NewRad Rad)
    ; check to modify point
    (if (> (length
      (member pcnt ModPts)) 0)
     (setq NewRad
       (+ Rad (* (sin (dtr rang))
       RadOff)))
    )
    (setq xpt (+ (nth 0 cpnt)
      (* NewRad (sin (dtr pang)))))
    (setq ypt (+ (nth 1 cpnt)
      (* NewRad (cos (dtr pang)))))
    (setq npnt
      (list xpt ypt LevelElev))
    ; add to mesh
    (command npnt)
    ; inc ang
    (setq pang (+ pang panginc))
    ; inc count
    (setq pcnt (+ pcnt 1))
   )
   ; inc offset angle
   (setq rang (+ rang ranginc))
   ; inc elev
   (setq LevelElev
     (+ LevelElev LevelHeight))
  )
  ; add top
  (setq npnt (list
    (nth 0 cpnt) (nth 1 cpnt)
    (- LevelElev LevelHeight)))
  (repeat (+ NumSides 1)
   (command npnt)
  )
  (setvar "CMDECHO" 1)
  (command ".VIEW" "swiso")
  (command ".ZOOM" "e")
  (command ".HIDE")
  (princ)
)
;---------------------------------
```

Tower sections from mathematical curves

For this series of variations, instead of using a polygon section, use a mathematical curve function to develop a section that can be modified by its dimensions. For example, for a Cardioid Curve, add function PROG10a using a copy of PROG03. The input already has a start and end radius.

For function PROG10a, replace the regular polygon-point computation with:

```
; compute point
(setq xpt (* 2 (* (/ Rad 4)
  (* (cos (dtr pang))
   (+ 1 (cos (dtr pang)))))))
(setq ypt (* 2 (* (/ Rad 4)
  (* (sin (dtr pang))
   (+ 1 (cos (dtr pang)))))))
(setq npnt
  (list xpt ypt LevelElev))
```

Add PROG10b, Geometric Pedal B Curve, using a copy of PROG03. For function PROG10b, replace the regular polygon-point computation with:

```
; compute point
(setq rval (+ 2.0 (* 1.0
  (expt (cos (dtr pang))
  (* 2 8.0)))))
(setq xpt (* (* rval (/ Rad 4))
   (cos (dtr pang))))
(setq ypt (* (* rval (/ Rad 4))
   (sin (dtr pang))))
(setq npnt
  (list xpt ypt LevelElev))
```

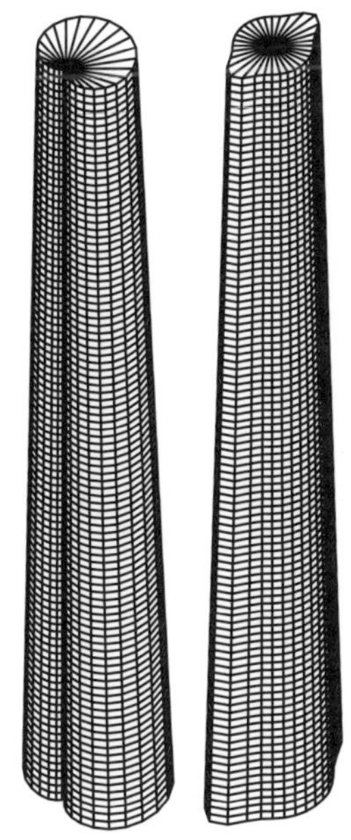

PROG10a and PROG10b: Cardioid and Geometric Pedal B Curve sections with thirty-two sides

Sample script file for PROG10a:

```
;---------------------------------
(prog10a)
; Layer name:
LAYER10a
; number of levels
100
; level height
10'
; number of sides
32
; radius start
120'
; radius end
80'
;---------------------------------
```

Completed function PROG10a:

```
;---------------------------------
(defun prog10a ()
 (graphscr)
 ; tower repeats
 ; Cardioid Curve for section
 ; x = 2 a cos t (1 + cos t)
 ; y = 2 a sin t (1 + cos t)
 (setvar "CMDECHO" 0)
 ; centerpoint
 (setq cpnt (list 0.0 0.0 0.0))
 ; get curve parameters
 (princ "\nProg10a - Tower")
 (setq TowerLayer
   (getstring
   "\nEnter layer name: "))
 (setq NumLevels
   (getint
   "\nEnter number of levels: "))
 (setq LevelHeight
   (getdist
   "\nEnter level height: "))
 (setq NumSides
   (getint
   "\nEnter number of curve
   sides: "))
 (setq RadStart
   (getdist "\nEnter start
   radius: "))
 (setq RadEnd
   (getdist "\nEnter radius end: "))
 ; clear layer
 (command ".LAYER" "THAW" "*"
   "ON" "*" "")
 (command ".LAYER"
   "MAKE" TowerLayer "")
 (command ".LAYER" "SET" 0 "")
 (command ".LAYER" "OFF" "@*"
   "FREEZE" "@*" "")
 (command ".LAYER" "THAW" TowerLayer
   "ON" TowerLayer
   "SET" TowerLayer "")
 (command ".ERASE" "ALL" "")
 ; set elev
 (setq LevelElev 0.0)
 ; start mesh
 (command ".3DMESH"
   (+ (+ NumLevels 1) 2)
   (+ NumSides 1))
 ; add bottom
 (setq npnt cpnt)
 (repeat (+ NumSides 1)
  (command npnt)
 )
 ; radius inc
 (setq RadInc
   (/ (- RadEnd RadStart)
   NumLevels))
 (setq Rad RadStart)
 ; create each level
 (repeat (+ NumLevels 1)
  ; draw polygon
  (setq panginc (/ 360.0 NumSides))
  (setq pang 0.0)
  (repeat (+ NumSides 1)
   ; compute point
   (setq xpt (* 2 (* (/ Rad 4)
     (* (cos (dtr pang))
     (+ 1 (cos (dtr pang)))))))
   (setq ypt (* 2 (* (/ Rad 4)
     (* (sin (dtr pang))
     (+ 1 (cos (dtr pang)))))))
   (setq npnt
     (list xpt ypt LevelElev))
   ; add to mesh
   (command npnt)
   ; inc ang
   (setq pang (+ pang panginc))
  )
  ; inc elev
  (setq LevelElev
    (+ LevelElev LevelHeight))
  ; inc radius
  (setq Rad (+ Rad RadInc))
 )
 ; add top
 (setq npnt (list
   (nth 0 cpnt) (nth 1 cpnt)
   (- LevelElev LevelHeight)))
 (repeat (+ NumSides 1)
  (command npnt)
 )
 (setvar "CMDECHO" 1)
 (command ".VIEW" "swiso")
 (command ".ZOOM" "e")
 (command ".HIDE")
 (princ)
)
;---------------------------------
```

Add function PROG10c, a Hippopede Curve with rotating section, using a copy of PROG04. For function PROG10c, replace the regular polygon-point computation with:

```
; compute point
(setq Xrad
  (/ XRadStart 2))
(setq YRad
  (* YRadFact XRad))
(setq xpt
  (* (* 2 (cos (dtr pang)))
  (sqrt (- (* XRad YRad)
  (* (expt YRad 2)
  (expt (sin (dtr pang)) 2))))))
(setq ypt
  (* (* 2 (sin (dtr pang)))
  (sqrt (- (* XRad YRad)
  (* (expt YRad 2)
  (expt (sin (dtr pang)) 2))))))
```

The input for radius is modified to:

```
(setq XRadStart
  (getdist "\nEnter X radius: "))
(setq YRadStart
  (getreal
  "\nEnter Y radius start factor: "))
(setq YRadEnd
  (getreal
  "\nEnter Y radius end factor: "))
```

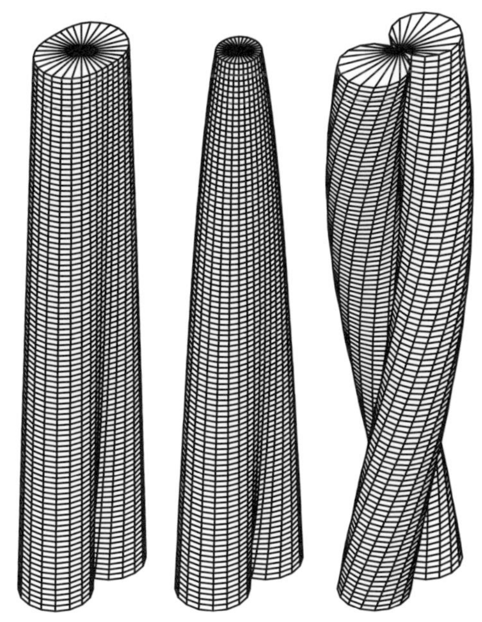

PROG10c: Hippopede Curve with thirty-two sides and changing radius and a rotation

Sample script file for PROG10c:

```
;----------------------------------
(prog10c)
; Layer name:
LAYER10c_3
; number of levels
100
; level height
10'
; number of sides
32
; radius X
120'
; radius Y start
1.0
; radius Y end
1.0
; rotation
180
;----------------------------------
```

Completed function PROG10c:

```
;---------------------------------
(defun prog10c ()
 (graphscr)
 ; tower repeats
 ; Hippopede curve for section
 ; x = (2 * COS t) * SQRT(
 ; (major radius * minor radius)
 ; - (minor radius^2 * SIN t^2))
 ; y = (2 * SIN t) * SQRT(
 ; (major radius * minor radius)
 ; - (minor radius^2 * SIN t^2))
 ; with rotation
 (setvar "CMDECHO" 0)
 ; centerpoint
 (setq cpnt (list 0.0 0.0 0.0))
 ; get curve parameters
 (princ "\nProg10c - Tower")
 (setq TowerLayer
   (getstring
   "\nEnter layer name: "))
 (setq NumLevels
   (getint
   "\nEnter number of levels: "))
 (setq LevelHeight
   (getdist
   "\nEnter level height: "))
 (setq NumSides
   (getint
   "\nEnter number of curve
   sides: "))
 (setq XRadStart
   (getdist "\nEnter X radius: "))
 (setq YRadStart
   (getreal
   "\nEnter Y radius start
   factor: "))
 (setq YRadEnd
   (getreal
   "\nEnter Y radius end
   factor: "))
 (setq RotTotal
   (getreal
   "\nEnter total rotation
   angle: "))
 ; clear layer
 (command ".LAYER" "THAW" "*"
  "ON" "*" "")
(command ".LAYER"
  "MAKE" TowerLayer "")
(command ".LAYER" "SET" 0 "")
(command ".LAYER" "OFF" "@*"
  "FREEZE" "@*" "")
(command ".LAYER" "THAW" TowerLayer
  "ON" TowerLayer
  "SET" TowerLayer "")
(command ".ERASE" "ALL" "")
; set elev
(setq LevelElev 0.0)
; start mesh
(command ".3DMESH"
  (+ (+ NumLevels 1) 2)
  (+ NumSides 1))
; add bottom
(setq npnt cpnt)
(repeat (+ NumSides 1)
 (command npnt)
)
; rotation inc
(setq RotInc
  (/ RotTotal NumLevels))
(setq Rotang 0.0)
; radius inc
(setq YRadInc
  (/ (- YRadEnd YRadStart)
  NumLevels))
(setq YRadFact YRadStart)
; create each level
(repeat (+ NumLevels 1)
 ; draw polygon
 (setq panginc (/ 360.0 NumSides))
 (setq pang 0.0)
 (repeat (+ NumSides 1)
  ; compute point
  (setq Xrad (/ XRadStart 2))
  (setq YRad (* YRadFact XRad))
  (setq xpt
    (* (* 2 (cos (dtr pang)))
    (sqrt (- (* XRad YRad)
    (* (expt YRad 2)
    (expt (sin (dtr pang)) 2))))))
  (setq ypt
    (* (* 2 (sin (dtr pang)))
    (sqrt (- (* XRad YRad)
    (* (expt YRad 2)
```

```
      (expt (sin (dtr pang)) 2))))))
    ; rotate
    (setq rxpt
      (- (* xpt (cos (dtr Rotang)))
      (* ypt (sin (dtr Rotang)))))
    (setq rypt
      (+ (* xpt (sin (dtr Rotang)))
      (* ypt (cos (dtr Rotang)))))
    (setq npnt
      (list rxpt rypt LevelElev))
    ; add to mesh
    (command npnt)
    ; inc ang
    (setq pang (+ pang panginc))
  )
  ; inc elev
  (setq LevelElev
    (+ LevelElev LevelHeight))
  ; inc radius
  (setq YRadFact
    (+ YRadFact YRadInc))
  ; inc rotation
  (setq Rotang (+ Rotang Rotinc))
 )
 ; add top
 (setq npnt (list
   (nth 0 cpnt) (nth 1 cpnt)
   (- LevelElev LevelHeight)))
 (repeat (+ NumSides 1)
  (command npnt)
 )
 (setvar "CMDECHO" 1)
 (command ".VIEW" "swiso")
 (command ".ZOOM" "e")
 (command ".HIDE")
 (princ)
)
;-----------------------------------
```

Add function PROG10d, a Curve of Convexities, using a copy of PROG03. This curve has parameters that control the opening of the pedals.

The input includes:

```
(setq Rad
  (getdist "\nEnter radius: "))
(setq NumPedals
  (getint
  "\nEnter number of pedals: "))
(setq cfactStart
  (getreal
  "\nEnter curve factor start: "))
(setq cfactEnd
  (getreal
  "\nEnter curve factor end: "))
```

For function PROG10d, replace the regular polygon-point computation with:

```
; compute point
(setq r (+ 1.0 (* cfact
  (cos (* (dtr pang) NumPedals)))))
(setq xpt (* (* r (* Rad 0.62))
   (cos (dtr pang))))
(setq ypt (* (* r (* Rad 0.62))
   (sin (dtr pang))))
(setq npnt
  (list xpt ypt LevelElev))
```

Instead of the radius being varied, the curve factor has a start and end value. Compute a curve-factor increment, starting value, and increment it after each floor. Note the shapes of the top and bottom floors.

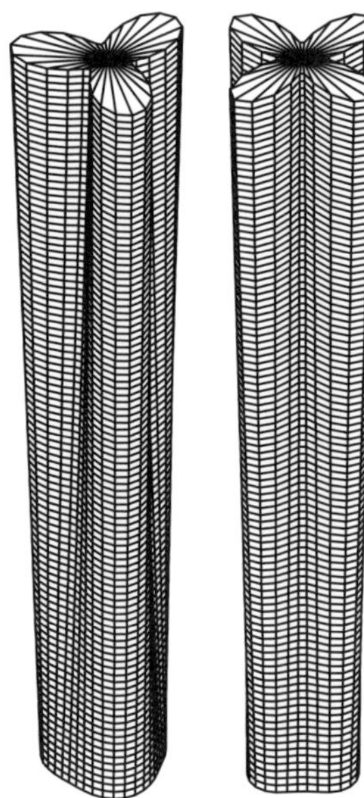

PROG10d: Curve of Convexities, thirty-six-sided polygon with three and four pedals and a changing curve factor

Sample script file for PROG10d:

```
;-----------------------------------
(prog10d)
; Layer name:
LAYER10d_1
; number of levels
100
; level height
10'
; number of sides
36
; radius X
120'
; pedals
3
; curve factor start
0.1
; curve factor end
0.6
;-----------------------------------
```

Completed function PROG10d:

```
;-----------------------------------
(defun prog10d ()
 (graphscr)
 ; tower repeats
 ; curve for section
 ; r = (1.0 +
 ; ((e * (cos t * pedals))) /  p
 ; x = (r * radius) * cos t
 ; y = (r * radius) * sin t
 (setvar "CMDECHO" 0)
 ; centerpoint
 (setq cpnt (list 0.0 0.0 0.0))
 ; get curve parameters
 (princ "\nProg10d - Tower")
 (setq TowerLayer
   (getstring
   "\nEnter layer name: "))
 (setq NumLevels
   (getint
   "\nEnter number of levels: "))
 (setq LevelHeight
   (getdist
   "\nEnter level height: "))
 (setq NumSides
   (getint
   "\nEnter number of curve
   sides: "))
 (setq Rad
   (getdist "\nEnter radius: "))
 (setq NumPedals
   (getint
   "\nEnter number of pedals: "))
 (setq cfactStart
   (getreal
   "\nEnter curve factor
   start: "))
 (setq cfactEnd
   (getreal
   "\nEnter curve factor end: "))
 ; clear layer
 (command ".LAYER" "THAW" "*"
   "ON" "*" "")
 (command ".LAYER"
   "MAKE" TowerLayer "")
 (command ".LAYER" "SET" 0 "")
 (command ".LAYER" "OFF" "@*"
```

```
  "FREEZE" "@*" "")
(command ".LAYER" "THAW" TowerLayer
  "ON" TowerLayer
  "SET" TowerLayer "")
(command ".ERASE" "ALL" "")
; set elev
(setq LevelElev 0.0)
; start mesh
(command ".3DMESH"
  (+ (+ NumLevels 1) 2)
  (+ NumSides 1))
; add bottom
(setq npnt cpnt)
(repeat (+ NumSides 1)
 (command npnt)
)
; radius inc
(setq cfactInc
  (/ (- cfactEnd cfactStart)
  NumLevels))
(setq cfact cfactStart)
; create each level
(repeat (+ NumLevels 1)
 ; draw polygon
 (setq panginc (/ 360.0 NumSides))
 (setq pang 0.0)
 (repeat (+ NumSides 1)
  ; compute point
  (setq r
    (+ 1.0  (* cfact (cos
    (* (dtr pang) NumPedals)))))
  (setq xpt
    (* (* r (* Rad 0.62))
    (cos (dtr pang))))
  (setq ypt
    (* (* r (* Rad 0.62))
    (sin (dtr pang))))
  (setq npnt
    (list xpt ypt LevelElev))
  ; add to mesh
  (command npnt)
  ; inc ang
  (setq pang (+ pang panginc))
 )
 ; inc elev
 (setq LevelElev
   (+ LevelElev LevelHeight))
 ; inc radius
  (setq cfact (+ cfact cfactInc))
 )
 ; add top
 (setq npnt (list
   (nth 0 cpnt) (nth 1 cpnt)
   (- LevelElev LevelHeight)))
 (repeat (+ NumSides 1)
  (command npnt)
 )
 (setvar "CMDECHO" 1)
 (command ".VIEW" "swiso")
 (command ".ZOOM" "e")
 (command ".HIDE")
 (princ)
)
;---------------------------------
```

Towers with partial polygon sections

The polygon definition for the tower section has a number of interesting parameters that can be specified and varied: radius, number of segments, and included angle. For function PROG11a, set an included angle for the polygon section at less than 360 degrees. Also include a rotation angle for twisting.

Add PROG011a using a copy of PROG04. Add the included angle for the polygon:

```
(setq AngSides
  (getreal
  "\nEnter total angle for polygon: "))
```

This angle is used in the computation of the polygon-angle increment. Also note that the first and last points for the polygon are the center of the polygon. This requires the 3DMESH command to be modified by adding two points to the section; before and after the floor section is computed, the centerpoint must also be added. The straight edges of the polygon section remain the same length throughout the repetition of floors.

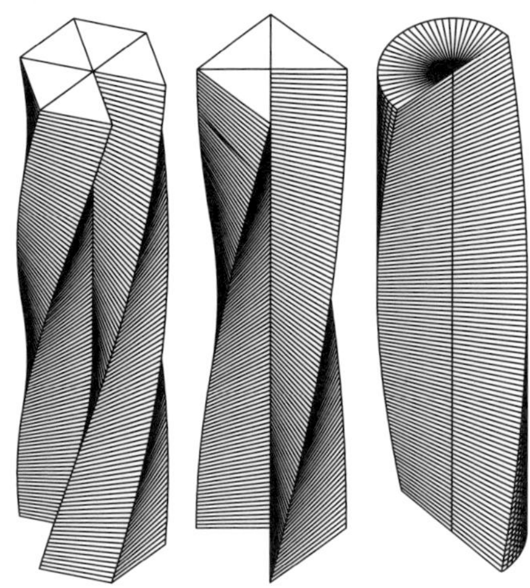

PROG11a: partial polygon sections with six, four, and thirty-two sides, rotated with different start angles

Sample script file for PROG11a:

```
;----------------------------------
(prog11a)
; Layer name:
LAYER11a_3
; number of levels
100
; level height
10'
; number of sides
32
; polygon angle
180
; radius start
120'
; rotation
90
;----------------------------------
```

Completed function PROG11a:

```
;----------------------------------
(defun prog11a ()
 (graphscr)
 ; tower repeats
 ; partial polygon section
 (setvar "CMDECHO" 0)
 ; centerpoint
 (setq cpnt (list 0.0 0.0 0.0))
 ; get tower parameters
 (princ "\nProg11a - Tower")
 (setq TowerLayer
   (getstring
   "\nEnter layer name: "))
 (setq NumLevels
   (getint
   "\nEnter number of levels: "))
 (setq LevelHeight
   (getdist
   "\nEnter level height: "))
 (setq NumSides
   (getint
   "\nEnter number of polygon
   sides: "))
 (setq AngSides
   (getreal
   "\nEnter total angle for
   polygon: "))
 (setq Rad
   (getdist "\nEnter radius: "))
 (setq RotTotal
   (getreal
   "\nEnter total rotation
   angle: "))
 ; clear layer
 (command ".LAYER" "THAW" "*"
   "ON" "*" "")
 (command ".LAYER"
   "MAKE" TowerLayer "")
 (command ".LAYER" "SET" 0 "")
 (command ".LAYER" "OFF" "@*"
   "FREEZE" "@*" "")
 (command ".LAYER" "THAW" TowerLayer
   "ON" TowerLayer
   "SET" TowerLayer "")
 (command ".ERASE" "ALL" "")
 ; set elev
```

```
(setq LevelElev 0.0)
; start mesh
(command ".3DMESH"
  (+ (+ NumLevels 1) 2)
  (+ (+ NumSides 1) 2))
; add bottom
(setq npnt cpnt)
(repeat (+ NumSides 3)
 (command npnt)
)
; rotation inc
(setq RotInc
  (/ RotTotal NumLevels))
(setq Rotang 0.0)
; create each level
(repeat (+ NumLevels 1)
 ; first center pt
 (setq fpnt (list
   (nth 0 cpnt) (nth 1 cpnt)
    LevelElev))
 (command fpnt)
 ; draw polygon
 (setq panginc
   (/ AngSides NumSides))
 (setq pang (/ panginc 2.0))
 (repeat (+ NumSides 1)
  ; compute point
  (setq xpt (+ (nth 0 cpnt)
    (* Rad (sin (dtr pang)))))
  (setq ypt (+ (nth 1 cpnt)
    (* Rad (cos (dtr pang)))))
  ; rotate
  (setq rxpt
    (- (* xpt (cos (dtr Rotang)))
    (* ypt (sin (dtr Rotang)))))
  (setq rypt
    (+ (* xpt (sin (dtr Rotang)))
    (* ypt (cos (dtr Rotang)))))
  (setq npnt
    (list rxpt rypt LevelElev))
  ; add to mesh
  (command npnt)
  ; inc ang
  (setq pang (+ pang panginc))
 )
 ; back to first pt
 (command fpnt)
 ; inc elev
 (setq LevelElev
   (+ LevelElev LevelHeight))
 ; inc rotation
 (setq Rotang (+ Rotang Rotinc))
)
; add top
(setq npnt (list
  (nth 0 cpnt) (nth 1 cpnt)
  (- LevelElev LevelHeight)))
(repeat (+ NumSides 3)
 (command npnt)
)
(setvar "CMDECHO" 1)
(command ".VIEW" "swiso")
(command ".ZOOM" "e")
(command ".HIDE")
(princ)
)
;---------------------------------
```

For function PROG11b, the polygon section has a start and end included angle; rotation is not included. Vary the included angle for each level. Add PROG011b using a copy of PROG03.

Add the included start and end angle for the polygon:

```
(setq AngStart
  (getreal
  "\nEnter start angle for polygon: "))
(setq AngEnd
  (getreal
  "\nEnter end angle for polygon: "))
```

Note that straight edges of the polygon section do not remain the same length throughout the repetition of floors.

Examples for PROG11b include: 270 to 180 degrees with 4 sides; and 288 to 180 degrees with 5 sides.

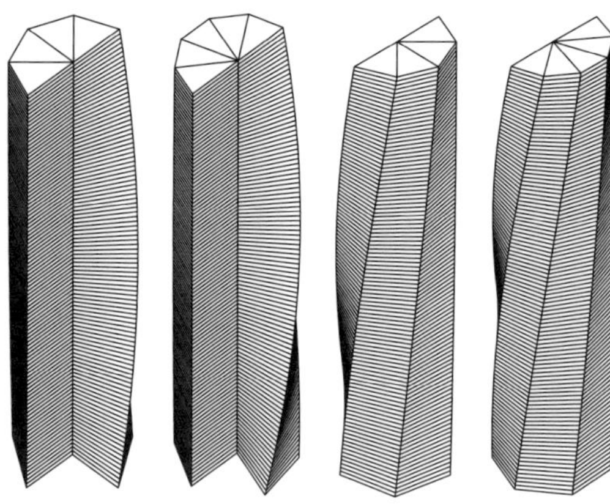

PROG11b: include partial polygons, front and rear views

Sample script file for PROG11b:

```
;---------------------------------
(prog11b)
; Layer name:
LAYER11b_1
; number of levels
100
; level height
10'
; number of sides
5
; start angle
288
; end angle
180
; radius
120'
;---------------------------------
```

Completed function PROG11b:

```
;---------------------------------
(defun prog11b ()
 (graphscr)
 ; tower repeats
 ; partial polygon section
 (setvar "CMDECHO" 0)
 ; centerpoint
 (setq cpnt (list 0.0 0.0 0.0))
 ; get curve parameters
 (princ "\nProg11b - Tower")
 (setq TowerLayer
   (getstring
   "\nEnter layer name: "))
 (setq NumLevels
   (getint
   "\nEnter number of levels: "))
 (setq LevelHeight
   (getdist
   "\nEnter level height: "))
 (setq NumSides
   (getint
   "\nEnter number of polygon
   sides: "))
 (setq AngStart
   (getreal
   "\nEnter start angle for
   polygon: "))
 (setq AngEnd
   (getreal
   "\nEnter end angle for
   polygon: "))
 (setq Rad
   (getdist "\nEnter radius: "))
 ; clear layer
 (command ".LAYER" "THAW" "*"
   "ON" "*" "")
 (command ".LAYER"
   "MAKE" TowerLayer "")
 (command ".LAYER" "SET" 0 "")
 (command ".LAYER" "OFF" "@*"
   "FREEZE" "@*" "")
 (command ".LAYER" "THAW" TowerLayer
   "ON" TowerLayer
   "SET" TowerLayer "")
 (command ".ERASE" "ALL" "")
 ; set elev
```

```
(setq LevelElev 0.0)
; start mesh
(command ".3DMESH"
  (+ (+ NumLevels 1) 2)
  (+ NumSides 3))
; add bottom
(setq npnt cpnt)
(repeat (+ NumSides 3)
 (command npnt)
)
; polygon ang inc
(setq AngInc
  (/ (- AngStart AngEnd)
  NumLevels))
(setq Polyang AngStart)
; create each level
(repeat (+ NumLevels 1)
 ; first center pt
 (setq fpnt (list
   (nth 0 cpnt) (nth 1 cpnt)
   LevelElev))
 (command fpnt)
 ; draw polygon
 (setq panginc
   (/ Polyang NumSides))
 (setq pang 0.0)
 (repeat (+ NumSides 1)
  ; compute point
  (setq xpt (+ (nth 0 cpnt)
    (* Rad (sin (dtr pang)))))
  (setq ypt (+ (nth 1 cpnt)
    (* Rad (cos (dtr pang)))))
  (setq npnt
    (list xpt ypt LevelElev))
  ; add to mesh
  (command npnt)
  ; inc ang
  (setq pang (+ pang panginc))
 )
 ; back to first pt
 (command fpnt)
 ; inc elev
 (setq LevelElev
   (+ LevelElev LevelHeight))
 ; inc polygon ang
 (setq Polyang (- Polyang AngInc))
)
; add top
(setq npnt (list
  (nth 0 cpnt) (nth 1 cpnt)
  (- LevelElev LevelHeight)))
(repeat (+ NumSides 3)
 (command npnt)
)
(setvar "CMDECHO" 1)
(command ".VIEW" "swiso")
(command ".ZOOM" "e")
(command ".HIDE")
(princ)
)
;---------------------------------
```

Tower section based on a list of points

All previous examples base the floor section of the tower on a regular geometric section, such as a polygon, circle, or ellipse. Any irregular closed section can also be considered if it is defined by a simple list of points.

Add function `PROG12` using a copy of `PROG04`. Accept a list of points and place them at each floor elevation. The radius and number of sides is replaced with input of the points.

The `read` function is used to convert the string to a list:

```
(setq BotSect
  (read (getstring
  "\nEnter bottom list of points: ")))
```

Four points, centered on `(0,0)` are entered on a single line as:

```
((-60.0 -60.0) (60.0 -60.0) (60.0 60.0)
  (-60.0 60.0) (-60.0 -60.0))
```

Points can be entered clockwise or counter-clockwise. It is best to set the center of these points at `(0,0)`. Make sure the first and last points are the same. Units are assumed to be in feet. The `nth` function is used to get the x and y coordinates, and the polygon section computations are replaced with extractions of points for the entered list.

The point computation is:

```
(setq npt 0)
(repeat npts
 ; get point
 (setq xpt (* 12
   (nth 0 (nth npt BotSect))))
 (setq ypt (* 12
   (nth 1 (nth npt BotSect))))
 ; rotate
 (setq rxpt
   (- (* xpt (cos (dtr Rotang)))
   (* ypt (sin (dtr Rotang)))))
 (setq rypt
   (+ (* xpt (sin (dtr Rotang)))
   (* ypt (cos (dtr Rotang)))))
 (setq npnt
   (list rxpt rypt LevelElev))
 ; add to mesh
 (command npnt)
 ; next pt
 (setq npt (+ npt 1))
)
```

The examples for PROG12 includes a square and cross shape, both rotated 90 degrees.

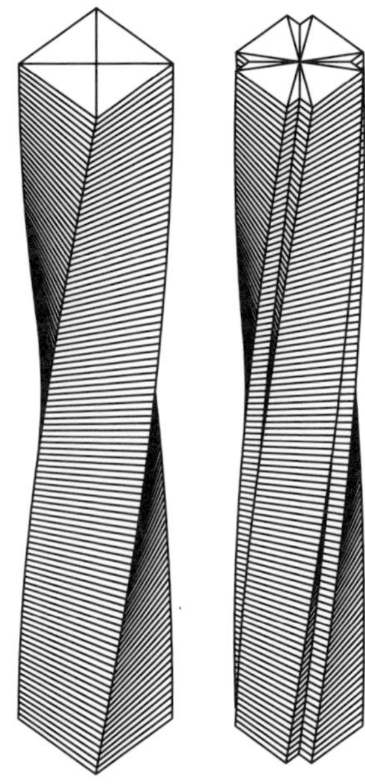

PROG12: section based on a list of points

Sample script files for PROG12:

```
;----------------------------------
(prog12)
; Layer name:
LAYER12_1
; number of levels
100
; level height
10'
; section pts - square
((-60.0 -60.0) (60.0 -60.0)
  (60.0 60.0) (-60.0 60.0)
  (-60.0 -60.0) )
; rotation
90
;----------------------------------
```

The list of section points is entered on a single line in the script file.

And:

```
;----------------------------------
(prog12)
; Layer name:
LAYER12_2
; number of levels
100
; level height
10'
; section pts - cross
((-40.0 -60.0) (40.0 -60.0) (40.0 -40.0)
  (60.0 -40.0) (60.0 40.0) (40.0 40.0)
  (40.0 60.0) (-40.0 60.0) (-40.0 40.0)
  (-60.0 40.0) (-60.0 -40.0) (-40.0 -40.0)
  (-40 -60.0))
; rotation
90
;----------------------------------
```

Completed function PROG12:

```
;----------------------------------
(defun prog12 ()
 (graphscr)
 ; tower repeats
 ; section from a list of points
 (setvar "CMDECHO" 0)
 ; centerpoint
 (setq cpnt (list 0.0 0.0 0.0))
 ; get curve parameters
 (princ "\nProg12 - Tower")
 (setq TowerLayer
   (getstring
   "\nEnter layer name: "))
 (setq NumLevels
   (getint
   "\nEnter number of levels: "))
 (setq LevelHeight
   (getdist
   "\nEnter level height: "))
 (setq BotSect
   (read (getstring
   "\nEnter bottom list of
   points: ")))
 (setq RotTotal
   (getreal "\nEnter total rotation
  angle: "))
; clear layer
(command ".LAYER" "THAW" "*"
  "ON" "*" "")
(command ".LAYER"
  "MAKE" TowerLayer "")
(command ".LAYER" "SET" 0 "")
(command ".LAYER" "OFF" "@*"
  "FREEZE" "@*" "")
(command ".LAYER" "THAW" TowerLayer
  "ON" TowerLayer
  "SET" TowerLayer "")
(command ".ERASE" "ALL" "")
; set elev
(setq LevelElev 0.0)
; rotation inc
(setq RotInc
  (/ RotTotal NumLevels))
(setq Rotang 0.0)
; points
(setq npts (length BotSect))
; start mesh
(command ".3DMESH"
  (+ (+ NumLevels 1) 2) npts)
; add bottom
(setq npnt cpnt)
(repeat npts
 (command npnt)
)
; create each level
(repeat (+ NumLevels 1)
 (setq npt 0)
 (repeat npts
  ; get point
  (setq xpt (* 12
    (nth 0 (nth npt BotSect))))
  (setq ypt (* 12
    (nth 1 (nth npt BotSect))))
  ; rotate
  (setq rxpt
    (- (* xpt (cos (dtr Rotang)))
    (* ypt (sin (dtr Rotang)))))
  (setq rypt
    (+ (* xpt (sin (dtr Rotang)))
    (* ypt (cos (dtr Rotang)))))
  (setq npnt
    (list rxpt rypt LevelElev))
  ; add to mesh
```

```
    (command npnt)
    ; next pt
    (setq npt (+ npt 1))
   )
   ; inc elev
   (setq LevelElev
     (+ LevelElev LevelHeight))
   (setq nlevel (+ nlevel 1))
   ; inc rotation
   (setq Rotang (+ Rotang Rotinc))
  )
  ; add top
  (setq npnt (list
    (nth 0 cpnt) (nth 1 cpnt)
    (- LevelElev LevelHeight)))
  (repeat npts
   (command npnt)
  )
  (setvar "CMDECHO" 1)
  (command ".VIEW" "swiso")
  (command ".ZOOM" "e")
  (command ".HIDE")
  (princ)
)
;----------------------------------
```

Morph one section into another

Add function PROG13 using a copy of PROG12. Accept two lists of points, one for the bottom section and one for the top section. Use these points to interpolate the points for every floor in-between.

A second set of points needs to be entered as:

```
(setq TopSect
  (read (getstring
  "\nEnter top list of points: ")))
```

Morph the bottom section of points into the top, by adding an incremental x- and y-offset at each level, based on the difference between every two corresponding points. Point 1 of the top list is morphed to point 1 of the bottom, point 2 to point 2, and so on. The level counter is used to compute an incremental change at each floor. Note that the morphing in this function requires that the two lists have the exact same number of coordinates. So how can you morph a square to a triangle? By morphing to the same coordinate value; point 3 morphs to point 3 and point 4 to point 4, but points 3 and 4 of the top list have the same values.

Using this approach, any closed shape consisting of straight lines can be morphed to any other closed shape. Any curved shape can be approximated with straight line segments. Also, midpoints or quarter-points on straight edges can be included so that individual facets can be modeled on a larger face.

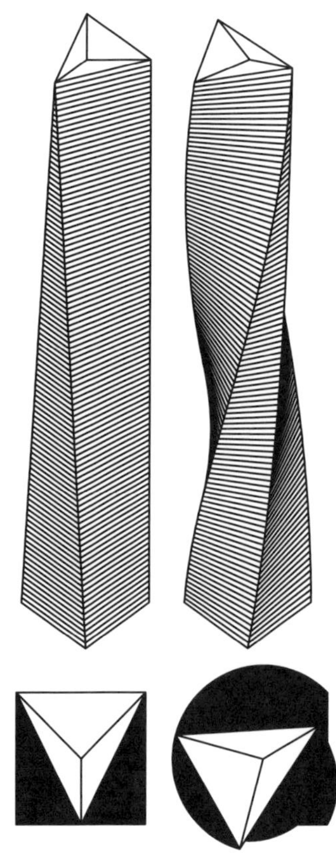

PROG13: morph a square to a triangle section, with and without rotation

Sample script files for PROG13:

```
;----------------------------------
(prog13)
; Layer name:
LAYER13_3
; number of levels
100
; level height
10'
; bottom list
((-60.0 -60.0) (60.0 -60.0) (60.0 60.0)
  (-60.0 60.0) (-60.0 -60.0))
;top list
5-104
((-60.0 -60.0) (60.0 -60.0) (00.0 60.0)
  (00.0 60.0) (-60.0 -60.0))
; rotation
120
;----------------------------------
```

Completed function PROG13:

```
;----------------------------------
(defun prog13 ()
 (graphscr)
 ; tower repeats
 ; morph from lists of points
 (setvar "CMDECHO" 0)
 ; centerpoint
 (setq cpnt (list 0.0 0.0 0.0))
 ; get curve parameters
 (princ "\nProg13 - Tower")
 (setq TowerLayer
   (getstring
   "\nEnter layer name: "))
 (setq NumLevels
   (getint
   "\nEnter number of levels: "))
 (setq LevelHeight
   (getdist
   "\nEnter level height: "))
 (setq BotSect
   (read (getstring
   "\nEnter bottom list of
   points: ")))
 (setq TopSect
   (read (getstring
   "\nEnter top list of points: ")))
 (setq RotTotal
   (getreal
   "\nEnter total rotation
   angle: "))
 ; clear layer
 (command ".LAYER" "THAW" "*"
   "ON" "*" "")
 (command ".LAYER"
   "MAKE" TowerLayer "")
 (command ".LAYER" "SET" 0 "")
 (command ".LAYER" "OFF" "@*"
   "FREEZE" "@*" "")
 (command ".LAYER" "THAW" TowerLayer
   "ON" TowerLayer
   "SET" TowerLayer "")
 (command ".ERASE" "ALL" "")
 ; set elev
 (setq LevelElev 0.0)
 ; points
 (setq npts (length BotSect))
 ; rotation inc
 (setq RotInc
   (/ RotTotal NumLevels))
 (setq Rotang 0.0)
 ; start mesh
 (command ".3DMESH"
   (+ (+ NumLevels 1) 2) npts)
 ; add bottom
 (setq npnt cpnt)
 (repeat npts
  (command npnt)
 )
 ; create each level
 (setq nlevel 0)
 (repeat (+ NumLevels 1)
  (setq npt 0)
  (repeat npts
   ; get point
   (setq xpt
     (nth 0 (nth npt BotSect)))
   (setq ypt
     (nth 1 (nth npt BotSect)))
   ; compute inc
   (setq xinc
     (/ (- (nth 0 (nth npt TopSect))
     (nth 0 (nth npt BotSect)))
```

```
      NumLevels))
    (setq yinc
      (/ (- (nth 1 (nth npt TopSect))
      (nth 1 (nth npt BotSect)))
      NumLevels))
    ; add to pt
    (setq xpt (+ (* xpt 12)
      (* (* xinc 12) nlevel)))
    (setq ypt (+ (* ypt 12)
      (* (* yinc 12) nlevel)))
    ; rotate
    (setq rxpt
      (- (* xpt (cos (dtr Rotang)))
      (* ypt (sin (dtr Rotang)))))
    (setq rypt
      (+ (* xpt (sin (dtr Rotang)))
      (* ypt (cos (dtr Rotang)))))
    (setq npnt
      (list rxpt rypt LevelElev))
    ; add to mesh
    (command npnt)
    ; next pt
    (setq npt (+ npt 1))
   )
   ; inc elev
   (setq LevelElev
     (+ LevelElev LevelHeight))
   (setq nlevel (+ nlevel 1))
   ; inc rotation
   (setq Rotang (+ Rotang Rotinc))
  )
  ; add top
  (setq npnt (list
    (nth 0 cpnt) (nth 1 cpnt)
    (- LevelElev LevelHeight)))
  (repeat npts
   (command npnt)
  )
  (setvar "CMDECHO" 1)
  (command ".VIEW" "swiso")
  (command ".ZOOM" "e")
  (command ".HIDE")
  (princ)
 )
;---------------------------------
```

Computing floor areas in the tower

All of these examples have focused on the tower's external form. Another capability that can be added is to compute the area of each floor as the section is being created.

Add function PROG14 using a copy of PROG04. Remove all lines of code related to the 3DMESH. For each polygon, construct a closed POLYLINE. Then use the AREA command to compute the area of the polyline. To extract the computed area, get the system variable area and accumulate it for a total floor area of the entire tower.

Note how the area of the last polyline drawn was found:

```
; get area
(command ".AREA"
  "o" "last")
; acum area
(setq FlrArea
  (/ (getvar "area") 144))
(setq TotalArea
  (+ TotalArea FlrArea))
```

At the end of the function, the total area is displayed:

```
(princ "\nTotal Area: ")
  (princ (rtos TotalArea 2 0))
  (princ " sqft")
```

The displayed result is:

```
>> Total Area: 826448 sqft
```

Function PROG14 also converts each POLYLINE into a REGION, a zero thickness solid, so that each floorplate can be displayed in hidden-line mode or as a rendered image.

To convert a POLYLINE to a REGION, use:

```
; convert to a region
(command ".REGION" "last" "")
```

When the area is computed, the perimeter is also computed and saved in a system variable.

To extract it, use:

```
(setq FlrPerm
  (/ (getvar "perimeter") 12))
```

This value, along with the floor-to-floor height, could be used to estimate the surface area of the exterior of the tower.

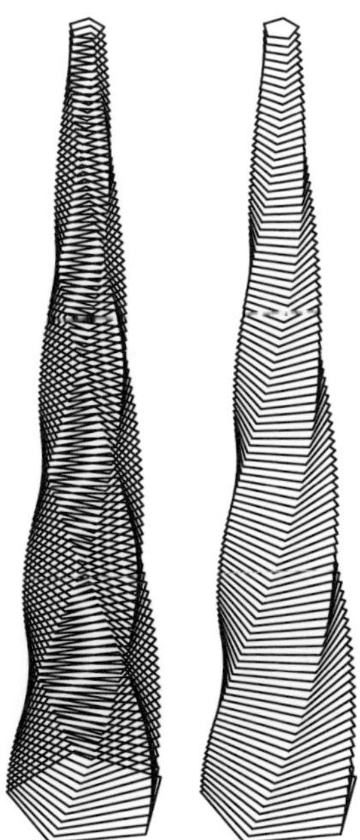

PROG14: floorplates as POLYLINEs and REGIONs

Sample script file for PROG14:

```
;---------------------------------
(prog14)
; Layer name:
LAYER14c
; number of levels
100
; level height
10'
; number polygon sides
5
; radius start
90'
; radius end
20'
; rotation
270
;---------------------------------
```

Completed function PROG14:

```
;---------------------------------
(defun prog14 ()
 (graphscr)
 ; tower by polygon repeats
 ; twist
 ; with areas
 (setvar "CMDECHO" 0)
 ; centerpoint
 (setq cpnt (list 0.0 0.0 0.0))
 ; get curve parameters
 (princ "\nProg14 - Tower")
 (setq TowerLayer
   (getstring
   "\nEnter layer name: "))
 (setq NumLevels
   (getint
   "\nEnter number of levels: "))
 (setq LevelHeight
   (getdist
   "\nEnter level height: "))
 (setq NumSides
   (getint
   "\nEnter number of polygon
   sides: "))
 (setq RadStart
   (getdist
```

```
  "\nEnter start radius: "))
(setq RadEnd
  (getdist
  "\nEnter end radius: "))
(setq RotTotal
  (getreal
  "\nEnter total rotation
  angle: "))
; clear layer
(command ".LAYER" "THAW" "*"
  "ON" "*" "")
(command ".LAYER"
  "MAKE" TowerLayer "")
(command ".LAYER" "SET" 0 "")
(command ".LAYER" "OFF" "@*"
  "FREEZE" "@*" "")
(command ".LAYER" "THAW" TowerLayer
  "ON" TowerLayer
  "SET" TowerLayer "")
(command ".ERASE" "ALL" "")
; set total area
(setq TotalArea 0.0)
; set elev
(setq LevelElev 0.0)
; radius inc
(setq RadInc
  (/ (- RadEnd RadStart)
  NumLevels))
(setq Rad RadStart)
; rotation inc
(setq RotInc
  (/ RotTotal NumLevels))
(setq Rotang 0.0)
; create each level
(repeat (+ NumLevels 1)
 ; draw polygon
 (setq panginc (/ 360.0 NumSides))
 (setq pang (/ panginc 2.0))
 (command ".PLINE")
 (repeat (+ NumSides 1)
  ; compute point
  (setq xpt (+ (nth 0 cpnt)
    (* Rad (sin (dtr pang)))))
  (setq ypt (+ (nth 1 cpnt)
    (* Rad (cos (dtr pang)))))
  ; rotate point
  (setq rxpt
    (- (* xpt (cos (dtr Rotang)))
    (* ypt (sin (dtr Rotang)))))
  (setq rypt
    (+ (* xpt (sin (dtr Rotang)))
    (* ypt (cos (dtr Rotang)))))
  (setq npnt
    (list rxpt rypt LevelElev))
  ; add to mesh
  (command npnt)
  ; inc ang
  (setq pang (+ pang panginc))
 )
 ; close PLINE
 (command "c")
 (command ".ZOOM" "e")
 ; get area
 (command ".AREA" "o" "last")
 ; acum area
 (setq FlrArea
   (/ (getvar "area") 144))
 (setq TotalArea
   (+ TotalArea FlrArea))
 ; convert to a region
 (command ".REGION" "last" "")
 ; inc radius
 (setq Rad (+ Rad RadInc))
 ; inc elev
 (setq LevelElev
   (+ LevelElev LevelHeight))
 ; inc rotation
 (setq Rotang (+ Rotang Rotinc))
)
; add top
(setq npnt (list
  (nth 0 cpnt) (nth 1 cpnt)
  (- LevelElev LevelHeight)))
(repeat (+ NumSides 1)
 (command npnt)
)
(command ".VIEW" "swiso")
(command ".ZOOM" "e")
(command ".HIDE")
(setvar "CMDECHO" 1)
(princ "\nTotal Area: ")
  (princ (rtos TotalArea 2 0))
  (princ " sqft")
(princ)
)
;---------------------------------
```

Combine tower forms

To be able to model tall buildings that include setbacks or have distinctive sections with shapes that do not blend together but are meant to be stacked, use the functions developed as a kit-of-parts for specifying each vertical section of a building.

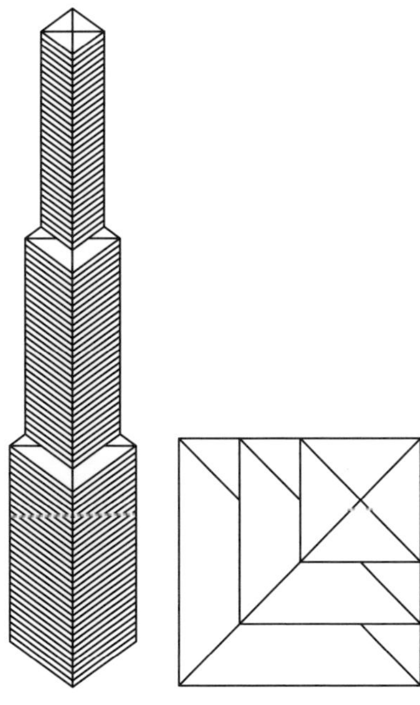

PROG15: setbacks with multiple sections combined

For example, to model a simple setback, with each section as a rectangle, convert the function PROG02 to a callable function PROG15.

Completed function PROG15:

```
;----------------------------------
(defun prog15 (cpnt NumLevels
  LevelHeight XSide YSide / npnt
  LevelElev pnt1 pnt2 pnt3 pnt4)
 ; tower rectangular section
 ; by center and sides
 ; set sides
 (setq NumSides 4)
 ; set elev
 (setq LevelElev (nth 2 cpnt))
 ; start mesh
 (command ".3DMESH"
   (+ (+ NumLevels 1) 2)
   (+ NumSides 1))
 ; add bottom
 (setq npnt cpnt)
 (repeat (+ NumSides 1)
  (command npnt)
 )
 ; create each level
 (repeat (+ NumLevels 1)
  ; compute rectangle points
  (setq pnt1 (list
    (- (nth 0 cpnt) (/ XSide 2.0))
    (- (nth 1 cpnt) (/ YSide 2.0))
    LevelElev))
  (setq pnt2 (list
    (+ (nth 0 cpnt) (/ XSide 2.0))
    (- (nth 1 cpnt) (/ YSide 2.0))
    LevelElev))
  (setq pnt3 (list
    (+ (nth 0 cpnt) (/ XSide 2.0))
    (+ (nth 1 cpnt) (/ YSide 2.0))
    LevelElev))
  (setq pnt4 (list
    (- (nth 0 cpnt) (/ XSide 2.0))
    (+ (nth 1 cpnt) (/ YSide 2.0))
    LevelElev))
  ; add to mesh
  (command pnt1 pnt2 pnt3 pnt4
    pnt1)
  ; inc elev
  (setq LevelElev
    (+ LevelElev LevelHeight))
 )
 ; add top
```

```
 (setq npnt (list
   (nth 0 cpnt) (nth 1 cpnt)
   (- LevelElev LevelHeight)))
 (repeat (+ NumSides 1)
  (command npnt)
 )
 (princ)
)
;-----------------------------------
```

With this function completed, another function DRWG15 is developed that assembles the sections using multiple calls to function PROG15.

Completed function DRWG15:

```
;-----------------------------------
(defun drwg15 ()
 ; step back square tower
 (setvar "CMDECHO" 0)
 ; get tower parameters
 (setq TowerLayer  "drwg15")
 ; clear layer
 (command ".LAYER" "THAW" "*"
   "ON" "*" "")
 (command ".LAYER"
   "MAKE" TowerLayer "")
 (command ".LAYER" "SET" 0 "")
 (command ".LAYER" "OFF" "@*"
   "FREEZE" "@*" "")
 (command ".LAYER" "THAW" TowerLayer
   "ON" TowerLayer
   "SET" TowerLayer "")
 (command ".ERASE" "ALL" "")
 ; set elev
 (setq LevelElev 0.0)
 (setq cpnt
   (list 0.0 0.0 LevelElev))
 ; base tower
 (prog15 cpnt 30 (* 10 12)
   (* 100 12) (* 100 12))
 ; first setback
 (setq LevelElev
   (+ LevelElev (* 30 (* 10 12))))
 (setq cpnt (list
   (* 12.5 12) (* 12.5 12)
   LevelElev))
 (prog15 cpnt 30 (* 10 12)
   (* 75 12) (* 75 12))
 ; second setback
 (setq LevelElev
   (+ LevelElev (* 30 (* 10 12))))
 (setq cpnt (list
   (* 25.0 12) (* 25.0 12)
   LevelElev))
 (prog15 cpnt 30 (* 10 12)
   (* 50 12) (* 50 12))
 (command ".VIEW" "swiso")
 (command ".ZOOM" "e")
 (command ".HIDE")
 (setvar "CMDECHO" 1)
 (princ)
)
;-----------------------------------
```

Note the settings of elevations from section to section. The center location for each rectangular section is adjusted so they all stack up in one corner. Also note that the section height and dimension values have been converted to feet.

Any of these individual functions can be converted to callable functions to model any possible tower configuration.

6.0

Randomness in architectural patterns and forms is not arbitrary. The following examples are based on defining a framework within which elements can be varied in a number of different ways. The framework forms the boundary conditions or limits. This approach attempts to implement an orderly disorder.

The examples in this chapter cover applications at a number of scales, as well as two- and three-dimensional patterns. Some of these aplications result in reliefs or laser cutting; others lead to small- and large-scale masses. With the evolution of automated fabrication, randomness can play an important role in defining patterns that seem to not repeat on themselves, at the same production cost of modular repeating patterns. In manufacturing the trend is from "many of one" to "one of many."

The first step in developing randomness is to compute a random number. Algorithms have been developed that can generate a series of numbers so that given any sequence—five, ten, or one hundred in a row—it would never repeat itself.

In AutoLISP the function `rn` computes a random number and returns a value from 0.0 to 1.0:

```
;----------------------------------
(defun rn (/ modulus multiplier
  increment random)
 (if (not rnseed))
   (setq rnseed (getvar "DATE")))
 (setq modulus   65536
   multiplier 25173
   increment  13849
   rnseed
     (rem (+ (* multiplier rnseed)
     increment) modulus)
   random    (/ rnseed modulus)
 )
)
;----------------------------------
```

This algorithm is based on the one presented in *Condensed Pascal* by Doug Cooper, (New York: W.W. Norton & Co., 1987).

Start a new drawing and set the units to architectural; set the grid to 1 foot and turn off all snaps and dynamic input.

Start a new AutoLISP file in the editor: `CH06A.LSP` and add function `rn`.

At the command line enter:

```
(rn)
```

Here are common examples of situations where a specific type of random number is required. Try executing these exercises a few times to see the results.

Generate random values from 0.0 to some maximum

```
;----------------------------------
(defun ex01 ()
 (repeat 10
  (setq rval (* (rn) 5.0))
  (princ rval) (princ " ")
 )
(princ)
)
;----------------------------------
```

Returns real numbers in the range of 0.0 to 5.0, note that 5.0 would only be generated if `(rn)` returned 1.0

```
;----------------------------------
(defun ex02 ()
 (repeat 10
  (setq rval (fix (* (rn) 5.0)))
  (princ rval) (princ " ")
 )
(princ)
)
;----------------------------------
```

Returns integer numbers in the range of 0 to 4.

```
;----------------------------------
(defun ex03 ()
 (repeat 10
  (setq rval (fix (* (rn) 5.99)))
  (princ rval) (princ " ")
 )
(princ)
)
;----------------------------------
```

Returns integer numbers in the range of 0 to 5.

Generate random values from a minimum to a maximum

```
;----------------------------------
(defun ex04 ()
 (setq vmin 5.0)
 (setq vmax 10.0)
 (repeat 10
  (setq vdiff (- vmax vmin))
  (setq rval
    (+ (* (rn) vdiff) vmin))
  (princ rval) (princ " ")
 )
(princ)
)
;----------------------------------
```

Generate random values, plus or minus some offset from a target value

```
;----------------------------------
(defun ex05 ()
 (setq targetval 10.0)
 (setq offsetval 2.0)
 (repeat 10
  (setq rval (+ (* (rn)
    (* offsetval 2))
    (- targetval offsetval)))
  (princ rval) (princ " ")
 )
(princ)
)
;----------------------------------
```

Generate a random value based on selection of a target value

```
;----------------------------------
(defun ex06 ()
 (repeat 10
  (setq n (fix (* (rn) 3.99)))
  (setq rval
    (nth n (list 0 90 180 270)))
  (princ rval) (princ " ")
 )
(princ)
)
;----------------------------------
```

Returns `n` for integers 0 to 3, `rval` for 0, 90, 180, or 270.

Generate a random value based on a selection of target values, with a greater probability of certain values

```
;----------------------------------
(defun ex07 ()
 (repeat 10
  (setq n (fix (* (rn) 5.99)))
  (setq rval
    (nth n (list 0 0 90
    180 180 270)))
  (princ rval) (princ " ")
 )
(princ)
)
;----------------------------------
```

Returns `n` for integers 0 to 5, `rval` for 0, 90, 180, or 270.

The same method can be used to select a specific dimension from a list.

For example:

```
;----------------------------------
(defun ex08 ()
 (repeat 10
  (setq n (fix (* (rn) 5.99)))
  (setq rval
    (nth n (list 0.25 0.50 0.75
    1.25 1.50 1.75)))
  (princ rval) (princ " ")
 )
(princ)
)
;----------------------------------
```

Generate a random value for some incremental amount

For example, any 60 degrees from 0 to 360:

```
;----------------------------------
(defun ex09 ()
 (repeat 10
  (setq rval
   (* (fix (* (rn) 6.99)) 60))
  (princ rval) (princ " ")
 )
(princ)
)
;----------------------------------
```

Returns integers 0, 60, 120, 180, 240, 300, or 360.

Seeding the random function

The random function is started with a "seed"—a variable the function checks for. If it is not defined, the seed is reset to the system-date value retrieved by the `getvar` function:

```
>> (rtos (getvar "date"))
"2453795.3584"
```

The date number represents: `<Julian day number>.<Decimal fraction of a day>`.

If you wish to use the same sequence of random numbers, then prior to the first call to the random function, set the random seed, where the variable `myseed` is any number you choose:

```
(setq rnseed myseed)
```

For example, execute this function:

```
;----------------------------------
(defun ex10 ()
 (setq rnseed 10.0)
 (repeat 10
  (setq rval
   (* (fix (* (rn) 6.99)) 60))
  (princ rval) (princ " ")
 )
(princ)
)
;----------------------------------
```

To return to have the seed value reset, use:

```
(setq rnseed nil)
```

The following examples focus on patterns that can be used as reliefs in architectural surfaces; in three dimensions, or as etching for two-dimensional patterns. Each is a single panel that can be dimensioned for a large area or used in a panel that repeats itself. A number of these examples combine all of the solid elements into one unit using the `UNION` command. A union is not needed if the panel is only being modeled for a rendering. If a hidden-line drawing is required for an automated fabrication system, such as a CNC-mill or 3-D printer, a union will be needed in most cases.

6.1 Random Relief Patterns from Basic Shapes

Draw a simple grid of squares

Add function PROG01, a simple program to draw an array of squares given their dimension and the number of times to repeat them in each direction. Each square is placed by its lower-left corner. Note where the x and y values start and where the increments occur.

Here is an outline for nested loops in the function:

```
; start Y coordinate
(repeat ytimes
  ; start X coordinate
  (repeat xtimes
   ; compute corner points
   ; draw rectangle
   ; increment X coordinate
  )
  ; increment Y coordinate
)
```

Using AutoCAD's RECTANGLE command, the points in the grid represent the lower-left corner of each square. To draw the square, the upper-right corner point also needs to be computed.

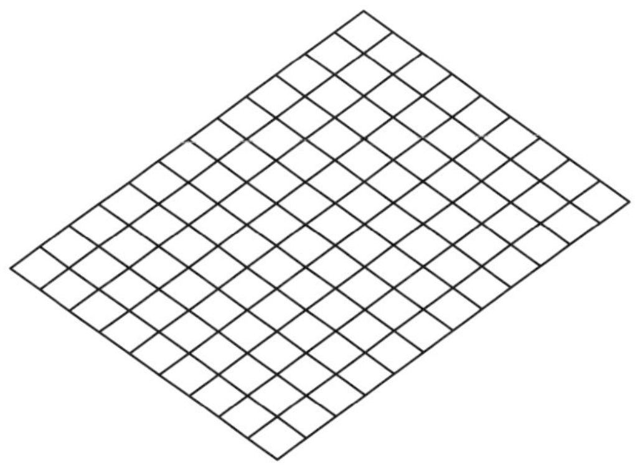

PROG01: grid of squares

Add functions dtr, rtd, and PROG01 to CH06A.LSP:

```
;----------------------------------
(defun dtr (a) (* pi (/ a 180.0)))
(defun rtd (a) (/ (* a 180.0) pi))
;----------------------------------
(defun prog01 ()
 (graphscr)
 (command ".ERASE" "all" "")
 ; set start point
 (setq pnt0 (list 0 0 0))
 (prompt "\nPROG01:")
 (setq xyside
   (getdist pnt0
   "\nEnter XY side:"))
 (setq xtimes
   (getint
   "\nEnter number X repeats:"))
 (setq ytimes
   (getint
   "\nEnter number Y repeats:"))
 ; start y location
 (setq yloc (nth 1 pnt0))
 (repeat ytimes
  ; start x location
  (setq xloc (nth 0 pnt0))
  (repeat xtimes
   ; lower corner pt
   (setq pnt1
     (list xloc yloc (nth 2 pnt0)))
   ; upper-right corner pt for
   ; rectangle
   (setq pnt2 (list
     (+ (nth 0 pnt1) xyside)
     (+ (nth 1 pnt1) xyside)
     (nth 2 pnt1)))
   ; draw rectangle
   (command ".RECTANGLE" pnt1 pnt2)
   ; inc x location
   (setq xloc (+ xloc xyside))
  )
  ; inc y location
  (setq yloc (+ yloc xyside))
  (command ".ZOOM" "e")
 )
 (princ)
)
;----------------------------------
```

Consider other alternatives for specifying this grid. The total length and width could be entered and the number of times for the repetition in each direction, then the dimension for the square could be computed; if not a square, then a rectangle.

Random-height rectangles in the grid

Add function PROG02. Extrude each square to a random height given a minimum and a maximum height. Once placed in the grid, UNION all of the squares.

Add:

```
(setq zmin
  (getdist
  "\nEnter min Z height: "))
(setq zmax
   (getdist
   "\nEnter max Z height: "))
```

Compute the height:

```
; compute height
(setq zheight
  (+ zmin (* (rn)
  (- zmax zmin))))
(command ".EXTRUDE"
  "last" "" zheight "")
```

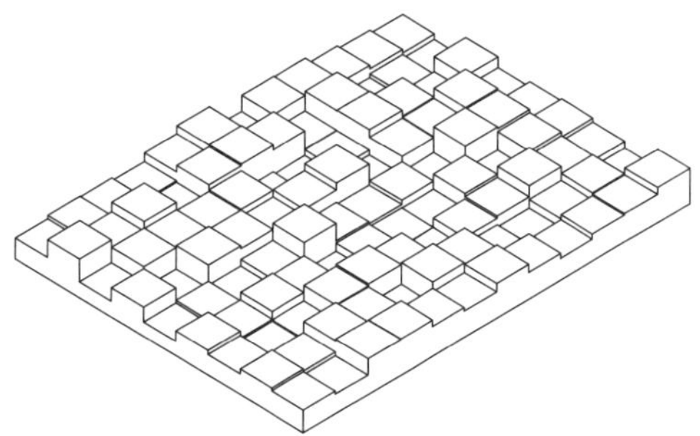

PROG02: repeated squares with random heights

Note that since the values can range anywhere from the minimum to the maximum entered, the height is very irregular.

Execute this function with the same values and you will see that the arrangement is different each time. The only way to reproduce the exact pattern is to use your own input seed for the random function.

Sample script file for PROG02:

```
;----------------------------------
(prog02)
;Enter XY side:
5
;Enter number X repeats:
12
;Enter number Y repeats:
9
;Enter min Z height:
1
;Enter max Z height:
5
view
swiso
hide
;----------------------------------
```

Completed function PROG02:

```
;----------------------------------
(defun prog02 ()
 (graphscr)
 (command ".ERASE" "all" "")
 ; set start point
 (setq pnt0 (list 0 0 0))
 (prompt "\nPROG02:")
 (setq xyside
   (getdist pnt0
   "\nEnter XY side:"))
 (setq xtimes
   (getint
   "\nEnter number X repeats:"))
 (setq ytimes
   (getint
   "\nEnter number Y repeats:"))
 (setq zmin
```

```
    (getdist
    "\nEnter min Z height: "))
  (setq zmax
    (getdist
    "\nEnter max Z height: "))
  ; start y location
  (setq yloc (nth 1 pnt0))
  (repeat ytimes
   ; start x location
   (setq xloc (nth 0 pnt0))
   (repeat xtimes
    ; lower corner pt
    (setq pnt1
      (list xloc yloc (nth 2 pnt0)))
    ; upper-right corner pt for
    ; rectangle
    (setq pnt2 (list
      (+ (nth 0 pnt1) xyside)
      (+ (nth 1 pnt1) xyside)
      (nth 2 pnt1)))
    ; draw rectangle
    (command ".RECTANGLE" pnt1 pnt2)
    ; compute height
    (setq zheight (+ zmin (* (rn)
      (- zmax zmin))))
    (command ".EXTRUDE"
      "last" "" zheight)
    ; versions prior to 2007 require
    ; the taper parameter
    ;(command ".EXTRUDE"
    ;  "last" "" zheight "")
    ; inc x location
    (setq xloc (+ xloc xyside))
   )
   ; inc y location
   (setq yloc (+ yloc xyside))
   (command ".ZOOM" "e")
  )
  ; union
  (command ".UNION" "all" "")
  (princ)
)
;-----------------------------------
```

Place random circles in the grid

In PROG02, we kept the dimensions of the square within the grid. Add function PROG03 using a copy of PROG02. Replace the RECTANGLE with a CIRCLE and try some values for the radius that are greater than the grid spacing. Add input for the circle radius. If the radius is the same size as or smaller than the grid spacing, gaps will form between the circles. To retain the arrangement as a single panel, place a rectangular base at one-half the minimum height in each grid location.

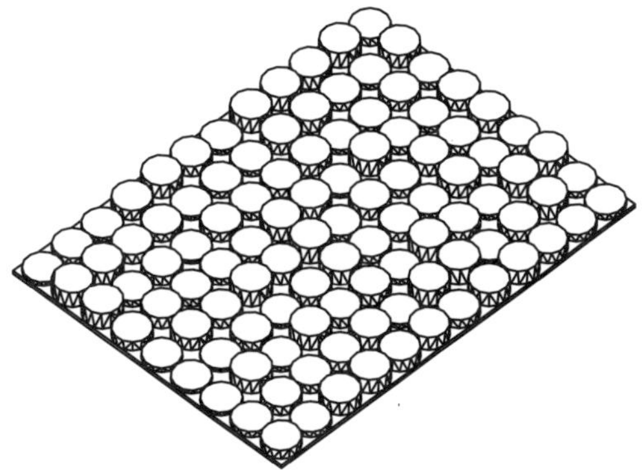

PROG03: repeated circles inside the grid

Sample script file for PROG03:

```
;-----------------------------------
(prog03)
;Enter XY side:
5
;Enter number X repeats:
12
;Enter number Y repeats:
9
;Enter min Z height:
1
;Enter max Z height:
3
```

```
;circle radius
2.5
view
swiso
hide
;---------------------------------
```

Completed function PROG03:

```
;---------------------------------
(defun prog03 ()
 (graphscr)
 (command ".ERASE" "all" "")
 ; set start point
 (setq pnt0 (list 0 0 0))
 (prompt "\nPROG03:")
 (setq xyside
   (getdist pnt0
   "\nEnter XY side:"))
 (setq xtimes
   (getint
   "\nEnter number X repeats:"))
 (setq ytimes
   (getint
   "\nEnter number Y repeats:"))
 (setq zmin
   (getdist
   "\nEnter min Z height: "))
 (setq zmax
   (getdist
   "\nEnter max Z height: "))
 (setq crad
   (getdist
   "\nEnter circle radius: "))
 ; start y location
 (setq yloc (nth 1 pnt0))
 (repeat ytimes
  ; start x location
  (setq xloc (nth 0 pnt0))
  (repeat xtimes
   ; lower corner pt
   (setq pnt1
     (list xloc yloc (nth 2 pnt0)))
   ; center of square
   (setq pnt2 (list
     (+ (nth 0 pnt1) (/ xyside 2))
     (+ (nth 1 pnt1) (/ xyside 2))
     (nth 2 pnt1)))
   ; draw circle
   (command ".CIRCLE" pnt2 crad)
   ; compute height
   (setq zheight (+ zmin (* (rn)
     (- zmax zmin))))
   (command ".EXTRUDE"
     "last" "" zheight)
   ; versions prior to 2007 require
   ; the taper parameter
   ;(command ".EXTRUDE"
   ;  "last" "" zheight "")
   ; base, upper-right corner pt for
   ; rectangle
   (setq pnt2 (list
     (+ (nth 0 pnt1) xyside)
     (+ (nth 1 pnt1) xyside)
     (nth 2 pnt1)))
   (command ".RECTANGLE" pnt1 pnt2)
   (command ".EXTRUDE"
     "last" "" (/ zmin 2))
   ; versions prior to 2007 require
   ; the taper parameter
   ;(command ".EXTRUDE"
     "last" "" (/ zmin 2) "")
   ; inc x location
   (setq xloc (+ xloc xyside))
  )
  ; inc y location
  (setq yloc (+ yloc xyside))
  (command ".ZOOM" "e")
 )
 ; union
 (command ".UNION" "all" "")
 (princ)
)
;---------------------------------
```

A more interesting arrangement is produced when the radius is greater than the grid spacing. In this example, the circle radius was changed to 3.5.

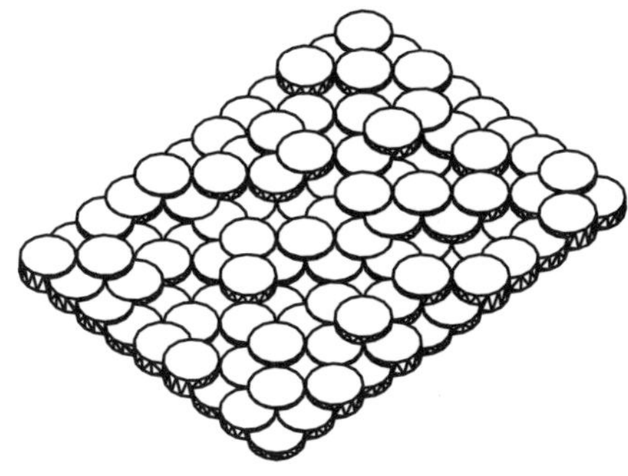

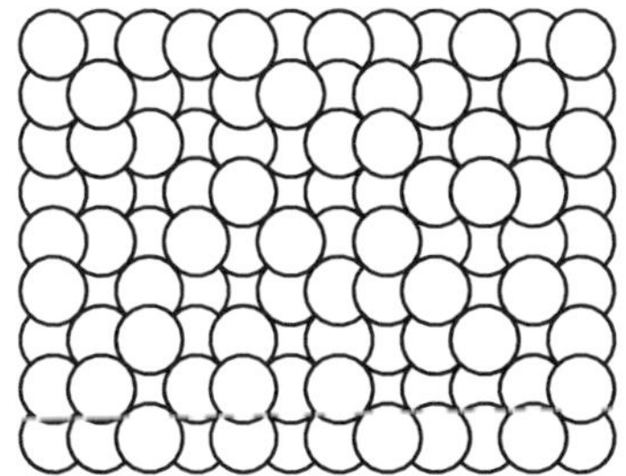

PROG03: repeated circles extending outside the grid

For a rendering, if the base and circles need to represent different materials, assign each to its own layer, using:

```
(command ".LAYER"
  "MAKE" "layername" "")
```

Place the LAYER command prior to the CIRCLE and RECTANGLE commands. Also, remove the UNION command at the end of the function.

Using other shapes inside the grid

Add function PROG04 using a copy of PROG03. Replace the circles with an n-sided polygon of your choice, by radius, inscribed in the square. You can include the number of sides as input. Once placed in the grid, UNION all of the polygons and the base. Note in the previous function that at the boundary the circles expanded outside the grid. If you were modeling a reproducable panel, the edges would not meet correctly. Also, this would not allow you to add a lip for fastening considerations. To solve this problem, use the SLICE command to trim the panel at the boundary.

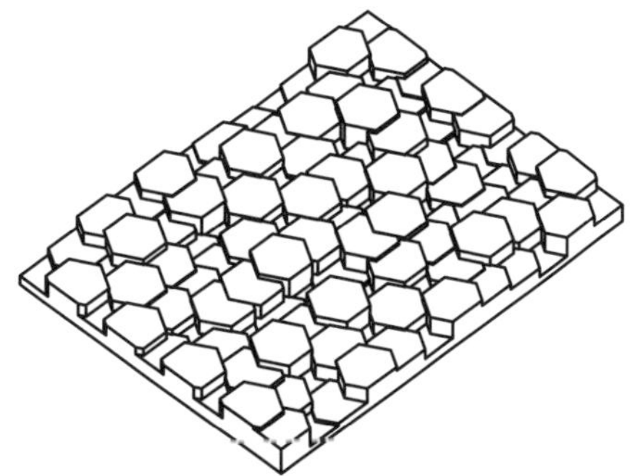

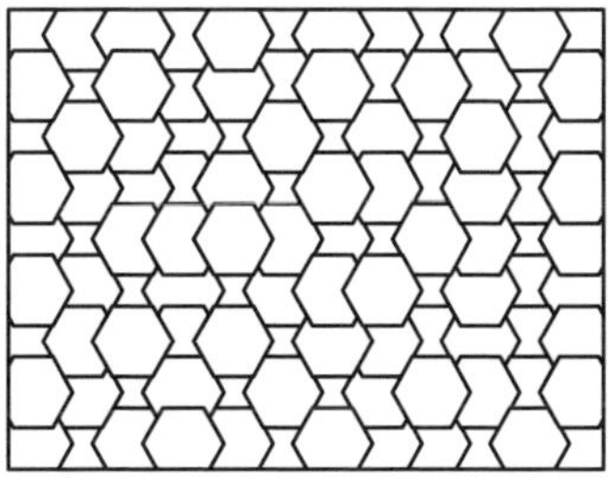

PROG04: repeated polygon, trimmed to edges

The SLICE command does not require the slicing plane to cross the entire object—just two points that lie on that plane. The third point in the command is some point on the side of the slicing plane representing that part of the object to be kept; in this case, it is the center of the boundary.

For example, the bottom edge is trimmed by:

```
; trim edges
  ; center of boundary
 (setq pntc (list
   (+ (nth 0 pnt0)
   (* (/ xtimes 2.0) xyside))
   (+ (nth 1 pnt0)
   (* (/ ytimes 2.0) xyside))
   (nth 2 pnt0)))
 ; bottom edge
 (setq pnt1 pnt0)
 (setq pnt2 (list
   (+ (nth 0 pnt1) xyside)
   (nth 1 pnt1) (nth 2 pnt1)))
 (command ".SLICE"
   "all" "" pnt1 pnt2 pntc)
```

Sample script file for PROG04:

```
;---------------------------------
(prog04)
;Enter XY side:
5
;Enter number X repeats:
12
;Enter number Y repeats:
9
;Enter min Z height:
1
;Enter max Z height:
5
;polygon sides
6
;polygon radius
4.0
view
swiso
hide
;---------------------------------
```

Completed function PROG04:

```
;---------------------------------
(defun prog04 ()
 (graphscr)
 (command ".ERASE" "all" "")
 ; set start point
 (setq pnt0 (list 0 0 0))
 (prompt "\nPROG04:")
 (setq xyside
   (getdist pnt0
   "\nEnter XY side:"))
 (setq xtimes
   (getint
   "\nEnter number X repeats:"))
 (setq ytimes
   (getint
   "\nEnter number Y repeats:"))
 (setq zmin
   (getdist
   "\nEnter min Z height: "))
 (setq zmax
   (getdist
   "\nEnter max Z height: "))
 (setq nsides
   (getint
   "\nEnter polygon sides:"))
 (setq crad
   (getdist
   "\nEnter polygon radius: "))
 ; start y location
 (setq yloc (nth 1 pnt0))
 (repeat ytimes
  ; start x location
  (setq xloc (nth 0 pnt0))
  (repeat xtimes
   ; lower corner pt
   (setq pnt1
     (list xloc yloc (nth 2 pnt0)))
   ; center of square
   (setq pnt2 (list
     (+ (nth 0 pnt1) (/ xyside 2))
     (+ (nth 1 pnt1) (/ xyside 2))
     (nth 2 pnt1)))
   ; draw polygon
   (command ".POLYGON"
     nsides pnt2 "I" crad)
   ; compute height
```

```
  (setq zheight (+ zmin (* (rn)
    (- zmax zmin))))
  (command ".EXTRUDE"
    "last" "" zheight)
  ; versions prior to 2007 require
  ; the taper parameter
  ;(command ".EXTRUDE"
  ;  "last" "" (/ zmin 2) "")
  ; base, upper-right corner pt for
  ; rectangle
  (setq pnt2 (list
    (+ (nth 0 pnt1) xyside)
    (+ (nth 1 pnt1) xyside)
    (nth 2 pnt1)))
  (command ".RECTANGLE" pnt1 pnt2)
  (command ".EXTRUDE"
    "last" "" (/ zmin 2))
  ; versions prior to 2007 require
  ; the taper parameter
  ;(command ".EXTRUDE"
  ;  "last" "" (/ zmin 2) "")
  ; inc x location
  (setq xloc (+ xloc xyside))
 )
 ; inc y location
 (setq yloc (+ yloc xyside))
 (command ".ZOOM" "e")
)
; union
(command ".UNION" "all" "")
; trim edges
; center of boundary
(setq pntc (list
  (+ (nth 0 pnt0)
  (* (/ xtimes 2.0) xyside))
  (+ (nth 1 pnt0)
  (* (/ ytimes 2.0) xyside))
  (nth 2 pnt0)))
; bottom edge
(setq pnt1 pnt0)
(setq pnt2 (list
  (+ (nth 0 pnt1) xyside)
  (nth 1 pnt1) (nth 2 pnt1)))
(command ".SLICE"
  "all" "" pnt1 pnt2 pntc)
; top edge
(setq pnt1 (list
  (nth 0 pnt0)
  (+ (nth 1 pnt0)
  (* ytimes xyside))
  (nth 2 pnt0)))
(setq pnt2 (list
  (+ (nth 0 pnt1) xyside)
  (nth 1 pnt1) (nth 2 pnt1)))
(command ".SLICE"
  "all" "" pnt1 pnt2 pntc)
; left edge
(setq pnt1 pnt0)
(setq pnt2 (list
  (nth 0 pnt1)
  (+ (nth 1 pnt1) xyside)
  (nth 2 pnt1)))
(command ".SLICE"
  "all" "" pnt1 pnt2 pntc)
; right edge
(setq pnt1 (list
  (+ (nth 0 pnt0)
  (* xtimes xyside))
  (nth 1 pnt0) (nth 2 pnt0)))
(setq pnt2 (list
  (nth 0 pnt1)
  (+ (nth 1 pnt1) xyside)
  (nth 2 pnt1)))
(command ".SLICE"
  "all" "" pnt1 pnt2 pntc)
 (princ)
)
;---------------------------------
```

Random heights from a list

In these examples, the heights extend over a range from a minimum to a maximum. The variety of heights is great. If the perforations are punched and not cut, the diameter of the punches could be limited. To better control the selection of heights, specify a list of possible heights.

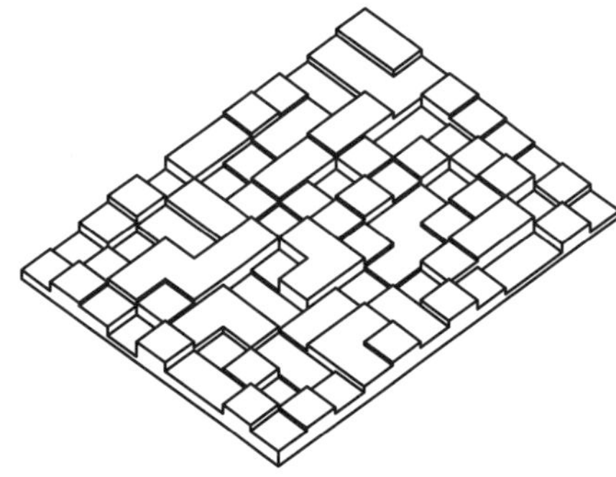

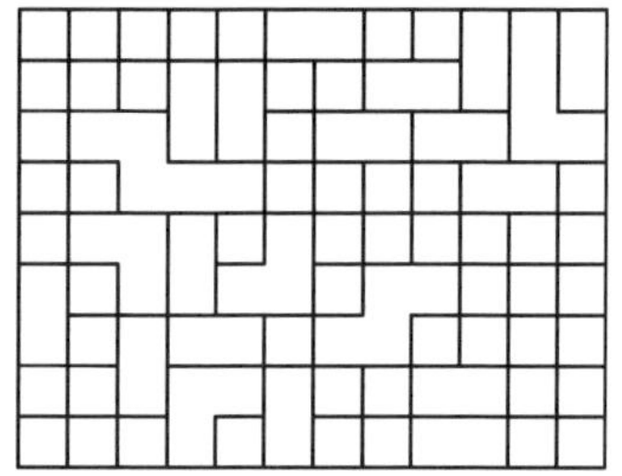

PROG05: random heights from a list

Add function PROG05 using a copy of PROG02. Remove input for the heights and add input for a list of heights:

```
(setq hlist
  (read (getstring
  "\nEnter height list:")))
```

The list would be entered as:

```
(1.0 1.5 2.0 2.5 3.0 3.5)
```

This list can have any number of valid heights in any order. The `read` function converts the entered string to a list. Once it is a list, an index to the list can be computed and the height extracted, using:

```
; compute height
(setq n (fix (* (rn)
  (- (length hlist) 0.1))))
(setq zheight
  (nth n hlist))
```

In this case, the `length` function determines that there are six members in the list. The index to the list has to be in the range of 0 to 5, so that the `nth` function can be used to extract the value. The length is decreased by 0.1, so that the `rn` function—which returns a value from 0.0 to 1.0—will never generate 6. The number generated from the random function is converted to an integer with the `fix` function, because the `nth` function only accepts integers. Since the heights are set consistently, where they match adjoining panels, the patterns take on a contiguous area, forming larger patterns. Instead of six selections, try fewer.

For fabrication purposes, let's assume the pattern is to be constructed of one-half-inch-thick tiles. After generating each height, the height value can be included at the center of the square by using:

```
; add height to model
(command ".TEXT" (list
  (+ (nth 0 pnt1) (/ xyside 10))
  (+ (nth 1 pnt1) (/ xyside 10))
  (nth 2 pnt1))
  (/ xyside 10) "0"
  (rtos zheight 2 2))
```

The text size and location within the grid is set to one-tenth the dimension of the grid spacing. Since the elevation of the text is 0.0, if the panel is plotted with `hide` on, the test is not visible; if plotted with `wireframe` on, it is visible.

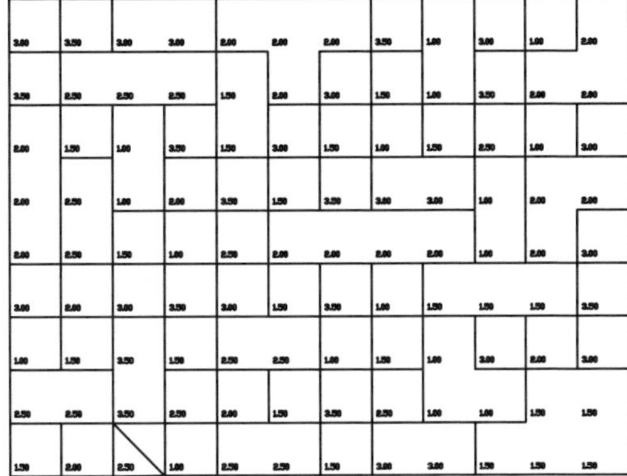

PROG05: with height values included

Sample script file for PROG05:

```
;----------------------------------
(prog05)
;Enter XY side:
5
;Enter number X repeats:
12
;Enter number Y repeats:
9
;Enter height list
(1.0 1.5 2.0 2.5 3.0 3.5)
view
swiso
hide
;----------------------------------
```

Completed function PROG05:

```
;----------------------------------
(defun prog05 ()
 (graphscr)
 (command ".ERASE" "all" "")
 ; set start point
 (setq pnt0 (list 0 0 0))
 (prompt "\nPROG05:")
 (setq xyside
   (getdist pnt0
   "\nEnter XY side:"))
 (setq xtimes
   (getint
   "\nEnter number X repeats:"))
 (setq ytimes
   (getint
   "\nEnter number Y repeats:"))
 (setq hlist
   (read (getstring
   "\nEnter height list:")))
 ; start y location
 (setq yloc (nth 1 pnt0))
 (repeat ytimes
  ; start x location
  (setq xloc (nth 0 pnt0))
  (repeat xtimes
   ; lower corner pt
   (setq pnt1
     (list xloc yloc (nth 2 pnt0)))
   ; upper corner of square
   (setq pnt2 (list
     (+ (nth 0 pnt1) xyside)
     (+ (nth 1 pnt1) xyside)
     (nth 2 pnt1)))
   ; draw rectangle
   (command ".RECTANGLE" pnt1 pnt2)
   ; compute height
   (setq n (fix (* (rn)
     (- (length hlist) 0.1))))
   (setq zheight (nth n hlist))
   (command ".EXTRUDE"
     "last" "" zheight)
   ; versions prior to 2007 require
   ; the taper parameter
   ;(command ".EXTRUDE"
```

```
    ;  "last" "" zheight "")
    ; add height to model
    (command ".TEXT" (list
      (+ (nth 0 pnt1) (/ xyside 10))
      (+ (nth 1 pnt1) (/ xyside 10))
      (nth 2 pnt1))
      (/ xyside 10) "0"
      (rtos zheight 2 2))
    ; inc x location
    (setq xloc (+ xloc xyside))
   )
   ; inc y location
   (setq yloc (+ yloc xyside))
   (command ".ZOOM" "e")
  )
  ; union
  (command ".UNION" "all" "")
  (princ)
)
;-----------------------------------
```

Add a random rotation

The next property of elements to vary in the grid is a random rotation. Add function PROG06 using a copy of PROG02. Include a random rotation for each square. Set the rotation to multiples of 45, 22.5, or 12.25 degrees, with rotation occurring at the center of each square. The angle multiple can be included as input. Optionally, because the rotation will leave gaps in the panel, add a base rectangle at each grid that is half of the minimum height. Also, the rotated rectangles can extend outside the grid boundary. Consider adding the boundary slice to the function.

Add input for the angle rotation as:

```
(setq angx
   (getreal
   "\nEnter angle multiple: "))
```

Compute the random rotation before the square is extruded as:

```
; rotate
(setq rotang
  (* (fix (* (rn) 10.0)) angx))
(command ".ROTATE"
  "last" "" pnt3 rotang)
```

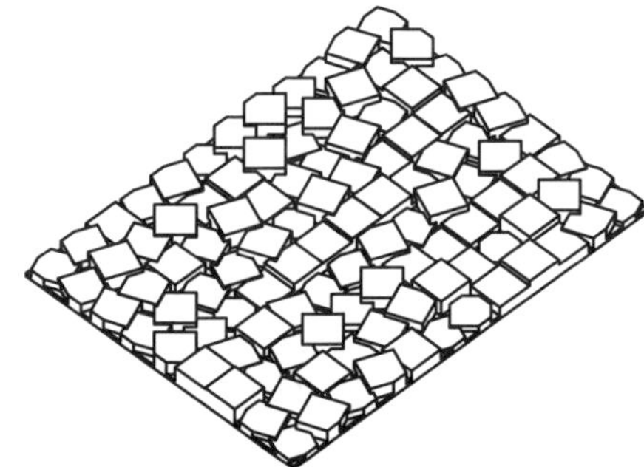

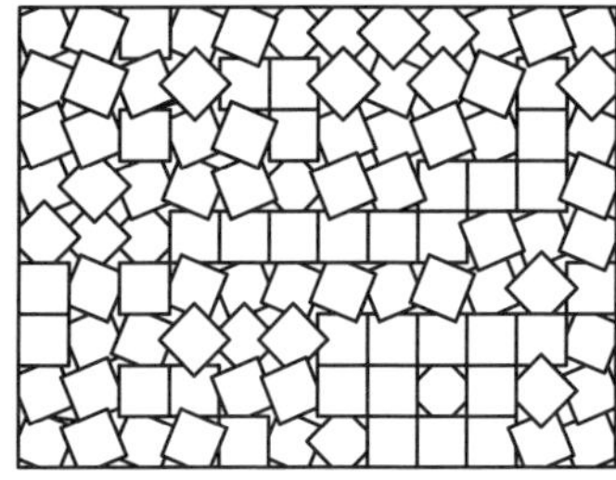

PROG06: randomly rotated squares

Sample script file for PROG06:

```
;-----------------------------------
(prog06)
;Enter XY side:
5
;Enter number X repeats:
12
;Enter number Y repeats:
```

```
9
; Z min
1.0
; Z max
3.0
;angle multiple
22.5
view
swiso
hide
;----------------------------------
```

Completed function PROG06:

```
;----------------------------------
(defun prog06 ()
 (graphscr)
 (command ".ERASE" "all" "")
 ; set start point
 (setq pnt0 (list 0 0 0))
 (prompt "\nPROG06:")
 (setq xyside
   (getdist pnt0
   "\nEnter XY side:"))
 (setq xtimes
   (getint
   "\nEnter number X repeats:"))
 (setq ytimes
   (getint
   "\nEnter number Y repeats:"))
 (setq zmin
   (getdist
   "\nEnter min Z height: "))
 (setq zmax
   (getdist
   "\nEnter max Z height: "))
 (setq angx
   (getreal
   "\nEnter angle multiple: "))
 ; start y location
 (setq yloc (nth 1 pnt0))
 (repeat ytimes
  ; start x location
  (setq xloc (nth 0 pnt0))
  (repeat xtimes
   ; lower corner pt
   (setq pnt1
     (list xloc yloc (nth 2 pnt0)))
   ; upper-right corner pt for
   ; rectangle
   (setq pnt2 (list
     (+ (nth 0 pnt1) xyside)
     (+ (nth 1 pnt1) xyside)
     (nth 2 pnt1)))
   ; draw rectangle
   (command ".RECTANGLE" pnt1 pnt2)
   ; center of square
   (setq pnt3 (list
     (+ (nth 0 pnt1) (/ xyside 2))
     (+ (nth 1 pnt1) (/ xyside 2))
     0))
   ; rotate
   (setq rotang
     (* (fix (* (rn) 10.0)) angx))
   (command ".ROTATE"
     "last" "" pnt3 rotang)
   ; compute height
   (setq zheight (+ zmin (* (rn)
     (- zmax zmin))))
   (command ".EXTRUDE"
     "last" "" zheight)
   ; versions prior to 2007 require
   ; the taper parameter
   ;(command ".EXTRUDE"
   ;  "last" "" zheight "")
   ; base
   (command ".RECTANGLE" pnt1 pnt2)
   (command ".EXTRUDE"
     "last" "" (/ zmin 2))
   ; versions prior to 2007 require
   ; the taper parameter
   ;(command ".EXTRUDE"
   ;  "last" "" (/ zmin 2) "")
   ; inc x location
   (setq xloc (+ xloc xyside))
  )
  ; inc y location
  (setq yloc (+ yloc xyside))
  (command ".ZOOM" "e")
 )
 ; union
 (command ".UNION" "all" "")
 ; trim edges
 ; center of boundary
 (setq pntc (list
```

```
    (+ (nth 0 pnt0)
    (* (/ xtimes 2.0) xyside))
    (+ (nth 1 pnt0)
    (* (/ ytimes 2.0) xyside))
    (nth 2 pnt0)))
  ; bottom edge
  (setq pnt1 pnt0)
  (setq pnt2 (list
    (+ (nth 0 pnt1) xyside)
    (nth 1 pnt1) (nth 2 pnt1)))
  (command ".SLICE"
     "all" "" pnt1 pnt2 pntc)
  ; top edge
  (setq pnt1 (list
    (nth 0 pnt0)
    (+ (nth 1 pnt0)
    (* ytimes xyside))
    (nth 2 pnt0)))
  (setq pnt2 (list
    (+ (nth 0 pnt1) xyside)
    (nth 1 pnt1) (nth 2 pnt1)))
  (command ".SLICE"
    "all" "" pnt1 pnt2 pntc)
  ; left edge
  (setq pnt1 pnt0)
  (setq pnt2 (list
    (nth 0 pnt1)
    (+ (nth 1 pnt1) xyside)
    (nth 2 pnt1)))
  (command ".SLICE"
    "all" "" pnt1 pnt2 pntc)
  ; right edge
  (setq pnt1 (list
    (+ (nth 0 pnt0)
    (* xtimes xyside))
    (nth 1 pnt0) (nth 2 pnt0)))
  (setq pnt2 (list
    (nth 0 pnt1)
    (+ (nth 1 pnt1) xyside)
    (nth 2 pnt1)))
  (command ".SLICE"
    "all" "" pnt1 pnt2 pntc)
  (princ)
)
;----------------------------------
```

Add function PROG06a. Add a random rotation to a copy of function PROG05, with selected heights from a list. For this example, only three heights were in the selection list and the rotation angle was based on a multiple of 45 degrees. With less rotation specified and a smaller number of heights, more contiguous areas are formed.

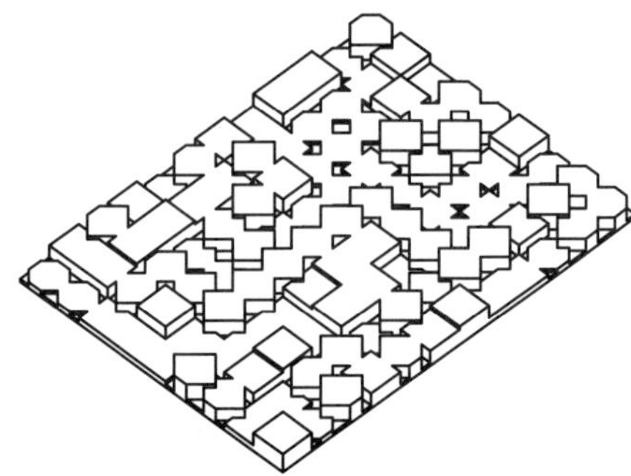

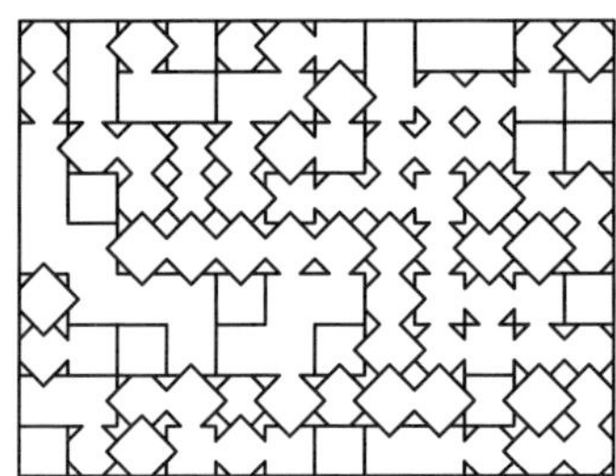

PROG06a: with random rotation and height list

Generating larger contiguous areas on random rotated squares

Add function PROG07 using a copy of PROG06. Generate the random rotation as a multiple of 45 degrees. If the rotation is a multiple of 90 degrees, set the height to the minimum; otherwise set the height to the maximum. The base surface should also be set to the minimum height.

Compute the random rotation and set the height as:

```
; rotate
(setq rotang
  (* (fix (* (rn) 4.99)) 45.0))
(command ".ROTATE"
  "last" "" pnt3 rotang)
; compute height
(if (= (rem rotang 90) 0)
 (setq zheight zmin)
 (setq zheight zmax)
)
```

The random rotation computation will generate the integers 0, 1, 2, 3, and 4 and the angles 0, 45, 90, 135, and 180 degrees. Note that the base surface is applied to all panels, even the ones that have non-90-degree rotation.

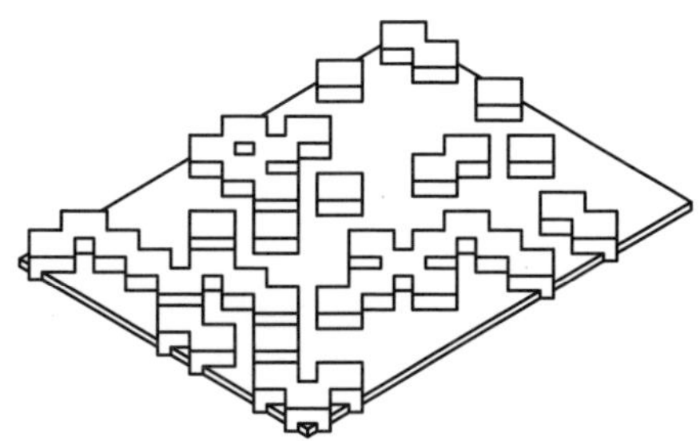

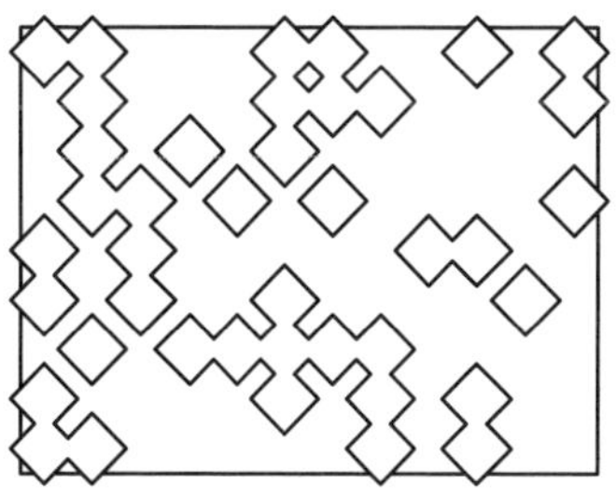

PROG07: squares with set heights based on rotation

Sample script file for PROG07:

```
;---------------------------------
(prog07)
;Enter XY side:
5
;Enter number X repeats:
12
;Enter number Y repeats:
9
; Z min
1.0
; Z max
3.0
view
swiso
hide
;---------------------------------
```

Completed function PROG07:

```
;---------------------------------
(defun prog07 ()
 (graphscr)
 (command ".ERASE" "all" "")
 ; set start point
 (setq pnt0 (list 0 0 0))
 (prompt "\nPROG07:")
 (setq xyside
   (getdist pnt0
   "\nEnter XY side:"))
 (setq xtimes
```

```
    (getint
    "\nEnter number X repeats:"))
  (setq ytimes
    (getint
    "\nEnter number Y repeats:"))
  (setq zmin
    (getdist
    "\nEnter min Z height: "))
  (setq zmax
    (getdist
    "\nEnter max Z height: "))
  ; start y location
  (setq yloc (nth 1 pnt0))
  (repeat ytimes
   ; start x location
   (setq xloc (nth 0 pnt0))
   (repeat xtimes
    ; lower corner pt
    (setq pnt1
      (list xloc yloc (nth 2 pnt0)))
    ; upper-right corner pt for
    ; rectangle
    (setq pnt2 (list
      (+ (nth 0 pnt1) xyside)
      (+ (nth 1 pnt1) xyside)
      (nth 2 pnt1)))
    ; draw rectangle
    (command ".RECTANGLE" pnt1 pnt2)
    ; center of square
    (setq pnt3 (list
      (+ (nth 0 pnt1) (/ xyside 2))
      (+ (nth 1 pnt1) (/ xyside 2))
      0))
    ; rotate
    (setq rotang
      (* (fix (* (rn) 4.99)) 45.0))
    (command ".ROTATE"
      "last" "" pnt3 rotang)
    ; compute height
    (if (= (rem rotang 90) 0)
     (setq zheight zmin)
     (setq zheight zmax)
    )
    (command ".EXTRUDE"
      "last" "" zheight)
    ; versions prior to 2007 require
    ; the taper parameter
    ;(command ".EXTRUDE"
    ;  "last" "" zheight "")
    ; base
    (command ".RECTANGLE" pnt1 pnt2)
    (command ".EXTRUDE"
      "last" "" zmin)
    ; versions prior to 2007 require
    ; the taper parameter
    ;(command ".EXTRUDE"
    ;  "last" "" zmin "")
    ; inc x location
    (setq xloc (+ xloc xyside))
   )
   ; inc y location
   (setq yloc (+ yloc xyside))
   (command ".ZOOM" "e")
  )
  ; union
  (command ".UNION" "all" "")
  (princ)
)
;----------------------------------
```

Generating larger contiguous areas on random rotated polygons

Add function PROG08 using a copy of PROG07. Set the shape to an n-sided polygon. To set the heights as in PROG07, add input for the number of sides, radius, rotation increment, and angle.

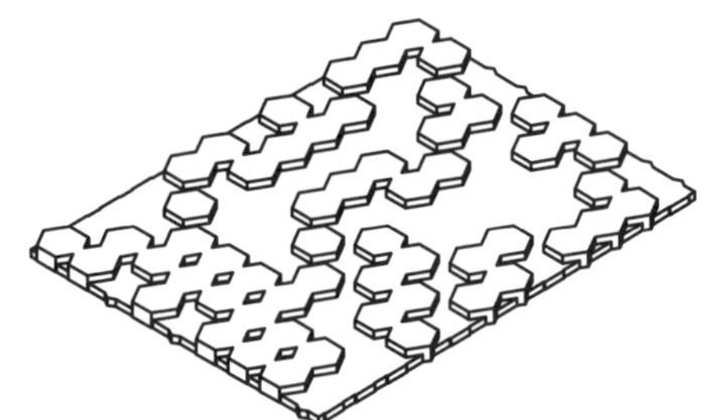

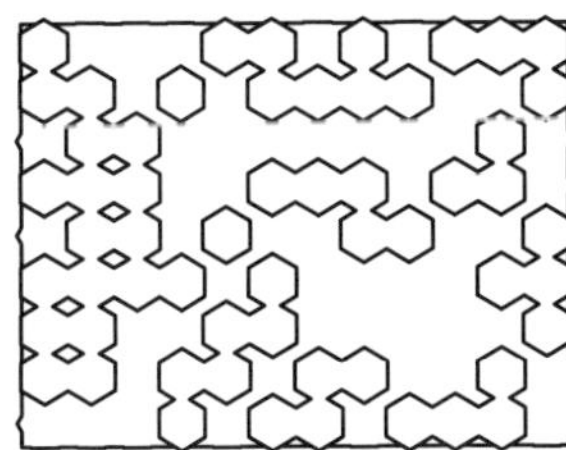

PROG08: polygons with set heights based on rotation

Sample script file for PROG08:

```
;-----------------------------------
(prog08)
;Enter XY side:
5
;Enter number X repeats:
12
;Enter number Y repeats:
9
;Enter min Z height:
1
;Enter max Z height:
2
;Enter polygon sides
6
;Enter polygon radius
3.0
;Enter rotation angle increment
30
;Enter height angle
60
view
swiso
hide
;-----------------------------------
```

Completed function PROG08:

```
;-----------------------------------
(defun prog08 ()
 (graphscr)
 (command “.ERASE” “all” “”)
 ; set start point
 (setq pnt0 (list 0 0 0))
 (prompt “\nPROG08:”)
 (setq xyside
   (getdist pnt0
   “\nEnter XY side:”))
 (setq xtimes
   (getint
   “\nEnter number X repeats:”))
 (setq ytimes
   (getint
   “\nEnter number Y repeats:”))
 (setq zmin
   (getdist
   “\nEnter min Z height: “))
 (setq zmax
   (getdist
   “\nEnter max Z height: “))
 (setq psides
   (getint
   “\nEnter number of polygon
   sides: “))
 (setq prad
   (getdist
   “\nEnter polygon radius: “))
 (setq pang
   (getreal
   “\nEnter rotation angle inc: “))
 (setq anghght
   (getint
   “\nEnter height angle: “))
 ; start y location
 (setq yloc (nth 1 pnt0))
 (repeat ytimes
  ; start x location
  (setq xloc (nth 0 pnt0))
  (repeat xtimes
   ; lower corner pt
   (setq pnt1
     (list xloc yloc (nth 2 pnt0)))
   ; center of square
   (setq pnt2 (list
```

```
    (+ (nth 0 pnt1) (/ xyside 2))
    (+ (nth 1 pnt1) (/ xyside 2))
    (nth 2 pnt1)))
  ; draw polygon
  (command ".POLYGON"
    psides pnt2 "I" prad)
  ; rotate
  (setq rotang
    (* (fix (* (rn) 360)) pang))
  (command ".ROTATE"
    "last" "" pnt2 rotang)
  ; compute height
  (if (= (rem rotang anghght) 0)
    (setq zheight zmin)
    (setq zheight zmax)
  )
  (command ".EXTRUDE"
    "last" "" zheight)
  ; versions prior to 2007 require
  ; the taper parameter
  ;(command ".EXTRUDE"
  ;  "last" "" zheight "")
  ; base
  ; upper-right corner pt for
  ; rectangle
  (setq pnt2 (list
    (+ (nth 0 pnt1) xyside)
    (+ (nth 1 pnt1) xyside)
    (nth 2 pnt1)))
  (command ".RECTANGLE" pnt1 pnt2)
  (command ".EXTRUDE"
    "last" "" zmin)
  ; versions prior to 2007 require
  ; the taper parameter
  ;(command ".EXTRUDE"
  ;  "last" "" zmin "")
  ; inc x location
  (setq xloc (+ xloc xyside))
 )
 ; inc y location
 (setq yloc (+ yloc xyside))
 (command ".ZOOM" "e")
)
; union
(command ".UNION" "all" "")
(princ)
)
;----------------------------------
```

Another example of random polygon rotation and placement is an overlapping triangle. Note that the height angle is set to a value that would never be satisfied. The only time the triangle is set to the minimum height is when the rotation angle is computed as zero.

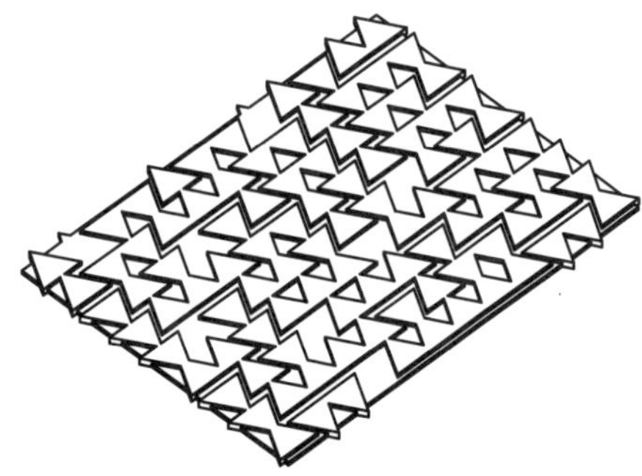

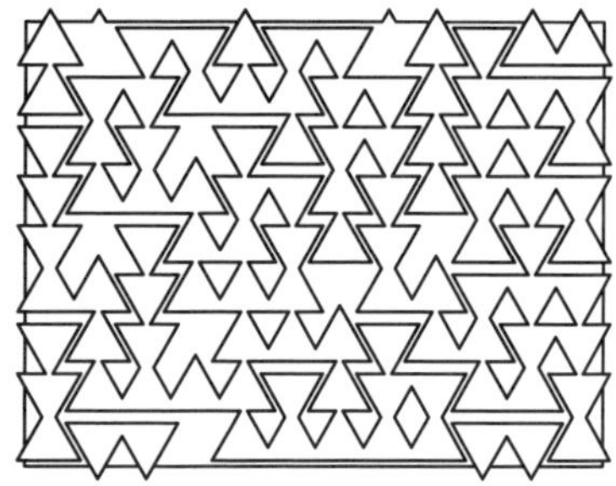

PROG08: overlapping triangles

Sample script file for PROG08:

```
;----------------------------------
(prog08)
;Enter XY side:
5
;Enter number X repeats:
12
;Enter number Y repeats:
9
```

```
;Enter min Z height:
0.5
;Enter max Z height:
1
;Enter polygon sides
3
;Enter poygon radius
3.75
;Enter rotation angle increment
60
;Enter height angle
9999
view
swiso
hide
;---------------------------------
```

Generate circles with random radii

In addition to height, another parameter to consider for random generation is the variety of possible dimensions for the shape being placed in the grid. Add function PROG08 using a copy of PROG03. Compute a randomly selected radius in the range of a minimum and maximum entered radius.

Replace the single radius input with:

```
(setq cradmin
  (getdist
  "\nEnter circle min radius: "))
(setq cradmax
  (getdist
  "\nEnter circle max radius: "))
```

Compute the random radius as:

```
; compute radius
(setq crad
  (+ cradmin (* (rn)
  (- cradmax cradmin))))
```

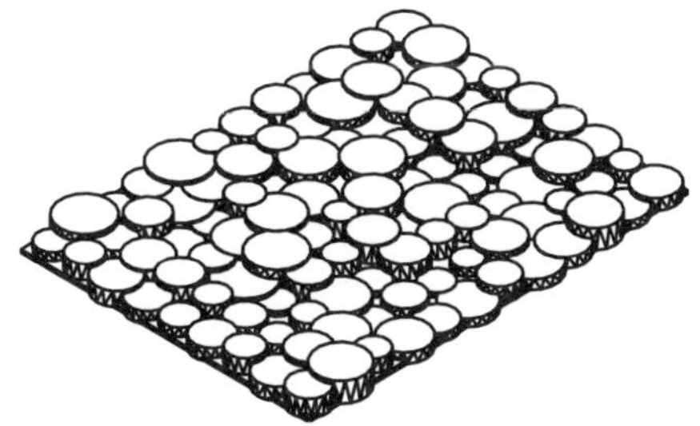

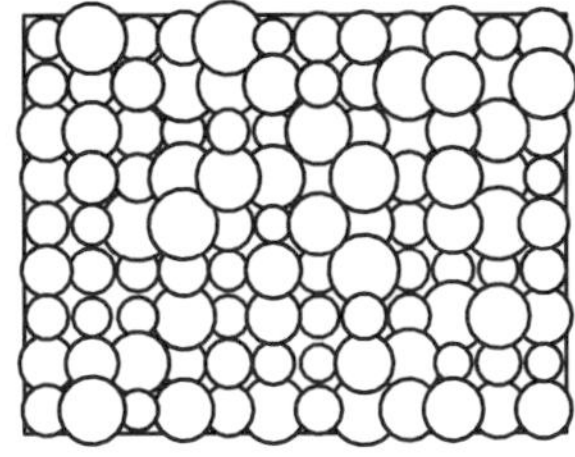

PROG09: circles with random radius and height

Sample script file for PROG09:

```
;---------------------------------
(prog09)
;Enter XY side:
5
;Enter number X repeats:
12
;Enter number Y repeats:
9
; Z min
1.0
; Z max
3.0
; radius min
2.0
; radius max
4.0
view
swiso
hide
;---------------------------------
```

Completed function PROG09:

```
;---------------------------------
(defun prog09 ()
 (graphscr)
 (command ".ERASE" "all" "")
 ; set start point
 (setq pnt0 (list 0 0 0))
 (prompt "\nPROG09:")
 (setq xyside
   (getdist pnt0
   "\nEnter XY side:"))
 (setq xtimes
   (getint
   "\nEnter number X repeats:"))
 (setq ytimes
   (getint
   "\nEnter number Y repeats:"))
 (setq zmin
   (getdist
   "\nEnter min Z height: "))
 (setq zmax
   (getdist
   "\nEnter max Z height: "))
 (setq cradmin
   (getdist
   "\nEnter circle min radius: "))
 (setq cradmax
   (getdist
   "\nEnter circle max radius: "))
 ; start y location
 (setq yloc (nth 1 pnt0))
 (repeat ytimes
  ; start x location
  (setq xloc (nth 0 pnt0))
  (repeat xtimes
   ; lower corner pt
   (setq pnt1
     (list xloc yloc (nth 2 pnt0)))
   ; center of square
   (setq pnt2 (list
     (+ (nth 0 pnt1) (/ xyside 2))
     (+ (nth 1 pnt1) (/ xyside 2))
     (nth 2 pnt1)))
   ; compute radius
   (setq crad (+ cradmin (* (rn)
     (- cradmax cradmin))))
   ; draw circle
   (command ".CIRCLE" pnt2 crad)
   ; compute height
   (setq zheight (+ zmin (* (rn)
     (- zmax zmin))))
   (command ".EXTRUDE"
     "last" "" zheight)
   ; versions prior to 2007 require
   ; the taper parameter
   ;(command ".EXTRUDE"
   ;  "last" "" zheight "")
   ; base
   ; upper-right corner pt for
   ; rectangle
   (setq pnt2 (list
     (+ (nth 0 pnt1) xyside)
     (+ (nth 1 pnt1) xyside)
     (nth 2 pnt1)))
   (command ".RECTANGLE" pnt1 pnt2)
   (command ".EXTRUDE"
     "last" "" (/ zmin 2))
   ; versions prior to 2007 require
   ; the taper parameter
   ;(command ".EXTRUDE"
   ;  "last" "" (/ zmin 2) "")
   ; inc x location
   (setq xloc (+ xloc xyside))
  )
  ; inc y location
  (setq yloc (+ yloc xyside))
  (command ".ZOOM" "e")
 )
 ; union
 (command ".UNION" "all" "")
 (princ)
)
;---------------------------------
```

Generate circles with random offsets

In addition to the height and radius, another parameter to consider for random generation is an offset of a shape from the center of the grid. Add function `PROG10` using a copy of `PROG09`. Compute a randomly selected offset in the x and y directions, from the center. Input maximum x and y offsets. Compute the offsets as either left or right, over or under, the center.

Input the maximum distance for the offsets:

```
(setq xoffmax
  (getdist
  "\nEnter max X offset: "))
(setq yoffmax
  (getdist
  "\nEnter max Y offset: "))
```

To compute the random offsets, half of the offset is subtracted from the center so that the range is left and right, above and below, as follows:

```
; center of square
(setq pnt2 (list
  (+ (nth 0 pnt1) (/ xyside 2))
  (+ (nth 1 pnt1) (/ xyside 2))
  (nth 2 pnt1)))
; X and Y offset
(setq xoff (- (* (rn)
  xoffmax) (/ xoffmax 2)))
(setq yoff (- (* (rn)
  yoffmax) (/ yoffmax 2)))
(setq pnt3 (list
  (+ (nth 0 pnt2) xoff)
  (+ (nth 1 pnt2) yoff)
  (nth 2 pnt2)))
```

Also change the height selection to a list of possible heights and set the base surface height to the first (and lowest) one in the list.

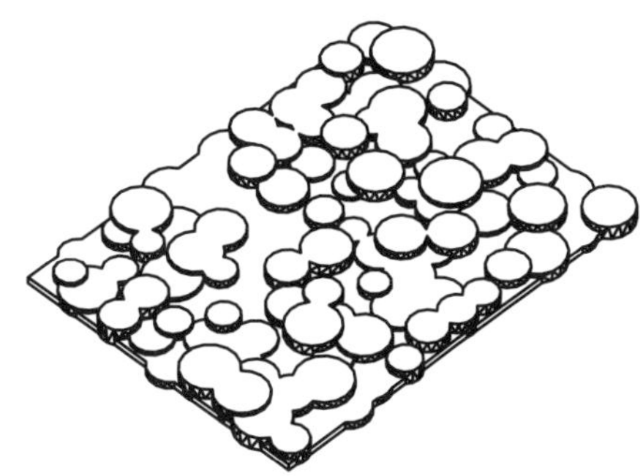

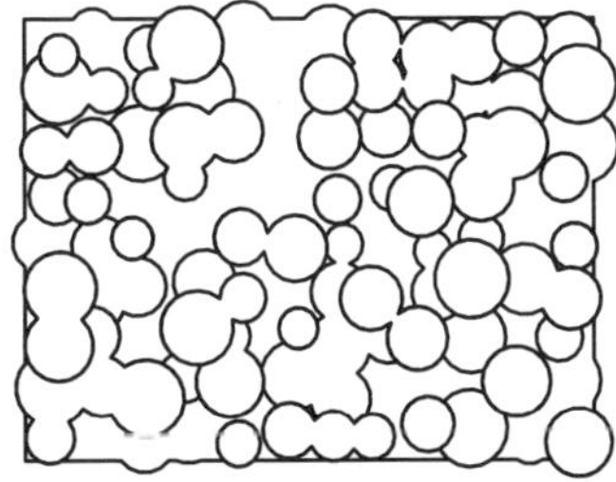

`PROG10`: circles with random radius, height, and offsets

Sample script file for `PROG10`:

```
;----------------------------------
(prog10)
;Enter XY side:
5
;Enter number X repeats:
12
;Enter number Y repeats:
9
;Enter radius min
2.0
;Enter radius max
4.0
;Enter max X offset
```

```
2.5
;Enter max Y offset
2.5
;Enter height list
(1.0 1.5 2.0 2.5)
view
swiso
hide
;---------------------------------
```

Completed function PROG10:

```
;---------------------------------
(defun prog10 ()
 (graphscr)
 (command ".ERASE" "all" "")
 ; set start point
 (setq pnt0 (list 0 0 0))
 (prompt "\nPROG10:")
 (setq xyside
   (getdist pnt0
   "\nEnter XY side:"))
 (setq xtimes
   (getint
   "\nEnter number X repeats:"))
 (setq ytimes
   (getint
   "\nEnter number Y repeats:"))
 (setq cradmin
   (getdist
   "\nEnter circle min radius: "))
 (setq cradmax
   (getdist
   "\nEnter circle max radius: "))
 (setq xoffmax
   (getdist
   "\nEnter max X offset: "))
 (setq yoffmax
   (getdist
   "\nEnter max Y offset: "))
 (setq hlist
   (read (getstring
   "\nEnter height list:")))
 ; start y location
 (setq yloc (nth 1 pnt0))
 (repeat ytimes
  ; start x location
 (setq xloc (nth 0 pnt0))
 (repeat xtimes
  ; lower corner pt
  (setq pnt1 (list xloc yloc 0))
  ; center of square
  (setq pnt2 (list
    (+ (nth 0 pnt1) (/ xyside 2))
    (+ (nth 1 pnt1) (/ xyside 2))
    (nth 2 pnt1)))
  ; X and Y offset
  (setq xoff (- (* (rn) xoffmax)
    (/ xoffmax 2)))
  (setq yoff (- (* (rn) yoffmax)
    (/ yoffmax 2)))
  (setq pnt3 (list
    (+ (nth 0 pnt2) xoff)
    (+ (nth 1 pnt2) yoff)
    (nth 2 pnt2)))
  ; compute radius
  (setq crad (+ cradmin (* (rn)
    (- cradmax cradmin))))
  ; draw circle
  (command ".CIRCLE" pnt3 crad)
  ; compute height
  (setq n (fix (* (rn)
    (- (length hlist) 0.1))))
  (setq zheight (nth n hlist))
  (command ".EXTRUDE"
    "last" "" zheight)
  ; versions prior to 2007 require
  ; the taper parameter
  ;(command ".EXTRUDE"
  ;  "last" "" zheight "")
  ; base
  ; upper-right corner pt for
  ; rectangle
  (setq pnt2 (list
    (+ (nth 0 pnt1) xyside)
    (+ (nth 1 pnt1) xyside)
    (nth 2 pnt1)))
  (command ".RECTANGLE" pnt1 pnt2)
  (command ".EXTRUDE"
    "last" "" (nth 0 hlist))
  ; versions prior to 2007 require
  ; the taper parameter
  ;(command ".EXTRUDE"
  ;  "last" "" (nth 0 hlist) "")
  ; inc x location
```

```
    (setq xloc (+ xloc xyside))
  )
  ; inc y location
  (setq yloc (+ yloc xyside))
  (command ".ZOOM" "e")
 )
 ; union
 (command ".UNION" "all" "")
 (princ)
)
;-----------------------------------
```

Creating a negative of the pattern

If the panel needs to be cast, the negative of the current pattern would have to be made.

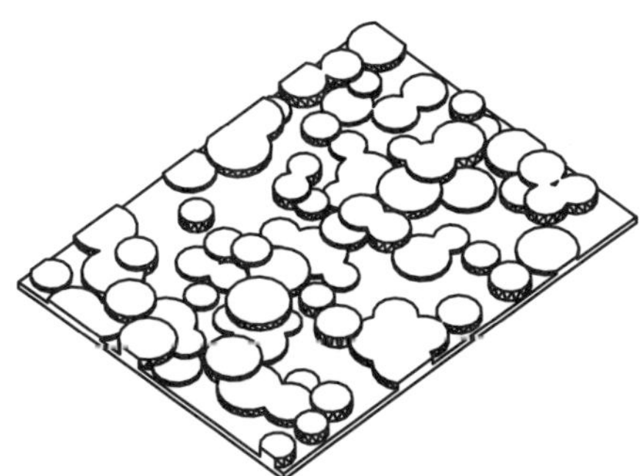

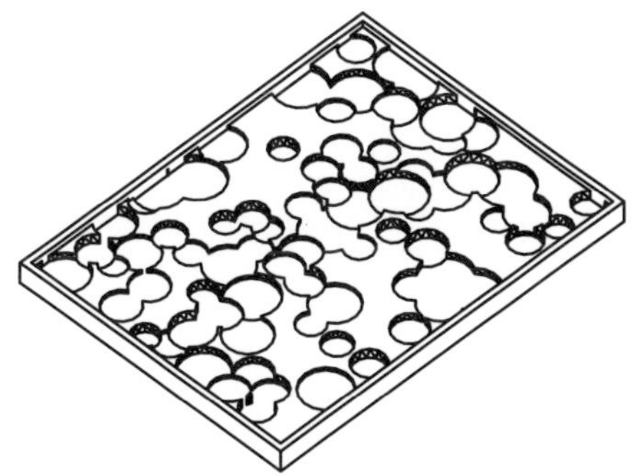

PROG11: positive and negative pattern

Add function PROG11 using a copy of PROG10. First add the section from PROG06 that trims the panel at the edges. To make a negative, make a copy of the panel, place the copy in a selection list, create a solid that is one inch larger than the panel, place it in a selection list, and subtract the two, rotating the negative portion so it faces up. Note that this function assumes that the highest height is the last in the list of heights.

Add the following after the UNION command:

```
; trim edges
 ; center of boundary
 (setq pntc (list
   (+ (nth 0 pnt0)
   (* (/ xtimes 2.0) xyside))
   (+ (nth 1 pnt0)
   (* (/ ytimes 2.0) xyside))
   (nth 2 pnt0)))
 ; bottom edge
 (setq pnt1 pnt0)
 (setq pnt2 (list
   (+ (nth 0 pnt1) xyside)
   (nth 1 pnt1) (nth 2 pnt1)))
 (command ".SLICE"
   "all" "" pnt1 pnt2 pntc)
 ; top edge
 (setq pnt1 (list
   (nth 0 pnt0) (+ (nth 1 pnt0)
   (* ytimes xyside))
   (nth 2 pnt0)))
 (setq pnt2 (list
   (+ (nth 0 pnt1) xyside)
   (nth 1 pnt1) (nth 2 pnt1)))
 (command ".SLICE"
   "all" "" pnt1 pnt2 pntc)
 ; left edge
 (setq pnt1 pnt0)
 (setq pnt2 (list
   (nth 0 pnt1)
   (+ (nth 1 pnt1) xyside)
   (nth 2 pnt1)))
 (command ".SLICE"
   "all" "" pnt1 pnt2 pntc)
 ; right edge
 (setq pnt1 (list
   (+ (nth 0 pnt0)
```

```
    (* xtimes xyside))
    (nth 1 pnt0) (nth 2 pnt0)))
  (setq pnt2 (list
    (nth 0 pnt1)
    (+ (nth 1 pnt1) xyside)
    (nth 2 pnt1)))
  (command ".SLICE"
    "all" "" pnt1 pnt2 pntc)
  ; make negative
  (command ".COPY"
    "last" "" pnt0 pnt0)
  (setq obj1 (ssadd (entlast)))
  (setq pnt1 (list
    (- (nth 0 pnt0) 1)
    (- (nth 1 pnt0) 1)
    (nth 2 pnt0)))
  (setq pnt2 (list
    (+ (+ (nth 0 pnt0)
    (* xtimes xyside)) 1)
    (+ (+ (nth 1 pnt0)
    (* ytimes xyside)) 1)
    (nth 2 pnt0)))
  (command ".RECTANGLE" pnt1 pnt2)
  (command ".ZOOM" "e")
  (command ".EXTRUDE"
    "last" "" (+ (last hlist) 1))
  ; versions prior to 2007 require
  ; the taper parameter
  ;(command ".EXTRUDE"
  ;  "last" "" (+ (last hlist) 1) "")
  (setq obj2 (ssadd (entlast)))
  ; subtract
  (command ".SUBTRACT"
    obj2 "" obj1 "")
  (command ".ROTATE3D"
    "last" "" "Y" pnt2 "180")
  (command ".ZOOM" "e")
```

Constructing random grid modules

In addition to basic shapes, consider constructing a module that can be assigned different heights and rotated to form larger patterns.

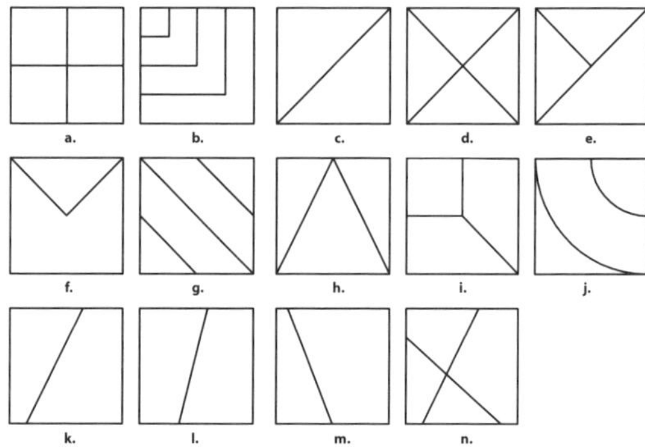

Sample of simple module constructions

For example, in `module a` consisting of four quarters, each separate quarter can be assigned a height; then the entire group can be rotated. The concept is to develop a panel that, when placed next to another panel, can form a larger pattern. Heights can be selected from a possible list of heights so that adjoining panels meet.

Add function `PROG12a` to implement `module a`, four quarters. Input a minimum and maximum height, assign each quarter one-fourth of the difference of the heights, clockwise or counterclockwise, starting with the minimum height. Randomly rotate each on a 90-degree increment.

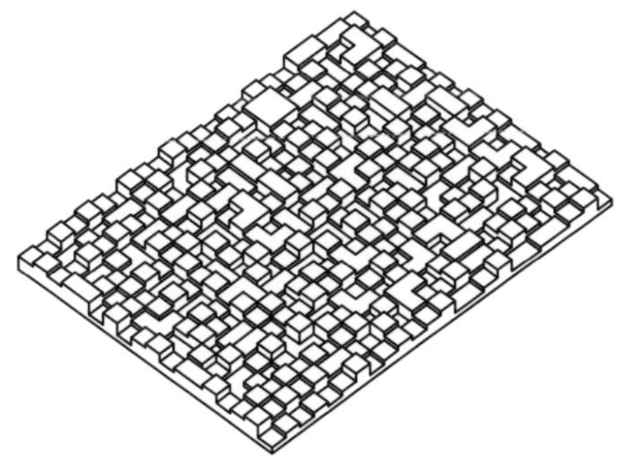

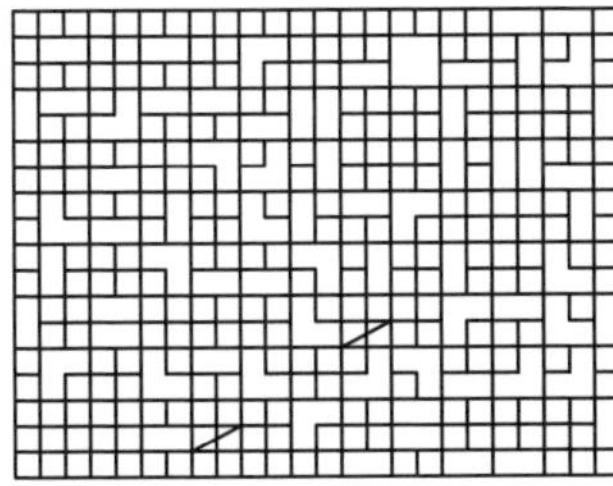

PROG12a: with four quarters module

Sample script file for PROG12a:

```
;---------------------------------
(prog12a)
;Enter XY side:
5
;Enter number X repeats:
12
;Enter number Y repeats:
9
;Enter min Z height:
1
;Enter max Z height:
3
view
swiso
hide
;---------------------------------
```

Completed function PROG12a:

```
;---------------------------------
(defun prog12a ()
 (graphscr)
 (command ".ERASE" "all" "")
 ; set start point
 (setq pnt0 (list 0 0 0))
 (prompt "\nPROG12a:")
 (setq xyside
   (getdist pnt0
   "\nEnter XY side:"))
 (setq xtimes
   (getint
   "\nEnter number X repeats:"))
 (setq ytimes
   (getint
   "\nEnter number Y repeats:"))
 (setq zmin
   (getdist
   "\nEnter min Z height: "))
 (setq zmax
   (getdist
   "\nEnter max Z height: "))
 ; z inc
 (setq zinc (/ (- zmax zmin) 3.0))
 ; start y location
 (setq yloc (nth 1 pnt0))
 (repeat ytimes
  ; start x location
  (setq xloc (nth 0 pnt0))
  (repeat xtimes
   (setq zheight zmin)
   ; first quad
   (setq pnt1
     (list xloc yloc (nth 2 pnt0)))
   (setq pnt2 (list
     (+ (nth 0 pnt1) (/ xyside 2))
     (+ (nth 1 pnt1) (/ xyside 2))
     (nth 2 pnt1)))
   ; draw rectangle
   (command ".RECTANGLE" pnt1 pnt2)
   (command ".EXTRUDE"
     "last" "" zheight)
   ; versions prior to 2007 require
   ; the taper parameter
   ;(command ".EXTRUDE"
   ;  "last" "" zheight "")
```

```
; add to list
(setq rlist (ssadd (entlast)))
; inc height
(setq zheight (+ zheight zinc))
; second quad
(setq pnt1 (list
  (+ xloc (/ xyside 2))
  yloc (nth 2 pnt0)))
(setq pnt2 (list
  (+ (nth 0 pnt1) (/ xyside 2))
  (+ (nth 1 pnt1) (/ xyside 2))
  (nth 2 pnt1)))
; draw rectangle
(command ".RECTANGLE" pnt1 pnt2)
(command ".EXTRUDE"
  "last" "" zheight)
; versions prior to 2007 require
; the taper parameter
;(command ".EXTRUDE"
;  "last" "" zheight "")
; add to list
(setq rlist
  (ssadd (entlast) rlist))
; inc height
(setq zheight (+ zheight zinc))
; third quad
(setq pnt1 (list
  (+ xloc (/ xyside 2))
  (+ yloc (/ xyside 2))
  (nth 2 pnt0)))
(setq pnt2 (list
  (+ (nth 0 pnt1) (/ xyside 2))
  (+ (nth 1 pnt1) (/ xyside 2))
  (nth 2 pnt1)))
; draw rectangle
(command ".RECTANGLE" pnt1 pnt2)
(command ".EXTRUDE"
  "last" "" zheight)
; versions prior to 2007 require
; the taper parameter
;(command ".EXTRUDE"
;  "last" "" zheight "")
; add to list
(setq rlist
  (ssadd (entlast) rlist))
; inc height
(setq zheight (+ zheight zinc))
; fourth quad
      (setq pnt1 (list
        xloc (+ yloc (/ xyside 2))
       (nth 2 pnt0)))
      (setq pnt2 (list
        (+ (nth 0 pnt1) (/ xyside 2))
        (+ (nth 1 pnt1) (/ xyside 2))
        (nth 2 pnt1)))
      ; draw rectangle
      (command ".RECTANGLE" pnt1 pnt2)
      (command ".EXTRUDE"
        "last" "" zheight)
      ; versions prior to 2007 require
      ; the taper parameter
      ;(command ".EXTRUDE"
      ;  "last" "" zheight "")
      ; add to list
      (setq rlist
        (ssadd (entlast) rlist))
      ; rotate
      (setq pnt3 (list
        (+ xloc (/ xyside 2))
        (+ yloc (/ xyside 2)) 0))
      (setq rotang
        (* (fix (* (rn) 4.99)) 90.0))
      (command ".ROTATE"
        rlist "" pnt3 rotang)
      ; inc x location
      (setq xloc (+ xloc xyside))
    )
    ; inc y location
    (setq yloc (+ yloc xyside))
    (command ".ZOOM" "e")
  )
  ; union
  (command ".UNION" "all" "")
  (princ)
)
;---------------------------------
```

Module b through i would be developed in a similar fashion. Module j is different because it consists of arcs.

Add function PROG12j using PROG12a. Construct module j, three arcs. Set the corner arcs to the minimum height and the middle arc to the maximum height. Review the sequence of options used in the POLYLINE command to create the arcs for each segment of the module and which points are needed define the arcs.

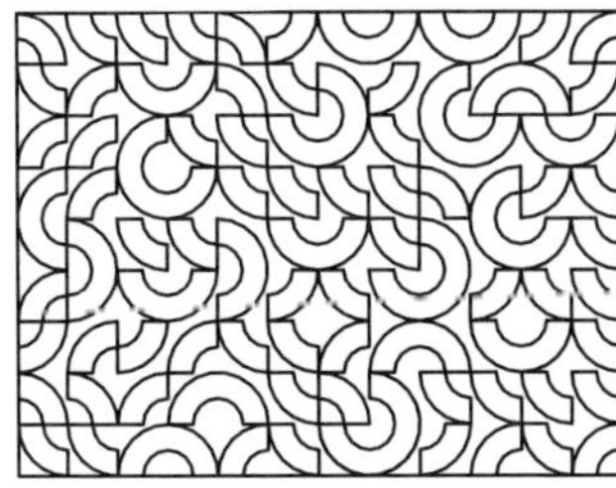

PROG12j: module with three arcs

Sample script file for PROG12j:

```
;-----------------------------------
(prog12j)
;Enter XY side:
5
;Enter number X repeats:
12
;Enter number Y repeats:
9
;Enter min Z height:
1
;Enter max Z height:
2
view
swiso
hide
;-----------------------------------
```

Completed function PROG12j:

```
;-----------------------------------
(defun prog12j ()
 (graphscr)
 (command ".ERASE" "all" "")
 ; set start point
 (setq pnt0 (list 0 0 0))
 (prompt "\nPROG12j:")
 (setq xyside
   (getdist pnt0
   "\nEnter XY side:"))
 (setq xtimes
   (getint
   "\nEnter number X repeats:"))
 (setq ytimes
   (getint
   "\nEnter number Y repeats:"))
 (setq zmin
   (getdist
   "\nEnter min Z height: "))
 (setq zmax
   (getdist
   "\nEnter max Z height: "))
 ; start y location
 (setq yloc (nth 1 pnt0))
 (repeat ytimes
  ; start x location
  (setq xloc (nth 0 pnt0))
  (repeat xtimes
   ; corner and arc points and
   ; center
   (setq pnt1
     (list xloc yloc (nth 2 pnt0)))
   (setq pnt2 (list
     (nth 0 pnt1)
     (+ (nth 1 pnt1) xyside)
     (nth 2 pnt1)))
   (setq pnt3 (list
```

```
    (+ (nth 0 pnt1) (/ xyside 2))
    (+ (nth 1 pnt1) xyside)
    (nth 2 pnt1)))
  (setq pnt4 (list
    (+ (nth 0 pnt1) xyside)
    (+ (nth 1 pnt1) xyside)
    (nth 2 pnt1)))
  (setq pnt5 (list
    (+ (nth 0 pnt1) xyside)
    (+ (nth 1 pnt1) (/ xyside 2))
    (nth 2 pnt1)))
  (setq pnt6 (list
    (+ (nth 0 pnt1) xyside)
    (nth 1 pnt1) (nth 2 pnt1)))
  (setq pnt7 (list
    (+ (nth 0 pnt1) (/ xyside 2))
    (+ (nth 1 pnt1) (/ xyside 2))
    (nth 2 pnt1)))
  ; upper right arc
  (command ".PLINE" pnt5 "a" "d"
    pnt7 pnt3 "l" pnt4 pnt5 "")
  (command ".EXTRUDE"
    "last" "" zmin)
  ; versions prior to 2007 require
  ; the taper parameter
  ;(command ".EXTRUDE"
  ;  "last" "" zmin "")
  ; add to list
  (setq rlist (ssadd (entlast)))
  ; middle arc
  (command ".PLINE" pnt6 "a" "d"
    pnt1 pnt2 "l" pnt3 "a"  "d"
    pnt7 pnt5 "l" pnt6 "")
  (command ".EXTRUDE"
    "last" ""  zmax)
  ; versions prior to 2007 require
  ; the taper parameter
  ;(command ".EXTRUDE"
  ;  "last" "" zmax "")
  ; add to list
  (setq rlist
    (ssadd (entlast) rlist))
  ; inc height
  (setq zheight (+ zheight zinc))
  ; lower left arc
  (command ".PLINE" pnt6 "a" "d"
    pnt1 pnt2 "l" pnt1 pnt6 "")
  (command ".EXTRUDE"
    "last" "" zmin)
  ; versions prior to 2007 require
  ; the taper parameter
  ;(command ".EXTRUDE"
  ;  "last" "" zmin "")
  ; add to list
  (setq rlist
    (ssadd (entlast) rlist))
  ; rotate
  (setq pnt8 (list
    (+ xloc (/ xyside 2))
    (+ yloc (/ xyside 2)) 0))
  (setq rotang
    (* (fix (* (rn) 4.99)) 90.0))
  (command ".ROTATE"
    rlist "" pnt8 rotang)
  ; inc x location
  (setq xloc (+ xloc xyside))
 )
 ; inc y location
 (setq yloc (+ yloc xyside))
 (command ".ZOOM" "e")
)
; union
(command ".UNION" "all" "")
(princ)
)
;---------------------------------
```

`Modules` `k` through `n` do not break the grid at the corners or midpoints. The ends of the bisecting lines are randomly selected along the edges. This random distance is based on the dimension of the grid.

A variety of approaches for computing random locations along one or both sides can be developed. One method is to enter a random dimension—less than the side dimension—to apply to the selection. Half of the remaining distance is the offset from the corner. This assures that the point never falls on the corners.

For `module k`, add `PROG12k` using a copy of `PROG12a`. For the random edge computation, use:

```
; random top edge
(setq xtoff
  (+ (/ (- xyside rdim) 2)
  (* (rn) rdim)))
; random bottom edge
(setq xboff
  (+ (/ (- xyside rdim) 2)
  (* (rn) rdim)))
```

This distance is the location of the bisecting line from the left side. Set the left segment to the minimum height and the right segment to the maximum height.

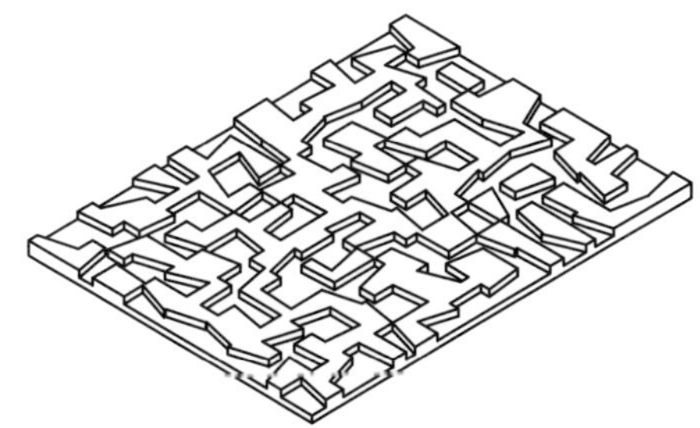

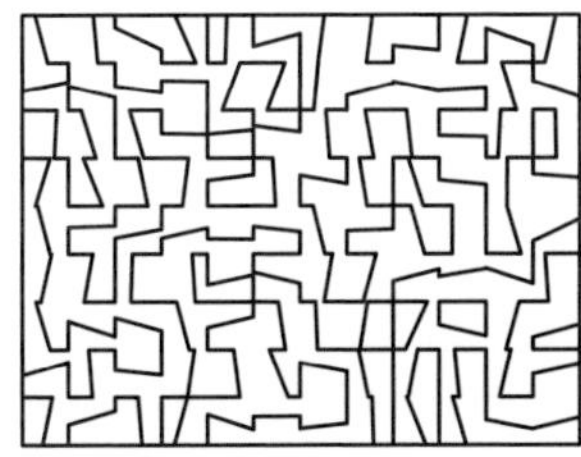

`PROG12k`: module with two random segments

Sample script file for `PROG12k`:

```
;-----------------------------------
(prog12k)
;Enter XY side:
5
;Enter number X repeats:
12
;Enter number Y repeats:
9
;Enter min Z height:
1
;Enter max Z height:
2
;Enter random dimension for edge
2.5
view
swiso
hide
;-----------------------------------
```

Completed function `PROG12k`:

```
;-----------------------------------
(defun prog12k ()
 (graphscr)
 (command ".ERASE" "all" "")
 ; set start point
 (setq pnt0 (list 0 0 0))
 (prompt "\nPROG12k:")
 (setq xyside
   (getdist pnt0
   "\nEnter XY side:"))
 (setq xtimes
   (getint
   "\nEnter number X repeats:"))
 (setq ytimes
   (getint
   "\nEnter number Y repeats:"))
 (setq zmin
   (getdist
   "\nEnter min Z height: "))
 (setq zmax
   (getdist
   "\nEnter max Z height: "))
 (setq rdim
   (getdist
```

```
    "\nEnter random dimension for
    edge: "))
  ; start y location
  (setq yloc (nth 1 pnt0))
  (repeat ytimes
   ; start x location
   (setq xloc (nth 0 pnt0))
   (repeat xtimes
    ; random top edge
    (setq xtoff
      (+ (/ (- xyside rdim) 2)
      (* (rn) rdim)))
    ; random bottom edge
    (setq xboff
      (+ (/ (- xyside rdim) 2)
      (* (rn) rdim)))
    ; left segment
    (setq pnt1
      (list xloc yloc (nth 2 pnt0)))
    (setq pnt2 (list
      (nth 0 pnt1)
      (+ (nth 1 pnt1) xyside)
      (nth 2 pnt1)))
    (setq pnt3 (list
      (+ (nth 0 pnt1) xtoff)
      (+ (nth 1 pnt1) xyside)
      (nth 2 pnt1)))
    (setq pnt4 (list
      (+ (nth 0 pnt1) xboff)
      (nth 1 pnt1) (nth 2 pnt1)))
    ; draw segment
    (command ".PLINE" pnt1 pnt2 pnt3
      pnt4 pnt1 "")
    (command ".EXTRUDE"
      "last" "" zmin)
    ; versions prior to 2007 require
    ; the taper parameter
    ;(command ".EXTRUDE"
    ;  "last" "" zmin "")
    ; add to list
    (setq rlist (ssadd (entlast)))
    ; right segment
    (setq pnt5 (list
      (+ (nth 0 pnt1) xyside)
      (+ (nth 1 pnt1) xyside)
      (nth 2 pnt1)))
    (setq pnt6 (list
      (+ (nth 0 pnt1) xyside)
      (nth 1 pnt1) (nth 2 pnt1)))
    ; draw segment
    (command ".PLINE" pnt3 pnt5 pnt6
      pnt4 pnt3 "")
    (command ".EXTRUDE"
      "last" "" zmax)
    ; versions prior to 2007 require
    ; the taper parameter
    ;(command ".EXTRUDE"
    ;  "last" "" zmax "")
    ; add to list
    (setq rlist
      (ssadd (entlast) rlist))
    ; rotate
    (setq pnt7 (list
      (+ xloc (/ xyside 2))
      (+ yloc (/ xyside 2)) 0))
    (setq rotang
      (* (fix (* (rn) 4.99)) 90.0))
    (command ".ROTATE"
      rlist "" pnt7 rotang)
    ; inc x location
    (setq xloc (+ xloc xyside))
   )
   ; inc y location
   (setq yloc (+ yloc xyside))
   (command ".ZOOM" "e")
  )
  ; union
  (command ".UNION" "all" "")
  (princ)
)
;---------------------------------
```

6.2 Random Relief Patterns of 3-D Shapes

Start a new drawing and set the units to architectural; set the grid to one foot and turn off all snaps and dynamic input. Start a new AutoLISP file in the editor: `CH06B.LSP`. Add functions `rn`, `dtr`, and `rtd` from `CH06A.LSP` in the previous section.

Generate an array of pyramid-shaped panels

Within each grid cell construct a pyramid, centered, with the edges meeting each corner on the rectangular panel.

Add function PROG01 using a copy of PROG01 from CH06A.LSP. Instead of incrementing the lower-left corner of the grid, this series will use the center of each grid cell. In this first version, construct the pyramid edges with only lines.

Review PROG01, including computations of the grid center and each pyramid edge. The bottom points of the pyramid, pnt1 through pnt4, start at the lower-left and proceed counterclockwise.

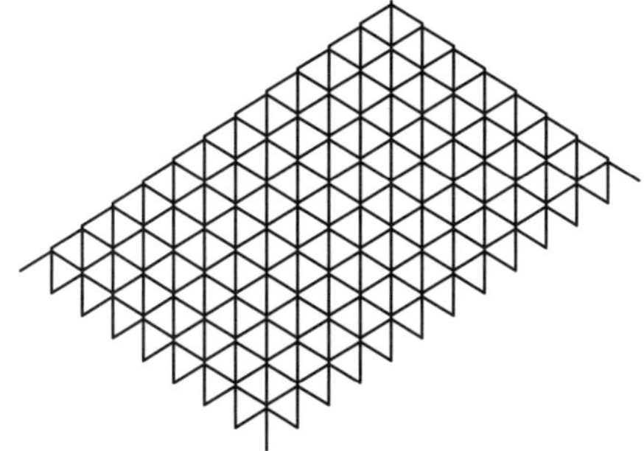

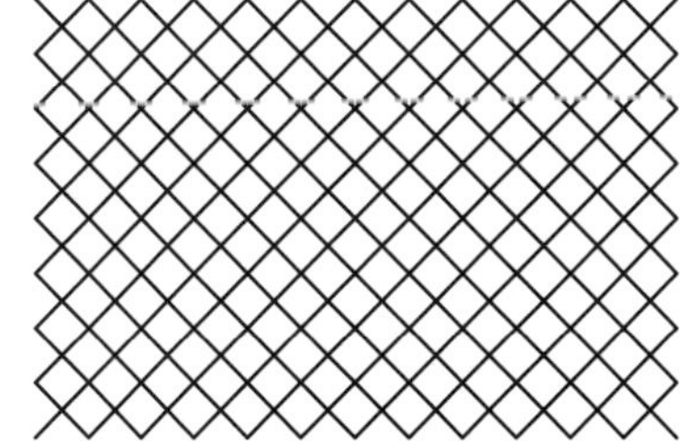

PROG01: pyramid panels constructed with lines

Sample script file for PROG01:

```
;---------------------------------
(prog01)
;Enter X side panel:
5
;Enter Y side panel:
5
;Enter number of X panels:
12
;Enter number of Y panels:
8
;Enter height:
3
view
swiso
hide
;---------------------------------
```

Completed function PROG01:

```
;---------------------------------
(defun prog01 ()
 (graphscr)
 (command ".ERASE" "all" "")
 ; pyramid panel
 ; lines only
 (setq pnt0 (list 0 0 0))
 (prompt "\nPROG01:")
 (setq xside
   (getdist pnt0
   "\nEnter X side panel:"))
 (setq yside
   (getdist pnt0
   "\nEnter Y side panel:"))
 (setq nx
   (getint
   "\nEnter number of X panels:"))
 (setq ny
   (getint
   "\nEnter number of Y panels:"))
 (setq zhgt
   (getdist pnt0 "\nEnter height:"))
 ; pyramidal panels - lines
 (setq ypos
   (+ (nth 1 pnt0) (/ yside 2)))
 (repeat ny
  (setq xpos
    (+ (nth 0 pnt0) (/ xside 2)))
  (repeat nx
   ; center top point
   (setq pntc
     (list xpos ypos zhgt))
   (setq pnt1 (list
     (- xpos (/ xside 2))
```

```
      (- ypos (/ yside 2)) 0.0))
    (setq pnt2 (list
      (+ xpos (/ xside 2))
      (- ypos (/ yside 2)) 0.0))
    (setq pnt3 (list
      (+ xpos (/ xside 2))
      (+ ypos (/ yside 2)) 0.0))
    (setq pnt4 (list
      (- xpos (/ xside 2))
      (+ ypos (/ yside 2)) 0.0))
    (command ".LINE" pntc pnt1 "")
    (command ".LINE" pntc pnt2 "")
    (command ".LINE" pntc pnt3 "")
    (command ".LINE" pntc pnt4 "")
    ; inc x
    (setq xpos (+ xpos xside))
  )
  ; inc y
  (setq ypos (+ ypos yside))
 )
 (command ".ZOOM" "e")
 (princ)
)
;-----------------------------------
```

Add function PROG01a using a copy of PROG01. Convert the line edges to four 3DFACES, individual surfaces each defined by four points. Each 3DFACE is entered counterclockwise as it faces you. Also add an additional 3DFACE to the underside of each pyramid.

Remove the LINE commands and replace them with:

```
; pyramid faces
(command ".3DFACE" pntc pnt1
  pnt2 pntc "")
(command ".3DFACE" pntc pnt2
  pnt3 pntc "")
(command ".3DFACE" pntc pnt3
  pnt4 pntc "")
(command ".3DFACE" pntc pnt4
  pnt1 pntc "")
; base
(command ".3DFACE" pnt4 pnt3
  pnt2 pnt1 "")
```

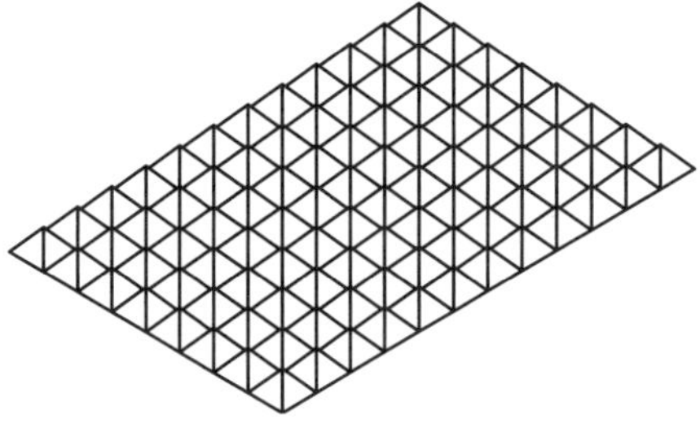

PROG01a: pyramid panels constructed with 3DFACES

Render these models to see the effect of lighting, shadows, and to determine the appropriate surface height.

Random offset the peak of the pyramid

Add function PROG02 using a copy of PROG01a. Add an xy-offset parameter controlled by random selection. The random offset is determined so that it is left and right, above and below, the centerpoint.

It is computed as:

```
; random X and Y offset
 (setq xoff (* (rn) xyoff))
 (setq yoff (* (rn) xyoff))
 ; center top point
 (setq pntc (list
   (+ (- xpos (/ xyoff 2)) xoff)
   (+ (- ypos (/ xyoff 2)) yoff)
   zhgt))
```

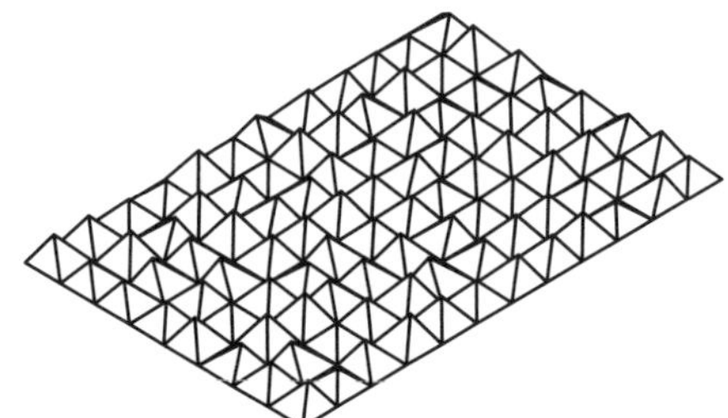

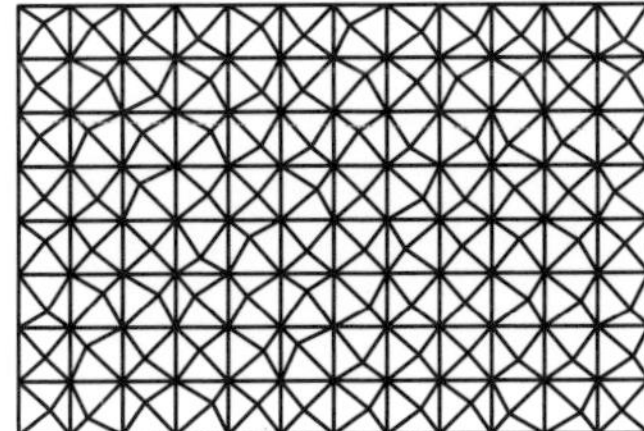

PROG02: pyramid panels with random center

Sample script file for PROG02:

```
;----------------------------------
(prog02)
;Enter X side panel:
5
;Enter Y side panel:
5
;Enter number of X panels:
12
;Enter number of Y panels:
8
;Enter height:
3
;Enter XY offset:
2
view
swiso
hide
;----------------------------------
```

Completed function PROG02:

```
;----------------------------------
(defun prog02 ()
 (graphscr)
 (command ".ERASE" "all" "")
 ; pyramid panel
 ; 3DFACEs
 (setq pnt0 (list 0 0 0))
 (prompt "\nPROG02:")
 (setq xside
    (getdist pnt0
    "\nEnter X side panel:"))
 (setq yside
   (getdist pnt0
   "\nEnter Y side panel:"))
 (setq nx
   (getint
   "\nEnter number of X panels:"))
 (setq ny
   (getint
   "\nEnter number of Y panels:"))
 (setq zhgt
   (getdist pnt0 "\nEnter height:"))
 (setq xyoff
   (getdist pnt0
   "\nEnter XY top offset:"))
 ; pyramidal panels - lines
 (setq ypos
   (+ (nth 1 pnt0) (/ yside 2)))
 (repeat ny
  (setq xpos
    (+ (nth 0 pnt0) (/ xside 2)))
  (repeat  nx
   ; random X and Y offset
   (setq xoff (* (rn) xyoff))
   (setq yoff (* (rn) xyoff))
   ; center top point
   (setq pntc (list
     (+ (- xpos (/ xyoff 2)) xoff)
     (+ (- ypos (/ xyoff 2)) yoff)
     zhgt))
   (setq pnt1 (list
     (- xpos (/ xside 2))
     (- ypos (/ yside 2)) 0.0))
   (setq pnt2 (list
     (+ xpos (/ xside 2))
     (- ypos (/ yside 2)) 0.0))
   (setq pnt3 (list
     (+ xpos (/ xside 2))
     (+ ypos (/ yside 2)) 0.0))
   (setq pnt4 (list
     (- xpos (/ xside 2))
     (+ ypos (/ yside 2)) 0.0))
   ; pyramid faces
   (command ".3DFACE" pntc pnt1
     pnt2 pntc "")
   (command ".3DFACE" pntc pnt2
     pnt3 pntc "")
   (command ".3DFACE" pntc pnt3
```

```
      pnt4 pntc "")
    (command ".3DFACE" pntc pnt4
      pnt1 pntc "")
    ; base
    (command ".3DFACE" pnt4 pnt3
      pnt2 pnt1 "")
    ; inc x
    (setq xpos (+ xpos xside))
   )
   ; inc y
   (setq ypos (+ ypos yside))
  )
  (command ".ZOOM" "e")
  (princ)
)
;----------------------------------
```

Random offset the peak of the pyramid within a circular path

Add function PROG03 using a copy of PROG02, so that the xy-offset parameter controls a circular path around the top centerpoint. Add an angle increment to determine the resolution of the path. Also, start each row with a randomly selected angle based on a multiple of the angle increment; this angle will start the circular-path offset.

In the sequences that follow, we will continue to control the amount and application of randomness so that structured and seemingly unstructured aspects of design are possible.

Compute a random angle-start, based on the entered angle increment, before the start of each row, enter:

```
; random angle start
(setq ang (* (fix (* (rn)
  (- (/ 360.0 xyang) 0.1)))
   xyang))
```

Compute the offset within a circular path:

```
; circular xy offset
(setq xypt (polar
  (list 0 0 0) (dtr ang) xyoff))
(setq xoff (nth 0 xypt))
(setq yoff (nth 1 xypt))
; top center pt
(setq pntc (list
  (+ xpos xoff)
  (+ ypos yoff) zhgt))
```

The angle is incremented within the grid cells in each row.

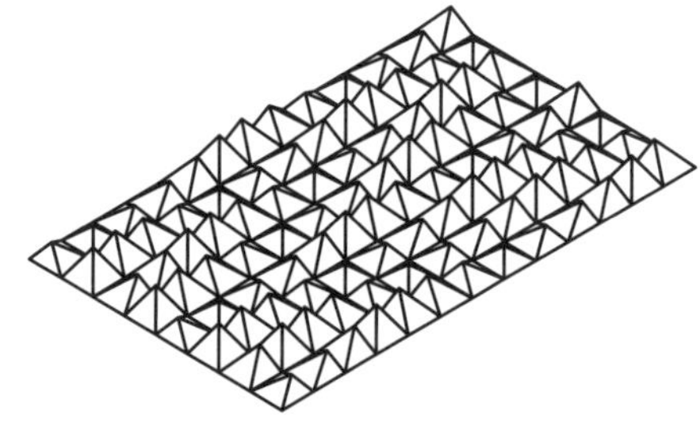

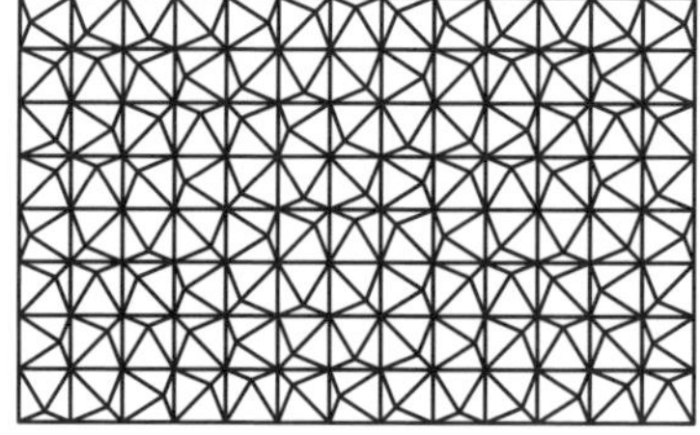

PROG03: pyramid panels with a circular path offset

Sample script file for PROG03:

```
;---------------------------------
(prog03)
;Enter X side panel:
5
;Enter Y side panel:
5
;Enter number of X panels:
13
;Enter number of Y panels:
8
;Enter height:
3
;Enter XY top offset:
1.5
;Enter XY top inc angle:
45
view
swiso
hide
;---------------------------------
```

Completed function PROG03:

```
;---------------------------------
(defun prog03 ()
 (graphscr)
 (command ".ERASE" "all" "")
 ; pyramid panel
 ; 3DFACEs
 (setq pnt0 (list 0 0 0))
 (prompt "\nPROG03:")
 (setq xside
   (getdist pnt0
   "\nEnter X side panel:"))
 (setq yside
   (getdist pnt0
   "\nEnter Y side panel:"))
 (setq nx
   (getint
   "\nEnter number of X panels:"))
 (setq ny
   (getint
   "\nEnter number of Y panels:"))
 (setq zhgt
   (getdist pnt0 "\nEnter height:"))
(setq xyoff
  (getdist pnt0
  "\nEnter XY top offset:"))
(setq xyang
  (getreal
  "\nEnter XY top inc angle:"))
; pyramidal panels - 3DFACEs
(setq ypos
  (+ (nth 1 pnt0) (/ yside 2)))
(repeat ny
 (setq xpos
   (+ (nth 0 pnt0) (/ xside 2)))
 ; random angle start
 (setq ang (* (fix (* (rn)
   (- (/ 360.0 xyang) 0.1)))
   xyang))
 (repeat nx
  ; circular xy offset
  (setq xypt (polar
    (list 0 0 0) (dtr ang) xyoff))
  (setq xoff (nth 0 xypt))
  (setq yoff (nth 1 xypt))
  ; top center pt
  (setq pntc (list
    (+ xpos xoff)
    (+ ypos yoff) zhgt))
  ; four bottom points
  (setq pnt1 (list
    (- xpos (/ xside 2))
    (- ypos (/ yside 2)) 0.0))
  (setq pnt2 (list
    (+ xpos (/ xside 2))
    (- ypos (/ yside 2)) 0.0))
  (setq pnt3 (list
    (+ xpos (/ xside 2))
    (+ ypos (/ yside 2)) 0.0))
  (setq pnt4 (list
    (- xpos (/ xside 2))
    (+ ypos (/ yside 2)) 0.0))
  ; pyramid faces
  (command ".3DFACE" pntc pnt1
    pnt2 pntc "")
  (command ".3DFACE" pntc pnt2
    pnt3 pntc "")
  (command ".3DFACE" pntc pnt3
    pnt4 pntc "")
  (command ".3DFACE" pntc pnt4
    pnt1 pntc "")
```

```
    ; base
    (command ".3DFACE" pnt4 pnt3
      pnt2 pnt1 "")
    ; inc x
    (setq xpos (+ xpos xside))
    ; inc angle
    (setq ang (+ ang xyang))
  )
  ; inc y
  (setq ypos (+ ypos yside))
 )
 (command ".ZOOM" "e")
 (princ)
)
;----------------------------------
```

Generate an array of truncated, pyramid-shaped panels

One variation of a pyramid-shaped panel is truncated with a flat top. Add function PROG04 using a copy of PROG01a. Create a truncated pyramid centered on each grid cell.

Review how the top and bottom points of the pyramid are computed and how each surface is defined.

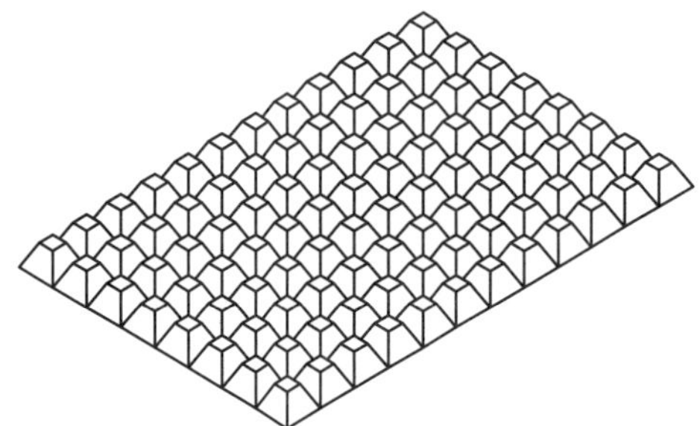

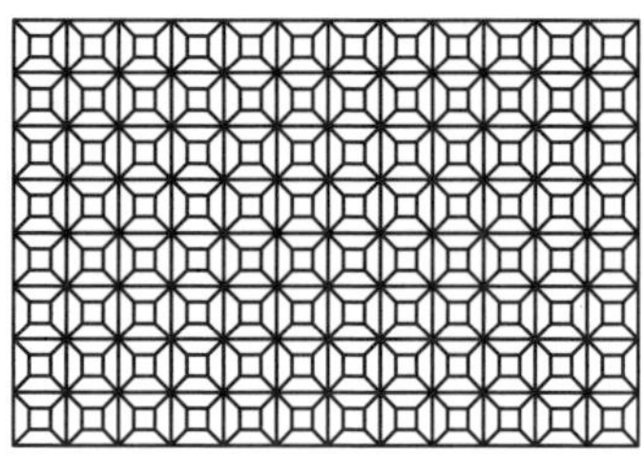

PROG04: truncated pyramid panels

Sample script file for PROG04:

```
;----------------------------------
(prog04)
;Enter X side panel:
5
;Enter Y side panel:
5
;Enter number of X panels:
12
;Enter number of Y panels:
8
;Enter height:
3
;Enter X dim of panel:
2
;Enter Y dim of panel:
2
view
swiso
hide
;----------------------------------
```

Completed function PROG04:

```
;----------------------------------
(defun prog04 ()
 (graphscr)
 (command ".ERASE" "all" "")
 ; square top, truncated pyramids
 ; 3DFACEs
 (setq pnt0 (list 0 0 0))
 (prompt "\nPROG04:")
 (setq xside
```

```
  (getdist pnt0
  "\nEnter X side panel:"))
(setq yside
  (getdist pnt0
  "\nEnter Y side panel:"))
(setq nx
  (getint
  "\nEnter number of X panels:"))
(setq ny
  (getint
  "\nEnter number of Y panels:"))
(setq zhgt
  (getdist pnt0 "\nEnter height:"))
(setq xdim
  (getdist pnt0
  "\nEnter X dim of panel:"))
(setq ydim
  (getdist pnt0
  "\nEnter Y dim of panel:"))
; rectangles panels - 3DFACES
(setq ypos
  (+ (nth 1 pnt0) (/ yside 2)))
(repeat ny
 (setq xpos
   (+ (nth 0 pnt0) (/ xside 2)))
 (repeat  nx
  ; top center pt
  (setq pntc
    (list xpos ypos zhgt))
  ; top pts
  (setq pntt1 (list
    (- (nth 0 pntc) (/ xdim 2))
    (- (nth 1 pntc) (/ ydim 2))
    (nth 2 pntc)))
  (setq pntt2 (list
    (+ (nth 0 pntc) (/ xdim 2))
    (- (nth 1 pntc) (/ ydim 2))
    (nth 2 pntc)))
  (setq pntt3 (list
    (+ (nth 0 pntc) (/ xdim 2))
    (+ (nth 1 pntc) (/ ydim 2))
    (nth 2 pntc)))
  (setq pntt4 (list
    (- (nth 0 pntc) (/ xdim 2))
    (+ (nth 1 pntc) (/ ydim 2))
    (nth 2 pntc)))
  ; bottom pts
  (setq pntb1 (list
    (- xpos (/ xside 2))
    (- ypos (/ yside 2)) 0.0))
  (setq pntb2 (list
    (+ xpos (/ xside 2))
    (- ypos (/ yside 2)) 0.0))
  (setq pntb3 (list
    (+ xpos (/ xside 2))
    (+ ypos (/ yside 2)) 0.0))
  (setq pntb4 (list
    (- xpos (/ xside 2))
    (+ ypos (/ yside 2)) 0.0))
  ; top
  (command ".3DFACE" pntt1 pntt2
    pntt3 pntt4 "")
  (command ".3DFACE" pntt1 pntb1
    pntb2 pntt2 "")
  ; sides
  (command ".3DFACE" pntt2 pntb2
    pntb3 pntt3 "")
  (command ".3DFACE" pntt3 pntb3
    pntb4 pntt4 "")
  (command ".3DFACE" pntt4 pntb4
    pntb1 pntt1 "")
  ; base
  (command ".3DFACE" pntb4 pntb3
    pntb2 pntb1 "")
  ; inc x
  (setq xpos (+ xpos xside))
 )
 ; inc y
 (setq ypos (+ ypos yside))
)
(command ".ZOOM" "e")
(princ)
)
;----------------------------------
```

Execute this function for a few different dimensions. The grid and the flat top can be square or rectangular; or one can be rectangular and the other square.

You can also vary this truncated pyramid panel by a random offset of the top surface or a random selection of height, as previously developed for other panel shapes. Taking advantage of the uniquely shaped pyramid, the top surface can be randomly offset to the corners of the grid cell.

Render these models to see the effect of lighting and the shadows cast to determine the appropriate surface height and dimensions.

Random offset for the top of the truncated pyramid

Add function PROG05 using a copy of PROG04. Randomly offset the top surface of the truncated pyramid so that it lies in one of the four corners. Since all of the pyramid's surfaces are determined by the top centerpoint, compute it based on the corner that the top will align to.

For example, compute the top-left corner using:

```
; random X and Y offset, select
; corner
(setq nc (fix (* (rn) 3.99)))
; top center pt based on corner
(if (= nc 0) (setq pntc (list
  (+ (- xpos (/ xside 2))
  (/ xdim 2))
  (+ (- ypos (/ yside 2))
  (/ ydim 2)) zhgt)))
```

The computation of variable nc determines which corner, numbered 0 to 3. Based on the corner number the centerpoint is computed.

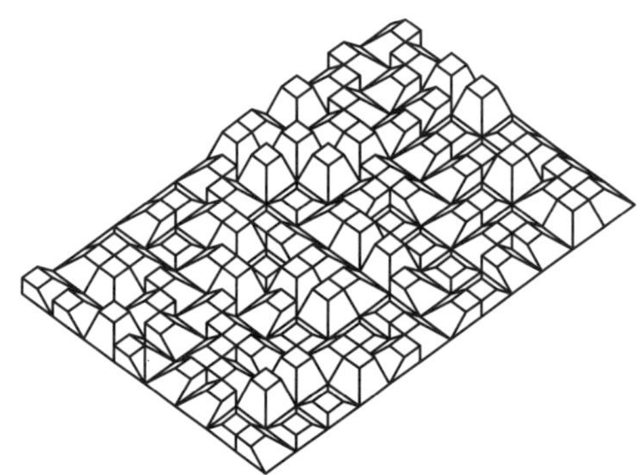

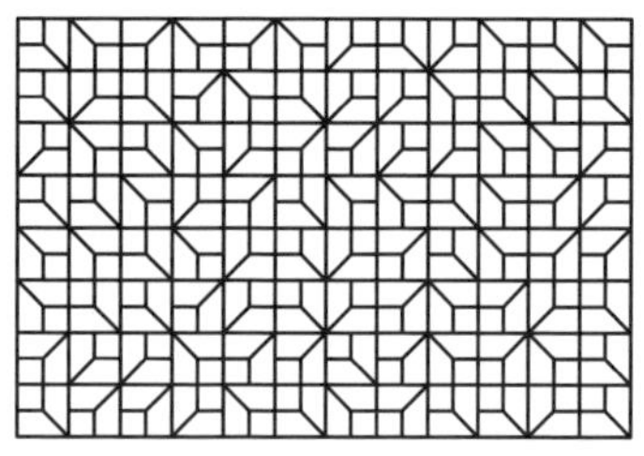

PROG05: truncated pyramid with random top offset

Sample script file for PROG05:

```
;----------------------------------
(prog05)
;Enter X side panel:
5
;Enter Y side panel:
5
;Enter number of X panels:
12
;Enter number of Y panels:
8
;Enter height:
2.5
;Enter X dim of panel:
2.5
;Enter Y dim of panel:
2.5
view
swiso
hide
;----------------------------------
```

Completed function PROG05:

```
;----------------------------------
(defun prog05 ()
 (graphscr)
 (command ".ERASE" "all" "")
 ; square top, truncated pyramids
 ; 3DFACEs
 ; random XY offset of top at the
 ;  corners
```

```
(setq pnt0 (list 0 0 0))
(prompt "\nPROG05:")
(setq xside
  (getdist pnt0
  "\nEnter X side panel:"))
(setq yside
  (getdist pnt0
  "\nEnter Y side panel:"))
(setq nx
  (getint
  "\nEnter number of X panels:"))
(setq ny
  (getint
  "\nEnter number of Y panels:"))
(setq zhgt
  (getdist pnt0 "\nEnter height:"))
(setq xdim
  (getdist pnt0
  "\nEnter X dim of panel:"))
(setq ydim
  (getdist pnt0
  "\nEnter Y dim of panel:"))
; rectangles panels - 3DFACES
(setq ypos
  (+ (nth 1 pnt0) (/ yside 2)))
(repeat ny
 (setq xpos
   (+ (nth 0 pnt0) (/ xside 2)))
 (repeat nx
  ; random X and Y offset, select
  ; corner
  (setq nc (fix (* (rn) 3.99)))
  ; top center pt based on corner
  (if (= nc 0) (setq pntc (list
    (+ (- xpos (/ xside 2))
    (/ xdim 2))
    (+ (- ypos (/ yside 2))
    (/ ydim 2)) zhgt)))
  (if (= nc 1) (setq pntc (list
    (- (+ xpos (/ xside 2))
    (/ xdim 2))
    (+ (- ypos (/ yside 2))
    (/ ydim 2)) zhgt)))
  (if (= nc 2) (setq pntc (list
    (- (+ xpos (/ xside 2))
    (/ xdim 2))
    (- (+ ypos (/ yside 2))
    (/ ydim 2)) zhgt)))
  (if (= nc 3) (setq pntc (list
    (+ (- xpos (/ xside 2))
    (/ xdim 2))
    (- (+ ypos (/ yside 2))
    (/ ydim 2)) zhgt)))
  ; top pts
  (setq pntt1 (list
    (- (nth 0 pntc) (/ xdim 2))
    (- (nth 1 pntc) (/ ydim 2))
    (nth 2 pntc)))
  (setq pntt2 (list
    (+ (nth 0 pntc) (/ xdim 2))
    (- (nth 1 pntc) (/ ydim 2))
    (nth 2 pntc)))
  (setq pntt3 (list
    (+ (nth 0 pntc) (/ xdim 2))
    (+ (nth 1 pntc) (/ ydim 2))
    (nth 2 pntc)))
  (setq pntt4 (list
    (- (nth 0 pntc) (/ xdim 2))
    (+ (nth 1 pntc) (/ ydim 2))
    (nth 2 pntc)))
  ; bottom pts
  (setq pntb1 (list
    (- xpos (/ xside 2))
    (- ypos (/ yside 2)) 0.0))
  (setq pntb2 (list
    (+ xpos (/ xside 2))
    (- ypos (/ yside 2)) 0.0))
  (setq pntb3 (list
    (+ xpos (/ xside 2))
    (+ ypos (/ yside 2)) 0.0))
  (setq pntb4 (list
    (- xpos (/ xside 2))
    (+ ypos (/ yside 2)) 0.0))
  ; top
  (command ".3DFACE" pntt1 pntt2
    pntt3 pntt4 "")
  (command ".3DFACE" pntt1 pntb1
    pntb2 pntt2 "")
  ; sides
  (command ".3DFACE" pntt2 pntb2
    pntb3 pntt3 "")
  (command ".3DFACE" pntt3 pntb3
    pntb4 pntt4 "")
  (command ".3DFACE" pntt4 pntb4
    pntb1 pntt1 "")
  ; base
```

```
    (command ".3DFACE" pntb4 pntb3
      pntb2 pntb1 "")
    ; inc x
    (setq xpos (+ xpos xside))
  )
  ; inc y
  (setq ypos (+ ypos yside))
 )
 (command ".ZOOM" "e")
 (princ)
)
;----------------------------------
```

An alternative method is to place the five 3DFACEs in a selection list and rotate them a random number of 90-degree increments.

Render these models to see the effect of lighting and the shadows cast to determine the appropriate surface height and dimensions.

Random dimensions for the top of the truncated pyramid

The main dimensioned parameter of the truncated pyramid is the top surface. Add function PROG06 using a copy of PROG04. Randomly vary the size of the top surface of each truncated pyramid within an entered minimum and maximum range.

The top dimensions are defined as minimum x and y values, with a single maximum value entered as:

```
(setq xdim
  (getdist pnt0
  "\nEnter min X dim of panel:"))
(setq ydim
  (getdist pnt0
  "\nEnter min Y dim of panel:"))
(setq mdim
  (getdist pnt0
  "\nEnter max panel size:"))
```

The random top dimension is then computed as:

```
; random top dimension
(setq moff
  (/ (* (rn) mdim) 2.0))
(setq xfdim (+ xdim moff))
(setq yfdim (+ ydim moff))
```

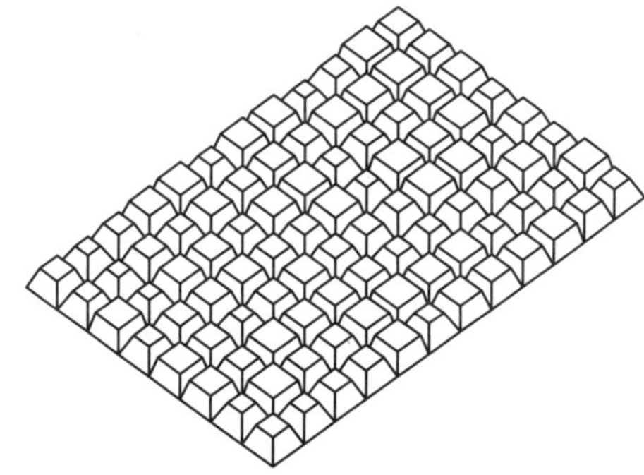

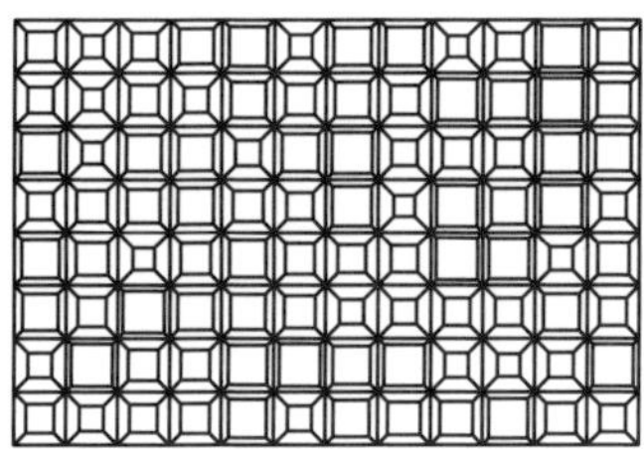

PROG06: truncated pyramid with random top dimension

Sample script file for PROG06:

```
;----------------------------------
(prog06)
;Enter X side panel:
5
;Enter Y side panel:
5
;Enter number of X panels:
12
;Enter number of Y panels:
8
;Enter height:
3
;Enter min X dim of panel:
2
;Enter min Y dim of panel:
2
;Enter max panel size:
4
view
swiso
hide
;----------------------------------
```

Completed function PROG06:

```
;----------------------------------
(defun prog06 ()
 (graphscr)
 (command ".ERASE" "all" "")
 ; square top, truncated pyramids
 ; 3DFACEs
 ; random top dimensions
 (setq pnt0 (list 0 0 0))
 (prompt "\nPROG06:")
 (setq xside
   (getdist pnt0
   "\nEnter X side panel:"))
 (setq yside
   (getdist pnt0
   "\nEnter Y side panel:"))
 (setq nx
   (getint
   "\nEnter number of X panels:"))
 (setq ny
   (getint
   "\nEnter number of Y panels:"))
 (setq zhgt
   (getdist pnt0 "\nEnter height:"))
 (setq xdim
   (getdist pnt0
   "\nEnter min X dim of panel:"))
 (setq ydim
   (getdist pnt0
   "\nEnter min Y dim of panel:"))
 (setq mdim
   (getdist pnt0
   "\nEnter max panel size:"))
 ; rectangles panels - 3DFACES
 (setq ypos
   (+ (nth 1 pnt0) (/ yside 2)))
 (repeat ny
  (setq xpos
    (+ (nth 0 pnt0) (/ xside 2)))
  (repeat  nx
   ; random top dimension
   (setq moff
     (/ (* (rn) mdim) 2.0))
   (setq xfdim (+ xdim moff))
   (setq yfdim (+ ydim moff))
   ; top center pt
   (setq pntc
     (list xpos ypos zhgt))
   ; top ptc
   (setq pntt1 (list
     (- (nth 0 pntc) (/ xfdim 2))
     (- (nth 1 pntc) (/ yfdim 2))
     (nth 2 pntc)))
   (setq pntt2 (list
     (+ (nth 0 pntc) (/ xfdim 2))
     (- (nth 1 pntc) (/ yfdim 2))
     (nth 2 pntc)))
   (setq pntt3 (list
     (+ (nth 0 pntc) (/ xfdim 2))
     (+ (nth 1 pntc) (/ yfdim 2))
     (nth 2 pntc)))
   (setq pntt4 (list
     (- (nth 0 pntc) (/ xfdim 2))
     (+ (nth 1 pntc) (/ yfdim 2))
     (nth 2 pntc)))
   ; bottom pts
   (setq pntb1 (list
     (- xpos (/ xside 2))
     (- ypos (/ yside 2)) 0.0))
```

```
    (setq pntb2 (list
      (+ xpos (/ xside 2))
      (- ypos (/ yside 2)) 0.0))
    (setq pntb3 (list
      (+ xpos (/ xside 2))
      (+ ypos (/ yside 2)) 0.0))
    (setq pntb4 (list
      (- xpos (/ xside 2))
      (+ ypos (/ yside 2)) 0.0))
    ; top
    (command ".3DFACE" pntt1 pntt2
      pntt3 pntt4 "")
    (command ".3DFACE" pntt1 pntb1
      pntb2 pntt2 "")
    ; sides
    (command ".3DFACE" pntt2 pntb2
      pntb3 pntt3 "")
    (command ".3DFACE" pntt3 pntb3
      pntb4 pntt4 "")
    (command ".3DFACE" pntt4 pntb4
      pntb1 pntt1 "")
    ; base
    (command ".3DFACE" pntb4 pntb3
      pntb2 pntb1 "")
    ; inc x
    (setq xpos (+ xpos xside))
   )
   ; inc y
   (setq ypos (+ ypos yside))
  )
  (command ".ZOOM" "e")
  (princ)
)
;----------------------------------
```

Another variation is to have the top surface be rectangular, not just always square, or to pick from a standard list of top dimensions.

6.3 Random Perforations

The examples in the previous two sections were based on building random forms from basic shapes. This section explores patterns used as arrangements for perforations or multilayered surfaces.

Start a new drawing and set the units to architectural; set the grid to 1 foot and turn off all snaps and dynamic input.

Start a new AutoLISP file in the editor CH06C.LSP. Add functions rn, dtr, and rtd from the previous section.

Simple perforations

Add function PROG01 using a copy of function PROG03 from CH06A.LSP. Draw a randomly sized circle in each grid cell. Enter the circle radius minimum and maximum.

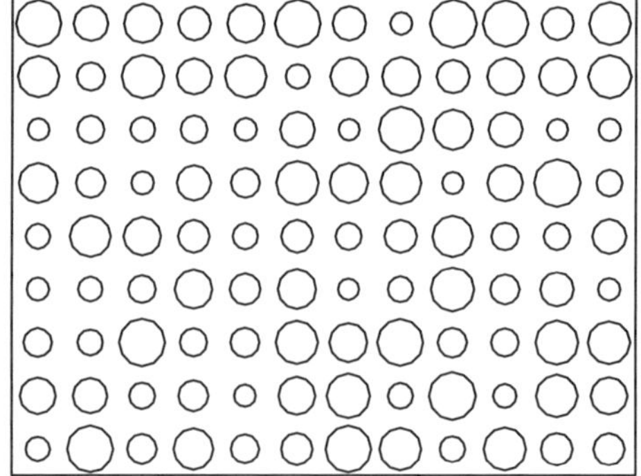

PROG01: simple perforations

Remove all EXTRUDE and UNION commands and base rectangle in each grid cell. Compute the circle radius in the same manner as the height:

```
; compute radius
(setq crad
  (+ cradmin (* (rn)
  (- cradmax cradmin))))
```

The radius of the circle should remain within the grid cell so that some material remains surrounding each opening.

The desired result is a drawing that only has cut lines for each circle and the border of the panel. (Imagine a sheet of paper with holes in it.) To model perforations in a solid panel, the concept is to draw the circles and convert them to REGIONs, two-dimensional solids. Then subtract the circles from a base representing the border of the panel. The result is one solid entity, a REGION. With the EXTRUDE command, it can also be given a thickness, if needed. A simpler approach is to draw each circle, and then surround it with a rectangle for the border, which would be adequate for laser-cutting purposes but could not be extruded to three dimensions. The use of two-dimensional solids will enable us to consider more complex border conditions in a later exercise.

To convert the circle to a solid, use:

```
; draw circle
(command ".CIRCLE" pnt2 crad)
(command ".ZOOM" "e")
; convert to region
(command ".REGION" "last" "")
```

To subtract the circles from the border, use:

```
; surface to be perforated
 (setq xmax (* xyside xtimes))
 (setq ymax (* xyside ytimes))
 (setq pnt1 (list
   (+ (nth 0 pnt0) xmax)
   (+ (nth 1 pnt0) ymax)))
 (command ".RECTANGLE" pnt0 pnt1)
 (command ".ZOOM" "e")
 ; convert to region
 (command ".REGION" "last" "")
 ; subtract openings
 (command ".SUBTRACT"
   "last" "" "all" "")
```

Sample script file for PROG01:

```
;----------------------------------
(prog01)
;Enter XY side:
5
;Enter number X repeats:
12
;Enter number Y repeats:
9
;Enter min radius:
1
;Enter max radius:
2.25
view
swiso
hide
;----------------------------------
```

Completed function PROG01:

```
;----------------------------------
(defun prog01 ()
 (graphscr)
 ; set start point
 (setq pnt0 (list 0 0 0))
 (prompt "\nPROG01:")
 (setq xyside
   (getdist pnt0
   "\nEnter XY side:"))
```

```
(setq xtimes
  (getint
  "\nEnter number X repeats:"))
(setq ytimes
  (getint
  "\nEnter number Y repeats:"))
(setq cradmin
  (getdist
  "\nEnter min radius: "))
(setq cradmax
  (getdist
  "\nEnter max radius: "))
(command ".ELEV" 0.0 0.0)
(command ".ERASE" "all" "")
; start y location
(setq yloc (nth 0 pnt0))
(repeat ytimes
 ; start x location
 (setq xloc (nth 1 pnt0))
 (repeat xtimes
  ; lower corner pt
  (setq pnt1
    (list xloc yloc (nth 2 pnt0)))
  ; center of square
  (setq pnt2 (list
    (+ (nth 0 pnt1) (/ xyside 2))
    (+ (nth 1 pnt1) (/ xyside 2))
    (nth 2 pnt1)))
  ; compute radius
  (setq crad
    (+ cradmin (* (rn)
    (- cradmax cradmin))))
  ; draw circle
  (command ".CIRCLE" pnt2 crad)
  (command ".ZOOM" "e")
  ; convert to region
  (command ".REGION" "last" "")
  ; inc x location
  (setq xloc (+ xloc xyside))
 )
 ; inc y location
 (setq yloc (+ yloc xyside))
 (command ".ZOOM" "e")
)
; surface to be perforated
(setq xmax (* xyside xtimes))
(setq ymax (* xyside ytimes))
(setq pnt1 (list
    (+ (nth 0 pnt0) xmax)
    (+ (nth 1 pnt0) ymax)))
  (command ".RECTANGLE" pnt0 pnt1)
  (command ".ZOOM" "e")
  ; convert to region
  (command ".REGION" "last" "")
  ; subtract openings
  (command ".SUBTRACT"
    "last" "" "all" "")
  (princ)
)
;----------------------------------
```

These perforations can be any basic shape: a circle, rectangle, polygon, or any polyline. They can be randomly sized, rotated, or offset, as shown in some of the previous examples. The amount remaining between perforations will depend on the material being perforated, its makeup, and thickness.

Sticks creating perforations

Another method of perforating a material is to design the material that is to remain, not the perforations. Create the positive of an image, remove the negative.

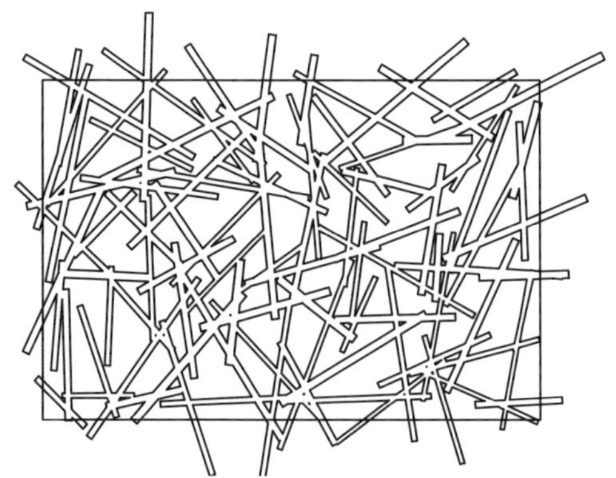

PROG02: random sticks

For this example, rotated sticks will be used. The dimensions of the sticks will be randomly selected along with an offset and rotation.

Add function PROG02 using function PROG01 expanded for an x- and y-panel size. Within each grid cell at the centerpoint, draw a rectangle as a POLYLINE converted to a REGION; once drawn, UNION them all. Randomly select the rectangle dimensions from a minimum and maximum. Also include a random angle rotation and a random x- and y-offset. Finally, draw a rectangle around the border of the panel, for reference.

All intersections of the sticks are created by making all the sticks into REGIONs and then UNIONing them together. The edges of the combined sticks are individual boundaries that either a laser cutter, waterjet, or a router could easily follow.

The random selection is computed as:

```
; random stick size, offset,
; and rotation
(setq xrside (+ xmin (* (rn)
  (- xmax xmin))))
(setq yrside (+ ymin (* (rn)
  (- ymax ymin))))
(setq xoff (* (rn) xyoff))
(setq yoff (* (rn) xyoff))
(setq rang (* (rn) rotang))
```

A three-dimensional version of this panel requires a simple EXTRUDE command after all the sticks are UNIONed. REGIONs as polylines can be extruded into three-dimensional solids.

Sample script file for PROG02:

```
;---------------------------------
(prog02)
;Enter X side panel:
5
;Enter Y side panel:
5
;Enter number of X panels:
12
;Enter number of Y panels:
8
;Enter X min rectangle:
0.5
;Enter X max rectangle:
1
;Enter Y min rectangle:
8
;Enter Y max rectangle:
24
;Enter XY offset:
1.5
;Enter rotation angle:
180
;---------------------------------
```

Completed function PROG02:

```
;---------------------------------
(defun prog02 ()
 (graphscr)
 ; random sticks
 (setq pnt0 (list 0 0 0))
 (prompt "\nPROG02:")
 (setq xside
   (getdist pnt0
   "\nEnter X side panel:"))
 (setq yside
   (getdist pnt0
   "\nEnter Y side panel:"))
 (setq xtimes
   (getint
   "\nEnter number of X panels:"))
 (setq ytimes
   (getint
   "\nEnter number of Y panels:"))
 (setq xmin
```

```
    (getdist pnt0
    "\nEnter X min rectangle:"))
  (setq xmax
    (getdist pnt0
    "\nEnter X max rectangle:"))
  (setq ymin
    (getdist pnt0
    "\nEnter Y min rectangle:"))
  (setq ymax
    (getdist pnt0
    "\nEnter Y max rectangle:"))
  (setq xyoff
    (getdist pnt0
    "\nEnter XY offset:"))
  (setq rotang
    (getreal
    "\nEnter rotation angle:"))
  (command ".ELEV" 0.0 0.0)
  (command ".ERASE" "all" "")
  ; start y location
  (setq ypos
    (+ (nth 1 pnt0) (/ yside 2)))
  (repeat ytimes
   ; start x location
   (setq xpos
     (+ (nth 0 pnt0) (/ xside 2)))
   (repeat xtimes
    ; random stick size, offset, and
    ; rotation
    (setq xrside (+ xmin
      (* (rn) (- xmax xmin))))
    (setq yrside (+ ymin
      (* (rn) (- ymax ymin))))
    (setq xoff (* (rn) xyoff))
    (setq yoff (* (rn) xyoff))
    (setq rang (* (rn) rotang))
    ; center pt
    (setq pntc (list
      (+ (- xpos (/ xyoff 2)) xoff)
      (+ (- ypos (/ xyoff 2)) yoff)))
    ; stick
    (setq pnt1 (list
      (- (nth 0 pntc) (/ xrside 2))
      (- (nth 1 pntc) (/ yrside 2))))
    (setq pnt2 (list
      (+ (nth 0 pntc) (/ xrside 2))
      (- (nth 1 pntc) (/ yrside 2))))
    (setq pnt3 (list
      (+ (nth 0 pntc) (/ xrside 2))
      (+ (nth 1 pntc) (/ yrside 2))))
    (setq pnt4 (list
      (- (nth 0 pntc) (/ xrside 2))
      (+ (nth 1 pntc) (/ yrside 2))))
    (command ".PLINE" pnt1 pnt2 pnt3
      pnt4 pnt1 "")
    (command ".ZOOM" "e")
    (command ".REGION" "last" "")
    (command ".ROTATE"
      "last" "" pntc rang)
    ; inc x
    (setq xpos (+ xpos xside))
   )
   ; inc y
   (setq ypos (+ ypos yside))
  )
  ; union regions
  (command ".UNION" "all" "")
  ; border
  (setq xmax (* xside xtimes))
  (setq ymax (* yside ytimes))
  (setq pnt1 (list
    (+ (nth 0 pnt0) xmax)
    (+ (nth 1 pnt0) ymax)))
  (command ".RECTANGLE" pnt0 pnt1)
  (command ".ZOOM" "e")
  (princ)
)
;---------------------------------
```

If this pattern along with its extensions beyond the border were to be laser-cut, then you would remove the border rectangle and use the remaining drawing for cutting. If you want the pattern to fit inside the border, then trim the sticks to the border.

Add function `PROG02a` using a copy of `PROG02`. Trim the sticks to the border edge.

Replace the section starting with the UNION command, and draw the border with:

```
; union regions
 (command ".UNION" "all" "")
 (setq obj1 (ssadd (entlast)))
 ; inside border
 (setq xmax (* xside xtimes))
 (setq ymax (* yside ytimes))
 (setq pnt1 (list
   (+ (nth 0 pnt0) xmax)
   (+ (nth 1 pnt0) ymax)))
 (command ".RECTANGLE" pnt0 pnt1)
 (command ".ZOOM" "e")
 (command ".REGION" "last" "")
 (setq obj2 (ssadd (entlast)))
 ; outside border
 (setq pnt2 (list
   (- (nth 0 pnt0) xmax)
   (- (nth 1 pnt0) ymax)))
 (setq pnt3 (list
   (+ (nth 0 pnt1) xmax)
   (+ (nth 1 pnt1) ymax)))
 (command ".RECTANGLE" pnt2 pnt3)
 (command ".ZOOM" "e")
 (command ".REGION" "last" "")
 (setq obj3 (ssadd (entlast)))
 ; make border
 (command ".SUBTRACT"
   obj3 "" obj2 "")
 (setq obj2 (ssadd (entlast)))
 ; subtract border from panel
 (command ".SUBTRACT"
   obj1 "" obj2 "")
 (command ".ZOOM" "e")
(princ)
```

A large thick frame is generated around the border as a REGION and then subtracted from the panel so that all stick edges are trimmed.

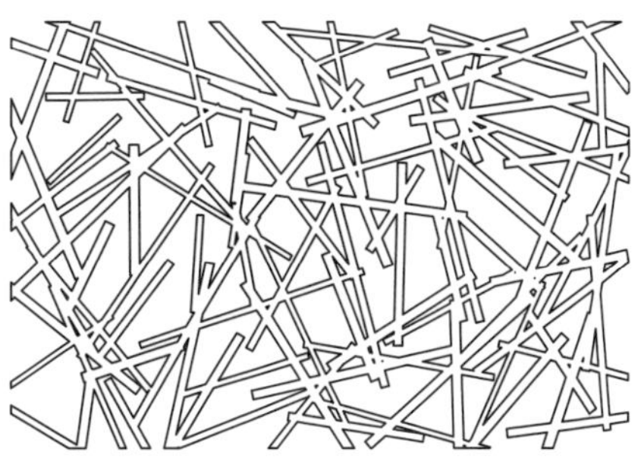

PROG02a: random sticks trimmed

Since we purposely made the sticks long enough to overlap, none are floating by themselves. Another version of this panel is to add a frame around the border so that areas between the sticks become perforations.

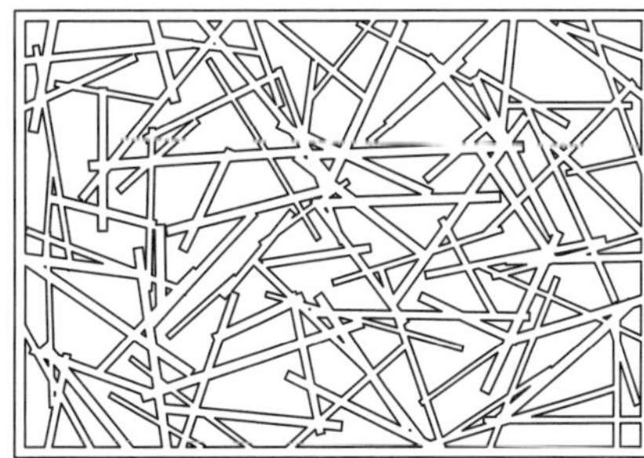

PROG02b: random sticks trimmed and framed

Add function PROG02b using a copy of PROG02. Trim the sticks to the border edge and add a one-inch-thick frame. The thickness of the frame can be set as input; also consider if the frame is inside or outside the entered panel's overall dimensions.

Replace the section starting with the UNION command and drawing the border with:

```
; union regions
 (command ".UNION" "all" "")
 (setq obj1 (ssadd (entlast)))
 ; inside border
 (setq xmax (* xside xtimes))
 (setq ymax (* yside ytimes))
 (setq pnt1 (list
   (+ (nth 0 pnt0) xmax)
   (+ (nth 1 pnt0) ymax)))
 (command ".RECTANGLE" pnt0 pnt1)
 (command ".ZOOM" "e")
 (command ".REGION" "last" "")
 (setq obj2 (ssadd (entlast)))
 ; outside border
 (setq pnt2 (list
   (- (nth 0 pnt0) xmax)
   (- (nth 1 pnt0) ymax)))
 (setq pnt3 (list
   (+ (nth 0 pnt1) xmax)
   (+ (nth 1 pnt1) ymax)))
 (command ".RECTANGLE" pnt2 pnt3)
 (command ".ZOOM" "e")
 (command ".REGION" "last" "")
 (setq obj3 (ssadd (entlast)))
 ; make border
 (command ".SUBTRACT"
   obj3 "" obj2 "")
 (setq obj2 (ssadd (entlast)))
 ; subtract border from panel
 (command ".SUBTRACT"
   obj1 "" obj2 "")
 (setq obj1 (ssadd (entlast)))
 ; make frame at border
 ; inside border
 (setq pnt1 (list xmax ymax))
 (command ".RECTANGLE" pnt0 pnt1)
 (command ".ZOOM" "e")
 (command ".REGION" "last" "")
 (setq obj2 (ssadd (entlast)))
 ; outside border
 (setq pnt2 (list
   (- (nth 0 pnt0) 1)
   (- (nth 1 pnt0) 1)))
 (setq pnt3 (list
   (+ (nth 0 pnt1) 1)
   (+ (nth 1 pnt1) 1)))
 (command ".RECTANGLE" pnt2 pnt3)
 (command ".ZOOM" "e")
 (command ".REGION" "last" "")
 (setq obj3 (ssadd (entlast)))
 ; make frame
 (command ".SUBTRACT"
   obj3 "" obj2 "")
 (setq obj2 (ssadd (entlast)))
 ; add to panel
 (command ".UNION" "all" "")
 (command ".ZOOM" "e")
 (princ)
```

A third alternative is to not trim the sticks, but to add a one-inch frame to the border.

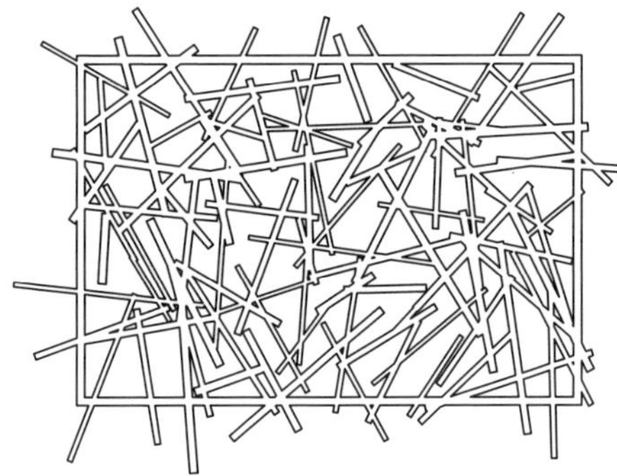

PROG02c: random sticks framed

Add function PROG02c using a copy of PROG02. Add a one-inch-thick frame to the panel.

Replace the section starting with the UNION command and drawing the border with:

```
; union regions
 (command ".UNION" "all" "")
 ; make frame at border
 ; inside border
 (setq xmax (* xside xtimes))
 (setq ymax (* yside ytimes))
 (setq pnt1 (list
   (+ (nth 0 pnt0) xmax)
   (+ (nth 1 pnt0) ymax)))
 (command ".RECTANGLE" pnt0 pnt1)
 (command ".ZOOM" "e")
 (command ".REGION" "last" "")
 (setq obj2 (ssadd (entlast)))
 ; outside border
 (setq pnt2 (list
   (- (nth 0 pnt0) 1)
   (- (nth 1 pnt0) 1)))
 (setq pnt3 (list
   (+ (nth 0 pnt1) 1)
   (+ (nth 1 pnt1) 1)))
 (command ".RECTANGLE" pnt2 pnt3)
 (command ".ZOOM" "e")
 (command ".REGION" "last" "")
 (setq obj3 (ssadd (entlast)))
 ; make frame
 (command ".SUBTRACT"
    obj3 "" obj2 "")
 (setq obj2 (ssadd (entlast)))
 ; add to panel
 (command ".UNION" "all" "")
 (command ".ZOOM" "e")
 (princ)
```

Random circular rings

Previously, the basic shapes that were randomly placed—circles and polygons—were solid shapes. They can also be represented in stick form, as rings. This enables you to design a more delicate element for forming reliefs, grilles, etchings, or perforations.

Add function PROG03 using a copy of PROG02a. Within each panel at the centerpoint, draw a ring as a REGION. Once they are all drawn, UNION them. Randomly select the rings' dimensions from a minimum and maximum. Also include a random x- and y-offset. Trim the rings to the panel edge.

The random parameters and the ring are constructed as:

```
; random ring size and offset
(setq rorad (+ romin
  (* (rn) (- romax romin))))
(setq risize (+ rsmin
  (* (rn) (- rsmax rsmin))))
(setq xoff (* (rn) xyoff))
(setq yoff (* (rn) xyoff))
; center pt
(setq pntc (list
  (+ (- xpos (/ xyoff 2)) xoff)
  (+ (- ypos (/ xyoff 2)) yoff)))
; make ring
(command ".CIRCLE" pntc rorad)
(command ".ZOOM" "e")
(command ".REGION" "last" "")
(setq obj1 (ssadd (entlast)))
(command ".CIRCLE"
  pntc (- rorad risize))
(command ".ZOOM" "e")
(command ".REGION" "last" "")
(setq obj2 (ssadd (entlast)))
(command ".SUBTRACT"
  obj1 "" obj2 "")
```

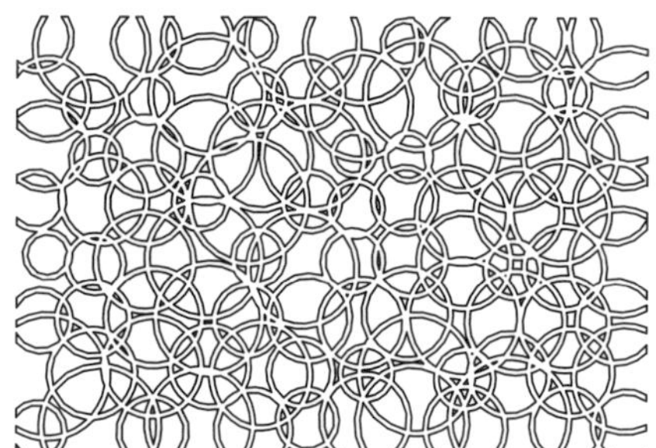

PROG03: random circular rings

Sample script file for PROG03:

```
;----------------------------------
(prog03)
;Enter X side panel:
5
;Enter Y side panel:
5
;Enter number of X panels:
12
;Enter number of Y panels:
8
;Enter ring radius outside min:
2
;Enter ring radius outside max:
6
;Enter ring size min:
0.5
;Enter ring size max:
0.5
;Enter XY offset:
1.5
;----------------------------------
```

Completed function PROG03:

```
;----------------------------------
(defun prog03 ()
 (graphscr)
 ; ring relief 2D version
 (setq pnt0 (list 0 0 0))
 (prompt "\nPROG03:")
(setq xside
  (getdist pnt0
  "\nEnter X side panel:"))
(setq yside
  (getdist pnt0
  "\nEnter Y side panel:"))
(setq xtimes
  (getint
  "\nEnter number of X panels:"))
(setq ytimes
  (getint
  "\nEnter number of Y panels:"))
(setq romin
  (getdist pnt0
  "\nEnter ring radius outside min:"))
(setq romax
  (getdist pnt0
  "\nEnter ring radius outside max:"))
(setq rsmin
  (getdist pnt0
  "\nEnter ring size min:"))
(setq rsmax
  (getdist pnt0
  "\nEnter ring size max:"))
(setq xyoff
  (getdist pnt0
  "\nEnter XY offset:"))
(command ".ELEV" 0.0 0.0)
(command ".ERASE" "all" "")
; rectangles panels
; start y location
(setq ypos
  (+ (nth 1 pnt0) (/ yside 2)))
(repeat ytimes
 ; start x location
 (setq xpos
   (+ (nth 0 pnt0) (/ xside 2)))
 (repeat xtimes
  ; random ring size and offset
  (setq rorad (+ romin
    (* (rn) (- romax romin))))
  (setq risize (+ rsmin
    (* (rn) (- rsmax rsmin))))
  (setq xoff (* (rn) xyoff))
  (setq yoff (* (rn) xyoff))
  ; center pt
  (setq pntc (list
    (+ (- xpos (/ xyoff 2)) xoff)
```

```
    (+ (- ypos (/ xyoff 2)) yoff)))
  ; make ring
  (command ".CIRCLE" pntc rorad)
  (command ".ZOOM" "e")
  (command ".REGION" "last" "")
  (setq obj1 (ssadd (entlast)))
  (command ".CIRCLE"
    pntc (- rorad risize))
  (command ".ZOOM" "e")
  (command ".REGION" "last" "")
  (setq obj2 (ssadd (entlast)))
  (command ".SUBTRACT"
    obj1 "" obj2 "")
  ; inc x
  (setq xpos (+ xpos xside))
 )
 ; inc y
 (setq ypos (+ ypos yside))
)
; union regions
(command ".UNION" "all" "")
(setq obj1 (ssadd (entlast)))
; inside border
(setq xmax (* xside xtimes))
(setq ymax (* yside ytimes))
(setq pnt1 (list
  (+ (nth 0 pnt0) xmax)
  (+ (nth 1 pnt0) ymax)))
(command ".RECTANGLE" pnt0 pnt1)
(command ".ZOOM" "e")
(command ".REGION" "last" "")
(setq obj2 (ssadd (entlast)))
; outside border
(setq pnt2 (list
  (- (nth 0 pnt0) xmax)
  (- (nth 1 pnt0) ymax)))
(setq pnt3 (list
  (+ (nth 0 pnt1) xmax)
  (+ (nth 1 pnt1) ymax)))
(command ".RECTANGLE" pnt2 pnt3)
(command ".ZOOM" "e")
(command ".REGION" "last" "")
(setq obj3 (ssadd (entlast)))
; make border
(command ".SUBTRACT"
   obj3 "" obj2 "")
(setq obj2 (ssadd (entlast)))
; subtract border from panel
 (command ".SUBTRACT"
   obj1 "" obj2 "")
 (command ".ZOOM" "e")
 (princ)
)
;---------------------------------
```

Vary the amount of randomness based on a distance relationship to the panel

Add function `PROG03a` using a copy of `PROG03`. The random offset is based on the distance from the center of the panel. The closer the ring is to the center, the greater the random offset.

The percentage of off-setting is computed using:

```
; center of panel
(setq cpt (list
  (+ (nth 0 pnt0) (/ xmax 2.0))
  (+ (nth 1 pnt0) (/ ymax 2.0))
  (nth 2 pnt0)))
; center pt
(setq pntc
  (list xpos ypos (nth 2 pnt0)))
; distance to center determines
; amount of offset
(setq xdist (abs (- (nth 0 pntc)
  (nth 0 cpt))))
(setq ydist (abs (- (nth 1 pntc)
  (nth 1 cpt))))
(setq xprct (- 1.0 (/ xdist
  (/ (- xmax xside) 2.0))))
(setq yprct (- 1.0 (/ ydist
  (/ (- ymax yside) 2.0))))
(setq xoff (* (rn)
  (* xprct xyoff)))
(setq yoff (* (rn)
  (* yprct xyoff)))
; redefine center pt
(setq pntc (list
  (+ (- xpos (/
  (* xyoff xprct) 2)) xoff)
  (+ (- ypos (/
  (* xyoff yprct) 2)) yoff)
  (nth 2 pnt0)))
```

Both the x and y distances are computed independently.

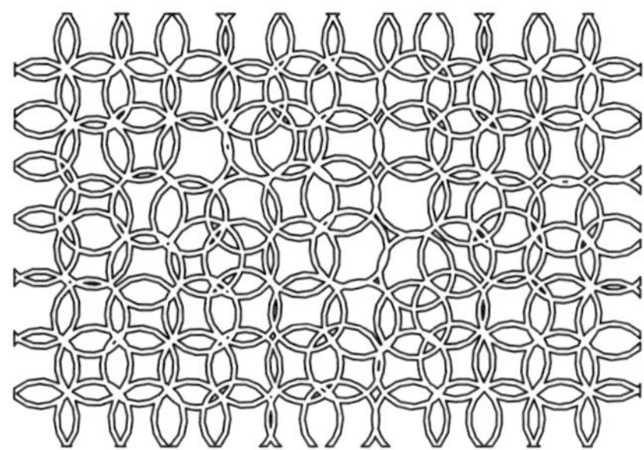

PROG03a: circular rings, increase randomness to center

Sample script file for PROG03a:

```
;---------------------------------
(prog03a)
;Enter X side panel:
5
;Enter Y side panel:
5
;Enter number of X panels:
12
;Enter number of Y panels:
8
;Enter ring radius outside min:
3.76
;Enter ring radius outside max:
3.76
;Enter ring size min:
0.5
;Enter ring size max:
0.5
;Enter XY offset:
3.0
;---------------------------------
```

Completed function PROG03a:

```
;---------------------------------
(defun prog03a ()
 (graphscr)
 ; ring relief 2D version
 (setq pnt0 (list 0 0 0))
 (prompt "\nPROG03a:")
 (setq xside
   (getdist pnt0
   "\nEnter X side panel:"))
 (setq yside
   (getdist pnt0
   "\nEnter Y side panel:"))
 (setq xtimes
   (getint
   "\nEnter number of X panels:"))
 (setq ytimes
   (getint
   "\nEnter number of Y panels:"))
 (setq romin
   (getdist pnt0
   "\nEnter ring radius outside min:"))
 (setq romax
   (getdist pnt0
   "\nEnter ring radius outside max:"))
 (setq rsmin
   (getdist pnt0
   "\nEnter ring size min:"))
 (setq rsmax
   (getdist pnt0
   "\nEnter ring size max:"))
 (setq xyoff
   (getdist pnt0
   "\nEnter XY offset:"))
 (command ".ELEV" 0.0 0.0)
 (command ".ERASE" "all" "")
 ;panel size
 (setq xmax (* xside xtimes))
 (setq ymax (* yside ytimes))
 ; start y location
 (setq ypos
   (+ (nth 1 pnt0) (/ yside 2)))
 (repeat ytimes
  ; start x location
  (setq xpos
    (+ (nth 0 pnt0) (/ xside 2)))
  (repeat xtimes
```

```
; random ring size and offset
(setq rorad (+ romin
  (* (rn) (- romax romin))))
(setq risize (+ rsmin
  (* (rn) (- rsmax rsmin))))
; center of panel
(setq cpt (list
  (+ (nth 0 pnt0) (/ xmax 2.0))
  (+ (nth 1 pnt0) (/ ymax 2.0))
  (nth 2 pnt0)))
; center pt
(setq pntc
  (list xpos ypos (nth 2 pnt0)))
; distance to center determines
; amount of offset
(setq xdist (abs (- (nth 0 pntc)
  (nth 0 cpt))))
(setq ydist (abs (- (nth 1 pntc)
  (nth 1 cpt))))
(setq xprct (- 1.0 (/ xdist
  (/ (- xmax xside) 2.0))))
(setq yprct (- 1.0 (/ ydist
  (/ (- ymax yside) 2.0))))
(setq xoff (* (rn)
  (* xprct xyoff)))
(setq yoff (* (rn)
  (* yprct xyoff)))
; redefine center pt
(setq pntc (list
  (+ (- xpos (/
  (* xyoff xprct) 2)) xoff)
  (+ (- ypos (/
  (* xyoff yprct) 2)) yoff)
  (nth 2 pnt0)))
; make ring
(command ".CIRCLE" pntc rorad)
(command ".ZOOM" "e")
(command ".REGION" "last" "")
(setq obj1 (ssadd (entlast)))
(command ".CIRCLE"
  pntc (- rorad risize))
(command ".ZOOM" "e")
(command ".REGION" "last" "")
(setq obj2 (ssadd (entlast)))
(command ".SUBTRACT"
  obj1 "" obj2 "")
; inc x
(setq xpos (+ xpos xside))
  )
  ; inc y
  (setq ypos (+ ypos yside))
 )
 ; union regions
 (command ".UNION" "all" "")
 (setq obj1 (ssadd (entlast)))
 ; inside border
 (setq pnt1 (list
   (+ (nth 0 pnt0) xmax)
   (+ (nth 1 pnt0) ymax)))
 (command ".RECTANGLE" pnt0 pnt1)
 (command ".ZOOM" "e")
 (command ".REGION" "last" "")
 (setq obj2 (ssadd (entlast)))
 ; outside border
 (setq pnt2 (list
   (- (nth 0 pnt0) xmax)
   (- (nth 1 pnt0) ymax)))
 (setq pnt3 (list
   (+ (nth 0 pnt1) xmax)
   (+ (nth 1 pnt1) ymax)))
 (command ".RECTANGLE" pnt2 pnt3)
 (command ".ZOOM" "e")
 (command ".REGION" "last" "")
 (setq obj3 (ssadd (entlast)))
 ; make border
 (command ".SUBTRACT"
    obj3 "" obj2 "")
 (setq obj2 (ssadd (entlast)))
 ; subtract border from panel
 (command ".SUBTRACT"
   obj1 "" obj2 "")
 (command ".ZOOM" "e")
 (princ)
)
;----------------------------------
```

Since randomness is considered for the x and y distances, some offset is computed, except for the corner-grid locations.

Add function PROG03b using a copy of PROG03a. Add a factor for controlling when distance applies to the computation of the offsets.

Add a distance factor:

```
(setq dfact
  (getreal "\nEnter distance factor:"))
```

Use this factor to check the x and y distances as percentages. If both are greater, then compute the offset; otherwise don't. The check occurs when the centerpoint is redefined:

```
; redefine center pt
(if (and (>= xprct dfact)
  (>= yprct dfact))
 (setq pntc (list
    (+ (- xpos (/ (* xyoff xprct)
    2)) xoff)
    (+ (- ypos (/ (* xyoff yprct)
    2)) yoff)
   (nth 2 pnt0)))
)
```

In this case, both have to be greater. For example, if the distance factor is set to 0.25, only grid locations within 25 percent of the maximum distance from the center will be offset; the others will not.

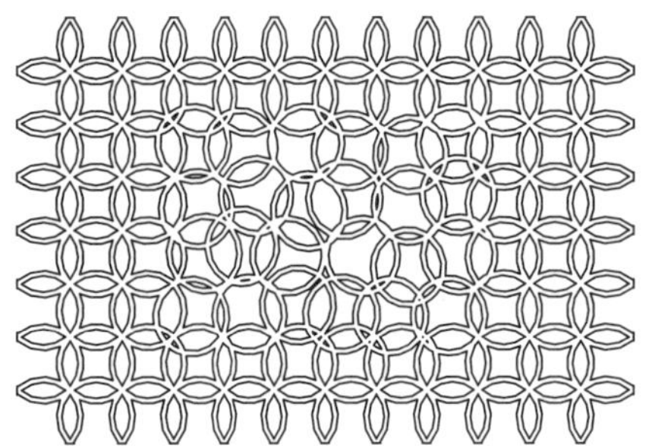

PROG03b: circular rings, selective increase of randomness to center

The result is that the rings remain unchanged along the edges. This enables you to control when the randomness begins. A value of 1.0 would leave all rings without an offset, and a value of 0.0 would offset all of them. In addition to the center, another option would be the distance to the right edge.

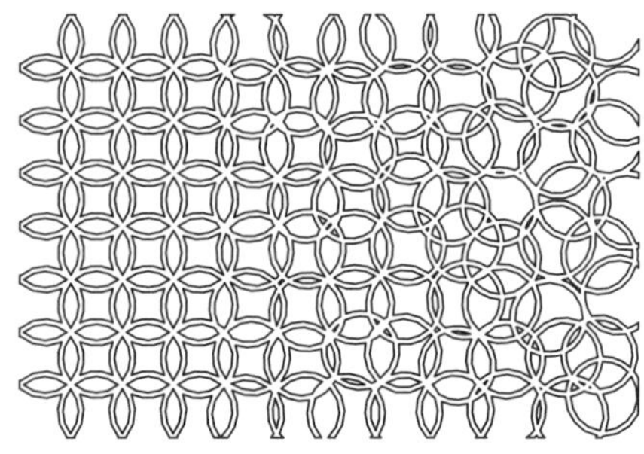

PROG03c: circular rings, selective increase in randomness to the right edge

Add function PROG03c using a copy of PROG03b. Modify the distance computation to consider randomness increasing from left to right, across the panel.

The distance computation would be modified to:

```
; right edge of panel
(setq cpt (list
  (+ (nth 0 pnt0) xmax)
  (+ (nth 1 pnt0) (/ ymax 2.0))
  (nth 2 pnt0)))
; center pt
(setq pntc
  (list xpos ypos (nth 2 pnt0)))
; distance to center determines
; amount of offset
(setq xdist (abs (- (nth 0 pntc)
  (nth 0 cpt))))
(setq xprct (- 1.0 (/ xdist
  (- xmax xside))))
(setq xoff (* (rn)
```

```
  (* xprct xyoff)))
(setq yoff (* (rn)
  (* xprct xyoff)))
; redefine center pt
(if (>= xprct dfact)
 (setq pntc (list
   (+ (- xpos (/ (* xyoff xprct)
   2)) xoff)
   (+ (- ypos (/ (* xyoff xprct)
   2)) yoff)
  (nth 2 pnt0)))
)
```

Both the x and y offsets would be controlled by only the x-distance to the right edge.

Sample script file for PROG03c:

```
;----------------------------------
(prog03c)
;Enter X side panel:
5
;Enter Y side panel:
5
;Enter number of X panels:
12
;Enter number of Y panels:
8
;Enter ring radius outside min:
3.76
;Enter ring radius outside max:
3.76
;Enter ring size min:
0.5
;Enter ring size max:
0.5
;Enter XY offset:
3.0
;Enter distance factor
0.25
;----------------------------------
```

Completed function PROG03c:

```
;----------------------------------
(defun prog03c ()
 (graphscr)
 ; ring relief 2D version
 (setq pnt0 (list 0 0 0))
 (prompt "\nPROG03c:")
 (setq xside
   (getdist pnt0
   "\nEnter X side panel:"))
 (setq yside
   (getdist pnt0
   "\nEnter Y side panel:"))
 (setq xtimes
   (getint
   "\nEnter number of X panels:"))
 (setq ytimes
   (getint
   "\nEnter number of Y panels:"))
 (setq romin
   (getdist pnt0
   "\nEnter ring radius outside
    min:"))
 (setq romax
   (getdist pnt0
   "\nEnter ring radius outside
    max:"))
 (setq rsmin
   (getdist pnt0
   "\nEnter ring size min:"))
 (setq rsmax
   (getdist pnt0
   "\nEnter ring size max:"))
 (setq xyoff
  (getdist pnt0
  "\nEnter XY offset:"))
 (setq dfact
   (getreal
   "\nEnter distance factor:"))
 (command ".ELEV" 0.0 0.0)
 (command ".ERASE" "all" "")
 ;panel size
 (setq xmax (* xside xtimes))
 (setq ymax (* yside ytimes))
 ; start y location
 (setq ypos
   (+ (nth 1 pnt0) (/ yside 2)))
```

```
(repeat ytimes
 ; start x location
 (setq xpos
   (+ (nth 0 pnt0) (/ xside 2)))
 (repeat xtimes
  ; random ring size and offset
  (setq rorad (+ romin
    (* (rn) (- romax romin))))
  (setq risize (+ rsmin
    (* (rn) (- rsmax rsmin))))
  ; right edge of panel
  (setq cpt (list
    (+ (nth 0 pnt0) xmax)
    (+ (nth 1 pnt0) (/ ymax 2.0))
    (nth 2 pnt0)))
  ; center pt
  (setq pntc
    (list xpos ypos (nth 2 pnt0)))
  ; distance to center determines
  ; amount of offset
  (setq xdist (abs (- (nth 0 pntc)
    (nth 0 cpt))))
  (setq xprct (- 1.0 (/ xdist
    (- xmax xside))))
  (setq xoff (* (rn)
    (* xprct xyoff)))
  (setq yoff (* (rn)
    (* xprct xyoff)))
  ; redefine center pt
  (if (>= xprct dfact)
   (setq pntc (list
     (+ (- xpos (/ (* xyoff xprct)
     2)) xoff)
     (+ (- ypos (/ (* xyoff xprct)
     2)) yoff)
    (nth 2 pnt0)))
  )
  ; make ring
  (command ".CIRCLE" pntc rorad)
  (command ".ZOOM" "e")
  (command ".REGION" "last" "")
  (setq obj1 (ssadd (entlast)))
  (command ".CIRCLE"
    pntc (- rorad risize))
  (command ".ZOOM" "e")
  (command ".REGION" "last" "")
  (setq obj2 (ssadd (entlast)))
  (command ".SUBTRACT"
    obj1 "" obj2 "")
  ; inc x
  (setq xpos (+ xpos xside))
 )
 ; inc y
 (setq ypos (+ ypos yside))
)
; union regions
(command ".UNION" "all" "")
(setq obj1 (ssadd (entlast)))
; inside border
(setq pnt1 (list
  (+ (nth 0 pnt0) xmax)
  (+ (nth 1 pnt0) ymax)))
(command ".RECTANGLE" pnt0 pnt1)
(command ".ZOOM" "e")
(command ".REGION" "last" "")
(setq obj2 (ssadd (entlast)))
; outside border
(setq pnt2 (list
  (- (nth 0 pnt0) xmax)
  (- (nth 1 pnt0) ymax)))
(setq pnt3 (list
  (+ (nth 0 pnt1) xmax)
  (+ (nth 1 pnt1) ymax)))
(command ".RECTANGLE" pnt2 pnt3)
(command ".ZOOM" "e")
(command ".REGION" "last" "")
(setq obj3 (ssadd (entlast)))
; make border
(command ".SUBTRACT"
  obj3 "" obj2 "")
(setq obj2 (ssadd (entlast)))
; subtract border from panel
(command ".SUBTRACT"
  obj1 "" obj2 "")
(command ".ZOOM" "e")
(princ)
)
;----------------------------------
```

In addition to the center and right edge, other options for increasing or decreasing randomness include: distance to one or more edges, a corner point, or a point of attraction. Try developing some of these on your own. Are other distance relationships possible?

Random polygonal rings

The previously explored random arrangements of circular rings can also be developed using a variety of polygons.

Add function PROG04 using a copy of PROG03. Within each panel at the centerpoint, draw a polygon as a ring, a REGION. Once all are drawn, UNION them. Include input for number of sides. Randomly select the rings' dimensions from a minimum and maximum. Also include a random x- and y-offset and rotation angle. Trim the rings to the panel edge. Include the one-inch frame at the border, as in function PROG02b.

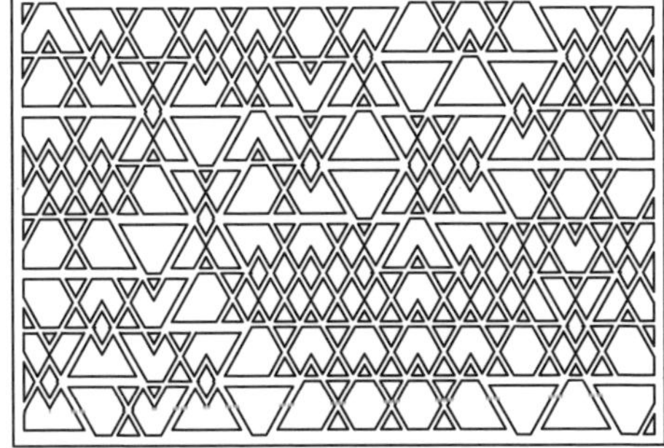

PROG04: polygonal rings, random triangles

The input values for these triangles were selected to overlap and form interesting patterns, in particular the size and rotation values.

Sample script file for PROG04:

```
;-----------------------------------
(prog04)
;Enter X side panel:
5
;Enter Y side panel:
5
;Enter number of X panels:
12
;Enter number of Y panels:
8
;Enter number of sides:
3
;Enter ring radius outside min:
2.5
;Enter ring radius outside max:
2.5
;Enter ring size min:
0.5
;Enter ring size max:
0.5
;Enter XY offset:
0
;Enter rotation:
60
;-----------------------------------
```

Completed function PROG04:

```
;-----------------------------------
(defun prog04 ()
 (graphscr)
 ; random sticks
 (setq pnt0 (list 0 0 0))
 (prompt "\nPROG04:")
 (setq xside
   (getdist pnt0
   "\nEnter X side panel:"))
 (setq yside
   (getdist pnt0
   "\nEnter Y side panel:"))
 (setq xtimes
   (getint
   "\nEnter number of X panels:"))
 (setq ytimes
   (getint
   "\nEnter number of Y panels:"))
 (setq nsides
   (getint
   "\nEnter number of sides for
    polygon:"))
 (setq romin
   (getdist pnt0
   "\nEnter ring radius outside
    min:"))
 (setq romax
```

```
  (getdist pnt0
  "\nEnter ring radius outside
   max:"))
(setq rsmin
  (getdist pnt0
  "\nEnter ring size min:"))
(setq rsmax
  (getdist pnt0
  "\nEnter ring size max:"))
(setq xyoff
  (getdist pnt0
  "\nEnter XY offset:"))
(setq rotang
  (getreal
  "\nEnter rotation angle:"))
(command ".ELEV" 0.0 0.0)
(command ".ERASE" "all" "")
; start y location
(setq ypos
  (+ (nth 1 pnt0) (/ yside 2)))
(repeat ytimes
 ; start x location
 (setq xpos
   (+ (nth 0 pnt0) (/ xside 2)))
 (repeat xtimes
  ; random polygon size, offset,
  ; and rotation
  (setq rorad (+ romin
    (* (rn) (- romax romin))))
  (setq risize (+ rsmin
    (* (rn) (- rsmax rsmin))))
  (setq xoff (* (rn) xyoff))
  (setq yoff (* (rn) xyoff))
  (setq rang (* (fix
    (* (rn) 360)) rotang))
  ; center pt
  (setq pntc (list
    (+ (- xpos (/ xyoff 2)) xoff)
    (+ (- ypos (/ xyoff 2)) yoff)))
  ; make ring
  (command ".POLYGON"
    nsides pntc "C" rorad)
  (command ".ZOOM" "e")
  (command ".REGION" "last" "")
  (setq obj1 (ssadd (entlast)))
  (command ".POLYGON"
    nsides pntc "C"
    (- rorad risize))
  (command ".ZOOM" "e")
  (command ".REGION" "last" "")
  (setq obj2 (ssadd (entlast)))
  (command ".SUBTRACT"
    obj1 "" obj2 "")
  (command ".ROTATE"
    "last" "" pntc rang)
  ; inc x
  (setq xpos (+ xpos xside))
 )
 ; inc y
 (setq ypos (+ ypos yside))
)
; union regions
(command ".UNION" "all" "")
(setq obj1 (ssadd (entlast)))
; inside border
(setq xmax (* xside xtimes))
(setq ymax (* yside ytimes))
(setq pnt1 (list
  (+ (nth 0 pnt0) xmax)
  (+ (nth 1 pnt0) ymax)))
(command ".RECTANGLE" pnt0 pnt1)
(command ".ZOOM" "e")
(command ".REGION" "last" "")
(setq obj2 (ssadd (entlast)))
; outside border
(setq pnt2 (list
  (- (nth 0 pnt0) xmax)
  (- (nth 1 pnt0) ymax)))
(setq pnt3 (list
  (+ (nth 0 pnt1) xmax)
  (+ (nth 1 pnt1) ymax)))
(command ".RECTANGLE" pnt2 pnt3)
(command ".ZOOM" "e")
(command ".REGION" "last" "")
(setq obj3 (ssadd (entlast)))
; make border
(command ".SUBTRACT"
  obj3 "" obj2 "")
(setq obj2 (ssadd (entlast)))
; subtract border from panel
(command ".SUBTRACT"
  obj1 "" obj2 "")
(setq obj1 (ssadd (entlast)))
; make frame at border
; inside border
(setq pnt1 (list
```

```
    (+ (nth 0 pnt0) xmax)
    (+ (nth 1 pnt0) ymax)))
  (command ".RECTANGLE" pnt0 pnt1)
  (command ".ZOOM" "e")
  (command ".REGION" "last" "")
  (setq obj2 (ssadd (entlast)))
  ; outside border
  (setq pnt2 (list
    (- (nth 0 pnt0) 1)
    (- (nth 1 pnt0) 1)))
  (setq pnt3 (list
    (+ (nth 0 pnt1) 1)
    (+ (nth 1 pnt1) 1)))
  (command ".RECTANGLE" pnt2 pnt3)
  (command ".ZOOM" "e")
  (command ".REGION" "last" "")
  (setq obj3 (ssadd (entlast)))
  ; make frame
  (command ".SUBTRACT"
    obj3 "" obj2 "")
  (setq obj2 (ssadd (entlast)))
  ; add to panel
  (command ".UNION" "all" "")
  (command ".ZOOM" "e")
  (princ)
)
;---------------------------------
```

Another example using function PROG04 is a four-sided polygon.

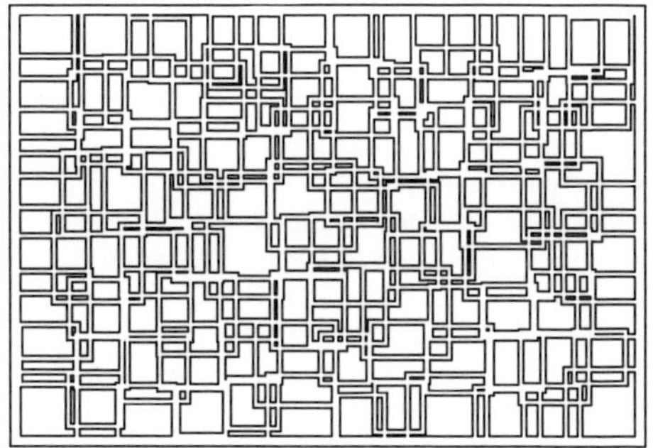

PROG04: polygonal rings, random rectangles

Sample script file for PROG04 with rectangles:

```
;---------------------------------
(prog04)
;Enter X side panel:
5
;Enter Y side panel:
5
;Enter number of X panels:
12
;Enter number of Y panels:
8
;Enter number of sides:
4
;Enter ring radius outside min:
2.5
;Enter ring radius outside max:
4.5
;Enter ring size min:
0.5
;Enter ring size max:
0.5
;Enter XY offset:
2.0
;Enter rotation:
0
;---------------------------------
```

Multilayer random patterns

To create a simple three-dimensional version of these random patterns, stack one atop another.

For example, function PROG03b could be executed to produce a circular ring pattern without randomness and then executed a second time with randomness. These then could be laser-cut and placed over each other.

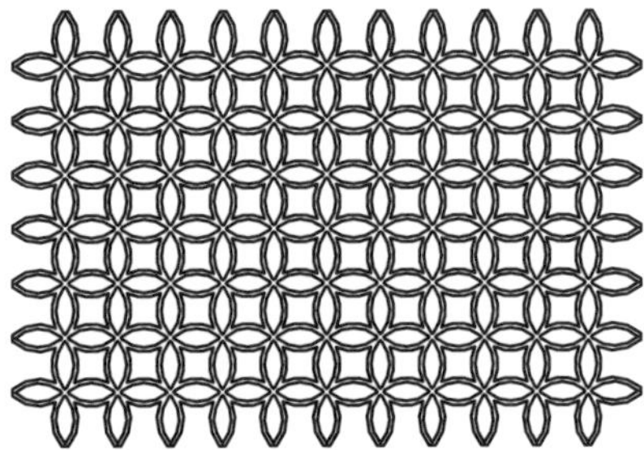

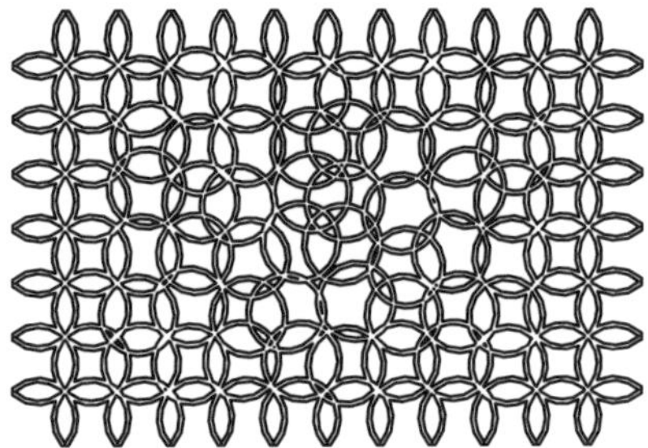

PROG03b: circular rings, multilayered

Sample script file for PROG03b, without randomness for the base layer:

```
;---------------------------------
(prog03b)
;Enter X side panel:
5
;Enter Y side panel:
5
;Enter number of X panels:
12
;Enter number of Y panels:
8
;Enter ring radius outside min:
3.76
;Enter ring radius outside max:
3.76
;Enter ring size min:
0.4
;Enter ring size max:
0.4
;Enter XY offset:
3.0
;Enter distance factor
1.0
;---------------------------------
```

For the second layer, the distance factor is changed to 0.25.

Another approach to generate three-dimensional multilayered patterns is to assign a random height layer to each circle.

Add function PROG05. Using a copy of PROG03, add a maximum height layer as input. For each circle generated, select a random height layer and place that circle in a separate selection list, up to the one selected. For example, if layer 3 was selected, the circle would be placed in selection lists 1, 2, and 3.

The selection lists separate each layer for trimming. Since multiple trims will be needed, a function DOTRIM is also added.

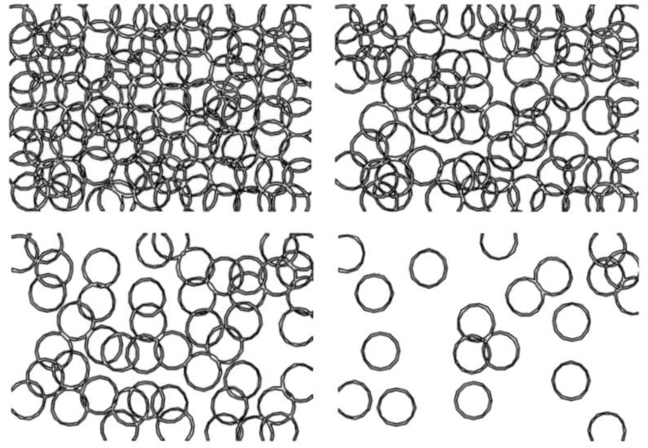

PROG05: circular rings on four layers

Sample script file for PROG05:

```
;---------------------------------
(prog05)
;Enter X side panel:
5
;Enter Y side panel:
5
;Enter number of X panels:
12
;Enter number of Y panels:
8
;Enter ring radius outside min:
3.76
;Enter ring radius outside max:
3.76
;Enter ring size min:
0.4
;Enter ring size max:
0.4
;Enter XY offset:
3.0
;Enter number of layers:
4
;---------------------------------
```

Completed function DOTRIM:

```
;---------------------------------
(defun dotrim ()
 ; inside border
 (setq pnt1 (list
   (+ (nth 0 pnt0) xmax)
   (+ (nth 1 pnt0) ymax)))
 (command ".RECTANGLE" pnt0 pnt1)
 (command ".ZOOM" "e")
 (command ".REGION" "last" "")
 (setq obj2 (ssadd (entlast)))
 ; outside border
 (setq pnt2 (list
   (- (nth 0 pnt0) xmax)
   (- (nth 1 pnt0) ymax)))
 (setq pnt3 (list
   (+ (nth 0 pnt1) xmax)
   (+ (nth 1 pnt1) ymax)))
 (command ".RECTANGLE" pnt2 pnt3)
 (command ".ZOOM" "e")
 (command ".REGION" "last" "")
 (setq obj3 (ssadd (entlast)))
 ; make border
 (command ".SUBTRACT"
   obj3 "" obj2 "")
 (setq obj2 (ssadd (entlast)))
 ; subtract border from panel
 (command ".SUBTRACT"
   obj1 "" obj2 "")
 (command ".ZOOM" "e")
 (princ)
)
;---------------------------------
```

Completed function PROG05:

```
;---------------------------------
(defun prog05 ()
 (graphscr)
 ; ring relief 2D version
 (setq pnt0 (list 0 0 0))
 (prompt "\nPROG05:")
 (setq xside
   (getdist pnt0
   "\nEnter X side panel:"))
 (setq yside
```

```
  (getdist pnt0
  "\nEnter Y side panel:"))
(setq xtimes
  (getint
  "\nEnter number of X panels:"))
(setq ytimes
  (getint
  "\nEnter number of Y panels:"))
(setq romin
  (getdist pnt0
  "\nEnter ring radius outside
   min:"))
(setq romax
  (getdist pnt0
  "\nEnter ring radius outside
   max:"))
(setq rsmin
  (getdist pnt0
  "\nEnter ring size min:"))
(setq rsmax
  (getdist pnt0
  "\nEnter ring size max:"))
(setq xyoff
  (getdist pnt0
  "\nEnter XY offset:"))
(setq nlayers
  (getint
  "\nEnter number of layers,
   1 to 4:"))
(command ".ELEV" 0.0 0.0)
(command ".ERASE" "all" "")
; selection lists
(setq layer01 (ssadd))
(setq layer02 (ssadd))
(setq layer03 (ssadd))
(setq layer04 (ssadd))
; panel dims
(setq xmax (* xside xtimes))
(setq ymax (* yside ytimes))
; start y location
(setq ypos
  (+ (nth 1 pnt0) (/ yside 2)))
(repeat ytimes
 ; start x location
 (setq xpos
   (+ (nth 0 pnt0) (/ xside 2)))
 (repeat xtimes
  ; random ring size and offset
  (setq rorad (+ romin
    (* (rn) (- romax romin))))
  (setq risize (+ rsmin
    (* (rn) (- rsmax rsmin))))
  (setq xoff (* (rn) xyoff))
  (setq yoff (* (rn) xyoff))
  (setq nlayer (+ (fix
    (* (rn) (- nlayers 0.1))) 1))
  ; center pt
  (setq pntc (list
    (+ (- xpos (/ xyoff 2)) xoff)
    (+ (- ypos (/ xyoff 2)) yoff)))
  ; make ring
  (command ".CIRCLE" pntc rorad)
  (command ".ZOOM" "e")
  (command ".REGION" "last" "")
  (setq obj1 (ssadd (entlast)))
  (command ".CIRCLE"
    pntc (- rorad risize))
  (command ".ZOOM" "e")
  (command ".REGION" "last" "")
  (setq obj2 (ssadd (entlast)))
  (command ".SUBTRACT"
    obj1 "" obj2 "")
  (setq layer01
    (ssadd (entlast) layer01))
  (if (>= nlayer 2) (progn
   (command ".COPY"
     "last" "" pntc pntc )
   (setq layer02
     (ssadd (entlast) layer02))
  ))
  (if (>= nlayer 3) (progn
   (command ".COPY"
     "last" "" pntc pntc )
   (setq layer03
     (ssadd (entlast) layer03))
  ))
  (if (>= nlayer 4) (progn
   (command ".COPY"
     "last" "" pntc pntc )
   (setq layer04
     (ssadd (entlast) layer04))
  ))
  ; inc x
  (setq xpos (+ xpos xside))
 )
 ; inc y
 (setq ypos (+ ypos yside))
)
```

```
 ; union and trim each layer
 (command ".ZOOM" "e")
 (setq obj1 layer01)
 (dotrim)
 (setq layers (ssadd (entlast)))
 (if (> nlayers 1) (progn
  (setq obj1 layer02)
  (dotrim)
  (setq layers
    (ssadd (entlast) layers))
 ))
 (if (> nlayers 2) (progn
  (setq obj1 layer03)
  (dotrim)
 ))
 (if (> nlayers 3) (progn
  (setq obj1 layer04)
  (dotrim)
 ))
 ; separate layers
 (setq layers (ssget "a"))
 (setq cnt 0)
 (repeat (sslength layers)
  (setq obj (ssname layers cnt))
  (setq pnt1 (list
    (- (nth 0 pnt0)
    (* (+ xmax xside)(+ cnt 1)))
    (nth 1 pnt0) (nth 2 pnt0)))
  (command ".MOVE"
    obj "" pnt0 pnt1)
  (command ".ZOOM" "e")
  (setq cnt (+ cnt 1))
 )
 (princ)
)
;----------------------------------
```

Review the method used to create and add the selection lists for each layer; the trimming sequence for each layer; how the layers are separated across the drawing. To separate them—each layer being a single region—the ssget function gathers all of the regions into a selection list, and the ssname function extracts each region from the list and moves it away from its original location in the drawing. Each of these layers can then be laser-cut and stacked over each other to form a variable three-dimensional version of the random circular rings.

Multiple random shapes

In addition to generating random variation of a single shape, multiple shapes can be randomly selected and placed.

Add function PROG06. Using a copy of PROG03, develop a number of different shapes. For example, a circle, triangle, square, or 5- and 6-sided polygons. Randomly select one of these using entered parameters to place it in the grid cell.

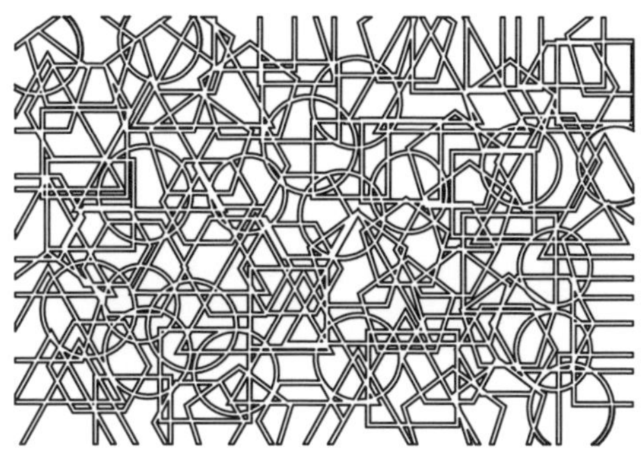

PROG06: multiple random shapes

Select one of the shapes, assuming there are five, and create the corresponding ring. If the first shape is a circle, use:

```
; select type of ring
(setq rtype (+ (fix
  (* (rn) 4.99)) 1))
(if (= rtype 1) (progn
 (command ".CIRCLE" pntc rorad)
 (command ".ZOOM" "e")
 (command ".REGION" "last" "")
 (setq obj1 (ssadd (entlast)))
 (command ".CIRCLE"
   pntc (- rorad risize))
 (command ".ZOOM" "e")
 (command ".REGION" "last" "")
 (setq obj2 (ssadd (entlast)))
 (command ".SUBTRACT"
```

```
    obj1 "" obj2 "")
))
; select type of ring
(setq rtype (+ (fix
   (* (rn) 4.99)) 1))
(if (= rtype 1) (progn
 (command ".CIRCLE" pntc rorad)
 (command ".ZOOM" "e")
 (command ".REGION" "last" "")
 (setq obj1 (ssadd (entlast)))
 (command ".CIRCLE"
    pntc (- rorad risize))
 (command ".ZOOM" "e")
 (command ".REGION" "last" "")
 (setq obj2 (ssadd (entlast)))
 (command ".SUBTRACT"
    obj1 "" obj2 "")
))
```

A random number from 0 to 4 is generated and then one is added to it, so the selection is based on numbers 1 through 5. Similar sections of code can be developed for each shape to be selected.

Sample script file for PROG06:

```
;----------------------------------
(prog06)
;Enter X side panel:
5
;Enter Y side panel:
5
;Enter number of X panels:
12
;Enter number of Y panels:
8
;Enter ring radius outside min:
3.76
;Enter ring radius outside max:
3.76
;Enter ring size min:
0.4
;Enter ring size max:
0.4
;Enter XY offset:
3.0
;----------------------------------
```

Completed function PROG06:

```
;----------------------------------
(defun prog06 ()
 (graphscr)
 ; ring relief 2D version
 (setq pnt0 (list 0 0 0))
 (prompt "\nPROG06:")
 (setq xside
   (getdist pnt0
   "\nEnter X side panel:"))
 (setq yside
   (getdist pnt0
   "\nEnter Y side panel:"))
 (setq xtimes
   (getint
   "\nEnter number of X panels:"))
 (setq ytimes
   (getint
   "\nEnter number of Y panels:"))
 (setq romin
   (getdist pnt0
   "\nEnter ring radius outside min:"))
 (setq romax
   (getdist pnt0
   "\nEnter ring radius outside max:"))
 (setq rsmin
   (getdist pnt0
   "\nEnter ring size min:"))
 (setq rsmax
   (getdist pnt0
   "\nEnter ring size max:"))
 (setq xyoff
   (getdist pnt0
   "\nEnter XY offset:"))
 (command ".ELEV" 0.0 0.0)
 (command ".ERASE" "all" "")
 ;panel size
 (setq xmax (* xside xtimes))
 (setq ymax (* yside ytimes))
 ; start y location
 (setq ypos
   (+ (nth 1 pnt0) (/ yside 2)))
 (repeat ytimes
  ; start x location
  (setq xpos
    (+ (nth 0 pnt0) (/ xside 2)))
  (repeat xtimes
```

```
; random ring size and offset
(setq rorad (+ romin
  (* (rn) (- romax romin))))
(setq risize (+ rsmin
  (* (rn) (- rsmax rsmin))))
(setq xoff (* (rn) xyoff))
(setq yoff (* (rn) xyoff))
; center pt
(setq pntc (list
  (+ (- xpos (/ xyoff 2)) xoff)
  (+ (- ypos (/ xyoff 2)) yoff)))
; select type of ring
(setq rtype (+ (fix
  (* (rn) 4.99)) 1))
(if (= rtype 1) (progn
 (command ".CIRCLE" pntc rorad)
 (command ".ZOOM" "e")
 (command ".REGION" "last" "")
 (setq obj1 (ssadd (entlast)))
 (command ".CIRCLE"
   pntc (- rorad risize))
 (command ".ZOOM" "e")
 (command ".REGION" "last" "")
 (setq obj2 (ssadd (entlast)))
 (command ".SUBTRACT"
   obj1 "" obj2 "")
))
(if (= rtype 2) (progn
 (command ".POLYGON"
   "3" pntc "C" rorad)
 (command ".ZOOM" "e")
 (command ".REGION" "last" "")
 (setq obj1 (ssadd (entlast)))
 (command ".POLYGON"
   "3" pntc "C" (- rorad risize))
 (command ".ZOOM" "e")
 (command ".REGION" "last" "")
 (setq obj2 (ssadd (entlast)))
 (command ".SUBTRACT"
   obj1 "" obj2 "")
))
(if (= rtype 3) (progn
 (command ".POLYGON"
   "4" pntc "C" rorad)
 (command ".ZOOM" "e")
 (command ".REGION" "last" "")
 (setq obj1 (ssadd (entlast)))
 (command ".POLYGON"
   "4" pntc "C" (- rorad risize))
 (command ".ZOOM" "e")
 (command ".REGION" "last" "")
 (setq obj2 (ssadd (entlast)))
 (command ".SUBTRACT"
   obj1 "" obj2 "")
))
(if (= rtype 4) (progn
 (command ".POLYGON"
   "5" pntc "C" rorad)
 (command ".ZOOM" "e")
 (command ".REGION" "last" "")
 (setq obj1 (ssadd (entlast)))
 (command ".POLYGON"
   "5" pntc "C" (- rorad risize))
 (command ".ZOOM" "e")
 (command ".REGION" "last" "")
 (setq obj2 (ssadd (entlast)))
 (command ".SUBTRACT"
   obj1 "" obj2 "")
))
(if (= rtype 5) (progn
 (command ".POLYGON"
   "6" pntc "C" rorad)
 (command ".ZOOM" "e")
 (command ".REGION" "last" "")
 (setq obj1 (ssadd (entlast)))
 (command ".POLYGON"
   "6" pntc "C" (- rorad risize))
 (command ".ZOOM" "e")
 (command ".REGION" "last" "")
 (setq obj2 (ssadd (entlast)))
 (command ".SUBTRACT"
   obj1 "" obj2 "")
))
; inc x
(setq xpos (+ xpos xside))
)
; inc y
(setq ypos (+ ypos yside))
)
; union regions
(command ".UNION" "all" "")
(setq obj1 (ssadd (entlast)))
; inside border
(setq pnt1 (list
  (+ (nth 0 pnt0) xmax)
  (+ (nth 1 pnt0) ymax)))
```

```
  (command ".RECTANGLE" pnt0 pnt1)
  (command ".ZOOM" "e")
  (command ".REGION" "last" "")
  (setq obj2 (ssadd (entlast)))
  ; outside border
  (setq pnt2 (list
    (- (nth 0 pnt0) xmax)
    (- (nth 1 pnt0) ymax)))
  (setq pnt3 (list
    (+ (nth 0 pnt1) xmax)
    (+ (nth 1 pnt1) ymax)))
  (command ".RECTANGLE" pnt2 pnt3)
  (command ".ZOOM" "e")
  (command ".REGION" "last" "")
  (setq obj3 (ssadd (entlast)))
  ; make border
  (command ".SUBTRACT"
    obj3 "" obj2 "")
  (setq obj2 (ssadd (entlast)))
  ; subtract border from panel
  (command ".SUBTRACT"
    obj1 "" obj2 "")
  (command ".ZOOM" "e")
  (princ)
)
;---------------------------------
```

There is an equal probability that any one of the defined shapes will be selected. If you would like to skew the chances of some being picked more often, then create a pick list and select from it.

For example, in the pick list:

```
( 1 1 1 1 2 3 3 3 4 5 )
```

The circle and rectangle have a higher chance of being picked.

Add function PROG06a. Using a copy of PROG06, make the shape selection from a pick list.

Add input from the list:

```
(setq plist
  (read (getstring
  "\nEnter random list of
selections:")))
```

Replace the selection of shape type with:

```
; select type of ring
(setq nlist (fix (* (rn)
  (- (length plist) 0.1))))
(setq rtype (nth nlist plist))
```

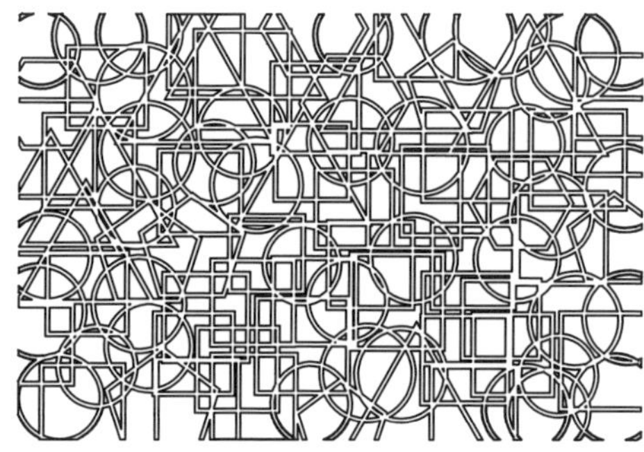

PROG06a: selective multiple random shapes

Sample script file for PROG06a:

```
;---------------------------------
(prog06a)
;Enter X side panel:
5
;Enter Y side panel:
5
;Enter number of X panels:
12
;Enter number of Y panels:
8
;Enter ring radius outside min:
3.76
```

```
;Enter ring radius outside max:
3.76
;Enter ring size min:
0.4
;Enter ring size max:
0.4
;Enter XY offset:
3.0
;Enter random selections:
( 1 1 1 1 2 3 3 3 4 5)
;---------------------------------
```

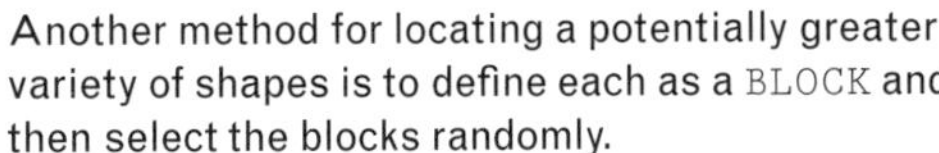

Another method for locating a potentially greater variety of shapes is to define each as a BLOCK and then select the blocks randomly.

Add function PROG06a. Using PROG06, randomly select a block that has been previously defined in the drawing.

In the drawing, create a series of blocks that are within a one-unit square and have their insert point in the center. If they are one unit in size, the INSERT command's scaling option can be used to size them. If you wish to make regions from them, define each block element as a region. The block names will be placed in a list for selection.

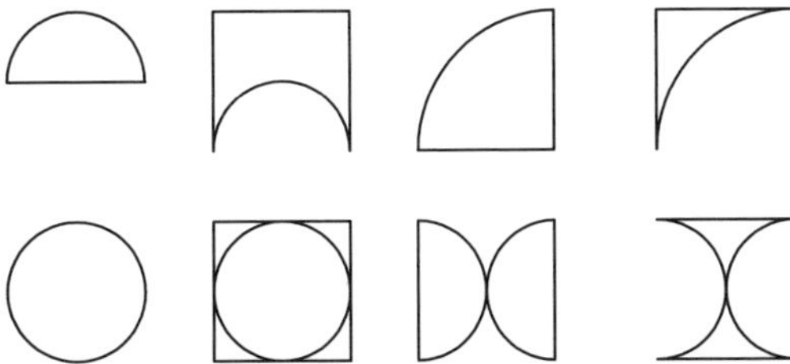

PROG06b: blocks to be placed randomly

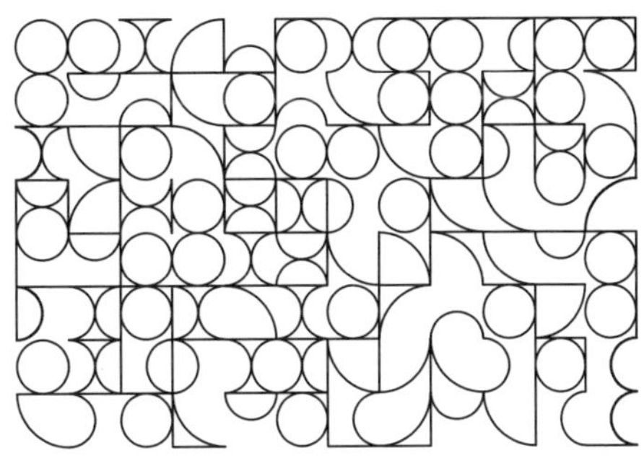

PROG06b: random blocks rotated

The blocks are selected from a pick list and then inserted, scaled, and rotated using:

```
; random rotation
(setq rang (* (fix
  (* (rn) 3.99)) 90))
; center pt
(setq pntc
  (list xpos ypos (nth 2 pnt0)))
; select block
(setq nlist (fix (* (rn)
  (- (length blist) 0.1))))
(setq nblock (nth nlist blist))
; get block
(command ".INSERT"
  nblock "s" xside pntc rang)
(command ".ZOOM" "e")
(command ".EXPLODE" "last")
```

The EXPLODE command is included so that all the regions can be unioned.

Sample script file for PROG06b:

```
;---------------------------------
(prog06b)
;Enter X side panel:
5
;Enter Y side panel:
5
;Enter number of X panels:
12
;Enter number of Y panels:
8
;Enter block names:
( "pat01" "pat02" "pat03" "pat04"
"pat05" "pat06""pat07" "pat08")
;---------------------------------
```

The block name list is entered on a single line in the script file.

Completed function PROG06b:

```
;---------------------------------
(defun prog06b ()
 (graphscr)
 ; ring relief 2D version
 (setq pnt0 (list 0 0 0))
 (prompt "\nPROG06b:")
 (setq xside
   (getdist pnt0
   "\nEnter X side panel:"))
 (setq yside
   (getdist pnt0
   "\nEnter Y side panel:"))
 (setq xtimes
   (getint
   "\nEnter number of X panels:"))
 (setq ytimes
   (getint
   "\nEnter number of Y panels:"))
 (setq blist
   (read (getstring
   "\nEnter random list of
    selections:")))
 (command ".ELEV" 0.0 0.0)
 (command ".ERASE" "all" "")
 ;panel size
 (setq xmax (* xside xtimes))
 (setq ymax (* yside ytimes))
 ; start y location
 (setq ypos
   (+ (nth 1 pnt0) (/ yside 2)))
 (repeat ytimes
  ; start x location
  (setq xpos
    (+ (nth 0 pnt0) (/ xside 2)))
  (repeat xtimes
   ; random rotation
   (setq rang (* (fix
     (* (rn) 3.99)) 90))
   ; center pt
   (setq pntc
     (list xpos ypos (nth 2 pnt0)))
   ; select type of ring
   (setq nlist (fix (* (rn)
     (- (length blist) 0.1))))
   (setq nblock (nth nlist blist))
   ; get block
   (command ".INSERT"
     nblock "s" xside pntc rang)
   (command ".ZOOM" "e")
   (command ".EXPLODE" "last")
   ; inc x
   (setq xpos (+ xpos xside))
  )
  ; inc y
  (setq ypos (+ ypos yside))
 )
 ; union regions
 (command ".UNION" "all" "")
 (setq obj1 (ssadd (entlast)))
 ; inside border
 (setq pnt1 (list
   (+ (nth 0 pnt0) xmax)
   (+ (nth 1 pnt0) ymax)))
 (command ".RECTANGLE" pnt0 pnt1)
 (command ".ZOOM" "e")
 (command ".REGION" "last" "")
 (setq obj2 (ssadd (entlast)))
 ; outside border
 (setq pnt2 (list
   (- (nth 0 pnt0) xmax)
   (- (nth 1 pnt0) ymax)))
 (setq pnt3 (list
   (+ (nth 0 pnt1) xmax)
```

```
    (+ (nth 1 pnt1) ymax)))
  (command ".RECTANGLE" pnt2 pnt3)
  (command ".ZOOM" "e")
  (command ".REGION" "last" "")
  (setq obj3 (ssadd (entlast)))
  ; make border
  (command ".SUBTRACT"
    obj3 "" obj2 "")
  (setq obj2 (ssadd (entlast)))
  ; subtract border from panel
  (command ".SUBTRACT"
    obj1 "" obj2 "")
  (command ".ZOOM" "e")
  (princ)
)
;-----------------------------------
```

Random perforations that fill a panel

All of the perforations developed so far have been within the grid framework. Another approach is to fill a panel with perforations that do not overlap.

Add function PROG07 to use the packed circle method to fill a panel with perforations.

An outline of the approach:

* Select a circle radius and location randomly.
* Check the distance to all other circles placed so that it is greater than the radius of any two, plus 10 percent, or some minimum spacing dimension.
* If the distance passes, draw the circle and add its location and radius to the list. Reset the failure counter; if not, add one to the failure counter.
* If enough failed, stop; otherwise, return to the first step.

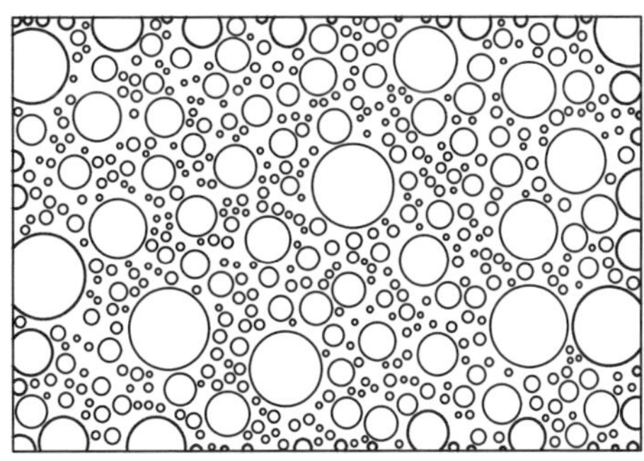

PROG07: random circles filling the panel

Radius and location are computed for a candidate circle, using:

```
; random circle size and location
(setq rad (+ rmin
  (* (rn) (- rmax rmin))))
(setq xpos (* (rn) xmax))
(setq ypos (* (rn) ymax))
; center pt
(setq pntc (list
  (+ (nth 0 pnt0) xpos)
  (+ (nth 1 pnt0) ypos)
  (nth 2 pnt0)))
```

The core computations entail checking the distance between the candidate circle and all circles already drawn. The distances between their centers are computed and must be at least 10 percent greater than the minimum radius entered. If every placed circle passes this test, then the candidate is drawn and added to the list to be checked on the next cycle. The distances are checked by:

```
; check prevision locations
(setq idraw 1)
(if (> ncircles 0) (progn
 (setq ic 0)
 (repeat ncircles
  (setq pntp
    (nth 0 (nth ic clist)))
  (setq radp
```

```
    (nth 1 (nth ic clist)))
  (setq cdist
    (distance pntp pntc))
  ; spacing of 10 percent
  (if (< (- cdist
    (* rmin 1.10))
    (+ rad radp)) (progn
   (setq idraw 0)
  ))
 (setq ic (+ ic 1))
 )
))
```

For each circle to be drawn, it is added to a list, which includes its location and radius:

```
; draw circle
(if (= idraw 1) (progn
 (command ".CIRCLE" pntc rad)
 (command ".REGION" "last" "")
 ; add to list: location and
 ; radius
 (setq clist (append
   (list (list pntc rad)) clist))
 (setq ncircles (+ ncircles 1))
 (setq ifail 0)
))
```

In this example, if a candidate is not found within 2,000 random generations, the function stops.

Sample script file for PROG07:

```
;----------------------------------
(prog07)
;Enter X side panel:
5
;Enter Y side panel:
5
;Enter number of X panels:
12
;Enter number of Y panels:
8
;Enter min radius:
0.25
;Enter max radius:
4.0
;----------------------------------
```

Completed function PROG07:

```
;----------------------------------
(defun prog07 ()
 (graphscr)
 ; packed circles
 ; random circle size
 (setq pnt0 (list 0 0 0))
 (prompt "\nPROG07:")
 (setq xside
   (getdist pnt0
    "\nEnter X side panel:"))
 (setq yside
   (getdist pnt0
   "\nEnter Y side panel:"))
 (setq xtimes
   (getint
   "\nEnter number of X panels:"))
 (setq ytimes
   (getint
   "\nEnter number of Y panels:"))
 (setq rmin
   (getdist pnt0
   "\nEnter min radius:"))
 (setq rmax
   (getdist pnt0
   "\nEnter max radius:"))
 (command ".ELEV" 0.0 0.0)
 (command ".ERASE" "all" "")
 ; count number of failures to
 ; stop at
 (setq nfails 2000)
 ; count of circles drawn
 (setq ncircles 0)
 ; list of placed circles
 (setq clist (list ))
 ; panel
 (setq xmax (* xside xtimes))
 (setq ymax (* yside ytimes))
 (command ".RECTANGLE"
   pnt0 (list (+ (nth 0 pnt0) xmax)
   (+ (nth 1 pnt0) ymax)))
 (command ".ZOOM" "e")
 ; packed circles
 (setq ido 1)
 (while (= ido 1)
  ; random circle size and location
  (setq rad (+ rmin
```

```
    (* (rn) (- rmax rmin))))
  (setq xpos (* (rn) xmax))
  (setq ypos (* (rn) ymax))
  ; center pt
  (setq pntc (list
    (+ (nth 0 pnt0) xpos)
    (+ (nth 1 pnt0) ypos)
    (nth 2 pnt0)))
  ; check prevision locations
  (setq idraw 1)
  (if (> ncircles 0) (progn
   (setq ic 0)
   (repeat ncircles
    (setq pntp
      (nth 0 (nth ic clist)))
    (setq radp
      (nth 1 (nth ic clist)))
    (setq cdist
      (distance pntp pntc))
    ; spacing of 10 percent
    (if (< (- cdist
      (* rmin 1.10))
      (+ rad radp)) (progn
     (setq idraw 0)
    ))
   (setq ic (+ ic 1))
   )
  ))
  ; failed
  (if (= idraw 0) (progn
   (setq ifail (+ ifail 1))
   (princ "\nFailed=")
     (princ ifail)
  ))
  ; draw circle
  (if (= idraw 1) (progn
   (command ".CIRCLE" pntc rad)
   (command ".REGION" "last" "")
   ; add to list: location and
   ; radius
   (setq clist (append
     (list (list pntc rad)) clist))
   (setq ncircles (+ ncircles 1))
   (setq ifail 0)
  ))
 ; check if to stop
 (if (> ifail nfails) (setq ido 0))
 )
 (command ".ZOOM" "e")
 ; union regions
 (command ".UNION" "all" "")
 (setq obj1 (ssadd (entlast)))
 ; inside border
 (setq pnt1 (list
   (+ (nth 0 pnt0) xmax)
   (+ (nth 1 pnt0) ymax)))
 (command ".RECTANGLE" pnt0 pnt1)
 (command ".ZOOM" "e")
 (command ".REGION" "last" "")
 (setq obj2 (ssadd (entlast)))
 ; outside border
 (setq pnt2 (list
   (- (nth 0 pnt0) xmax)
   (- (nth 1 pnt0) ymax)))
 (setq pnt3 (list
   (+ (nth 0 pnt1) xmax)
   (+ (nth 1 pnt1) ymax)))
 (command ".RECTANGLE" pnt2 pnt3)
 (command ".ZOOM" "e")
 (command ".REGION" "last" "")
 (setq obj3 (ssadd (entlast)))
 ; make border
 (command ".SUBTRACT"
   obj3 "" obj2 "")
 (setq obj2 (ssadd (entlast)))
 ; subtract border from panel
 (command ".SUBTRACT"
   obj1 "" obj2 "")
 (command ".ZOOM" "e")
 (princ)
)
;---------------------------------
```

Other possible considerations:

* Area of coverage: sum the area of the circles placed compared to the total surface area, and use a target-filled area to stop generation.
* Uneven distribution of circle sizes: select specific sizes from a list.
* After half of the failures, reduce the maximum circle size by half.

* To develop a similar method for other shapes, such as squares, rectangles, and triangles, (rotated or not rotated) requires checking intersections of the proposed shape, line by line, against ones already placed.

6.4 Random Surface Constructions

This section explores methods for distorting a surface by applying random values to it.

Start a new drawing and set the units to architectural. Set the grid to 1 foot, and turn off all snaps and dynamic input.

Start a new AutoLISP file in the editor CH06D.LSP. Add functions rn, dtr, and rtd from the previous section.

Simple mesh with random heights

Add function PROG01 to compute a set of grid points; use those locations along with a random height to create a 3DMESH, a single surface.

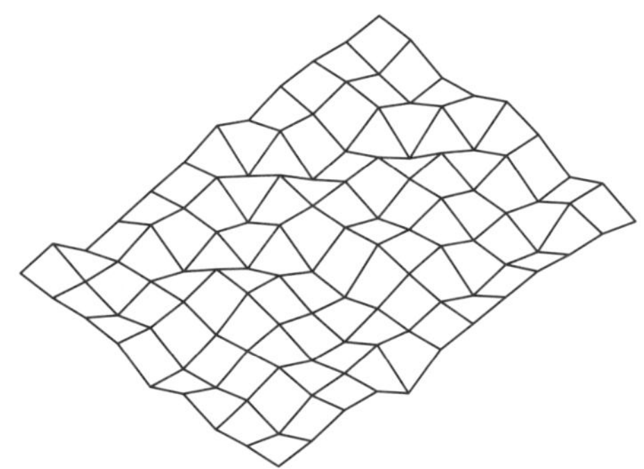

PROG01: simple mesh with random heights

The number of points in the x- and y-direction will determine how smooth the mesh will be. Since it is a single entity, most rendering methods will render it as one smooth surface.

The height of each mesh point is computed as:

```
; grid pt
(setq pnt1 (list xloc yloc 0))
; compute height
(setq zheight (* (rn) maxheight))
; grid pt
(setq pnt2 (list
  (nth 0 pnt1)
  (nth 1 pnt1) zheight))
; add mesh pt
(command pnt2)
```

Sample script file for PROG01:

```
;----------------------------------
(prog01)
;Enter X side:
5
;Enter Y side:
5
;Enter number X repeats:
12
;Enter number Y repeats:
9
;Enter maximum height:
5.0
;----------------------------------
```

Completed function PROG01:

```
;----------------------------------
(defun prog01 ()
 (graphscr)
 (command ".ERASE" "all" "")
 ; set start point
 (setq pnt0 (list 0 0 0))
 (prompt "\nPROG01:")
 (setq xside
   (getdist pnt0
   "\nEnter X side:"))
 (setq yside
   (getdist pnt0
   "\nEnter Y side:"))
 (setq xtimes
   (getint
   "\nEnter number X repeats:"))
 (setq ytimes
```

```
    (getint
    "\nEnter number Y repeats:"))
  (setq maxheight
    (getdist pnt0
    "\nEnter maximum height:"))
  ; start mesh
  (command ".3DMESH" ytimes xtimes)
  ; start y location
  (setq yloc (nth 1 pnt0))
  (repeat ytimes
   ; start x location
   (setq xloc (nth 0 pnt0))
   (repeat xtimes
    ; grid pt
    (setq pnt1 (list xloc yloc 0))
    ; compute height
    (setq zheight (* (rn) maxheight))
    ; grid pt
    (setq pnt2 (list
      (nth 0 pnt1)
      (nth 1 pnt1) zheight))
    ; add mesh pt
    (command pnt2)
    ; inc x location
    (setq xloc (+ xloc xside))
   )
   ; inc y location
   (setq yloc (+ yloc yside))
  )
  (command ".ZOOM" "e")
  (princ)
)
;-----------------------------------
```

Taper edge of mesh

The border points in this mesh have random heights. Modify the function to set the edge points to an elevation of zero.

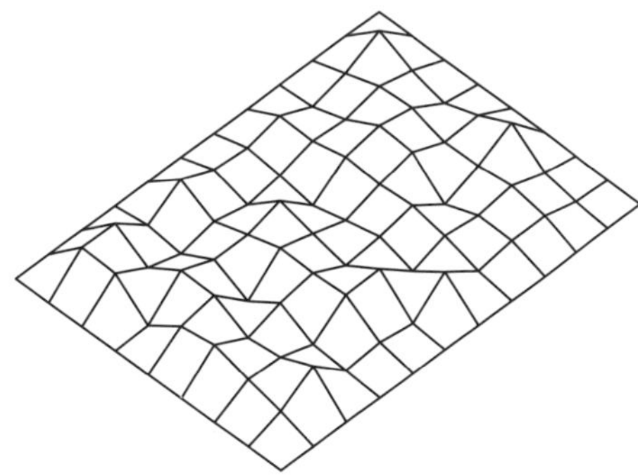

PROG02: mesh with edge elevations set at zero

Add function PROG02. Using a copy of PROG01, modify the height on the edges to zero.

Add a counter for the x and y locations. When the counter is either at the first x- or y-location, or at the last x- or y-location, set the z-height to 0.0; otherwise, set z to a random height, as before.

The random height is computed as:

```
 ; compute height
(if (or (or (or (= ynum 1)
   (= ynum ytimes)) (= xnum 1))
   (= xnum xtimes))
  (setq zheight 0.0)
  (setq zheight
    (* (rn) maxheight))
)
```

Sample script file for PROG02:

```
;----------------------------------
(prog02)
;Enter X side:
5
;Enter Y side:
5
;Enter number X repeats:
12
;Enter number Y repeats:
9
;Enter maximum height:
5.0
;----------------------------------
```

Completed function PROG02:

```
;----------------------------------
(defun prog02 ()
 (graphscr)
 (command ".ERASE" "all" "")
 ; set start point
 (setq pnt0 (list 0 0 0))
 (prompt "\nPROG02:")
 (setq xside
   (getdist pnt0
   "\nEnter X side:"))
 (setq yside
   (getdist pnt0
   "\nEnter Y side:"))
 (setq xtimes
   (getint
   "\nEnter number X repeats:"))
 (setq ytimes
   (getint
   "\nEnter number Y repeats:"))
 (setq maxheight
   (getdist pnt0
   "\nEnter maximum height:"))
 ; start mesh
 (command ".3DMESH" ytimes xtimes)
 ; start y location
 (setq yloc (nth 1 pnt0))
 (setq ynum 1)
 (repeat ytimes
  ; start x location
  (setq xloc (nth 0 pnt0))
  (setq xnum 1)
  (repeat xtimes
   ; grid pt
   (setq pnt1 (list xloc yloc 0))
   ; compute height
   (if (or (or (or (= ynum 1)
     (= ynum ytimes)) (= xnum 1))
     (= xnum xtimes))
    (setq zheight 0.0)
    (setq zheight
      (* (rn) maxheight))
   )
   ; grid pt
   (setq pnt2 (list
     (nth 0 pnt1)
     (nth 1 pnt1) zheight))
   ; add mesh pt
   (command pnt2)
   ; inc x location
   (setq xloc (+ xloc xside))
   (setq xnum (+ xnum 1))
  )
  ; inc y location
  (setq yloc (+ yloc yside))
  (setq ynum (+ ynum 1))
 )
 (command ".ZOOM" "e")
 (princ)
)
;----------------------------------
```

Most of the following examples will compute some random variation of a height value. In addition to a height value, a random xy-offset could also be included.

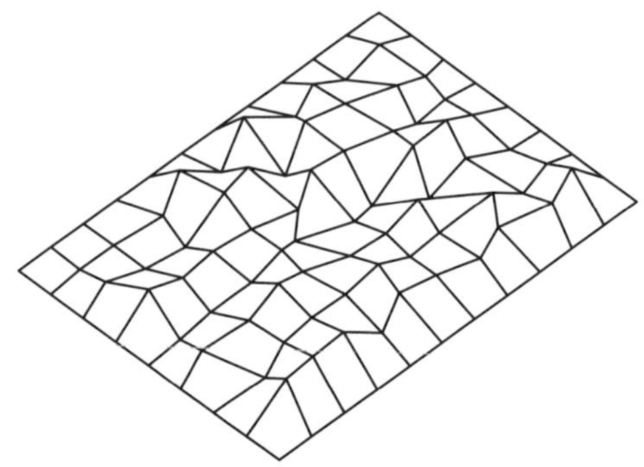

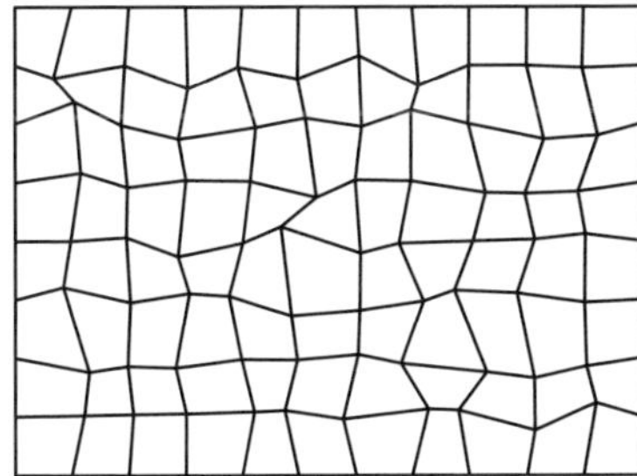

PROG02a: mesh with a random xy-offset

Add function PROG02a. Using a copy of PROG02, randomly compute an xy-offset based on an input maximum, as:

```
; compute height
(if (or (or (or (= ynum 1)
  (= ynum ytimes)) (= xnum 1))
  (= xnum xtimes))
 (progn
  (setq zheight 0.0)
  (setq xoff 0.0)
  (setq yoff 0.0)
 )
 (progn
  (setq zheight
    (* (rn) maxheight))
  (setq opnt (polar
    (list 0 0 0)
    (dtr (* (rn) 360.0))
    (* (rn) maxoffset)))
  (setq xoff (nth 0 opnt))
  (setq yoff (nth 1 opnt))
 )
)
```

At the edge, the offset is set to zero. For interior points, a coordinate is computed based on a random angle and distance. This method gives a random point that can either be left or right, above or below, the computed grid point.

This application of a random value could also be used in two-dimensional tiling patterns by randomly breaking up a large panel into smaller pieces.

Sample script file for PROG02a:

```
;----------------------------------
(prog02a)
;Enter X side:
5
;Enter Y side:
5
;Enter number X repeats:
12
;Enter number Y repeats:
9
;Enter height:
5.0
;Enter maximum XY offset
2.0
;----------------------------------
```

Completed function PROG02a:

```
;----------------------------------
(defun prog02a ()
 (graphscr)
 (command ".ERASE" "all" "")
 ; set start point
 (setq pnt0 (list 0 0 0))
 (prompt "\nPROG02a:")
 (setq xside
   (getdist pnt0
   "\nEnter X side:"))
 (setq yside
   (getdist pnt0
   "\nEnter Y side:"))
 (setq xtimes
   (getint
   "\nEnter number X repeats:"))
 (setq ytimes
   (getint
   "\nEnter number Y repeats:"))
 (setq maxheight
   (getdist pnt0
   "\nEnter maximum height:"))
 (setq maxoffset
   (getdist pnt0
   "\nEnter maximum XY offset:"))
```

```
  ; start mesh
  (command ".3DMESH" ytimes xtimes)
  ; start y location
  (setq yloc (nth 1 pnt0))
  (setq ynum 1)
  (repeat ytimes
   ; start x location
   (setq xloc (nth 0 pnt0))
   (setq xnum 1)
   (repeat xtimes
    ; grid pt
    (setq pnt1 (list xloc yloc 0))
    ; compute height
    (if (or (or (or (= ynum 1)
      (= ynum ytimes)) (= xnum 1))
      (= xnum xtimes))
     (progn
      (setq zheight 0.0)
      (setq xoff 0.0)
      (setq yoff 0.0)
     )
     (progn
      (setq zheight
        (* (rn) maxheight))
      (setq opnt (polar
        (list 0 0 0)
        (dtr (* (rn) 360.0))
        (* (rn) maxoffset)))
      (setq xoff (nth 0 opnt))
      (setq yoff (nth 1 opnt))
     )
    )
    ; grid pt
    (setq pnt2 (list
      (+ (nth 0 pnt1) xoff)
      (+ (nth 1 pnt1) yoff)
      zheight))
    ; add mesh pt
    (command pnt2)
    ; inc x location
    (setq xloc (+ xloc xside))
    (setq xnum (+ xnum 1))
   )
   ; inc y location
   (setq yloc (+ yloc yside))
   (setq ynum (+ ynum 1))
  )
  (command ".ZOOM" "e")
  (princ)
)
;---------------------------------
```

Add bottom to a tapered mesh

Note that this mesh does not have a bottom surface, just a top surface that tapers to the edges. To add the bottom, increase the number of mesh points in the x-direction by 1. For each row, capture the first computed point. When the row is complete, add it to the mesh. This closes the underside of the mesh.

Add function PROG03. Using a copy of PROG02, add the bottom of the mesh.

PROG03: mesh with a bottom included

Modify the start of the mesh:

```
; start mesh
(command ".3DMESH"
  ytimes (+ xtimes 1))
```

After the mesh point is added, use:

```
; add 3DMESH pt
(command pnt2)
; save first pt
(if (= xnum 1)
  (setq pnt3 pnt2))
```

After the x-row completes, add the first point to the mesh. The mesh is now watertight and can be used in a number of rapid-prototyping systems to construct a physical model.

Sample script file for PROG03:

```
;---------------------------------
(prog03)
;Enter X side:
5
;Enter Y side:
5
;Enter number X repeats:
12
;Enter number Y repeats:
9
;Enter maximum height:
5.0
;---------------------------------
```

Completed function PROG03:

```
;---------------------------------
(defun prog03 ()
 (graphscr)
 (command ".ERASE" "all" "")
 ; set start point
 (setq pnt0 (list 0 0 0))
 (prompt "\nPROG03:")
 (setq xside
   (getdist pnt0
   "\nEnter X side:"))
 (setq yside
   (getdist pnt0
   "\nEnter Y side:"))
 (setq xtimes
   (getint
   "\nEnter number X repeats:"))
 (setq ytimes
   (getint
   "\nEnter number Y repeats:"))
 (setq maxheight
   (getdist pnt0
   "\nEnter maximum height:"))
 ; start mesh
 (command ".3DMESH"
   ytimes (+ xtimes 1))
 ; start y location
 (setq yloc (nth 1 pnt0))
 (setq ynum 1)
 (repeat ytimes
   ; start x location
   (setq xloc (nth 0 pnt0))
   (setq xnum 1)
   (repeat xtimes
    ; grid pt
    (setq pnt1 (list xloc yloc 0))
    ; compute height
    (if (or (or (or (= ynum 1)
      (= ynum ytimes)) (= xnum 1))
      (= xnum xtimes))
     (setq zheight 0.0)
     (setq zheight
       (* (rn) maxheight))
    )
    ; grid pt
    (setq pnt2 (list
      (nth 0 pnt1)
      (nth 1 pnt1) zheight))
    ; add mesh pt
    (command pnt2)
    ; save first pt
    (if (= xnum 1) (setq pnt3 pnt2))
    ; inc x location
    (setq xloc (+ xloc xside))
    (setq xnum (+ xnum 1))
   )
   ; repeat first point
   (command pnt3)
   ; inc y location
   (setq yloc (+ yloc yside))
   (setq ynum (+ ynum 1))
 )
 (command ".ZOOM" "e")
 (princ)
)
;---------------------------------
```

Vertical edges of the mesh

Another way to handle the edge is to have the mesh sides be vertical, not just taper off, as they do now.

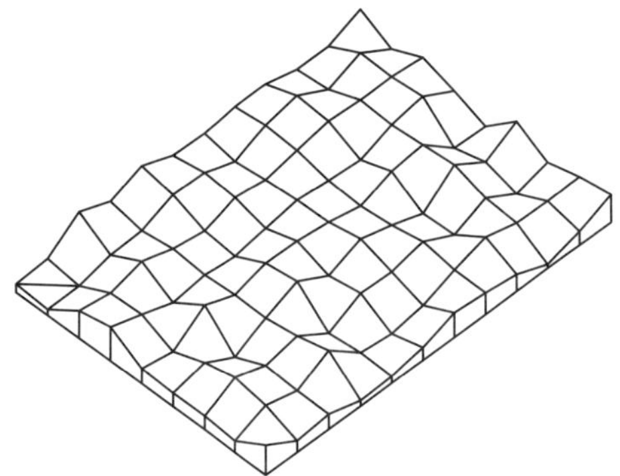

PROG04: mesh with vertical sides

Add function PROG04 using a copy of PROG01. To include the sides, add two more mesh rows and columns to the grid to account for side points:

```
; start mesh
(command ".3DMESH"
  (+ ytimes 2) (+ xtimes 2))
```

Each loop is also increased by 2 times.

The sides need to be located directly along the edge, at the first and last row and column of random heights. For the location increment, only increment the location if the x- and y-counter is after the first row and column or before the last row and column.

For example:

```
; inc x location
(if (and (> xnum 1)
   (< xnum (- (+ xtimes 2) 1)))
 (setq xloc (+ xloc xside))
)
```

As the edge may have a 0.0 height, also input a z-minimum value and add it to compute the random height. The random value will be between the maximum and minimum heights, as:

```
; compute height
(if (or (or (or (= ynum 1)
  (= ynum (+ ytimes 2)))
  (= xnum 1))
  (= xnum (+ xtimes 2)))
 (setq zheight 0.0)
 (setq zheight (+ (* (rn)
   (- maxheight minheight))
   minheight))
)
```

Sample script file for PROG04:

```
;---------------------------------
(prog04)
;Enter X side:
5
;Enter Y side:
5
;Enter number X repeats:
12
;Enter number Y repeats:
9
;Enter maximum height:
5.0
;Enter minimum height:
0.5
;---------------------------------
```

Completed function PROG04:

```
;---------------------------------
(defun prog04 ()
 (graphscr)
 (command ".ERASE" "all" "")
 ; set start point
 (setq pnt0 (list 0 0 0))
 (prompt "\nPROG04:")
 (setq xside
   (getdist pnt0
   "\nEnter X side:"))
 (setq yside
   (getdist pnt0
   "\nEnter Y side:"))
 (setq xtimes
   (getint
   "\nEnter number X repeats:"))
 (setq ytimes
   (getint
   "\nEnter number Y repeats:"))
 (setq maxheight
   (getdist pnt0
   "\nEnter maximum height:"))
 (setq minheight
   (getdist pnt0
   "\nEnter minimum height:"))
 ; start mesh
 (command ".3DMESH"
   (+ ytimes 2) (+ xtimes 2))
 ; start y location
 (setq yloc (nth 1 pnt0))
 (setq ynum 1)
 (repeat (+ ytimes 2)
  ; start x location
  (setq xloc (nth 0 pnt0))
  (setq xnum 1)
  (repeat (+ xtimes 2)
   ; grid pt
   (setq pnt1 (list xloc yloc 0))
   ; compute height
   (if (or (or (or (= ynum 1)
     (= ynum (+ ytimes 2)))
     (= xnum 1))
     (= xnum (+ xtimes 2)))
    (setq zheight 0.0)
    (setq zheight (+ (* (rn)
      (- maxheight minheight))
      minheight))
   )
   ; grid pt
   (setq pnt2 (list
     (nth 0 pnt1) (nth 1 pnt1)
     zheight))
   ; add mesh pt
   (command pnt2)
   ; inc x location
   (if (and (> xnum 1)
     (< xnum (- (+ xtimes 2) 1)))
    (setq xloc (+ xloc xside))
   )
   (setq xnum (+ xnum 1))
  )
  ; inc y location
  (if (and (> ynum 1)
    (< ynum (- (+ ytimes 2) 1)))
   (setq yloc (+ yloc yside))
  )
  (setq ynum (+ ynum 1))
 )
 (command ".ZOOM" "e")
 (princ)
)
;---------------------------------
```

Add bottom to vertical-edged mesh

Add function PROG05. Using a copy of PROG04, add the bottom surface as in PROG03.

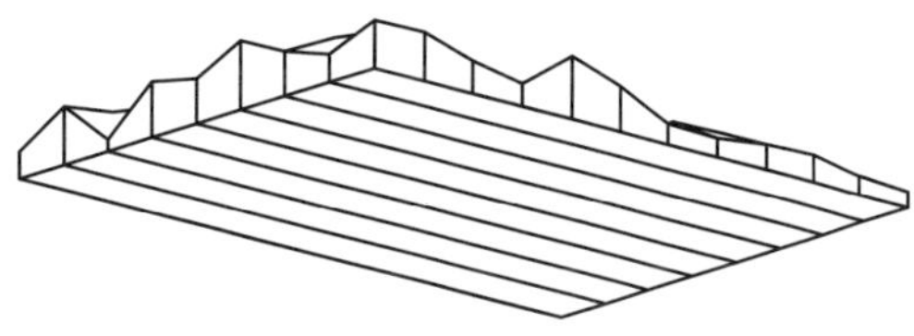

PROG05: mesh with vertical sides and bottom

Sample script file for PROG05:

```
;----------------------------------
(prog05)
;Enter X side:
5
;Enter Y side:
5
;Enter number X repeats:
12
;Enter number Y repeats:
9
;Enter maximum height:
5.0
;Enter minimum height:
0.5
;----------------------------------
```

Completed function PROG05:

```
;----------------------------------
(defun prog05 ()
 (graphscr)
 (command ".ERASE" "all" "")
 ; set start point
 (setq pnt0 (list 0 0 0))
 (prompt "\nPROG05:")
 (setq xside
   (getdist pnt0
   "\nEnter X side:"))
 (setq yside
   (getdist pnt0
   "\nEnter Y side:"))
 (setq xtimes
   (getint
   "\nEnter number X repeats:"))
 (setq ytimes
   (getint
   "\nEnter number Y repeats:"))
 (setq maxheight
   (getdist pnt0
   "\nEnter maximum height:"))
 (setq minheight
   (getdist pnt0
   "\nEnter minimum height:"))
 ; start mesh
 (command ".3DMESH"
   (+ ytimes 2) (+ (+ xtimes 2) 1))
 ; start y location
 (setq yloc (nth 1 pnt0))
 (setq ynum 1)
 (repeat (+ ytimes 2)
  ; start x location
  (setq xloc (nth 0 pnt0))
  (setq xnum 1)
  (repeat (+ xtimes 2)
   ; grid pt
   (setq pnt1 (list xloc yloc 0))
   ; compute height
   (if (or (or (or (= ynum 1)
     (= ynum (+ ytimes 2)))
     (= xnum 1))
     (= xnum (+ xtimes 2)))
    (setq zheight 0.0)
    (setq zheight (+ (* (rn)
      (- maxheight minheight))
      minheight))
   )
   ; grid pt
   (setq pnt2 (list
     (nth 0 pnt1) (nth 1 pnt1) zheight))
   ; add mesh pt
   (command pnt2)
   ; save first pt
   (if (= xnum 1) (setq pnt3 pnt2))
   ; inc x location
   (if (and (> xnum 1)
     (< xnum (- (+ xtimes 2) 1)))
    (setq xloc (+ xloc xside))
   )
   (setq xnum (+ xnum 1))
  )
  ; repeat first point
  (command pnt3)
  ; inc y location
  (if (and (> ynum 1)
    (< ynum (- (+ ytimes 2) 1)))
   (setq yloc (+ yloc yside))
  )
  (setq ynum (+ ynum 1))
 )
 (command ".ZOOM" "e")
 (princ)
)
;----------------------------------
```

Vary the amount of randomness by distance

Add function PROG06. Using a copy of PROG05, compute a random height based on the x-distance of each location relative to the distance to the right edge. The closer to the right edge, the greater the height.

The only modification is the random height computation, which changes to:

```
; compute height
(if (or (or (or (= ynum 1)
  (= ynum (+ ytimes 2)))
  (= xnum 1))
  (= xnum (+ xtimes 2)))
 (setq zheight 0.0)
 (setq zheight (+ (* (rn)
   (* (/ xloc (* xside xtimes))
   (- maxheight minheight)))
   minheight))
)
```

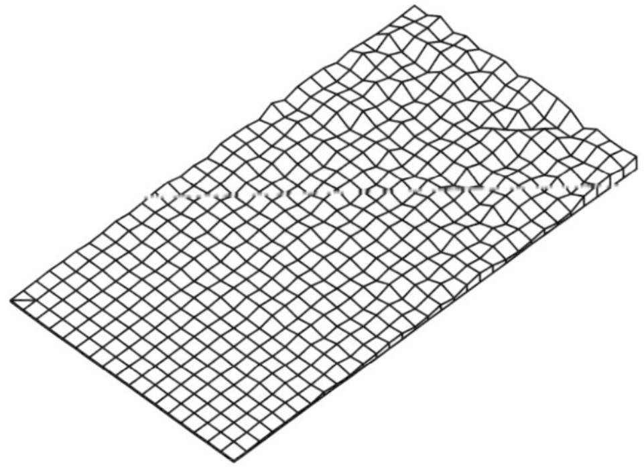

PROG06: mesh with increased randomness

The sample script file for PROG06 is the same as the one for PROG05, except the size of the mesh doubles to 24 by 18.

Develop other methods to vary the distribution of randomness.

* Distance from another edge; increasing or decreasing
* Distance from a corner; increasing or decreasing
* Distance from the center; increasing or decreasing
* Distance from any entered coordinate; increasing or decreasing

Vary the amount of randomness by a mathematical function

To simply increase or decrease the rate of randomness, the random height can be based on a mathematical function.

Add function PROG07. Using a copy of PROG06, compute the random height based on the mathematical function sine.

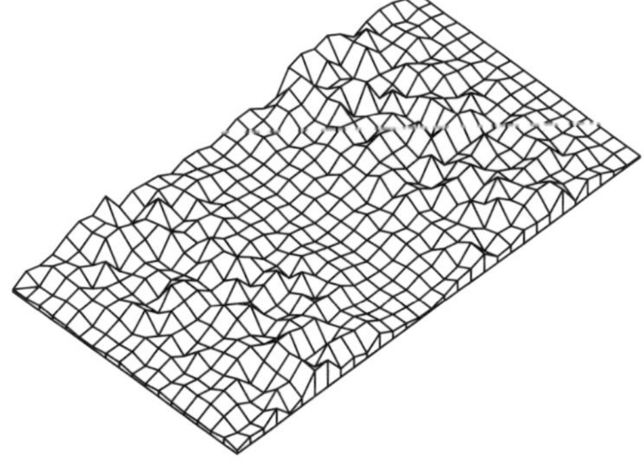

PROG07: mesh with randomness by a mathematical function

Compute the random height as:

```
; compute height
(if (or (or (or (= ynum 1)
  (= ynum (+ ytimes 2)))
  (= xnum 1))
  (= xnum (+ xtimes 2)))
 (setq zheight 0.0)
 (setq zheight (+ (* (rn)
   (* (abs (sin (dtr ang)))
   (- maxheight minheight)))
   minheight))
)
```

In this example, the absolute value of the sine curve will cover 360 degrees in each row. Add an angle and angle increment; start the angle at zero and increment it at each position along the x-axis. In this case, include the absolute value so that negative values are not computed.

Sample script file for PROG07:

```
;----------------------------------
(prog07)
;Enter X side:
5
;Enter Y side:
5
;Enter number X repeats:
12
;Enter number Y repeats:
9
;Enter maximum height:
5.0
;Enter minimum height:
0.5
;----------------------------------
```

Completed function PROG07:

```
;----------------------------------
(defun prog07 ()
 (graphscr)
 (command ".ERASE" "all" "")
 ; set start point
 (setq pnt0 (list 0 0 0))
 (prompt "\nPROG07:")
 (setq xside
   (getdist pnt0
   "\nEnter X side:"))
 (setq yside
   (getdist pnt0
   "\nEnter Y side:"))
 (setq xtimes
   (getint
   "\nEnter number X repeats:"))
 (setq ytimes
   (getint
   "\nEnter number Y repeats:"))
 (setq maxheight
   (getdist pnt0
   "\nEnter maximum height:"))
 (setq minheight
   (getdist pnt0
   "\nEnter minimum height:"))
 ; start mesh
 (command ".3DMESH"
   (+ ytimes 2) (+ (+ xtimes 2) 1))
 ; start y location
 (setq yloc (nth 1 pnt0))
 (setq ynum 1)
 (repeat (+ ytimes 2)
  ; ang start and inc
  (setq ang 0.0)
  (setq anginc (/ 360.0 xtimes))
  ; start x location
  (setq xloc (nth 0 pnt0))
  (setq xnum 1)
  (repeat (+ xtimes 2)
   ; grid pt
   (setq pnt1 (list xloc yloc 0))
   ; compute height
   (if (or (or (or (= ynum 1)
     (= ynum (+ ytimes 2)))
     (= xnum 1))
     (= xnum (+ xtimes 2)))
```

```
      (setq zheight 0.0)
      (setq zheight (+ (* (rn)
        (* (abs (sin (dtr ang)))
        (- maxheight minheight)))
        minheight))
    )
    ; grid pt
    (setq pnt2 (list
      (nth 0 pnt1) (nth 1 pnt1)
      zheight))
    ; add mesh pt
    (command pnt2)
    ; save first pt
    (if (= xnum 1) (setq pnt3 pnt2))
    ; inc x location
    (if (and (> xnum 1)
      (< xnum (- (+ xtimes 2) 1)))
     (setq xloc (+ xloc xside))
    )
    (setq xnum (+ xnum 1))
    ; inc angle
    (setq ang (+ ang anginc))
   )
   ; repeat first point
   (command pnt3)
   ; inc y location
   (if (and (> ynum 1)
     (< ynum (- (+ ytimes 2) 1)))
    (setq yloc (+ yloc yside))
   )
   (setq ynum (+ ynum 1))
  )
  (command ".ZOOM" "e")
  (princ)
)
;-----------------------------------
```

Random selection of a mathematical function

To generate a smoother surface variation, use a mathematical function for the heights, but for each row start the function with a different randomly selected starting angle and the total number of degrees it will cover.

Add function PROG08. Using a copy of PROG07, randomly select the starting angle and total angle for the height to be varied.

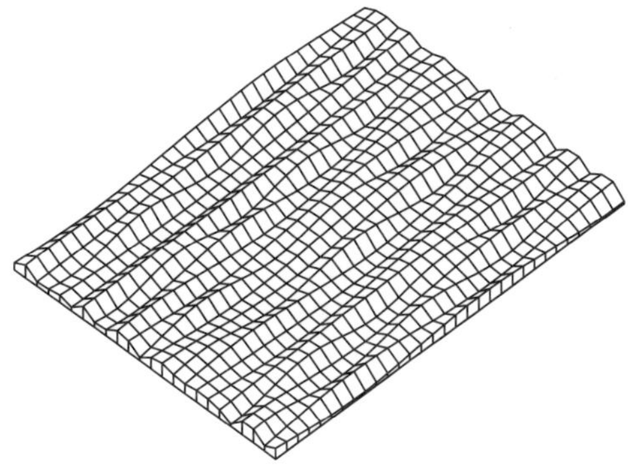

PROG08: mesh with randomness varying a mathematical function

At the start of each row, compute a random starting angle and a random total degrees based on an entered angle increment, as:

```
; ang start and inc
(setq ang (* (fix (* (rn)
  12.0)) xanginc))
(setq totalang (* (fix (* (rn)
  24.0)) xanginc))
(setq anginc
  (/ totalang xtimes)
```

The constants 12.0 and 24.0 are used to compute a random multiplier for the angle increment. Any constant could be used.

To relate the multiplier to the angle increment directly, so it generates 0 to 360 degrees, use:

```
(setq multi (+ (/ 360.0 xanginc) 0.99))
```

The height is then computed as:

```
; compute height
(if (or (or (or (= ynum 1)
  (= ynum (+ ytimes 2)))
  (= xnum 1))
  (= xnum (+ xtimes 2)))
 (setq zheight 0.0)
 (setq zheight
   (+ (* (sin (dtr ang))
   (- maxheight minheight))
   minheight))
)
```

Sample script file for PROG08:

```
;----------------------------------
(prog08)
;Enter X side:
5
;Enter Y side:
5
;Enter number X repeats:
32
;Enter number Y repeats:
24
;Enter maximum height:
6.0
;Enter minimum height:
3.5
;Enter angle increment:
45
;----------------------------------
```

Completed function PROG08:

```
;----------------------------------
(defun prog08 ()
 (graphscr)
 (command ".ERASE" "all" "")
 ; set start point
 (setq pnt0 (list 0 0 0))
 (prompt "\nPROG08:")
 (setq xside
   (getdist pnt0
   "\nEnter X side:"))
 (setq yside
   (getdist pnt0
   "\nEnter Y side:"))
 (setq xtimes
   (getint
   "\nEnter number X repeats:"))
 (setq ytimes
   (getint
   "\nEnter number Y repeats:"))
 (setq maxheight
   (getdist pnt0
   "\nEnter maximum height:"))
 (setq minheight
   (getdist pnt0
   "\nEnter minimum height:"))
 (setq xanginc
   (getint
   "\nEnter angle increment:"))
 ; start mesh
 (command ".3DMESH"
   (+ ytimes 2) (+ (+ xtimes 2) 1))
 ; start y location
 (setq yloc (nth 1 pnt0))
 (setq ynum 1)
 (repeat (+ ytimes 2)
  ; ang start and inc
  (setq ang (* (fix
    (* (rn) 12.0)) xanginc))
  (setq totalang (* (fix
    (* (rn) 24.0)) xanginc))
  (setq anginc (/ totalang xtimes))
  ; start x location
  (setq xloc (nth 0 pnt0))
  (setq xnum 1)
  (repeat (+ xtimes 2)
   ; grid pt
   (setq pnt1 (list xloc yloc 0))
   ; compute height
   (if (or (or (or (= ynum 1)
     (= ynum (+ ytimes 2)))
     (= xnum 1))
     (= xnum (+ xtimes 2)))
    (setq zheight 0.0)
    (setq zheight
      (+ (* (sin (dtr ang))
      (- maxheight minheight))
      minheight))
   )
```

```
    ; grid pt
    (setq pnt2 (list
      (nth 0 pnt1) (nth 1 pnt1)
      zheight))
    ; add mesh pt
    (command pnt2)
    ; save first pt
    (if (= xnum 1) (setq pnt3 pnt2))
    ; inc x location
    (if (and (> xnum 1)
      (< xnum (- (+ xtimes 2) 1)))
     (setq xloc (+ xloc xside))
    )
    (setq xnum (+ xnum 1))
    ; inc angle
    (setq ang (+ ang anginc))
   )
   ; repeat first point
   (command pnt3)
   ; inc y location
   (if (and (> ynum 1)
     (< ynum (- (+ ytimes 2) 1)))
    (setq yloc (+ yloc yside))
   )
   (setq ynum (+ ynum 1))
  )
  (command ".ZOOM" "e")
  (princ)
)
;-----------------------------------
```

Set edge heights on the mesh

The heights of the edges are randomly computed and will vary. Compute the edge height so that panels can be placed adjacent to each other with no variation in heights.

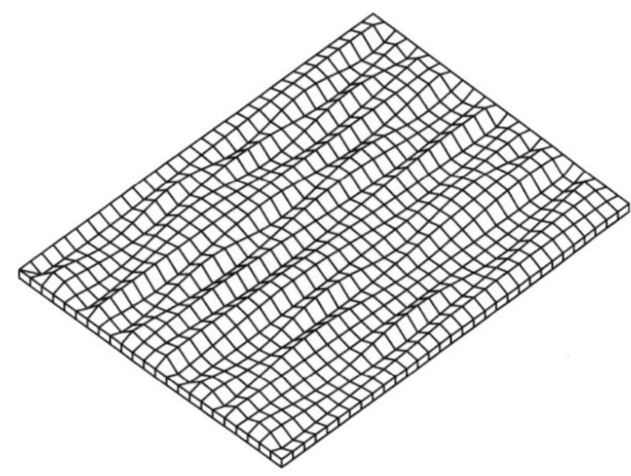

PROG09: mesh with a set edge height

Add function PROG09. Using a copy of PROG08, set each edge to the minimum height; this forms a straight edge for the panels to be placed adjacent to each other.

The computation of the height is as follows, including checking the outside edges to set their height.

After:

```
; compute height
(if (or (or (or (= ynum 1)
  (= ynum (+ ytimes 2)))
  (= xnum 1))
  (= xnum (+ xtimes 2)))
 (progn
  (setq zheight 0.0)
  (setq yoff 0.0)
)
 (setq zheight
   (+ (* (sin (dtr ang))
   (- maxheight minheight))
   minheight))
)
```

Add:

```
; near edge
(if (and (= ynum 2) (> xnum 1)
  (< xnum (+ xtimes 2)))
 (progn
  (setq zheight minheight)
  (setq yoff 0.0)
))
; far edge
(if (and (= ynum (+ ytimes 1))
  (> xnum 1)
  (< xnum (+ xtimes 2)))
 (progn
  (setq zheight minheight)
  (setq yoff 0.0)
))
; left edge
(if (and (= xnum 2) (> ynum 1)
  (< ynum (+ ytimes 2)))
 (progn
  (setq zheight minheight)
  (setq yoff 0.0)
))
; right edge
(if (and (= xnum (+ xtimes 1))
  (> ynum 1) (< ynum (+ ytimes 2)))
 (progn
  (setq zheight minheight)
  (setq yoff 0.0)
))
```

An additional variation using a curve to control the height is to have it control a y-offset of each edge point.

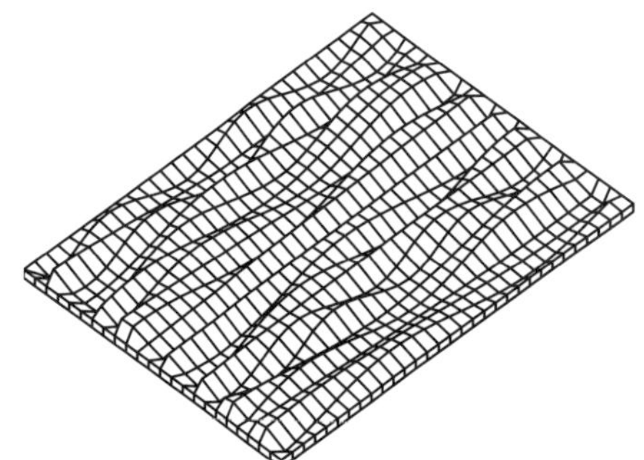

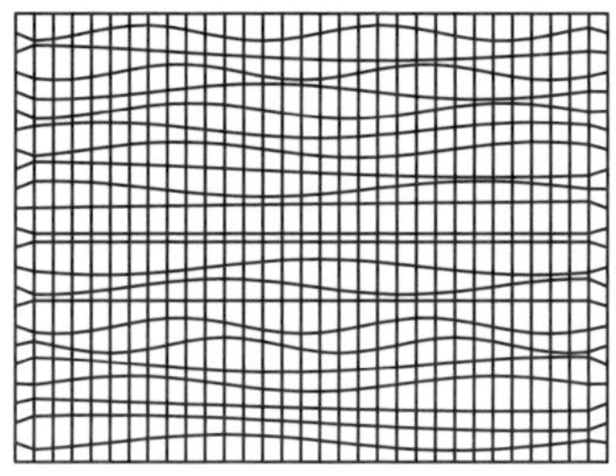

PROG09a: mesh with y-offset

Add function PROG09a. Using a copy of PROG9, add input for a maximum y-offset, and compute the offset for each point using the same method as the height.

For example:

```
; compute Y offset
(setq yoff
  (* (sin (dtr ang)) maxyoff))
```

This offset would be added to the mesh point as:

```
; grid pt
(setq pnt2 (list
  (nth 0 pnt1)
  (+ (nth 1 pnt1) yoff)
   zheight))
```

Review function PROG09a and note how the y-offset is reset when an edge point is found.

Sample script file for PROG09a:

```
;----------------------------------
(prog09a)
;Enter X side:
5
;Enter Y side:
5
;Enter number X repeats:
32
;Enter number Y repeats:
24
;Enter maximum height:
6.0
;Enter minimum height:
3.5
;Enter angle increment:
45
;Enter maximum Y offset
2.0
;----------------------------------
```

Completed function PROG09a:

```
;----------------------------------
(defun prog09a ()
 (graphscr)
 (command ".ERASE" "all" "")
 ; set start point
 (setq pnt0 (list 0 0 0))
 (prompt "\nPROG09a:")
 (setq xside
   (getdist pnt0
   "\nEnter X side:"))
 (setq yside
   (getdist pnt0
   "\nEnter Y side:"))
 (setq xtimes
   (getint
   "\nEnter number X repeats:"))
 (setq ytimes
   (getint
   "\nEnter number Y repeats:"))
 (setq maxheight
   (getdist pnt0
   "\nEnter maximum height:"))
 (setq minheight
   (getdist pnt0
   "\nEnter minimum height:"))
(setq xanginc
   (getint
   "\nEnter angle increment:"))
(setq maxyoff
   (getdist
   "\nEnter maximum Y offset:"))
; start mesh
(command ".3DMESH"
   (+ ytimes 2) (+ (+ xtimes 2) 1))
; start y location
(setq yloc (nth 1 pnt0))
(setq ynum 1)
(repeat (+ ytimes 2)
 ; ang start and inc
 (setq ang (* (fix
   (* (rn) 12.0)) xanginc))
 (setq totalang (* (fix
   (* (rn) 24.0)) xanginc))
 (setq anginc (/ totalang xtimes))
 ; start x location
 (setq xloc (nth 0 pnt0))
 (setq xnum 1)
 (repeat (+ xtimes 2)
  ; grid pt
  (setq pnt1 (list xloc yloc 0))
  ; compute Y offset
  (setq yoff
    (* (sin (dtr ang)) maxyoff))
  ; compute height
  (if (or (or (or (= ynum 1)
    (= ynum (+ ytimes 2)))
    (= xnum 1))
    (= xnum (+ xtimes 2)))
   (progn
    (setq zheight 0.0)
    (setq yoff 0.0)
  )
   (setq zheight
     (+ (* (sin (dtr ang))
     (- maxheight minheight))
     minheight))
  )
  ; near edge
  (if (and (= ynum 2) (> xnum 1)
    (< xnum (+ xtimes 2)))
   (progn
```

```
      (setq zheight minheight)
      (setq yoff 0.0)
    ))
    ; far edge
    (if (and (= ynum (+ ytimes 1))
      (> xnum 1)
      (< xnum (+ xtimes 2)))
     (progn
      (setq zheight minheight)
      (setq yoff 0.0)
    ))
    ; left edge
    (if (and (= xnum 2) (> ynum 1)
      (< ynum (+ ytimes 2)))
     (progn
      (setq zheight minheight)
      (setq yoff 0.0)
    ))
    ; right edge
    (if (and (= xnum (+ xtimes 1))
      (> ynum 1) (< ynum (+ ytimes 2)))
     (progn
      (setq zheight minheight)
      (setq yoff 0.0)
    ))
    ; grid pt
    (setq pnt2 (list
      (nth 0 pnt1)
      (+ (nth 1 pnt1) yoff) zheight))
    ; add mesh pt
    (command pnt2)
    ; save first pt
    (if (= xnum 1) (setq pnt3 pnt2))
    ; inc x location
    (if (and (> xnum 1)
      (< xnum (- (+ xtimes 2) 1)))
     (setq xloc (+ xloc xside))
    )
    (setq xnum (+ xnum 1))
    ; inc angle
    (setq ang (+ ang anginc))
  )
  ; repeat first point
  (command pnt3)
  ; inc y location
  (if (and (> ynum 1)
    (< ynum (- (+ ytimes 2) 1)))
   (setq yloc (+ yloc yside))
  )
   (setq ynum (+ ynum 1))
 )
 (command ".ZOOM" "e")
 (princ)
)
;----------------------------------
```

Selection of multiple mathematical functions

Additional variations can be included by randomly selecting a different mathematical function to compute the heights.

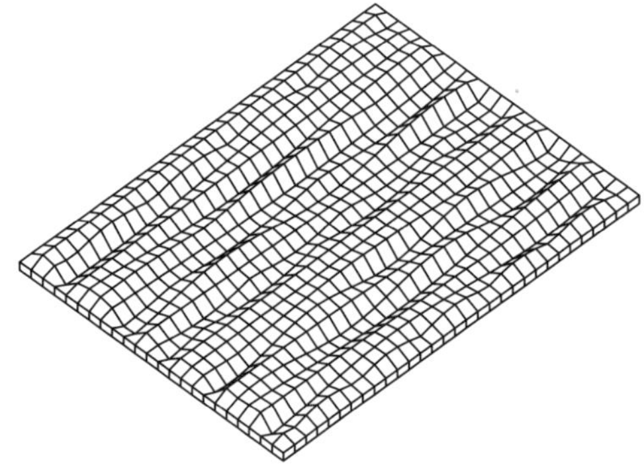

PROG10: mesh using multiple mathematical functions

Add PROG10. Using a copy of PROG09, add the random selection of a function to control the mesh height. Include 4 to 6 functions; select one at the start of each row. One of the function selections should have the height constant.

The function is selected randomly by number as:

```
; select function
(setq nfunc (+ (fix
  (* (rn) 6.99)) 1))
```

Each is selected for height computation as:

```
(progn
 (setq zmaxoff
   (- maxheight minheight))
 (if (= nfunc 1) (setq zoff
   (* zmaxoff 0.5)))
 (if (= nfunc 2) (setq zoff
   (* (sin (dtr ang))
     zmaxoff)))
 (if (= nfunc 3) (setq zoff
   (* (abs (sin (dtr ang)))
   zmaxoff)))
 (if (= nfunc 4) (setq zoff
   (* (* (abs (sin (dtr ang)))
   zmaxoff) -1)))
 (if (= nfunc 5) (setq zoff
   (* (cos (dtr ang))
   zmaxoff)))
 (if (= nfunc 6) (setq zoff
   (* (abs (cos (dtr ang)))
   zmaxoff)))
 (if (= nfunc 7) (setq zoff
   (* (* (abs (cos (dtr ang)))
   zmaxoff) -1)))
 (setq zheight
   (+ minheight zoff))
)
)
```

Sample script file for PROG10:

```
;---------------------------------
(prog10)
;Enter X side:
5
;Enter Y side:
5
;Enter number X repeats:
32
;Enter number Y repeats:
24
;Enter maximum height:
6.5
;Enter minimum height:
3.5
;Enter angle increment:
45
;---------------------------------
```

Completed function PROG10:

```
;---------------------------------
(defun prog10 ()
 (graphscr)
 (command ".ERASE" "all" "")
 ; set start point
 (setq pnt0 (list 0 0 0))
 (prompt "\nPROG10:")
 (setq xside
   (getdist pnt0
   "\nEnter X side:"))
 (setq yside
   (getdist pnt0
   "\nEnter Y side:"))
 (setq xtimes
   (getint
   "\nEnter number X repeats:"))
 (setq ytimes
   (getint
   "\nEnter number Y repeats:"))
 (setq maxheight
   (getdist pnt0
   "\nEnter maximum height:"))
 (setq minheight
   (getdist pnt0
   "\nEnter minimum height:"))
 (setq xanginc
   (getint
   "\nEnter angle increment:"))
 ; start mesh
 (command ".3DMESH"
   (+ ytimes 2) (+ (+ xtimes 2) 1))
 ; start y location
 (setq yloc (nth 1 pnt0))
 (setq ynum 1)
 (repeat (+ ytimes 2)
  ; ang start and inc
  (setq ang (* (fix
    (* (rn) 12.0)) xanginc))
  (setq totalang (* (fix
    (* (rn) 24.0)) xanginc))
  (setq anginc (/ totalang xtimes))
  ; select function
  (setq nfunc (+ (fix
    (* (rn) 6.99)) 1))
  ; start x location
  (setq xloc (nth 0 pnt0))
  (setq xnum 1)
```

```
(repeat (+ xtimes 2)
 ; grid pt
 (setq pnt1 (list xloc yloc 0))
 ; compute height
 (if (or (or (or (= ynum 1)
    (= ynum (+ ytimes 2)))
    (= xnum 1))
    (= xnum (+ xtimes 2)))
  (progn
   (setq zheight 0.0)
  )
  (progn
   (setq zmaxoff
     (- maxheight minheight))
   (if (= nfunc 1) (setq zoff
     (* zmaxoff 0.5)))
   (if (= nfunc 2) (setq zoff
     (* (sin (dtr ang))
       zmaxoff)))
   (if (= nfunc 3) (setq zoff
     (* (abs (sin (dtr ang)))
     zmaxoff)))
   (if (= nfunc 4) (setq zoff
     (* (* (abs (sin (dtr ang)))
     zmaxoff) -1)))
   (if (= nfunc 5) (setq zoff
     (* (cos (dtr ang))
     zmaxoff)))
   (if (= nfunc 6) (setq zoff
     (* (abs (cos (dtr ang)))
     zmaxoff)))
   (if (= nfunc 7) (setq zoff
     (* (* (abs (cos (dtr ang)))
     zmaxoff) -1)))
   (setq zheight
     (+ minheight zoff))
  )
 )
 ; near edge
 (if (and (= ynum 2) (> xnum 1)
   (< xnum (+ xtimes 2)))
  (setq zheight minheight)
 )
 ; far edge
 (if (and (= ynum (+ ytimes 1))
   (> xnum 1)
   (< xnum (+ xtimes 2)))
  (setq zheight minheight)
 )
   ; left edge
   (if (and (= xnum 2) (> ynum 1)
     (< ynum (+ ytimes 2)))
    (setq zheight minheight)
   )
   ; right edge
   (if (and (= xnum (+ xtimes 1))
     (> ynum 1)
     (< ynum (+ ytimes 2)))
    (setq zheight minheight)
   )
   ; grid pt
   (setq pnt2 (list
     (nth 0 pnt1) (nth 1 pnt1)
     zheight))
   ; add mesh pt
   (command pnt2)
   ; save first pt
   (if (= xnum 1) (setq pnt3 pnt2))
   ; inc x location
   (if (and (> xnum 1)
     (< xnum (- (+ xtimes 2) 1)))
    (setq xloc (+ xloc xside))
   )
   (setq xnum (+ xnum 1))
   ; inc angle
   (setq ang (+ ang anginc))
  )
  ; repeat first point
  (command pnt3)
  ; inc y location
  (if (and (> ynum 1)
    (< ynum (- (+ ytimes 2) 1)))
   (setq yloc (+ yloc yside))
  )
  (setq ynum (+ ynum 1))
 )
 (command ".ZOOM" "e")
 (princ)
)
;---------------------------------
```

Construct a simple vertical mesh

Using function PROG01 in this series, reconstruct it so that the y-axis is the z-axis, and the x-axis is based on radial measure. The normally horizontal mesh can now be cylindrical.

The input changes to number of radial points and number of points along the height.

Add function PROG11. Construct a simple cylinder based on the entered height and radius.

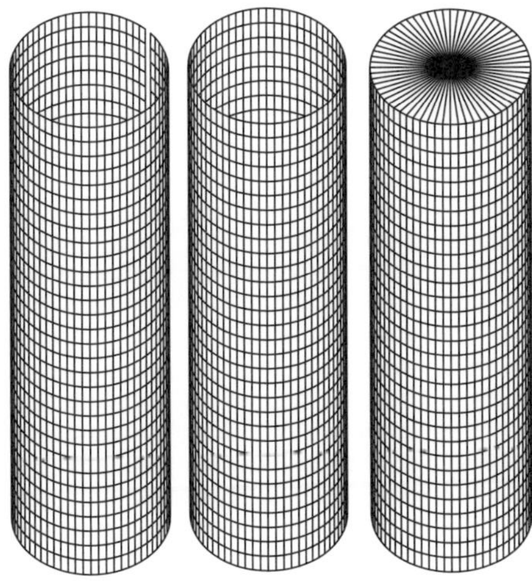

PROG11, 11a and 11b: vertical mesh, open, closed, and with a top and bottom

Review function PROG11, including: input parameters, computing the height and radial increments, computation of the radial distance, and incrementing the angle and height.

Sample script file for PROG11:

```
;----------------------------------
(prog11)
;Enter number radial points:
64
;Enter number Z points:
32
;Enter maximum height:
12
;Enter radius:
1.5
;----------------------------------
```

Completed function PROG11:

```
;----------------------------------
(defun prog11 ()
 (graphscr)
 (command ".ERASE" "all" "")
 ; set start point
 (setq pnt0 (list 0 0 0))
 (prompt "\nPROG11:")
 (setq rtimes
   (getint
   "\nEnter number radial points:"))
 (setq ztimes
   (getint
   "\nEnter number Z points:"))
 (setq maxheight
   (getdist pnt0
   "\nEnter maximum height:"))
 (setq crad
   (getdist pnt0
   "\nEnter radius:"))
 ; Z inc
 (setq zinc (/ maxheight ztimes))
 (command ".3DMESH" ztimes rtimes)
 ; start z location
 (setq zloc (nth 2 pnt0))
 (repeat ztimes
  ; start radial location
  (setq rang 0.0)
  (setq ranginc (/ 360.0 rtimes))
  (repeat rtimes
   ; radial distance
   (setq xoff
```

```
      (* crad (cos (dtr rang))))
    (setq yoff
      (* crad (sin (dtr rang))))
    ; grid pt
    (setq npnt (list
      (+ (nth 0 pnt0) xoff)
      (+ (nth 1 pnt0) yoff) zloc))
    ; add mesh pt
    (command npnt)
    ; inc radial location
    (setq rang (+ rang ranginc))
   )
   ; inc z location
   (setq zloc (+ zloc zinc))
  )
  (command ".ZOOM" "e")
  (princ)
)
;---------------------------------
```

Note that the mesh does not meet back at the start.

Add function PROG11a. Using a copy of PROG11, capture the first point and add it to the mesh after each radial set of points completes. Add a counter to the radial points to determine when the first one computes. Increase the number of radial points in the mesh by one.

Completed function PROG11a:

```
;---------------------------------
(defun prog11a ()
  (graphscr)
  (command ".ERASE" "all" "")
  ; set start point
  (setq pnt0 (list 0 0 0))
  (prompt "\nPROG11a:")
  (setq rtimes
    (getint
    "\nEnter number radial points:"))
  (setq ztimes
    (getint
    "\nEnter number Z points:"))
  (setq maxheight
    (getdist pnt0
    "\nEnter maximum height:"))
  (setq crad
    (getdist pnt0
    "\nEnter radius:"))
  ; Z inc
  (setq zinc (/ maxheight ztimes))
  (command ".3DMESH"
    ztimes (+ rtimes 1))
  ; start z location
  (setq zloc (nth 2 pnt0))
  (repeat ztimes
   ; start radial location
   (setq rang 0.0)
   (setq ranginc (/ 360.0 rtimes))
   (setq rnum 1)
   (repeat rtimes
    ; radial distance
    (setq xoff
      (* crad (cos (dtr rang))))
    (setq yoff
      (* crad (sin (dtr rang))))
    ; grid pt
    (setq npnt (list
      (+ (nth 0 pnt0) xoff)
     (+ (nth 1 pnt0) yoff) zloc))
    ; add mesh pt
    (command npnt)
    ; save first pt
    (if (= rnum 1) (setq fpnt npnt))
    ; inc radial location
    (setq rang (+ rang ranginc))
    (setq rnum (+ rnum 1))
   )
   ; add first pt
   (command fpnt)
   ; inc z location
   (setq zloc (+ zloc zinc))
  )
  (command ".ZOOM" "e")
  (princ)
)
;---------------------------------
```

The mesh also requires bottom and top surfaces.

Add function PROG11b. Using PROG11a, add a top and bottom to the mesh. Before the first set of radial points and after the last set, add the centerpoint to the mesh. Increase the number of z-points to the mesh by two.

Completed function PROG11b:

```
;-----------------------------------
(defun prog11b ()
 (graphscr)
 (command ".ERASE" "all" "")
 ; set start point
 (setq pnt0 (list 0 0 0))
 (prompt "\nPROG11b:")
 (setq rtimes
   (getint
   "\nEnter number radial points:"))
 (setq ztimes
   (getint
   "\nEnter number Z points:"))
 (setq maxheight
   (getdist pnt0
   "\nEnter maximum height:"))
 (setq crad
   (getdist pnt0
   "\nEnter radius:"))
 ; Z inc
 (setq zinc (/ maxheight ztimes))
 (command ".3DMESH"
   (+ ztimes 2) (+ rtimes 1))
 ; bottom pts
 (repeat (+ rtimes 1)
  (command pnt0)
 )
 ; start z location
 (setq zloc (nth 2 pnt0))
 (repeat ztimes
  ; start radial location
  (setq rang 0.0)
  (setq ranginc (/ 360.0 rtimes))
  (setq rnum 1)
  (repeat rtimes
   ; radial distance
   (setq xoff
     (* crad (cos (dtr rang))))
   (setq yoff
     (* crad (sin (dtr rang))))
   ; grid pt
   (setq npnt (list
     (+ (nth 0 pnt0) xoff)
     (+ (nth 1 pnt0) yoff) zloc))
   ; add mesh pt
   (command npnt)
   ; save first pt
   (if (= rnum 1) (setq fpnt npnt))
   ; inc radial location
   (setq rang (+ rang ranginc))
   (setq rnum (+ rnum 1))
  )
  ; add first pt
  (command fpnt)
  ; inc z location
  (setq zloc (+ zloc zinc))
 )
 ; bottom pts
 (repeat (+ rtimes 1)
  (command (list
    (nth 0 pnt0) (nth 1 pnt0)
    (- zloc zinc)))
 )
 (command ".ZOOM" "e")
 (princ)
)
;-----------------------------------
```

Random variation in radius for the vertical mesh

With a completed vertical mesh, add a radial offset based on a mathematical function, similar to the method used in PROG08.

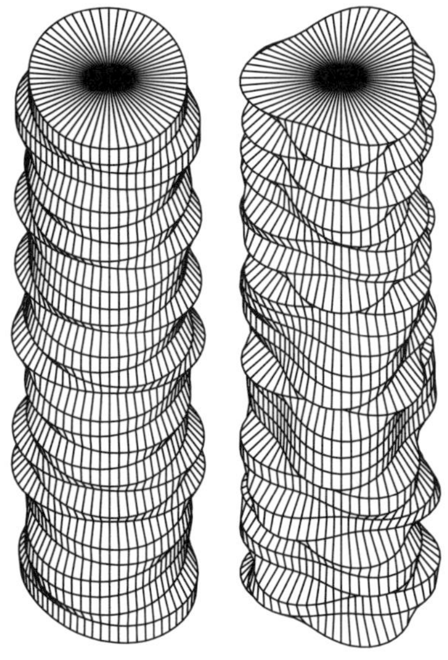

PROG12: random variation of a radius offset

Add function PROG12. Using a copy of PROG11b, add input for a radius offset, starting angle increment, and number of 360-degree cycles for the sine curve to cover.

Compute the offset angle increment as:

```
; offset ang
(setq sang (* (fix (* (rn)
  24)) fanginc))
(setq sanginc
  (/ (* 360.0 fcycles) rtimes))
```

Compute a new radius with the offset included based on the sine curve, using:

```
; radial distance
(setq nrad (+ crad
  (* (sin (dtr sang)) cradoff)))
(setq xoff
  (* nrad (cos (dtr rang))))
(setq yoff
  (* nrad (sin (dtr rang))))
```

Note that some values for the number of cycles may generate a bump at the closure of the mesh, as the first point meets the last point.

A simple alternative to vary the curve even more is to randomly select the number of 360-degree cycles based on a maximum number of cycles. In this case, the number of cycles is the same for every radial series of points.

Sample script file for PROG12:

```
;-----------------------------------
(prog12)
;Enter number radial points:
64
;Enter number Z points:
32
;Enter maximum height:
12
;Enter radius:
1.5
;Enter radius offset:
0.15
;Enter starting angle increment:
10
;Enter total angle cycles:
2.0
;-----------------------------------
```

The second example used a radius offset of 0.25 and number of cycles as 3.0.

Completed function PROG12:

```
;----------------------------------
(defun prog12 ()
 (graphscr)
 (command ".ERASE" "all" "")
 ; set start point
 (setq pnt0 (list 0 0 0))
 (prompt "\nPROG12:")
 (setq rtimes
   (getint
   "\nEnter number radial points:"))
 (setq ztimes
   (getint
   "\nEnter number Z points:"))
 (setq maxheight
   (getdist pnt0
   "\nEnter maximum height:"))
 (setq crad
   (getdist pnt0
   "\nEnter radius:"))
 (setq cradoff
   (getdist pnt0
   "\nEnter radius offset:"))
 (setq fanginc
   (getint
   "\Enter starting angle
    increment:"))
 (setq fcycles
   (getreal
   "\Enter total angle cycles:"))
 ; Z inc
 (setq zinc (/ maxheight ztimes))
 (command ".3DMESH"
   (+ ztimes 2) (+ rtimes 1))
 ; bottom pts
 (repeat (+ rtimes 1)
  (command pnt0)
 )
 ; start z location
 (setq zloc (nth 2 pnt0))
 (repeat ztimes
  ; offset ang
  (setq sang (* (fix
    (* (rn) 24)) fanginc))
  (setq sanginc
    (/ (* 360.0 fcycles) rtimes))
  ; start radial location
  (setq rang 0.0)
  (setq ranginc (/ 360.0 rtimes))
  (setq rnum 1)
  (repeat rtimes
   ; radial distance
   (setq nrad (+ crad
     (* (sin (dtr sang)) cradoff)))
   (setq xoff
     (* nrad (cos (dtr rang))))
   (setq yoff
     (* nrad (sin (dtr rang))))
   ; grid pt
   (setq npnt (list
     (+ (nth 0 pnt0) xoff)
     (+ (nth 1 pnt0) yoff) zloc))
   ; add mesh pt
   (command npnt)
   ; save first pt
   (if (= rnum 1) (setq fpnt npnt))
   ; inc radial location
   (setq rang (+ rang ranginc))
   (setq rnum (+ rnum 1))
   (setq sang (+ sang sanginc))
  )
  ; add first pt
  (command fpnt)
  ; inc z location
  (setq zloc (+ zloc zinc))
 )
 ; bottom pts
 (repeat (+ rtimes 1)
  (command (list
    (nth 0 pnt0) (nth 1 pnt0)
    (- zloc zinc)))
 )
 (command ".ZOOM" "e")
 (princ)
)
;----------------------------------
```

Modify the direction of the random variation for the vertical mesh

In the previous example, the sine-curve offset was for the radial series of points around the cylinder. Flip the curve so that random changes move along the vertical axis of the cylinder.

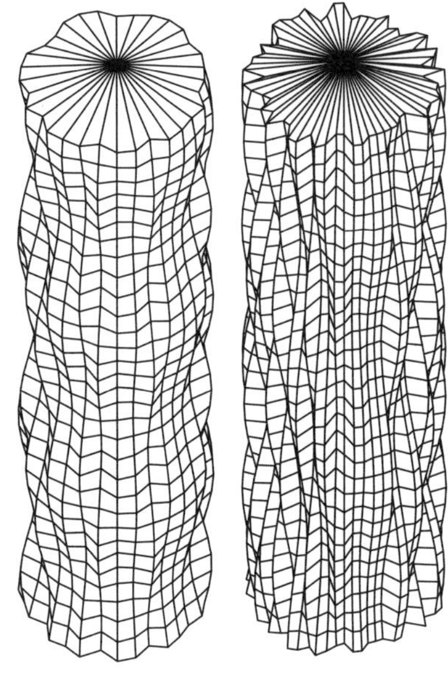

PROG13: vertical random variation of radius offset

Add function PROG13. Using a copy of PROG12, switch the loop parameters so that the outside loop controls the change in sine curve.

Review PROG13 on how the direction was switched from horizontal rings to vertical folds along the cylinder.

Sample script file for PROG13:

```
;-----------------------------------
(prog13)
;Enter number radial points:
32
;Enter number Z points:
32
;Enter maximum height:
12
;Enter radius:
1.5
;Enter radius offset:
0.15
;Enter starting angle increment:
10
;Enter total angle cycles:
3.0
;-----------------------------------
```

Completed function PROG13:

```
;-----------------------------------
(defun prog13 ()
 (graphscr)
 (command ".ERASE" "all" "")
 ; set start point
 (setq pnt0 (list 0 0 0))
 (prompt "\nPROG13:")
 (setq rtimes
   (getint
   "\nEnter number radial points:"))
 (setq ztimes
   (getint
   "\nEnter number Z points:"))
 (setq maxheight
   (getdist pnt0
   "\nEnter maximum height:"))
 (setq crad
   (getdist pnt0
   "\nEnter radius:"))
 (setq cradoff
   (getdist pnt0
   "\nEnter radius offset:"))
 (setq fanginc
   (getint
   "\Enter starting angle
```

```
    increment:"))
(setq fcycles
  (getreal
  "\Enter total angle cycles:"))
; Z inc
(setq zinc (/ maxheight ztimes))
(command ".3DMESH"
  (+ rtimes 1) (+ ztimes 2))
; start radial location
(setq rnum 1)
(setq rang 0.0)
(setq ranginc (/ 360.0 rtimes))
(repeat (+ rtimes 1)
 ; bottom pt
 (command pnt0)
 ; start z location
 (setq znum 1)
 (setq zloc (nth 2 pnt0))
 (setq sang (* (fix
   (* (rn) 24)) fanginc))
 (setq sanginc
   (/ (* 360.0 fcycles) ztimes))
 ; save first angle
 (if (= rnum 1) (setq fsang sang))
 ; check for last segment
 (if (= rnum (+ rtimes 1)) (progn
  (setq rang 0.0)
  (setq sang fsang)
 ))
 (repeat ztimes
  ; radial distance
  (setq nrad (+ crad
    (* (sin (dtr sang)) cradoff)))
  (setq xoff
    (* nrad (cos (dtr rang))))
  (setq yoff
    (* nrad (sin (dtr rang))))
  ; grid pt
  (setq npnt (list
    (+ (nth 0 pnt0) xoff)
    (+ (nth 1 pnt0) yoff) zloc))
  ; add mesh pt
  (command npnt)
  ; inc height location
  (setq znum (+ znum 1))
  (setq zloc (+ zloc zinc))
  (setq sang (+ sang sanginc))
 )
  ; inc radial location
  (setq rnum (+ rnum 1))
  (setq rang (+ rang ranginc))
  ; top pt
  (command (list
    (nth 0 pnt0) (nth 1 pnt0)
    (* zinc ztimes)))
 )
 (command ".ZOOM" "e")
 (princ)
)
;----------------------------------
```

Generating an elliptical cylindrical mesh

As in previous examples using radial computations, the circular section can be easily changed to an elliptical section.

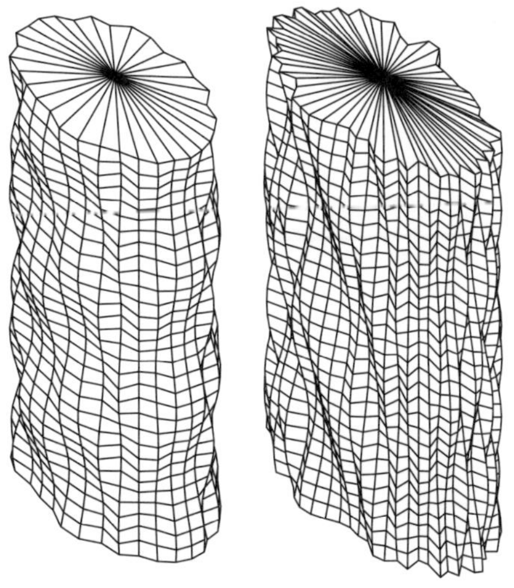

PROG14: elliptical-vertical random variation of radius offset

Add function PROG14. Using a copy of PROG13, convert the circular radial computation to an elliptical one.

Another version would be to use a copy of PROG12, horizontal rings.

Add input for radii x and y, then modify the radial-point computation to:

```
; radial distance
(setq nxrad (+ cxrad
  (* (sin (dtr sang)) cradoff)))
(setq nyrad (+ cyrad
(* (sin (dtr sang)) cradoff)))
(setq xoff (* nxrad
  (cos (dtr rang))))
(setq yoff (* nyrad
  (sin (dtr rang))))
; grid pt
(setq npnt (list
  (+ (nth 0 pnt0) xoff)
  (+ (nth 1 pnt0) yoff) zloc))
```

Sample script file for PROG14:

```
;---------------------------------
(prog14)
;Enter number radial points:
32
;Enter number Z points:
32
;Enter maximum height:
12
;Enter X radius:
1.5
;Enter Y radius:
2.5
;Enter radius offset:
0.15
;Enter starting angle increment:
10
;Enter total angle cycles:
3.0
;---------------------------------
```

Completed function PROG14:

```
;---------------------------------
(defun prog14 ()
 (graphscr)
 (command ".ERASE" "all" "")
 ; set start point
 (setq pnt0 (list 0 0 0))
 (prompt "\nPROG14:")
 (setq rtimes
   (getint
   "\nEnter number radial points:"))
 (setq ztimes
   (getint
   "\nEnter number Z points:"))
 (setq maxheight
   (getdist pnt0
   "\nEnter maximum height:"))
 (setq cxrad
   (getdist pnt0
   "\nEnter X radius:"))
 (setq cyrad
   (getdist pnt0
   "\nEnter Y radius:"))
 (setq cradoff
   (getdist pnt0
   "\nEnter radius offset:"))
 (setq fanginc
  (getint
  "\Enter starting angle
   increment:"))
 (setq fcycles
   (getreal
   "\Enter total angle cycles:"))
 ; Z inc
 (setq zinc (/ maxheight ztimes))
 (command ".3DMESH"
   (+ rtimes 1) (+ ztimes 2))
 ; start radial location
 (setq rnum 1)
 (setq rang 0.0)
 (setq ranginc (/ 360.0 rtimes))
 (repeat (+ rtimes 1)
  ; bottom pt
  (command pnt0)
  ; start z location
  (setq znum 1)
  (setq zloc (nth 2 pnt0))
```

```
  (setq sang (* (fix
    (* (rn) 24)) fanginc))
  (setq sanginc
    (/ (* 360.0 fcycles) ztimes))
  ; save first angle
  (if (= rnum 1) (setq fsang sang))
  ; check for last segment
  (if (= rnum (+ rtimes 1)) (progn
   (setq rang 0.0)
   (setq sang fsang)
  ))
  (repeat ztimes
   ; radial distance
   (setq nxrad (+ cxrad
     (* (sin (dtr sang)) cradoff)))
   (setq nyrad (+ cyrad
     (* (sin (dtr sang)) cradoff)))
   (setq xoff (* nxrad
     (cos (dtr rang))))
   (setq yoff (* nyrad
     (sin (dtr rang))))
   ; grid pt
   (setq npnt (list
     (+ (nth 0 pnt0) xoff)
     (+ (nth 1 pnt0) yoff) zloc))
   ; add mesh pt
   (command npnt)
   ; inc height location
   (setq znum (+ znum 1))
   (setq zloc (+ zloc zinc))
   (setq sang (+ sang sanginc))
  )
  ; inc radial location
  (setq rnum (+ rnum 1))
  (setq rang (+ rang ranginc))
  ; top pt
  (command (list
    (nth 0 pnt0) (nth 1 pnt0)
    (* zinc ztimes)))
 )
 (command ".ZOOM" "e")
 (princ)
)
;----------------------------------
```

6.5 Random Floor Constructions

This section explores methods for distorting a building-floor edge by applying random elements to it.

Start a new drawing and set the units to architectural. Set the grid to 1 foot, and turn off all snaps and dynamic input.

Start a new AutoLISP file in the editor: `CH06E.LSP`. Add functions `rn`, `dtr`, and `rtd` from the previous section.

A number of different approaches can be taken to articulate an elevation of a building: as a surface, as a total mass, or floor-by-floor.

Random elevation pattern using a square

This first pattern will be created by simply placing a randomly rotated square at the edge of each floorplate.

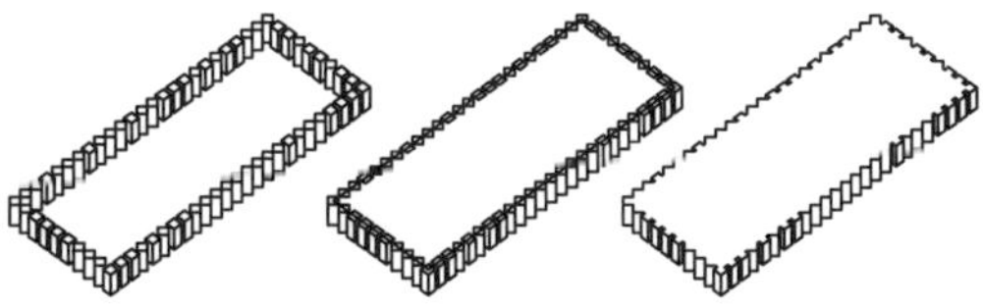

`PROG01`: development of random squares at floor edge

Add `PROG01` using a copy of `PROG01` in `CH06A.LSP`. The edge locations are generated by computing all grid points but placing the square at locations at the edge of the floor. The first loop is the repetition in height. Each floor level is computed and a floor block is placed. Then the x and y locations are generated, placing a square at the edges. The block is required since it is possible that gaps will form next to each square.

A selection list is started for each level, for the block and the edge squares, so they can be UNIONed at each level.

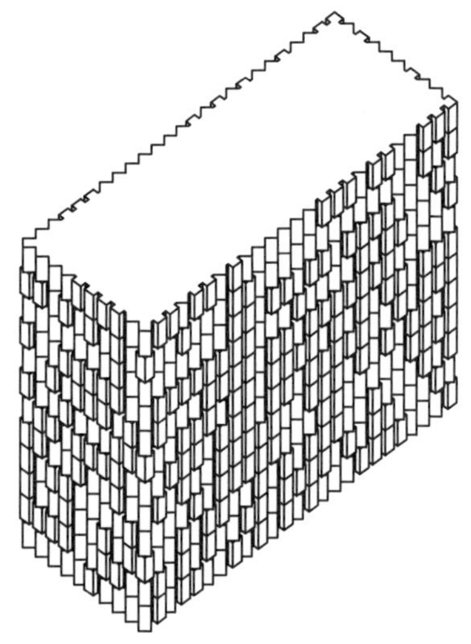

PROG01: completed random squares at floor edge

Sample script file for PROG01:

```
;----------------------------------
(prog01)
;Enter XY side:
5
;Enter number X repeats:
25
;Enter number Y repeats:
10
;Enter Z height:
9.5
;Enter number of levels:
12
;Enter angle multiple:
45
;----------------------------------
```

Completed function PROG01:

```
;----------------------------------
(defun prog01 ()
 (graphscr)
 (command ".ERASE" "all" "")
 ; set start point
 (setq pnt0 (list 0 0 0))
 (prompt "\nPROG01:")
 (setq xyside
   (getdist pnt0
   "\nEnter XY side:"))
 (setq xtimes
   (getint
   "\nEnter number X repeats:"))
 (setq ytimes
   (getint
   "\nEnter number Y repeats:"))
 (setq zheight
   (getdist "\Enter Z height: "))
 (setq nlevels
   (getint
   "\Enter number of levels: "))
 (setq angz
   (getreal
   "\Enter angle multiple: "))
 ; start Z location
 (setq zelev 0.0)
 (repeat nlevels
  ; level block
  (setq pnt1 (list
    (+ (nth 0 pnt0) (/ xyside 2.0))
    (+ (nth 1 pnt0) (/ xyside 2.0))
    zelev))
  (setq pnt2 (list
    (+ (nth 0 pnt1)
    (- (* xtimes xyside) xyside))
    (+ (nth 1 pnt1)
    (- (* ytimes xyside) xyside))
    zelev))
  (command ".RECTANGLE" pnt1 pnt2)
  (command ".ZOOM" "e")
  (command ".EXTRUDE"
    "last" "" zheight)
  ; versions prior to 2007
  ; require taper parameter
  ;(command ".EXTRUDE"
  ;  "last" "" zheight "")
```

```
    ; add to level list
    (setq llist (ssadd (entlast)))
    ; start y location
    (setq ynum 1)
    (setq yloc (nth 1 pnt0))
    (repeat ytimes
     ; start x location
     (setq xnum 1)
     (setq xloc (nth 0 pnt0))
     (repeat xtimes
      ; only if at edge
      (if (or (= ynum 1)
        (= ynum ytimes) (= xnum 1)
        (= xnum xtimes))
       (progn
        ; lower corner pt
        (setq pnt1
          (list xloc yloc zelev))
        ; center of grid
        (setq pnt2 (list
          (+ (nth 0 pnt1)
          (/ xyside 2))
          (+ (nth 1 pnt1)
          (/ xyside 2)) zelev))
        ; rotate ang
        (setq rotang (* (fix
          (* (rn) 10.0)) angz))
        ; draw rectangle
        (command ".POLYGON"
          "4" pnt2 "I" (/ xyside 2.0))
        (command ".ZOOM" "e")
        (command ".ROTATE"
          "last" "" pnt2 rotang)
        ; extrude to height
        (command ".EXTRUDE"
          "last" "" zheight)
        ; versions prior to 2007
        ; require taper parameter
        ;(command ".EXTRUDE"
        ;  "last" "" zheight "")
        ; add to selection list
        (setq llist
          (ssadd (entlast) llist))
      ))
      ; inc x location
      (setq xloc (+ xloc xyside))
      (setq xnum (+ xnum 1))
     )
     ; inc y location
     (setq yloc (+ yloc xyside))
     (setq ynum (+ ynum 1))
    )
    ; union level
    (command ".UNION" llist "")
    ; inc levels elev
    (setq zelev (+ zelev zheight))
  )
  (princ)
)
;----------------------------------
```

Review PROG01 for structure: how the edge locations were determined and use of the selection list to UNION each floor level.

To further add variation to the edge of the floor and define design constraints, only include squares that are increments of the entered angle, and do not place a square on any of the four corners. This develops a better corner condition and also larger open areas on each floor elevation.

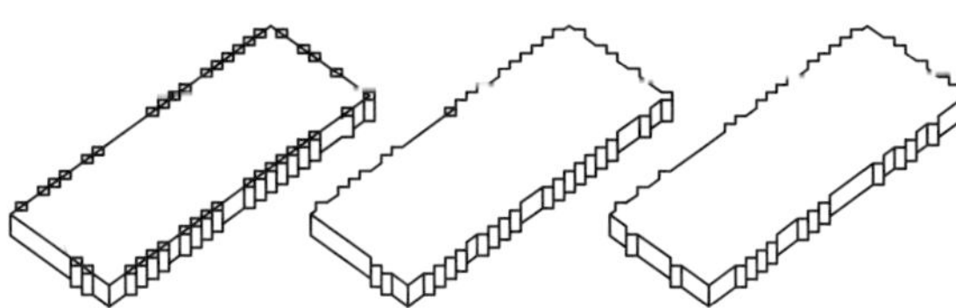

PROG01a: development of additional design constraints on a floor edge

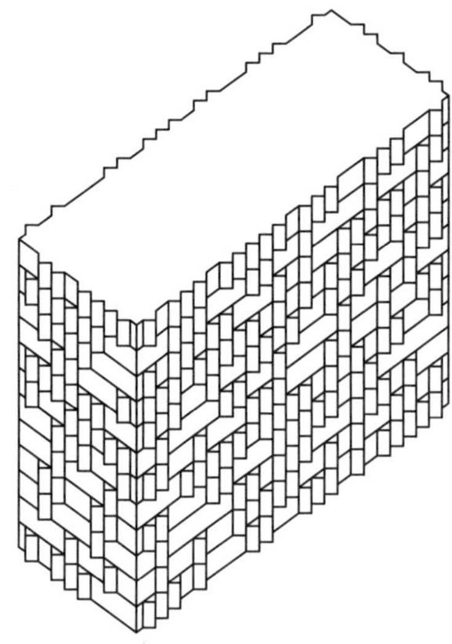

PROG01a: completed random squares at floor edge

Consider the condition at ground level and how a lobby could be added. Also begin to develop your own set of architectural issues that could be addressed.

Completed function PROG01a:

```
;----------------------------------
(defun prog01a ()
 (graphscr)
 (command ".ERASE" "all" "")
 ; set start point
 (setq pnt0 (list 0 0 0))
 (prompt "\nPROG01a:")
 (setq xyside
   (getdist pnt0
   "\nEnter XY side:"))
 (setq xtimes
   (getint
   "\nEnter number X repeats:"))
 (setq ytimes
   (getint
   "\nEnter number Y repeats:"))
(setq zheight
  (getdist
  "\Enter Z height: "))
(setq nlevels
  (getint
  "\Enter number of levels: "))
(setq angz
  (getreal
  "\Enter angle multiple: "))
; start Z location
(setq zelev 0.0)
(repeat nlevels
 ; level block
 (setq pnt1 (list
   (+ (nth 0 pnt0)
   (/ xyside 2.0))
   (+ (nth 1 pnt0)
   (/ xyside 2.0)) zelev))
 (setq pnt2 (list
   (+ (nth 0 pnt1)
   (- (* xtimes xyside) xyside))
   (+ (nth 1 pnt1)
   (- (* ytimes xyside) xyside))
   zelev))
 (command ".RECTANGLE" pnt1 pnt2)
 (command ".ZOOM" "e")
 (command ".EXTRUDE"
   "last" "" zheight)
 ; versions prior to 2007
 ; require taper parameter
 ;(command ".EXTRUDE"
 ;  "last" "" zheight "")
 ; add to level list
 (setq llist (ssadd (entlast)))
 ; start y location
 (setq ynum 1)
 (setq yloc 0)
 (repeat ytimes
  ; start x location
  (setq xnum 1)
  (setq xloc 0)
  (repeat xtimes
   ; only if at edge
   (if (or (or (or (= ynum 1)
     (= ynum ytimes)) (= xnum 1))
     (= xnum xtimes))
    (progn
     ; lower corner pt
```

```
  (setq pnt1
    (list xloc yloc zelev))
  ; center of grid
  (setq pnt2 (list
    (+ (nth 0 pnt1)
    (/ xyside 2))
    (+ (nth 1 pnt1)
    (/ xyside 2)) zelev))
  ; flag to draw
  (setq ido 1)
  ; rotate ang
  (setq rotang (* (fix
    (* (rn) 10.0)) angz))
  ; check rotation
  (if (= (rem rotang 90) 0)
    (setq ido 0))
  ; check for corners
  (if (and (= ynum 1)
    (= xnum 1)) (setq ido 0))
  (if (and (= ynum 1)
    (= xnum xtimes))
    (setq ido 0))
  (if (and (= xnum 1)
    (= ynum ytimes))
    (setq ido 0))
  (if (and (= xnum xtimes)
    (= ynum ytimes))
    (setq ido 0))
  ; check flag
  (if (= ido 1) (progn
   ; draw rectangle
   (command ".POLYGON"
     "4" pnt2 "I" (/ xyside 2.0))
   (command ".ZOOM" "e")
   (command ".ROTATE"
     "last" "" pnt2 rotang)
   ; extrude to height
   (command ".EXTRUDE"
     "last" "" zheight)
   ; versions prior to 2007
   ; require taper parameter
   ;(command ".EXTRUDE"
   ;  "last" "" zheight "")
   ; add to selection list
   (setq llist
     (ssadd (entlast) llist))
  ))
))
       ; inc x location
       (setq xloc (+ xloc xyside))
       (setq xnum (+ xnum 1))
      )
      ; inc y location
      (setq yloc (+ yloc xyside))
      (setq ynum (+ ynum 1))
    )
    ; union level
    (command ".UNION" llist "")
    ; inc levels elev
    (setq zelev (+ zelev zheight))
  )
  (princ)
)
;----------------------------------
```

Review PROG01a for using a drawing flag to determine if all conditions are met when including a specific square. The flag is set to draw, and then conditions are checked to see if it should not be drawn. This is a common technique for handling multiple conditions that are computed or determined in a variety of ways.

Additional architectural elements could also be considered in a similar fashion.

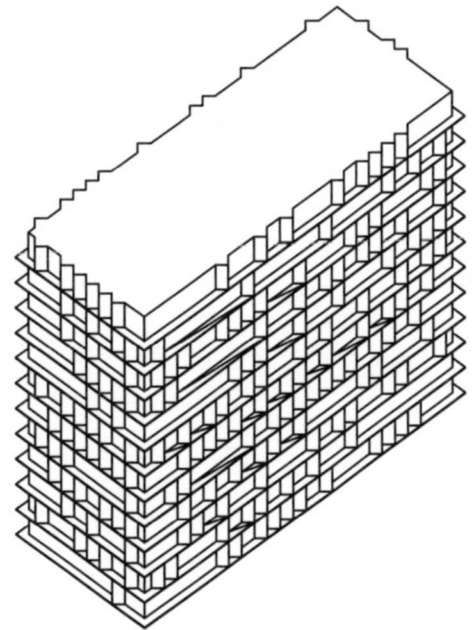

PROG016: floor slab, included

Add PROG01b. Using a copy of PROG01a, add a floor slab to each level. Consider the condition at the first and last levels, where the floor/roof becomes an overhang/balcony.

Add input for a slab thickness. After the floor block is placed, add the slab:

```
; add slab
(setq pnt1 (list
  (nth 0 pnt0) (nth 1 pnt0)
  zelev))
(setq pnt2 (list
  (+ (nth 0 pnt1)
  (* xtimes xyside))
  (+ (nth 1 pnt1)
  (* ytimes xyside)) zelev))
(command ".RECTANGLE" pnt1 pnt2)
(command ".EXTRUDE"
  "last" "" zthk)
; versions prior to 2007
; require taper parameter
;(command ".EXTRUDE"
;  "last" "" zheight "")
; add to level list
(setq llist
  (ssadd (entlast) llist))
```

Sample script file for PROG01b:

```
;----------------------------------
(prog01b)
;Enter XY side:
5
;Enter number X repeats:
25
;Enter number Y repeats:
10
;Enter Z height:
9.5
;Enter slab thickness:
0.25
;Enter number of levels:
12
;Enter angle multiple:
45
;----------------------------------
```

Random elevation pattern using any polygon

Replace the square with any n-sided polygon to randomly articulate the floor elevation.

Add PROG02. Using a copy of PROG01a or PROG01b, add input for the number of sides in the polygon, radius, and an angle for excluding rotations.

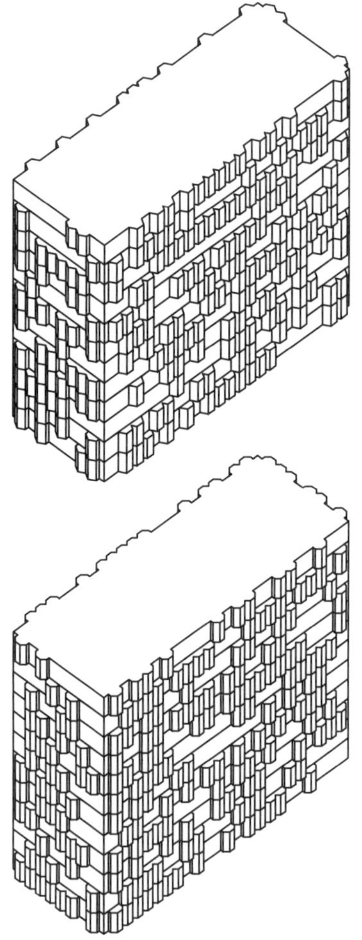

PROG02: random polygons at edge

Sample script files for PROG02:

```
;---------------------------------
(prog02)
;Enter XY side:
5
;Enter number X repeats:
25
;Enter number Y repeats:
10
;Enter Z height:
9.5
;Enter number of levels:
12
;Enter polygon sides:
6
;Enter polygon radius:
3.0
;Enter angle multiple:
60
;Enter angle multiple to exclude:
120
;---------------------------------
```

```
;---------------------------------
(prog02)
;Enter XY side:
5
;Enter number X repeats:
25
;Enter number Y repeats:
10
;Enter Z height:
9.5
;Enter number of levels:
12
;Enter polygon sides:
8
;Enter polygon radius:
3.0
;Enter angle multiple:
45
;Enter angle multiple to exclude:
90
;---------------------------------
```

Completed function PROG02:

```
;---------------------------------
(defun prog02 ()
 (graphscr)
 (command ".ERASE" "all" "")
 ; set start point
 (setq pnt0 (list 0 0 0))
 (prompt "\nPROG02:")
 (setq xyside
   (getdist pnt0
   "\nEnter XY side:"))
 (setq xtimes
   (getint
   "\nEnter number X repeats:"))
 (setq ytimes
   (getint
   "\nEnter number Y repeats:"))
 (setq zheight
   (getdist "\Enter Z height: "))
 (setq nlevels
   (getint
   "\Enter number of levels: "))
 (setq psides
   (getint
   "\Enter polygon sides: "))
 (setq prad
   (getdist
   "\Enter polygon radius: "))
 (setq angz
   (getreal
   "\Enter angle multiple: "))
 (setq angzx
   (getreal
   "\Enter angle multiple to
    exclude: "))
 ; start Z location
 (setq zelev 0.0)
 (repeat nlevels
  ; level block
  (setq pnt1 (list
    (+ (nth 0 pnt0)
    (/ xyside 2.0))
    (+ (nth 1 pnt0)
    (/ xyside 2.0)) zelev))
  (setq pnt2 (list
    (+ (nth 0 pnt1)
    (- (* xtimes xyside) xyside))
```

```
  (+ (nth 1 pnt1)
  (- (* ytimes xyside) xyside))
  zelev))
(command ".RECTANGLE" pnt1 pnt2)
(command ".ZOOM" "e")
(command ".EXTRUDE"
  "last" "" zheight)
; versions prior to 2007
; require taper parameter
;(command ".EXTRUDE"
;  "last" "" zheight "")
; add to level list
(setq llist (ssadd (entlast)))
; start y location
(setq ynum 1)
(setq yloc 0)
(repeat ytimes
 ; start x location
 (setq xnum 1)
 (setq xloc 0)
 (repeat xtimes
  ; only if at edge
  (if (or (or (or (= ynum 1)
    (= ynum ytimes)) (= xnum 1))
    (= xnum xtimes))
   (progn
    ; lower corner pt
    (setq pnt1
      (list xloc yloc zelev))
    ; center of grid
    (setq pnt2 (list
      (+ (nth 0 pnt1)
      (/ xyside 2))
      (+ (nth 1 pnt1)
      (/ xyside 2)) zelev))
    ; flag to draw
    (setq ido 1)
    ; rotate ang
    (setq rotang (* (fix
      (* (rn) 10.0)) angz))
    ; check rotation
    (if (= (rem rotang angzx) 0)
      (setq ido 0))
    ; check for corners
    (if (and (= ynum 1)
      (= xnum 1)) (setq ido 0))
    (if (and (= ynum 1)
      (= xnum xtimes))
      (setq ido 0))
    (if (and (= xnum 1)
      (= ynum ytimes))
      (setq ido 0))
    (if (and (= xnum xtimes)
      (= ynum ytimes))
      (setq ido 0))
    ; check flag
    (if (= ido 1) (progn
     ; draw rectangle
     (command ".POLYGON"
       psides pnt2 "I" prad)
     (command ".ZOOM" "e")
     (command ".ROTATE"
       "last" "" pnt2 rotang)
     ; extrude to height
     (command ".EXTRUDE"
       "last" "" zheight)
     ; versions prior to 2007
     ; require taper parameter
     ;(command ".EXTRUDE"
     ;  "last" "" zheight "")
     ; add to selection list
     (setq llist
       (ssadd (entlast) llist))
    ))
   ))
   ; inc x location
   (setq xloc (+ xloc xyside))
   (setq xnum (+ xnum 1))
  )
  ; inc y location
  (setq yloc (+ yloc xyside))
  (setq ynum (+ ynum 1))
 )
 ; union level
 (command ".UNION" llist "")
 ; inc levels elev
 (setq zelev (+ zelev zheight))
)
(princ)
)
;---------------------------------
```

Random elevation pattern using a circle

Replace the square with a circle to randomly articulate the floor elevation.

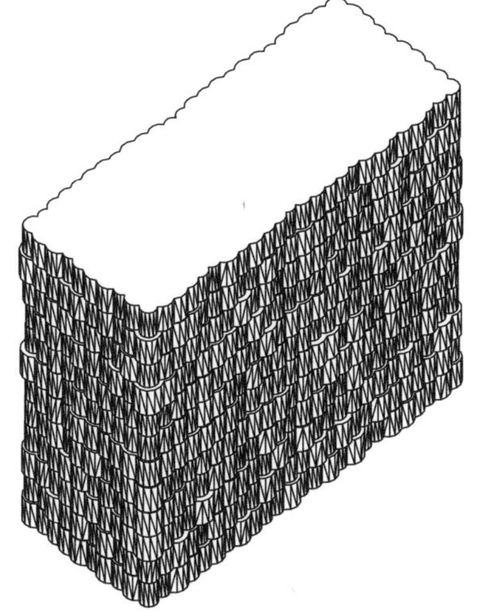

PROG03: random-radius circles at floor edge

Add PROG03. Using a copy of PROG01a or PROG01b, add input for the minimum and maximum circle radius. Remove input for the angle rotation.

Compute a random radius for each circle from the values entered, as:

```
; compute radius
(setq crad (+ cradmin (* (rn)
  (- cradmax cradmin))))
```

Sample script file for PROG03:

```
;-----------------------------------
(prog03)
;Enter XY side:
5
;Enter number X repeats:
25
;Enter number Y repeats:
10
;Enter Z height:
9.5
;Enter number of levels:
12
;Enter circle min radius:
2.5
;Enter circle max radius:
4.5
;-----------------------------------
```

Completed function PROG03:

```
;-----------------------------------
(defun prog03 ()
 (graphscr)
 (command ".ERASE" "all" "")
 ; set start point
 (setq pnt0 (list 0 0 0))
 (prompt "\nPROG03:")
 (setq xyside
   (getdist pnt0
   "\nEnter XY side:"))
 (setq xtimes
   (getint
   "\nEnter number X repeats:"))
 (setq ytimes
   (getint
   "\nEnter number Y repeats:"))
 (setq zheight
   (getdist "\Enter Z height: "))
 (setq nlevels
   (getint
   "\Enter number of levels: "))
 (setq cradmin
   (getdist
   "\Enter circle min radius: "))
 (setq cradmax
```

```
  (getdist
  "\Enter circle max radius: "))
; start Z location
(setq zelev 0.0)
(repeat nlevels
 ; level block
 (setq pnt1 (list
   (+ (nth 0 pnt0) (/ xyside 2.0))
   (+ (nth 1 pnt0) (/ xyside 2.0))
   zelev))
 (setq pnt2 (list
   (+ (nth 0 pnt1)
   (- (* xtimes xyside) xyside))
   (+ (nth 1 pnt1)
   (- (* ytimes xyside) xyside))
   zelev))
 (command ".RECTANGLE" pnt1 pnt2)
 (command ".ZOOM" "e")
 (command ".EXTRUDE"
   "last" "" zheight)
 ; versions prior to 2007 require
 ; the taper parameter
 ;(command ".EXTRUDE"
 ;  "last" "" zheight "")
 ; add to level list
 (setq llist (ssadd (entlast)))
 ; start y location
 (setq ynum 1)
 (setq yloc 0)
 (repeat ytimes
  ; start x location
  (setq xnum 1)
  (setq xloc 0)
  (repeat xtimes
   ; only if at edge
   (if (or (or (or (= ynum 1)
     (= ynum ytimes)) (= xnum 1))
     (= xnum xtimes))
    (progn
     ; lower corner pt
     (setq pnt1 (
       list xloc yloc zelev))
     ; center of grid
     (setq pnt2 (list
       (+ (nth 0 pnt1)
       (/ xyside 2))
       (+ (nth 1 pnt1)
       (/ xyside 2)) zelev))
     ; compute radius
     (setq crad
       (+ cradmin (* (rn)
       (- cradmax cradmin))))
     ; draw circle
     (command ".CIRCLE" pnt2 crad)
     (command ".ZOOM" "e")
     ; extrude to height
     (command ".EXTRUDE"
       "last" "" zheight)
     ; versions prior to 2007
     ; require taper parameter
     ;(command ".EXTRUDE"
     ;  "last" "" zheight "")
     ; add to selection list
     (setq llist
       (ssadd (entlast) llist))
   ))
   ; inc x location
   (setq xloc (+ xloc xyside))
   (setq xnum (+ xnum 1))
  )
  ; inc y location
  (setq yloc (+ yloc xyside))
  (setq ynum (+ ynum 1))
 )
 ; union level
 (command ".UNION" llist "")
 ; inc levels elev
 (setq zelev (+ zelev zheight))
)
(princ)
)
;---------------------------------
```

Add PROG03a, a variation of PROG03. Instead of basing the entire floor massing on the random circle, use it for a floor slab only. The floor massing is constant.

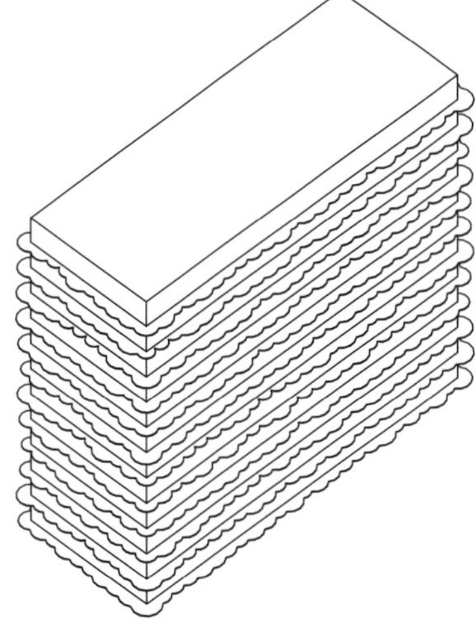

PROG03a: random-radius circles at floor-slab edge

Add input for the floor-slab thickness, and replace extrude-to-floor height with slab thickness:

```
; extrude to slab thickness
(command ".EXTRUDE"
  "last" "" zthk)
```

Another variation would be to combine the circular floor elevation with the circular floor slab.

Sample script files for PROG03a:

```
;----------------------------------
(prog03a)
;Enter XY side:
5
;Enter number X repeats:
25
;Enter number Y repeats:
10
;Enter Z height:
9.5
;Enter slab thickness:
0.25
;Enter number of levels:
12
;Enter circle min radius:
2.5
;Enter circle max radius:
4.5
;----------------------------------
```

Articulate a single floor edge

Using the sine function, articulate the front edge of each floorplate.

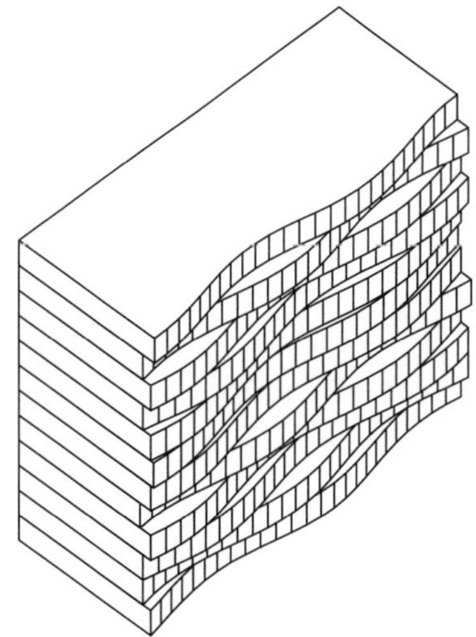

PROG04: random sine curve for the front edge

Add PROG04. Randomly select the start angle based on the entered angle multiple. Instead of placing elements along the edges of a grid, each floor is generated as a polyline that can be extruded to the floor height. The sides and back are straight lines. The front is a sine curve based on grid spacing and number of parameters. A y-offset is included to determine the extent of the curve, as well as the number of curve cycles for determining the curve-angle range.

Sample script file for PROG04:

```
;---------------------------------
(prog04)
;Enter XY side:
5
;Enter number X repeats:
25
;Enter number Y repeats:
10
;Enter Z height:
9.5
;Enter number of levels:
12
;Enter max Y offset:
3.0
;Enter angle multiple:
30
;Enter number of curve cycles:
1.5
;---------------------------------
```

Completed function PROG04:

```
;---------------------------------
(defun prog04 ()
 (graphscr)
 (command ".ERASE" "all" "")
 ; set start point
 (setq pnt0 (list 0 0 0))
 (prompt "\nPROG04:")
 (setq xyside
   (getdist pnt0
   "\nEnter XY side:"))
 (setq xtimes
   (getint
   "\nEnter number X repeats:"))
 (setq ytimes
   (getint
   "\nEnter number Y repeats:"))
 (setq zheight
   (getdist "\Enter Z height: "))
 (setq nlevels
   (getint
   "\Enter number of levels: "))
 (setq ymaxoff
   (getdist
   "\Enter max Y offset: "))
 (setq angy
   (getreal
   "\Enter angle multiple: "))
 (setq ycycles
   (getreal
   "\Enter number of curve
    cycles: "))
 ; start Z location
 (setq zelev 0.0)
 (repeat nlevels
  ; start edge
  (command ".PLINE")
  ; curve angles
  (setq xang (* (fix
    (* (rn) 24)) angy))
  (setq xanginc
    (/ (* 360.0 ycycles) xtimes))
  (setq xloc (nth 0 pnt0))
  (setq yloc (nth 1 pnt0))
  (setq xnum 1)
  (repeat (+ xtimes 1)
   ; compute Y offset based on
   ; curve
   (setq yoff
     (* (sin (dtr xang)) ymaxoff))
   (setq npnt (list
     xloc (+ yloc yoff) zelev))
   (command npnt)
   ; save first pt
   (if (= xnum 1) (setq fpnt npnt))
   ; inc x location and angs
   (setq xloc (+ xloc xyside))
   (setq xang (+ xang xanginc))
   (setq xnum (+ xnum 1))
  )
  ; level corner pts
```

```
  (setq pnt1 (list
    (+ (nth 0 pnt0)
    (* xtimes xyside))
    (+ (nth 1 pnt0)
    (* ytimes xyside)) zelev))
  (setq pnt2 (list
    (nth 0 pnt0)
    (+ (nth 1 pnt0)
    (* ytimes xyside)) zelev))
  (command pnt1 pnt2 fpnt)
  ; close polyline
  (command "c")
  (command ".ZOOM" "e")
  ; extrude to height
  (command ".EXTRUDE"
    "last" "" zheight)
  ; versions prior to 2007
  ; require taper parameter
  ;(command ".EXTRUDE"
  ;  "last" "" zheight "")
  ; inc levels elev
  (setq zelev (+ zelev zheight))
 )
 (princ)
)
;---------------------------------
```

Review PROG04: the structure, how the floor boundary is defined as a polyline, and computation of the back edges.

The number of cycles for the angle range could also be selected randomly.

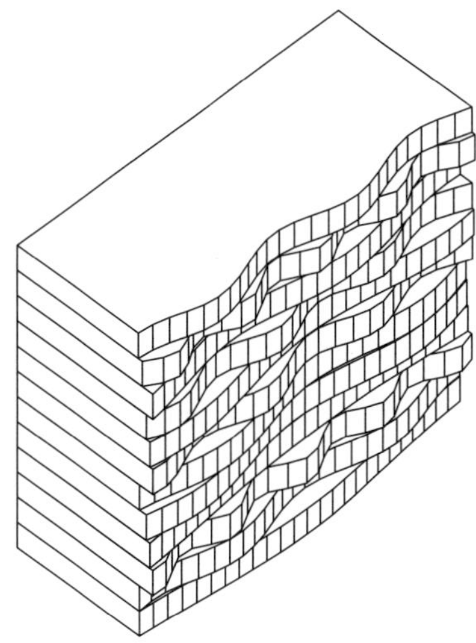

PROG04a: random start and range for the sine curve

Add PROG04a. Using a copy of PROG04, change the total angle selection by including a random computation.

Change:

```
; curve angles
(setq xang (* (fix (* (rn)
  24)) angy))
(setq xanginc
  (/ (* 360.0 ycycles) xtimes))
```

To:

```
; curve angles
(setq xang (* (fix (* (rn)
  24)) angy))
(setq xanginc
  (/ (* 360.0 (+ (* (rn)
  ycycles) 0.5)) xtimes))
```

Sample script file for PROG04a:

```
;----------------------------------
(prog04a)
;Enter XY side:
5
;Enter number X repeats:
25
;Enter number Y repeats:
10
;Enter Z height:
9.5
;Enter number of levels:
12
;Enter max Y offset:
3.0
;Enter angle multiple:
30
;Enter number of curve cycles:
4.0
;----------------------------------
```

As in a previous example, articulate the slab of each floor and keep the floor elevation constant.

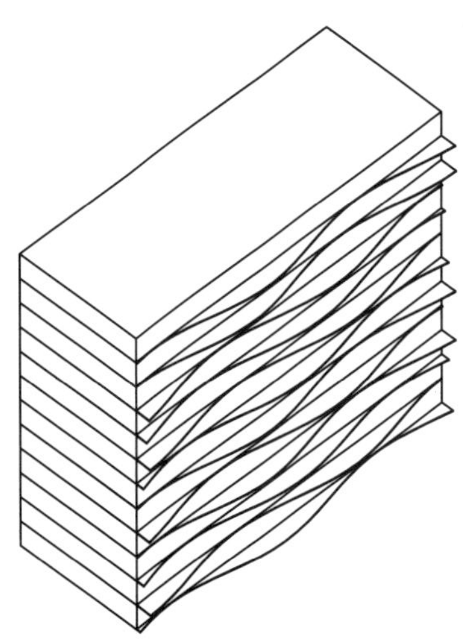

PROG04b: add floor slab

Add PROG04b. Using a copy of PROG04 or PROG04a, add input for slab thickness. Add floor mass after the slab is extruded. In this example, as in the others, the slab and floor masses are unioned. If this model is to be rendered, then union would not be required, and each element would be assigned to a different layer for material application (one for the floor mass and the other for the slab).

Sample script files for PROG04b:

```
;----------------------------------
(prog04b)
;Enter XY side:
5
;Enter number X repeats:
25
;Enter number Y repeats:
10
;Enter Z height:
9.5
;Enter slab thickness:
0.25
;Enter number of levels:
12
;Enter max Y offset:
3.0
;Enter angle multiple:
30
;Enter number of curve cycles:
1.5
;----------------------------------
```

Completed function PROG04b:

```
;----------------------------------
(defun prog04b ()
 (graphscr)
 (command ".ERASE" "all" "")
 ; set start point
 (setq pnt0 (list 0 0 0))
 (prompt "\nPROG04b:")
 (setq xyside
   (getdist pnt0
   "\nEnter XY side:"))
 (setq xtimes
   (getint
   "\nEnter number X repeats:"))
 (setq ytimes
```

```
  (getint
  "\nEnter number Y repeats:"))
(setq zheight
  (getdist "\Enter Z height: "))
(setq zthk
  (getdist
  "\Enter slab thickness: "))
(setq nlevels
  (getint
  "\Enter number of levels: "))
(setq ymaxoff
  (getdist
  "\Enter max Y offset: "))
(setq angy
  (getreal
  "\Enter angle multiple: "))
(setq ycycles
  (getreal
  "\Enter number of curve
   cycles: "))
; start Z location
(setq zelev 0.0)
(repeat nlevels
 ; start edge
 (command ".PLINE")
 ; curve angles
 (setq xang
   (* (fix (* (rn) 24)) angy))
 (setq xanginc
   (/ (* 360.0 ycycles) xtimes))
 (setq xloc (nth 0 pnt0))
 (setq yloc (nth 1 pnt0))
 (setq xnum 1)
 (repeat (+ xtimes 1)
  ; compute Y offset based on
  ; curve
  (setq yoff
    (* (sin (dtr xang)) ymaxoff))
  (setq npnt (list
    xloc (+ yloc yoff) zelev))
  (command npnt)
  ; save first pt
  (if (= xnum 1) (setq fpnt npnt))
  ; inc x location and angs
  (setq xloc (+ xloc xyside))
  (setq xang (+ xang xanginc))
  (setq xnum (+ xnum 1))
 )
 ; level corner pts
 (setq pnt1 (list
   (+ (nth 0 pnt0)
   (* xtimes xyside))
   (+ (nth 1 pnt0)
   (* ytimes xyside)) zelev))
 (setq pnt2 (list
   (nth 0 pnt0) (+ (nth 1 pnt0)
   (* ytimes xyside)) zelev))
 (command pnt1 pnt2 fpnt)
 ; close polyline
 (command "c")
 (command ".ZOOM" "e")
 ; extrude to height
 (command ".EXTRUDE"
   "last" "" zthk)
 ; versions prior to 2007
 ; require taper parameter
 ;(command ".EXTRUDE"
 ;  "last" "" zthk "")
 ; add to list
 (setq llist (ssadd (entlast)))
 ; floor mass
 (setq pnt1 (list
   (nth 0 pnt0)
   (+ (nth 1 pnt0) ymaxoff)
   zelev))
 (setq pnt2 (list
   (+ (nth 0 pnt0)
   (* xtimes xyside))
   (+ (nth 1 pnt0)
   (* ytimes xyside)) zelev))
 (command ".RECTANGLE" pnt1 pnt2)
 ; extrude to height
 (command ".EXTRUDE"
   "last" "" zheight)
 ; versions prior to 2007
 ; require taper parameter
 ;(command ".EXTRUDE"
 ;  "last" "" zheight "")
 ; add to list
 (setq llist
   (ssadd (entlast) llist))
 ; union level
 (command ".UNION" llist "")
 ; inc levels elev
 (setq zelev (+ zelev zheight))
)
(princ)
)
;---------------------------------
```

To further control the edge of the slab, consider a sequence of curves based on a random start.

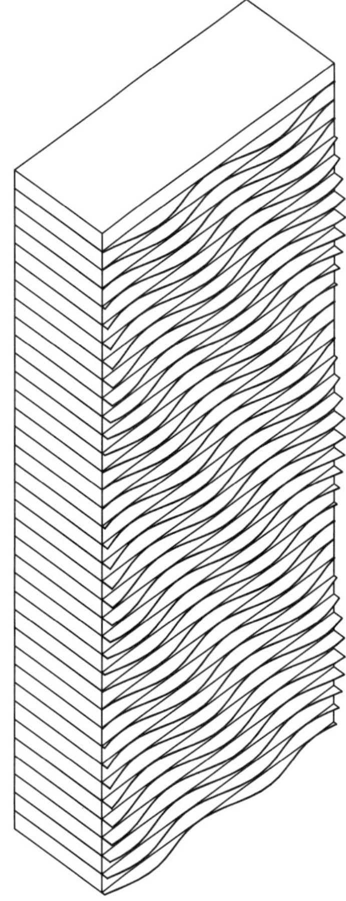

PROG04c: sequence of curves

Add PROG04c. Using a copy of PROG04b, select the starting random angle before the first level. After a level completes, increment the starting value by the entered angle multiple. Use that angle to start each level.

Sample script file for PROG04c:

```
;----------------------------------
(prog04c)
;Enter XY side:
5
;Enter number X repeats:
25
;Enter number Y repeats:
10
;Enter Z height:
9.5
;Enter slab thickness:
0.25
;Enter number of levels:
36
;Enter max Y offset:
3.0
;Enter angle multiple:
30
;Enter number of curve cycles:
2.0
;----------------------------------
```

Completed function PROG04c:

```
;----------------------------------
(defun prog04c ()
 (graphscr)
 (command ".ERASE" "all" "")
 ; set start point
 (setq pnt0 (list 0 0 0))
 (prompt "\nPROG04c:")
 (setq xyside
   (getdist pnt0
   "\nEnter XY side:"))
 (setq xtimes
   (getint
   "\nEnter number X repeats:"))
 (setq ytimes
   (getint
   "\nEnter number Y repeats:"))
 (setq zheight
   (getdist "\Enter Z height: "))
 (setq zthk
   (getdist
   "\Enter slab thickness: "))
```

```
(setq nlevels
  (getint
  "\Enter number of levels: "))
(setq ymaxoff
  (getdist
  "\Enter max Y offset: "))
(setq angy
  (getreal
  "\Enter angle multiple: "))
(setq ycycles
  (getreal
  "\Enter number of curve
   cycles: "))
; start Z location
(setq zelev 0.0)
; starting curve angle
(setq sxang
  (* (fix (* (rn) 24)) angy))
(repeat nlevels
 ; start edge
 (command ".PLINE")
 ; curve angles
 (setq xang sxang)
 (setq xanginc
   (/ (* 360.0 ycycles) xtimes))
 (setq xloc (nth 0 pnt0))
 (setq yloc (nth 1 pnt0))
 (setq xnum 1)
 (repeat (+ xtimes 1)
  ; compute Y offset based on
  ; curve
  (setq yoff
    (* (sin (dtr xang)) ymaxoff))
  (setq npnt (list
    xloc (+ yloc yoff) zelev))
  (command npnt)
  ; save first pt
  (if (= xnum 1) (setq fpnt npnt))
  ; inc x location and angs
  (setq xloc (+ xloc xyside))
  (setq xang (+ xang xanginc))
  (setq xnum (+ xnum 1))
 )
 ; level corner pts
 (setq pnt1 (list
   (+ (nth 0 pnt0)
   (* xtimes xyside))
   (+ (nth 1 pnt0)
   (* ytimes xyside)) zelev))
 (setq pnt2 (list
   (nth 0 pnt0)
   (+ (nth 1 pnt0)
   (* ytimes xyside)) zelev))
 (command pnt1 pnt2 fpnt)
 ; close polyline
 (command "c")
 (command ".ZOOM" "e")
 ; extrude to height
 (command ".EXTRUDE"
   "last" "" zthk)
 ; versions prior to 2007
 ; require taper parameter
 ;(command ".EXTRUDE"
 ;  "last" "" zthk "")
 ; add to list
 (setq llist (ssadd (entlast)))
 ; floor mass
 (setq pnt1 (list
   (nth 0 pnt0)
   (+ (nth 1 pnt0) ymaxoff)
   zelev))
 (setq pnt2 (list
   (+ (nth 0 pnt0)
   (* xtimes xyside))
   (+ (nth 1 pnt0)
   (* ytimes xyside)) zelev))
 (command ".RECTANGLE" pnt1 pnt2)
 ; extrude to height
 (command ".EXTRUDE"
   "last" "" zheight)
 ; versions prior to 2007
 ; require taper parameter
 ;(command ".EXTRUDE"
   "last" "" zheight "")
 ; add to list
 (setq llist
   (ssadd (entlast) llist))
 ; union level
 (command ".UNION" llist "")
 ; inc levels elev
 (setq zelev (+ zelev zheight))
 ; inc ang
 (setq sxang (+ sxang angy))
)
(princ)
)
;-----------------------------------
```

Review how the random angle is selected, how it is set for each level, and how it is incremented after a level.

Articulate all floor edges

The previous set of examples used a rectangular floorplate for applying a single, randomly curved edge.

Other basic shapes, such as an ellipse, enable us to randomly control the entire floor-slab edge. With each floorplate modeled as a POLYLINE, the area of each floor can also be computed.

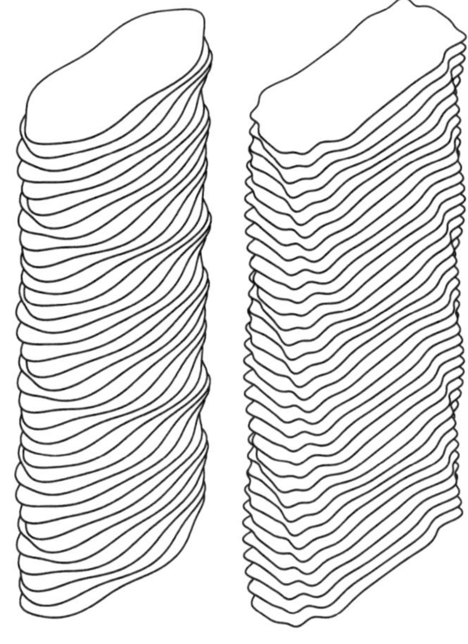

PROG05 and PROG05a: elliptical and superelliptical floor edge

Add PROG05 using a copy of PROG04c. Replace the rectangular polyline with a curved edge and an ellipse. Input is changed to overall dimensions; the number of segments is computed to set the smoothness of the edge; and the elliptical curve equation is used to compute the edge points.

The y-offset from the ellipse is computed as:

```
; radius offset
(setq roff
  (* (+ (sin (dtr (* xang 2)))
  (sin (dtr (* xang 3))))
  ymaxoff))
; ellipse
(setq xoff
  (* (+ radx roff)
  (cos (dtr rang))))
(setq yoff
  (* (+ rady roff)
  (sin (dtr rang))))
(setq npnt (list
  (+ xloc xoff)
  (+ yloc yoff) zelev))
(command npnt)
```

Note that only the floor slab is included in this example.

Also note how the area of each floor is computed and accumulated, using:

```
; compute area
(command ".AREA" "o" "last")
(setq flrarea
  (/ (getvar "AREA") 144))
(setq flrperm
  (/ (getvar "PERIMETER") 12))
; acum floor and building surface
(setq totalarea
  (+ totalarea flrarea))
(setq totalperm
  (+ totalperm flrperm))
```

Many other curve equations could be used to compute the radius offset from the ellipse.

Sample script file for PROG05:

```
;----------------------------------
(prog05)
;Enter X distance:
125
;Enter Y distance:
50
;Enter Z height:
9.5
;Enter slab thickness:
0.25
;Enter number of levels:
36
;Enter max Y offset:
1.5
;Enter angle multiple:
30
;Enter number of curve cycles:
2.0
;----------------------------------
```

Completed function PROG05:

```
;----------------------------------
(defun prog05 ()
 (graphscr)
 (command ".ERASE" "all" "")
 ; set start point
 (setq pnt0 (list 0 0 0))
 (prompt "\nPROG05:")
 (setq radx
   (/ (getdist
   "\nEnter X distance:") 2))
 (setq rady
   (/ (getdist
   "\nEnter Y distance:") 2))
 (setq zheight
   (getdist
   "\Enter Z height: "))
 (setq zthk
   (getdist
   "\Enter slab thickness: "))
 (setq nlevels
   (getint
   "\Enter number of levels: "))
 (setq ymaxoff
   (getdist
   "\Enter max Y offset: "))
 (setq angy
   (getreal
   "\Enter angle multiple: "))
 (setq ycycles
   (getreal
   "\Enter number of curve
    cycles: "))
 ; segments
 (setq xtimes (fix (/ 360.0 2)))
 ; start angle
 (setq sxang
   (* (fix (* (rn) 24)) angy))
 (setq xanginc
   (/ (* 360.0 ycycles) xtimes))
 ; start Z location
 (setq zelev 0.0)
 (setq xloc (nth 0 pnt0))
 (setq yloc (nth 1 pnt0))
 ; total area and perimeter
 (setq totalarea 0.0)
 (setq totalperm 0.0)
 (repeat nlevels
  ; start outline
  (command ".PLINE")
  ; curve face start x location
  (setq xang sxang)
  (setq rang 0.0)
  (setq ranginc (/ 360.0 xtimes))
  (setq xnum 1)
  (repeat (+ xtimes 1)
   ; radius offset
   (setq roff
     (* (+ (sin (dtr (* xang 2)))
     (sin (dtr (* xang 3))))
     ymaxoff))
   ; ellipse
   (setq xoff
     (* (+ radx roff)
     (cos (dtr rang))))
   (setq yoff
     (* (+ rady roff)
     (sin (dtr rang))))
   (setq npnt (list
     (+ xloc xoff)
     (+ yloc yoff) zelev))
   (command npnt)
```

```
    ; save first pt
    (if (= xnum 1) (setq fpnt npnt))
    ; inc segment
    (setq rang (+ rang ranginc))
    (setq xang (+ xang xanginc))
    (setq xnum (+ xnum 1))
  )
  ; close
  (command "c")
  (command ".ZOOM" "e")
  ; compute area
  (command ".AREA" "o" "last")
  (setq flrarea
    (/ (getvar "AREA") 144))
  (setq flrperm
    (/ (getvar "PERIMETER") 12))
  ; acum floor and building surface
  (setq totalarea
    (+ totalarea flrarea))
  (setq totalperm
    (+ totalperm flrperm))
  ; extrude to height
  (command ".EXTRUDE"
    "last" "" zthk)
  ; versions prior to 2007
  ; require taper parameter
  ;(command ".EXTRUDE"
  ;  "last" "" zheight "")
  ; inc levels elev
  (setq zelev (+ zelev zheight))
  ; inc start angle
  (setq sxang (+ sxang angy))
 )
 (princ "\nTotal area: ")
   (princ (rtos totalarea 2 0))
 (princ "  Perimeter: ")
   (princ (rtos totalperm 2 0))
 (princ)
)
;---------------------------------
```

Another shape to consider is the superellipse, or Lame Curve, which generates a rounded rectangle.

Add PROG05a using a copy of PROG05. Change the elliptical curve to the superellipse, and change the radius-offset curve.

Replace the radius-offset and ellipse computations with:

```
; radius offset
(setq roff
  (* (+ (sin (dtr xang))
  (sin (dtr (* xang 2))))
  ymaxoff))
; superellipse
(setq xoff
  (* (+ radx roff)
  (* (expt (abs
  (cos (dtr rang))) 0.5)
  (sign (cos (dtr rang))))))
(setq yoff
  (* (+ rady roff)
  (* (expt (abs
  (sin (dtr rang))) 0.5)
  (sign (sin (dtr rang))))))
(setq npnt (list
  (+ xloc xoff)
  (+ yloc yoff) zelev))
(command npnt)
```

Also include the sign function:

```
;---------------------------------
(defun sign (a) (if (< a 0.0)
  (- 0 1.0) (+ 0 1.0)))
;---------------------------------
```

Sample script file for PROG05a:

```
;---------------------------------
(prog05a)
;Enter X distance:
125
;Enter Y distance:
50
;Enter Z height:
9.5
;Enter slab thickness:
```

```
0.25
;Enter number of levels:
36
;Enter max Y offset:
1.0
;Enter angle multiple:
30
;Enter number of curve cycles:
3.0
;-----------------------------------
```

Repeated random floorplates

In the previous examples, a set of random selections were made at each floor level. Another approach is to create a single floor randomly and then repeat it vertically.

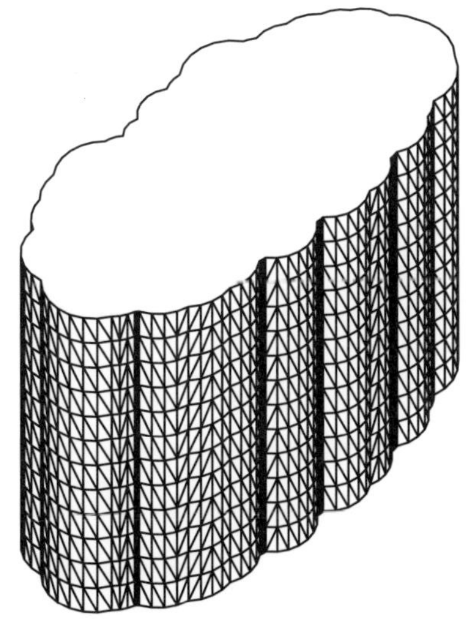

PROG06: elliptical series of random circles

Add function PROG06. Using the concepts in the last few functions, generate a series of randomly sized circles along the edge of an ellipse. Extrude to a floor height and then, using the COPY command, repeat it vertically for the entered number of levels.

Sample script file for PROG06:

```
;-----------------------------------
(prog06)
;Enter X distance:
125
;Enter Y distance:
50
;Enter Z height:
9.5
;Enter number of levels:
12
;Enter number of locations:
36
;Enter min radius:
6.0
;Enter max radius:
15.0
;-----------------------------------
```

Completed function PROG06:

```
;-----------------------------------
(defun prog06 ()
 (graphscr)
 (command ".ERASE" "all" "")
 ; set start point
 (setq pnt0 (list 0 0 0))
 (prompt "\nPROG06:")
 (setq radx
   (/ (getdist
   "\nEnter X distance:") 2))
 (setq rady
   (/ (getdist
   "\nEnter Y distance:") 2))
 (setq zheight
   (getdist "\Enter Z height: "))
 (setq nlevels
   (getint
   "\Enter number of levels: "))
 (setq nlocs
   (getint
   "\Enter number of locations: "))
 (setq cradmin
   (getdist "\Enter min radius: "))
 (setq cradmax
   (getdist "\Enter max radius: "))
 ; locations along ellipse
```

```
(setq rang 0.0)
(setq ranginc (/ 360.0 nlocs))
(setq xloc (nth 0 pnt0))
(setq yloc (nth 1 pnt0))
(repeat nlocs
 ; ellipse
 (setq xoff
   (* radx (cos (dtr rang))))
 (setq yoff
   (* rady (sin (dtr rang))))
 (setq pntc (list
   (+ xloc xoff)
   (+ yloc yoff) 0.0))
 ; radius
 (setq crad
   (+ cradmin (* (rn)
   (- cradmax cradmin))))
 (command ".CIRCLE" pntc crad)
 ; extrude to height
 (command ".EXTRUDE"
   "last" "" zheight)
 ; versions prior to 2007
 ; require taper parameter
 ;(command ".EXTRUDE"
 ;  "last" "" zheight "")
 (command ".ZOOM" "e")
 ; inc ang location
 (setq rang (+ rang ranginc))
)
; center core
(command ".ELLIPSE"
  "c" pnt0 (list radx 0 0) rady)
; extrude to height
(command ".EXTRUDE"
  "last" "" zheight)
; versions prior to 2007
; require taper parameter
;(command ".EXTRUDE"
;  "last" "" zheight "")
; union all
(command ".UNION" "all" "")
; copy to full height
(setq llist (ssadd (entlast)))
; set above first copy
(setq zelev zheight)
(repeat (- nlevels 1)
 (command ".COPY"
   llist "" pnt0
    (list (nth 0 pnt0)
    (nth 1 pnt0) zelev))
  (command ".ZOOM" "e")
  ; inc height
  (setq zelev (+ zelev zheight))
 )
 (princ)
)
;---------------------------------
```

Review the structure of function PROG06: how the points along the ellipse are computed, how the circles are placed, the inclusion of an elliptical core to tie the individual circles together, and repetition of the floor with the COPY command.

Following the same concept, randomly select a starting and ending level along the elliptical path.

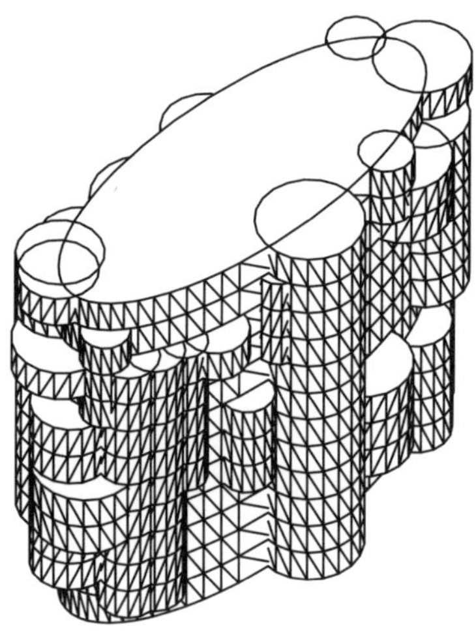

PROG06a: elliptical series of random circles, varied heights

Add function PROG06a using a copy of PROG06. Copy a randomly sized circle to a set of selected levels; also add an elliptical floor mass at each level.

Sample script file for PROG06a:

```
;----------------------------------
(prog06a)
;Enter X distance:
125
;Enter Y distance:
50
;Enter Z height:
9.5
;Enter number of levels:
12
;Enter number of locations:
36
;Enter min radius:
6.0
;Enter max radius:
15.0
;----------------------------------
```

Completed function PROG06a:

```
;----------------------------------
(defun prog06a ()
 (graphscr)
 (command ".ERASE" "all" "")
 ; set start point
 (setq pnt0 (list 0 0 0))
 (prompt "\nPROG06a:")
 (setq radx
   (/ (getdist
   "\nEnter X distance:") 2))
 (setq rady
   (/ (getdist
   "\nEnter Y distance:") 2))
 (setq zheight
   (getdist "\Enter Z height: "))
 (setq nlevels
   (getint
   "\Enter number of levels: "))
 (setq nlocs
   (getint
   "\Enter number of locations: "))
 (setq cradmin
   (getdist
   "\Enter min radius: "))
 (setq cradmax
   (getdist
   "\Enter max radius: "))
; locations along ellipse
(setq rang 0.0)
(setq ranginc (/ 360.0 nlocs))
(setq xloc (nth 0 pnt0))
(setq yloc (nth 1 pnt0))
(repeat nlocs
 ; ellipse
 (setq xoff
   (* radx (cos (dtr rang))))
 (setq yoff
   (* rady (sin (dtr rang))))
 ; radius
 (setq crad
   (+ cradmin (* (rn)
   (- cradmax cradmin))))
 ; get bottom elev
 (setq slevel
   (fix (* (rn) nlevels)))
 (setq nlevel
   (+ (fix (* (rn)
   (- nlevels slevel))) 1))
 (setq zelev (* slevel zheight))
 (repeat nlevel
  (setq pntc (list
    (+ xloc xoff)
    (+ yloc yoff) zelev))
  (command ".CIRCLE" pntc crad)
  ; extrude to height
  (command ".EXTRUDE"
    "last" "" zheight)
  ; versions prior to 2007
  ; require taper parameter
  ;(command ".EXTRUDE"
  ;  "last" "" zheight "")
  (command ".ZOOM" "e")
  (setq zelev (+ zelev zheight))
 )
 ; inc x location
 (setq rang (+ rang ranginc))
)
; center core
(setq zelev 0.0)
(repeat nlevels
 (command ".ELLIPSE"
   "c" (list (nth 0 pnt0)
   (nth 1 pnt0) zelev)
```

```
    (list radx 0 zelev) rady)
  (command ".EXTRUDE"
    "last" "" zheight)
  ; versions prior to 2007
  ; require taper parameter
  ;(command ".EXTRUDE"
  ;  "last" "" zheight "")
  (setq zelev (+ zelev zheight))
 )
 (princ)
)
;----------------------------------
```

Review the structure of function PROG06a: how each circle and cylinder is repeated vertically and the addition of the elliptical core to tie the cylinders together.

Repeated random building masses along a path

In the previous examples, a set of random selections were made at each floor level or individual areas of floors. Another approach is to create larger masses composing the building form.

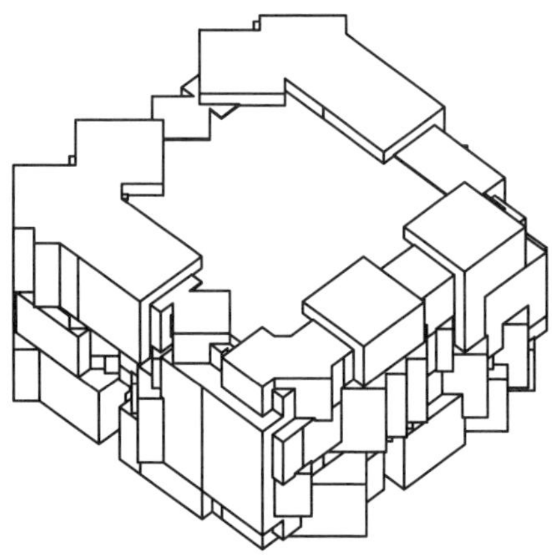

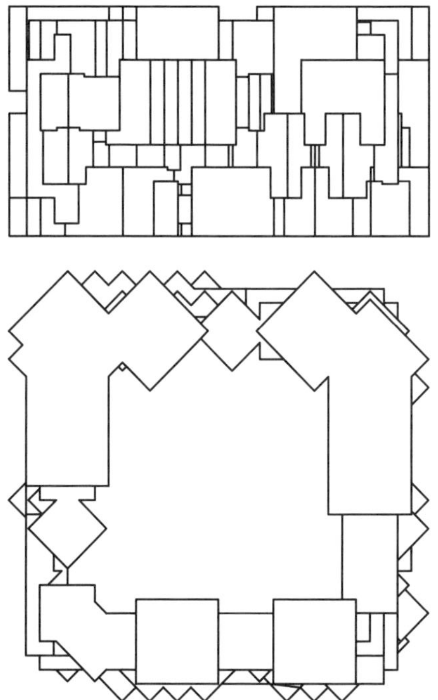

PROG07: random building masses along a rectangular edge

Add function PROG07 using a copy of PROG03. Place randomly sized cubes along a rectangular edge, including random size and rotation. UNION all cubes by level and then UNION all the levels. Finally, since some of the cubes extend below ground level, slice off those below a zero elevation.

The random cube size is computed as a multiple of the grid, using:

```
; cube dimension
(setq cx (+ cminx (* (fix (* (rn)
  (/ (- cmaxx cminx)
  xyside))) xyside)))
```

The cube is generated using the BOX command:

```
; draw cube
(command ".BOX"
  "ce" pnt2 "c" cx)
```

The cube is rotated using the ROTATE3D command:

```
; rotate
(command ".ROTATE3D"
  "last" "" "z" pnt2
  (+ crang 0.0001))
```

Note that this rotation is around the z-axis, but x and y are also available. Also note that the rotation angle is computed so that it is neither zero nor a multiple of 360 degrees.

The mass below the ground elevation is removed using the SLICE command:

```
; slice at ground
(command ".SLICE"
  "all" "" "XY"
  (list 0 0 0) (list 0 0 1))
```

Sample script file for PROG07:

```
;----------------------------------
(prog07)
;Enter XY side:
5
;Enter number X repeats:
12
;Enter number Y repeats:
12
;Enter Z height:
9.5
;Enter number of levels:
4
;Enter cube min size:
5.0
;Enter cube max size:
20.0
;Enter angle increment
45.0
;----------------------------------
```

Include the following at the very end of the LSP file to load the ROTATE3D command:

```
;----------------------------------
; load solid modeling DLL
(arxload "geom3d")
;----------------------------------
```

Completed function PROG07:

```
;----------------------------------
(defun prog07 ()
 (graphscr)
 (command ".ERASE" "all" "")
 ; set start point
 (setq pnt0 (list 0 0 0))
 (prompt "\nPROG07:")
 (setq xyside
   (getdist pnt0
   "\nEnter XY side:"))
 (setq xtimes
   (getint
   "\nEnter number X repeats:"))
 (setq ytimes
   (getint
   "\nEnter number Y repeats:"))
 (setq zheight
   (getdist "\nEnter Z height: "))
 (setq nlevels
   (getint
   "\nEnter number of levels: "))
 (setq cminx
   (getdist
   "\nEnter cube min size: "))
 (setq cmaxx
   (getdist
   "\nEnter cube max size: "))
 (setq angrot
   (getreal
   "\Enter angle multiple: "))
 ; start Z location
 (setq zelev 0.0)
 (repeat nlevels
  ; level block
  (setq pnt1 (list
    (+ (nth 0 pnt0) (/ xyside 2.0))
    (+ (nth 1 pnt0) (/ xyside 2.0))
    zelev))
```

```
(setq pnt2 (list
  (+ (nth 0 pnt1)
  (- (* xtimes xyside) xyside))
  (+ (nth 1 pnt1)
  (- (* ytimes xyside) xyside))
  zelev))
(command ".RECTANGLE" pnt1 pnt2)
(command ".ZOOM" "e")
(command ".EXTRUDE"
  "last" "" zheight)
; versions prior to 2007
; require taper parameter
;(command ".EXTRUDE"
;  "last" "" zheight "")
(setq llist (ssadd (entlast)))
; start y location
(setq ynum 1)
(setq yloc 0)
(repeat ytimes
 ; start x location
 (setq xnum 1)
 (setq xloc 0)
 (repeat xtimes
  (if (or (or (or (= ynum 1)
    (= ynum ytimes)) (= xnum 1))
    (= xnum xtimes))
   (progn
    ; lower corner pt
    (setq pnt1
      (list xloc yloc zelev))
    ; center of module
    (setq pnt2 (list
      (+ (nth 0 pnt1)
      (/ xyside 2))
      (+ (nth 1 pnt1)
      (/ xyside 2))
      (+ zelev (/ zheight 2))))
    ; cube dimension
    (setq cx
      (+ cminx (* (fix (* (rn)
      (+ (/ (- cmaxx cminx)
      xyside) 1))) xyside)))
    ; rotation
    (setq crang
      (* (fix (* (rn) angrot))
      angrot))
    ; draw cube
    (command ".BOX"
      "ce" pnt2 "c" cx)
    (command ".ZOOM" "e")
    ; rotate
    (command ".ROTATE3D"
      "last" "" "z" pnt2
      (+ crang 0.0001))
    ; add to list
    (setq llist
      (ssadd (entlast) llist))
   ))
  ; inc x location
  (setq xloc (+ xloc xyside))
  (setq xnum (+ xnum 1))
 )
 ; union level
 (command ".UNION" "all" "")
 ; inc y location
 (setq yloc (+ yloc xyside))
 (setq ynum (+ ynum 1))
)
; inc levels elev
(setq zelev (+ zelev zheight))
)
; union cubes
(command ".UNION" "all" "")
; slice at ground
(command ".SLICE"
  "all" "" "XY" (list 0 0 0)
  (list 0 0 1))
(princ)
)
;---------------------------------
```

An alternative is using a nonrectangular edge

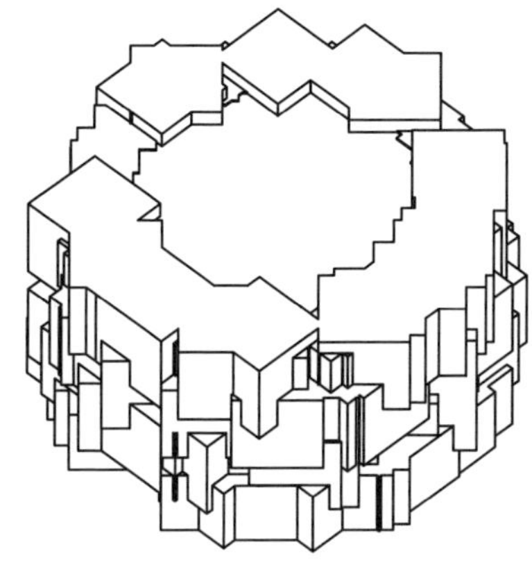

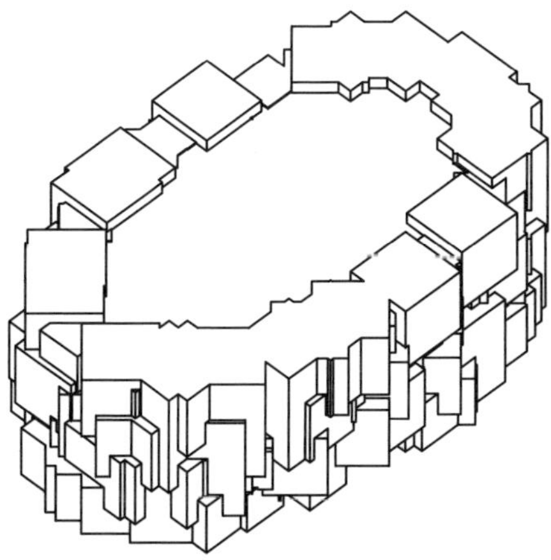

PROG07a: random building masses along an elliptical edge

Add function PROG07a. Using a copy of PROG07 and the computations in PROG06a for an elliptical path, place the random cubes along circular and elliptical paths.

Sample script file for PROG07a:

```
;-----------------------------
(prog07a)
;Enter XY side:
5
;Enter X radius:
100
;Enter Y radius:
60
;Enter Z height:
9.5
;Enter number of levels:
4
;Enter number of locations:
64
;Enter cube min size:
5.0
;Enter cube max size:
20.0
;Enter angle increment
45.0
;---------------------------------
```

Completed function PROG07a:

```
;---------------------------------
(defun prog07a ()
 (graphscr)
 (command ".ERASE" "all" "")
 ; set start point
 (setq pnt0 (list 0 0 0))
 (prompt "\nPROG07a:")
 (setq xyside
   (getdist pnt0
   "\nEnter XY side:"))
 (setq radx
   (/ (getdist
   "\nEnter X distance:") 2))
 (setq rady
   (/ (getdist
   "\nEnter Y distance:") 2))
 (setq zheight
   (getdist "\nEnter Z height: "))
 (setq nlevels
   (getint
   "\nEnter number of levels: "))
```

```
(setq nlocs
  (getint
  "\Enter number of locations: "))
(setq cminx
  (getdist
  "\nEnter cube min size: "))
(setq cmaxx
  (getdist
  "\nEnter cube max size: "))
(setq angrot
  (getreal
  "\Enter angle multiple: "))
; start Z location
(setq zelev 0.0)
(repeat nlevels
 ; level block
 (command ".ELLIPSE"
   "c" (list (nth 0 pnt0)
   (nth 1 pnt0) zelev)
   (list radx 0 zelev) rady)
 (command ".ZOOM" "e")
 (command ".EXTRUDE"
   "last" "" zheight)
 ; versions prior to 2007
 ; require taper parameter
 ;(command ".EXTRUDE"
 ;  "last" "" zheight "")
 (setq llist (ssadd (entlast)))
 ; locations along ellipse
 (setq rang 0.0)
 (setq ranginc (/ 360.0 nlocs))
 (setq xloc (nth 0 pnt0))
 (setq yloc (nth 1 pnt0))
 (repeat nlocs
  ; ellipse
  (setq xoff
    (* radx (cos (dtr rang))))
  (setq yoff
    (* rady (sin (dtr rang))))
  ; center of module
  (setq pnt2 (list
    (+ xloc xoff)
    (+ yloc yoff)
    (+ zelev (/ zheight 2))))
  ; cube dimension
  (setq cx
    (+ cminx (* (fix (* (rn)
    (+ (/ (- cmaxx cminx)
    xyside) 1))) xyside)))
  ; rotation
  (setq crang
    (* (fix (* (rn) angrot))
    angrot))
  ; draw cube
  (command ".BOX"
    "ce" pnt2 "c" cx)
  (command ".ZOOM" "e")
  ; rotate
  (command ".ROTATE3D"
    "last" "" "z" pnt2
    (+ crang 0.0001))
  ; add to list
  (setq llist
    (ssadd (entlast) llist))
  ; inc ang
  (setq rang (+ rang ranginc))
 )
 ; union level
 (command ".UNION" "all" "")
 ; inc levels elev
 (setq zelev (+ zelev zheight))
)
; union cubes
(command ".UNION" "all" "")
; slice at ground
(command ".SLICE"
  "all" "" "XY" (list 0 0 0)
  (list 0 0 1))
(princ)
)
;----------------------------------
```

Consider other closed mathematical curves that could be used as paths for generating random elements. These examples used cubes; consider other three-dimensional shapes that could be placed.

Since all elements in the last series were constructed as solids, use the SECTION command to generate floor plans for each level.

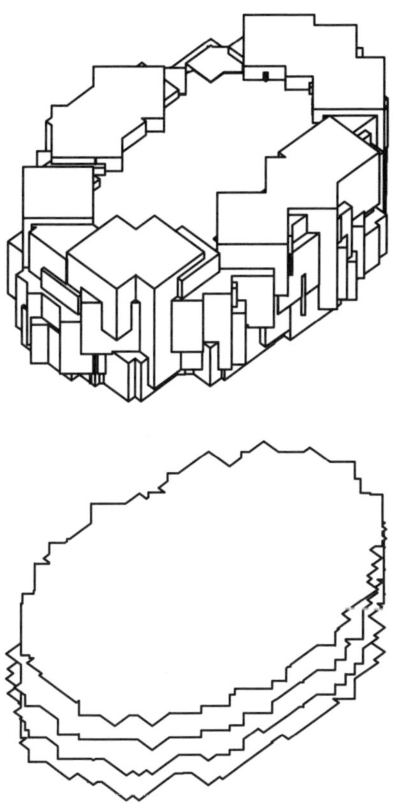

PROG07b: random building masses with floor plans

Add function PROG07b. Using a copy of PROG07a, add the generation of floor plans and total area.

After the SLICE command, add the following:

```
; generate floor plans
 (setq totalarea 0.0)
 (setq totalperm 0.0)
 (setq zelev 0.0)
 (repeat nlevels
  ; get section
  (command ".SECTION"
    "all" "" "xy" (list 0 0 zelev))
  ; move it
  (command ".MOVE"
    "last" "" (list 0 0 zelev)
    (list (+ (nth 0 pnt0)
    (* radx 3.0)) (nth 1 pnt0)
    zelev))
  ; compute area
  (command ".AREA" "o" "last")
  (setq flrarea
    (/ (getvar "AREA") 144))
  (setq flrperm
    (/ (getvar "PERIMETER") 12))
  ; acum floor and building
  ; surface
  (setq totalarea
    (+ totalarea flrarea))
  (setq totalperm
    (+ totalperm flrperm))
  ; inc height
  (setq zelev (+ zelev zheight))
 )
(command ".ZOOM" "e")
 (princ "\nTotal area: ")
   (princ (rtos totalarea 2 0))
 (princ "  Perimeter: ")
   (princ (rtos totalperm 2 0))
```

Same script file as in PROG07a.

Randomly repeated building masses

In the previous approach, as in many others we've covered, a path was used as framework to generate random forms. A more random approach would be to generate random elements within a boundary.

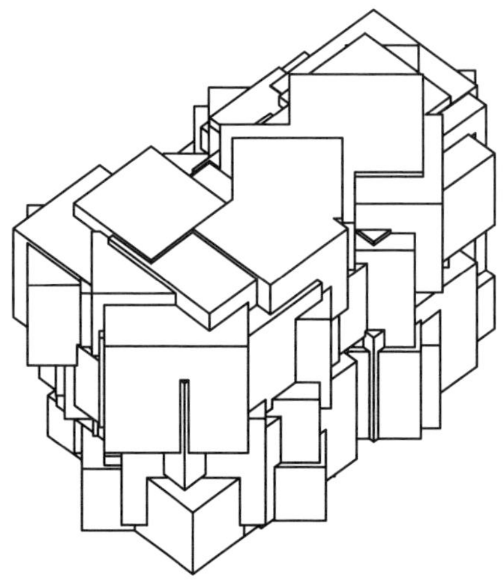

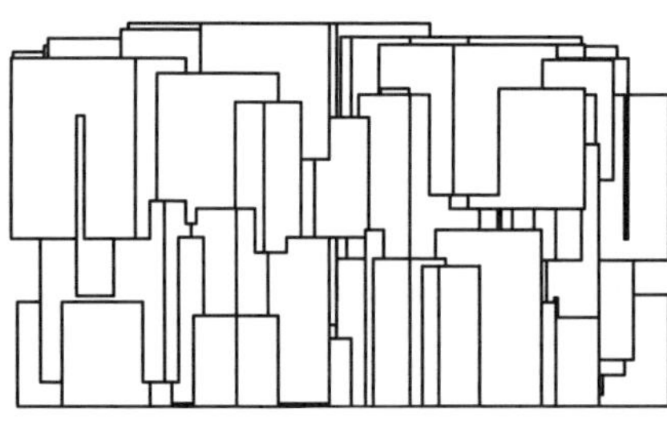

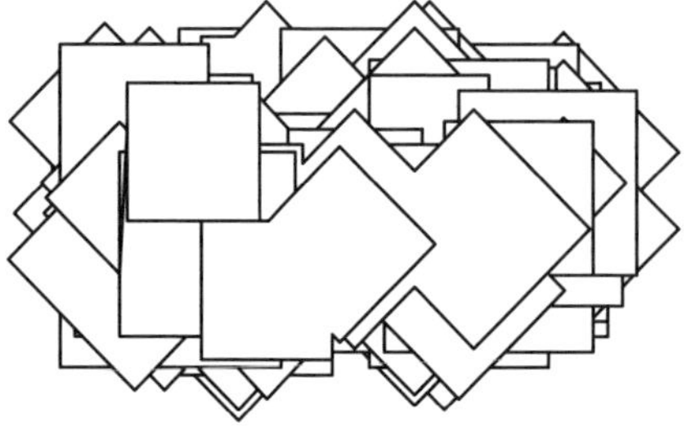

PROG08: random building masses within a boundary

Add function PROG08. Using a copy of PROG07, generate some number of random cubes within the entered boundaries.

A random location for the cube is computed using the grid module and floor height:

```
; random location
(setq xoff
  (* (fix (* (rn) xtimes))
  xyside))
(setq yoff
  (* (fix (* (rn) ytimes))
  xyside))
(setq zelev
  (* (fix (* (rn) nlevels))
  zheight))
```

These dimensions are also used as modules to place the cubes.

Sample script file for PROG08:

```
;-----------------------------------
(prog08)
;Enter XY side:
5
;Enter number X repeats:
32
;Enter number Y repeats:
12
;Enter Z height:
9.5
;Enter number of levels:
12
;Enter cube min size:
10.0
;Enter cube max size:
60.0
;Enter angle increment
45.0
;Enter number of random placements:
256
;-----------------------------------
```

Completed function PROG08:

```
;-----------------------------------
(defun prog08 ()
 (graphscr)
 (command ".ERASE" "all" "")
 ; set start point
 (setq pnt0 (list 0 0 0))
 (prompt "\nPROG08:")
 (setq xyside
   (getdist pnt0
   "\nEnter XY side:"))
 (setq xtimes
   (getint
   "\nEnter number X repeats:"))
 (setq ytimes
   (getint
   "\nEnter number Y repeats:"))
 (setq zheight
   (getdist "\nEnter Z height: "))
 (setq nlevels
   (getint
   "\nEnter number of levels: "))
 (setq cminx
   (getdist
   "\nEnter cube min size: "))
 (setq cmaxx
   (getdist
   "\nEnter cube max size: "))
 (setq angrot
   (getreal
   "\Enter angle multiple: "))
 (setq ntimes
   (getint
   "\nEnter number of random
    placements: "))
 ; number of placements
 (repeat ntimes
  ; random location
  (setq xoff
    (* (fix (* (rn) xtimes))
    xyside))
  (setq yoff
    (* (fix (* (rn) ytimes))
    xyside))
  (setq zelev
    (* (fix (* (rn) nlevels))
    zheight))
  ; center of module
  (setq pnt2 (list
    (+ (nth 0 pnt0) xoff)
    (+ (nth 1 pnt0) yoff)
    (+ (nth 2 pnt0) zelev)))
  ; cube dimension
  (setq cx
    (+ cminx
    (* (fix (* (rn)
    (+ (/ (- cmaxx cminx)
    xyside) 1))) xyside)))
  ; rotation
  (setq crang
    (* (fix (* (rn) angrot))
    angrot))
  ; draw cube
  (command ".BOX"
    "ce" pnt2 "c" cx)
  (command ".ZOOM" "e")
  ; rotate
  (command ".ROTATE3D"
    "last" "" "z" pnt2
    (+ crang 0.0001))
 )
 ; union cubes
 (command ".UNION" "all" "")
 ; slice at ground
 (command ".SLICE"
   "all" "" "XY" (list 0 0 0)
   (list 0 0 1))
 (princ)
)
;-----------------------------------
```

Many of the cubes extend outside the boundary, consider trimming the cubes to the boundary edge.

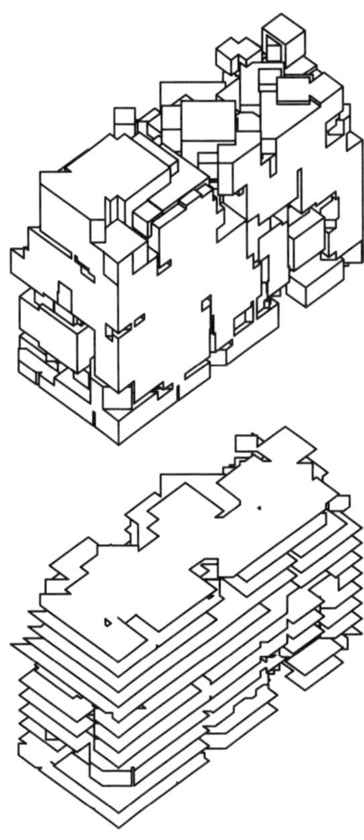

PROG08a: random building masses within a trimmed boundary

Add function PROG08a. Using a copy of PROG08, trim the cubes to the four sides of the boundary and generate floor plans for the building mass.

Sample script file for PROG08a:

```
;---------------------------------
(prog08a)
;Enter XY side:
5
;Enter number X repeats:
32
;Enter number Y repeats:
12
;Enter Z height:
9.5
;Enter number of levels:
12
;Enter cube min size:
10.0
;Enter cube max size:
30.0
;Enter angle increment
45.0
;Enter number of random placements:
256
;---------------------------------
```

Completed function PROG08a:

```
;---------------------------------
(defun prog08a ()
 (graphscr)
 (command ".ERASE" "all" "")
 ; set start point
 (setq pnt0 (list 0 0 0))
 (prompt "\nPROG08a:")
 (setq xyside
   (getdist pnt0
   "\nEnter XY side:"))
 (setq xtimes
   (getint
   "\nEnter number X repeats:"))
 (setq ytimes
   (getint
   "\nEnter number Y repeats:"))
 (setq zheight
   (getdist "\nEnter Z height: "))
 (setq nlevels
   (getint
   "\nEnter number of levels: "))
```

```
(setq cminx
  (getdist
  "\nEnter cube min size: "))
(setq cmaxx
  (getdist
  "\nEnter cube max size: "))
(setq angrot
  (getreal
  "\Enter angle multiple: "))
(setq ntimes
  (getint
  "\nEnter number of random
   placements: "))
; number of placements
(repeat ntimes
 ; random location
 (setq xoff
   (* (fix (* (rn) xtimes))
   xyside))
 (setq yoff
   (* (fix (* (rn) ytimes))
   xyside))
 (setq zelev
   (* (fix (* (rn) nlevels))
   zheight))
 ; center of module
 (setq pnt2 (list
   (+ (nth 0 pnt0) xoff)
   (+ (nth 1 pnt0) yoff)
   (+ (nth 2 pnt0) zelev)))
 ; cube dimension
 (setq cx
   (+ cminx (* (fix (* (rn)
   (+ (/ (- cmaxx cminx)
   xyside) 1))) xyside)))
 ; rotation
 (setq crang
   (* (fix (* (rn) angrot))
   angrot))
 ; draw cube
 (command ".BOX"
   "ce" pnt2 "c" cx)
 (command ".ZOOM" "e")
 ; rotate
 (command ".ROTATE3D"
   "last" "" "z" pnt2
   (+ crang 0.0001))
)
; union cubes
(command ".UNION" "all" "")
; slice at ground
(command ".SLICE"
  "all" "" "XY"
  (list 0 0 0) (list 0 0 1))
; slice at sides
(command ".SLICE"
  "all" "" "YZ"
  (list 0 0 0) (list 1 0 0))
(command ".SLICE"
  "all" "" "ZX"
  (list 0 0 0) (list 0 1 0))
(command ".SLICE"
  "all" "" "YZ"
  (list (* xtimes xyside) 0 0)
  (list 1 0 0))
(command ".SLICE"
  "all" "" "ZX"
  (list 0 (* ytimes xyside) 0)
  (list 0 1 0))
; generate floor plans
(setq totalarea 0.0)
(setq totalperm 0.0)
(setq zelev 0.0)
(repeat nlevels
 ; get section
 (command ".SECTION"
   "all" "" "xy"
   (list 0 0 zelev))
 ; move it
 (command ".MOVE"
   "last" "" (list 0 0 zelev)
   (list (+ (nth 0 pnt0)
   (* (* xyside xtimes) 1.5))
   (nth 1 pnt0) zelev))
 ; compute area
 (command ".AREA" "o" "last")
 (setq flrarea
   (/ (getvar "AREA") 144))
 (setq flrperm
   (/ (getvar "PERIMETER") 12))
 ; acum floor and building
 ; surface
 (setq totalarea
   (+ totalarea flrarea))
 (setq totalperm
   (+ totalperm flrperm))
```

```
  ; inc height
  (setq zelev (+ zelev zheight))
 )
 (command ".ZOOM" "e")
 (princ "\nTotal area: ")
   (princ (rtos totalarea 2 0))
 (princ "  Perimeter: ")
   (princ (rtos totalperm 2 0))
 (princ)
)
;---------------------------------
```

Consider other three-dimensional shapes that could be randomly placed. Also consider other controls for better organizing randomness.

7.0

A variety of drawings and models can be created from data values collected from the environment or from other sources. One common example is topographic data, a series of x, y, and z values that can be represented as a three-dimensional surface. Numeric data, images, and text all have the same potential to create forms.

7.1 Constructions from Weather Data

Numeric data is available from a number of sources, including those that represent measurements of the environment.

Weather is available in Typical Meteorological Year (TMY) format. A TMY is a data set that includes hourly values of solar radiation and meteorological elements for a one-year period. It consists of months selected from individual years and concatenated to form a complete year. The intended use is for computer simulations of solar energy conversion and building systems; the energy analysis software program DOE2 uses this data. For more information on these files and the data they contain, search the web for the National Solar Radiation Data Base (NSRDB) and the file format TMY2.

Weather data sets are available for over 200 locations. The TMY2 data sets and manual were produced by the National Renewable Energy Laboratory's (NREL) Analytic Studies Division under the Resource Assessment Program, which is funded and monitored by the United States Department of Energy's Office of Solar Energy Conversion.

For these examples, the data set for Chicago, `94846.exe`, is uncompressed to `94846.tm2`. This file can be viewed with Microsoft Notepad. If you wish to use the TMY3 file format, the data field discussed will have to be adjusted to meet TMY3 specifications or use the TMY3 to TMY4 conversion utility.

Reading and writing data files

Start a new drawing and set the units to architectural; set the grid to 1 foot, and turn off all snaps and dynamic input.

Start a new AutoLISP file in the editor `CH07A.LSP` and add functions `dtr` and `rtd`.

The first step will be to extract data from the TMY2 file. The first line in the file is an identification and can be ignored:

```
94846 CHICAGO                    IL   -6 N 41
47 W   87 45    190
```

The remaining lines consist of weather data for every day and every hour for a full year; January 1 reads:

```
Characters 1-50:
 86010101000000000000?000
00?00000?00000?00000?0000
Characters 51-100:
0?00000?009A709A7-122A7-1
61A7073A70995A7270A7026A7
Characters 101-142
0241A702743A7099999999900
4E7090F8000A701E7
```

The data of greatest interest for construction can be found in these locations:

```
Characters:
004 - 005 Month, 1-12
006 - 007 Day, 1-31
008 - 009 Hour, 1-24
068 - 071 Dry bulb temperature in
  tenths of degrees Celsius
074 - 077 Dew point temperature in
  tenths of degrees Celsius
080 - 082 Relative humidity in
  percent
085 - 088 Atmospheric pressure at
  station in millibars
091 - 093 Wind direction in degrees,
  0-360, N = 0 or 360, E = 90,
  S = 180,W = 270
096 - 098 Wind speed in tenths of
  meters per second
124 - 126 Precipitable water in
  millimeters
134 - 136 Snow depth in centimeters
```

Add function PROG01 to read each line in the file and display the data values listed on the previous page:

```
;-----------------------------------
(defun prog01 ()
 (graphscr)
 (princ "\nProg01:")
 ; file to read
 (setq fh1 (open
   "C:\\TMY2_data\\94846.tm2" "r"))
 (while fh1
  (setq nline (read-line fh1))
  (if nline
   (progn
    (princ "\n")(princ nline)
   )
   (setq fh1 (close fh1))
  )
 )
 (textscr)
 (princ)
)
;-----------------------------------
```

Execute PROG01 from the command line. The last two lines on the text screen will read:

```
 68123123000000000000?00000?00000?00000?0
0000?00000?00000?007
A706A7-211A7-272A7058A70999A7260A7082A7006
4A700579A70999099949003
E7090F8010A700E7
 68123124000000000000?00000?00000?00000?0
0000?00000?00000?010
A707A7-211A7-272A7058A71000A7270A7088A7006
4A700579A70999999949003
E7090F8010A700E7
```

Review the structure of PROG01.

The data file is opened using:

```
(setq fh1 (open
   "C:\\TMY2_data\\94846.tm2" "r"))
```

The option r opens the file for reading. The variable fh1 represents the "handle" for the actual file being opened. If the file is not found, fh1 would be set to nil. The double back slashes are required in the path's filename.

To read a complete line from the file as a string, use:

```
(setq nline (read-line fh1))
```

When the end of file is reached, the variable nline will be set to nil.

To display the line from the file, use:

```
(princ "\n") (princ nline)
```

To close the file, use:

```
(setq fh1 (close fh1))
```

The next step is to read only the data needed.

Add function PROG01a. Using a copy of PROG01, extract from the line only the portions that contain the information of interest.

Completed function PROG01a:

```
;-----------------------------------
(defun prog01a ()
 (graphscr)
 (princ "\nProg01a:")
 ; file to read
 (setq fh1 (open
   "C:\\TMY2_data\\94846.tm2" "r"))
 (while fh1
  (setq nline (read-line fh1))
  (if nline
   (progn
    ; 004 - 005 Month, 1-12
    (princ (atoi (substr nline 4 2)))
      (princ " ")
    ; 006 - 007 Day, 1-31
    (princ (atoi (substr nline 6 2)))
      (princ " ")
```

```
    ; 008 - 009 Hour, 1-24
    (princ (atoi (substr nline 8 2)))
      (princ " ")
    ; 068 - 071 Dry bulb temperature
    ;  in tenths of degrees Celsius
    (princ (/ (atof
      (substr nline 68 4)) 10.0))
      (princ " ")
    ; 074 - 077 Dew point temperature
    ;  in tenths of Celisue
    (princ (/ (atof
      (substr nline 74 4)) 10.0))
      (princ " ")
    ; 080 - 082 Relative humidity
    ;  in percent
    (princ (atoi
      (substr nline 80 3)))
      (princ " ")
    ; 085 - 088 Atmospheric pressure
    ;  at station in millibars
    (princ (atoi
      (substr nline 85 4)))
      (princ " ")
    ; 091 - 093 Wind direction in
    ;  degrees, 0-360
    (princ (atoi
      (substr nline 91 3)))
      (princ " ")
    ; 096 - 098 Wind speed in tenths
    ;  of meters per second
    (princ (/ (atof
      (substr nline 96 3)) 10.0))
      (princ " ")
    ; 124 - 126 Precipitable water
    ;  in millimeters
    (princ (atoi
      (substr nline 124 3)))
      (princ " ")
    ; 134 - 136 Snow depth in
    ;  centimeters
    (princ (atoi
      (substr nline 134 3)))
    (princ "\n")
   )
   (setq fh1 (close fh1))
  )
 )
 (textscr)
 (princ)
)
;-----------------------------------
```

Each data value is extracted from the input string and converted to its appropriate integer or real value.

Execute PROG01a from the command line; the data for December 31 should read as:

```
12  31  1  -11.7  -14.4  80  994  260
6.7  5  10
12  31  2  -14.4  -17.2  79  994  270  4.1
4  10
12  31  3  -15.6  -18.9  76  996  240
4.1  4  10
12  31  4  -18.9  -21.7  79  997  250
10.3  4  10
12  31  5  -21.1  -27.2  58  999  240
8.2  3  10
12  31  6  -21.7  -27.8  58  999  250
8.2  3  10
12  31  7  -22.2  -28.3  58  1000  250
8.2  3  10
12  31  8  -22.8  -28.9  57  1001  260
9.3  3  10
12  31  9  -22.2  -28.3  58  1002  270
9.8  3  10
12  31  10  -21.1  -27.8  55  1001  260
7.7  3  10
12  31  11  -20.6  -28.3  50  1001  270
8.2  3  10
12  31  12  -20.0  -28.3  47  1000  260
8.8  3  10
12  31  13  -18.9  -27.2  48  1000  250
7.2  3  10
12  31  14  -18.9  -26.7  51  999  240
7.2  3  10
12  31  15  -18.3  -26.7  48  999  250
9.3  3  10
12  31  16  -18.3  -25.6  53  998  240
8.2  3  10
12  31  17  -18.3  -25.0  56  999  250
7.7  3  10
12  31  18  -18.9  -25.0  59  999  270
10.3  3  10
12  31  19  -20.0  -28.3  48  1000  270
9.3  3  10
12  31  20  -21.1  -28.9  50  1000  270
7.7  3  10
12  31  21  -21.7  -28.9  52  999  250
7.7  3  10
12  31  22  -21.7  -28.3  55  998  270
7.7  3  10
```

```
12   31   23   -21.1   -27.2   58   999   260
8.2   3   10
12   31   24   -21.1   -27.2   58   1000   270
8.8   3   10
```

To create drawings or models, the PROG01a function can be used to extract the data when needed, but our approach will be to first filter and prepare the data; then create a new file that contains only the data needed from the original set, in a form that is easy to use.

Add function PROG01b. Using a copy of PROG01a, copy the data values needed into a new file.

Completed function PROG01b:

```
;-----------------------------------
(defun prog01b ()
 (graphscr)
 (princ "\nProg01b:")
 ; file to write
 (setq fh2 (open
   "C:\\TMY2_data\\Chicago.txt" "w"))
 ; file to read
 (setq fh1 (open
   "C:\\TMY2_data\\94846.tm2" "r"))
 ; read first line and ignore
 (if (/= fh1)
   (setq nline (read-line fh1)))
 (while fh1
  (setq nline (read-line fh1))
  (if nline
   (progn
    ; 004 - 005 Month, 1-12
    (princ (atoi
      (substr nline 4 2)) fh2)
      (princ " " fh2)
    ; 006 - 007 Day, 1-31
    (princ (atoi
      (substr nline 6 2)) fh2)
      (princ " " fh2)
    ; 008 - 009 Hour, 1-24
    (princ (atoi
      (substr nline 8 2)) fh2)
      (princ " " fh2)
    ; 068 - 071 Dry bulb temperature
    ;  in tenths of degrees Celsius
    ; to Fahrenheit
    (setq val (+ (/ (* (/ (atof
      (substr nline 68 4)) 10.0) 9.0)
      5.0) 32))
    (princ val fh2) (princ " " fh2)
    ; 074 - 077 Dew point temperature
    ;  in tenths of
    ;  Celsius
    ; to Fahrenheit
    (setq val (+ (/ (* (/ (atof
      (substr nline 74 4)) 10.0) 9.0)
      5.0) 32))
    (princ val fh2) (princ " " fh2)
    ; 080 - 082 Relative humidity
    ;  in percent
    (princ (atoi
      (substr nline 80 3)) fh2)
      (princ " " fh2)
    ; 085 - 088 Atmospheric pressure
    ;  at station in millibars
    (princ (atoi
      (substr nline 85 4)) fh2)
      (princ " " fh2)
    ; 091 - 093 Wind direction in
    ;  degrees, 0-360
    (princ (atoi
      (substr nline 91 3)) fh2)
      (princ " " fh2)
    ; 096 - 098 Wind speed in tenths
    ;  of meters per second
    ; to miles/hr
    (setq val (* (/ (atof
      (substr nline 96 3)) 10.0)
      2.236))
    (princ val fh2) (princ " " fh2)
    ; 124 - 126 Precipitable water
    ;  in millimeters
    ; to inches
    (setq val (* (atoi
      (substr nline 124 3)) 0.03937))
    (princ val fh2) (princ " " fh2)
    ; 134 - 136 Snow depth in
    ;  centimeters
    ; to inches
    (setq val (* (atoi
      (substr nline 134 3)) 0.3937))
    (princ val fh2)
    (princ "\n" fh2)
   )
  (setq fh1 (close fh1))
 )
```

```
    )
    (setq fh2 (close fh2))
    (princ)
)
;----------------------------------
```

The output file is opened with:

```
(setq fh2 (open
    "C:\\TMY2_data\\Chicago.txt" "w"))
```

The option w opens the file for writing. If the file does not already exist, it will be created. If it does exist, it will be written over with new data.

To write data, the file handle is added to the princ function. For example:

```
; 124 - 126 Precipitable water
;  in millimeters
; to inches
 (setq val (* (atoi
  (substr nline 124 3)) 0.03937))
 (princ val fh2) (princ " " fh2)
```

Spaces are placed between data values and the princ function writes a new line character so the next data value is on a new line.

Note that the original values from the TMY2 file have been converted to other units.

Execute PROG01b from the command line. Once completed, open the file Chicago.txt using Microsoft Notepad.

The data for December 31 should read as:

```
12  31  1  10.94  6.08  80  994  260
14.9812  0.19685  3.937
12  31  2  6.08  1.04  79  994  270
9.1676  0.15748  3.937
12  31  3  3.92  -2.02  76  996  240
9.1676  0.15748  3.937
12  31  4  -2.02  -7.06  79  997  250
23.0308  0.15748  3.937
12  31  5  -5.98  -16.96  58  999  240
18.3352  0.11811  3.937
12  31  6  -7.06  -18.04  58  999  250
18.3352  0.11811  3.937
12  31  7  -7.96  -18.94  58  1000  250
18.3352  0.11811  3.937
12  31  8  -9.04  -20.02  57  1001  260
20.7948  0.11811  3.937
12  31  9  -7.96  -18.94  58  1002  270
21.9128  0.11811  3.937
12  31  10  -5.98  -18.04  55  1001  260
17.2172  0.11811  3.937
12  31  11  -5.08  -18.94  50  1001  270
18.3352  0.11811  3.937
12  31  12  -4.0  -18.94  47  1000  260
19.6768  0.11811  3.937
12  31  13  -2.02  -16.96  48  1000  250
16.0992  0.11811  3.937
12  31  14  -2.02  -16.06  51  999  240
16.0992  0.11811  3.937
12  31  15  -0.94  -16.06  48  999  250
20.7948  0.11811  3.937
12  31  16  -0.94  -14.08  53  998  240
18.3352  0.11811  3.937
12  31  17  -0.94  -13.0  56  999  250
17.2172  0.11811  3.937
12  31  18  -2.02  -13.0  59  999  270
23.0308  0.11811  3.937
12  31  19  -4.0  -18.94  48  1000  270
20.7948  0.11811  3.937
12  31  20  -5.98  -20.02  50  1000  270
17.2172  0.11811  3.937
12  31  21  -7.06  -20.02  52  999  250
17.2172  0.11811  3.937
12  31  22  -7.06  -18.94  55  998  270
17.2172  0.11811  3.937
12  31  23  -5.98  -16.96  58  999  260
18.3352  0.11811  3.937
12  31  24  -5.98  -16.96  58  1000  270
19.6768  0.11811  3.937
```

Other variations of the file can also be written, such as the average temperature by day or high and low temperatures for every day.

For these types of files, values separated by at least one space can also be created using any spreadsheet software capable of saving a file in MS-DOS text format. If the data contains commas, replace the commas with spaces.

Add function PROG01c. Using a copy of PROG0b, write a file that only computes the average temperature for each day.

Completed function PROG01c:

```
;-----------------------------------
(defun prog01c ()
 (graphscr)
 (princ "\nProg01c:")
 ; file to write
 (setq fh2 (open
   "C:\\TMY2_data\\Chicago03.txt"
   "w"))
 ; file to read
 (setq fh1 (open
   "C:\\TMY2_data\\94846.tm2" "r"))
 ; set total temp
 (setq totaltemp 0.0)
 ; set high/low temp
 (setq hightemp -9999.0)
 (setq lowtemp 9999.0)
 ; read first line and ignore
 (if (/= fh1)
   (setq nline (read-line fh1)))
 (while fh1
  (setq nline (read-line fh1))
  (if nline
   (progn
    ; 004 - 005 Month, 1-12
    (setq nmonth (atoi
      (substr nline 4 2)))
    ; 006 - 007 Day, 1-31
    (setq nday (atoi
      (substr nline 6 2)))
    ; 008 - 009 Hour, 1-24
    (setq nhour
      (atoi (substr nline 8 2)))
    ; 068 - 071 Dry bulb temperature
    ;  in tenths of degrees Celsius
    ; to Fahrenheit
    (setq tempval (+ (/ (* (/ (atof
      (substr nline 68 4)) 10.0) 9.0)
      5.0) 32))
    ; acum temp
    (setq totaltemp
      (+ totaltemp tempval))
    ; check temp
    (if (> tempval hightemp)
      (setq hightemp tempval))
    (if (< tempval lowtemp)
      (setq lowtemp tempval))
    ; check hour
    (if (= nhour 24) (progn
     ; compute average
     (setq avgtemp (/ totaltemp 24))
     ; write to file
     (princ nmonth fh2)
       (princ " " fh2)
     (princ nday fh2)
       (princ " " fh2)
     (princ avgtemp fh2)
       (princ " " fh2)
     (princ lowtemp fh2)
       (princ " " fh2)
     (princ hightemp fh2)
     (princ "\n" fh2)
     ; reset total temp
     (setq totaltemp 0.0)
     ; reset high/low temp
     (setq hightemp -9999.0)
     (setq lowtemp 9999.0)
    ))
   )
   (setq fh1 (close fh1))
  )
 )
 (setq fh2 (close fh2))
 (princ)
)
;-----------------------------------
```

Review how the temperature is extracted and collected to compute the average, as well as the high and low for each day.

Execute PROG01c from the command line. Once complete, open the file Chicago03.txt with Microsoft Notepad.

The data for December should read:

```
12  1   35.255   33.8   37.04
12  2   37.4975   35.06   41.0
12  3   38.2025   35.06   42.98
12  4   37.22   35.06   41.0
12  5   27.125   21.92   32.0
12  6   21.6725   17.06   32.0
12  7   20.4725   14.0   30.02
12  8   20.18   12.92   30.02
12  9   26.48   15.98   32.0
12  10   30.905   28.04   35.06
12  11   39.41   24.98   51.08
12  12   50.1125   48.02   53.06
12  13   25.37   17.96   44.96
12  14   18.8225   12.92   24.08
12  15   22.8275   19.04   26.96
12  16   23.45   17.96   32.0
12  17   26.9675   17.06   35.06
12  18   35.0075   32.0   37.04
12  19   36.65   30.92   46.04
12  20   31.0175   26.06   33.08
12  21   29.06   21.92   33.08
12  22   33.425   24.98   37.94
12  23   23.2325   15.98   28.04
12  24   11.6975   5.0   15.98
12  25   9.1475   -0.04   17.96
12  26   27.08   19.04   35.06
12  27   39.1625   35.06   42.98
12  28   30.17   21.92   37.94
12  29   18.0275   12.02   23.0
12  30   27.05   15.08   35.06
12  31   -3.295   -9.04   10.94
```

In both the Chicago.txt and Chicago03.txt files, data is not in a fixed field-width format. When data is in a fixed field-width format, methods that work well are conversions of string positions to numeric values.

When a data file has individual line entries of information but the numeric values are only separated by blank spaces, another method can be used.

Add function PROG01d. Using a copy of PROG01, modify it to read the text files previously created and display the individual fields.

Since the data values are not in the same position, do not have the same length, and are separated by at least one blank space, we can convert the string input to a list and then use the nth function to extract any value we need.

The conversion from a string to a list is completed with:

```
(setq datalist (read
  (strcat "(" nline ")")))
```

The read function converts the string (with the opening and closing parentheses) to a list.

This method still requires that each entry in the data file have the same number of values and that they be in the same order from left to right. The first member in the list index is zero.

To extract the temperature, use:

```
(nth 3 datalist)
```

Completed function PROG01d:

```
;-----------------------------------
(defun prog01d ()
 (graphscr)
 (princ "\nProg01d:")
 ; file to read
 (setq fh1 (open
   "C:\\TMY2_data\\Chicago.txt"
   "r"))
 (while fh1
  (setq nline (read-line fh1))
  (if nline
   (progn
    (setq datalist (read
      (strcat "(" nline ")")))
    (princ "\n") (princ datalist)
   )
   (setq fh1 (close fh1))
```

```
  )
 )
 (textscr)
 (princ)
)
;-----------------------------------
```

Execute PROG01d from the command line.

The data for December 31 should read as the lists:

```
(12 31 1 10.94 6.08 80 994 260 14.9812
0.19685 3.937)
(12 31 2 6.08 1.04 79 994 270 9.1676
0.15748 3.937)
(12 31 3 3.92 -2.02 76 996 240 9.1676
0.15748 3.937)
(12 31 4 -2.02 -7.06 79 997 250 23.0308
0.15748 3.937)
(12 31 5 -5.98 -16.96 58 999 240 18.3352
0.11811 3.937)
(12 31 6 -7.06 -18.04 58 999 250 18.3352
0.11811 3.937)
(12 31 7 -7.96 -18.94 58 1000 250 18.3352
0.11811 3.937)
(12 31 8 -9.04 -20.02 57 1001 260 20.7948
0.11811 3.937)
(12 31 9 -7.96 -18.94 58 1002 270 21.9128
0.11811 3.937)
(12 31 10 -5.98 -18.04 55 1001 260 17.2172
0.11811 3.937)
(12 31 11 -5.08 -18.94 50 1001 270 18.3352
0.11811 3.937)
(12 31 12 -4.0 -18.94 47 1000 260 19.6768
0.11811 3.937)
(12 31 13 -2.02 -16.96 48 1000 250 16.0992
0.11811 3.937)
(12 31 14 -2.02 -16.06 51 999 240 16.0992
0.11811 3.937)
(12 31 15 -0.94 -16.06 48 999 250 20.7948
0.11811 3.937)
(12 31 16 -0.94 -14.08 53 998 240 18.3352
0.11811 3.937)
(12 31 17 -0.94 -13.0 56 999 250 17.2172
0.11811 3.937)
(12 31 18 -2.02 -13.0 59 999 270 23.0308
0.11811 3.937)
(12 31 19 -4.0 -18.94 48 1000 270 20.7948
0.11811 3.937)
(12 31 20 -5.98 -20.02 50 1000 270 17.2172
0.11811 3.937)
(12 31 21 -7.06 -20.02 52 999 250 17.2172
0.11811 3.937)
(12 31 22 -7.06 -18.94 55 998 270 17.2172
0.11811 3.937)
(12 31 23 -5.98 -16.96 58 999 260 18.3352
0.11811 3.937)
(12 31 24 -5.98 -16.96 58 1000 270 19.6768
0.11811 3.937)
```

Construct a mesh from weather data

Using the data file `Chicago.txt`, edit the file in Microsoft Notepad, delete all entries except for the month of January. Save the file as `Chicago01.txt`.

To convert the temperature data for January to a mesh, the following assignments will be made:

```
Day = X value
Hour = Y value
Temperature = Z value
```

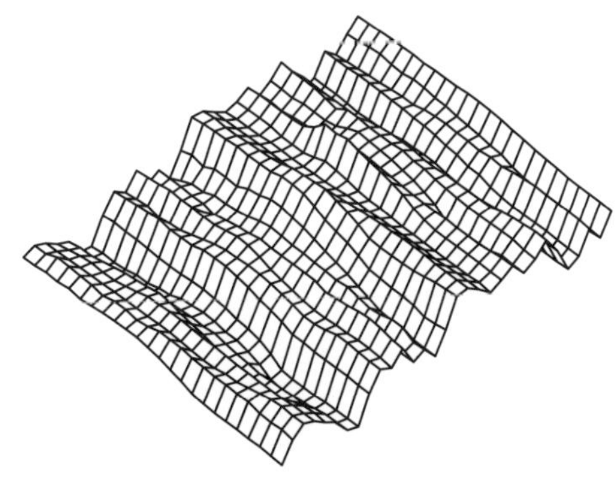

PROG02: January temperature mesh

Add function PROG02. Using a copy of PROG01d, add the day, month, and dry bulb temperature as points in a 3DMESH.

Add the start of the 3DMESH command before the loop:

```
(command ".3DMESH" "31" "24")
```

Each point in the mesh is specified as:

```
(setq pt (list
  (nth 1 datalist)
  (nth 2 datalist)
  (* (nth 3 datalist) 0.1)))
(command pt)
```

Completed function PROG02:

```
;-----------------------------------
(defun prog02 ()
 (graphscr)
 (command ".ERASE" "ALL" "")
 (princ "\nProg02:")
 ; file to read
 (setq fh1 (open
   "C:\\TMY2_data\\Chicago01.txt"
   "r"))
 ; start mesh
 (command ".3DMESH" "31" "24")
 (while fh1
  (setq nline (read-line fh1))
  (if nline
   (progn
    (setq datalist
      (read (strcat "(" nline ")")))
    ; add pt to mesh
    (setq pt (list
      (nth 1 datalist)
      (nth 2 datalist)
      (* (nth 3 datalist) 0.1)))
    (command pt)
   )
   (setq fh1 (close fh1))
  )
 )
 (command ".ZOOM" "e")
 (princ)
)
;-----------------------------------
```

Execute PROG02 from the command line.

Note the translation of data, the order read, and the axes the points are placed along. Also notice the z-value has been scaled by a value of 0.1, but there are no scale factors on the x or y values.

Set the z-scale as required or set a scale for the x and y values. Given it is January in Chicago, note that some temperature values are positive, some are negative.

The entire year of data could also be represented as a mesh.

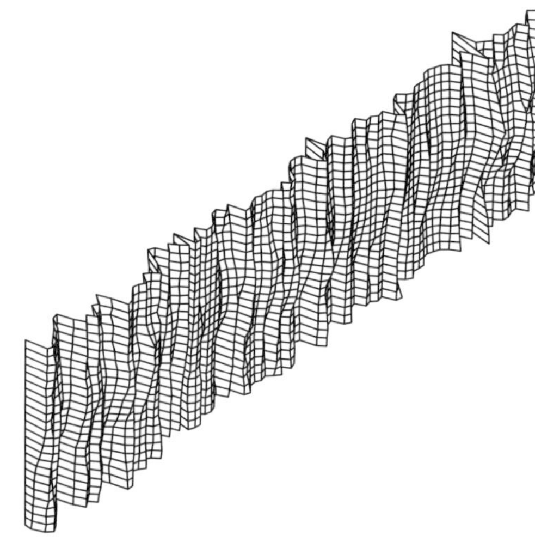

PROG02a: entire year of temperature data

Add function PROG02a. Using a copy of PROG02, read the entire year of data and create a mesh for each month.

Completed function PROG02a:

```
;----------------------------------
(defun prog02a ()
 (graphscr)
 (command ".ERASE" "ALL" "")
 (princ "\nProg02a:")
 ; file to read
 (setq fh1 (open
   "C:\\TMY2_data\\Chicago.txt"
   "r"))
 ; months
 (setq months (list 0 31 28 31 30 31
   30 31 31 30 31 30 31))
 (setq nday 1)
 (setq nmonth 1)
 (repeat 12
  (setq ndays (nth nmonth months))
  (command ".3DMESH"
    (+ ndays 2) "24")
  ; add first pts in month
  (setq nhour 1)
  (repeat 24
   (command (list
     (* nday 0.025) nhour 0.0))
   (setq nhour (+ nhour 1))
  )
  (setq nday (+ nday 1))
  (repeat ndays
   (repeat 24
    (setq nline (read-line fh1))
    (if nline
     (progn
      (setq datalist (read
        (strcat "(" nline ")")))
      (setq pt (list
        (* nday 0.025)
        (nth 2 datalist)
        (* (nth 3 datalist)
        0.075) ))
      (command pt)
      (setq nday (+ nday 1))
     )
     (setq fh1 (close fh1))
    )
   )
  )
  ; add last pts in month
  (setq nhour 1)
  (repeat 24
   (command (list
     (* nday 0.025) nhour 0.0))
   (setq nhour (+ nhour 1))
  )
  (setq nday (+ nday 1))
  ; inc month
  (setq nmonth (+ nmonth 1))
 )
 ; rotate to vertical
 (command ".ROTATE3D"
   "all" "" "x" "0,0,0" "90")
 (princ)
)
;----------------------------------
```

Note that reading of data for the year is set by the number of months, days, and hours. Prior to and after each month, points are generated to a common location. This serves as a transition between months.

Also note that a day counter, variable ndays, increments along the x-axis to set the x-dimension of the meshes. A scale factor is included for both the x and y locations. An alternative method is to include a length and height for the entire year to fit into. Then compute the scales accordingly.

Each monthly mesh is created flat. Then all of the meshes are rotated to a vertical position.

A variation of the first mesh includes the edges and bottom.

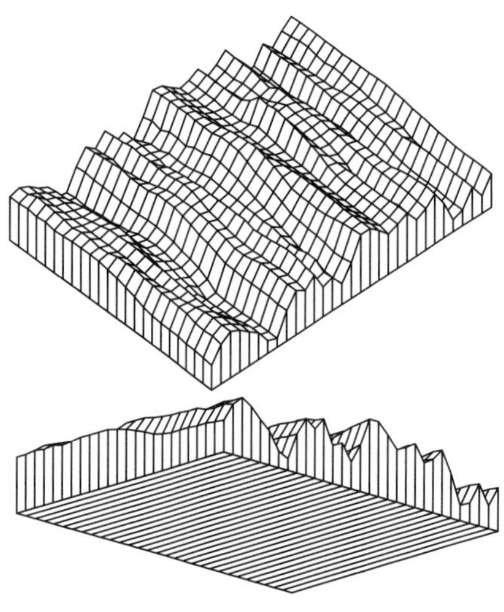

PROG02b: January temperature mesh with edges and bottom

Add function PROG02b. Using a copy of PROG02 and the mesh concepts presented in Chapter 6, add the edges and bottom surfaces. Also add input for a temperature scale and a minimum value. The minimum value will set the edges above any low points in the data.

Sample script file for PROG02b:

```
;-----------------------------------
(prog02b)
;Enter Z scale
0.1
;Enter Z minimum:
1.5
;-----------------------------------
```

Completed function PROG02b:

```
;-----------------------------------
(defun prog02b ()
 (graphscr)
 (command ".ERASE" "ALL" "")
 (princ "\nProg02b:")
 (setq zscale
   (getdist "\nEnter Z scale: "))
 (setq zmin
   (getdist
   "\nEnter minimum Z value: "))
 ; file to read
 (setq fh1 (open
   "C:\\TMY2_data\\Chicago01.txt"
   "r"))
 ; start mesh
 (command ".3DMESH"
   (+ 31 2) (+ 24 3))
 (while fh1
  (setq nline (read-line fh1))
  (if nline
   (progn
    (setq datalist
      (read (strcat "(" nline ")")))
    (setq nday (nth 1 datalist))
    (setq nhour (nth 2 datalist))
    ; add pt to mesh
    (setq pt (list
      nday nhour
      (+ (* (nth 3 datalist)
      zscale) zmin)))
    ; check for first edge
    (if (and (= nday 1)
      (= nhour 1)) (progn
     (setq ihour 1)
     (command (list nday ihour 0))
     (repeat 24
      (command (list nday ihour 0))
      (setq ihour (+ ihour 1))
     )
     (command (list nday 24 0))
     (command (list nday 1 0))
    ))
    ; save first pt
    (if (= nhour 1) (progn
     (setq fpt (list nday nhour 0))
     (command fpt)
```

```
      ))
      (command pt)
      ; add first pt
      (if (= nhour 24) (progn
       (command (list nday nhour 0))
       (command fpt)
      ))
      ; check for last edge
      (if (and (= nday 31)
        (= nhour 24)) (progn
       (setq ihour 1)
       (command (list nday ihour 0))
       (repeat 24
        (command (list nday ihour 0))
        (setq ihour (+ ihour 1))
       )
       (command (list nday 24 0))
       (command (list nday 1 0))
      ))
     )
     (setq fh1 (close fh1))
    )
   )
  (command ".ZOOM" "e")
  (princ)
)
;-----------------------------------
```

Review the approach used in PROG02b to include the edge and bottom surfaces in the mesh.

A variation of the mesh is to create sections that could be printed, laser-cut, or CNC-routed to develop templates for formwork.

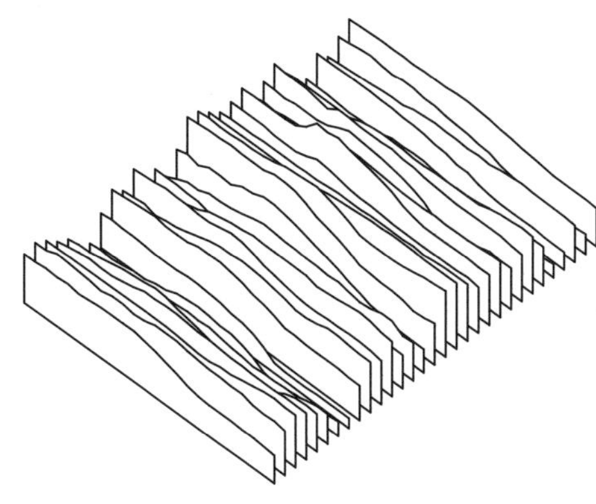

PROG02c: January temperature sections

Add function PROG02c. Using a copy of PROG02, create a section for each day. Add a z-scale factor and a z-minimum value so that the section points do not fall below zero elevation.

Sample script file for PROG02c:

```
;-----------------------------------
(prog02c)
;Enter Z scale
0.1
;Enter Z minimum:
1.5
;-----------------------------------
```

Completed function PROG02c:

```
;-----------------------------------
(defun prog02c ()
 (graphscr)
 (command ".ERASE" "ALL" "")
 (princ "\nProg02c:")
 (setq zscale
```

```
    (getdist "\nEnter Z scale: "))
  (setq zmin
    (getdist
    "\nEnter minimum Z value: "))
  ; file to read
  (setq fh1 (open
    "C:\\TMY2_data\\Chicago01.txt"
    "r"))
  ; start mesh
  (while fh1
   (setq nline (read-line fh1))
   (if nline
    (progn
     (setq datalist
       (read (strcat "(" nline ")")))
     ; add pt to section
     (setq pt (list
       (nth 1 datalist)
       (nth 2 datalist)
       (+ (* (nth 3 datalist)
       zscale) zmin)))
     ; start
     (if (= (nth 2 datalist) 1)
      (command ".3DPOLY"
        (list (nth 1 datalist)
        (nth 2 datalist) 0)))
     (command pt)
     (if (= (nth 2 datalist) 24)
       (progn
      (command
        (list (nth 1 datalist)
        (nth 2 datalist) 0) "c")
      (command ".ZOOM" "e")
      (command ".REGION" "last" "")
     ))
    )
    (setq fh1 (close fh1))
   )
  )
  (command ".ZOOM" "e")
  (princ)
)
;-----------------------------------
```

Note the use of 3DPOLY instead of PLINE to create each section, and its conversion to a REGION. The RECION conversion is optional.

Consider expanding this function to lay the sections out next to each other for laser-cutting.

Construct a relief from weather data

Convert the temperature data for January to a series of cubes. Use the same day and hour to locate the center of the cube, and use the temperature as the height.

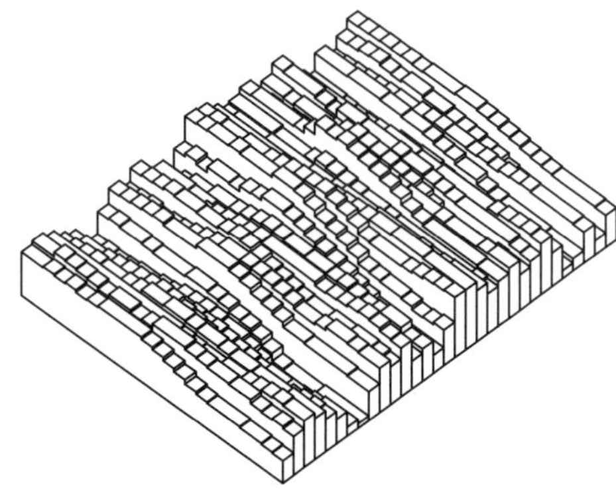

PROG03: January temperature relief

Add function PROG03. Using a copy of PROG02, set the x and y locations for each cube, and use a selection list to UNION each 24 hours together. Include scale factors for the x, y, and z values; also use a z-minimum so that negative values do not project below zero elevation.

The selection of the minimum z-value would have to be determined by inspection, since the lowest temperature in the data set has yet to be found.

Sample script file for PROG03:

```
;-----------------------------------
(prog03)
;Enter XY scale:
5
;Enter Z scale:
0.5
;Enter minimum Z value:
5.0
;-----------------------------------
```

Completed function PROG03:

```
;-----------------------------------
(defun prog03 ()
 (graphscr)
 (command ".ERASE" "ALL" "")
 (princ "\nProg03:")
 (setq xyscale
   (getdist "\nEnter XY scale: "))
 (setq zscale
   (getdist "\nEnter Z scale: "))
 (setq zmin
   (getdist
   "\nEnter minimum Z value: "))
 ; selection list
 (setq llist (ssadd))
 ; file to read
 (setq fhl (open
   "C:\\TMY2_data\\Chicago01.txt"
   "r"))
 (while fhl
  (setq nline (read-line fhl))
  (if nline
   (progn
    (setq datalist
      (read (strcat "(" nline ")")))
    ; construct cube at pt
    (setq nday (nth 1 datalist))
    (setq xpt (* nday xyscale))
    (setq nhour (nth 2 datalist))
    (setq ypt (* nhour xyscale))
    (setq ntemp (nth 3 datalist))
    (setq zpt
      (+ (* ntemp zscale) zmin))
    ; center pt
    (setq pntc (list xpt ypt 0.0))
    ; draw polygon
    (command ".POLYGON"
      "4" pntc "C" (/ xyscale 2.0))
    (command ".ZOOM" "e")
    (command ".EXTRUDE"
      "last" "" zpt)
    ; add to list
    (setq llist
      (ssadd (entlast) llist))
    ; versions prior to 2007 require
    ; the taper parameter
    ;(command ".EXTRUDE"
    ;  "last" "" zpt "")
    ; check if day completed
    (if (= nhour 24) (progn
     (command ".UNION" llist "")
     (setq llist (ssadd))
    ))
   )
   (setq fhl (close fhl))
  )
 )
 (command ".ZOOM" "e")
 (command ".BREP" "all" "")
 (command ".UNION" "all" "")
 (princ)
)
;-----------------------------------
```

If a final UNION command is desired and it results in an error because of the large number of individual solids or if you are using version 2007 or later, the SOLIDHIST system variable can be used to turn off HISTORY and complete the UNION; you can also use the BREP command to turn off history.

To UNION all days together, insert after the final ZOOM command:

```
(command ".BREP" "all" "")
(command ".UNION" "all" "")
```

As explored in the section on random constructions, a variety of shapes can be used instead of the cube. Try others.

Weather data also contains values that can be used for representing dimensions other than height.

Create perforations from weather data

Some weather data values can be used as radii in a perforation pattern to show the difference between the lowest and highest values, such as temperature.

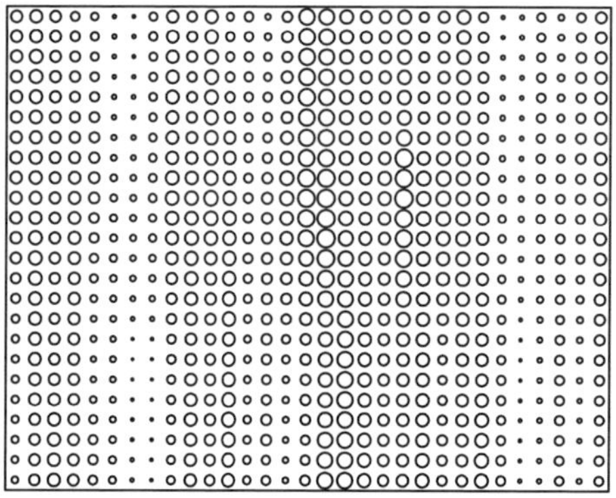

PROG04: January temperature perforations

Add function PROG04. Using a copy of PROG03, remove all three-dimensional commands, except the POLYGON command. Either increase the number of sides for it or replace it with a CIRCLE command to represent a perforation.

For the perforations to be correctly sized, the lowest and highest temperature values need to be found first, so that the temperature, when converted to a radius, leaves some material between the openings.

One method is to read the data file twice: once to get the minimum and maximum temperatures and a second time to draw the circles.

Also add a rectangle to show the boundary of the perforations.

Sample script file for PROG04:

```
;-----------------------------------
(prog04)
;Enter XY scale:
5
;Enter minimum radius percent:
0.10
;-----------------------------------
```

Completed function PROG04:

```
;-----------------------------------
(defun prog04 ()
 (graphscr)
 (command ".ERASE" "ALL" "")
 (princ "\nProg04:")
 (setq xyscale
   (getdist "\nEnter XY scale: "))
 (setq cmin
   (getdist
   "\nEnter minimum radius
    percent: "))
 ; file to read
 (setq fhl (open
   "C:\\TMY2_data\\Chicago01.txt"
   "r"))
 ; min/max
 (setq hightemp -9999.0)
 (setq lowtemp 9999.0)
 (while fhl
  (setq nline (read-line fhl))
  (if nline
   (progn
    (setq datalist
      (read (strcat "(" nline ")")))
    (setq ntemp (nth 3 datalist))
    ; check min/max
    (if (> ntemp hightemp)
      (setq hightemp ntemp))
    (if (< ntemp lowtemp)
      (setq lowtemp ntemp))
   )
   (setq fhl (close fhl))
  )
 )
 ; temp diff
 (setq difftemp (- hightemp lowtemp))
```

```
 ; min radius
 (setq minrad
   (* (/ xyscale 2.0) cmin))
 ; radius diff
 (setq raddiff
   (- (* (/ xyscale 2.0) 0.90)
   minrad))
 ; file to read
 (setq fh1 (open
   "C:\\TMY2_data\\Chicago01.txt"
   "r"))
 (while fh1
  (setq nline (read-line fh1))
  (if nline
   (progn
    (setq datalist
      (read (strcat "(" nline ")")))
    ; construct circle at pt
    (setq nday (nth 1 datalist))
    (setq xpt (* nday xyscale))
    (setq nhour (nth 2 datalist))
    (setq ypt (* nhour xyscale))
    (setq ntemp (nth 3 datalist))
    ; compute radius
    (setq crad
      (+ minrad (* (/ (abs
      (- lowtemp ntemp)) difftemp)
      raddiff)))
    ; center pt
    (setq pntc (list xpt ypt 0.0))
    ; draw circle
    (command ".CIRCLE" pntc crad)
    (command ".ZOOM" "e")
   )
   (setq fh1 (close fh1))
  )
 )
 ; boundary
 (setq pnt0 (list
   (/ xyscale 2.0)
   (/ xyscale 2.0) 0))
 (setq pnt1 (list
   (+ (nth 0 pnt0) (* 31 xyscale))
   (+ (nth 1 pnt0) (* 24 xyscale))
   0))
 (command ".RECTANGLE" pnt0 pnt1)
 (command ".ZOOM" "e")
 (princ)
)
;----------------------------------
```

To size each perforation, the difference in temperature and minimum and maximum radii are computed. This computation assumes that 10 percent of the spacing between openings will remain:

```
; temp diff
 (setq difftemp (- hightemp lowtemp))
 ; min radius
 (setq minrad
   (* (/ xyscale 2.0) cmin))
 ; radius diff
 (setq raddiff
   (- (* (/ xyscale 2.0) 0.90)
   minrad))
```

For each temperature, the radius is computed proportional to the maximum difference in temperature and radius, then the minimum radius is added:

```
; compute radius
(setq crad
  (+ minrad (* (/ (abs
  (- lowtemp ntemp)) difftemp)
  raddiff)))
```

Another method is to read the file once, find the minimum and maximum values, and place the temperature values into a list. The second part of the function uses the list to draw the circles.

Add function `PROG04a`. Using `PROG04`, create a list to capture the data. Then draw the circles.

The list is started as:

```
; set list
(setq plist (list ))
```

Each data point is appended to the list as:

```
(setq pt (list
  (nth 1 datalist)
  (nth 2 datalist)
  (nth 3 datalist)))
; add pt to list
(setq plist
  (append plist (list pt)))
```

The point is extracted from the list by position:

```
; construct circle at pt
(setq nday (nth 0 (nth cnt plist)))
(setq xpt (* nday xyscale))
(setq nhour (nth 1 (nth cnt plist)))
(setq ypt (* nhour xyscale))
(setq ntemp (nth 2 (nth cnt plist)))
```

The variable `cnt` is incremented through the length of the list.

The script file is the same as in `PROG04`.

Completed function `PROG04a`:

```
;-----------------------------------
(defun prog04a ()
 (graphscr)
 (command ".ERASE" "ALL" "")
 (princ "\nProg04a:")
 (setq xyscale
   (getdist "\nEnter XY scale: "))
 (setq cmin
   (getdist
   "\nEnter minimum radius
    percent: "))
 ; file to read
 (setq fh1 (open
   "C:\\TMY2_data\\Chicago01.txt"
   "r"))
 ; min/max
 (setq hightemp -9999.0)
 (setq lowtemp 9999.0)
 ; set list
 (setq plist (list ))
(while fh1
 (setq nline (read-line fh1))
 (if nline
  (progn
   (setq datalist
     (read (strcat "(" nline ")")))
   (setq ntemp (nth 3 datalist))
   ; check min/max
   (if (> ntemp hightemp)
     (setq hightemp ntemp))
   (if (< ntemp lowtemp)
     (setq lowtemp ntemp))
   (setq pt (list
     (nth 1 datalist)
     (nth 2 datalist)
     (nth 3 datalist)))
   ; add pt to list
   (setq plist
     (append plist (list pt)))
  )
  (setq fh1 (close fh1))
 )
)
; temp diff
(setq difftemp (- hightemp lowtemp))
; min radius
(setq minrad
  (* (/ xyscale 2.0) cmin))
; radius diff
(setq raddiff
  (- (* (/ xyscale 2.0) 0.90)
  minrad))
; list counter
(setq cnt 0)
(repeat (length plist)
 ; construct circle at pt
 (setq nday (nth 0 (nth cnt plist)))
 (setq xpt (* nday xyscale))
 (setq nhour (nth 1 (nth cnt plist)))
 (setq ypt (* nhour xyscale))
 (setq ntemp (nth 2 (nth cnt plist)))
 ; compute radius
 (setq crad
   (+ minrad (* (/ (abs
   (- lowtemp ntemp)) difftemp)
   raddiff)))
 ; center pt
 (setq pntc (list xpt ypt 0.0))
```

```
    ; draw circle
    (command ".CIRCLE" pntc crad)
    (command ".ZOOM" "e")
    ; next pos in list
    (setq cnt (+ cnt 1))
  )
  ; boundary
  (setq pnt0 (list
     (/ xyscale 2.0)
     (/ xyscale 2.0) 0))
  (setq pnt1 (list
    (+ (nth 0 pnt0) (* 31 xyscale))
    (+ (nth 1 pnt0) (* 24 xyscale))
    0))
  (command ".RECTANGLE" pnt0 pnt1)
  (command ".ZOOM" "e")
  (princ)
)
;-----------------------------------
```

Create a perforation pattern based on the direction and speed of wind

Add PROG04b. Using a copy of PROG04a, replace temperature with the direction and speed of wind.

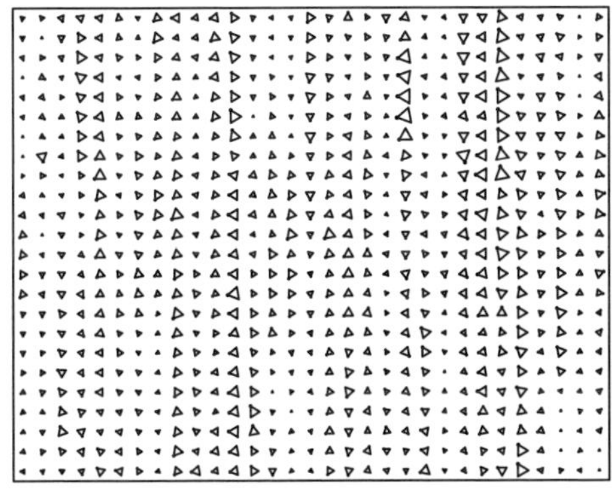

PROG04b: January wind direction and speed perforations

The wind direction is in degrees: 0–360, where north is 0 or 360, east is 90, south is 180, and west is 270 degrees. A rotated triangle will be used to show direction.

The triangle is rotated by:

```
; rotate triangle
(setq rotang (* ndir -1))
(command ".ROTATE"
  "last" "" pntc rotang)
```

Since the triangle is symmetrical, a small circle is added to the point showing the direction:

```
; add marker
(setq cpt (polar
  pntc (dtr (+ rotang 90)) crad))
(command ".CIRCLE"
  cpt (* crad 0.15))
```

Other changes in this function are related to replacing temperature with wind speed. Review these.

The script file is the same as in PROG04.

Completed function PROG04b:

```
;-----------------------------------
(defun prog04b ()
 (graphscr)
 (command ".ERASE" "ALL" "")
 (princ "\nProg04b:")
 (setq xyscale
   (getdist "\nEnter XY scale: "))
 (setq cmin
   (getdist
   "\nEnter minimum radius
    percent: "))
 ; file to read
 (setq fh1 (open
   "C:\\TMY2_data\\Chicago01.txt"
   "r"))
 ; min/max
 (setq highspeed -9999.0)
 (setq lowspeed 9999.0)
```

```
; set list
(setq plist (list ))
(while fh1
 (setq nline (read-line fh1))
 (if nline
  (progn
   (setq datalist
     (read (strcat "(" nline ")")))
   (setq nspeed (nth 8 datalist))
   ; check min/max
   (if (> nspeed highspeed)
     (setq highspeed nspeed))
   (if (< nspeed lowspeed)
     (setq lowspeed nspeed))
   (setq pt (list
     (nth 1 datalist)
     (nth 2 datalist)
     (nth 7 datalist)
     (nth 8 datalist)))
   ; add pt to list
   (setq plist
     (append plist (list pt)))
  )
  (setq fh1 (close fh1))
 )
)
; temp diff
(setq diffspeed
  (- highspeed lowspeed))
; min radius
(setq minrad
  (* (/ xyscale 2.0) cmin))
; radius diff
(setq raddiff
  (- (* (/ xyscale 2.0) 0.90)
  minrad))
; list counter
(setq cnt 0)
(repeat (length plist)
 ; construct circle at pt
 (setq nday (nth 0 (nth cnt plist)))
 (setq xpt (* nday xyscale))
 (setq nhour (nth 1 (nth cnt plist)))
 (setq ypt (* nhour xyscale))
 (setq ndir (nth 2 (nth cnt plist)))
 (setq nspeed (nth 3 (nth cnt plist)))
 ; compute radius
 (setq crad
   (+ minrad (* (/ (abs
     (- lowspeed nspeed)) diffspeed)
     raddiff)))
   ; center pt
   (setq pntc (list xpt ypt 0.0))
   ; draw triangle
   (command ".POLYGON"
     "3" pntc "i" crad)
   (command ".ZOOM" "e")
   ; rotate triangle
   (setq rotang (* ndir -1))
   (command ".ROTATE"
     "last" "" pntc rotang)
   ; add marker
   (setq cpt (polar
     pntc (dtr (+ rotang 90)) crad))
   (command ".CIRCLE"
     cpt (* crad 0.15))
   ; next pos in list
   (setq cnt (+ cnt 1))
  )
  ; boundary
  (setq pnt0 (list
    (/ xyscale 2.0)
    (/ xyscale 2.0) 0))
  (setq pnt1 (list
    (+ (nth 0 pnt0) (* 31 xyscale))
    (+ (nth 1 pnt0) (* 24 xyscale))
    0))
  (command ".RECTANGLE" pnt0 pnt1)
  (command ".ZOOM" "e")
  (princ)
)
;----------------------------------
```

Create a cylindrical mesh from weather data

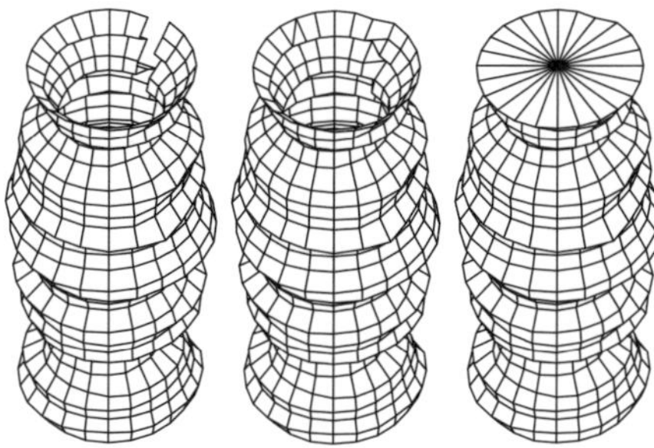

PROG05, 5a, and 5b: January temperature as a cylindrical mesh

Add function PROG05. Using PROG02, wrap the mesh around a cylinder with the radius representing temperature.

Assume the radius of the cylinder is based on twenty-four hours with the scaled temperature value added to it.

To convert to cylindrical coordinates, x and y are based on the radius, hours, and temperature; z is based on the day.

Given that the circumference of a circle is c=pi(2r) and the radius is r=c/(2pi), the minimum radius of the mesh is:

```
; radius and angle inc based on
; 24 hours
(setq rad (/ 24.0 (* 2 pi)))
(setq anginc (/ 360.0 24))
```

The point on the cylinder is then computed as:

```
; radius is hours plus
; temperature
(setq xpt (* (+ rad
  (* (nth 3 datalist) 0.075))
  (cos (dtr
  (* anginc (nth 2 datalist))))))
(setq ypt (* (+ rad
  (* (nth 3 datalist) 0.0751))
  (sin (dtr
  (* anginc (nth 2 datalist))))))
; height is day
(setq zpt (- (nth 1 datalist) 1))
(setq pt (list xpt ypt zpt))
(command pt)
```

The z-elevation is adjusted so that day one is at zero elevation.

Execute PROG05 from the command line.

Completed function PROG05:

```
;-----------------------------------
(defun prog05 ()
 (graphscr)
 (command ".ERASE" "ALL" "")
 (princ "\nProg05:")
 ; file to read
 (setq fhl (open
   "C:\\TMY2_data\\Chicago01.txt"
   "r"))
 ; radius and angle inc based on
 ; 24 hours
 (setq rad (/ 24.0 (* 2 pi)))
 (setq anginc (/ 360.0 24))
 ; start mesh
 (command ".3DMESH" "31" "24")
 (while fhl
  (setq nline (read-line fhl))
  (if nline
   (progn
    (setq datalist
      (read (strcat "(" nline ")")))
    ; radius is hours plus
    ; temperature
    (setq xpt (* (+ rad
      (* (nth 3 datalist) 0.075))
      (cos (dtr
      (* anginc (nth 2 datalist))))))
    (setq ypt (* (+ rad
      (* (nth 3 datalist) 0.0751))
      (sin (dtr
      (* anginc (nth 2 datalist))))))
```

```
    ; height is day
    (setq zpt (- (nth 1 datalist) 1))
    (setq pt (list xpt ypt zpt))
    (command pt)
   )
   (setq fh1 (close fh1))
  )
 )
 (command ".ZOOM" "e")
 (princ)
)
;-----------------------------------
```

Notice the mesh does not meet. Add the last remaining section.

Add function PROG05a. Using a copy of PROG05, change the hour mesh number by one, in the start of the 3DMESH command. Save the first hour point and add the first point to the mesh after the twenty-four-hour point.

Execute PROG05a from the command line.

Completed function PROG05a:

```
;-----------------------------------
(defun prog05a ()
 (graphscr)
 (command ".ERASE" "ALL" "")
 (princ "\nProg05a:")
 ; file to read
 (setq fh1 (open
   "C:\\TMY2_data\\Chicago01.txt"
   "r"))
 ; radius and angle inc based on
 ; 24 hours
 (setq rad (/ 24.0 (* 2 pi)))
 (setq anginc (/ 360.0 24))
 ; start mesh
 (command ".3DMESH" "31" (+ 24 1))
 (while fh1
  (setq nline (read-line fh1))
  (if nline
   (progn
    (setq datalist
      (read (strcat "(" nline ")")))
    ; radius is hours plus
    ; temperature
    (setq xpt (* (+ rad
      (* (nth 3 datalist) 0.075))
      (cos (dtr
      (* anginc (nth 2 datalist))))))
    (setq ypt (* (+ rad
      (* (nth 3 datalist) 0.075))
      (sin (dtr
      (* anginc (nth 2 datalist))))))
    ; height is day
    (setq zpt (- (nth 1 datalist) 1))
    (setq pt (list xpt ypt zpt))
    ; save first pt
    (if (= (nth 2 datalist) 1)
      (setq fpt pt))
    (command pt)
    ; close mesh
    (if (= (nth 2 datalist) 24)
      (command fpt))
   )
   (setq fh1 (close fh1))
  )
 )
 (command ".ZOOM" "e")
 (princ)
)
;-----------------------------------
```

The final change is to add a bottom and top to the mesh.

Add function PROG05b. Using a copy of PROG05a, increase the 3DMESH command for two more days of points. Before and after the hour mesh points, add the bottom and top points.

Execute PROG05b from the command line.

Completed function PROG05b:

```
;-----------------------------------
(defun prog05b ()
 (graphscr)
 (command ".ERASE" "ALL" "")
 (princ "\nProg05b:")
 ; file to read
 (setq fh1 (open
   "C:\\TMY2_data\\Chicago01.txt"
```

```
    "r"))
  ; radius and angle inc based on
  ;  24 hours
  (setq rad (/ 24.0 (* 2 pi)))
  (setq anginc (/ 360.0 24))
  ; start mesh
  (command ".3DMESH"
    (+ 31 2) (+ 24 1))
  ; bottom
  (repeat (+ 24 1)
   (command (list 0 0 0))
  )
  (while fh1
   (setq nline (read-line fh1))
   (if nline
    (progn
     (setq datalist
       (read (strcat "(" nline ")")))
     ; radius is hours plus
     ; temperature
     (setq xpt (* (+ rad
       (* (nth 3 datalist) 0.075))
       (cos (dtr
       (* anginc (nth 2 datalist))))))
     (setq ypt (* (+ rad
       (* (nth 3 datalist) 0.075))
       (sin (dtr
       (* anginc (nth 2 datalist))))))
     ; height is day
     (setq zpt (- (nth 1 datalist) 1))
     (setq pt (list xpt ypt zpt))
     ; save first pt
     (if (= (nth 2 datalist) 1)
       (setq fpt pt))
     (command pt)
     ; close mesh
     (if (= (nth 2 datalist) 24)
       (command fpt))
    )
    (setq fh1 (close fh1))
   )
  )
  ; top
  (repeat (+ 24 1)
   (command (list 0 0 zpt))
  )
  (command ".ZOOM" "e")
  (princ)
)
;-----------------------------------
```

As in the horizontal mesh, sections were created. In the cylindrical mesh, sections can also be created as the basis for creating patterns for laser-cutting, including a cutting layout.

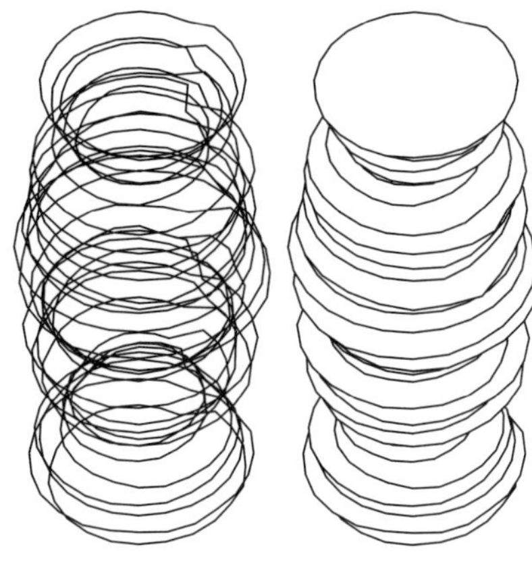

PROG05c: January temperature as circular sections

Add function PROG05c. Using a copy of PROG05a, create each set of hours as a 3DPOLY. These could also be converted to REGIONs.

Execute PROG05c from the command line.

Completed function PROG05c:

```
;-----------------------------------
(defun prog05c ()
 (graphscr)
 (command ".ERASE" "ALL" "")
 (princ "\nProg05c:")
 ; file to read
 (setq fh1 (open
   "C:\\TMY2_data\\Chicago01.txt"
   "r"))
 ; radius and angle inc based on
 ; 24 hours
 (setq rad (/ 24.0 (* 2 pi)))
 (setq anginc (/ 360.0 24))
```

```
  (while fhl
   (setq nline (read-line fhl))
   (if nline
    (progn
     (setq datalist
       (read (strcat "(" nline ")")))
     ; radius is hours plus
     ; temperature
     (setq xpt (* (+ rad
       (* (nth 3 datalist) 0.075))
       (cos (dtr
       (* anginc (nth 2 datalist))))))
     (setq ypt (* (+ rad
       (* (nth 3 datalist) 0.075))
       (sin (dtr
       (* anginc (nth 2 datalist))))))
     ; height is day
     (setq zpt (- (nth 1 datalist) 1))
     (setq pt (list xpt ypt zpt))
     ; first pt start polyline
     (if (= (nth 2 datalist) 1)
       (command ".3DPOLY"))
     (command pt)
     ; close polyline
     (if (= (nth 2 datalist) 24)
       (progn
      (command "c")
      (command ".ZOOM" "e")
      (command ".REGION" "last" "")
     ))
    )
    (setq fhl (close fhl))
   )
  )
  (command ".ZOOM" "e")
  (princ)
)
;-----------------------------------
```

The natural order of weather data files lends itself to a mesh consisting of the number of days in the month times 24. What if we wanted to create the reverse of the mesh: 24 times the number of days in the month? This will enable hours to be placed vertically, and the radius to be based on the number of days in the month.

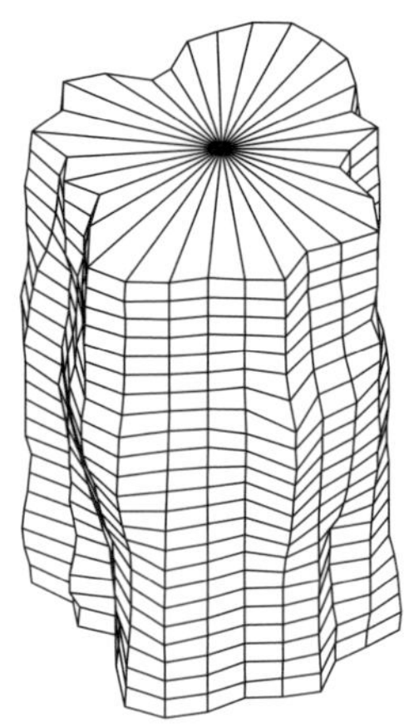

PROG05d: January temperature, represented vertically

Add function PROG05d. Start by using copies of PROG05b and PROG04a modified for the cylindrical mesh. The data-set file has to be read and the coordinates placed into a list that can be extracted in the order of hour and day, not day and hour.

Review how the list was made and how each coordinate was extracted. At the command line enter:

```
>> (setq plist (list
  (list (list 1 1) 10)
  (list (list 1 5) 20)
  (list (list 2 1) 30)))
(((1 1) 10) ((1 5) 20) ((2 1) 30))

>> (nth 2 plist)
((2 1) 30)

>> (assoc (list 2 1) plist)
((2 1) 30)

>> (cdr (assoc (list 2 1)
  plist))
(30)

>> (car (cdr (assoc (list 2 1)
```

```
  plist)))
30

>> (nth 1 (assoc (list 2 1)
  plist))
30
```

For example, each point and temperature is saved as day and hour, then temperature: `((2 1) 30)`; `(2 1)`. The first list, `(2 1)`, can be used as an index to extract the temperature needed, in any order required.

Execute `PROG05d` from the command line.

Completed function `PROG05d`:

```
;-----------------------------------
(defun prog05d ()
 (graphscr)
 (command ".ERASE" "ALL" "")
 (princ "\nProg05d:")
 ; file to read
 (setq fhl (open
   "C:\\TMY2_data\\Chicago01.txt"
   "r"))
 ; set list
 (setq plist (list ))
 (while fhl
  (setq nline (read-line fhl))
  (if nline
   (progn
    (setq datalist
      (read (strcat "(" nline ")")))
    (setq pt (list (list
      (nth 1 datalist)
      (nth 2 datalist))
      (nth 3 datalist)))
    ; add pt to list
    (setq plist
      (append plist (list pt)))
   )
   (setq fhl (close fhl))
  )
 )
 ; radius and angle inc based on
 ; 24 hours
 (setq rad (/ 31.0 (* 2 pi)))
 (setq anginc (/ 360.0 31))
 ; start mesh
 (command ".3DMESH"
   (+ 24 2) (+ 31 1))
 ; bottom
 (repeat (+ 31 1)
  (command (list 0 0 0))
 )
 ; hour count
 (setq hcnt 1)
 (repeat 24
  ; day count
  (setq dcnt 1)
  (repeat 31
   ; get temperature
   (setq ntemp (nth 1
     (assoc (list dcnt hcnt)
     plist)))
   ; radius is day plus temperature
   (setq xpt (* (+ rad
     (* ntemp 0.075))
     (cos (dtr (* anginc dcnt)))))
   (setq ypt (* (+ rad
     (* ntemp 0.075))
     (sin (dtr (* anginc dcnt)))))
   ; height is hour
   (setq zpt (- hcnt 1))
   (setq pt (list xpt ypt zpt))
   ; get first pt
   (if (= dcnt 1) (setq fpt pt))
   (command pt)
   ; check for last pt, connect to
   ; first pt
   (if (= dcnt 31) (command fpt))
   ; inc day
   (setq dcnt (+ dcnt 1))
  )
  ; inc hour
  (setq hcnt (+ hcnt 1))
 )
 ; top
 (repeat (+ 31 1)
  (command (list 0 0 zpt))
 )
 (command ".ZOOM" "e")
 (princ)
)
;-----------------------------------
```

Review PROG05d, including how the temperature list was made, as well as the loops for hours and days.

The temperature is extracted using:

```
; get temperature
(setq ntemp (nth 1 (assoc
  (list dcnt hcnt) plist)))
```

Consider adding input to scale the height and diameter to actual dimensions. This version scales the temperature, but the unit of measure for the day and hour is still one unit.

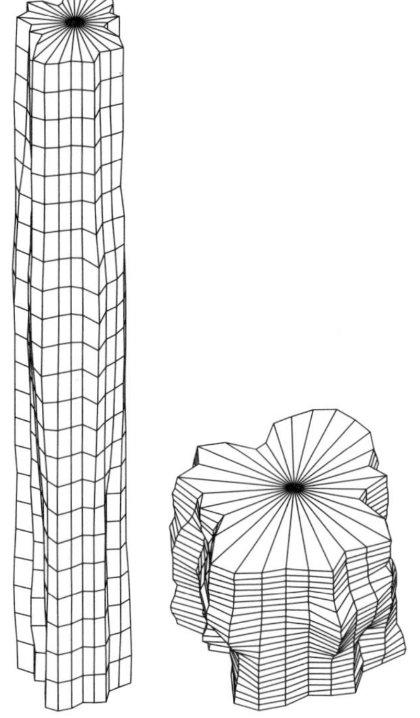

PROG05e: January temperature, represented vertically to scale

Add function PROG05e. Using a copy of PROG05d, modify the scale of the radius and height to actual dimensions. Add input for height and minimum and maximum radii. The temperature change will be reflected in the difference in radius.

The scales are computed as:

```
; height scale
(setq hscale
  (/ zheight (- 24 1)))
; radius
(setq tscale
  (/ (- cradmax cradmin)
  (- tmax tmin)))
```

The point is scaled by:

```
; radius is day plus temperature
(setq xpt (* (+ cradmin
  (* (abs (- tmin ntemp)) tscale))
  (cos (dtr (* anginc dcnt)))))
(setq ypt (* (+ cradmin
  (* (abs (- tmin ntemp)) tscale))
  (sin (dtr (* anginc dcnt)))))
; height is hour
(setq zpt (* (- hcnt 1) hscale))
```

Sample script file of PROG05e:

```
;----------------------------------
(prog05e)
;Enter height:
12'
;Enter min radius:
4"
;Enter max radius:
12'
;----------------------------------
```

Completed function `PROG05e`:

```
;-----------------------------------
(defun prog05e ()
 (graphscr)
 (command ".ERASE" "ALL" "")
 (princ "\nProg05e:")
 (setq zheight
   (getdist "\nEnter height: "))
 (setq cradmin
   (getdist "\nEnter min radius: "))
 (setq cradmax
   (getdist "\nEnter max radius: "))
 ; file to read
 (setq fhl (open
   "C:\\TMY2_data\\Chicago01.txt"
   "r"))
 ; set list
 (setq plist (list ))
 ; min/max temp
 (setq tmin 9999.0)
 (setq tmax -9999.0)
 (while fhl
  (setq nline (read-line fhl))
  (if nline
   (progn
    (setq datalist
      (read (strcat "(" nline ")")))
    (setq pt (list (list
      (nth 1 datalist)
      (nth 2 datalist))
      (nth 3 datalist)))
    ; add pt to list
    (setq plist
      (append plist (list pt)))
    ; check for min/max
    (if (> (nth 3 datalist) tmax)
      (setq tmax (nth 3 datalist)))
    (if (< (nth 3 datalist) tmin)
      (setq tmin (nth 3 datalist)))
   )
   (setq fhl (close fhl))
  )
 )
 ; height scale
 (setq hscale (/ zheight (- 24 1)))
 ; radius
 (setq tscale
   (/ (- cradmax cradmin)
   (- tmax tmin)))
 ; radius and angle inc based on
 ; 31 days
 (setq anginc (/ 360.0 31))
 ; start mesh
 (command ".3DMESH"
   (+ 24 2) (+ 31 1))
 ; bottom
 (repeat (+ 31 1)
  (command (list 0 0 0))
 )
 ; hour count
 (setq hcnt 1)
 (repeat 24
  ; day count
  (setq dcnt 1)
  (repeat 31
   ; get temperature
   (setq ntemp (nth 1
     (assoc (list dcnt hcnt)
     plist)))
   ; radius is day plus temperature
   (setq xpt (* (+ cradmin
     (* (abs (- tmin ntemp)) tscale))
     (cos (dtr (* anginc dcnt)))))
   (setq ypt (* (+ cradmin
     (* (abs (- tmin ntemp)) tscale))
     (sin (dtr (* anginc dcnt)))))
   ; height is hour
   (setq zpt (* ( hcnt 1) hscale))
   (setq pt (list xpt ypt zpt))
   ; get first pt
   (if (= dcnt 1) (setq fpt pt))
   (command pt)
   ; check for last pt, connect to
   ; first pt
   (if (= dcnt 31) (command fpt))
   ; inc day
   (setq dcnt (+ dcnt 1))
  )
  ; inc hour
  (setq hcnt (+ hcnt 1))
 )
 ; top
 (repeat (+ 31 1)
  (command (list 0 0 zpt))
 )
 (command ".ZOOM" "e")
 (princ)
)
;-----------------------------------
```

Convert the mesh to a radial relief

Instead of cylindrical projection, simply lay out all points in a series of twenty-four concentric circles. Since the data set is January, each circle represents 31 days, so the hours are placed in a radial fashion across the circles.

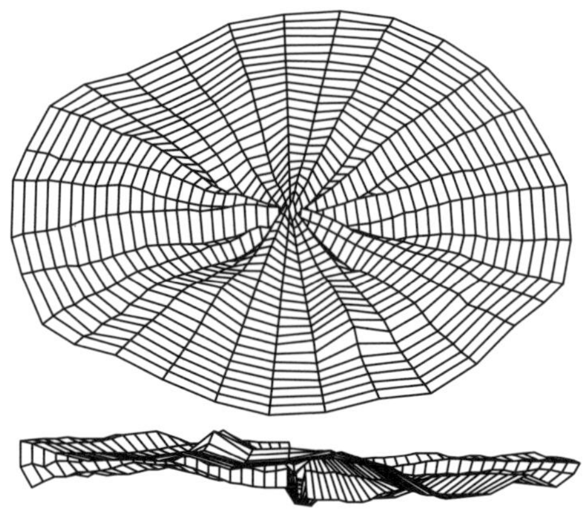

PROG06: January temperature, represented in a radial pattern

The coordinates are computed as:

```
xpt = hour(cos dayangle)
ypt = hour(sin dayangle)
zpt = temperature
```

Add function PROG06. Using a copy of PROG05d, remove the bottom and top points for the mesh and modify the radial computations.

Execute PROG06 from the command line.

Completed function PROG06:

```
;-----------------------------------
(defun prog06 ()
 (graphscr)
 (command ".ERASE" "ALL" "")
 (princ "\nProg06:")
 ; file to read
 (setq fh1 (open
   "C:\\TMY2_data\\Chicago01.txt"
   "r"))
 ; set list
 (setq plist (list ))
 (while fh1
  (setq nline (read-line fh1))
  (if nline
   (progn
    (setq datalist
      (read (strcat "(" nline ")")))
    (setq pt (list (list
      (nth 1 datalist)
      (nth 2 datalist))
      (nth 3 datalist)))
    ; add pt to list
    (setq plist
      (append plist (list pt)))
   )
   (setq fh1 (close fh1))
  )
 )
 ; radius and angle inc based on
 ; 24 hours
 (setq rad (/ 31.0 (* 2 pi)))
 (setq anginc (/ 360.0 31))
 ; start mesh
 (command ".3DMESH"
   (+ 24 0) (+ 31 1))
 ; hour count
 (setq hcnt 1)
 (repeat 24
  ; day count
  (setq dcnt 1)
  (repeat 31
   ; get temperature
   (setq ntemp (nth 1
     (assoc (list dcnt hcnt)
     plist)))
   ; radius is hours
```

```
    (setq xpt (* hcnt (cos
      (dtr (* anginc dcnt)))))
    (setq ypt (* hcnt (sin
      (dtr (* anginc dcnt)))))
    ; height is temperature
    (setq zpt (* ntemp 0.1))
    (setq pt (list xpt ypt zpt))
    ; get first pt
    (if (= dcnt 1) (setq fpt pt))
    (command pt)
    ; check for last pt, connect to
    ; first pt
    (if (= dcnt 31) (command fpt))
    ; inc day
    (setq dcnt (+ dcnt 1))
  )
  ; inc hour
  (setq hcnt (+ hcnt 1))
 )
 (command ".ZOOM" "e")
 (princ)
)
;-----------------------------------
```

Review PROG06, including loops for the hours and days and the radial computations, using:

```
; get temperature
(setq ntemp (nth 1 (assoc
  (list dcnt hcnt) plist)))
; radius is hours
(setq xpt (* hcnt
  (cos (dtr (* anginc dcnt)))))
(setq ypt (* hcnt
  (sin (dtr (* anginc dcnt)))))
; height is temperature
(setq zpt (* ntemp 0.1))
```

Since the center radius starts at one hour, there is a small opening. To close it, one hour is subtracted from each hour value, or a constant is added if a larger opening is desired.

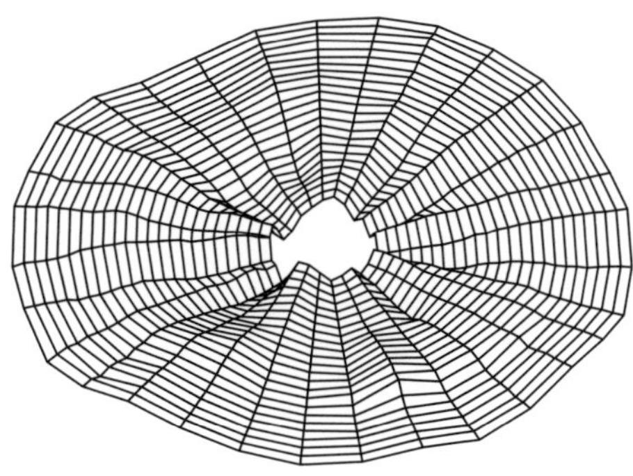

PROG06a: January temperature, represented in a radial pattern wih a variable opening

Add function PROG06a. Using a copy of PROG06, add an offset to the hour and the radial computation to adjust the center opening.

To close or open, use:

```
; radius is hours
(setq xpt (* (+ hcnt coff)
  (cos (dtr (* anginc dcnt)))))
(setq ypt (* (+ hcnt coff)
  (sin (dtr (* anginc dcnt)))))
```

Where the variable coff can be set to -1 or some positive value.

Execute PROG06a from the command line.

Since temperatures are all different at the first hour, the centerpoint is not exactly the same for each day.

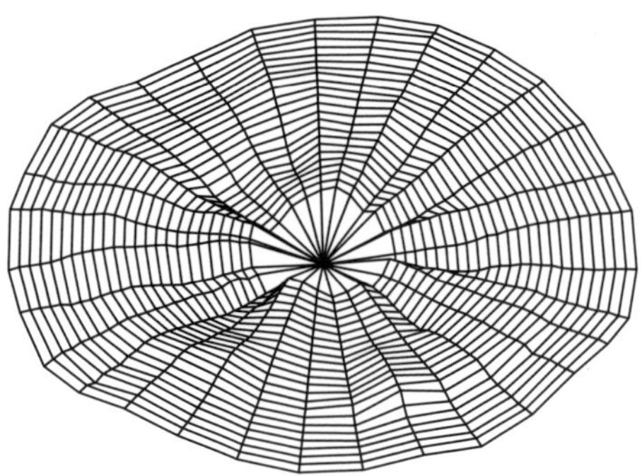

PROG06b: January temperature, represented in a radial pattern with a common center

Add function PROG06b. Using a copy of PROG06a, set the center to a common point, 0.0, as the first point in each radial line. Then add an offset for the center to control the opening size.

The centerpoint is added using:

```
; start mesh
(command
  ".3DMESH" (+ 24 1) (+ 31 1))
; center
(repeat (+ 31 1)
  (command (list 0 0 0))
)
```

Execute PROG06b from the command line.

Completed function PROG06b:

```
;-----------------------------------
(defun prog06b ()
 (graphscr)
 (command ".ERASE" "ALL" "")
(princ "\nProg06b:")
; file to read
(setq fh1 (open
  "C:\\TMY2_data\\Chicago01.txt"
  "r"))
; set list
(setq plist (list ))
(while fh1
 (setq nline (read-line fh1))
 (if nline
  (progn
   (setq datalist
     (read (strcat "(" nline ")")))
   (setq pt (list (list
     (nth 1 datalist)
     (nth 2 datalist))
     (nth 3 datalist)))
   ; add pt to list
   (setq plist
     (append plist (list pt)))
  )
  (setq fh1 (close fh1))
 )
)
; radius and angle inc based on
; 24 hours
(setq rad (/ 31.0 (* 2 pi)))
(setq anginc (/ 360.0 31))
; center offset
(setq coff 6.0)
; start mesh
(command ".3DMESH"
  (+ 24 1) (+ 31 1))
; center
(repeat (+ 31 1)
 (command (list 0 0 0))
)
; hour count
(setq hcnt 1)
(repeat 24
 ; day count
 (setq dcnt 1)
 (repeat 31
  ; get temperature
  (setq ntemp (nth 1
    (assoc (list dcnt hcnt)
    plist)))
  ; radius is hours
```

```
    (setq xpt (* (+ hcnt coff) (cos
      (dtr (* anginc dcnt)))))
    (setq ypt (* (+ hcnt coff) (sin
      (dtr (* anginc dcnt)))))
    ; height is temperature
    (setq zpt (* ntemp 0.1))
    (setq pt (list xpt ypt zpt))
    ; get first pt
    (if (= dcnt 1) (setq fpt pt))
    (command pt)
    ; check for last pt, connect to
    ; first pt
    (if (= dcnt 31) (command fpt))
    ; inc day
    (setq dcnt (+ dcnt 1))
   )
   ; inc hour
   (setq hcnt (+ hcnt 1))
  )
  (command ".ZOOM" "e")
  (princ)
)
;-----------------------------------
```

Convert the circular pattern to elliptical

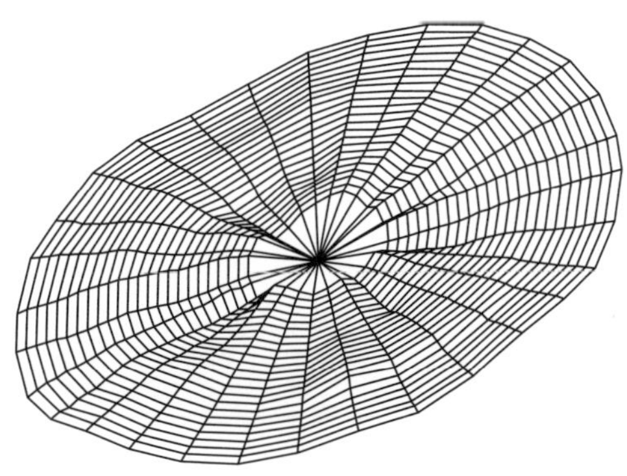

PROG06c: January temperature, represented in an elliptical pattern

Add function PROG06c. Using a copy of PROG06b, modify the radial computations to change the x- or y-radius to elliptical.

The radial computation could simply include a radius factor, using:

```
; radius is hours
(setq xpt (* (* (+ hcnt coff) 1.50)
  (cos (dtr (* anginc dcnt)))))
(setq ypt (* (+ hcnt coff)
  (sin (dtr (* anginc dcnt)))))
```

Execute PROG06c from the command line.

The previous meshes were modeled as single surfaces. Complete the mesh with sides and a bottom.

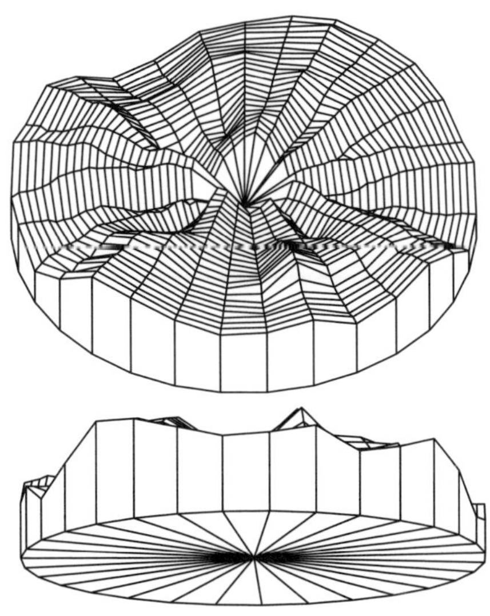

PROG06d: January temperature, represented in a radial pattern with edges and bottom

Add function PROG06d. Using a copy of PROG06b or PROG06c, add an additional series of points for the edge and bottom.

The edge points are added as:

```
; edge
 (setq dcnt 1)
 (repeat 31
  (setq xpt (* (+ 24 coff)
    (cos (dtr (* anginc dcnt)))))
  (setq ypt (* (+ 24 coff)
    (sin (dtr (* anginc dcnt)))))
  (setq pt (list xpt ypt 0))
  ; get first pt
  (if (= dcnt 1) (setq fpt pt))
  (command pt)
  ; check for last pt, connect to
  ; first pt
  (if (= dcnt 31) (command fpt))
  (setq dcnt (+ dcnt 1))
 )
 ; bottom
 (repeat (+ 31 1)
  (command (list 0 0 0))
 )
```

A z-scale and a z-minimum were added to define the edge height. The centerpoint on the top is set to the z-minimum elevation. As with other meshes we have closed, this mesh is ready for use with rapid-prototyping systems to create three-dimensional models.

Sample script file of PROG06d:

```
;----------------------------------
(prog06d)
;Enter Z scale:
0.2
;Enter Z minimum:
4.0
;----------------------------------
```

Completed function PROG06d:

```
;----------------------------------
(defun prog06d ()
 (graphscr)
 (command ".ERASE" "ALL" "")
 (princ "\nProg06d:")
 (setq zscale
   (getdist "\nEnter Z scale: "))
 (setq zmin
   (getdist
   "\nEnter minimum Z value: "))
 ; file to read
 (setq fh1 (open
   "C:\\TMY2_data\\Chicago01.txt"
   "r"))
 ; set list
 (setq plist (list ))
 (while fh1
  (setq nline (read-line fh1))
  (if nline
   (progn
    (setq datalist
      (read (strcat "(" nline ")")))
    (setq pt (list (list
      (nth 1 datalist)
      (nth 2 datalist))
      (nth 3 datalist)))
    ; add pt to list
    (setq plist
      (append plist (list pt)))
   )
   (setq fh1 (close fh1))
  )
 )
 ; radius and angle inc based on
 ; 24 hours
 (setq rad (/ 31.0 (* 2 pi)))
 (setq anginc (/ 360.0 31))
 ; center offset
 (setq coff 6.0)
 ; start mesh
 (command ".3DMESH"
   (+ 24 3) (+ 31 1))
 ; center
 (repeat (+ 31 1)
  (command (list 0 0 zmin))
 )
```

```
; hour count
(setq hcnt 1)
(repeat 24
 ; day count
 (setq dcnt 1)
 (repeat 31
  ; get temperature
  (setq ntemp (nth 1
    (assoc (list dcnt hcnt)
    plist)))
  ; radius is hours
  (setq xpt
    (* (+ hcnt coff)
    (cos (dtr (* anginc dcnt)))))
  (setq ypt
    (* (+ hcnt coff)
    (sin (dtr (* anginc dcnt)))))
  ; height is temperature
  (setq zpt
    (+ (* ntemp zscale) zmin))
  (setq pt (list xpt ypt zpt))
  ; get first pt
  (if (= dcnt 1) (setq fpt pt))
  (command pt)
  ; check for last pt, connect to
  ; first pt
  (if (= dcnt 31) (command fpt))
  ; inc day
  (setq dcnt (+ dcnt 1))
 )
 ; inc hour
 (setq hcnt (+ hcnt 1))
)
; edge
(setq dcnt 1)
(repeat 31
 (setq xpt (* (+ 24 coff)
   (cos (dtr (* anginc dcnt)))))
 (setq ypt (* (+ 24 coff)
   (sin (dtr (* anginc dcnt)))))
 (setq pt (list xpt ypt 0))
 ; get first pt
 (if (= dcnt 1) (setq fpt pt))
 (command pt)
 ; check for last pt, connect to
 ; first pt
 (if (= dcnt 31) (command fpt))
 (setq dcnt (+ dcnt 1))
 )
 ; bottom
 (repeat (+ 31 1)
  (command (list 0 0 0))
 )
 (command ".ZOOM" "e")
 (princ)
)
;-----------------------------------
```

Convert a mesh to a spherical pattern

Instead of a radial relief pattern, convert the mesh to a spherical projection.

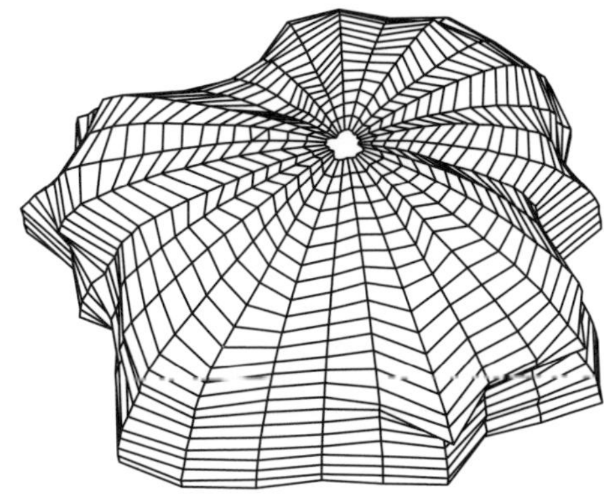

PROG07: January temperature, represented as a spherical mesh

Add function PROG07. Using a copy of PROG06, replace the radial computations with spherical ones, and add radius and angle increments for both hours and days.

The spherical coordinates are computed as:

```
xpt = hrad(cos hang)(sin vang)
ypt = hrad(sin hang)(sin vang)
zpt = vrad(cos vang)
```

Whereas `hrad` and `hang` are horizontal radii (hour plus temperature) and cover 360 degrees, `vrad` and `vang` are vertical radii (days) and cover 90 degrees.

The radius and angle increments are computed as:

```
; radius and angle inc based on
; days and hours
(setq hrad (/ 24.0 (* 2 pi)))
(setq hanginc (/ 90.0 24))
(setq drad (/ 31.0 (* 2 pi)))
(setq danginc (/ 360.0 31))
```

Each point is computed as:

```
(setq xpt
  (* (* (+ drad (* ntemp 0.075))
  (cos (dtr (* danginc dcnt))))
  (sin (dtr (* hanginc hcnt)))))
(setq ypt
  (* (* (+ drad (* ntemp 0.075))
  (sin (dtr (* danginc dcnt))))
  (sin (dtr (* hanginc hcnt)))))
(setq zpt (* hrad
  (cos (dtr (* hanginc hcnt)))))
```

The temperature value is scaled.

Execute `PROG07` from the command line.

Completed function `PROG07`:

```
;-----------------------------------
(defun prog07 ()
 (graphscr)
 (command ".ERASE" "ALL" "")
 (princ "\nProg07:")
 ; file to read
 (setq fhl (open
   "C:\\TMY2_data\\Chicago01.txt"
   "r"))
 ; set list
 (setq plist (list ))
 (while fhl
  (setq nline (read-line fhl))
  (if nline
   (progn
    (setq datalist
      (read (strcat "(" nline ")")))
    (setq pt (list (list
      (nth 1 datalist)
      (nth 2 datalist))
      (nth 3 datalist)))
    ; add pt to list
    (setq plist
      (append plist (list pt)))
   )
   (setq fhl (close fhl))
  )
 )
 ; radius and angle inc based on
 ; 24 hours
 (setq hrad (/ 24.0 (* 2 pi)))
 (setq hanginc (/ 90.0 24))
 (setq drad (/ 31.0 (* 2 pi)))
 (setq danginc (/ 360.0 31))
 ; start mesh
 (command ".3DMESH"
   (+ 24 0) (+ 31 1))
 ; hour count
 (setq hcnt 1)
 (repeat 24
  ; day count
  (setq dcnt 1)
  (repeat 31
   ; get temperature
   (setq ntemp (nth 1
     (assoc (list dcnt hcnt) plist)))
   (setq xpt
     (* (* (+ drad (* ntemp 0.075))
     (cos (dtr (* danginc dcnt))))
     (sin (dtr (* hanginc hcnt)))))
   (setq ypt
     (* (* (+ drad (* ntemp 0.075))
     (sin (dtr (* danginc dcnt))))
     (sin (dtr (* hanginc hcnt)))))
   (setq zpt (* hrad
     (cos (dtr (* hanginc hcnt)))))
   (setq pt (list xpt ypt zpt))
   ; get first pt
   (if (= dcnt 1) (setq fpt pt))
   (command pt)
   ; check for last pt, connect to
```

```
    ; first pt
    (if (= dcnt 31) (command fpt))
    ; inc day
    (setq dcnt (+ dcnt 1))
   )
   ; inc hour
   (setq hcnt (+ hcnt 1))
  )
  (command ".ZOOM" "e")
  (princ)
)
;-----------------------------------
```

Review PROG07, including setting the day and hour radii and angle increment, as well as the computation of spherical points.

Consider adding an offset angle so that the vertical angle would be less than 90 degrees. The result is an opening at the top.

The computation would be:

```
; radius and angle inc
; based on 24 hours
(setq openang 20)
(setq hrad (/ 24.0 (* 2 pi)))
(setq hanginc
  (/ (- 90.0 openang) 24))
```

Another alternative is to use 180 degrees for the vertical angle, instead of 90 degrees.

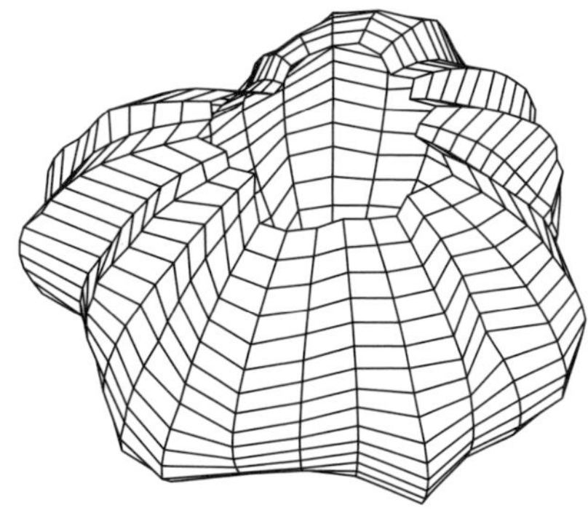

PROG07a: January temperature, presented as a full spherical mesh

Add function PROG07a. Using a copy of PROG07, add an opening angle and change the vertical angle to generate a full sphere.

The computation would be:

```
; radius and angle inc
; based on 24 hours
(setq openang 20)
(setq hrad (/ 24.0 (* 2 pi)))
(setq hanginc
  (/ (- 180.0 openang) 24))
```

And the spherical computation is:

```
; get temperature
(setq ntemp (nth 1
  (assoc (list dcnt hcnt)
  plist)))
(setq xpt
  (* (* (+ drad (* ntemp 0.075))
  (cos (dtr (* danginc dcnt))))
  (sin (dtr (+ (* hanginc hcnt)
  openang)))))
```

```
(setq ypt
  (* (* (+ drad (* ntemp 0.075))
  (sin (dtr (* danginc dcnt))))
  (sin (dtr (+ (* hanginc hcnt)
  openang)))))
(setq zpt (* hrad
  (cos (dtr (+ (* hanginc hcnt)
  openang)))))
```

Execute PROG07a from the command line.

Completed function PROG07a:

```
;-----------------------------------
(defun prog07a ()
 (graphscr)
 (command ".ERASE" "ALL" "")
 (princ "\nProg07a:")
 ; file to read
 (setq fh1 (open
   "C:\\TMY2_data\\Chicago01.txt"
   "r"))
 ; set list
 (setq plist (list ))
 (while fh1
  (setq nline (read-line fh1))
  (if nline
   (progn
    (setq datalist
      (read (strcat "(" nline ")")))
    (setq pt (list (list
      (nth 1 datalist)
      (nth 2 datalist))
      (nth 3 datalist)))
    ; add pt to list
    (setq plist
      (append plist (list pt)))
   )
   (setq fh1 (close fh1))
  )
 )
 ; radius and angle inc based on
 ; 24 hours
 (setq openang 20)
 (setq hrad (/ 24.0 (* 2 pi)))
 (setq hanginc
   (/ (- 180.0 openang) 24))
 (setq drad (/ 31.0 (* 2 pi)))
 (setq danginc (/ 360.0 31))
 ; start mesh
 (command ".3DMESH"
   (+ 24 0) (+ 31 1))
 ; hour count
 (setq hcnt 1)
 (repeat 24
  ; day count
  (setq dcnt 1)
  (repeat 31
   ; get temperature
   (setq ntemp (nth 1
     (assoc (list dcnt hcnt)
     plist)))
   (setq xpt
     (* (* (+ drad (* ntemp 0.075))
     (cos (dtr (* danginc dcnt))))
     (sin (dtr (+ (* hanginc hcnt)
     openang)))))
   (setq ypt
     (* (* (+ drad (* ntemp 0.075))
     (sin (dtr (* danginc dcnt))))
     (sin (dtr (+ (* hanginc hcnt)
     openang)))))
   (setq zpt (* hrad
      (cos (dtr (+ (* hanginc hcnt)
      openang)))))
   (setq pt (list xpt ypt zpt))
   ; get first pt
   (if (= dcnt 1) (setq fpt pt))
   (command pt)
   ; check for last pt, connect to
   ; first pt
   (if (= dcnt 31) (command fpt))
   ; inc day
   (setq dcnt (+ dcnt 1))
  )
  ; inc hour
  (setq hcnt (+ hcnt 1))
 )
 (command ".ZOOM" "e")
 (princ)
)
;-----------------------------------
```

Explore other numeric data sets, such as population, frequency of use, travel times or natural or artificial light levels. Each has the potential to generate a unique form.

7.2 Constructions from Images

Another source of data is an image. An image differs from weather data in that it already has a visual representation. With weather data, we had to explore different ways of expressing the data values. This is not the case with images.

Convert an image to points

An image consists of a set of pixels organized in rows and columns, each having an RGB value with red, green, and blue color components. The row and column values locate a point in a grid, and the color value can act as an elevation. Each RGB component value ranges from 0 to 255. We can also convert the RGB value to a grayscale value. This gives a single value for each location, rather than three individual values.

The first step is to develop a function that takes an image file and converts it to a form that is better suited for interpretation. The image file type we will be using is BMP, a common bitmap format.

For example, this grayscale image of Ludwig Mies van der Rohe that can be converted to a file of pixel values.

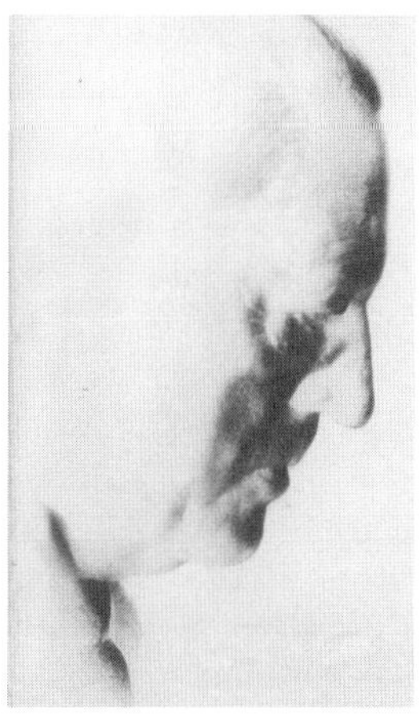

Image of Ludwig Mies van der Rohe

The first 10 pixels in row 0 would be:

```
149255024
000000033033033033
001000028028028028
002000026026026026
003000025025025025
004000025025025025
005000025025025025
006000026026026026
007000026026026026
008000025025025025
009000025025025025
```

The first line of values consists of the width, height, and the color mode of the image: 149 by 255, at 24-bit color.

For each pixel, a separate line is included that consists of an x- and y-location, RGB color values, and its grayscale value. These are all in fields of three characters, all integer values.

The PROG01 function accepts the names for a BMP image and the resulting PTS file.

For example, the script file for PROG01 would be:

```
;-----------------------------------
(prog01)
; BMP filename:
c:\bmp_data\mies01.bmp
; PTS filename:
c:\bmp_data\mies01.bmp.pts
;-----------------------------------
```

The PROG01 function accepts only BMP images saved in the 24-bit color mode and in the Microsoft Windows file format. Always set the image to 24-bit color, even if it is actually grayscale or black and white. The image size is limited to 255 by 255 pixels.

The image can be filtered and adjusted to highlight the content. For images with very strong content, use brightness and contrast and convert it to grayscale or black and white. Consider inverting the colors or grayscale values. Also, orient the image so that the height is y and the width is x.

Image data is stored in order by row and column. For example, x is the width and y is the height. The normal origin, the (0,0) pixel, for an image is the upper-left corner. In function PROG01, this has been changed to the lower-left corner for our purposes. The RGB and grayscale values have been inverted so that white is 000 and black is 255. White represents the lowest elevation and black represents the highest.

PROG01 demonstrates how the read-char function can be used to read binary files. The BMP file format is openly published, so determining the file format was easily accomplished.

Start a new drawing and set the units to architectural; set the grid to 1 foot, and turn off all snaps and dynamic input.

Since a large number of drawing elements will be generated, also consider turning off the UNDO feature. Start a new AutoLISP file in the editor CH07B.LSP, and add functions dtr, rtd, and PROG01.

Completed function PROG01:

```
;-----------------------------------
(defun prog01 ()
 ; convert BMP file to PTS file
 (setvar "CMDECHO" 0)
 (setq iname
   (getstring
   "\nEnter BMP filename: "))
 (setq fh1 (open iname "r"))
 (setq oname
   (getstring
   "\nEnter PTS filename: "))
 (setq fh2 (open oname "w"))
 ; BMP Header 1
 (setq h1list (list ))
 (repeat 14
  (setq nchar (read-char fh1))
  (setq h1list
    (append h1list (list nchar)))
 )
 ; MP Header 2
 (setq h2list (list ))
 (repeat 40
  (setq nchar (read-char fh1))
  (setq h2list
    (append h2list (list nchar)))
 )
 ; width, height, colors
 (setq iw (nth 4 h2list))
 (setq ih (nth 8 h2list))
 (setq ic (nth 14 h2list))
 ; write PTS header info
 (princ (substr (rtos
   (+ 1000 iw) 2 0) 2 3) fh2)
 (princ (substr (rtos
   (+ 1000 ih) 2 0) 2 3) fh2)
 (princ (substr (rtos
   (+ 1000 ic) 2 0) 2 3) fh2)
 (princ "\n" fh2)
 ; get pixels
 (setq nh 0)
 (repeat ih
  (setq nw 0)
  (repeat iw
   ; get RGB value
   (setq rval (read-char fh1))
```

```
    (setq gval (read-char fh1))
    (setq bval (read-char fh1))
    ; compute grayscale value
    (setq gsval
      (fix (+ (* 0.3 rval)
      (* 0.59 gval) (* 0.11 bval))))
    ; write to file
    (princ (substr (rtos
      (+ 1000 nw) 2 0) 2 3) fh2)
    (princ (substr (rtos
      (+ 1000 nh) 2 0) 2 3) fh2)
    (princ (substr (rtos
      (+ 1000 (- 255 rval)) 2 0) 2 3)
      fh2)
    (princ (substr (rtos
      (+ 1000 (- 255 gval)) 2 0) 2 3)
      fh2)
    (princ (substr (rtos
      (+ 1000 (- 255 bval)) 2 0) 2 3)
      fh2)
    (princ (substr (rtos
      (+ 1000 (- 255 gsval)) 2 0) 2 3)
      fh2)
    (princ "\n" fh2)
    (setq nw (+ nw 1))
  )
  ; skip padding
  (if (/= (fix (/ (* iw 3.0) 4))
     (/ (* iw 3.0) 4)) (progn
    (repeat (- 4 (rem (* iw 3) 4))
     (setq nchar (read-char fh1))
    )
  ))
  (setq nh (+ nh 1))
 )
 ; close files
 (close fh1)
 (close fh2)
 (princ "\nFile created: ")
   (princ oname)
 (princ "\nBMP Width: ") (princ iw)
   (princ " Height: ") (princ ih)
   (princ " Colors: ") (princ ic)
 (setvar "CMDECHO" 1)
 (princ)
)
;----------------------------------
```

Pixels as drawings

One method for interpreting image data is to use graphic elements that can be etched or printed onto a surface or as perforations.

For example, each pixel can be represented as a circle.

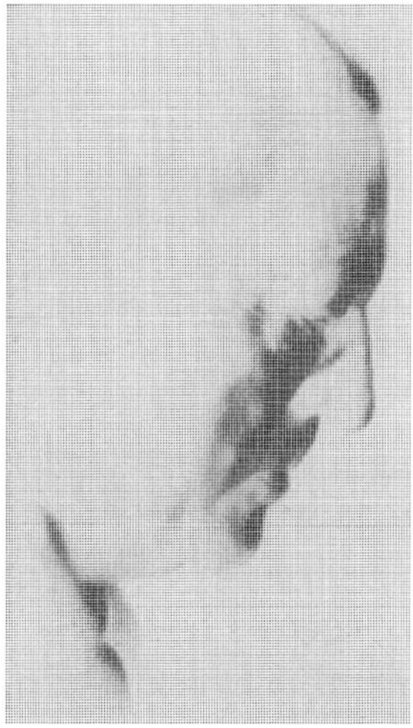

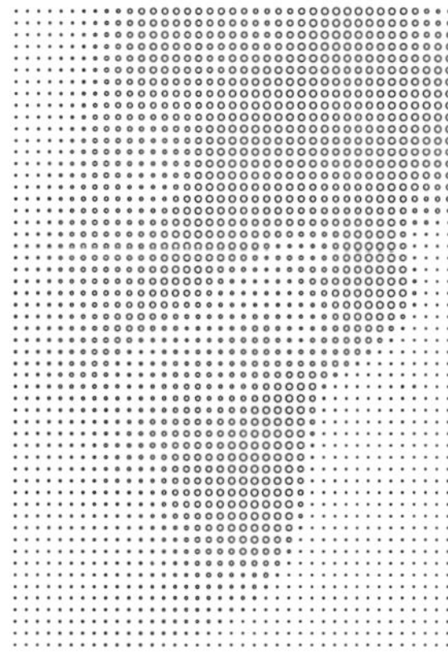

PROG02: pixels hollow as circles

Add function PROG02 to represent each pixel as a circle. Include a module size for the x- and y-spacing of pixels, and minimum and maximum circle sizes. The grayscale value will determine the radius of the circle.

Function PROG02 reads the first record of the file and extracts the width, height, and number of colors, using:

```
; header record
(setq dataline
  (read-line fh1))
(setq wmax
  (atoi (substr dataline 1 3)))
(setq hmax
  (atoi (substr dataline 4 3)))
(setq ncolors
  (atoi (substr dataline 7 3)))
```

Each of the remaining records contains the x and y locations and the RGB and grayscale values of each pixel, using:

```
; get pts record
(setq dataline
  (read-line fh1))
; Y and X location
(setq xpt
  (atoi (substr dataline 1 3)))
(setq ypt
  (atoi (substr dataline 4 3)))
; RGB and grayscale values
(setq rcolor
  (atoi (substr dataline 7 3)))
(setq gcolor
  (atoi (substr dataline 10 3)))
(setq bcolor
  (atoi (substr dataline 13 3)))
(setq gscolor
  (atoi (substr dataline 16 3)))
```

The radius of the circle is proportional to the grayscale value and it is based on the circle's minimum and maximum sizes. A minimum radius is included so that the circle radius is never set to zero.

Radius is computed as:

```
; convert grayscale to percent
(setq gsprct (/ gscolor 255.0))
; radius
(setq rad (+ cmin
  (* (- cmax cmin) gsprct)))
```

Sample script file for PROG02:

```
;----------------------------------
(prog02)
; PTS filename:
c:\bmp_data\mies01.bmp.pts
;Enter module size:
5.0
;Enter maximum circle radius:
2.4
;Enter minimum circle radius:
0.25
;----------------------------------
```

Completed function PROG02:

```
;----------------------------------
(defun prog02 ()
 ; 2D circle at each point
 ; diameter based grayscale value
 (setvar "CMDECHO" 0)
 (command ".ERASE" "all" "")
 (princ "\nProg02:")
 (setq fname
   (getstring
   "\nEnter PTS filename: "))
 (setq fh1 (open fname "r"))
 (setq mod
   (getdist "\nEnter module size: "))
 ; convert BMP file to PTS file
 (setq cmax
   (getdist
   "\nEnter maximum circle size: "))
```

```
  (setq cmin
    (getdist
    "\nEnter minimum circle size: "))
  ; header record
  (setq dataline (read-line fh1))
  (setq wmax
    (atoi (substr dataline 1 3)))
  (setq hmax
    (atoi (substr dataline 4 3)))
  (setq ncolors
    (atoi (substr dataline 7 3)))
  (repeat hmax
   (repeat wmax
    ; get pts record
    (setq dataline (read-line fh1))
    ; X and Y location
    (setq xpt
      (atoi (substr dataline 1 3)))
    (setq ypt
      (atoi (substr dataline 4 3)))
    ; RGB and grayscale values
    (setq rcolor
      (atoi (substr dataline 7 3)))
    (setq gcolor
      (atoi (substr dataline 10 3)))
    (setq bcolor
      (atoi (substr dataline 13 3)))
    (setq gscolor
      (atoi (substr dataline 16 3)))
    ; xy coords
    (setq ptx (* xpt mod))
    (setq pty (* ypt mod))
    ; centerpoint
    (setq cpt (list ptx pty))
    ; convert grayscale to percent
    (setq gsprct (/ gscolor 255.0))
    ; radius
    (setq rad (+ cmin
      (* (- cmax cmin) gsprct)))
    ; circle
    (command ".CIRCLE" cpt rad)
   )
  )
  (close fh1)
  (command ".ZOOM" "e")
  (setvar "CMDECHO" 1)
  (princ)
)
;----------------------------------
```

Circles, as well as other basic shapes, can be used as graphic elements to be etched or drawn in a surface. The drawings could also represent cuts for perforations.

In the following two examples, a circle and square have a solid fill to highlight their sizes.

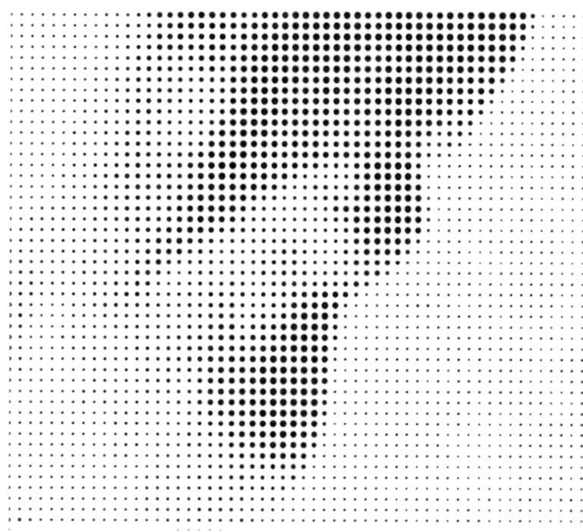

PROG02a: pixels as filled circles

Add function PROG02a. Using a copy of PROG02, fill all circles by adding the following after the ZOOM command:

```
; fill the circles
(command ".FILL" "on")
(command ".HATCH" "solid" "all" "")
```

Use the same script file as for PROG02.

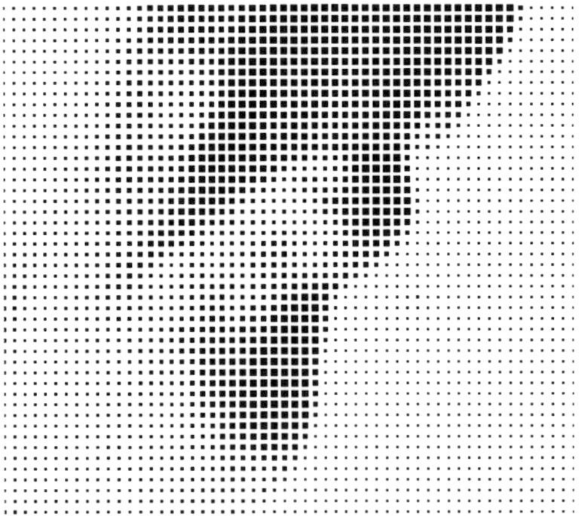

PROG02b: pixels as filled squares

Add function PROG02b. Using a copy of PROG02a, display squares by replacing the CIRCLE command with:

```
; square
(command ".POLYGON"
  "4" cpt "c" rad)
```

Use the same script file as for PROG02.

PROG02c: pixels as rotated filled squares

Add function PROG02c to display rotated squares. Using a copy of PROG02b, add a rotation of 45 degrees to the POLYGON command:

```
; square
(command ".POLYGON"
  "4" cpt "c" rad)
(command ".ZOOM" "e")
(command ".ROTATE"
  "last" "" cpt "45")
```

Use the same script file as for PROG02.

For perforations, any of the above can be used with the fill removed. For print or etching applications, the fill can be used, or at larger scales, the line thickness can be adjusted. In addition to simple shapes, the density of color can be represented by a series of concentric circles, squares, or any other shape, including simple lines, horizontal or vertical.

Explore other methods to show intensity of color

In these examples, the entire range of color and grayscale values were considered and 256 possible sizes. If perforations are planned, the number of possible sizes might be limited due to the punch or drill bit available. Graphically, you might also want to limit the circle sizes.

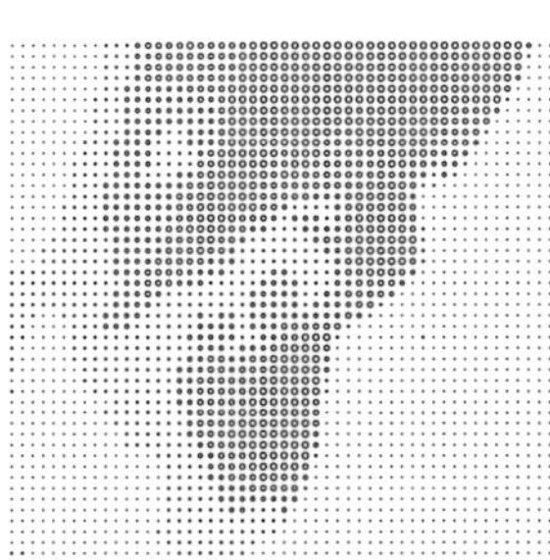

PROG02d: pixels at fixed radius

Add function PROG02d. Using a copy of PROG02, include input for the number of levels the color should be set at.

The list is input as:

```
(setq cradlist
  (read (getstring
  "\nEnter radius list: ")))
; levels
(setq nlevels (length cradlist))
```

The read function coverts the getstring results to a list. The number of levels is the number of sizes in the list.

The grayscale value is converted to a level and radius, using:

```
; convert to level
(setq gslevel (fix
  (/ gscolor (/ 256.0 nlevels))))
; radius
(setq rad (nth gslevel cradlist))
```

Sample script file for PROG02d:

```
;-----------------------------------
(prog02d)
; PTS filename:
c:\bmp_data\mies01.bmp.pts
;Enter module size:
5.0
;Enter radius list:
(0.25 0.5 1.0 1.25 1.5 1.75 2.0 2.25)
;-----------------------------------
```

Completed function PROG02d:

```
;-----------------------------------
(defun prog02d ()
 ; 2D circle at each point
 ; diameter based grayscale value
 (setvar "CMDECHO" 0)
 (command ".ERASE" "all" "")
```

```
(princ "\nProg02d:")
(setq fname
  (getstring
  "\nEnter PTS filename: "))
(setq fhl (open fname "r"))
(setq mod
   (getdist
   "\nEnter module size: "))
(setq cradlist
  (read (getstring
  "\nEnter radius list: ")))
; levels
(setq nlevels (length cradlist))
; header record
(setq dataline (read-line fhl))
(setq wmax
  (atoi (substr dataline 1 3)))
(setq hmax
  (atoi (substr dataline 4 3)))
(setq ncolors
  (atoi (substr dataline 7 3)))
(repeat hmax
 (repeat wmax
  ; get pts record
  (setq dataline (read-line fhl))
  ; X and Y location
  (setq xpt
    (atoi (substr dataline 1 3)))
  (setq ypt
    (atoi (substr dataline 4 3)))
  ; RGB and grayscale values
  (setq rcolor
    (atoi (substr dataline 7 3)))
  (setq gcolor
    (atoi (substr dataline 10 3)))
  (setq bcolor
    (atoi (substr dataline 13 3)))
  (setq gscolor
    (atoi (substr dataline 16 3)))
  ; xy coords
  (setq ptx (* xpt mod))
  (setq pty (* ypt mod))
  ; centerpoint
  (setq cpt (list ptx pty))
  ; convert to level
  (setq gslevel (fix
    (/ gscolor (/ 256.0 nlevels))))
  ; radius
  (setq rad (nth gslevel cradlist))
  ; circle
  (command ".CIRCLE" cpt rad)
 )
)
(close fhl)
(command ".ZOOM" "e")
(setvar "CMDECHO" 1)
(princ)
)
;-----------------------------------
```

Function PROG02d could also include the fill. A lower number of levels used will reduce the image to an abstraction of itself. Explore the possible images that could be created by controlling the number of color levels.

The same method can be used to insert a block from a list of blocks, representing a specific symbol for each level of gray. The blocks could represent symbols for intensity or be iconic for the project. Once the block name is selected, use the INSERT command to scale and place it.

Another series of drawings can be created from color images, when RGB values are considered. This would be the same as color separation: an image using only the red color-component value, another using the green component value, and still another using the blue component value.

Construct a relief from an image

Pixel value can also be used for the physical height of a series of squares placed at each location.

Using `clouds01.bmp`:

Image of clouds

Script file to convert image to points:

```
;----------------------------------
(prog01)
; BMP filename:
c:\bmp_data\clouds01.bmp
; PTS filename:
c:\bmp_data\clouds01.bmp.pts
;----------------------------------
```

The `clouds01.bmp` file is 50 by 33 pixels.

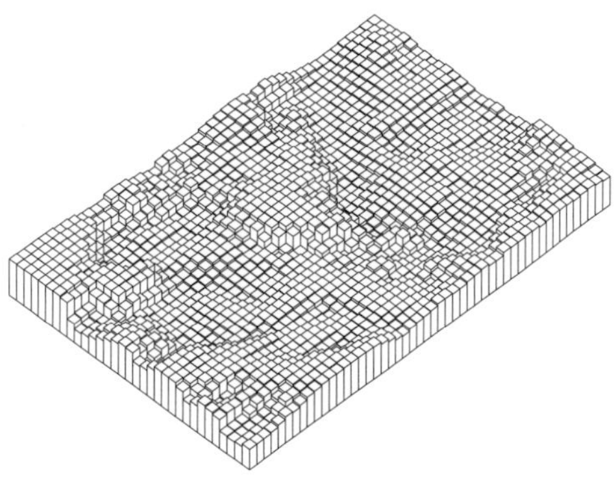

PROG03: clouds image as a relief

The clouds are white in this image. Invert the grayscale so that they become the primary elements. The inversion can be done with any image processing software, or built into function PROG03.

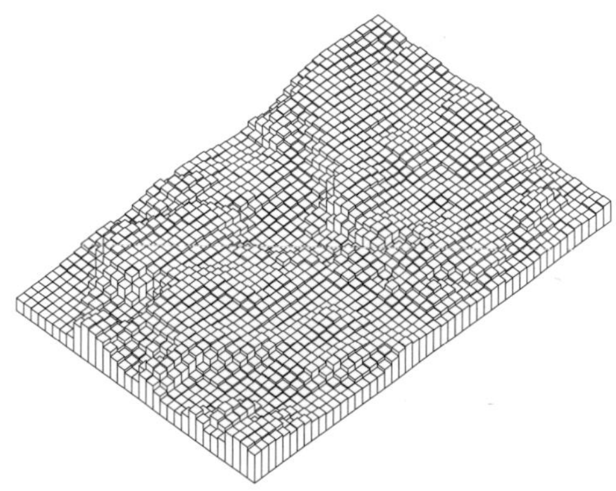

PROG03: clouds image as an inverted relief

Add function PROG03. Using a copy of PROG02, place a square at each pixel location and set the height by the grayscale value. Input minimum and maximum heights.

To compute the height of each square with a grayscale inversion, use:

```
; convert inverted grayscale
; to percent
(setq gsprct
  (/ (- 255 gscolor) 255.0))
; height
(setq zheight (+ zmin
  (* (- zmax zmin) gsprct)))
; square
(command ".POLYGON"
  "4" cpt "C" (/ mod 2.0))
(command ".ZOOM" "e")
(command ".EXTRUDE"
  "last" "" zheight)
; versions prior to 2007 require
; the taper parameter
;(command ".EXTRUDE"
;  "last" "" zheight "")
```

Sample script file for PROG03:

```
;----------------------------------
(prog03)
; PTS filename:
c:\bmp_data\clouds01.bmp.pts
;Enter module size:
5.0
;Enter Z maximum:
30.0
;Enter Z minimum:
2.5
;----------------------------------
```

Completed function PROG03:

```
;----------------------------------
(defun prog03 ()
 ; 3D square at each point
 ; diameter based grayscale value
 (setvar "CMDECHO" 0)
 (command ".ERASE" "all" "")
 (princ "\nProg03:")
 (setq fname
   (getstring
   "\nEnter PTS filename: "))
 (setq fhl (open fname "r"))
 (setq mod
   (getdist "\nEnter module size: "))
 (setq zmax
   (read (getstring
   "\nEnter Z maximum: ")))
 (setq zmin
    (read (getstring
    "\nEnter Z minimum: ")))
 ; levels
 (setq nlevels (length cradlist))
 ; header record
 (setq dataline (read-line fhl))
 (setq wmax
   (atoi (substr dataline 1 3)))
 (setq hmax
   (atoi (substr dataline 4 3)))
 (setq ncolors
   (atoi (substr dataline 7 3)))
 (repeat hmax
  (repeat wmax
   ; get pts record
   (setq dataline (read-line fhl))
   ; X and Y location
   (setq xpt
     (atoi (substr dataline 1 3)))
   (setq ypt
     (atoi (substr dataline 4 3)))
   ; RGB and grayscale values
   (setq rcolor
     (atoi (substr dataline 7 3)))
   (setq gcolor
     (atoi (substr dataline 10 3)))
   (setq bcolor
     (atoi (substr dataline 13 3)))
   (setq gscolor
```

```
      (atoi (substr dataline 16 3)))
    ; xy coords
    (setq ptx (* xpt mod))
    (setq pty (* ypt mod))
    ; centerpoint
    (setq cpt (list ptx pty))
    ; convert inverted grayscale
    ; to percent
    (setq gsprct
      (/ (- 255 gscolor) 255.0))
    ; height
    (setq zheight (+ zmin
      (* (- zmax zmin) gsprct)))
    ; square
    (command ".POLYGON"
      "4" cpt "C" (/ mod 2.0))
    (command ".ZOOM" "e")
    (command ".EXTRUDE"
      "last" "" zheight)
    ; versions prior to 2007 require
    ; the taper parameter
    ;(command ".EXTRUDE"
    ;  "last" "" zheight "")
  )
 )
 (close fhl)
 (command ".ZOOM" "e")
 (setvar "CMDECHO" 1)
 (princ)
)
;-----------------------------------
```

Large areas of contiguous squares can be developed if a limited range of heights is used.

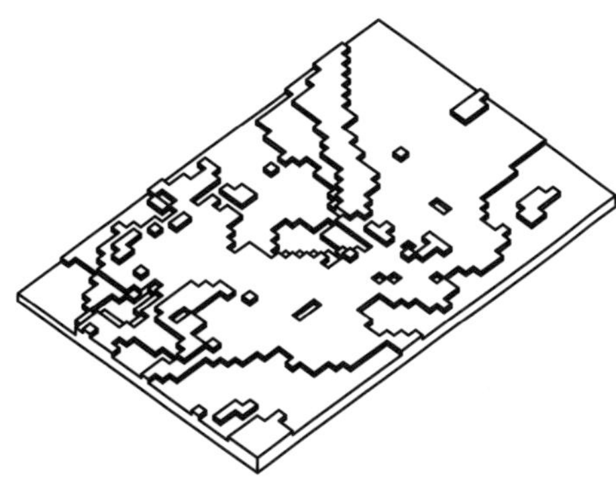

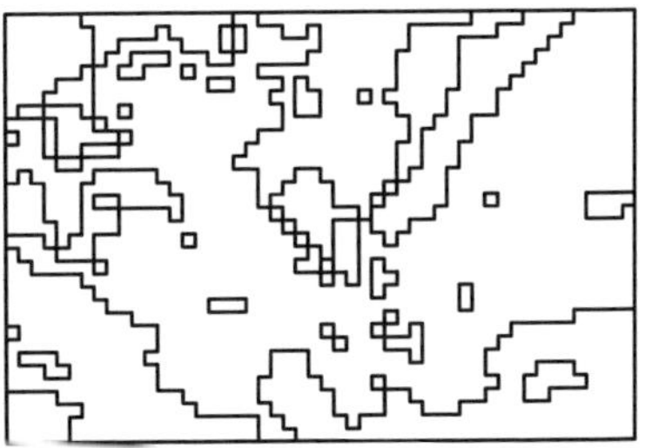

PROG03a: clouds image as an inverted relief using a list of heights

Add function PROG03a. Using a copy of PROG03, include a height list and UNION all the squares into a single solid.

The height is computed as:

```
; convert to level
(setq gslevel (fix
  (/ (- 255 gscolor)
  (/ 256.0 nlevels))))
; height
(setq zheight
  (nth gslevel zheightlist))
(command ".POLYGON"
```

```
  "4" cpt "C" (/ mod 2.0))
(command ".ZOOM" "e")
(command ".EXTRUDE"
  "last" "" zheight)
; versions prior to 2007 require
; the taper parameter
;(command ".EXTRUDE"
;  "last" "" zheight "")
```

Sample script file for PROG03a:

```
;-----------------------------------
(prog03a)
; PTS filename:
c:\bmp_data\clouds01.bmp.pts
;Enter module size:
5.0
;Enter height list:
(5.0 7.5 10.0 12.5)
;-----------------------------------
```

Completed function PROG03a:

```
;-----------------------------------
(defun prog03a ()
 ; 3D square at each point
 ; diameter based grayscale value
 (setvar "CMDECHO" 0)
 (command ".ERASE" "all" "")
 (princ "\nProg03a:")
 (setq fname
   (getstring
   "\nEnter PTS filename: "))
 (setq fh1 (open fname "r"))
 (setq mod
   (getdist "\nEnter module size: "))
 (setq zheightlist
   (read (getstring
   "\nEnter height list: ")))
 ; levels
 (setq nlevels (length zheightlist))
 ; header record
 (setq dataline (read-line fh1))
 (setq wmax
   (atoi (substr dataline 1 3)))
 (setq hmax
   (atoi (substr dataline 4 3)))
 (setq ncolors
   (atoi (substr dataline 7 3)))
 (repeat hmax
  (repeat wmax
   ; get pts record
   (setq dataline (read-line fh1))
   ; X and Y location
   (setq xpt (atoi
     (substr dataline 1 3)))
   (setq ypt
     (atoi (substr dataline 4 3)))
   ; RGB and grayscale values
   (setq rcolor
     (atoi (substr dataline 7 3)))
   (setq gcolor
     (atoi (substr dataline 10 3)))
   (setq bcolor
     (atoi (substr dataline 13 3)))
   (setq gscolor
     (atoi (substr dataline 16 3)))
   ; xy coords
   (setq ptx (* xpt mod))
   (setq pty (* ypt mod))
   ; centerpoint
   (setq cpt (list ptx pty))
   ; convert to level
   (setq gslevel (fix
     (/ (- 255 gscolor)
     (/ 256.0 nlevels))))
   ; height
   (setq zheight
     (nth gslevel zheightlist))
   (command ".POLYGON"
     "4" cpt "C" (/ mod 2.0))
   (command ".ZOOM" "e")
   (command ".EXTRUDE"
     "last" "" zheight)
   ; versions prior to 2007 require
   ; the taper parameter
   ;(command ".EXTRUDE"
   ;  "last" "" zheight "")
  )
 )
 (close fh1)
 (command ".ZOOM" "e")
 (command ".BREP" "all" "")
 (command ".UNION" "all" "")
 (setvar "CMDECHO" 1)
 (princ)
)
;-----------------------------------
```

In addition to using the BREP command to turn off solid history, or setting the SOLIDHIST system variable to 0; in the UNDO command, select Auto and Off to turn off the undo feature and to decrease file size and processing time.

Construct a simple mesh from an image

The pixel color value as height can also be used to create a mesh, as in previous examples shown for weather data.

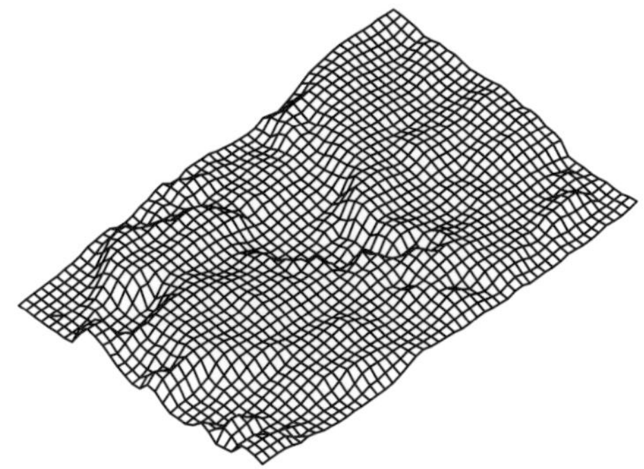

PROG04: clouds image as a mesh

Add function PROG04. Using a copy of PROG03, compute the height and place the point into a mesh. Input a maximum height for scaling the grayscale values. Note that a 000 grayscale value will be a 0.0 height.

The mesh is started as:

```
; start mesh
(command ".3DMESH" hmax wmax)
```

The mesh point is computed as:

```
; convert inverted grayscale to
; percent
(setq gsprct
  (/ (- 255 gscolor) 255.0))
; height
(setq zheight (* zmax gsprct))
; mesh point
(setq cpt (list ptx pty zheight))
(command cpt)
```

Sample script file for PROG04:

```
;-----------------------------------
(prog04)
; PTS filename:
c:\bmp_data\clouds01.bmp.pts
;Enter module size:
5.0
;Enter maximum height:
30.0
;-----------------------------------
```

Completed function PROG04:

```
;-----------------------------------
(defun prog04 ()
 ; 3D mesh
 ; height based grayscale value
 (setvar "CMDECHO" 0)
 (command ".ERASE" "all" "")
 (princ "\nProg04:")
 (setq fname
   (getstring
   "\nEnter PTS filename: "))
 (setq fhl (open fname "r"))
 (setq mod
   (getdist "\nEnter module size: "))
 (setq zmax
  (getdist
  "\nEnter maximum height: "))
 ; header record
 (setq dataline (read-line fhl))
 (setq wmax
   (atoi (substr dataline 1 3)))
 (setq hmax
   (atoi (substr dataline 4 3)))
 (setq ncolors
   (atoi (substr dataline 7 3)))
```

```
  ; start mesh
  (command ".3DMESH" hmax wmax)
  (repeat hmax
   (repeat wmax
    ; get pts record
    (setq dataline (read-line fh1))
    ; X and Y location
    (setq xpt
      (atoi (substr dataline 1 3)))
    (setq ypt
      (atoi (substr dataline 4 3)))
    ; RGB and grayscale values
    (setq rcolor
      (atoi (substr dataline 7 3)))
    (setq gcolor
      (atoi (substr dataline 10 3)))
    (setq bcolor
      (atoi (substr dataline 13 3)))
    (setq gscolor
      (atoi (substr dataline 16 3)))
    ; xy coords
    (setq ptx (* xpt mod))
    (setq pty (* ypt mod))
    ; centerpoint
    (setq cpt (list ptx pty))
    ; convert inverted grayscale to
    ; percent
    (setq gsprct
      (/ (- 255 gscolor) 255.0))
    ; height
    (setq zheight (* zmax gsprct))
    ; mesh point
    (setq cpt (list ptx pty zheight))
    (command cpt)
   )
  )
  (close fh1)
  (command ".ZOOM" "e")
  (setvar "CMDECHO" 1)
  (princ)
)
;-----------------------------------
```

Complete the mesh by adding sides and a bottom.

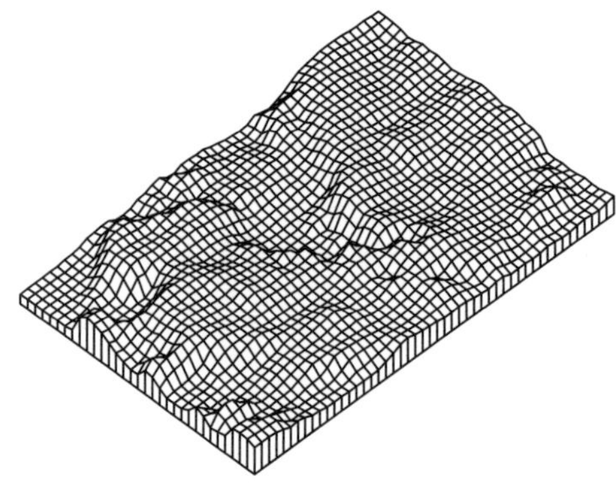

PROG04a: clouds image as a mesh with sides and bottom

Add function PROG04a. Using a copy of PROG04 and the method in the previous example for closing a mesh, add the sides and bottom.

Note that the first row and column start at 0, not 1, as in previous data-file examples.

Sample script file for PROG04a:

```
;-----------------------------------
(prog04a)
; PTS filename:
c:\bmp_data\clouds01.bmp.pts
;Enter module size:
5.0
;Enter maximum height:
30.0
;Enter maximum height:
2.5
;-----------------------------------
```

Completed function PROG04a:

```
;---------------------------------
(defun prog04a ()
 (setvar "CMDECHO" 0)
 (command ".ERASE" "all" "")
 (princ "\nProg04a:")
 (setq fname
   (getstring
   "\nEnter PTS filename: "))
 (setq fhl (open fname "r"))
 (setq mod
   (getdist "\nEnter module size: "))
 (setq zmax
   (getdist
   "\nEnter maximum height: "))
 (setq zmin
   (getdist
   "\nEnter minimum height: "))
 ; header record
 (setq dataline (read-line fhl))
 (setq wmax
   (atoi (substr dataline 1 3)))
 (setq hmax
   (atoi (substr dataline 4 3)))
 (setq ncolors
   (atoi (substr dataline 7 3)))
 ; start mesh
 (command ".3DMESH"
   (+ hmax 2) (+ wmax 3))
 (repeat hmax
  (repeat wmax
   ; get pts record
   (setq dataline (read-line fhl))
   ; X and Y location
   (setq xpt
     (atoi (substr dataline 1 3)))
   (setq ypt
     (atoi (substr dataline 4 3)))
   ; RGB and grayscale values
   (setq rcolor
     (atoi (substr dataline 7 3)))
   (setq gcolor
     (atoi (substr dataline 10 3)))
   (setq bcolor
     (atoi (substr dataline 13 3)))
   (setq gscolor
     (atoi (substr dataline 16 3)))
; xy coords
(setq ptx (* xpt mod))
(setq pty (* ypt mod))
; centerpoint
(setq cpt (list ptx pty))
; convert inverted grayscale to
; percent
(setq gsprct
  (/ (- 255 gscolor) 255.0))
; height
(setq zheight
  (+ zmin (* zmax gsprct)))
; mesh point
(setq cpt (list ptx pty zheight))
; check for first edge
(if (and (= xpt 0) (= ypt 0))
  (progn
 (setq iw 0)
 (command (list
   (* iw mod) (* ypt mod) 0))
 (repeat wmax
  (command (list
    (* iw mod) (* ypt mod) 0))
  (setq iw (+ iw 1))
 )
 (command (list
   (* (- wmax 1) mod)
   (* ypt mod) 0))
 (command (list
   (* 0 mod) (* ypt mod) 0))
))
; save first pt
(if (= xpt 0) (progn
 (setq fpt (list ptx pty 0))
 (command fpt)
))
(command cpt)
; add first pt
(if (= xpt (- wmax 1)) (progn
 (command (list ptx pty 0))
 (command fpt)
))
; check for last edge
(if (and (= ypt (- hmax 1))
  (= xpt (- wmax 1))) (progn
 (setq iw 0)
 (command (list
   (* iw mod) (* ypt mod) 0))
```

```
     (repeat wmax
      (command (list
        (* iw mod) (* ypt mod) 0))
      (setq iw (+ iw 1))
     )
     (command (list
       (* (- wmax 1) mod)
       (* ypt mod) 0))
     (command (list
       (* 0 mod) (* ypt mod) 0))
    ))
   )
  )
  (setq fh1 (close fh1))
  (command ".ZOOM" "e")
  (setvar "CMDECHO" 1)
  (princ)
 )
;-----------------------------------
```

Create a cylindrical mesh from an image

The pixel-color value as offset can also be used to create a cylindrical mesh, as in previous examples shown using weather data.

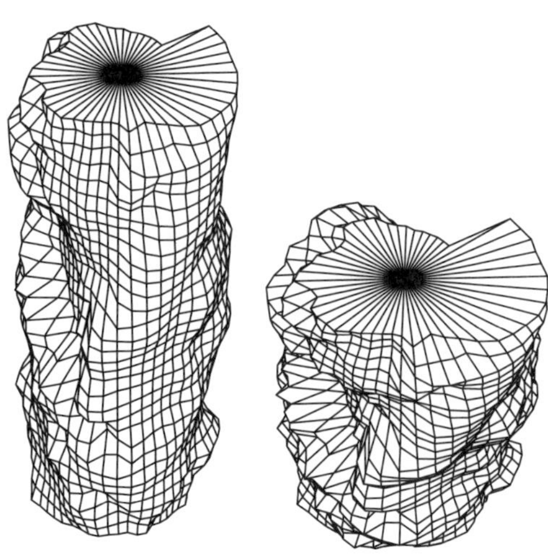

PROG05: clouds image as cylindrical meshes

Add function PROG05. Using a copy of PROG04a, add the cylindrical projection computations for the radius and height.

The computation of the radius is:

```
; convert inverted grayscale to
; percent
(setq gsprct
  (/ (- 255 gscolor) 255.0))
; radius
(setq rad
  (+ rmin (* rmax gsprct)))
; radius is hours plus
; temperature
(setq rxpt (* rad
  (cos (dtr (* anginc xpt)))))
(setq rypt (* rad
  (sin (dtr (* anginc xpt)))))
; height
(setq rzpt pty)
(setq cpt (list rxpt rypt rzpt))
```

Sample script file for PROG05:

```
;-----------------------------------
(prog05)
; PTS filename:
c:\bmp_data\clouds01.bmp.pts
;Enter module size:
5.0
;Enter maximum radius:
30.0
;Enter maximum radius:
10.0
;-----------------------------------
```

Completed function PROG05:

```
;-----------------------------------
(defun prog05 ()
 (setvar "CMDECHO" 0)
 (command ".ERASE" "all" "")
 (princ "\nProg05:")
 (setq fname
   (getstring
```

```
  "\nEnter PTS filename: "))
(setq fhl (open fname "r"))
(setq mod
  (getdist "\nEnter module size: "))
(setq rmax
  (getdist
  "\nEnter maximum radius: "))
(setq rmin
  (getdist
  "\nEnter minimum radius: "))
; header record
(setq dataline (read-line fhl))
(setq wmax
  (atoi (substr dataline 1 3)))
(setq hmax
  (atoi (substr dataline 4 3)))
(setq ncolors
  (atoi (substr dataline 7 3)))
; angle inc
(setq anginc (/ 360.0 wmax))
; start mesh
(command ".3DMESH"
  (+ hmax 2) (+ wmax 1))
; bottom
(repeat (+ wmax 1)
 (command (list 0 0 0))
)
(repeat hmax
 (repeat wmax
  ; get pts record
  (setq dataline (read-line fhl))
  ; X and Y location
  (setq xpt
    (atoi (substr dataline 1 3)))
  (setq ypt
    (atoi (substr dataline 4 3)))
  ; RGB and grayscale values
  (setq rcolor
    (atoi (substr dataline 7 3)))
  (setq gcolor
    (atoi (substr dataline 10 3)))
  (setq bcolor
    (atoi (substr dataline 13 3)))
  (setq gscolor
    (atoi (substr dataline 16 3)))
  ; xy coords
  (setq ptx (* xpt mod))
  (setq pty (* ypt mod))
  ; convert inverted grayscale to
  ; percent
  (setq gsprct
    (/ (- 255 gscolor) 255.0))
  ; radius
  (setq rad
    (+ rmin (* rmax gsprct)))
  ; radius is hours plus
  ; temperature
  (setq rxpt (* rad
    (cos (dtr (* anginc xpt)))))
  (setq rypt (* rad
    (sin (dtr (* anginc xpt)))))
  ; height
  (setq rzpt pty)
  (setq cpt (list rxpt rypt rzpt))
  ; save first pt
  (if (= xpt 0) (setq fpt cpt))
  (command cpt)
  ; add first pt
  (if (= xpt (- wmax 1))
    (command fpt))
 )
)
; bottom
(repeat (+ wmax 1)
 (command (list 0 0 rzpt))
)
(setq fhl (close fhl))
(command ".ZOOM" "e")
(setvar "CMDECHO" 1)
(princ)
)
;----------------------------------
```

Create a spherical mesh from an image

The pixel-color value as offset for a cylindrical mesh can be extended to a spherical projection, as shown in the example using weather data.

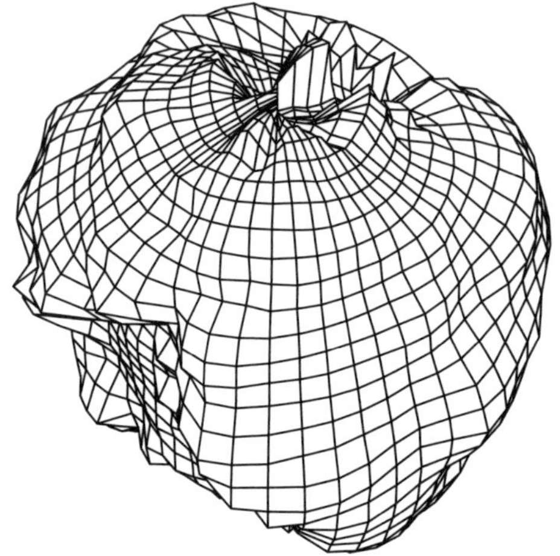

PROG06: clouds image as a spherical mesh

Add function PROG06. Using a copy of PROG05, convert the cylindrical projection computations for the radius and height to spherical.

The computation of the radius is:

```
; convert inverted grayscale to
; percent
(setq gsprct
  (/ (- 255 gscolor) 255.0))
; radius
(setq rad
  (+ rmin (* rmax gsprct)))
; radius is hours plus
; temperature
(setq rxpt (* (* rad
  (cos (dtr (* wanginc xpt))))
  (sin (dtr (* hanginc ypt)))))
(setq rypt (* (* rad
  (sin (dtr (* wanginc xpt))))
  (sin (dtr (* hanginc ypt)))))
(setq rzpt (* rad
  (cos (dtr (* hanginc ypt)))))
(setq cpt (list rxpt rypt rzpt))
```

Sample script file for PROG06:

```
;-----------------------------------
(prog06)
; PTS filename:
c:\bmp_data\clouds01.bmp.pts
;Enter module size:
5.0
;Enter maximum radius:
30.0
;Enter maximum radius:
20.0
;-----------------------------------
```

Completed function PROG06:

```
;-----------------------------------
(defun prog06 ()
 (setvar "CMDECHO" 0)
 (command ".ERASE" "all" "")
 (princ "\nProg06:")
 (setq fname
   (getstring
   "\nEnter PTS filename: "))
 (setq fhl (open fname "r"))
 (setq mod
   (getdist "\nEnter module size: "))
 (setq rmax
   (getdist
   "\nEnter maximum radius: "))
 (setq rmin
   (getdist
   "\nEnter minimum radius: "))
 ; header record
 (setq dataline (read-line fhl))
 (setq wmax
   (atoi (substr dataline 1 3)))
 (setq hmax
   (atoi (substr dataline 4 3)))
```

```
(setq ncolors
  (atoi (substr dataline 7 3)))
; angle inc
(setq wanginc (/ 360.0 wmax))
(setq hanginc (/ 180.0 hmax))
; start mesh
(command ".3DMESH"
  (+ hmax 2) (+ wmax 1))
; top
(repeat (+ wmax 1)
 (command (list 0 0 rmax))
)
(repeat hmax
 (repeat wmax
  ; get pts record
  (setq dataline (read-line fh1))
  ; X and Y location
  (setq xpt
    (atoi (substr dataline 1 3)))
  (setq ypt
    (atoi (substr dataline 4 3)))
  ; RGB and grayscale values
  (setq rcolor
    (atoi (substr dataline 7 3)))
  (setq gcolor
    (atoi (substr dataline 10 3)))
  (setq bcolor
    (atoi (substr dataline 13 3)))
  (setq gscolor
    (atoi (substr dataline 16 3)))
  ; xy coords
  (setq ptx (* xpt mod))
  (setq pty (* ypt mod))
  ; convert inverted grayscale to
  ; percent
  (setq gsprct
    (/ (- 255 gscolor) 255.0))
  ; radius
  (setq rad
    (+ rmin (* rmax gsprct)))
  ; radius is hours plus
  ; temperature
  (setq rxpt (* (* rad
    (cos (dtr (* wanginc xpt))))
    (sin (dtr (* hanginc ypt)))))
  (setq rypt (* (* rad
    (sin (dtr (* wanginc xpt))))
    (sin (dtr (* hanginc ypt)))))
  (setq rzpt (* rad
    (cos (dtr (* hanginc ypt)))))
  (setq cpt (list rxpt rypt rzpt))
  ; save first pt
  (if (= xpt 0) (setq fpt cpt))
  (command cpt)
  ; add first pt
  (if (= xpt (- wmax 1))
    (command fpt))
 )
)
; bottom
(repeat (+ wmax 1)
 (command (list 0 0 (* rmax -1)))
)
(setq fh1 (close fh1))
(command ".ZOOM" "e")
(setvar "CMDECHO" 1)
(princ)
)
;-----------------------------------
```

Explore other images, including ones that are directly related to the project site or that represent the business of the client, as well as images that are totally abstract or fanciful.

ACKNOWLEDGMENTS

This workbook is based on the many notes I developed for ARCH 429, a course in CAD programming and form generation that was first offered in the spring of 1995 at the Illinois Institute of Technology (IIT), College of Architecture, in Chicago. Some of the advanced material contained in the text came from my work advising students enrolled in the MArch and PhD programs; some came from workshops conducted for architectural firms or from my own research. Many thanks to all the students who have challenged me to continually develop new approaches and new material. Thanks to Dean George Schipporeit, Dean Donna Robertson, and Dr. Mahjoub Elnimeiri for their continued support. Thanks to the team at Princeton Architectural Press, editor Laurie Manfra, and designer Arnoud Verhaeghe.

A very special thanks to my wife, Corinne, for her support and understanding as this book was being completed, exactly the same time that we were preparing for our wedding. Thank you also to our children Alexis, Catherine, and James, and granddaughter Makayla for always keeping me level-headed and grounded.

ADDITIONAL READING

Abelson, Harold and Andrea A. diSessa. *Turtle Geometry: the Computer as a Medium for Exploring Mathematics.* Cambridge, MA: MIT Press, 1981.

Aranda, Benjamin and Chris Lasch. *Pamphlet Architecture 27: Tooling.* New York: Princeton Architectural Press, 2006.

Bertol, Daniela. *Visualizing With CAD: An Auto CAD Exploration of Geometric and Architectural Forms.* Santa Clara, CA: Telos, 1994.

Clayson, James. *Visual Modeling with Logo: A Structured Approach to Seeing.* Cambridge, MA: MIT Press, 1988.

Dixon, Robert. *Mathographics.* New York: Dover Publications, 1991.

Ferre, Albert, Irene Hwang, Tomoko Sakamoto, Anna Tetas, Michael Kubo, and Ramon Prat, eds. *Verb Natures.* Barcelona: Actar, 2006.

Hensel, Michael, Achim Menges, and Michael Weinstock. "Emergence: Morphogenetic Design Strategies." *Architectural Design* 74, no. 3 (May/June 2004).

Kramer, William. *Understanding AutoLISP: Programming for Productivity.* Albany, NY: Delmar, 1993.

Lawrence, J. Dennis. *A Catalog of Special Plane Curves.* New York: Dover Publications, 1972.

Leach, Neil, David Turnbull, and Chris Williams, eds. *Digital Tectonics.* Hoboken, NJ: Wiley-Academy, 2004.

Maeda, John. *Creative Code.* New York: Thames & Hudson, 2004.

Maeda, John. *Design By Numbers.* Cambridge, MA: MIT Press, 1999.

Mitchell, William J., Robin S. Liggett, and Thomas Kvan. *The Art of Computer Graphics Programming: A Structured Introduction for Architects and Designers.* New York: Van Nostrand Reinhold, 1987.

Rahim, Ali. *Catalytic Formations.* London: Taylor & Francis, 2006.

Rahim, Ali and Hina Jamelle. "Elegance." *Architectural Design* 77, no. 1 (January/February 2007).

Rawls, Rod and Mark Hagen. *AutoLISP Programming Principles and Techniques.* Tinley Park, IL: Goodheart-Willcox, 1998.

Schmitt, Gerhard. *Microcomputer Aided Design: For Architects and Designers.* New York: Wiley, 1988.

Silver, Mike. "Programming Cultures: Architecture, Art and Science in the Age of Software Development." *Architectural Design* 76, no. 4 (July/August 2006).

Terzidis, Kostas. *Algorithmic Architecture.* Oxford: Architectural Press, 2006.